THE OXFORD HANDBOOK OF

PHILOSOPHY
OF POLITICAL
SCIENCE

THE OXFORD HANDBOOK OF

PHILOSOPHY OF POLITICAL SCIENCE

Edited by
HAROLD KINCAID
and
JEROEN VAN BOUWEL

OXFORD
UNIVERSITY PRESS

OXFORD
UNIVERSITY PRESS

Oxford University Press is a department of the University of Oxford. It furthers
the University's objective of excellence in research, scholarship, and education
by publishing worldwide. Oxford is a registered trade mark of Oxford University
Press in the UK and certain other countries.

Published in the United States of America by Oxford University Press
198 Madison Avenue, New York, NY 10016, United States of America.

Library of Congress Cataloging-in-Publication Data
Names: Kincaid, Harold, 1952– editor. | Bouwel, Jeroen van, editor.
Title: The Oxford handbook of philosophy of political science /
[edited by Harold Kincaid and Jeroen Van Bouwel].
Description: New York, NY : Oxford University Press, [2023] |
Includes bibliographical references and index. |
Identifiers: LCCN 2022029518 (print) | LCCN 2022029519 (ebook) |
ISBN 9780197519806 (hardback) | ISBN 9780197519820 (epub) |
ISBN 9780197519837
Subjects: LCSH: Political science—Philosophy.
Classification: LCC JA71 .O947 2022 (print) | LCC JA71 (ebook) |
DDC 320.01—dc23/eng/20220816
LC record available at https://lccn.loc.gov/2022029518
LC ebook record available at https://lccn.loc.gov/2022029519

DOI: 10.1093/oxfordhb/9780197519806.001.0001

1 3 5 7 9 8 6 4 2

Printed by Marquis, Canada

Harold:
To Don Ross, for many years of intellectual inspiration and friendship

Jeroen:
To my parents, Marie-Thérèse Greefs and Jo Van Bouwel,
for supporting me unconditionally.

TABLE OF CONTENTS

PART 1. ANALYZING BASIC FRAMEWORKS IN POLITICAL SCIENCE

PART 2. METHODS IN POLITICAL SCIENCE, DEBATES, AND RECONCILIATIONS

PART 3. PURPOSES AND USES OF POLITICAL SCIENCE

PART 4. POLITICAL SCIENCE IN SOCIETY: VALUES, EXPERTISE, AND PROGRESS

ACKNOWLEDGMENTS

SPECIAL thanks go to Amy Mazur who provided enthusiastic support for this Philosophy of Political Science (PoPS) project and helped organize and fund the workshop held at Washington State University in the fall of 2019, at which a major subset of the chapters was presented. We thank the School of Politics, Philosophy, and Public Affairs (Steven Stehr, Director), Foley Institute of Public Policy (Cornell Clayton, Director), and the Claudius O. and Mary W. Johnson Distinguished Professorship of Political Science for funding along with the School of Economics, University of Cape Town, as well as the Faculty of Arts and Philosophy, Ghent University. Also, thanks to Sofia Blanco Sequeiros, Francesco Guala, and Erik Angner for their reviewing work, and to all the contributors to the volume, almost all of whom also did some reviewing, which was one way to increase interactions between political scientists and philosophers. Jeroen would like to thank his sons Adrian and Max for their entertainment (especially during the COVID-19 lockdowns) and Linnéa for continuing encouragement and support.

LIST OF FIGURES, TABLES AND BOXES

Figures

Tables

List of Boxes

List of Contributors

N. Emrah Aydinonat (PhD, Docent) is a researcher working at the Faculty of Social Sciences, University of Helsinki. He is one of the editors of the *Journal of Economic Methodology*. His research interests include the practices of modeling and explanation in the social sciences and the theories of institutions. Aydinonat is the author of *The Invisible Hand in Economics* (Routledge, 2008).

Andrew Bennett is Professor of Government at Georgetown University and author, with Alexander George, of *Case Studies and Theory Development in the Social Sciences* (MIT Press, 2005). He is also coeditor, with Jeffrey Checkel, of *Process Tracing: From Metaphor to Analytic Tool* (Cambridge, 2014) and President of the Consortium on Qualitative Research Methods, which organizes the annual Institute on Qualitative and Multimethod Research (IQMR) at Syracuse University.

Fred Chernoff is Harvey Picker Professor of International Relations, Colgate University, Hamilton, NY. His most recent book is *Explanation and Progress in Security Studies* (Stanford, 2014). His publications have appeared in such journals as *International Studies Quarterly*, *Journal of Conflict Resolution*, *International Theory*, *European Journal of International Relations*, *Philosophical Quarterly*, *Analysis*, and *Mind*. He holds doctoral degrees in political science (Yale) and philosophy (Johns Hopkins). He has held faculty posts at Yale, Brown, and Wesleyan Universities, and research positions at the International Institute of Strategic Studies (London), Norwegian Institute of International Affairs (Oslo), and the Rand Corporation.

Christopher Clarke is a senior research associate at the University of Cambridge (CRASSH) and an assistant professor at Erasmus University Rotterdam (School of Philosophy). He works on the nature of causal explanation and causal inference, especially in political science and economics.

Sharon Crasnow is Distinguished Professor Emerita, Norco College in Southern California. Her research is on methodological issues in the social sciences with a focus on political science. She has published work in this area in *Philosophy of the Social Sciences*, *Philosophy of Science*, *Studies in History and Philosophy of Science*, and *Synthese*. She also works on feminist philosophy of science and epistemology and is a coeditor (with Kristen Intemann) of *The Routledge Handbook of Feminist Philosophy of Science*.

Keith Dowding is Distinguished Professor Political Science and Political Philosophy at the Australian National University. He has published over a hundred articles in leading political science and political philosophy journals and over a dozen books including *The Philosophy and Methods of Political Science*, *Rational Choice and Political Power*, and *It's the Government, Stupid*.

Gary Goertz is Professor of Political Science at the Kroc Center for International Peace Studies at Notre Dame University. He is the author or editor of nine books and more than fifty articles and chapters on topics of international institutions, methodology, and conflict studies. His methodological research focuses on concepts and measurement along with set theoretic approaches, including "Explaining War and Peace: Case Studies and Necessary Condition Counterfactuals," (2007), "Politics, Gender, and Concepts: Theory and Methodology" (2008), "A Tale of Two Cultures: Qualitative and Quantitative Research in the Social Sciences" (2012), and "Multimethod Research, Causal Mechanisms, and Case Studies: The Research Triad" (2017). The completely revised and rewritten edition of his (2005) concept book "Social science concepts and measurement" was published by Princeton in 2020.

Stephan Haggard is Krause Distinguished Professor at the School of Global Policy and Strategy at the University of California San Diego. His publications on international political economy include *Pathways from the Periphery: The Newly Industrializing Countries in the International System* (Cornell University Press, 1990); *The Political Economy of the Asian Financial Crisis* (Institute for International Economics, 2000); and *Developmental States* (Cambridge University Press, 2018). His work with Robert Kaufman on democratization, inequality, and social policy includes *The Political Economy of Democratic Transitions* (Princeton University Press, 1995); *Democracy, Development and Welfare States: Latin America, East Asia, Eastern Europe* (Princeton, 2008); *Dictators and Democrats: Masses, Elites and Regime Change* (Princeton, 2016) and *Backsliding: Democratic Regress in the Contemporary World* (Cambridge, 2020). His work on North Korea with Marcus Noland includes *Famine in North Korea* (Columbia University Press, 2007); *Witness to Transformation: Refugee Insights into North Korea* (Peterson Institute for International Economics, 2011); and *Hard Target: Sanctions, Inducements and the Case of North Korea* (Stanford University Press, 2017).

David Henderson is Robert R. Chambers Professor of Philosophy at the University of Nebraska, Lincoln. His research interests include the philosophy of social science and epistemology—and the present work brings together these interests. His works include *Interpretation and Explanation in the Human Sciences* (State University of New York Press, 1993) and (with Terry Horgan) *The Epistemological Spectrum: At the Interface of Cognitive Science and Conceptual Analysis* (Oxford University Press, 2011). Recent work has been focused on social norms and epistemic norms—for example, "Are Epistemic Norms Fundamentally Social Norms?" (*Episteme*, 2020). He coedited and contributed to *The Routledge Handbook in Social Epistemology* (2019, with Miranda Fricker, David Henderson, Peter Graham, and Nikolaj Pedersen) and (with John Greco) *Epistemic Evaluation: Point and Purpose in Epistemology* (Oxford University Press, 2015).

Catherine Herfeld is an assistant professor of social theory and philosophy of the social sciences at the University of Zurich, Switzerland. Her research falls into the fields of philosophy and history of the social sciences, in particular economics.

Season Hoard is Associate Professor jointly appointed in the School of Politics, Philosophy, and Public Affairs and the Division of Governmental Studies and Services (DGSS) at Washington State University. She has a PhD in political science from Washington State University, and her areas of expertise include gender and politics, comparative politics, public policy, and applied social science research. Dr. Hoard helps provide applied research and program evaluation support for governmental agencies and nonprofit organizations in the United States. She has numerous publications focused on applied research methods and public policy, including recent publications in *American Political Science Review*, *Community Development, Politics and Life Sciences, Politics, Groups, and Identities, Biomass and Bioenergy* and the *International Journal of Aviation Management*.

Andre Hofmeyr is Associate Professor in the School of Economics at the University of Cape Town, and the Director of the Research Unit in Behavioural Economics and Neuroeconomics (RUBEN). He is an experimental economist who specializes in decision theory, game theory, experimental economic methodology, and structural econometrics. He is an associate editor of *Cognitive Processing*, and has recently published articles in *Experimental Economics, Journal of Behavioral and Experimental Economics, Journal of Economic Methodology*, and *Southern Economic Journal*, along with a commentary forthcoming in *Behavioral and Brain Sciences*.

Laci Hubbard Mattix is Assistant Professor (career track) in the School of Politics, Philosophy, and Public Affairs at Washington State University. She specializes in political theory and philosophy. Her work intersects critical theory, feminist theory, and ethics. She has published numerous book chapters on these issues as well as articles in *Essays in Philosophy* and *Transportation in the City*.

María Jiménez-Buedo is an associate professor at the Department of Logic, History and Philosophy of Science at UNED in Madrid. She works in the philosophy of the social sciences, with an emphasis on methodological issues. Her recent work focuses on experimental methods in the social sciences.

Peter John is Professor of Public Policy at King's College London. He is interested in how to involve citizens in public policy and in randomized controlled trials. His books include *Field Experiments in Political Science and Public Policy* (Routledge, 2017), *How Far to Nudge* (Edward Elgar, 2018), and his coauthored *Nudge, Nudge, Think, Think Experimenting with Ways to Change Citizen Behaviour* (Manchester University Press, 2019, 2nd ed.).

Jonathan Michael Kaplan is a professor in the philosophy program at Oregon State University, where he has taught since 2003. His primary research areas are political philosophy and the philosophy of biology. Recently, he has worked on the relationship between contemporary genomic technologies and arguments surrounding claims about the biological nature of human "races," as well as on issues emerging from recent research on the social determinants of health.

Harold Kincaid is Emeritus Professor in the School of Economics at the University of Cape Town. His research concerns issues in the philosophy of science and philosophy of social and behavioral science as well as experimental work in economics on, among other things, risk and time attitudes, trust and addiction. He is the author or editor of thirteen books (starting with *The Philosophical Foundations of the Social Sciences: Analyzing Controversies in Social Research*, Cambridge, 1996) and many journal articles and book chapters. Recent or forthcoming work includes the *Elgar Companion to Philosophy of Economics* with Don Ross (Elgar, 2021) and articles or book chapters on objectivity in the social sciences, improving causal inference in economics, the role of mechanisms in the social sciences, agent-based models, classifying mental disorders, the risk-trust confound, and prospect theory.

Jaakko Kuorikoski is an associate professor of practical philosophy at the University of Helsinki. His main areas of specialization are philosophy of economics and philosophy of social sciences, and he has published widely on scientific explanation, modeling, simulation, and causal reasoning.

Janet Lawler is a doctoral student in the Department of Politics at the University of Virginia, working on theories and implications of how new technologies alter public space and discourse.

Caterina Marchionni is University Researcher in the unit of practical philosophy and a member of TINT at the University of Helsinki. She specializes in the methodology and epistemology of science, in particular of economics and the social sciences. Caterina has published widely on scientific explanation, modelling, and interdisciplinarity. .

Johannes Marx is a professor of political theory at the University of Bamberg, Germany. His research falls into the fields of political philosophy, philosophy of social sciences, agent-based modeling, and political economy.

Amy G. Mazur is Claudius O. and Mary W. Johnson Distinguished Professor in Political Science at Washington State University and an Associate Researcher at LIEPP at Sciences Po, Paris. Her research and teaching interests focus on comparative feminist policy issues with a particular emphasis on France and comparative methodology. Her recent books include *The Politics of State Feminism: Innovation in Comparative Research* (with Dorothy McBride, Temple University Press, 2010) and *Gender Equality and Policy Implementation in the Corporate World: Making Democracy Work in Business* (edited with Isabelle Engeli, Oxford University Press, forthcoming). She has published in *French Politics, European Journal of Politics and Gender, Comparative European Politics, Revue Française de Science Politique, Politics and Gender, Political Research Quarterly, Journal of Women, Politics and Policy, PS: Political Science,* and *Politics, Groups and Identities.* She is currently co-convening, with Isabelle Engeli (Exeter University), the Gender Equality Policy in Practice Network (GEPP) as well as GEPP-Equal Employment and GEPP-France. She is Lead Editor of *French Politics* and a fellow-in-residence for the Global Contestations of Gender and Women's Rights at Bielefeld University.

Benjamin Mishkin is a doctoral candidate in political science at Georgetown University where he studies American foreign policy, civil-military relations, and bureaucratic politics. He also maintains interests in the study of political violence and qualitative methods.

Samantha Noll is an assistant professor in the School of Politics, Philosophy, and Public Affairs (PPPA) at Washington State University. She is also the bioethicist affiliated with the Functional Genomics Initiative, which applies genome editing in agriculture research. Her research agenda focuses on teasing out ethical, social, and environmental implications of agriculture biotechnology, food systems, and other technological innovations. Noll publishes widely on values and agriculture, local food movements, and the application of genomics technology.

Robert Northcott is Reader in Philosophy at Birkbeck College, London. He has published extensively on the philosophy of economics and other sciences, and on causation and causal explanation. He is currently working on a book that will develop a systematic position on the methodology of nonlaboratory sciences. He was founding coeditor of the *Elements* series in Philosophy of Science (Cambridge University Press), and is Honorary Secretary of the British Society for the Philosophy of Science.

Miquel Pellicer is Professor for Inequality and Poverty at the University of Marburg. He works on inequality, political behavior, and development. His articles have appeared, among others, in *Perspectives on Politics, Quarterly Journal of Political Science, Political Research Quarterly*, and the *Journal of Development Economics*.

Julian Reiss is Professor and Head of the Institute of Philosophy and Scientific Method at Johannes Kepler University Linz. He is the author of *Error in Economics* (2008), *Philosophy of Economics* (2013), *Causation, Evidence, and Inference* (2015), and seventy journal articles and book chapters on topics in general philosophy of science and philosophy of the biomedical and social sciences. He is a past president of the International Network for Economic Method (INEM).

Benoît Rihoux is a full professor in comparative politics at the University of Louvain (UCLouvain, Belgium), where he chairs the Centre for Political Science and Comparative Politics (CESPOL). His substantive research interests comprise among others political parties, political behavior, organizational change, social movements, gender and politics, and professional ethics. He plays a leading role in the development of configurational comparative methods and QCA (Qualitative Comparative Analysis) and coordinates the interdisciplinary COMPASSS global network (http://www.compasss.org) in that field. He has published multiple pieces around QCA: review pieces, empirical applications in diverse fields, and a reference textbook (Sage, 2009; with Charles Ragin). He is also strongly involved in research methods training as joint Academic Coordinator of MethodsNET, the Methods Excellence Network (https://www.methodsnet.org/home).

Don Ross is Professor and Head of the School of Society, Politics, and Ethics, University College Cork (Ireland); Professor in the School of Economics, University of Cape Town (South Africa); and Program Director for Methodology at the Center for Economic Analysis of Risk, Robinson College of Business, Georgia State University (United States). His current areas of research are the experimental economics of risk and time preferences; the economics of addiction and gambling; economic behavior in nonhuman animals; scientific metaphysics; and economic optimization of road networks in Africa. He is the author of many articles and chapters, and author or editor of fourteen books, including *Economic Theory and Cognitive Science: Microexplanation* (MIT Press, 2005); *Every Thing Must Go: Metaphysics Naturalised* (with James Ladyman, Oxford University Press, 2007); and *Philosophy of Economics* (Palgrave Macmillan, 2014). He is currently writing a book on the evolution of human risk management (with Glenn Harrison) and another on generalization of conditional game theory for application to economic choice experiments (with Wynn Stirling).

Federica Russo is a philosopher of science and technology based at the University of Amsterdam. She has a long-standing interest in social science methodology, and she wrote extensively about causal modelling, explanation, and evidence in the social, biomedical, and policy sciences. Among her contributions, *Causality and Causal Modelling in the Social Sciences. Measuring Variations* (Springer, 2009), *Causality: Philosophical Theory*

Meets Scientific Practice (Oxford University Press, 2014, with Phyllis Illari), and *Evaluating Evidence of Mechanisms in Medicine: Principles and Procedures* (Springer, 2018, a coauthored monograph of the EBM + group). Together with Phyllis Illari, she is editor-in-chief of the *European Journal for Philosophy of Science.*

Attilia Ruzzene is a postdoctoral researcher at the University of Bergamo. She obtained her first PhD in economics at the University of Torino and a PhD in philosophy at the Erasmus University in Rotterdam. She has been teaching courses on the philosophy of science, economics, and social sciences at the Erasmus University Rotterdam, Witten/ Herdecke University, and University of Bologna.Her research currently focuses on a variety of qualitative perspectives for the study of organizational phenomena which include causal-mechanistic reasoning, the practice approach, and visual analysis. She has long lasting interest in issues related to causal inference in case-study research and the use of case-study evidence for policy making.

Stephen Schneider is a fellow at the Carl R. Woese Institute for Genomic Biology at the University of Illinois at Urbana-Champaign. He works in the area of political psychology and has published articles examining how lay attributions for traits and behaviors influence tolerance, how threat influences conspiracy theory endorsement, and what role the behavioral immune system plays in support for refugee resettlement programs among others.

Wynn C. Stirling is an emeritus professor of Electrical and Computer Engineering at Brigham Young University. His current research interests are game theory, stochastic processes, and control theory. He received his Bachelor of Arts in Mathematics and Master of Science in Electrical Engineering from the University of Utah in 1969 and 1971, respectively, and his PhD in Electrical Engineering from Stanford University in 1983. Dr. Stirling is the author or many articles and chapters, is a co-author of *Mathematical Methods and Algorithms for Signal Processing* (Prentice Hall, 2000), and is the author of *Satisficing Games and Decision Making* (Cambridge, 2003), *Theory of Conditional Games* (Cambridge, 2012), and *Theory of Social Choice on Networks* (Cambridge, 2016). He is working with Don Ross on a book on applications of conditional game theory to economics.

Luca Tummolini is Senior Researcher at the Institute of Cognitive Sciences and Technologies of the Italian Research Council in Rome and Associated Researcher at the Institute for Future Studies in Sweden. He obtained his PhD in Cognitive Science from the University of Siena in 2010. His research interests are in social interaction and the cognitive mechanisms that enable humans to flexibly coordinate and collaborate with one another: from shared deliberation in small groups to conformity with population-wide regularities like conventions and social norms. He is also interested in using game theory to develop a common framework between the cognitive and the social sciences. He has published in philosophy, psychology, economics, and computer science journals. He is the author of more than fifty articles and coeditor of three books.

Jeroen Van Bouwel is a senior researcher at the *Centre for Logic and Philosophy of Science* and a visiting professor in the *Department of Philosophy and Moral Science* at Ghent University. His research areas include philosophy of the social sciences, social epistemology, and the relations between science and democracy. He has published work in these areas in, inter alia, *Philosophy of the Social Sciences, Economics & Philosophy, Social Epistemology,*

Perspectives on Science, History and Theory, Journal for General Philosophy of Science, and numerous collected volumes, handbooks, and encyclopedias. His books include *The Social Sciences and Democracy* (Palgrave, 2009, editor) and *Scientific Explanation* (Springer, 2013, coauthored with Erik Weber and Leen De Vreese).

David Waldner is Associate Professor in the Department of Politics at the University of Virginia. His empirical work focuses on the intersection of political and economic development; his methods writings focus on qualitative causal inference.

Eva Wegner is Professor of Comparative Politics at the University of Marburg. Her research focuses on political behavior and accountability in the Middle East and sub-Saharan Africa. Her work has appeared in *Perspectives on Politics, Journal of Conflict Resolution*, the *International Political Science Review*, and *Party Politics*, among others.

Petri Ylikoski is Professor of Science and Technology Studies at University of Helsinki. His research interests include theories of explanation and evidence, science studies, and social theory. His current research focuses on the foundations of mechanism-based social science, institutional epistemology, and the social consequences of artificial intelligence.

Julie Zahle is Professor in the Department of Philosophy at University of Bergen. Previously, she taught at Durham University and University of Copenhagen. She received her PhD from the History and Philosophy of Science Department at the University of Pittsburgh in 2009. Her research areas include the philosophy of qualitative methods, values and objectivity in social science, the individualism-holism debate, and social theories of practices.

Jesús Zamora-Bonilla is a philosopher and economist, and a professor of philosophy of science at UNED (Madrid). He is the coeditor of *The Sage Handbook of Philosophy of Social Sciences*, and author of numerous papers on rationality, normativity, scientific realism, verisimilitude, economics of scientific knowledge, and other topics, published in journals like *Synthese, Philosophy of Science, Erkenntnis, Journal of Economic Methodology, Philosophy of Social Sciences, Economics & Philosophy, Theoria, Episteme*, and *Perspectives on Science*.

CHAPTER 1

PUTTING PHILOSOPHY OF POLITICAL SCIENCE ON THE MAP

HAROLD KINCAID AND JEROEN VAN BOUWEL

1. WHY *PHILOSOPHY OF POLITICAL SCIENCE*?

OVER the last several decades, research in political science has expanded enormously, leading to much improved statistical testing (abetted by vast increases in computational technologies), innovative methods for dealing with small-N data, sophisticated formal models, experimental work on political behavior, biological and psychological perspectives on voting behavior, identification of exposed biases in political analysis, and much more.

This rich body of research raises numerous philosophical issues. However, these philosophy of science issues raised by political science have only gotten scattered and little organized attention; there is no field that labels itself *Philosophy of Political Science*. This is in contrast to, for example, economics which has two journals (*Journal of Economic Methodology* and *Economics & Philosophy*) and an international organization (*International Network for Economic Methodology*). The general philosophy of social science also has a solid institutional embedding with the journal *Philosophy of the Social Sciences* (Sage) and several formal groups (like the *Philosophy of Social Science Roundtable*, the *European Network for the Philosophy of the Social Sciences*, and the *Asian Network for Philosophy of the Social Sciences*). Sociology and anthropology are addressed in Turner and Risjord (2006) *Philosophy of Anthropology and Sociology: A Volume in the Handbook of the Philosophy of Science Series*, and history has its own journals such as the *Journal of the Philosophy of History* and *History & Theory*.

The philosophical issues raised by political science research are just as pressing and vibrant as those raised in these more organized fields; some of the issues are unique to political science, and others are general philosophy of social science issues that have not been much considered in relation to political science research. To give those issues the attention they deserve, this volume seeks to increase the currently scarce interaction between philosophers of science and political scientists and aims at fostering a field that labels itself *Philosophy of Political Science*, creating a fruitful meeting place for further develop-ment of ideas in philosophy of science and political science.[1]

2. HOW DOES THIS VOLUME APPROACH *PHILOSOPHY OF POLITICAL SCIENCE?*

In this volume an intellectually diverse group of philosophers of science and political scientists takes on a set of these Philosophy of Political Science (PoPS) issues. When we started compiling this volume we made a decision to focus on empirical political science and not on normative political theory. Normative political theory has of course received much philosophical attention. Thus, we decided rather to stick to issues that are tradi-tionally covered by philosophy of science and not venture into political philosophy.[2] The list of topics included reflects in part the interests of those willing and able to contribute (with COVID-19 hitting the world when the final versions of the manuscripts were being written and reviewed). However, we are confident that the volume addresses key issues in PoPS and that it will increase the interaction between philosophers of science and political scientists—it has already done so in the organizing of the volume.[3]

Our emphasis on the increased interaction between political scientists and philosophers of science flows from the perspective that motivates and structures this volume, namely a naturalist philosophy of science. Naturalism means here that philosophy of science is con-tinuous with and part of science, and, therefore, close to and informed by actual scientific practice. It denies that there is something special about the social world that would make it unamenable to scientific investigation. Neither is there something special about philosophy that would make it independent or prior to the sciences, including social sciences.

Following this naturalist approach, we consider PoPS to be a meeting place. On the one hand, it helps to increase philosophy of science sophistication in political science. The many political scientists interested in methodology (broadly conceived) might advance their re-search by being more cognizant of developments in philosophy of science. On the other hand, our naturalist approach says that philosophers of science must look carefully at actual political science research and learn from it to further develop their own ideas (for example think about the use of "diversity," "representation," "democratic," and so on, in discussions of scientific practice). Furthermore, political scientists have also been quite innovative in thinking about methodology, and philosophy of science has not generally built on these advancements to its detriment. For example, the application of Boolean and fuzzy set anal-ysis to complex causality and classification (Ragin 1987) has not found its way into philo-sophical discussions of these issues.

We have asked contributors to use examples from and stick closely to the actual prac-tice of political science, a test against which the philosophy of the discipline can be devel-oped and evaluated. Moreover, many of the contributors are practicing political scientists, and several chapters have been written by combined forces of political scientists and philosophers. Furthermore, by getting the contributors to comment upon each other's work, we ensured that the political scientists got feedback in developing the philosophy of science issues and that the philosophers' take on the political science is on track, thus strengthening the emerging community of philosophers of political science. Finally, in line with our approach, we emphasize that philosophy of science is something scientists themselves sometimes do, just as science is something that philosophers of science may do. This makes for PoPS to be part of ongoing scientific controversies and part of the process of settling those issues.

3. WHAT ARE THE ISSUES IN PHILOSOPHY OF POLITICAL SCIENCE?

What are the issues that PoPS might address? From the *Political Science* side, there are many aspects one can focus on. Political science is a complex system that involves a community of scientists engaged in research using scientific methods in order to produce new knowledge. As a label, "political science" may refer to a social institution, the research process, the (community of) researchers, the method of inquiry, the end product, i.e., political science knowledge, and other aspects.

That multilayered system has itself gone through a historical development, from the statism at the time of the discipline's early professionalization, via the pluralism of the 1920s and the behavioralism of the 1950s, to the Caucus for a New Political Science of the late 1960s and the Perestroika of the early 2000s with their challenges to primacy of value-free quantitative and formal modeling (cf. Dryzek 2006). Political science also crystallized into various subdisciplines like comparative politics, international relations, domestic politics, political theory, public administration, political economy, and so on. These are some key transformations in the internal history of the discipline. In addition, there is also the boundary work that goes on, and the conflicts and opportunities that arise in interacting with other disciplines that study the social world, such as sociology, economics, history, or anthropology, a much discussed issue for the social sciences more generally (Wallerstein 1996). Given that political scientists have been venturing both into the more so-called *nomothetic* approaches (for example, in political economy) as well as into more *ideographic* ones (for example, in diplomatic history or ethnographic studies more generally), and combinations thereof, intersections with adjacent disciplines have been many. The details of the history of the political science discipline and the internal and external demarcation from its neighboring disciplines is beyond our purview here, but the point is that there are many aspects of the practice of political science that deserve a philosophical analysis—both in political science's historical development as well as in its contemporary formations.

From the *Philosophy of Science* side, we can build on work by philosophers of science with the goal of helping political scientists to address philosophical and methodological issues that arise in the practice of research. Recent philosophy of science as a discipline has mainly focused on the quality of scientific knowledge, but has also paid attention to the processes and conditions of the production and application of that knowledge. Analyzing those processes and conditions may involve looking at particular research methods, the social-epistemic make-up of a discipline, the relations between different scientific fields, the aims or requirements steering the scientific research, and the use of scientific knowledge, not only its efficacy but also its legitimacy. Legitimacy questions concerning the application of scientific knowledge might concern, for example, possible harmful side-effect of applying specific findings, comparison with alternative methods for reaching similar aims, or the fair sharing of the benefits of scientific research. Typical topics in contemporary philosophy of science are the process and value of experimentation, evidence amalgamation, evidence-based deliberation, the transferability of case-based knowledge, mechanisms, causal pluralism, the accuracy and adequacy of scientific models, expertise and lay citizen's input, values in science and policy making, and so on (cf. Humphreys 2016).

We favor a naturalist approach in line with most of contemporary philosophy of science. It is more productive to directly engage with the study of human behavior, institutions, and society, rather than rely on philosophical intuitions and ponder a priori—autonomously from scientific investigation—how to study the social world and wonder whether the social sciences can become "real" sciences. Contemporary philosophy of science supports an approach that studies scientific practices and remains informed about and participates in developments in the sciences. This approach requires more constructive interactions between philosophers and scientists, which may include joint research, peer review, and mutual criticism.

What would such constructive interactions look like in the case of political science? What would the dialogue between them—the typical *Philosophy of Political Science* issues—be like? Let us start with a (obviously nonexhaustive) list of possible issues:

- What should be the aims of political science?
- What are and should be the most important topics of political science research?
- What are the characteristics of good political science knowledge?
- Can political science knowledge be objective?
- How do we establish facts about the political world?
- What methods are most appropriate for political science research?
- What steps should the research process take in order to get to the best knowledge possible?
- How should we measure progress in political science research?
- Should there be restrictions in the application of political science knowledge?
- How should the community of political scientists be organized in order to obtain the best political science knowledge possible?
- What kind of interdisciplinarity is most beneficial for political science research?
- What is the role of values in political science?
- Is political science biased? If so, where and how?
- What is the best route to fruitfully involve other scientific disciplines, researchers or citizens?
- How could the epistemic benefits of political science research best be shared?

If we structure these possible issues and understandings of PoPS in relation to different stages of the research process, we can distinguish (at least) five questions:

(a) Where to look (from)?
(b) What to study?
(c) Why study?
(d) How to study?

(e) Who to involve in studying?

Question (a), where to look (from), is linked to the different frameworks, lenses, perspectives, approaches, research traditions, and vantage points we encounter in the study of politics, including the meaning and use of concepts in political science, the choice of the unit and level of analysis, the theoretical characterization (philosophical anthropology) of the agent, and the understanding of agency-structure relations among other things. These topics are central in part 1 of the volume, "Analyzing Basic Frameworks in Political Science."

Question (b), what to study, asks what the important research questions in political science should be as well as how to make those decisions, who decides what research questions should (not) be prioritized, how a particular object of study is to be delineated, and what the scope of inquiry should be? The selection of research questions is, *inter alia*, discussed in part 4.

Question (c), why study, concerns what the purposes/aims/goals of research are. The answer(s) to that question could be, for example, *to explain* political phenomena, *to predict*, *to give policy advice*, *to understand* the limits on (possible) political change, *to preserve* or *to criticize* the status quo, *to create* new forms of political community, and so on. Robert Cox (1981, 128) emphasized that "theory is always *for* someone and *for* some purpose," where he saw a clear divide between political science research with a "problem-solving" purpose—ensuring existing political arrangement to function smoothly—and research with a broader, "critical" purpose reflecting on how the political order came into being, changed over time and may change again in desired ways in the future. Another researcher considering different aims of political science research is Steve Smith (1996, 13): "Theories do not simply explain or predict, they tell us what possibilities exist for human action and intervention; they define not merely our explanatory possibilities, but also our ethical and practical horizons." Therefore, making the epistemic and other interests underlying the research questions explicit might help us understand the dynamics of political science as a discipline. Some of these kinds of topics will be discussed in part 3, "Purposes and Uses of Political Science."

Question (d), how to study, asks what is the appropriate method to answer research questions (also taking into account the purposes of researching those specific questions)? There are obviously some links between (b) "what to study" and (d) "how to study." For example, some specialists working with a specific method are driven to apply the method to as many as questions as possible (and select topics to study accordingly), and others have urgent questions but are lacking an appropriate or a well-developed method to answer them and have to rely on unsatisfying existing methods. We think a broad agreement could be found that having a toolkit containing a lot of well-developed methods would be best in order to answer as many questions as possible in the best way possible, but once you get to the details of what that implies, a lot of trade-offs have to be made. This as well as other related topics are discussed in part 2, "Methods in Political Science, Debates, and Reconciliations."

Question (e) concerns who to involve in the study, who participates in the research and how is the community of political science researchers best organized in order to best answer the research questions at hand? When addressing a research question, do you stick to the institutionalized discipline of political science or do you include other disciplines, other social scientists? Are there sharply defined boundaries of the political science discipline, do you involve lay citizens, whose values should be prioritized, how to foster constructive criticism, how to discuss the applications of the research results, and so on? These type of questions, closely related to the field of social epistemology, have received a lot of attention recently and are some of the topics discussed in part 4, "Political Science in Society: Values, Expertise, and Progress."

We believe that a systematic reflection on questions (a) to (e) will help us to understand what is involved in providing successful accounts of political phenomena.

4. THE STRUCTURE OF THE VOLUME

Let us now sketch briefly how this volume contributes to that systematic reflection by giving a short introduction to its different parts.

Part 1: Analyzing Basic Frameworks in Political Science

Part 1 discusses various broad frameworks used in the study of political phenomena. By frameworks we mean things such as perspectives that help organize inquiry by providing categorizations and identifying the main causes to be studied. Frameworks can be all-encompassing, determining vocabulary, theoretical relations, legitimate questions, scientific standards, appropriate methods and so on, or can be as simple as just an unordered list of variables to focus on. The different frameworks represented in this section generally fall somewhere in the middle of this continuum. They identify variables to be studied and potential relations among them. The chapters of Part 1 critically discuss some such frameworks in political science, analyzing their commitments and potential evidence. Sociobiological approaches, explanation via norms and game theory, rational choice, institutional analysis, collective action, and notions of mechanisms are the main topics.

Kaplan (Chapter 2) and Henderson and Schneider (Chapter 3) discuss biological approaches to political behavior. Kaplan, a major contributor to debates in philosophy of biology over genetic explanations (Kaplan 2000), focuses on biological explanations of political attitudes. He sorts out various differences in claims by proponents of "genopolitics" and then relates them to the general problem recognized in biology and philosophy of biology of explaining complex, environmentally dependent traits in genetic terms. Henderson and Schneider likewise consider biological (not necessarily genetic) explanations of political attitudes. They do so by using ideas from the large literature on the role of mechanisms in explanation, largely developed in the philosophy of biology. Surveying a substantial body of political science research focusing on biological and psychological underpinnings of political attitudes, they outline the implicit mechanistic models that are being proposed. The result is a hopefully clearer understanding of the debates and potential explanatory virtues and weaknesses.

Explanations of political phenomena via the behavior of maximizing individuals are the frameworks taken up by Herfeld and Marx (Chapter 4) and Ross, Stirling and Tummolini (Chapter 5). Herfeld and Marx look at a multiple interpretations of rational choice theory in political science and different explanatory purposes it might fill. Assessments of rational choice theory need to in particular consider whether rational choice accounts are supposed to be psychologically realistic theories and whether they are accounts of individual or group behavior. The differences matter. Ross et al. discuss norms from a game theory perspective, particularly a conditional game theory perspective where norms are produced as preferences of individuals that are influenced by their interaction with others. Those preferences need not be strictly self-interested ones and are the traits of networks, not individuals alone. These chapters show how explicitly and rigorously analyzing the characteristics of the agent making rational choices matters greatly and small differences in philosophical anthropology might lead to very different findings in political science.

Frameworks relying on collective and institutional analysis are discussed in Chapter 6 by Aydinonat and Ylikoski and in Chapter 7 by Zamora-Bonilla. Aydinonat and Ylikoski discuss the problem of accounting for endogenous institutional change, looking particularly at broad equilibrium game theory perspectives. Game theory accounts of endogenous change have clear difficulties, and explaining institutional change is in general an open challenge for political science. Zamora-Bonilla continues the section with a historical survey of analytic approaches to collective choice, insightful in grasping how political scientists can conceive of necessarily collective decisions in very different ways as seen from different formal theoretical frameworks.

Thus, Part I moves from frameworks focusing on the most individual factors, namely, genetic makeup and other biological characteristics to increasingly social and collective approaches to political behavior. The general thrust is that all the approaches are partial and at best incomplete, with concrete assessments depending on specific details according to varying contexts. In the closing chapter of Part 1, Bennett and Mishkin (Chapter 8) address the plethora of viable alternative frameworks to explain political phenomena by introducing a taxonomy organizing nineteen kinds of theories about causal mechanisms. Reviewing within-agent, agent-agent, agent-structure, structure-agent, and structure-structure theories on ideas, material power, and institutions, they present the reader with a helpful guide to ensure no sensible alternative explanatory framework is being left out in researching political phenomena.

Part 2: Methods in Political Science, Debates, and Reconciliations

Part 2 considers a variety of issues in political science methodology. There has been an explosion of interesting methodological work in political science in the past two decades. Over the same time, there has been a general convergence in philosophy of science that is both postpositivist and post-Kuhnian, rejecting both simple-minded science as logic assumptions and pictures of science as nothing but rhetorical narratives. The chapters in Part 2 are largely about tying these two trends together in useful ways.

Debates over concept delineation and measurement is part of any methodological debate. Crasnow in Chapter 9 takes up explicating and measuring one of the most fundamental concepts of political science—democracy. She carefully lays out the multiple decisions that have to be made, the role that values seem inevitably to play, and routes to objectivity. Pragmatic validation of measures in terms of robust generalizations is one appealing route.

Zahle in Chapter 10 takes up the project of clarifying the idea of qualitative research in political science. Using ethnography, process tracing, and qualitative comparative analysis as test cases, she identifies four different senses of qualitative research and shows that they do not agree on which of the test cases is or is not qualitative research. This need not be a criticism, but it does suggest that many debates in political science over qualitative versus quantitative research may be misformulated or misguided.

The quantitative versus qualitative debate is also addressed by Lawler and Waldner in Chapter 11, but in the more general form of the interpretivism or positivism debate. They reject traditional notions of "positivism" as outdated and put in its place inferentialism, the idea that a main goal of science, especially political science, is causal inference, not the universal laws of the positivists. Causal inference as now done by political science relies often on "thick" descriptions and multiple interpretation via models; Lawler and Waldner show through several nice empirical examples that interpretivist studies do make causal claims. The positivist–interpretivist divide may not be such a divide after all in current political science research.

The next three chapters in Part 2 are mainly about using mixed evidence, both qualitative and quantitative, case study and large-N. Using the notion of "foliated pluralism" (Ruphy 2011) from philosophy of science, Russo and Rihoux argue in Chapter 12 that Qualitative Comparative Analysis (QCA) goes beyond the qualitative–quantitative divide, provides a successful case of using mixed methods, and provides numerous epistemic benefits in political science research. In Chapter 13, Kuorikoski and Marchionni focus specifically on mixed methods. They first identify three different epistemic virtues (triangulation, integration, and security) that supposedly come from having a variety of evidence and analyze three different mixed methods approaches in political science (nested analysis, set-theoretic multimethod research, and Bayesian approaches), assessing how well they embody the three virtues of evidential variety. They show how to dissolve some worries about incommensurability of evidence sources in political science and identify an ongoing problem from ignoring internal validity questions.

Goertz and Haggard in Chapter 14 look at new developments where case studies are done in large numbers, thus producing what they call large-N qualitative analysis (LNQA). The methodology behind such approaches has not previously be outlined explicitly. Using the famous study by Acemoglu and Robinson (2006) on the economic origins of dictatorship and democracy and two more recent books that employ LNQA, they show how this approach can begin to be fruitfully analyzed and explained using the mechanistic explanation perspective in recent philosophy of science. They give clear ideas about when LNQA might succeed or fail, but conclude much more analysis needs to be done.

The discussions by Clarke and by Dowding in Chapters 15 and 16 drill in on process tracing specifically. Clarke runs through a variety of different elements that get associated with process tracing, but seldom in a fully clear and explicit way. Some proposed criteria for process tracing are too weak, some too restrictive, and others plausible but vacuous. Clarke lays these out with care. Though that taxonomy is progress, Clarke grants that how process tracing is supposed to confirm causal claims without using standard regression assumptions like unit homogeneity remains very much an open question. Dowding likewise argues that process tracing has to be more carefully specified to be assessed. Process tracing evidence is not a competitor to large-N analysis but rather operates at a different level of detail—mechanistic processes. The case studies of process tracing can show that particular mechanisms are operative, but cannot establish generalizations.

Part 2 ends with the most "positivist" trend in political science research—experiments. John discusses experiments in the field in Chapter 17, particularly randomized controlled trials (RCTs), and Hofmeyr and Kincaid discuss lab experiments in political science in Chapter 18. John, a longtime user of RCTs in political science, traces the obvious advantages and the extent of RCTs in political science research. He then looks at criticisms—some old, some new—about the usefulness of RCTs in the social sciences. John argues convincingly on our view that the kinds of problems raised are instances of problems that face all social science evidence, not just RCTs. He grants that there are currently some zealots, now known as *randomistas*, who may overlook the real complexities that face inference from RCTs and in that sense the critics have a point. However, the point should be not to abandon RCTs in political science but instead to be aware of their potential difficulties and address them.

Finally, Hofmeyr and Kincaid look at lab experiments in political science. They provide a taxonomy of kinds of lab experiments in political science and provide a table classifying all the papers in the *Journal of Experimental Political Science* since its inception. Their focus is on political science experiments in what they call the experimental economics tradition that always provide incentivized choices. Hofmeyr and Kincaid then outline in considerable detail the latest best thinking about how economic experiments ought to be done. Experiments involve a number of independent parts, but Hofmeyr and Kincaid point out the resulting holistic nature of testing does not mean those individual parts cannot be given independent evidence. They then assess all the economic type experiments in their table for the extent to which they meet the ideal standards. As in experimental economics itself, there is likely room for improvement in the practice of experimental political science.

Part 3: Purposes and Uses of Political Science

As discussed above, there are many purposes for studying political phenomena. In a general way, one can distinguish, for example, seeking explanation, prediction, understanding, policy advice, critique, and so on. This might be all too obvious an observation, but it is important to scrutinize how it impacts actual political science research. All too often we think in terms of knowledge as ultimately an accurate and complete representation of the topic we want to study, and that we should evaluate knowledge accordingly. However, there seems to be a growing recognition that knowledge (be it models, explanations, etc.) is selected (and evaluated) on its ability to answer questions of interest, on its *adequacy* for purpose, more than merely on *accuracy*, on some overall fit with observational data or conformity with the world. Models are not only representations, but also tools used for particular epistemic and practical purposes, as Parker (2020, 459) writes: "It readily accounts for some prima facie puzzling features of modeling practice, including the fact that modelers sometimes misrepresent a target, even when they could avoid doing so; judicious misrepresentation can promote the achievement of some epistemic and practical aims." Similarly, scientific explanation and understanding bear a relation to both the *world* and to the *explainees* and *understandees* which implies that scientists have to trade-off between accuracy and adequacy (see, for example, Van Bouwel 2009). Clarifying how objects of study in political science are being delineated in light of purposes and uses seems to be a pursuit PoPS can contribute to.

Thus, specific purposes play a role in identifying, selecting, and deselecting (making abstraction of) aspects of the phenomenon that will be investigated. This is nicely illustrated in Chapter 19 on clientelism. Kincaid, Pellicer, and Wegner spell out how different perspectives and definitions of clientelism separate researchers in that area. These differences in perspectives and definitions reflect the underlying diversity of phenomena as well as the different purposes researchers have, which are often linked to specific empirical projects and are context specific. Although the plurality of definitions is often considered a shortcoming that requires a solution, this plurality—picking out different aspects of the phenomenon—is not necessarily contradictory or incompatible, and rather useful for different purposes. The chapter illustrates how applying a philosophy of science perspective might help with explicating the diversity and give structure to the plurality in the study of clientelism. It also urges researchers to become more explicit about their own purposes and how a specific setup of research is linked to a specific aim.

The contextuality and plurality we find in clientelism research—and across political science research more broadly—raises questions about the extent to which the results of specific studies can be extrapolated to other contexts and inform, for instance, policy making. One way in which scientists and philosophers have been addressing this question is by distinguishing between *internal* and *external validity*, where the former refers to the validity of the results of one's own particular experiment or study, while the latter stipulates the extent to which results from one's experiment or study can be generalized to other groups or situations. In Chapter 20, Jiménez-Buedo carefully analyzes the notion of *external validity* in philosophy and political science: first, the historical changes in its use; second, the philosophical issues in relation to the difficulties of extrapolation, in particular, the difficulties of extrapolating the results of RCTs; and, third, some conceptual unclarities and ambiguities surrounding *external validity*, which calls for using the notion cautiously.

Assessing external validity is a challenge, but hard to avoid when making policy claims and giving policy advice; one has to assess the efficacy of a policy intervention. In Chapter 21, Ruzzene studies the interplay between what she calls the policy mechanisms—explicated by *process tracing*—bringing about the outcome of interest, and the context in which the mechanism is situated—explicated by *process embedding*. Context matters in assessing whether the original and target context are equivalent enough for the mechanism to be portable from original to target, for case-based knowledge to be transferable. If they are not equivalent enough, having contextual knowledge might enable us to find effective ways to modify and adapt the policy mechanism to the characteristics of the target setting. This is nicely illustrated with examples of political science research on civil wars.

Political scientist might not only help policy makers by imparting apt interventions, they also might inform policy by making predictions. In Chapter 22, Northcott discusses the difficulty of prediction. In political science, the focus is often on contextual historical work, rather than prediction due to the ubiquity of causal fragility, underdetermination, and noise. If prediction is our purpose, we should expect warranted forward-looking predictions and interventions for policy to be narrow-scope (rather than wide-scope), because they require confirmed causal knowledge (local knowledge might be detailed enough to establish that there are few significant unmodeled causes, that there is sufficient causal stability, and that outcomes are predictable at all in the sense of not being too sensitive to unknowable details).

These philosophical points are brought out by a discussion of Donatella della Porta's work on political violence.

Aspects of causality, prediction, and extrapolation have received a lot of attention in philosophy of science in exploring the best ways for science to inform policy makers. Political scientists may benefit from this philosophy of science literature to articulate the opportunities and limitations of different tools for the attainment of our various goals, trading-off between accuracy and adequacy in light of our purposes and uses.

Part 4: Political Science in Society: Values, Expertise, and Progress

The dynamics of political science research are arguably greatly influenced by its social environment. This might show itself in the selection of research problems and in deciding what is significant or important enough to study according to various groups in society. It might also impact the preference for or "success" of certain theories or methods, for example, the post–World War II development of rational choice theory in the West in a Cold War setting (cf. Amadae 2003). This does not necessarily imply that a preferred theory, like rational choice theory in this case, would not have some inherent epistemic qualities that could explain its success, but it does tell us something about the distribution of attention, i.e., which approaches get more attention (and funding) than others (being ignored) and how that is related to dominant forces in society.

Being more aware of this social embeddedness of political science makes us pay more attention to issues such as who, or what procedure, decides what the important research questions are. Next, taking into account the social dynamics of scientific disciplines also requires scrutiny of the availability of theories and methods; are different approaches getting equal chances to being developed rigorously, being taught to students, or obtain funding? Much of the philosophy of science literature discussing these issues finds its roots in feminism. In chapter 23, Hoard, Hubbard-Mattix, Mazur, and Noll present the epistemological diversity of feminist approaches, with all of them bringing attention to research questions that had been long ignored. The authors deplore the lack of uptake of this rich feminist political science by the nonfeminist world of political science and, sensitive to both the underlying power structures and intersectional biases reified in feminist as well as nonfeminist research, argue for taking feminist approaches in political science more seriously.

The next chapter by Van Bouwel has a similar focus on the epistemic importance of social interaction among different approaches and research communities. Philosophers of science and social epistemologist have shown how the quality of scientific knowledge depends on more than individual genius, pointing to the role social-epistemic processes and conditions play. This work aims to provide directions for the improvement of our collective epistemic practices and institutions, identifying the conditions for optimizing the productivity of science. Along those lines, Van Bouwel reviews different strategies philosophers have developed in order to deal with values in science, while defending strategies that go beyond the individual researcher focusing on social-epistemic practices in Chapter 24. He discusses *transparency*, *representativeness*, and *citizen engagement* as strategies, using examples taken from contemporary political science debates in order to examine how dealing with values plays out in practice. Engaging political scientists to question how best to deal with value influences in science might help us to further develop these strategies as well as the science and values debate in general, which would benefit from more political analysis.

In Chapter 25, Kincaid also scrutinizes debates about values. He argues for tackling value issues as local, contingent, and empirical questions, rather than as a general, grand episte-mological question. Moreover, he shows how many of the debates concerning values and value freedom have been muddled and often involved caricatures, in particular in rela-tion to *positivism*. By carefully considering the critiques of positivism formulated by anti-positivists in political science, he shows how these critiques have little to do with what real *positivists* claimed. Subsequently, he presents a contemporary philosophy of science which avoids these caricatures and illustrates how it can be helpful in political science research.

In Chapter 26, Reiss considers how value judgments are deeply entangled with more purely scientific questions in technical-evaluative decisions—those decisions that do not merely depend on technical considerations concerning causality and efficacy but also on evaluative considerations concerning efficiency, the weighting of costs and benefits, the handling of risk and uncertainty, and the desirability of policy ends. When scientists are being called upon as experts by policy makers to give advice, the advice mostly concerns issues of such a technical-evaluative nature. This raises some questions about the role of sci-entific experts in a democratic society, for example, if expert opinions are given any weight in technical-evaluative decision-making, experts might wield illegitimate power (i.e., they would contribute twice to political outcomes: first, as voters, and second, as advisors, while in a liberal democracy citizens should participate equally in political matters). Furthermore, giving special weight to expert opinions might infringe on the idea of state neutrality in lib-eral democracies. How to address these questions and what should be the exact division of labor between experts and policy makers?

Given the role of value judgments in political science highlighted in the earlier chapters as well as the plurality and contextuality, one might wonder whether there has been, or can be, progress made in political science and, if so, how would we measure that? In Chapter 27, Chernoff addresses these questions by examining the democratic peace debate in International Relations. He lays out key elements of the debate between liberalism and realism over the connection between democracy and peace and progress therein, and, next, considers con-structivist worries that cast doubt on whether there is legitimate progress in political science akin to that in the natural sciences. The chapter seeks to show how some of the constructivist criticisms capture something of real importance, but that a proper perspective on their claims does not necessarily show a divergence with the natural sciences, thereby explicating how pragmatist contextualism deepens researchers' understanding of questions at issue and holds potential for cumulation and approach-to-consensus, what could be a measure for progress.

5.   CONCLUSION

Doing science always implies making philosophical choices and assumptions—ontological, conceptual, methodological, purposive, value-based, and so on. Some of these choices and assumptions are made explicitly and deliberately, others are implicit or unwitting—acquired via education, professional practice, or disciplinary traditions. PoPS might help to explicate, critically examine, challenge, in some cases replace, the choices and assumptions made, in order to avoid doctrinaire positions, reveal competing perspectives, ensure scientific advancement, or, just be aware of how assumptions play a role in evaluating science.

One cannot expect the reflection on these philosophical choices and assumptions in political science research to be the task of the individual scientists alone. Instead, we can create a meeting place where scientific communities critically discuss these issues and philosophers of science contribute to this process engaging with researchers in discussions about the philosophical foundations of their practice, frameworks, methods, purposes, and values. Thus PoPS can help to increase focus, pool expertise, bundle efforts, and bring fresh ideas to questions concerning political science. Social scientists in general should profit from this, for example, for economists, political science is often the place to go when looking for alternatives to the dominant quantitative methods and frameworks in their field.

As the volume will illustrate, some of the PoPS topics have been discussed by political scientists before, but here we have applied a consistent philosophy of science point of view aiming to contribute to political science in (1) the clarification of political science's concepts and frameworks; (2) the critical assessment and systematic comparison of political science's methods; (3) exploring how specific purposes play a role in identifying, selecting, and deselecting aspects of the phenomena investigated as well as the opportunities and limitations this implies for using political science knowledge; (4) analyzing the interactions between political science and society scrutinizing the social dimensions of scientific practice as well as the value judgments present in political science. In short, the volume offers good examples of the direction that we would like to see: philosophically informed scientists and scientifically informed philosophers of science who are prepared to debate with each other on topics that are highly relevant to both.

NOTES

1. That a *Philosophy of Political Science* field is missing was discussed before by Verbeek and McIntyre (2017) and Herfeld (2017). There are, however, some publications that use the label of the field; see, for example, Dowding (2016) and Lock (1987).
2. This is just a pragmatic choice. We do not want to suggest that there is no overlap or cross-fertilization between empirical political science and political theory. There certainly is, but analyzing that would require a second handbook.
3. A major subset of the papers was presented at a workshop around the volume held at Washington State University in 2019. Also, most contributors to the volume have been reviewers on other chapters. So organizing the volume intentionally involved making for interactions between political scientists and philosophers of science.

REFERENCES

Acemoglu, Daron, and James Robinson. 2006. *Economic Origins of Dictatorship and Democracy*. Cambridge: Cambridge University Press.

Amadae, Sonja. 2003. *Rationalizing Capitalist Democracy. The Cold War Origins of Rational Choice Liberalism*. Chicago: University of Chicago Press.

Cox, Robert. 1981. "Social Forces, States and World Orders: Beyond International Relations Theory." *Millennium* x no. 2: 126–155.

Dowding, Keith. 2016. *The Philosophy and Methods of Political Science*. London: Palgrave.

Dryzek, John. 2006. "Revolutions without Enemies: Key Transformations in Political Science." *American Political Science Review* 100, no. 4: 487–492.

Herfeld, Catherine. 2017. "Philosophie der Politikwissenschaft." In *Grundriss Wissenschaftsphilosophie: Die Philosophie der Einzelwissenschaften*, edited by Simon Lohse and Thomas Reydon, 615–650. Hamburg: Felix Meiner Verlag.

Humphreys, Paul, ed. 2016. *The Oxford Handbook of Philosophy of Science*. Oxford: Oxford University Press.

Kaplan, Jonathan. 2000. *The Limits and Lies of Human Genetic Research: Dangers for Social Policy*. London: Routledge.

Lock, Grahame. 1987. *Filosofie van de Politieke Wetenschappen*. Leiden: Martinus Nijhoff.

Parker, Wendy. 2020. "Model Evaluation: An Adequacy-for-Purpose View." *Philosophy of Science* 87, no. 3: 457–477.

Ragin, Charles C. 1987. *The Comparative Method: Moving Beyond Qualitative and Quantitative Strategies*. Oakland, CA: University of California Press.

Ruphy, Stéphanie. 2011. "From Hacking's Plurality of Styles of Scientific Reasoning to "Foliated" Pluralism: A Philosophically Robust Form of Ontologico-Methodological Pluralism." *Philosophy of Science* 78, no. 5: 1212–1222.

Smith, Steve. 1996. "Positivism and Beyond." In *International Theory: Positivism and Beyond*, edited by Steve Smith, Ken Booth, and Marysia Zalewski, 11–44. Cambridge: Cambridge University Press.

Turner, Stephen and Mark Risjord. 2006. *Philosophy of Anthropology and Sociology: A Volume in the Handbook of the Philosophy of Science Series*. Amsterdam, North Holland: Elsevier.

Van Bouwel, Jeroen. 2009. "Understanding in Political Science: The Plurality of Epistemic Interests." In *Scientific Understanding: Philosophical Perspectives*, edited by Henk de Regt, Sabina Leonelli and Kai Eigner, 298–313. Pittsburgh: University of Pittsburgh Press.

Verbeeck, Bruno and Lee McIntyre. 2017. "Why Is There no Philosophy of Political Science?" In *The Routledge Companion to Philosophy of Social Science*, edited by Lee McIntyre and Alexander Rosenberg, 433–447. London: Routledge.

Wallerstein, Immanuel, ed. 1996. *Open the Social Sciences: Report of the Gulbenkian Commission on the Restructuring of the Social Sciences*. Stanford, CA: Stanford University Press.

PART 1

··

ANALYZING BASIC FRAMEWORKS IN POLITICAL SCIENCE

··

PART 1, *Analyzing Basic Frameworks in Political Science*, clarifies and evaluates various broad frameworks used in the study of political phenomena. These frameworks can be understood as lenses/perspectives that help organize inquiry by providing categorizations and identifying the main causes to be studied. Sometimes they are all-encompassing, determining vocabulary, theoretical relations, legitimate questions, scientific standards, appropriate methods, and so on; sometimes they are just an unordered list of variables to focus on. The chapters of Part 1 analyze commitments and potential evidence of sociobiological approaches, explanation via norms and game theory, rational choice approaches, institutional explanations, collective action theories, and notions of mechanisms. The discussion begins with frameworks focusing on lower-level individual factors, such as genetic makeup, other biological characteristics, and rational choice, and then moves to increasingly larger social and collective factors affecting political behavior and organization. The concluding chapter of this part offers a taxonomy of viable alternative frameworks to tackle political phenomena and provides a helpful guide to the reader of the numerous alternative explanatory frameworks available.

CHAPTER 2

···

THE BIOLOGY OF POLITICS: SOME LIMITATIONS AND REASONS FOR CAUTION

···

JONATHAN MICHAEL KAPLAN

I. INTRODUCTION: GENOPOLITICS AND ITS CHALLENGES

···

IN his "Ten Misconceptions Concerning Neurobiology and Politics," John Hibbing issues the following challenge:

> I respect those who question the value of using biological concepts to better understanding political orientations and the political arena. They should continue to speak out. But the quality of the dialogue would be improved if they made clearer the stage at which they fall off the wagon. (2013, 485)

Part of the goal of this chapter is to try to unravel just what the particular "wagon" in question entails, and at what places there are good reasons to abandon it, or at least to follow its path only with real caution. I will first lay out what I take to be the major projects of "genopolitics"—the application of biological research as an attempt to understand variation in political attitudes (including political ideology). I will note the areas where most of the researchers involved in these projects agree and some of the places where their views pull apart. I will then review the places in this project where there are reasonable objections, either to the reliability of the research itself, or to the interpretations of the research, and what implications these objections might have for the project as a whole.

In the end, I want to suggest that while there are some reasons to be skeptical of the reliability of some of the biological and psychological research on which the "genopolitics" project relies, the main reasons for caution involve the fundamental limitations of the more general project of attempting to explain (or otherwise understand) complex human behaviors by reference to low-level biological (including genetic) systems.[1] One aspect of this emerges from recognizing the enormous variation in how particular "political ideologies" play out over space and time, suggesting that the genopolitics project will always be limited to examining variation *within* a limited range of currently extant social and political environments; like many studies that try to tie variations in complex behaviors to lower-level phenomena, while finding associations to within-population variation may be of some value, if it comes at the cost of ignoring between-population differences, it likely misses the places where most of the variation in fact lies, and hence where radical change is possible.[2] Another of these serious limitations emerges from the realization that human behavior genetics, for all its successes, has itself been forced to grapple with the disappointing conclusion that while it is relatively easy to find (weak) associations between particular genetic markers and complex human behaviors, elucidating the pathways between these in ways that would be helpful to generating real understanding is likely impossible. The project of illuminating our political landscape by reference to our genes runs up on the rocks of the complexity of the pathways between genes and complex human behaviors. This complexity poses not merely a methodological problem, but a likely insurmountable conceptual barrier in all but the very simplest cases (which do not include anything about political ideology).

II. The "Genopolitics" Project(s)

Two of the main proponents of "genopolitics"—Hibbing and Jost—would likely reject the title "genopolitics," arguing that the name reduces the project to linking genetic variation to political ideology, and that this is only a very small part of the project of understanding variation in political ideology by reference to variation in biological systems at work at a variety of levels. Nevertheless, the name seems to have stuck; readers should keep in mind, however, that the project is broader than that name might suggest. In its most general form, "genopolitics" makes the following claims:

(1) Political ideology is heritable—variation in the political ideology held within a particular population is associated with genetic variation in that population. [In some published work, particular links to individual genes supposedly associated with nontrivial proportions of the variation are proposed as well.]

(2) Variation in political ideology in the social realm can, in part, be explained by (or is at least associated with) people's different biologically mediated responses to certain kinds of stimuli (e.g., conservatives are on average more sensitive to disgust, have a higher level of negativity bias, lower levels of novelty seeking, etc.).

(3) In conjunction with the developmental environment encountered, differences in genetic endowments produce differences in neurobiology that (at least partially) explain the above differences in biologically mediated responses to certain sorts of stimuli.

(4) These (different) dispositions in (2) are the products of adaptive evolution, and were fitness-enhancing during some significant—relevant period of human evolution (the two main hypotheses are balancing selection for the presence of both in a population, or periods of directional selection for one or the other).

In its earliest incarnations, the focus of genopolitics was explicitly on the first claim— that political ideology is heritable—and on the fourth claim that there was adaptive (evolutionary) significance to this fact. For example, two of the earlier papers on these topics were Alford and Hibbing's (2004) "The Origin of Politics: An Evolutionary Theory of Political Behavior," and Alford, Funk, and Hibbing's (2005) "Are Political Orientations Genetically Transmitted?" The latter paper is generally credited with bringing genopolitics into the mainstream, and is focused almost entirely on heritability estimates for a variety of "political attitudes" (responses to survey questions about issues that social conservatives and social liberals tended to disagree about when the surveys were conducted), and the discussion of some candidate genes. But the importance of this paper to the project cannot really be understood outside of the context of their 2004 paper, which posits that humans evolved to be "wary cooperators" and that there was adaptive significance to traits like "conservativism."

In later work, Hibbing distances his project from the focus on heritability and on genes more generally. In "Ten Misconceptions Concerning Neurobiology and Politics," the first misconception addressed is "Biology Is Genetics" (2013, 476); Hibbing stresses that in his view, the important point is that there are biological correlates to political ideology, and not the precise etiology of those biological correlates. A biological correlate could be interesting, and explanatory of differences in political ideology, he argues, without itself being genetically mediated in any important or interesting sense. Without the focus on genes, however, the evolutionary accounts are unlikely to be compelling; the research groups associated with John Jost and Peter Hatemi, for example, both focus on evolutionary accounts in their later research, and need something to link those accounts to contemporary differences in biologically mediated responses to stimuli. If the biological differences are not linked in important ways to genetic differences, it is hard to see how any traditional account of those biological differences being produced by natural selection could be explanatory. While cultural evolution, and extended inheritance more generally (e.g., Fuentes 2016), might provide an in-principle way out of this problem, it seems clear that the kind of fitness-enhancing natural selection that these groups are appealing to is meant to have changes in gene frequencies mediated by selection at their base.

The aforementioned interpretation of the genopolitics project is also the interpretation used in popularizations of the account. Such popularizations have appeared in articles in such places as *The Atlantic, The Washington Post, Forbes, The New York Times, Mother Jones, Psychology Today*, and many others. In its popular form, the focus tends to be on the link between genes and political ideology, with articles claiming, for example, that "Your Genes Tell You How to Vote" (Mooney 2013) or that "people's political beliefs are predetermined at birth" (Judis 2014). But many of these articles tie the genopolitics project into the increased polarization of US politics; Avi Tuschman, for example, provides a story in terms of increased assertive mating leading to an increasingly polarized population (2014), and Sebastian Junger (2019) takes the genopolitics project as explaining why societies need both liberals and conservatives to thrive.

Linking the genopolitics project to contemporary concerns about polarization is not, however, limited to popularizers. In their 2005 piece, Alford, Funk, and Hibbing suggested that

> recognizing that our political antagonists probably have a different genetic predisposition to people, life, human nature, and politics may serve to ease frustrations and, eventually, to improve communications across the chasm. . . . As loathe as contextualists and absolutists are to admit it, the presence of the other orientation may make a society stronger. (166)

While this is not a central tenant of the genopolitics project, that it continues to be brought up suggests that it at least forms some part of the appeal.

To return to Hibbing's challenge, then, what are the weaknesses in genopolitics project as described? In the following sections, I will summarize what I take to be some of the key weaknesses of these steps in the genopolitics project. Finally, I will reflect briefly on the limitations inherent in the project more generally, focusing on the ways in which its explanatory project misses some of the most important variation in the political landscape.

III. POLITICAL IDEOLOGY AND PSYCHOLOGY: PEOPLE'S POLITICAL IDEOLOGY IS ASSOCIATED WITH OTHER (NONIDEOLOGICAL) PSYCHOLOGICAL TRAITS (THAT ARE THEMSELVES THE PRODUCT OF BIOLOGICALLY MEDIATED RESPONSES TO CERTAIN KINDS OF STIMULI)

The first step on the "genopolitics" path is one that it shares with those researchers working on the relationship between moral psychology and political science, namely, an attempt to link people's political ideologies to psychological traits not directly related to political ideology per se. The two most common findings for proponents of genopolitics to cite are that conservatives are more sensitive to disgust—to disgusting stimuli—and that conservatives have a higher level of "negativity bias" (and/or especially sensitivity to perceived threats; see, e.g., Jost 2017; Hibbing, Smith, and Alford 2014; and Schreiber et al. 2013; etc.). These psychological tendencies, it is argued, might seem broadly "apolitical" but in fact are closely associated with traits that are more straightforwardly ideological in a political sense, such as generally favoring traditions as a guide to social conduct, having a preference for authoritarianism in social organizations, tending to fear or dislike nongroup members and to favor harsher punishments for rule-breakers, and shying away from compromise as solutions to social problems.

Jonathan Haidt is perhaps the most famous researcher associated with these projects, and his 2001 paper with Mathew Hersh, "Sexual Morality: The Cultures and Emotions of Conservatives and Liberals," is a clear predecessor of genopolitics' attention to disgust sensitivity as a predictor of political ideology. But in that paper, Haidt and Hersh use the "culture wars" to frame the issue, and explicitly treat peoples' affective reactions to situations as at least in part products of the cultures in which they were brought up; note, for example, that they bring up the differences in disgust sensitivity (as well as what participants find disgusting) between Brazilians and Americans, as well as between Brazilians with relatively lower versus relatively higher socioeconomic status (Haidt and Hersh 2001, 193–194). While Haidt and his colleagues take disgust itself to be at least in part a product of adaptive evolution (pathogen avoidance), they also stress the aspects of it that they think are best explained via cultural and not (only) biological evolution (see, e.g., Rozin and Haidt 2013).

Some of the issues other researchers have raised with the genopolitics program start at this level. The first issue is whether "political ideologies" form the right kind of coherent phenotype that it makes sense to explain in these terms. Another is whether sensitivity to disgust (say) or a negativity bias can be explanatory in cases where whether or not something is perceived as disgusting, or whether it is seen as a threat, varies based on socially contingent factors. Both these concerns are in key ways about the locality of explanations, and whether explanations that don't generalize outside of the relatively narrow contexts in which they were developed should be seen as satisfying in the political sciences.

In the case of negativity bias and disgust, one criticism of the genopolitics program is precisely that there is often no way, outside of the very particular social and political context in which it occurs, to determine if something will be perceived by conservatives (say) as threatening or disgusting. With respect to negativity bias and threats, as Charney notes "the same state of affairs" can be seen as either negative or positive, depending both on the social context and one's ideological leanings (2014, 311). In the US context, for conservatives, limiting women's access to reproductive health care, and especially to abortion, is often framed as a positive, whereas for liberals it is a serious threat; conversely, expanded access to abortion services and birth control is often seen by conservatives as a threat, whereas to liberals it would generally be viewed as positive (Charney 2014, 311). In general, one often needs to know where one stands on an issue to know whether a particular change is a threat or not, and where one stands is often precisely the question at issue with a "left/right" split.

With respect to disgust, we can see both synchronic and diachronic differences in people's responses that are socially conditioned. For the first, it is instructive to look at an attempt by Rozin, Haidt, and others to check their "paper and pencil" disgust scale against behavioral measures (see Rozin et al. 1999). In these tests, after taking the pencil and paper test that they had developed and been using, participants were asked if they were willing to handle disgusting objects in increasingly intimate ways. Here, in analyzing their data, Rozin et al. removed the participant response to handling Nazi memorabilia from the test, as whether a participant self-identified as Jewish made an enormous difference to how willing they were to handle the object (which Rozin et al. was using as a proxy measure for being disgusted; 1999, 340). While it is possible that ideologically conservative participants who self-identified as Jewish would have reacted more strongly to the Nazi memorabilia than those who were ideologically liberal, the "Jewish/non-Jewish" axis is clearly doing much of the work here, and if the population were taken as a whole, how disgusting one found the objects would be a poor predictor of one's political ideology (but a better predictor of whether or not one self-identified as Jewish).

Thinking about changes over time, the enormous change in attitudes toward same-sex marriage (and "gay rights" more generally) is instructive. As late as 2004, around 60% of Americans were opposed to same-sex marriage, and only 30% supported it; by 2018, the numbers had flipped, with around 60% supporting it, and only 30% opposed (Pew Research Center 2019). What accounted for this dramatic flip? While support for gay rights is heritable, and has a genetic component (see Alford, Funk, and Hibbing 2005), any claim that involved changing allele frequencies in the population would be silly, as would any claims that involved changes in what fraction of people in the population were more or less sensitive to disgust in general. Rather, research suggests that many people in the United States that *used to* find the thought of homosexual sex disgusting, and hence opposed same-sex marriage, no longer do. It may be the case that conservatives are, on average, more sensitive to disgust (perhaps in the moral realm) than are liberals, but in order to explain conservative opposition to same-sex marriage, one needs to explain why (some) conservatives found, through the early 2000s, homosexuality "disgusting," and to explain why far fewer conservatives today are so opposed, one needs to explain why they at some point *stopped* finding it disgusting. Curiously, the second question is easier to answer than the first. Researchers attribute the change in attitude in part to the "normalization" of gay relationships in the media, and to more people having friends, family members, and acquaintances who self-identified as homosexual (see, e.g., Lee and Mutz 2019); other researchers point toward for example the rise of internet porn use, which was prospectively associated with increased tolerance for homosexuals (especially among men; Write and Randall 2014).[3]

The issue of "ideological phenotypes" is similarly contentious. Proponents of genopolitics argue that the basic outlines of "conservative" and "liberal" thought are more or less universal—that in every society, there will be some people who generally favor traditions as a guide to social conduct, tend toward authoritarianism, fear or dislike of nongroup members, favor harsher punishments for rule-breakers, and shy away from compromise as solutions to social problems, and others who generally lean the other way on these "bedrock" issues (see Smith et al. 2011, 381). The exact details will of course vary—at some point in French history, say, the mid-eighteenth century, "conservatives" on this scheme might have supported the monarchy, and "liberals" might have been for limiting its power, whereas explicit support of a monarchy in the United States has traditionally been very limited. But people in society will vary along those lines, and preferences for those positions will tend to align in similar ways. Other researchers argue that this way of conceptualizing ideology is of limited value.

One might for example question the ways in which different elements of political ideology "hang together" or fail to. In this chapter, I have deliberately focused on genopolitics as it relates to ideology in the so-called *cultural* (or "social") dimension, rather than the fiscal dimension. One reason for not tackling both is that the positions that in the United States "hang together" as social, cultural, and fiscal conservatism do not go together in all, or even most, other cultures (see Malka et al. 2014; Malka et al. 2017; Federico and Malka 2018). Malka et al. note that "valuing conformity, security, and tradition over self-direction and stimulation" is predictive of cultural conservatism, but (weakly) predictive of (what would in the US context be) "left-wing economic attitudes" (2014, 1031); Malka et al. (2017) extends this work and concludes that "it is more common for culturally and economically right-wing attitudes to correlate *negatively* with each other" (1, emphasis in original). So presumably "the same" psychological tendencies that lead to one set of ideological attitudes in one culture may lead to different ones in different cultures! While there are no doubt explanations for the differences (the particulars of present or recent past modes of social organization, etc.), these will not have anything to do with differences in genetic endowments.

Finally, it is worth noting that while there have been a number of studies linking these psychological tendencies to political ideology, and meta-analyses of some of the basic results suggest that they are reasonably robust, other aspects of this research have not been as successfully replicated. So some articles in genopolitics stress "subthreshold" effects—for example, that people exposed to disgusting stimuli will tend to answer surveys in a more conservative way than those who are exposed to pleasant or neutral stimuli (Hibbing,

Smith, and Alford 2014, 299); however, replication attempts (see, e.g., Ghelfi et al. 2018) and systematic literature reviews of this phenomena (see, e.g., Landy and Goodwin 2015) have found little or no evidence for its existence, though as always, others argue that the systematic reviews and replication attempts missed key elements and that the evidence for the effect is stronger than those analyses would suggest (see, e.g., Schnall et al. 2015). Other studies have failed to successfully replicate some of Haidt's basic work on moral foundations theory, on which this aspect of the genopolitics project rests (see, e.g., Frimer 2019). In the end, the basic result that in the contemporary US context, conservatives are for example on average more sensitive to disgust, have a higher level of negativity bias, and are more sensitive to perceived threats, is probably sound. But many of the related studies, especially those that have not had successful robust replication attempts, should be regarded with some skepticism.

IV. NEUROBIOLOGY AND ENDOPHENOTYPES: MECHANISM AND BIOLOGICAL RESPONSE

The primary neurobiological associations that genopolitics proponents rely on are related to the limbic system; a key claim is that the amygdala is larger and more active in conservatives, and that the insula and anterior cingulate cortex are larger and more active in liberals, and that these differences in part explain the differences in the more basic psychological traits that are associated with conservative and liberal ideologies (e.g., the claim that the more active amygdala is what determines heightened sensitivity to threats and disgust; see, e.g., Kanai et al. 2011; Jost et al. 2014; Hibbing, Smith, and Alford 2014; Nam et al. 2018; etc.).

On the one hand, the idea that systematic differences in, for example, reactivity would be associated with systematic differences in brains is not surprising; insofar as our brains are the source of our behaviors, differences in the latter must be reflected in differences in the former (though this trite observation does not guarantee the kinds of systematic differences that are at issue here). On the other hand, this part of the program is perhaps the most problematic from the point of view of the reliability of the research, and the gap between its aspirations and our current technical abilities.

While some of the key findings have not been subject to attempts to replicate, those that have been so subjected have not fared well, and in general, attempts to link general behavioral patterns to differences in neurobiology (activation or gray-matter size) as revealed by fMRI and similar techniques have proven to be particularly susceptible to replication problems. So for example, Masouleh et al. (2019) conclude that most apparently successful attempts to link differences in psychological phenotypes to variations in brain structure will fail to replicate in independent samples, and most of those that do will have initially significantly overestimated effect sizes. Boekel et al. 2015 attempted to replicate a number of studies, including several of the studies associated with Kanai (whose work on political orientation, moral values, and empathy is often cited by proponents of genopolitics); most of the reported effects could not be successfully replicated, and in many cases the evidence generated spoke actively against the effects initially reported. While Boekel et al. 2015 has been criticized sharply for being underpowered (see, e.g., Muhlert et al. 2016), as well as for some methodological decisions (see, e.g., Kanai 2016), the fact remains that many apparent clear successes linking particular differences in fMRI responses and/or brain volumes to specific psychological traits have proven harder to replicate than proponents have wanted to admit.

More generally, researchers like Littvay (2011) argue that attempts to tie political ideology to genetics via psychological and neurophysiological mechanisms are perhaps premature, with one major gap obvious at the level of neurophysiology. To successfully tie neurophysiology to ideology, Littvay suggests, requires that we identify the "endophenotypes" that link the high-level behavior in which we are interested to lower levels:

> Endophenotypes can be thought of as the decomposition of behavioral symptoms into more stable causes with clearer physiological and genetic foundations. It can also be thought of as steps backwards in the physiological pathway that begins with the protein coding of gene expression that, through the complex neurological pathway, manifests itself as behavior. (Littvay 2011, 109–110)

Littvay notes that "unfortunately, we are doing very poorly when we try to explain political behavior through these physiological mechanisms" (2011, 211). The mechanisms we do find, Littvay notes, are associated with at most a tiny fraction of the variation in the trait that we had hoped to explain. As we will see below, heritability estimates of "political ideology" are reasonably high (as they are for almost all complex behaviors); but if the neurological mechanisms we find are associated with only a tiny fraction of that, we are clearly missing something. Littvay expresses some hope that the matter might be conceptual—we might merely need to better operationalize some of the key associations, so that we are studying whatever the lower-level psychological traits clearly tied to neurophysiological differences are, that are actually doing the work. But nearly a decade of research since then has failed to meaningfully move the needle on finding traits that have these sorts of relationships.

Finally, there is the so-called "chicken or egg" problem; Jost, Noorbaloochi, and Bavel (2014) argue that we are currently unable to establish whether differences in neurobiology *cause* differences in ideological stances, or are themselves *caused by* the adoption of different ideological stances. Jost et al. (2014) suggest that the most likely pattern is a kind of feedback loop, where a person's inherent tendency towards being more reactive to fear (say) results in their selecting media and other environmental influences that reinforce that tendency, and increases their reactivity (Jost, Noorbaloochi, and Bavel 2014; Jost et al. 2014).

The possibility that there is actively created covariation between biologically mediated preferences and environments that encourage and reinforce those tendencies is a serious one, and, as the next section on heritability makes clear, it underwrites one of the common objections to treating estimates of the heritability of human behaviors as measuring the extent to which differences in genetic endowments cause differences in phenotypic outcomes. Where what would otherwise be minor differences in preferences, abilities, or tendencies are systematically sorted (including self-sorting) into very different environments, very large differences in outcomes can be the result. But in these cases, the claim that it is the genetic differences that are driving the differences in outcome can seem, from some critical perspectives, at best strained.

V. "Everything Is Heritable": Genopolitics and Human Behavior Genetics

The paper usually credited with bringing genopolitics into the mainstream, Alford, Funk, and Hibbing's (2005) "Are Political Orientations Genetically Transmitted?," was concerned almost entirely with the heritability of positions associated with political ideologies, and with finding genes associated with those same ideological positions. They cite research finding nonzero heritability for basically all the items surveyed, including attitude to school prayer, "gay rights," divorce, and a host of others. Much of the surprise evinced by these results, however, seems odd in light of Eric Turkheimer's (2000) classic paper, "Three Laws of Behavior Genetics and What They Mean." The first law of behavior genetics, as Turkheimer puts it, is that "all human behavioral traits are heritable" (2000, 160). While this "law" isn't *quite* universal, it very nearly is. Indeed, the basic idea, that the vast majority of human behavioral traits that are measurable and that vary within particular populations have a substantial heritable component, had already been treated as a well-established fact in the human behavior genetics community long before Turkheimer named it. By 2005, when Alford, Funk, and Hibbing were writing, only someone very much unaware of the results of contemporary behavior genetics would have been willing to bet *against* finding substantial heritability for almost any behavioral trait or behavior-based outcome that one can identify within a particular population!

But while most human behavior genetics researchers accept the first law of behavior genetics, some have not fully internalized the problematic implications of this result. If *everything* is heritable, then something's being heritable tells us rather less than we might have suspected. It is true that performance on IQ tests is heritable, as is susceptibility to most mental illnesses, but then, so is TV-watching behavior, and one's chances of getting divorced (see, e.g., Johnson et al. 2009). *That* something is heritable tell us little about what role genetic differences actual play in the production of the different traits, and little (indeed, more or less nothing) about how malleable the trait in question is, either at the individual or the population level.

Heritability is a technical concept—it is, strictly speaking, the proportion of the variance in the trait in question that is associated with genetic variation, in that population, at that time. Most heritability estimates in the literature are generated by comparing how similar *monozygotic* ("identical") twins are to each other to how similar *dizygotic* (nonidentical but same-sex) twins are. Under the assumption that same-sex dizygotic twins experience a developmental environment that is relevantly similar to the development environment shared by monozygotic twins, the heritability of the trait in question can be calculated straightforwardly (see Box 2.1). But note well that the question of whether or not a trait is heritable *simpliciter* is nonsensical—all one can ever say is that this particular trait is heritable (or not) in this particular population, with this particular distribution of genotypes, into this particular range of developmental environments. Change any of these and the heritability of the trait in question can (and often does) change as well (see Box 2.2).

It is unsurprising that political ideology is heritable, but *that* it is heritable tells us little about it. One of the hopes of human behavior genetics had been that the heritability of traits would be found to be the result of a relatively small number of genes with reasonably sized

Box 2.1   Heritability

A trait is heritable if offspring resemble their parents with respect to that trait more than they resemble the population at large. Technically, heritability is the proportion of the variance of the trait in that population that is associated with genetic variation in that population. In its simplest conceptual form, it is derived from the following analysis of variance:

$$V_P = V_G + V_E$$

The variance of the phenotype (V_P) is equal to the variance associated with the genetic differences (V_G), and the variance associated with environmental differences (V_E).
Heritability is then:

$$h = V_G / V_P$$

This is *broad-sense* heritability, as it includes all effects attributable to genetic differences, however they are realized. *Narrow-sense* heritability, on the other hand, includes only the effects of those genetic differences that contribute to the variance in an additive fashion (V_A). This excludes interactions between genes and other genes (if you include both dominance effects here as well as epistatic interactions; otherwise, these should be broken out further), interactions between genes and the developmental environment, and the covariance of genes with environments. The more complete analysis of variance accounting for these different factors, then, is

$$V_P = V_A + V_{GxG} + V_{GxE} + V_{COV(G,E)} + V_E$$

When heritability is calculated with twin studies, the assumption is made that monozygotic (identical) twins and dizygotic twins share the same familial environment, but differ in that monozygotic twins share all their genes, and dizygotic only half. Heritability, then, can be calculated by comparing the similarity of monozygotic to that of dizygotic twins; insofar as monozygotic twins are more similar to each other than are dizygotic twins, heritability is higher. On the ACE model, the outcome for each twin is assumed to be due to additive genetic factors (A), the environment that they share by virtue of sharing a family environment (C), and the environment that is not shared within a family (E); on this model, heritability can be calculated as twice the difference between the similarity of the monozygotic and dizygotic twins.

There are a number of issues that can raised about the reliability of these estimates, and in particular the assumption that gene-gene interactions, gene-environment interactions, and the covariance between genes and environments are of negligible importance is certainly dubious. Nevertheless, while twin-based studies may systematical over-estimate heritability (see, e.g., Feldman and Ramachandran 2018), it seems likely that most of the traits identified as having a significant heritable component really do so.

Readers interested in more of the technical details and philosophical implications might start with the Stanford Encyclopedia of Philosophy's recently updated entry on "Heritability" (Downes and Matthews 2020), which provides an excellent overview.

effects—so if a trait was say 50 percent heritable (as most human behavioral traits are, more or less), we'd find, say, a few dozen genes with reasonable effect sizes (say, each was associated with between one and a few percent of the total variation), which together accounted for some significant portion of the total heritability. Alas, this proved not to be the case; complex human behavioral traits (and indeed, even many seemingly simple physical traits) turned out to be massively polygenic (influenced by many many genes), and the effect sizes of individual genes associated with variations in the trait turned out to be minuscule.[4]

Box 2.2 Heritability, Causation, and Malleability

That a trait is heritable provides little information about how genes influence the development of the trait, and little information about how malleable the trait might be. As Lewontin noted forcefully in his famous "The Analysis of Variance and the Analysis of Causes" (1974), heritability is not a measure of how "genetic" a trait is, nor even the extent to which differences in genes cause differences in phenotypic outcomes, at least if we understand "cause" here in more or less ordinary ways.

One of the key ways in which heritability estimates in humans are likely misleading if understood to be about genetic causation (in some ordinary sense) is the likelihood that development is very often a matter of genetic and environment covarying in important ways. So consider the following example, based on one by James Flynn (2012). Someone who likes playing basketball, and starts out relatively good at it compared to their peers, is much more likely to practice basketball, engage in specialized training to become better at basketball, and hence become an excellent basketball player, than is someone is who does not enjoy the game, and who starts out showing little promise. But if we ask *why* the first player ends up so much better than the second—what made the first player such a superior player—surely the right answer is that it is *mostly* the practice and the training in which they, but not the second player, engaged. Nevertheless, a heritability estimate generated from looking at twins, say, would simply note how much more likely it is that monozygotic twins end up with similar levels of basketball ability than it is that dizygotic twins end up with similar levels of ability. *If*, as seems very likely, monozygotic twins are somewhat more likely to both show similar levels of interest, and similar early promise, because they share identical genetic backgrounds, then they will be that much more likely to practice similar amounts, get the same levels of training, and so forth. And those similarities will show up as genetic in a heritability study—the different genetic backgrounds result in a (rough) sorting into different environments, and while it is the different environments that do most of the work producing the key differences in phenotypes that we measure, heritability estimates will "fold" any work that environments do that systematically covary with genetic variation into the variance associated with that genetic variation, and hence into the heritability estimate.

More generally, that a trait is highly heritable in one set of environments says nothing about how sensitive that trait is other developmental environments. Even if height is almost entirely heritable within one developmental environment (as it is in say contemporary rich western societies), in a different developmental environment (say, one with significantly poorer nutrition), realized height could be very different indeed; despite the high heritability of height *within* populations, women in south Korea gained over 20cm (about 8″) over the last 100 years (see NCD-RisC 2016), while the population remained genetically very similar.

So while genome-wide association studies on traits like political ideology find "hits"— regions where particular genetic markers are associated with variation in the trait in the question—even putting all the hits together, very little of the variation is accounted for. While part of this may be blamed on the strict statistical standards adopted to avoid the risk that most "hits" will be false positives, even when these standards are relaxed and all associations, no matter how weak, are used to create "polygenic scores," these scores are associated with far less of the variance than heritability estimates would suggest. This gap can no longer be blamed on underpowered studies; while ever-larger studies (the largest GWAS studies now use over one million genomes) have found more markers associated with the traits in question, and raised the proportion of the variance associated with all the identifiable genetic variation somewhat, more of the heritability remains unassociated with this variation than with it. This is the so-called "missing heritability problem" (see Matthews and Turkheimer 2019)—while there are a number of proposed solutions, none of them has gained widespread support in the behavior genetics community.

These issues with heritability and gene-finding are relevant to the question of where one might wish to be cautious in supporting the genopolitics project in at least several ways. The first is obvious—*that* political ideology and related traits is heritable is not a surprising finding, nor does it imply anything in particular about how "genetic" political ideology is, nor anything much about how malleable it might be. The other is perhaps less so, and has to do with the proposed pathways. The basic idea was supposed to be that the heritability of political ideology would be associated with genes that influenced the development of basic neurobiological systems, and that differences in these systems than influenced basic psychological—physiological responses, and that these then led to one rather than another set of political—ideological views being adopted. But those proposed pathways have proven impossible to untangle, and each link in it is very weak—so despite the relatively high heritability of political ideology on the social dimension, very few genes can be found, and very little of the heritability can be successfully associated with genetic markers. And while we have found some genes, the way in which these might influence the development of the kinds of neurobiological systems (systems whose variation might influence the right sorts of psychological traits) remains more or less entirely opaque. And even assuming, rather optimistically, that at least some of the neurobiological studies turn out to be reliably replicable, these will, again, account for, at most, a small portion of the differences in basic psychological responses that, it is argued, drive people to adopt different ideological stances. Rather than tracing the causal pathway backward onto ever more basic ground, each step losses information, and seems particularly weak. And note that, by the first law of behavior genetics, we can be confident that while political ideology is heritable, so too will be sensitivity to disgust, and negativity bias. If sensitivity to disgust is associated with political ideology, then any genes that are associated with the former will be with the latter. And should, for example, amygdala activity level prove to be in fact associated with sensitivity to disgust, there is no doubt that it, too, will be heritable. And so on.

In any end, the "gene" element might be the weakest part of genopolitics. That conservative resistance to marriage equality is driven partly by disgust is an interesting finding; that both of these are heritable is not, and that with sufficiently massive samples, GWAS can find genetic markers that are associated with these traits is also of at most very limited interest. The claim that at some point, by studying the role that different alleles play in development, we will be able to understand the differences in tendencies to engage in particular kinds of complex behaviors, is looking increasingly implausible.

VI. EVOLUTION AND ADAPTATION: STORY-TELLING AND EVIDENCE

The last step in the genopolitics project is exploring the adaptive significance of the traits in question; in particular, some of the key supporters propose that there has been active selection for maintaining variation in the ideological stances themselves. For example, Alford, Funk, and Hibbing write that

> The exciting next step is to understand the reason such distinct orientations have evolved and lasted. . . . The benefits of genetic variation are most easily observed in the ability of differential immune systems to prevent a group of organisms from being completely wiped out by a single pathogen, but it is easy to imagine how sociopolitical variation could also create more viable groups. In fact, computer simulations give support to the hypothesis that divergent individual-level social behaviors, such as cooperation and defection, are beneficial at the group level (Hammond 2000). As loathe as contextualists and absolutists are to admit it, the presence of the other orientation may make a society stronger. (2005, 166)

Obviously, the supporters are not claiming that there was balancing selection during our evolutionary history to maintain a mix of people who, for example, support expanded access to medical insurance and those to oppose such an expansion, or those who support reproductive rights for women and those who oppose such rights. Rather, the idea is *either* that there had at some point been balancing selection for those more basic psychological traits (e.g., disgust sensitivity and threat sensitivity), or for a mix of individuals who supported some more basic elements of social organization rather than the other (authoritarianism versus less hierarchical organizations, etc.).

For the first interpretation, that selection worked on the more basic psychological traits, there might have been balancing selection to favor a particular mix of individuals who are relatively more sensitive and relatively less sensitive to disgust, or a mix of individuals who are relatively more inclined to perceive threats and downsides, and those who were relatively less so-inclined. The idea, apparently, is that having some people who are particularly sensitive to perceived threats (and disgust) is important for pointing out potential dangers; having others who are much less sensitive to those and more inclined toward novelty seeking is important for pointing toward potential important improvements. That people with these different adaptive psychological tendencies systematically prefer different modes of social organization would be, on this view, a mere side-effect—these tendencies were selected *for* their roles in avoiding disaster and discovering new opportunities. But given the availability of different modes of social organization, people with one set of tendencies ended up tending to prefer one rather than the other. Insofar as one thought, for example, that the range of options for social organization throughout much of human history was perhaps relatively limited, this model might seem particularly appealing.

On the second interpretation, on the other hand, selection *of* the different psychological traits would have been in service of selection *for* the different political ideologies themselves, where these are understood as a preference for particular kinds of social organization. That there was a selective advantage to having a mix of people within a society who prefer stronger leaders, the maintenance of tradition, feared outsiders, and so forth, and those who were inclined in the other direction on these issues, was on this view the reason that these traits were all maintained by balancing selection during human evolution, and the psychological traits that point in these directions were (merely) the mechanisms by which these traits were realized.

However, testing such adaptive hypotheses in humans is difficult or impossible—as Jost, Sapolsky, and Nam (2018) note, the kinds of rigorous tests of claims regarding the evolutionary etiology of traits used to evaluate such hypotheses are "typically not available to evolutionary social psychologists" (4). Part of the problem is that testing adaptive hypotheses on humans more generally presents special difficulties; many of the ways in which evidence for the adaptive significance of a trait is established are either impossible for ethical (as well as practical reasons), or unavailable because of the relatively lack of closely related species in which particular selective pressures are either shared or not. But as Jost, Sapolsky, and Nam note, hypotheses about the adaptive significance of human behaviors are especially difficult to test, as the evolution of behaviors usually does not leave the kinds of traces that the evolution of physical traits sometimes leave (2018, 4). The existence of people who vary in how sensitive they are to disgust, and the heritability of disgust, may be an example of balancing selection (or group selection of some sort). But it might also be mere "noise" around the basic evolved response of disgust for pathogen avoidance; the development, within a particular social and cultural context, of the complex behavioral repertoires involved in disgust, might simply be relatively poorly canalized. For someone living in a traditional hunter–gatherer society, it might not matter very much whether their disgust response was relatively more or less sensitive, as long it fell within a certain acceptable range (within a range that for example didn't get them killed particularly more often by consuming putrid food, nor resulted in their suffering from malnutrition due to being an overly picky eater). In both cases, disgust sensitivity would vary, and be heritable. We have, unfortunately, no one way of knowing which story is right.

VII. FINAL THOUGHTS: POLITICAL POLARIZATION AND GENOPOLITICS

One element present in both popular accounts of genopolitics, and in the writings of the researchers themselves, is that genopolitics might help us to understand some of the roots of political polarization, and help defuse or reduce the intensity of political polarization. To return to the Alford, Funk, and Hibbing (2005) article, recall that they end by noting that "recognizing that our political antagonists probably have a different genetic predisposition to people, life, human nature, and politics may serve to ease frustrations and, eventually, to improve communications across the chasm" (156). And this line is picked up and repeated by popular accounts; Junger (2019), writing for *The Washington Post*, claims that

> the real threat to the country, of course, is bellicose, divisive rhetoric. But this is where evolution might throw Americans a lifeline. . . . If liberalism and conservatism are partly rooted in genetics, then those worldviews had to have been adaptive—and necessary—in our evolutionary past. That means that neither political party can accuse the other of being illegitimate or inherently immoral; we are the way we are for good reason.

While these claims are not, on one interpretation, part of the genopolitics project strictly speaking, the way in which they go wrong is illustrative of one of genopolitics most serious weaknesses, namely, its failure to take seriously the locality of its particular results.

As Charney (2014) suggests, what counts as liberal or conservative would seem to vary widely with the details of the political circumstances; Charney notes that the definitions given by Hibbing, Smith, and Alford (2014) can be evoked to describe particular movements as "liberal" or "conservative" where other, more conventional understandings of those same movements would put them in the other category (310). But more generally, the idea that the heritability of a trait could tell us anything about the moral status of different versions of the trait is misguided in the extreme.

Recall the first law of behavior genetics: everything is heritable. The authors suggest that recognizing that support of right- or left-leaning policies in the United States is heritable might make us more understanding of people that hold the other view, and reveals that those views have some legitimacy (perhaps because they are products of evolution). But of course, the ubiquity of heritability implies that support for massively illegitimate, for actually *evil*, regimes must also have been heritable. The Nazis, famously, did not slaughter six million Jews without the support of a significant portion of the German population, but non-Jewish Germans were not universal in their support, or degree of support, for genocidal policies. And based on what we know about the behavior genetics, anyone who would bet against a tendency to support the Nazi regime being heritable would be making a very foolish bet indeed. What does the fact that support of the Nazi regime was heritable imply about its legitimacy? Surely the answer must be "nothing at all." Similarly, if support for the Khmer Rouge did not have a heritable component, it would a very rare trait indeed. But the most serious problems facing Cambodia during the rise of the Khmer Rouge, were not one of "increasingly bellicose rhetoric" but rather one of a political movement actively planning to commit genocide. I hope that it is obvious that whether or not the tendency to support a particular genocidal regime is associated with an increased sensitivity to disgust, or with increased novelty seeking, matters not a whit to the moral status of such support.

It may be the case that there is some dimension of preference for ways of organizing social life on which there is systematic variation in most societies, and where this variation usually falls out along an axis that we would recognize as ranging between "conservative" and "liberal." But even if that is true, this says little about what kinds of social organization are possible. In societies that have instituted extensive paid leave for new parents after the birth or adoption of a child, the arguments may be about how women and men should divide the paid time off, and whether using state policy to try to make childbirth and care less economically disadvantageous for women is an appropriate goal (see, e.g., Yle Uutiset 2019, reporting on proposed changes in Finland's policy that would aim to promote gender equality, as well as the well-being of the children). In another society, the arguments may be about whether it is legitimate to attempt to discourage refugees by forcefully separating children from their parents, and then systematically denying those children access to basic human needs (Dickerson 2019; BBC News 2019; UN News 2019). That in both cases there is a "conservative" and a "liberal" position tells us nothing about how understanding we should be of someone who takes the other side in a political argument, and nothing about the moral legitimacy of "the other side," the heritability of political ideology notwithstanding.

Whatever other successes genopolitics has, it is unlikely to be helpful at reducing polarization, or increasingly cross-ideological understanding. Whether or not a particular political agenda is legitimate, or morally reprehensible, depends on the details of the agenda, and not on the heritability of the traits that lead to some people being more likely to sign onto that agenda than are others. Nor can the genopolitics project help us understand why some options are available within a particular society rather than others—why in some societies there are debates about how much and why to increase social support for new parents, and in others, about the legitimacy of separating refugee children from their parents, and denying them access to basic human needs. Insofar as part of the project of political science is to understand why some political positions are available within particular societies at particular times, and how the range of political possibilities expands or contracts, genopolitics will likely be of little help.

ACKNOWLEDGMENTS

Drafts of this work were presented at the *Philosophy and Methodology of Political Science Workshop* at Washington State University in September 2019, and at a talk to the University of Utah's Philosophy Department in February 2020, and I thank the participants for their thoughtful questions and criticisms. In addition, I benefited from conservations with David Henderson, who also provided important feedback on drafts, as did Jeroen van Bouwel, and Melinda Bonnie Fagan, who I thank as well.

NOTES

1. For an overview of some of these techniques and their limitations for explaining complex human behaviors, see Longino (2014).
2. There is an important similarity here to Rose's classic distinction in epidemiology between the "causes of cases" and the "causes of incidence"—while both are important, as Rose notes, the largest gains in population-level health outcomes tend to come work modifying the risk factors associated with the latter, rather than the former (Rose 2001).
3. While the researchers involved did not explore this issue in any detail, a likely pathway here would seem to be a desensitization of (male) conservatives' disgust response to anal sex with increased exposure to internet pornography.
4. Note that another weakness of the empirical research on which the genopolitics project has often relied is precisely the fondness for early articles to cite research suggesting the existence of single genes with apparently sizeable effects, effects that we now have good reason to think don't exist. For example, Alford, Funk, and Hibbing (2005) devote an entire section of their paper to the 5-HTT region, which at the time was thought to be associated with a variety of personality traits and psychiatric conditions. But more recent meta-analyses have revealed that essentially all of those associations were spurious, and that most of the studies were so grossly underpowered that they had essentially no chance of finding true positives in any event (see Border et al. 2019); while not all the purported associations cited by Alford, Funk, and Hibbing were included in this analysis, the chances seem very good that *any* purported associations between complex behaviors and particular genes or genetic regions based on research done before the age of massive (at least tens of thousands, and preferably hundreds of thousands, of individuals) GWAS are also spurious.

REFERENCES

Alford, John R., and John R. Hibbing. 2004. "The Origin of Politics: An Evolutionary Theory of Political Behavior." *Perspectives on Politics* 2, no. 4: 707–723.

Alford, John R., Carolyn L. Funk, and John R. Hibbing. 2005. "Are Political Orientations Genetically Transmitted?" *American Political Science Review* 99, no. 2: 153–167.

BBC News (no byline) 2019. "Migrant Children in the US: The Bigger Picture Explained." Accessed January 4, 2020. https://www.bbc.com/news/world-us-canada-44532437.

Boekel, Wouter, Eric-Jan Wagenmakers, Luam Belay, Josine Verhagen, Scott Brown, and Birte U. Forstmann. 2015. "A Purely Confirmatory Replication Study of Structural Brain-Behavior Correlations." *Cortex* 66: 115–133.

Border, Richard, Emma C. Johnson, Luke M. Evans, Andrew Smolen, Noah Berley, Patrick F. Sullivan, and Matthew C. Keller. 2019. "No Support for Historical Candidate Gene or Candidate Gene-By-Interaction Hypotheses for Major Depression Across Multiple Large Samples." *American Journal of Psychiatry* 176, no. 5: 376–387.

Charney, Evan. 2014. "Conservatives, Liberals, and 'The Negative.'" *Behavioral and Brain Sciences* 37, no. 3: 310–311.

Dickerson, Caitlin. 2019. "'There Is a Stench': Soiled Clothes and No Baths for Migrant Children at a Texas Center." *The New York Times*. Accessed January 4, 2020. https://www.nytimes.com/2019/06/21/us/migrant-children-border-soap.html.

Downes, Stephen M. and Matthews, Lucas. 2020. "Heritability," In *The Stanford Encyclopedia of Philosophy* (Spring 2020 Edition), Edward N. Zalta (ed.). Standford, CA: Metaphysics Research Lab, Stanford University. Accessed June 6, 2020. https://plato.stanford.edu/archives/spr2020/entries/heredity/.

Federico, Christopher M., and Ariel Malka. 2018. "The Contingent, Contextual Nature of the Relationship Between Needs for Security and Certainty and Political Preferences: Evidence and Implications." *Political Psychology* 39: 3–48.

Feldman, Marcus W., and Sohini Ramachandran. 2018. "Missing Compared to What? Revisiting Heritability, Genes and Culture." *Philosophical Transactions of the Royal Society B: Biological Sciences* 373, no. 1743: 20170064.

Flynn, James, Micahel F. Shaughnessy, and Susan W. Fulgham. 2012. "An Interview with Jim Flynn about the Flynn Effect." *North American Journal of Psychology* 14, no. 1: 24–38.

Frimer, Jeremy A. 2019. "Do Liberals and Conservatives Use Different Moral Languages? Two Replications and Six Extensions of Graham, Haidt, and Nosek's (2009) Moral Text Analysis." *Journal of Research in Personality* 84: 103906.

Fuentes, Agustin. 2016. "The Extended Evolutionary Synthesis, Ethnography, and the Human Niche: Toward an Integrated Anthropology." *Current Anthropology* 57, no. S13: S13–S26.

Ghelfi, Eric, Cody D. Christopherson, Heather L. Urry, Richie L. Lenne, Nicole Legate, Mary Ann Fischer, Fieke MA Wagemans et al. 2018. "Reexamining the Effect of Gustatory Disgust on Moral Judgment: A Multi-Lab Direct Replication of Eskine, Kacinik, and Prinz (2011)." *Advances in Methods and Practices in Psychological Science* 3, no. 1: 3–32.

Haidt, Jonathan, and Matthew A. Hersh. 2001. "Sexual Morality: The Cultures and Emotions of Conservatives and Liberals." *Journal of Applied Social Psychology* 31, no. 1: 191–221.

Hammond, Ross. 2000. *Endogenous transition dynamics in corruption: An agent-based computer model*. Washington (DC): Center on Social and Economic Dynamics.

Hibbing, John R. 2013. "Ten Misconceptions Concerning Neurobiology and Politics." *Perspectives on Politics* 11, no. 2: 475–489.

Hibbing, John R., Kevin B. Smith, and John R. Alford. 2014. "Differences in Negativity Bias Underlie Variations in Political Ideology." *Behavioral and Brain Sciences* 37, no. 3: 297–350.

Johnson, Wendy, Eric Turkheimer, Irving I. Gottesman, and Thomas J. Bouchard Jr. 2009. "Beyond Heritability: Twin Studies in Behavioral Research." *Current Directions in Psychological Science* 18, no. 4: 217–220.

Jost, John T. 2017. "Ideological Asymmetries and the Essence of Political Psychology." *Political Psychology* 38, no. 2: 167–208.

Jost, John T., H. Hannah Nam, David M. Amodio, and Jay J. Van Bavel. 2014. "Political Neuroscience: The Beginning of a Beautiful Friendship." *Political Psychology* 35: 3–42.

Jost, John T., Sharareh Noorbaloochi, and Jay J. Van Bavel. 2014. "The "Chicken-and-Egg" Problem in Political Neuroscience." *Behavioral and Brain Sciences* 37, no. 3: 317–318.

Jost, John T., Robert M. Sapolsky, and H. Hannah Nam. 2018. "Speculations on the evolutionary origins of system justification." *Evolutionary Psychology* 16, no. 2: 1474704918765342.

Judis, John B. 2014. "Are Political Beliefs Predetermined at Birth? A Weird New Social Science Tries to Explain our Polarized Politics." *The New Republic*. Accessed November 10, 2019. https://newrepublic.com/article/119794/genopolitics-social-science-and-origin-political-beliefs.

Junger, Sebastian. 2019. "Our Politics Are in Our DNA. That's a Good Thing." *The Washington Post*. Accessed November 10, 2019. https://www.washingtonpost.com/opinions/our-polit ics-are-in-our-dna-thats-a-good-thing/2019/07/05/c4d8579e-984d-11e9-830a-21b9b36b64a d_story.html?fbclid=IwAR1cJvc3blDXl96K9w_NEkJaL1XR40Dn2V3A8kl5IOOXH9gx 03ZvCRNyj2g&noredirect=on.

Kanai, Ryota, Tom Feilden, Colin Firth, and Geraint Rees. 2011. "Political Orientations Are Correlated with Brain Structure in Young Adults." *Current Biology* 21, no. 8: 677–680.

Kanai, Ryota. 2016. "Open Questions in Conducting Confirmatory Replication Studies: Commentary on Boekel et al., 2015." *Cortex: A Journal Devoted to the Study of the Nervous System and Behavior* 74: 343–347.

Landy, Justin F., and Geoffrey P. Goodwin. 2015. "Does Incidental Disgust Amplify Moral Judgment? A Meta-Analytic Review of Experimental Evidence." *Perspectives on Psychological Science* 10, no. 4: 518–536.

Lee, Hye-Yon and Diana C. Mutz. 2019. "Changing Attitudes Toward Same-Sex Marriage: A Three-Wave Panel Study." *Political Behavior* 41: 701–722.

Lewontin, Richard C. 1974. "The Analysis of Variance and the Analysis of Causes." *American Journal of Human Genetics* 26, no. 3: 400–411.

Littvay, Levente. 2011. "Measuring Social and Political Phenotypes." In *Biology and Politics: The Cutting Edge*, edited by Steven A. Peterson and Albert Somit, 97–114. Bingley: Emerald.

Longino, Helen E. 2014. *Studying Human Behavior: How Scientists Investigate Aggression and Sexuality*. Chicago: University of Chicago Press.

Malka, Ariel, Christopher J. Soto, Michael Inzlicht, and Yphtach Lelkes. 2014. "Do Needs for Security and Certainty Predict Cultural and Economic Conservatism? A Cross-National Analysis." *Journal of Personality and Social Psychology* 106, no. 6: 1031.

Malka, Ariel, Yphtach Lelkes, and Christopher J. Soto. 2017. "Are Cultural and Economic Conservatism Positively Correlated? A Large-Scale Cross-National Test." *British Journal of Political Science* 49, no. 3: 1045–1069.

Masouleh, Shahrzad Kharabian, Simon B. Eickhoff, Felix Hoffstaedter, Sarah Genon, and Alzheimer's Disease Neuroimaging Initiative. 2019. "Empirical Examination of the Replicability of Associations between Brain Structure and Psychological Variables." *eLife* 8: e43464.

Matthews, Lucas J., and Eric Turkheimer. 2019. "Across the Great Divide: Pluralism and the Hunt for Missing Heritability." *Synthese* 198 no. 3: 2297–2311.

Mooney, Chris. 2013. "Your Genes Tell How to Vote." *Mother Jones*. Accessed November 10, 2019. https://www.motherjones.com/politics/2013/12/genetics-twins-politics-religion/.

Muhlert, Nils, and Gerard R. Ridgway. 2016. "Failed Replications, Contributing Factors and Careful Interpretations: Commentary on "A Purely Confirmatory Replication Study of Structural Brain-Behaviour Correlations" by Boekel et al., 2015." *Cortex* 74: 338.

Nam, H. Hannah, John T. Jost, Lisa Kaggen, Daniel Campbell-Meiklejohn, and Jay J. Van Bavel. 2018. "Amygdala Structure and the Tendency to Regard the Social System as Legitimate and Desirable." *Nature Human Behaviour* 2, no. 2: 133.

NCD Risk Factor Collaboration (NCD-RisC). 2016. "A Century of Trends in Adult Human Height." *eLife*, 5, no. e13410. doi:10.7554/eLife.13410.

Pew Research Center. 2019. "Attitudes on Same-Sex Marriage." Accessed December 16, 2019. https://www.pewforum.org/fact-sheet/changing-attitudes-on-gay-marriage/.

Rose, Geoffrey. 2001. "Sick Individuals and Sick Populations." *International Journal of Epidemiology* 30, no. 3: 427–432.

Rozin, Paul, and Jonathan Haidt. 2013. "The Domains of Disgust and Their Origins: Contrasting Biological and Cultural Evolutionary Accounts." *Trends in Cognitive Sciences* 17, no. 8: 367–368.

Rozin, Paul, Jonathan Haidt, Clark McCauley, Lance Dunlop, and Michelle Ashmore. 1999. "Individual Differences in Disgust Sensitivity: Comparisons and Evaluations of Paper-and-Pencil Versus Behavioral Measures." *Journal of Research in Personality* 33, no. 3: 330–351.

Schnall, Simone, Jonathan Haidt, Gerald L. Clore, and Alexander H. Jordan. 2015. "Landy and Goodwin Confirmed Most of Our Findings Then Drew the Wrong Conclusions." *Perspectives on Psychological Science*, 10, no. 4: 537–538.

Schreiber, Darren, Greg Fonzo, Alan N. Simmons, Christopher T. Dawes, Taru Flagan, James H. Fowler, and Martin P. Paulus. 2013. "Red Brain, Blue Brain: Evaluative Processes Differ in Democrats and Republicans." *PLoS one* 8, no. 2: e52970.

Smith, Kevin B., Douglas R. Oxley, Matthew V. Hibbing, John R. Alford, and John R. Hibbing. 2011. "Linking Genetics and Political Attitudes: Reconceptualizing Political Ideology." *Political Psychology* 32, no. 3: 369–397.

Turkheimer, Eric. 2000. "Three Laws of Behavior Genetics and What They Mean." *Current Directions in Psychological Science* 9, no. 5: 160–164.

Tuschman, Avi. 2014. "Why Americans Are So Polarized: Education and Evolution." *The Atlantic*. Accessed November 10, 2019. https://www.theatlantic.com/politics/archive/2014/02/why-americans-are-so-polarized-education-and-evolution/284098/.

Wright, Paul J. and Ashley K. Randall. 2014. "Pornography Consumption, Education, and Support for Same-Sex Marriage Among Adult U.S. Males." *Communication Research* 41, no. 5: 665–689.

UN News (no byline). 2019. "UN Rights Chief 'Appalled' by US Border Detention Conditions, Says Holding Migrant Children May Violate International Law." Accessed January 4, 2020. https://news.un.org/en/story/2019/07/1041991.

Yle Uutiset (no byline). 2020. "Finland's Parental Leave Reform Proposal to Promote Gender Equality." January 4, 2020. https://yle.fi/uutiset/osasto/news/finlands_parental_leave_reform_proposal_to_promote_gender_equality/10828028.

CHAPTER 3

....

THE BIOLOGICAL ASPECTS
OF POLITICAL ATTITUDES

....

DAVID HENDERSON AND STEPHEN SCHNEIDER

TOPIC

....

SEVERAL sets of investigators have recently undertaken projects exploring how biological differences and closely related psychological tendencies may give rise to differing political and social orientations. One finds a flowering of work on the matter in recent political science and closely related fields. We discuss some central recent work and, drawing on a framework from the philosophy of biology, suggest a general philosophical perspective on this work.

APPROACH

....

We draw on the philosophical framework developed in the work of philosophers such as Bechtel and Richardson (1993), Craver and Darden (2013), Darden (2007), and Machamer et al. (2000) who have focused on mechanistic explanation in biology (and fields such as psychology, cognitive science, and related special sciences). Mechanisms, in the sense we are concerned with here, "are entities and activities organized such that they are productive of regular changes from start or set-up to finish or termination conditions" (Craver and Darden 2013: 15). Recent work seeking to understand biological aspects of the formation of political/social attitudes can be understood as early steps in a project of mechanistic understanding—one that has some encouraging empirical results to its credit. Craver and Darden's (2013) account of mechanistic investigation and explanation highlights the interrelated tasks that investigators pursue in identifying and understanding a mechanism. Investigators begin by characterizing a phenomenon to be understood (but, of course, as work then proceeds, they may need to refine this characterization in empirically informed ways). Subsequent developments may be understood as a matter of sketching and refining schema characterizing the mechanism that makes for the phenomena of interest.

Mechanism schemata serve to represent the entities, their organization, and their activities, in order to account for the regularity that is the phenomenon. In progressively sketching a schema, one draws on emerging empirical information and a range of background understandings of related mechanisms. Repeatedly, one seeks to evaluate the schema as sketched (and its alternatives) and one searches for empirically constrained ways of refining schemata. The phenomena may be more or less precisely characterized at any one point, and typically would be susceptable to more precise characterizaton as inquiry proceeds. One's understanding of a mechanism may be more or less sketchy—and the project is one of making it progressively less sketchy, yielding a series of more empirically powerful sketches. In the early going, the entities and activities comprised in a mechanism may be only roughly understood—and treated as functional black boxes (or dark gray boxes). If investigators are barking up what is ultimately the right schematic tree, more satisfying understanding will come as one replaces black boxes with "gray boxes," and ultimately "glass boxes"—as one comes to possess a detailed understanding of the working of the modules in their sketch. Commonly, an understanding of these modules of the mechanism will turn on ideas and results developed by multiple disciplines—so that an understanding of the mechanism and the phenomena to which it gives rise involves theorizing that has a rich interfield character.

In drawing on the mechanistic model of explanation we are not thinking of it as a model of a kind of explanation that is distinct from explanations involving counterfactual supporting generalizations. The motivation of those developing the mechanistic model of explanation may have included the concern to get away from endless debates about what makes a generalization a "law." But one can, we think, escape that debate in other ways. As urged by Woodward (2000), one can sit aside talk of laws, and characterize the kind of more or less invariant generalizations that seem common in much explanatory practice in the sciences. Compatibly with this, one can reflect on the kinds of explanatory understanding of systems that is afforded by mechanistic models such as those discussed by Craver and Darden (2013). Invariant generalizations are found throughout such models. Generalizations with a fitting degree of invariance characterize what Craver and Darden would term the "activities" of the entities in a mechanistic model.

We should also caution against an overreading of talk of a *mechanistic* model. The kind of mechanistic explanation that is envisioned here does not require that everything be traced at the level of basic physics—it is not mechanistic in that sense. Machamer et al. (2000: 17, 22) argue that mechanism schema count as complete insofar as their account of entities and their activities "bottom out" in a class of causal relationships with few remaining anomalies. That is to say that what counts as an acceptable bottom level for purposes of a discipline or domain will turn on where one does not need to proceed to yet more fundamental levels in order to resolve troubling anomalies. For example, biochemists generally do not need to push beyond chemistry to take up the most fundamental physics. (Again, one is reminded of Woodward's [2000] account of causation in terms of acceptable invariance in a domain.) The work by political scientists (and political psychologists, and fellow travelers) discussed here suggest that an adequate understanding of how people in a population form their political stances out of the ideas and models that they encounter will need to come to terms with the effects of heritable biological variation within such populations—variation, for example, in the excitability of structures within the amygdala and insula. The question then becomes, once these processes conditioned by these variations are studied, what anomalies will remain, and which will call for boxes of different kinds.

The above characterizes the explanatory understanding sought in pursuing a mechanistic account, and one should hasten to add that one's understanding should be multiply empirically constrained and informed.

A CRUDE CHARACTERIZATION OF THE
PHENOMENA OF INTEREST

Twin studies suggest that dispositions regarding political orientations concerning a number of important issue domains show a significant heritability (Alford et al. 2005; Block and Block 2006; Hatemi 2013; Oskarsson et al. 2014). However, as argued in Kaplan (2000), heritability is a statistical measure that leaves one with daunting issues regarding what it reveals beyond the correlation involving variance in the relevant phenotypes, genetic features, and environmental features within the population from which the sample is drawn. As Kaplan (2000, 38) notes, as a general matter, "knowing the heritability of a trait within a population will not permit you to make predictions about what will happen if changes occur in either the environment, the genetic distributions, or the way that the population is distributed with respect to the environment." In effect one cannot thereby answer the sorts of why questions or what-if-things-had-been-different questions that are associated with causal knowledge. Twin studies commonly have more specific sources of uncertainty. One should not, for example, understand the results in the twin studies as probative regarding whether variations in political stances were to be explained partly in terms of genetic similarities and differences as opposed to very early environmental similarities and differences—most do not begin to discriminate between the variation in genes and the associated variation in gestational environment (shared by monozygotic twins)[1]. For multiple reasons, then, one should be careful not to overread the heritability found in the twin studies. It is at most a prompt for investigation concerning what biological factors—perhaps genetic, perhaps in gestational environment—give rise to intermediate cognitive or conative tendencies that interact with the environment to give rise to the correlated political differences. Might there be biologically rooted dispositions—likely heritable in the way that complex traits are heritable—that would incline differing agents to develop or adopt corresponding ranges of political preferences—selecting, as it were, from the social-political ideas on offer in agents' environments?

Work by Hibbing, Smith, Alford, and their collaborators provide evidence indicating that specific physiological/psychological tendencies that vary across individuals are correlated with political orientations.[2] They suggest that certain physiological differences within populations may make for differential responsiveness to classes of cues—with the result that important features of those agents' social and political environment have differing affective salience for different agents. Agents who differ on these physiological dimensions experience their social and political environments differently and are thereby led to construct or adopt differing social and political understandings or orientations. These physiological differences, their correlations with political preferences, and their causal consequences might be studied in ways that do not necessitate resolving the above qualms about the significance of heritability—and doing so would perhaps help to understand what lies behind those heritability results. The stability and hierarchy concerns that are characteristic of political conservatism seems particularly in focus in the writings of some researchers—and here threat sensitivity associated with changes to the status quo come into focus. Other lines of research indicate that political stances also are impacted by reactions that might be broadly understood as sensitive to contamination or impurity—and here a role for disgust responses also comes into focus. For many purposes, one will not need to proceed to decompose these modules into modules at yet lower levels—chemical or ultimately physical. Such decomposition can be added when it matters, of course. (It is worth noting that the causal role envisioned just now for physiological and related psychological factors does not require that one thinks that these things are themselves determined by genetic as opposed to embryonic or such early developmental factors; see for example, Hibbing [2013, 476–478].)

We thus have empirical reason to begin to characterize a phenomenon and to sketch the mechanism at play. The phenomenon very crudely characterized is the formation by agents of social-political preferences or stances in response to their social settings. Of course, differences in agents' "trajectories" through their social world—the differing "circles they run in," and differences in the ideas espoused by those nearest to them in various respects—certainly are significant. But, as just noted, there may be biological parameters the values of which condition the differential attractiveness of certain ideas to various agents. As a result, given a roughly parallel trajectory, agents alike with respect to such biological parameters would tend to be more alike with respect to their social-political attitudes or preferences than would agents relatively unlike in these biological parameters. Finally, the evidence assembled by Hibbing, Smith, Alford and others suggests at least some of the significant biological bases are those making for differently strong affective responses: the reactivity of structures such as the amygdala and the insula. This suggests a preliminary characterization of the phenomena of interest as in Figure 3.1.

So, the phenomenon of interest in much of this work is one that takes as input culturally encountered models and practices (together with what justification is commonly encountered in connection with these) and yields as output political preferences or stances. Further, as indicated already, there seems to be a significant intermediate module: agents' various affective responses—aversions or attractions—to various practices and various envisioned outcomes. The evidence from twin studies suggests that there is some early onset biological variation making for variation in these affective responses. Differences in

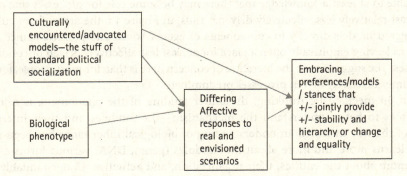

FIGURE 3.1. A preliminary characterization of the phenomena

such responses is hypothesized to be highly significant in the cognitive/conative processes by which agents come to form and maintain their social-political stances. Note also that the model as represented in Figure 3.1 does not commit to the claim that all social factors giving rise to agents' political preference work by way of cognitive processing turning on affective responses. The model only posits affective responses as featuring in an important causal route or set of routes. To reflect this, we have included an arrow in Figure 3.1 to acknowledge that perhaps some of the operative cognitive processes might include those that do not turn on an affective component. For example, it seems plausible that a given agent might arrive at some generalization concerning the surrounding society (one that counts as, or constrains, an element in that agent's political stance), and that the agent might do so by way of cognitive processes that were not paradigmatically affectively driven. The agent might be an investigator using careful sampling and statistical methods, and who is thereby led to the generalization in question. The model as here represented posits an important place for affectively driven or conditioned cognitive processes, while leaving open some place for less affectively motivated cognition. Here it seems worthwhile to distinguish two matters: (a) whether all social-political concepts come to be "affectively loaded" so that occurrent judgments featuring those concepts automatically elicit an affective response, and (b) whether all formation of beliefs about matters formulated in affectively loaded conceptual terms need be arise out of processes that are significantly responsive to the affective loading. While work such as Lodge and Taber (2005) speak more directly to the first issue, they may be commonly taken to support conclusions about the second. The model being sketched here indicates that automatic affective responses makes for a powerful background motivated resistance to arguments with affectively dissonant conclusions—and might forestall or delay the acceptance of a conclusion, or inhibit attention to conflicting information. Such affective headwinds and tailwinds might make a significant difference in what arises out of the composite cognitive processes in play in individuals. One might also note that motivations can vary across cases or contexts within a given agent's biography. Thus, Druckman (2012; see also Kunda 1990) suggests that, in cases and contexts, agents can be moved by a kind of "accuracy motivation," rather than more paradigmatically "affective motivations." When this obtains, there would presumably be less of a tendency for certain forms of affective bias. (Here again, one is reminded of two-system ideas familiar from cognitive psychology (see, for example, Kahneman and Frederick 2005). While positing an important place for affectively driven processes in the formation of political stances, it seems reasonable to at least acknowledge that there may be some role for processes that are not, or at least relatively less, affectively driven.[3] Thus, in Figure 3.1, the arrow from culturally encountered models directly to components of agents' social and political stances, is intended as leaving empirically open a place for at least less affectively driven or conditioned processes. The suggestion in the literature of concern here is that, for most people, for much of the time, affectively driven processes predominate.

Often, in mechanistic thinking, the understanding of the phenomena is refined as one comes to better understand the mechanism—the modules and their interaction. Think of the way in which an understanding of biological inheritance has been refined as one learns more and more about the modules (genes, DNA, various forms of RNA, etc.)—more about the entities, their organization, and activities. Understandably, given our initial crude characterization of the phenomena of interest (in Figure 3.1), work has concentrated on refining this sketch of the mechanism—developing reasonable and empirically suggested hypotheses concerning the biological character of the heritable phenotypes, how these give rise to different ranges of affective responses, and how these make for a tendency for individuals to embrace different social/political preferences and stances. The political study of biological aspects of the development of political attitudes have commonly sought to refine our understanding of this phenomena by developing an empirically refined sketch of the mechanism—one affording a more fine-grained model of the mechanism at work.

Some Development

We now focus on largely complementary lines of development found in the work of two sets of investigators.

Hibbing, Smith, and Alford provide evidence indicating that specific physiological/psychological tendencies that vary across individuals are correlated with political orientations. They argue that some physiological factors vary across agents within populations, making for differential responsiveness to classes of cues—with the result that important features of those agents' social and political environment have different affective salience for different agents. Agents differing on these physiological dimensions experience their social and political environments differently and are led to construct or embrace differing social and political understandings or orientations:

> The logic for our approach is straightforward. Life is about encounters: sights, sounds, smells, imaginings, objects, and people. These encounters are indisputably physiological and psychological because the systems employed to sense, process, formulate, and execute a response to stimuli are psychological and physiological. Equally indisputable is the existence of individual-level variation in these physiological and psychological mechanisms. Even if a stimulus is identical, one individual will sense, process, and respond to it differently than another. (Hibbing et al. 2014a, 298–299)

The idea is that agents' differing political orientations are rooted in more or less automatic cognitive and conative reactions. Various measures indicate that liberals and conservatives tend to differ in their physiological responsiveness to stimuli that are generally understood to be aversive—conservatives react more strongly to a range of stimuli that are generally evaluated as threatening or disgusting (including stimuli that are not generally understood to be of a political nature; Smith et al. 2011). Standard psychological measures of attention show that their attention is drawn to and captured by aversive stimuli more than is the attention of liberals:

> Thus, it is reasonable to hypothesize that individuals who are physiologically and psychologically responsive to negative stimuli will tend to endorse public policies that minimize tangible threats by giving prominence to past, traditional solutions, by limiting human discretion, . . . by being protective, by promoting in-groups relative to out-groups, and by embracing strong, unifying policies and authority figures. (Hibbing et al. 2014a: 304)

That is, the issue orientations characteristic of conservatives are those to which their physiological/psychological characteristics (as a statistical matter) would reasonably incline them:

In sum, we posit that, due in all likelihood to a combination of genetic, early developmental, and later environmental factors, people's physiological and deep psychological responses to negative life situations vary widely. These variations, in turn, encourage but certainly do not mandate particular social tendencies and, more to the point of this article, particular political beliefs. Both degree of negativity bias and political dispositions obviously can change over the course of a lifetime but both change rather grudgingly and stability is more common than wild fluctuation. (Hibbing et al. 2014a: 304)

Of course, it should not be news to any scientifically alive contemporary that biological systems are at work in political agents. Of course, biological processes are in play conditioning and even realizing all agents' psychological responses—these biopsychological processes make a difference for agents' cognitive and conative processes, and all social and political preferences and stances are realized in agents' physiological states. We all recognize in a general way the dependencies of political and social matters on the choices of various distributed, situated, interacting agents, and the dependencies of agents' choices on their psychological responses to their social and nonsocial world, and the dependencies of agents' psychological responses on the activity of their biological (neurological and physiological) systems, and the dependencies of such on organized chemical processes. All this is of a piece with standing contemporary understandings of the pervasive dependencies between features at various levels of organization in the complex systems making up our political, social, psychological, biological, chemical, and ultimately physical world. Such generalities are not the advertised news in the biological political science discussed here.

Hibbing, Smith, and Alford's point is more focused. There seem to be significant systematic differences across agents in the workings of several psycho-biological systems. Thus, there are differences in the respective strengths of approach-mediating and the avoidance-mediating components of agents' limbic system and resulting activity in their sympathetic nervous systems—and there are differences in the class of environmental matters to which such systems are responsive. As a general matter, all human agents tend to respond more strongly to aversive stimuli than to attractive stimuli. But, there are differences across agents in the degree to which physiological/psychological responses to aversive stimuli tend to be more pronounced than the responses to attracting stimuli. Such differences in the relative strengths of avoidance and attraction responses, such degrees of physiological and psychological responsiveness have now been shown to be correlated with differences in social and political preferences and stances. Those with stronger avoidance reactions tend to have more conservative social-political preferences, practices, and affiliations—and the correlation is strongest in the case of social issues rather than economic issues (Hibbing et al. 2014a: 305–306, 37–41).

Doubtless, in the course of an individual agent's life, that agent learns to perceive threat or defilement in certain things in contrast to other things. But, this is different from being systematically more attentive and responsive to threats or to disgusting things. The first is a matter of a shaping of the agent's innate threat or disgust reactions—a matter of the agent's sympathetic nervous system coming to be responsive to particular classes of things. The second is a matter of the differences across agents in the relative strength of (or general reactivity of) their individual biological attraction and avoidance systems. It is said that "some people are more attuned to potential threats, more sensitive to sources of contagion, and more desirous of in-group protection" (Hibbing et al. 2014a: 303). Humans generally show some cognitive negativity bias—that is, a range of common cognitive processes, commonly those termed heuristics, are more responsive to the possibility of aversive outcomes than to attractive outcomes. This may be the result of some degree of selective attention, or to something on the order of framing effects. Whatever the specific cognitive processes in play, they commonly have the result of being more responsive to losses or cost. Term this apparent overweighting a negativity bias. Now, such a bias in one's cognitive processes—a general negativity bias in agents' cognitive processes—would seem to interact with differences in agents' affective responses. There would then be a stronger negativity bias (a greater effective bias) on the part of those with generally stronger aversive affective responses. So, the differences in dispositions to aversive affective responses posited here would make for a difference in the strength of agents' negativity biases. This, the different degrees of negativity bias—and not merely differences in particulars found to be aversive—is correlated with, or varies with, conservatism/liberalism.

Such differences in the strength of agents' aversive affective responses are a function of deep biological differences, rooted in differences in the sensitivity of the approach and avoidance components of the limbic system and sympathetic nervous system. Such differences tend to arise early in development—prior to any significant political socialization—and to be stable across lifetimes (presumably absent special cases of prolonged strong stress or trauma). The suggestion then is that agents with relatively strong biologically rooted negativity biases are causally inclined to formulate or embrace political ideologies that promise more protection with respect to ranges of aversive (threatening and/or disgusting) phenomena (Hibbing et al. 2014b: 334–336). Socialization would plausibly also play a role—as it presents agents with already formulated alternatives for social and political life that may seem to the differing agents to be more or less satisfactory in view of their underlying responsiveness to aversive phenomena. But, it is said, the biological/psychological bases just indicated are central to a deep causal dynamic accounting for the tendency of agents to form or adopt political orientations commonly classified as conservative or liberal.

On this account, there is a strong causal arrow running from variation in biological-psychological processes making for varying affective responses to variation in political orientations. Biological differences predispose otherwise similarly environmentally situated agents to arrive at systematically differing political orientations and positions—and this involves a suite of more or less common cognitive processes that are themselves more responsive to aversively gauged outcomes than to attractive outcome. If one is born with (or comes to have) the biological tendency to respond relatively strongly to common aversive stimuli (more strongly than average), and one thus has a relatively strong negativity bias to one's rudimentary cognitive/conative processing, then one is likely to cobble together more conservative political orientations out of one's conditioned perceptions of threats and opportunities. One is likely to develop conservative orientations—relatively threat- and disgust-responsive positions favoring what, in one's setting, amount to traditional (cultural and societal) preferences. One likely is strongly attracted to stability of extant practices and hierarchies.[4]

Two points are worth emphasizing in connection with the last paragraph. First, it should be acknowledged that there are multiple ways of understanding the liberal/conservative dimension in political or social ideology. It is common enough to think of conservatism (or liberalism) in terms of a constellation of issue positions embraced within a given community at a time. On this understanding, conservative (or liberal) ideology in one community/time may involve a rather different thing than the conservative (or liberal) ideology at a different community/time—thus, what counts as conservative is local to that setting. Hibbing, Smith, and their collaborators are, we think, interested in a less local understanding of the liberal/conservative dimension. One might think of it as an underlying liberal/conservative dimension. They envision a dimension in the responses that are attuned to some underlying problems characteristic of human social life (matters such as coordination on extant practices, openness to modification of extant practices and relations, and comfort with degrees of hierarchical organization; see also Jost et al. 2014b: 16–20). Again, the idea is that variation on the biological aspects mentioned here conditions the attraction or repulsion that agents have to the alternatives presented in the agent's cultural/political context.

Second, one might worry that the explanation of a political stance afforded in one context—say the United States in 2019—does not "travel" to explanation of that political stance in a different context. In the one context, the stance might espouse hierarchical arrangements that are familiar and safe for the relevant agents, while those arrangements would perhaps be strange and threatening to agents in a different context (where less hierarchical practices are familiar). In contrast, the explanations envisioned by Hibbing, Smith, and collaborators have to do with dimensions of affective responses that vary in parallel ways across the various contexts. In addition to a dimension keyed to stability and hierarchy, they also take notice of dimensions of affective response involving disgust, which have been noted to be associated with social conservativism. Tybur et al. (2009) present evidence for an adaptionist model of disgust sensitivity in which such sensitivity is keyed to "three specialized domains" of adaptive significance: "pathogen disgust, which motivates the avoidance of infectious microorganisms; sexual disgust, which motivates the avoidance of sexual partners and behaviors that would jeopardize one's long-term reproductive success; and moral disgust, which motivates the avoidance of social norm violators." Certainly, disgust with social norm violations would help to make sense of the correlations that are found between disgust reactivity and social conservativism. Across various cases, there is variation in discomfort with unfamiliar arrangements, and in openness to change, in comfort with hierarchical social structures, or in disgust of various sorts. The relevantly conservative ideologies in a social-political context are those clusters of positions cobbled together in a way that cleave to the more familiar and hierarchical arrangements and practices among those espoused in a setting (and to what are to the agent the less disgust-provoking practices). There is reason to think that explanations at this level "travel" in the sense that there may well be a parallel mechanistic explanation to be had for the more conservative stances in differing contexts. Of course, what constellation of policies and practices counts as conservative in one setting, say the United States, can be different from the constellation counting as conservative in the Russian Federation, or Pakistan.

Now, to be clear, negativity bias looks to be a general cognitive tendency of all human agents: "Negativity bias is the principle that 'negative events are more salient, potent, dominant in combinations, and generally efficacious than positive events'" (Hibbing et al. 2014a: 303, here quoting Rozin and Rozyman 2001). As Kahneman and Tversky (2000) and Kahneman and Frederick (2005) note, such a cognitive weighting of losses is a pervasive aspect of human cognitive heuristics. As we understand what is proposed, what distinguishes many with conservative leanings from many with liberal leanings is not this heuristic itself—think of it as a module representing the cognitive uptake of input in the form of affective response, one that weights the negative or aversive input marginally more.

Rather, what seems to be differing across agents is the strength of the aversive affective input into their heuristic processing.

Drawing on their own work and work by numerous others, Hibbing, Smith, and their various collaborators can marshal significant empirical support for their refined modules. Central here are the correlations they have shown to obtain between social-political attitudes and individuals' differing reactivity to threats generally (this is the basis for boxes in Figure 3.2 having to do with the strength of individuals' threat and disgust sensitivities and with the differing affective responses occasioned as they move through their social-political environment). They assemble a range of the relevant empirical work—and they note the results of brain imaging and of measures of sympathetic nervous system response strength elicited by presentations of threatening and nonthreatening nonpolitical images (and to disgust-inducing and nondisgust-inducing images). The degree of excitability of individuals' threat responses is significantly correlated with the political orientations as independently measured (see in particular (Dodd et al. 2012). They also note the range of work in psychology and physiology into which their own results fit to make a powerful package.

We are reminded of Craver and Dardin's general observation about the range of information bearing on the informed sketching of a model for a mechanism: "The point is that biologists typically begin their search for mechanisms in an intellectual cornucopia of general knowledge that restricts the space of possible mechanisms and focuses attention on a few or a handful of key live possibilities" (2013: 69). In a parallel fashion, Hibbing et al. can draw on an impressive range of work in cognitive psychology characterizing a general negativity bias. This bias suggests a prominent "live possibility": negativity bias amplifies the greater negative affective responses exhibited by those who seem drawn to conservative social-political stances. With stronger negative responses generally comes a more

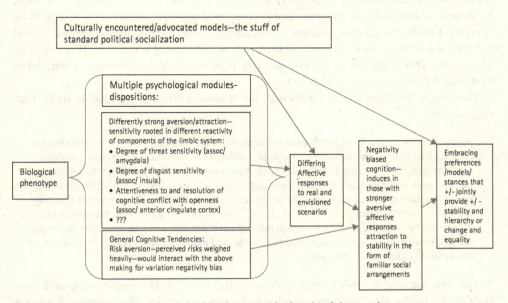

FIGURE 3.2. Hibbing, Smith, and Alford—a rough sketch of the mechanism

sustained attention to the threatening or disgusting provocation (the policy or practice to which they react) and greater accommodation of this in the development of standing political preferences. Others have noted that one might think of the negativity bias in terms of a framing effect—so that some agents would have a greater tendency to frame choices in terms of losses rather than gains (Coe et al. 2017). The suggestion is that the more conservative members of the population do not merely tend to fixate longer on the threats or disgusts that may be in the offing, but that they tend to frame choices in differing ways, calling into play those processes familiar from background cognitive psychology (Kahneman and Frederick 2005). Presumably, across repeated episodes, such framing leaves a residue of either settled opinion and/or habits of framing issues in settled ways—and in such a manner, agents come to cobble together political stances. Thus, in Figure 3.2, we represent Hibbing, Smith, and Alford's empirically and theoretically informed sketch of the mechanism accounting for the phenomena of interest.

Let us now focus on a second group of researchers who advance a closely related sketch of the mechanism accounting for the phenomena of interest (Carney et al. 2008; Jost et al. 2003; Jost and Amodio 2012; Jost et al. 2014a; Jost et al. 2014b; Jost et al. 2018). Their approach is largely compatible with, and supportive of, the work just discussed, while providing for some variations in our understanding. Generally, it suggests a picture in which differences in ideology arise as a result of a kind of motivated cognition in which rudimentary biological differences make for differences in affective attractions and aversions, and accordingly make attractive general constellations of political stances. Individuals are thus motivated to cobble together a political orientation that suits their felt needs. Carney et al. (2008) provide evidence that liberal and conservative political orientation are correlated with individual differences in two of personality psychology's "big five" dimensions. Openness to experience looks to be generally higher among liberals, while conscientiousness looks to be somewhat higher among conservatives. Here, they "conceptualize political ideology in terms of one's relative position on an abstract left–right (or liberal–conservative) dimension that is comprised of two core aspects that tend to be correlated with one another, namely: (a) acceptance versus rejection of inequality and (b) preference for social change vs. preservation of the societal status quo" (Carney et al. 2008: 808). This treatment of the relevant left–right dimension seems largely parallel to that reflected in our earlier discussion.

Thinking of what matters to agents with the relevant associated personality traits, they suggest that

> political conservatism is an ideological belief system that consists of two core components, resistance to change and opposition to equality, which serve to reduce uncertainty and threat. The idea is that there is an especially good fit between needs to reduce uncertainty and threat, on one hand, and resistance to change and acceptance of inequality, on the other, insofar as preserving the status quo allows one to maintain what is familiar and known while rejecting the risky, uncertain prospect of social change. The broader argument is that ideological differences between right and left have psychological roots: stability and hierarchy generally provide reassurance and structure, whereas change and equality imply greater chaos and unpredictability. (Jost et al. 2007: 990).

Notice the convergence with central ideas in the work of Hibbing, Smith, and their collaborators—the positions were developed largely in parallel. The convergence is yet deeper, as Jost and his collaborators note that the relevant motivating personality traits are likely heritable in some measure and certainly develop early and commonly are stable features within individual biographies. This leads this team of political psychologists to think that they are having a hand in "the beginnings of a beautiful friendship between neuroscience, political psychology, and political science" (Jost et al. 2014b: 3; see also John T. Jost et al. 2018). That is, they conclude that the psychological dimensions they see as motivating the formation of political orientations themselves spring from biological underpinnings. They celebrate two aspects of this friendship. One is the theoretical advances that arise when one is able to account for the dynamics of political preferences in light of an interplay involving personality needs and biological differences. (Of course, the resulting political and social stances are understood to result from motivated cognition responding to alternatives on offer in the agents' social-political settings. So there is no suggestion that political stances are to be explained by biology or the related psychological factors alone.) The second is worth more articulation than has been given it to this point in our discussion: neurobiological tools allow investigators a richer access to cognitive dynamics—certainly richer than what might be afforded by survey instruments alone. In agreement, Hibbing (2013) points out that this range of tools is complementary. As Jost et al. (2014b: 28) emphasize, this richness of tools affords the opportunity for a "collaborative cross-examination of neural and behavioral interpretations." Jost et al. (2014b: 5) provide a particularly rich and accessible overview of the emerging field of political neuroscience. In their overview, they distinguish "four areas of empirical inquiry that account for most of the publicly available research in political neuroscience: (1) racial prejudice and intergroup relations; (2) the existence of partisan bias and motivated political cognition; (3) the nature of left–right differences in political orientation; and (4) the dimensional structure of political attitudes." We here have focused on work in area (3).

Again, it will be notable how much background causal information, from various related disciplines, is invoked in these projects. In the philosophy of science, it has become common to note that many disciplines develop theories for phenomenon that turn on processes at various levels. Biological theorizing commonly deploys information about processes at various physical, molecular, systemic, and environmental levels. Geologists note the multidisciplinary character of their investigations. This is a source of epistemic strength. We suggest that biological political and social science looks to be another case: it pursues an "interfield theory" to tease out the causal dependencies working with information about causal processes at multiple levels (cf. Darden and Maull 1977; Darden 2006). For example, the responsiveness of neural structures such as the amygdala and insula to general and social or political prompts suggest that variations in threat and disgust responses may be involved in agents' motivated political cognition. But, such structures function in a diversity of kinds of tasks, and well-designed experiments can help to interpret the neuroscientific evidence. Of course, such experiments build on extant psychological theory and evidence. Significant issues include (a) the extent to which features such as sensitivity to threat, comfort with change, and with hierarchical social structures, and others posited as pivotal in motivating the cobbling together of political stances are themselves robust, or slow to change, so that they would serve in stretches of stance-formation; and (b) the extent to which these features themselves result from some combination of genetic or very early developmental factors. Scientific understanding indicating a genetic and/or early developmental basis for such features, and for their robustness, support or qualify the general understanding on offer. The interfield character of much of the relevant work is reflected in this characterization from Jost et al. (2014b: 4): "Political neuroscience is an interdisciplinary venture that tackles questions of mutual interest to political scientists and psychologists by drawing, at least in part, on the theories, methods, and assumptions of biology, especially neuroscience."

If one were seeking to diagram a sketch of the mechanism responsible for the formation of political stances or preferences as it is presented by Jost and his collaborators, it would look strikingly similar to what emerged from the work of Hibbing, Smith, Alford, and their collaborators. To some extent, both teams seek to draw on a similar range of psychological modules—having a central place for forms of motivated cognition and negativity bias. Both see the differences in the motivated cognition of liberals and conservatives as revolving around individual differences in threat sensitivity and disgust sensitivity. Both understand conservatives to be commonly rather more moved by aversive affective dispositions and to find comfort in the stability of familiar forms of social organization—including familiar hierarchies. Both see liberals as being more open to social change, perhaps militating against familiar hierarchies. Both understand the mechanisms behind the motivated cognition to be commonly working subpersonally—and the whole shebang as rooted in heritable traits. Both see political preferences as resulting from a significant gene-culture interaction. Jost and collaborators treat this as a matter of variation on phenotypic personality traits, understood as a matter of location along two dimensions of standard personality psychology: openness to experience and conscientiousness (Carney et al. 2008). It is not altogether clear just how central this personality framework is in their subsequent work, but it is clear that in subsequent work, the resulting political stances are understood in terms of two dimensions: (a) there are stances that cleave to the kind of stability afforded by familiar hierarchies (from among the alternatives on cultural offer in a setting) and these are those to which those on the political/social right are drawn, and (b) there are stances that are more welcoming of change (promising greater equality or diversity—although, perhaps greater unpredictability), and these generally hold more attraction in the motivated thinking of those on the left.

While differences in general threat and disgust sensitivity play an important role in the accounts on offer by various teams, we should note that many investigators are concerned to understand ways in which the perception of threats and the like may involve mechanisms and dispositions that themselves are tuned to distinctively social matters. For example, in a recent programmatic discussion Jost, Sapolsky, and Nam (2018) emphasize several respects in which humans seem to be evolved for life in groups in which members cooperate. In such groups, tracking in social networks, responsiveness to hierarchies, and social sentiments conducive to cooperation would be important. Plausibly, one will find variation among individuals with respect to the their sensitivity to such matters—think of the kind of variation explored by moral psychologists such as Haidt (2012). Thus, people may differ, not simply in their general responsiveness to threat, but more specifically, in the extent to which their threat sensitivity interacts with sensitivities to how things stand with respect to various social dimensions—they may differ in their "psychological orientation favoring maintenance of the status quo, which requires vigilance to markers of dominance (and potential changes to dominance rankings) as well as an affinity for hierarchical social arrangements" (Jost et al. 2018: 10). Interestingly, the amygdala features especially prominently when such social matters are in view. They cite evidence that larger bilateral gray matter volume in the amygdala was associated with better performance on a task in which participants were required to learn the relative ranks of members in a novel hierarchical social system" (Jost et al. 2018: 8). (Amygdala volume was unrelated to performance on a learning task involving a nonsocial hierarchy.)

Of course, life in human groups commonly involves marking off an "us" from several "thems"—and distinctive forms of social organization or status relations may be important here. Those who deal less readily with cognitive conflict and fluidity may be particularly threatened when differing social organizations—with differing normative demands—are entertained. There is said to be evidence that liberals do tend to have more gray matter volume in their anterior cingulate—which is involved in monitoring and responding to cognitive conflict (Amodio et al. 2007; Jost et al. 2018: 7–8). Those so equipped may find thinking about alternative political and social arrangements and practices easier and less threatening. Jost et al. (2014b: 12–16) suggest that such differences may make for differences in the extent to which agents are motivated to partisan defense of the policies and practices favored by the agent's own group, and to the extent to which agents readily expose themselves to information not favorable to their views, and to simulate the thinking of others.

It would be desirable to ultimately develop an understanding of how similarities and variation on these matters feature in the evolution of human social cognition (involving group identification, hierarchy tracking, cooperation, limited social flexibility, and the like). Jost, Sapolsky, and Nam (2018: 4–5) suggest that this will likely involve multilevel selection, including cultural group selection. A strong case can be made here, and such an account would further deepen and constrain understandings of the biological character of the mechanisms and psychological modules by which agents manage their social life—including the ways in which they respond to real and imagined threats (Henrich et al. 2004; Henrich and Henrich 2007; Richerson and Boyd 2005; Sober and Wilson 1998; Wilson and Wilson 2007).

Of course, were the biological/psychological understanding of the dynamics of social/ political stance development (presented here) to be embedded in an understanding of cultural group selection, one would need to expand our diagrams of the models presented here. This would itself involve boxes and arrows reflecting evolutionary bases for the ranges of variation in biological phenotypes to be found in the human population—and the account would likely afford greater constraint on the mechanistic model explicated here. It would also involve further modules (boxes and arrow) for the processes giving rise to the culturally encountered models to which agents respond affectively. Some of these modules and arrows would turn on cultural group selection impacting the range of biological variations in place in human groups. At present, this is a project for future research—and we do not pursue such widening of the mechanistic model here. Instead, we merely leave the reader with a diagram (Figure 3.3) representing composite understanding of the mechanism of political attitude production. This represents the phenomena as understood in the central literature on which we have focused. Doubtless, this model should be understood as merely a beginning—subject to much further development in light of the several scienific fields treating of the genetic, developmental, and psychological processes touched upon in the model represented in Figure 3.3.

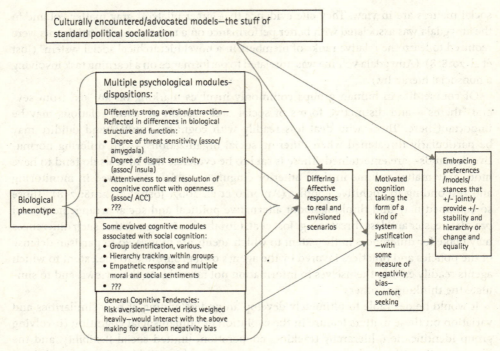

FIGURE 3.3. Diagram of the refined sketch

Notes

1. The point is recognized by John Hibbing (2013) who points to Carol Prescott, Ronald Johnson, and John Mcardle (1999).
2. In most of the literature on which we focus in this discussion, liberal and conservative stances tend to be measured in one of two ways. The first uses some variant of the Wilson-Patterson Attitude Inventory. Here one presents subjects with short stimulus phrases and elicit from them agreement (agree or yes), disagreement (disagree or no), or no response (uncertain or don't know). Multiple, culturally suggested elicitors should be employed, and these may reflect what may be multiple dimensions of conservatism or liberalism. Some may reflect economically centered conservatism or liberalism—for example, *capitalism, property tax, socialism,* or *unions*. Others may reflect more socially centered conservatism—perhaps *segregation, women's liberation, abortion,* or *divorce*. A Wilson-Patterson inventory will include a bank of elicitors, commonly twenty or more (the Wilson-Patterson inventory [1968] used fifty items) and the items can be chosen to account for political contexts in differing countries (although doing so also makes for difficulties in generalizing across applications). For examples of the use of such instruments, see Peter K. Hatemi (2013: 8); John R. Alford, Carolyn L. Funk, and John R. Hibbing (2005: 157–158); and John R. Hibbing, Kevin B. Smith, and John R. Alford (2014b: 38–39). The second general method is to ask subjects to simply self-report their location on "the" liberal/conservative spectrum. Thus, John T. Jost et al. (2014b: 19) indicates that their work commonly has measured political orientation on a scale ranging from −5

("extremely liberal") to 5 ("extremely conservative"). Using the Wilson-Patterson inventory has several advantages. For one, it does not suppose that there is simply one liberal conservative dimension and can afford some basis for disambiguating the phenomena.

3. One of the present authors has been interested in the ways in which epistemic norms—norms for how one ought to form beliefs—can be understood drawing on the literature on social norms of various stripes (see, for example, David Henderson 2020). Social norms are commonly keyed to social expectations (for adherence, and for expected normative evaluations) had by others in the relevant community. Even were those norms concerned with the production of true or accurate beliefs, adherence is at least marginally motivated by rewards (such as praise and status) and punishments (gossip, blame, and marginalization). This seems true of scientific communities. So, belief formation constrained by such norms is itself at least marginally affectively driven, although it is not affectively driven in the paradigmatic sense at issue in the literature under discussion.

4. As John Hibbing has emphasized to us in conversation, talk of an attraction to "stability," insofar as it is associated with "extant practices" and arrangements is doubtless something of an over-simplification. It is clear that some conservative concerns have to do with a picture of past practices—and may look to an equilibrium that never obtained, or if it obtained, did not obtain in the lived experience of the relevant agents.

REFERENCES

Alford, John R., Funk, Carolyn L., and Hibbing, John R. (2005), 'Are Political Orientations Genetically Transmitted?' *American Political Science Review*, 99 (2), 153–167.

Amodio, David M., Jost, John T., Masters, Sarah L., and Yee, Cindy M. (2007), 'Neurocognitive Correlates of Liberalism and Conservatism.' *Nature Neuroscience*, 10, 1246–1247.

Bechtel, William and Richardson, Robert (1993), *Discovering Complexity: Decomposition and Localization as Strategies in Scientific Research* (Princeton: Princeton University Press).

Block, Jack and Block, Jeanne H. (2006), 'Nursery School Personality and Political Orientation Two Decades Later.' *Journal of Research in Personality*, 40, 734–749.

Carney, Dana R., Jost, John T., Gosling, Samuel D., and Potter, Jeff (2008), 'The Secret Lives of Liberals and Conservatives: Personality Profiles, Interaction Styles, and the Things They Leave Behind.' *Political Psychology*, 29 (6), 807–840.

Coe, Chelsea, Canelo, S. Canelo, Vue, Kau, Hibbing, Matthew V., and Nicholson, Stephen (2017), 'The Physiological of Framing Effects: Threat Sensitivity and the Persuasiveness of Political Arguments.' *The Journal of Politics*, 79 (4), 1465–1468.

Craver, Carl and Darden, Lindley (2013), *In Search of Mechanisms: Discoveries across the Life Sciences* (Chicago: University of Chicago Press).

Darden, Lindley (2006), *Reasoning in Biological Discoveries: Essays on Mechanisms, Interfield Relations, and Anomaly Resolution* (Cambridge: Cambridge University Press).

Darden, Lindley (2007), 'Mechanisms and Models.' In *The Cambridge Companion to the Philosophy of Biology* (Cambridge: Cambridge University Press).

Darden, Lindley and Maull, Nancy (1977), 'Interfield Theories.' *Philosophy of Science*, 44, 43–64.

Dodd, Michael, Balzer, Amanda, Jacobs, Carly, Gruszczynski, Michael, Smith, Kevin, and Hibbing, John (2012), 'The Political Left Rolls with the Good: The Political Right Confronts the Bad.' *Philosophical Transactions of the Royal Society B: Biological Sciences*, 367, 640–649.

Druckman, James N. (2012), 'The Politics of Motivation.' *Critical Review*, 24 (2), 199–216.

Haidt, Jonathan (2012), *The Righteous Mind: Why Good People Are Divided by Politics and Religion* (1st edn.; New York: Pantheon Books), xvii.

Hatemi, Peter K. (2013), 'The Influence of Major Life Events on Economic Attitudes in a World of Gene-Environment Interplay.' *American Journal of Political Science*, 57 (1), 987–1007.

Henderson, David (2020), 'Are Epistemic Norms Fundamentally Social Norms?' *Episteme*, 17 (Special Issue 3: Epistemic Norms as Social Norms Conference), 281–300.

Henrich, Joseph., Boyd, Robert, Bowles, Samuel, Camerer, Colin, Fehr, Ernst, and Gintis, Herbert (eds.) (2004), *Foundations of Human Sociality: Economic Experiments and Ethographic Evidence from Fifteen Small-Scale Societies* (Oxford: Oxford University Press).

Henrich, Natalie and Henrich, Joseph (2007), *Why Humans Cooperate: A Cultural and Evolutionary Explanation* (Evolution and cognition; New York: Oxford University Press) xi, 267 p.

Hibbing, John (2013), 'Ten Misconceptions Concerning Neurobiology and Politics.' *Perspectives on Politics*, 11 (2), 475–489.

Hibbing, John R., Smith, Kevin B., and Alford, John R. (2014a), 'Differences in Negativity Bias Underlie Variations in Political Ideology.' *Behavioral & Brain Sciences*, 37 (3), 297–307.

Hibbing, John R., Smith, Kevin B., and Alford, John R. (2014b), 'Negativity Bias and Political Preferences: A Response to Commentators.' *Behavioral & Brain Sciences*, 37 (3), 333–350.

Jost, John and Amodio, David (2012), 'Political Ideology as Motivated Social Cognition: Behavioral and Neuroscientific Evidence.' *Motivation & Emotion*, 36 (1), 55–64.

Jost, John T, Noorbaloochi, Sharareh, and Van Bavel, Jay J. (2014a), 'The "Chicken-and-Egg" Problem in Political Neuroscience.' *Brain and Behavioral Science*, 37, 317–318.

Jost, John T., Sapolsky, Robert M., and Nam, H. Hannah (2018), 'Speculations on the Evolutionary Origins of System Justification.' *Evolutionary Psychology*, 16 (2), 1–1.

Jost, John T., Glaser, J., Kruglanski, A. W., and Sulloway, F. (2003), 'Political Conservatism and Motivated Social Cognition.' *Psychological Bulletin*, 129, 339–375.

Jost, John T., Nam, H. Hannah, Amodio, David M., and Van Bavel, Jay J. (2014b), 'Political Neuroscience: The Beginning of a Beautiful Friendship.' *Political Psychology*, 35, 3–42.

Jost, John. T., Napier, Jamie L., Thorisdottir, Hulda, Gosling, Samuel D., Palfai, Tibor P., and Ostafin, Brian (2007), 'Are Needs to Manage Uncertainty and Threat Associated with Political Conservatism or Ideological Extremity?' *Personality and Social Psychology Bulletin*, 33, 989–1007.

Kahneman, Daniel and Tversky, Amos (2000), *Choices, Values, and Frames* (Cambridge: Cambridge University Press) xx, 840 p.

Kahneman, Daniel and Frederick, Shane (2005), 'A Model of Heuristic Judgment.' In K. Holyoak and R. Morrison (eds.), *The Cambridge Handbook of Thinking and Reasoning* (New York: Cambridge University Press), 267–293.

Kaplan, Jonathan Michael (2000), *The Limits and Lies of Human Genetic Research* (New York: Routledge).

Kunda, Ziva (1990), 'The Case for Motivated Reasoning.' *Psychological Bulletin*, 108 (3), 480–498.

Lodge, Milton and Taber, Charles (2005), 'The Automaticity of Affect for Political Leaders, Groups, and Issues: An Experitial Test of the Hot Cognition Hypothesis.' *Political Psychology*, 26 (3), 455–482.

Machamer, Peter, Darden, Lindley, and Craver, Carl F. (2000), 'Thinking about Mechanisms.' *Philosophy of Science*, 67 (1), 1–25.

Oskarsson, S, Cesarini, D, and Johannesson, M (2014), 'Pre-Birth Factors, Post-Birth Factors, and Voting: Evidence from Swedish Adoption Data.' *American Political Science Review*, 108 (I), 71–87.

Prescott, Carol, Johnson, Ronald, and McArdle, John (1999), 'Chorion Type as a Possible Influence on the Results and Interpretation of Twin Study Data.' *Twin Research*, 2, 244–249.

Richerson, Peter. J. and Boyd, Robert (2005), *Not by Genes Alone: How Culture Transformed Human Evolution* (Chicago: University of Chicago Press).

Rozin, R. and Royzman, E. B. (2001), 'Negativity Bias, Negativity Dominance, and Contagion.' *Personality and Social Psychology Review*, (4), 296–320.

Smith, Kevin B., Oxley, Douglas R., Hibbing, Matthew V., Alford, John R., and Hibbing, John R. (2011), 'Linking Genetics and Political Attitudes: Reconceptualizing Political Ideology', *Political Psychology*, 32 (3), 369–397.

Sober, Elliott and Wilson, David Sloan (1998), *Unto others: the evolution and psychology of unselfish behavior* (Cambridge, MA: Harvard University Press) 394 p.

Tybur, Joshua M., Lieberman, Debra, and Griskevicius, Vladas (2009), 'Microbes, Mating, and Morality: Individual Differences in Three Functional Domains of Disgust.' *Journal of Personality and Social Psychology*, 97 (1), 103–122.

Wilson, David Sloan and Wilson, Edward O. (2007), 'Rethinking the Theoretical Foundations of Sociobiology.' *Quarterly Review of Biology*, 82, 327–348.

Woodward, James (2000), 'Explanation and Invariance in the Special Sciences', *British Journal for the Philosophy of Science*, 51 (2), 197–254.

CHAPTER 4

RATIONAL CHOICE EXPLANATIONS IN POLITICAL SCIENCE

CATHERINE HERFELD AND JOHANNES MARX

1. INTRODUCTION

RATIONAL choice theories (RCTs) are important in every social science. Political science is no exception. At least since the 1970s, they have been a central component of American political science, first in the field of international relations and later in comparative political science (Elster 2000, 685; Green & Shapiro 1999, 12; Moon 1991, 50). Nowadays, this certainly holds true for all of Western political science.

The scope of RCTs in political science is broad, ranging from the modeling of individual behavior at the microlevel, such as the voting behavior of citizens (Downs 1957a, 1957b; Lewis-Beck & Stegmaier 2007), to the analysis of phenomena at the mesolevel, such as coalition formation (Strøm 1997; Schofield 1993; Hardin 1976; Riker 1962), associations or organizations (Olson 1965, 1982; Andeweg et al. 2011; Shepsle 1989), to the study of political actors and processes at the macrolevel, such as the behavior of states or international organizations as well as the functioning of the international system itself (Tsebelis 2002; Bueno de Mesquita et al. 2005; Koremenos et al. 2001; Snidal 2002).

RCTs are applied to a wide range of political phenomena. However, the usefulness of core variants, namely game theory and decision theory, is still controversial and has been discussed extensively (Green & Shapiro 1994, 1995, 1999; Hardin 1990; Johnson 1993, 2002, 2010; MacDonald 2003; Mansbridge 1995; Monroe & Hill Maher 1995; Monroe 1997; Riker 1995; Shapiro 2004; Zuckert 1995). One important, yet unsettled, issue has been the usefulness of RCTs to explain phenomena relevant for political scientists. Opponents of RCTs deny altogether that they can successfully explain the behavior of political actors (e.g., Hoggett & Thompson 2012; Bunge 1995), one reason being that the empirical adequacy of their behavioral assumptions has been questioned. Critics call for an "affective turn" in political science, demanding an approach to political behavior that includes emotions and other psychological variables to improve the explanatory power of RCTs.[1]

Less drastically but likewise convinced of themselves, proponents of RCTs point to the success in applying RCTs in political science. Those proponents, however, disagree about how the "success" of RCTs should be understood. They can be divided into two camps, realists and instrumentalists. Realists (e.g., Hechter & Kanazawa 1997; Opp 2019) take explanatory power to be the standard for success. On their view, RCTs are without doubt successful in explaining political and social behavior, such as the origins, course, and forms of political protests (e.g., Opp 2019). By taking a realist stance, they consider RCTs to be explanatory in that they identify the causally relevant variables in bringing this behavior about. Those realists apply what has been called "empirical variants" of RCTs (e.g., Opp 2009, 2011). They proceed inductively insofar as the core concepts of RCTs, such as preferences and constraints, are interpreted as variables that should be directly observable and as such have turned out to be empirically correct. Such variants of RCTs make ontological claims about psychological mechanisms. In this view, RCTs are successful in political science because they offer causal explanations.[2]

In contrast, instrumentalists doubt that explanatory power is an appropriate measure for the success of RCTs altogether. By taking an instrumentalist stance, they commit to the main assumptions of RCTs but argue that those assumptions should not be understood as ontological claims about human psychology. Instead, they take RCTs to be a set of analytical tools that we arrive at deductively, on the basis of some standard political science theories (e.g., Olson 1965; Downs 1957a). In these what we will call "analytical variants" of RCTs, it is typically assumed that all actors maximize preferences, such as economic benefit or power, are fully informed, and are strictly self-interested (Olson 1965; Downs 1957a; see Opp 2009, 174). Those analytical variants are mainly used for predictions and the empirical and theoretical analysis of structural characteristics of macrolevel patterns. The argument is that as long as RCTs work well as an instrument for the purpose at hand, its core concepts, such as preferences and constraints, may be idealized or even empirically wrong. In this view, RCTs are successful because of their predictive power, although their central assumptions are not empirically informed.[3]

In this chapter, we want to push the debate about the usefulness of RCTs in political science one step further. Besides surveying the literature, our goal is to further clarify the explanatory role of RCTs in political science (for a similar discussion, see also Lovett 2006). While we position ourselves closer to the realist camp, we suggest taking a pragmatic stance toward the usefulness of RCTs for explanation in political science. We address the question whether there are conditions under which analytical models of RCTs used mainly by instrumentalists can also be useful from the realist perspective. To motivate this question, we start with an observation that is underappreciated so far, namely that the disagreement between instrumentalists and realists partly originates in the fact that they understand and apply RCTs in political science differently because they often target distinct phenomena. When realists claim successful applications of RCTs, they refer to the empirical variants to explain the political behavior of individual agents. In contrast, when instrumentalists claim successful applications of RCTs, they refer to analytical variants of RCTs to predict the behavior of collective actors, such as political parties, governments, coalitions, the state, and other political organizations. Given that realists and instrumentalists are thereby involved in different kinds of epistemic activities, we explore the idea that each variant of RCTs might be useful for different explanatory purposes in political science.

Because RCTs mostly ground causal explanations in political science, we address the question about the conditions under which analytical models of RCTs can be considered useful from the realist perspective by first analyzing how analytical and empirical variants of RCTs are actually used by political scientists to offer explanations. As different kinds of phenomena are considered relevant in political science, we show that their explanation requires different explanatory modes. We argue that those explanatory modes raise in turn distinct explanatory demands toward RCTs. Depending on the *explanandum*, empirical and analytical variants of RCTs can fulfill those demands in different ways. The distinction between kinds of *explananda* requiring distinct explanatory modes has not been acknowledged so far in the debate about the usefulness of RCTs. Exploring this distinction and its implications is the main goal of this chapter. This would enable a more nuanced and problem-oriented appraisal of rational choice theories in political science. Another implication of our discussion is that a broader concept of explanation would be advisable in political science.

A number of qualifications are in order. First, and most importantly, we exclusively focus on explanations that include an agent component as one of their core building blocks. That does not commit us to a strict version of methodological individualism because our focus on the microlevel is not constrained to the behavior of individual agents. Rather, it includes the behavior of collective actors as well. In other words, we do not discuss explanations that do not refer to any agents (individual or collective) at all.

Second, while RCTs are often discussed in political science as a monolithic and unified theory, in reality, practitioners mostly accept some but not all features of RCTs (e.g., Green & Shapiro 1994). Approaching RCTs from the practitioner's side requires acknowledging that there are different variants of RCTs—decision and game theory being two examples— that are conceptually and methodologically distinct (e.g., Herfeld 2020). As we will see below, while they have some family resemblance, they are applied to distinct problems in political science, they vary in how they interpret the main theoretical concepts, and they differ in how they are integrated into other theoretical frameworks, among other things.

Third, political science is an integrative discipline. It relies on methods imported from other fields. Political scientists apply formal-mathematical, simulational, quantitative, qualitative, and other empirical methods, thereby drawing on direct interviews and questionnaires, lab and field experiments, general political theories, (social) network analysis, and statistical techniques, among others (Box-Steffensmeier et al. 2008). While RCTs are often used as stand-alone approaches, they are regularly also an integral part of other methods and play a unique epistemic role in all of them. For example, RCTs are used in simulations to analyze the normative effects of rational strategies in iterated bargaining games (Klein et al. 2018). Here, we focus on the uses of RCTs for explanatory purposes only. Because not all of political science aims at giving explanations, our selection of issues concerning the use of RCTs in political science is therefore partial.

Finally, RCTs play a crucial role in (normative) political theory and political philosophy, which are themselves branches of political science (Berlin 1999; Dryzek et al. 2006; Kogelmann & Gaus 2017; Neal 1988; White & Moon 2004). Given their theoretical and normative interest, political theorists do not use RCTs to answer empirical questions or, more specifically, provide explanations. They use them as normative accounts that can support actors in realizing the rational course of behavior (e.g., Hardin 1993; Anand et al. 2009; Marx & Tiefensee 2015). Although an important research area, we neither discuss the specific uses of RCTs interpreted as normative theories, nor do we discuss their usefulness in political theory and political philosophy.

2. RATIONAL CHOICE THEORIES
IN POLITICAL SCIENCE

In this section, we address what most political scientists take to be the main components of RCTs.

The main characteristic of all variants of RCTs is that they account for human behavior in terms of rational behavior; they differ only in the way they interpret the concept of rationality. Furthermore, all variants of RCTs give a formal-mathematical, mostly axiomatic representation of rational decision-making and social interaction (Arrow 1958; Herne & Setälä 2004; Riker 1995). More specifically, RCTs have usually the form of an axiomatically grounded utility theory, drawing on a set of core concepts, mainly preferences and utility, to conceptualize the idea of rational decision-making. Most political scientists accept the formal requirements for the structure of preferences and beliefs from expected utility theory. Those requirements specify what makes an agent holding those preferences and beliefs rational (Marx & Tiefensee 2015, 514; Green & Shapiro 1994).[4]

Furthermore, there are a set of commitments that best characterize the theoretical core of RCTs in political science. Three commitments are particularly important. They are not the only way to characterize RCTs (see, e.g., Herfeld 2020). However, they are fulfilled by all RCTs in political science (e.g., Elster 1988; Klein et al. 2020). Most variants of RCTs in political science share this core, in that this is where they have some family resemblances. These are:

(1) A commitment to the principle that agents maximize their (expected) utility when choosing one option over another (*principle of [expected] utility*), with the concept of utility in most variants grounded in a concept of preferences.
(2) A commitment to the assumption that preferences are the defining factor of an agent's action as intentional.
(3) A commitment to the assumption that restrictions impose external conditions on behavior.

That action is understood as intentional is the key element underlying those commitments in political science. An intentional action is defined as goal-oriented behavior that ought to be distinguished from mere bodily movements by the fact that it has been brought about by some motive of the agent (Davidson 1963; Elster 1988; Weber 1980 [1921]). More specifically, intentionality is specified by a desire-belief couple that constitutes the motive leading the agent to perform the behavior in question. Desires are the main determinants of an action in light of the agent's beliefs and the information available. In RCTs, desires are formally represented by the concept of preferences. It is assumed that an actor ranks the options available to her according to their (expected) benefits based on her preferences. She chooses the option that promises her the greatest (expected) benefit.

"Benefit" is formally represented by the concept of utility. The concept of utility is flexible in that the ranking of options can be based on any kind of preference ordering. For example, we can distinguish between preference orderings that represent selfish and materially oriented interests and other-regarding interests (Riker 1995, 37; Sen 2005); an altruistic actor would rank her options differently than an egoistic actor in that the option that has the highest benefit for others would be highest on the altruist's ranking, while the option that has the highest benefit for the agent herself would be highest on the egoist's ranking. This difference in interests reflects in different preference orderings. In the first case, the altruistic action would promise the highest utility and would thus be ranked highest. In the second case, the action that best helps the actor pursue her egoistic interests would be ranked highest.

While the content of the preference concept is left open, the application of RCTs presupposes its specification via an interpretation. Furthermore, applying RCTs require that, among other things, the level of information, and the various goals and institutional limitations of the actor are made explicit (e.g., Johnson 1996, 86). Here is where empirical and analytical variants of RCTs depart. While defenders of analytical variants argue that the interpretation of core concepts, such as preferences, are informed by theory, proponents of empirical variants argue that how, for instance, the preference ordering of an agent looks cannot be decided on purely theoretical grounds but is an empirical question.

What is theoretically determined in both variants is a small set of minimal consistency requirements imposed on the preference order. They are described by a set of pre-defined axioms that give structure to an agent's preferences. The two most common axioms are transitivity and completeness. Transitivity requires that if an agent prefers A to B and B to C, then she also prefers A to C.[5] Completeness requires that the agent comparatively ranks any option that is subject to an agent's preference ordering. As such, every option can be rank-ordered. If those axioms are satisfied, a representation theorem can be proved, which formally represents the agent's preferences by a utility function. Depending on whether the utility function should be ordinal or cardinal, further conditions are sometimes required to derive the respective representations of an agent's preference ordering.

When rationality is in the first step defined by the set of axioms imposed on a preference ordering, political scientists speak of a formal as opposed to a substantive concept of rationality, since no interpretation has yet been given that specifies the content of the preferences. This formal concept rests upon a minimal understanding of rational behavior because rationality is solely defined in terms of the formal properties securing the consistency of the preferences (Green & Shapiro 1994; Herne & Setälä 2004; Monroe 1991). While the axiom system is selected on a priori grounds in both empirical and analytical variants of RCTs, the distinction between both variants manifests itself in how those axioms and the respective concepts, such as preferences, are interpreted (see also Arrow 1958). Some scholars defend them as reasonable characteristics of a rational agent and justify them by means of plausibility arguments or as grounded in theory; this is typical for analytical variants. Others justify them empirically, which is typical for the empirical variants of RCTs.[6]

Another way to look at this is to acknowledge that the specification of preferences and other concepts ultimately depends on the problem each variant is applied to and, thereby, on the type of agent—individual or collective—that is analyzed. This decision is usually made on the basis of plausibility considerations. Analytical variants addressing the problem of explaining the behavior of collective actors are mostly grounded in the assumption that such agents pursue their personal interests (*self-interest assumption*). For example, in analyses of party behavior in election campaigns, the primary goal of a party is taken to be its own election victory. Parties are assumed to choose their campaign strategy, their political program, and staffing in such a way that they maximize their votes and thus the party's political power. At the level of collective political actors, this assumption is considered plausible. Even if the problem is to explain the behavior of the individual politician, it has also been sometimes considered plausible that politicians pursue the strategy that increases their chances of securing a political office. In turn, proponents of empirical variants that aim at explaining individual behavior could argue that politicians can also be intrinsically motivated to fight for their ideas and represent the will of the majority of the people. Such an assumption would then require further empirical justification in political science.

Applying RCTs for explanation also requires specifying the agent's beliefs, the information she has available, and the restrictions she confronts. Analytical variants are largely used for problems in which it can be assumed that beliefs are determined by structural features of the environment or play no role whatsoever in bringing about the behavior. For example, in a simple variant of RCTs, a decision theory under certainty, it is assumed that an actor has full information which she is also able to cognitively process. It is assumed that actors are only restricted by external constraints. Those can be material (e.g., a budget), immaterial (e.g., existing norms), institutional (e.g., legal rules), etc. Again, in analytical variants, those assumptions are theoretically justified; beliefs or restrictions are not identified by doing empirical research.

Proponents of empirical variants have argued that such assumptions are empirically unfounded and therefore unjustified. For instance, voters make their decisions about candidates, parties, or election programs based on incomplete information and in light of uncertainty about the future (Green & Shapiro 1999, 30). Moreover, information seeking, for example, by a voter about a political candidate or program can itself be interpreted as a rational decision (Elster 1988). Acquiring information will result in search costs. Thus, a rational actor will collect information only until the benefit of additional information equals the cost of acquiring it. Proponents of empirical variants thus argue that further specifications of beliefs and the information available have to be grounded in and thus justified by empirical research into people's actual beliefs, the way they collect information, and how they learn over time.

There are two other variants of RCTs that are used to explain decision-making: under risk and under uncertainty. While in the second variant, the actor does not know the probabilities of the various outcomes of her actions, the numerical probabilities are known in the former variant. This is why the expected utility of each option can be calculated. Decision theory under uncertainty—when probabilities are not known—does not play a major role in empirical research in political science; usually, subjective probabilities are given.[7] Decision theory under risk is the standard model for realists in political science. When given an empirical interpretation, it is considered to be one main empirical variant of RCTs. In this case, the principle of expected utility is assumed to be the choice rule guiding the decision of a rational agent in such a way that she always chooses that option for which she calculated the highest subjective expected utility.

In expected utility theory, the restrictions an agent confronts in a particular decision situation are reflected in the actor's beliefs regarding the probability of the desired outcomes actually occurring. Such restrictions can be material (e.g., income, financial costs) or immaterial (e.g., informal sanctions or other immaterial costs; Marx & Tiefensee 2015). Even if the probabilities represent the actor's subjective beliefs, there are further theoretical conditions that are relevant: For example, the probabilities of the mutually exclusive outcomes must add up to 100 percent. However, what matters is that when it is used as an empirical variant, those desires and beliefs are taken to be about actual mental states.

In sum, political scientists accept three rationality requirements in RCTs that result from the three aforementioned commitments that specify which rationality requirements must be met by the constitutive components of RCTs: The first requirement concerns the relationship between desires/beliefs and the performed action, which is fixed by the above-mentioned principle of (expected) utility. The second requirement refers to preferences and defines specific conditions that a set of preferences should fulfill. The third requirement is connected to the beliefs an agent holds. As mentioned before, specifications must be made explicit for RCTs to be applicable. While the first requirement fixes the core of RCTs, the second and third are auxiliary requirements that help political scientists apply RCTs in a specific case. Analytical and empirical variants differ in how the second and third requirements should be met and justified.

3. Instrumentalism, Realism, and the *Explananda* of Political Science

That offering causal explanations is an essential goal of political science (Brady 2008) is not an uncontroversial position (e.g., Johnson 2014). However, a large part of the debate in political science discusses RCTs as a set of approaches that are supposed to offer such causal explanations (Green & Shapiro 1994). In the following, we suggest that the debate around the usefulness of RCTs in such explanations would benefit from distinguishing between empirical and analytical variants of RCTs in order to assess their usefulness in light of the phenomenon to be explained. To see the importance of separating different *explananda* in political science, we review how political scientists themselves frame the debate. In their discussions around RCTs, political scientists strongly uphold a distinction between scientific realism and what they call instrumental-empiricism. These positions represent competing views about the aims of political science (MacDonald 2003; Marx & Tiefensee 2015).

Generally speaking, for scientific realists, the aim of science is to discover new truths about the world, to uncover the subtle causal processes and regularities underlying social reality by using theories that offer causal explanations of those processes and regularities. The best means to do that is with theories that make "statements about real entities and processes"—observable or unobservable—that affect the phenomenon in question (MacDonald 2003, 554).[8] In this view, RCTs and their assumptions make ontological claims about causal relationships. More specifically, the realist is primarily interested in causally explaining instances of human behavior. Taking human behavior as the phenomenon to be explained raises specific explanatory demands toward RCTs. Because realists award priority to the epistemic goal of finding the *real* causes behind behavior, they often interpret the conceptual ingredients of RCTs to refer to unobservable yet actually existing entities or as describing causal mechanisms that connect individuals' motives and behavior. For example, they take the choice rules employed in RCTs to make claims about actual but unobservable thought processes of human beings. Asking for a theory that captures the causes that actually operate in the world, they reject a theory grounded in descriptively inadequate psychological assumptions about those mechanisms.

In contrast, for instrumentalist-empiricists science takes an operational turn. Their criterion for good theories is their ability to generate predictions about observable phenomena that can be verified empirically. Theories and their assumptions are selected for their generalizability and their ability to enable testable predictions of a variety of observable phenomena. Instrumentalists consider this goal possible because the abstract concepts of a theory can be clearly specified by measurable and observable indicators and thereby allow for falsification (MacDonald 2003, 553). In this view, theoretical concepts do not refer to entities that necessarily have ontological status; it is either assumed that those entities do not exist or that, because they are not observable, scientists remain agnostic about them. Along the same lines, RCTs serve as instruments, deductive tools, or heuristic devices to enable predictions.

In political science, instrumentalists are frequently concerned with making predictions about behavioral changes that occur under external constraints. The instrumentalist argues that because those behavioral changes can be traced back to changes in the environment, a theoretical description of the actual thought processes of the individual is not relevant. This argument becomes stronger when the phenomenon to be predicted is the behavior of collective actors. Because collective actors do not have mental states, the attribution of mental states to actors such as governments is at best instrumentally useful. As such, RCTs do not need to, and in the latter case also cannot meet the explanatory demand of providing a proper description of the causal processes behind the behavior of such actors. Therefore, a critique of unrealistic psychological assumptions becomes forceless and is viewed as misplaced.

While we side with the realist when it comes to the goals of political science, we nevertheless take the instrumentalist arguments to be instructive for thinking about RC-explanations in political science. We take those arguments to suggest that the concept of causal explanation used in political science might be too narrowly focused on identifying stable generalizations and the actual causal mechanisms underlying those generalizations. As we will see in the remainder of this chapter, for some phenomena—especially the behavior of collective actors as well as for patterns resulting from complex interaction processes—actual causal processes cannot be easily identified. When it comes to the prediction of social patterns, for example, the causal process underlying them is often so complex that we confront epistemic limitations to identify it. We thereby often fail to give an explanation in terms of the real causes underlying the pattern. While realists aim at causally explaining such patterns, the question is how this goal can be reconciled with the (epistemic) limitations that we confront when providing such explanations. We hope to learn something from the instrumentalist for thinking about this question because those are part of the phenomena to which instrumentalists apply RCTs.

One first step toward this goal is acknowledging one insight from the instrumentalist-realist dichotomy. In political science, the commitment to either an empirical variant or an analytical variant of RCTs frequently corresponds to different problems political scientists address. The assessments of RCTs diverge not only because realists and instrumentalists hold different views about the goals of science. Their views also diverge because they focus on different phenomena that they take to be interesting in political science. We can roughly identify two kinds of *explananda* in political science, namely, (1) behavior of actors, whereby we can distinguish between (a) human behavior, such as for instance the behavior of politicians, bureaucrats, or leaders of political movements, etc., and (b) the behavior of collective or institutionalized actors, such as governments, political parties, associations, or lobby groups; and (2) the social patterns resulting from the behavior of both kinds of actors. Examples of the latter are the emergence of social movements or aggregate voting patterns. They are often observable in the form of robust empirical regularities that result from more or less complex interaction processes.

As we will see below, there are different modes of explanation that are adopted to explain those phenomena. More specifically, which mode of explanation political scientists adopt depends on the *explanandum* in question. Depending on the respective explanatory mode, different explanatory demands are ultimately raised toward RCTs. For distinct *explananda*, different levels of abstraction are necessary to adequately capture the relevant causal relations. We can distinguish at least two explanatory modes in political science that draw on RCTs, namely what Satz and Ferejohn (1994) call psychological explanations and structural explanations.[9] Psychological explanations are the mode for causally explaining behavior in terms of an agent's mental processes. Structural explanations, in contrast, explain behavior in terms of the constraints and incentives set by the environment.

One difference between both explanatory modes lies precisely in the kind of causal relations that are relevant to explain behavior or the patterns emerging from it. When giving psychological explanations of human behavior, RCTs need to describe the actual reasoning processes of human agents (Satz & Ferejohn 1994, 73). The explanatory demand toward RCTs is that it gives an adequate psychological representation of the relation between mental states and choice. It requires what Satz and Ferejohn call an "internalist interpretation." RCTs, thus, make claims about the causal relation between mental states and choices. Such an internalist interpretation is compatible with a realist account according to which human behavior can be causally explained by recourse to psychological mechanisms that are in turn formally represented by some variant of RCTs. When political scientists explain the behavior of individual agents, they often draw on this model of explanation.

When political scientists explain the behavior of collective actors, they often draw on the mode of structural explanations. In such explanations, RCTs do not refer to the individual agent. While being constituted by individual agents, collective actors are modeled as actors in their own right. As long as this is how they are modeled, mental factors can at best be ascribed to individuals within the collective actor.[10] This is why it is seen to be plausible that only structural features are considered in the explanations of the behavior of collective actors. Whether structural factors are causally relevant for bringing the behavior about, however, depends on the degree to which the structure has an effect on the behavior. If behavior is heavily constrained by the structure, then the causal relations between the structure and the behavior are explanatorily relevant, more so than relations between mental states and individual behavior. The explanatory demand toward RCTs in those kinds of explanations is to contribute to a description of the mechanism operating between the causally relevant structure and behavior, not to describe any psychological mechanisms in detail.

In such explanations, Satz and Ferejohn (1994) speak of a "moderate externalist inter-pretation" of RCTs. While this interpretation is still compatible with realism about mental states and accepts the possibility for psychological explanation, mental states do not have to be part of an explanation of human action (Satz & Ferejohn 1994, 76). Rather, mental states are imputed to an individual by his or her position in the structure surrounding it. As such, the technical apparatus of RCTs does not have to map onto human psychology because mental states are not the relevant explanatory variables and are therefore not needed to give good explanations. Satz and Ferejohn argue that in such explanations, it is best if RCTs take a perspective external to the agent; they must only bear some semantic relation to in-dividual behavior and show that behavior is consistent with the mental states presupposed by RCTs. That is different from being an internalist about RCTs.

Specifying such a semantic relationship suffices for RCT-explanations that refer to the behavior of collective actors. In such explanations, the principle of (expected) utility, for ex-ample, is understood as a hypothesis of actors behaving as if maximizing their preferences. As such, moderate externalism is to be distinguished from a radical externalist interpre-tation of RCTs along the lines of a behavioristic theory. Radical externalism denies the existence and the causal efficacy of mental states altogether. From that perspective, RCTs are taken to make no claims whatsoever about the agent's psychology but only set some requirements on observable behavior.[11] Because the radical externalist denies the existence and causal efficacy of mental states (Ferejohn & Satz 1994, 74), RCTs on this interpretation are typically not used for causal explanations of behavior.[12]

At this point, it should be noted that the *explananda* in political science are not restricted to the level of either individual or collective actors. As mentioned earlier, political science as a social science is primarily concerned with explaining macrolevel phenomena. Certainly, the step of modeling the consequences of individual actions at the macrolevel is the biggest challenge for the formulation of causal explanations with RCTs that political scientists face. This is because in order to use a microlevel theory for the explanation of macrolevel phenomena, the interplay between macrolevel and microlevel should be modeled; both levels must be considered and integrated meaningfully into one framework. Depending on whether we ask a realist or an instrumentalist, such a framework requires different levels of specification regarding how the microlevel and the macrolevel interact, e.g., what the ag-gregation process looks like.

The extent to which this should be done is not agreed upon. While instrumentalists do not necessarily require a detailed description of the aggregation process in order to make predictions about the resulting pattern, most realists demand a detailed description not only of the relevant causal processes on the level of the individual but also of the aggre-gation process. For example, Opp (2019) illustrates a realist view of RCTs in analyzing the emergence of social protests. In addition to psychologically interpreted RCTs, his explana-tion also requires an empirically valid assessment of the aggregation processes by which individual actions result in the *explanandum* at the macrolevel. Apart from purely additive aggregation mechanisms (e.g., each voter counts as one), there are also complex aggrega-tion rules with threshold values (e.g., the success of political riots) or feedback loops (e.g., segregation processes) that have to be adequately captured by the theory.

A realist perspective appears feasible only under certain conditions. Political scientists can cope with this epistemological problem posed by the aggregation process as long as the agents' behavior can be aggregated by simple additive mechanisms. For example, political scientists can focus on the microlevel when they explain the political support for parties in a country or voting patterns. In this case, we can simply add the voting behavior of all individuals. Another strategy to deal with this problem is to focus on situations characterized by strong evolutionary pressure in which only some strategies survive in the long run. In those cases, the aggregation process is easily accessible. Finally, political scientists can cope with the problem in situations where strong institutional structures influence the aggregation process in that they strongly constrain the set of feasible social phenomena that could possibly result. For example, such constraints can ensure that certain actions do not have to be considered in the aggregation process (e.g., if ballot papers are filled out incorrectly or if a certain threshold of necessary votes to enter parliament has not been reached by the parties).

What matters in the case of such social patterns as *explananda* of political science is that a clear-cut decision either for realism or instrumentalism and thus for psychological explanations or structural explanations is not possible. Instead, the aggregation process has to be considered carefully in order to address the question of what is feasible and at which part of the process we can be realist or instrumentalist about RCTs. This is why in the following, we will focus primarily on the behavior of individual and of collective actors as the *explananda* for which RC-explanations are given.

In order to systematically reconstruct the different variants of RCTs in light of diverging explanatory demands, we draw on Coleman's boat. Prominently formulated by the sociologist James Coleman (1986, 1990), this is a scheme that allows us to discuss how the differences and similarities in explanatory demands toward RCTs play out in the application of RCTs in light of both kinds of *explananda*. For instance, depending on the *explanandum*, we need to ascribe psychologically informed assumptions to actors or not. Moreover, the *explanandum* frequently fixes the interpretation and methodological status of RCTs, as an internalist or externalist account.[13] Coleman's boat also reveals that RC-explanations of social phenomena, whether they are provided in an internalist or externalist mode, face the aggregation problem such that social patterns can be causally explained.

Generally, Coleman's boat specifies all the parts relevant for explaining social phenomena located on the macrolevel through individual and collective actors' (inter-) actions.[14] As shown in Figure 4.1, the scheme specifies social facts and explanatory relations based on causal dependencies at different steps of the explanation: in step (1), the social-structural conditions within which an agent is embedded are specified; in step (2), a set of explanatory relations are specified that describe how properties of the social structure causally

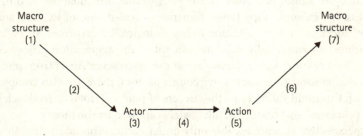

FIGURE 4.1. Coleman's boat (Coleman 1986, 1322, taken from Klein, Marx & Fischbach 2018, 12).

influence the individual actor and their properties, such as their desires and beliefs. In line with Siegwart Lindenberg's terminology (1981), we label the statements about those explanatory relations *bridge assumptions*.

Step (3) specifies the properties of agents with their perceptions and decision-making capacity. Those properties encompass beliefs, desires, habits, heuristics, goals, values, etc. Here, it must also be specified whether it is an individual or a collective actor. Step (4) specifies how agents choose their actions. The scheme allows for modeling such choices in any plausible way, including by using RCTs. Importantly, specifications in step (3) and step (4) do not necessarily refer to individual agents but also to collective agents. In that sense, the notion of microlevel is flexible in that it refers to the level of agency and not necessarily to the individual level (see also Ylikoski 2016, 6). In step (5), the behavioral outcome at the microlevel is specified. In step (6) the aggregation process is to be specified to describe the (intended or unintended) consequences of the agents' behavior on the social structure. In step (7), the updated social pattern is to be described.

In the following, we use Coleman's boat to further discuss how the uses and interpretations of RCTs for causal explanation in political science depend on the *explanandum* political scientists target and explain the consequences for the scope, power, and pitfalls of using RCTs for explanations in political science. We will see that separating human behavior and the behavior of collective actors as distinct *explananda* has implications for the explanatory demands raised toward RCTs in political science.

4. Explanations of Individual Behavior and their Challenges

Prima facie, the core of an RC-explanation refers to the level of the individual agent since the aforementioned conditions of RCTs specify an agent's behavior. One might, therefore, expect that RCTs lend themselves more naturally to explain human behavior and thereby fulfill the demands raised by psychological explanations. Political scientists apply RCTs to explain the behavior of individual agents, such as that of a single voter or a politician. As political scientists take RCTs to be an intention-based approach that causally explains human behavior, this has also been thought of as intentional explanations that identify the intention of the actor. Intentions, consisting of beliefs and desires, are interpreted as mental states that constitute reasons for an actor to behave in a certain way.

Realists are particularly prone to offer intentional explanations of individual behavior, when using RCTs (Elster 1988; Riker 1995). With regard to her goal, a rational actor always chooses the action she considers to be the best possible means of achieving her goals. Sometimes the relationship between intention and observed behavior is even considered to be lawful or at least understood as describing a robust and stable regularity. RCTs are then interpreted as psychological theories that refer to the mental states of individuals specifying the mechanism behind this regularity (see Bevir 2008; Green & Shapiro 1994, 20).

When reasons are interpreted as causes, RCTs offer causal explanations of individual behavior. On that interpretation, the actor's reason for an action causes him to perform that action; as such, the reason causally explains the action (Davidson 1963; Elster 1988;

Hedström 2005). For example, a presidential candidate's search for direct contact with the people can be explained by identifying his desires (he wants to win the election) and his beliefs (he believes he will get votes through direct contact with the people during the election campaign). This desire/belief-couple provides him with a reason to directly get in touch with people and thereby causes his behavior. In this view, intentional explanations are psychological explanations.[15]

Reconstructing this explanation in terms of the framework of Coleman's boat clarifies the explanatory demands that such an RC-explanation must meet for the realist: an explanation is valid if and only if the agent whose behavior we want to explain actually holds the relevant desires and beliefs that RCTs are postulating. The bridge assumptions in step 2 explicitly link features of the social structure to the agent's desires and beliefs. As such, they have to be empirically supported. Beliefs and desires are then assumed to have caused the action. The causal mechanism between desires/beliefs and behavior is specified in step 4.

The first challenge for such explanations using RCTs is that the political scientist has to refer to the existence of unobservable entities—intentions—which are difficult to measure. One way to bypass this challenge is by assuming loose preference categories as reasons for action for specific social groups and derive patterns of behavior of those groups. However, such categories are often justified in an ad hoc manner. For instance, political scientists might assume that the group of low-income employees are more likely to vote for conservative parties or that all political leaders prefer to stay in office and believe that they need the support of the electorate to do so (Downs 1957a). Based on such assumptions and the vague preference and belief categories underlying them, political scientists provide explanations of a specific voting pattern (see also Bevir 2008). Thus, given that they are based on imprecise or sometimes even false descriptions of causally effective beliefs and preferences, it is questionable whether such explanations can be taken to causally explain an individual's voting behavior.

Another common way in political science to measure intentions is to use survey instruments and ask actors directly about their desires and beliefs. This approach also faces several difficulties, one being that it is not clear to what extent general information about intentions gathered by surveys are relevant for identifying the intentions behind concrete actions that take place in a specific situational setting and at a different time than the survey (Zaller & Feldman 1992).

A potential solution to this first challenge has been that political scientists draw on revealed preference theory, another variant of RCTs from economics that was originally motivated to avoid making explicit assumptions about human psychology (Samuelson 1938). It is based on the idea that choices are consistent. Consistency is ensured by the so-called weak axiom of revealed preference. It says that if a voter prefers candidate A over candidate B in the election today, he will not vote for candidate B in the next election if candidate A is also available for election. While some defenders of revealed preference theory take the observation of choice to be sufficient for the analysis, recent proponents (e.g., Samuelson 1987) have gone one step further in arguing that from choice behavior, we can learn something about an agent's preferences. Because the voter is assumed to have stable preferences that lead him to behave consistently over time, we can use the observation of his past choices to predict his future behavior and potentially even get information about his political preferences.

The move toward revealed preference theory also faces problems, one being that the consistency assumption is a non-trivial assumption in political science. Politicians, lobby groups, voters, etc. may have reason to hide their true preferences, which is a phenomenon that is denied on most interpretations of revealed preference theory (Elster 1986). For instance, governments might frequently have strategic reasons for hiding their true preferences in international negotiations. It is thus questionable whether a revealed preference variant of RCTs can provide a causal explanation of some kinds of political behavior.

A second challenge for RCTs in fulfilling the explanatory demands for psychological explanations is that the empirical validity of the principle of (expected) utility as one main ingredient to describe the causal process behind individual behavior has been challenged (Kirchgässner 2008, 661 ff.). Psychological and neuroscientific results as well as experimental research in behavioral economics suggest that RCTs make unrealistic assumptions about psychological mechanisms, cognitive skills, and evaluative judgments (e.g., Kahneman 2003; Kahneman & Tversky 1979). Simon (1959) had already argued famously that individuals do not maximize their utility but are rather satisficers, i.e., they choose the action that, as the first and best possibility, fulfills the respective purpose. Along similar lines, Gigerenzer et al. (1999) have shown that limited rational behavior can even be beneficial to an individual. The debate about whether, and if so to which extent, RCTs and suggested alternatives, such as cumulative prospect theory, can be supported by empirical evidence is ongoing (e.g., Harrison & Swarthout 2016). Yet, those results have provoked the question whether the principle of expected utility can be used for causal explanation. They have frequently been taken to speak in favor of a theory that captures the actual causes behind human decision-making to better fulfill the explanatory demand raised by psychological explanations.

One way to cope with this second challenge is by committing to an externalist interpretation of RCTs (MacDonald 2003). However, this would strengthen the view of the instrumentalist that the primary criterion for their evaluation is their predictive power (cf. also Friedman 2008 [1953]). A counterargument raised by the realist against this move has been motivated by the question of how empirically inadequate assumptions can be permanently justified when predicting human behavior. If the theory does not describe causal relationships between mental states and behavior, then the selection of assumptions, as well as the theory itself, appears arbitrary. This may be acceptable as long as more or less precise predictions are made. However, if the causal structure behind the to-be-predicted behavior changes and if it possibly affects the behavior itself, then the theory would become useless also for predictions. The instrumentalist would not accept the conclusion of this argument. Yet, instrumentalists in political science have so far not given plausible reasons for why predictions turn out to be accurate for reasons other than that they are grounded in a theory that rests upon a set of assumptions approximating the actual causal structure behind the phenomenon to be predicted.

Another strategy has been to discuss the extent to which behavioral anomalies arise because of the fact that the relationship between desires, beliefs and actions does not meet the requirement of rationality (e.g., Opp 2020). In cases in which some of the requirements regarding beliefs or desires are violated, the core of RCTs would still be intact, and anomalies are grounded in violations of auxiliary assumptions (see Lakatos 1980; Watkins 2002). Following this line of reasoning, criticisms of RCTs grounded in psychological research give reason to discuss the empirical adequacy of auxiliary assumptions of RCTs but not to immediately reject RCTs as a whole.

A third challenge for using RCTs for psychological explanations concerns the relationship between theory and empirical observation. As mentioned before, mental states such as desires are unobservable. Because of the difficulties in measuring them, their specification is not easily possible. However, political scientists have argued that access to human intentions is possible through introspection and empathy (Riker 1995). A political scientist makes plausible assumptions about an actor's intentions, formulates predictions about her actions, and compares them with reality. If the action occurs as predicted, she has explained the action. Otherwise the assumptions about intentions have to be modified until the prediction matches the behavior observed (Riker 1995, 26). This process of testing and revision could not be accomplished without a theory.

RCTs have been used for such testing and revising purposes. Riker's discussion of the so-called "paradox of voter participation" is a case in point. RCTs are used here to analyze why voters go to the polls to vote for their favorite candidate (see also Kirchgässner 2008). Since Downs (1957a, b), voter participation has been formulated as a problem of collective action. The candidate's election is conceptualized as a public good: nobody can be excluded from its consumption, and there is no rivalry regarding its consumption. Whether citizens can consume the benefits (B) of the electoral victory is, therefore, independent of their vote. Furthermore, the probability that a single vote is decisive for the outcome of an election is close to zero. Consequently, an individual has no incentive to vote because she will benefit from her candidate's electoral victory no matter what.

Downs formulates the decision problem of a voter as follows: N is the expected utility of the electoral victory of the desired candidate minus the expected utility from the electoral victory of the undesired candidate. The rational voter knows that the probability p, with which her vote decides the outcome of the election, is insignificant. The benefits (B) and costs (C) of voting are included in the calculation of the citizen. The citizen will vote only if her overall expected utility (U) is higher than her expected cost:

$$p * N + B > C.$$

If $U = (p * N + B) < 0$, then the citizen will rely on her fellow citizens and free-ride. Since p is small, especially in the case of a high voter turnout, her expected costs of voting will be higher than the expected utility, even if she has a clear preference ordering regarding her candidates. Since her vote does not have a decisive influence on the outcome, she will minimize her costs and not vote while still benefiting from the advantages of the election outcome. RCTs thus predict a meager voter turnout.

This prediction differs from the observation that there is usually a high voter turnout. To explain that turnout, Riker integrates the idea that voters benefit from the very act of voting. He does so by adding further variables to the equation, such as doing one's civic duty (D):

$$p * N + B + D > C.$$

Riker and Ordeshook (1968) then show that an increase in D also increases voter turnout. On this basis, the modified theory can explain and predict a high voter turnout.

Riker and Ordeshook defend their strategy by pointing out the difficulty of possible alternative strategies, such as establishing indicators for motivations like "the duty to perform," collecting survey data, or using any other method to measure political preferences. Apart from the difficulties discussed above, another challenge of directly questioning or randomly conducting surveys is that the true preferences can be obscured, distorted, or concealed by false reports. This is particularly prevalent in political science since actors in a political context, be they candidates or voters, often have incentives to hide their true preferences.

Riker and Ordeshook's rescue attempts exemplify a methodological strategy of post hoc theory building. In the process of testing and revising RCTs, this is still common in political science (Green & Shapiro 1999, 47). Observations that contradict the theory's predictions are often not accepted as anomalies of the theory, which would lead to its replacement. Rather, the assumptions are modified such that the same theory can also explain the data that previously challenged it. The concept of utility can be reinterpreted on an ad hoc basis; almost anything that we can imagine introspectively can be assumed to influence utility. This, in turn, questions whether generalizations about voting behavior and its causes grounded in RCTs are justified and fruitful as well as whether empirically justified modifications are indeed possible.

An argument against such moves is that if no attempt is made to quantify the costs and benefits and weigh them against each other, the theory neither has explanatory nor predictive power. Depending on its assumptions, any behavior can arbitrarily be reconstructed as rational. What remains is, at best, a tautology whose scope of validity is in flux. Moreover, such ad hoc modifications have been criticized as reflecting the "theoretical convictions [of the scientist] to provide the necessary evidence to support the theory" (Green & Shapiro 1999, 70). Finally, the empirical content of RCTs can no longer be used as a decisive selection criterion for them. This is because with each ad hoc modification the boundary for clearly determining their empirical content becomes increasingly fuzzy.

Ad hoc modification is not a necessary solution strategy for addressing this last challenge. To give causal explanations of voter participation by using RCTs, Ferejohn and Fiorina (1974) take a different route by considering voting behavior under uncertain conditions. In such situations, the voter cannot calculate the probabilities of a candidate's electoral victory; she has to make her voting decision under uncertainty. They suggest applying the so-called minimax-regret criterion as a decision rule. According to this rule, the voter minimizes the possibility of realizing the option he prefers the least. In order to prevent the election of the least preferred candidate, i.e., the subjectively worst outcome, the voter has an incentive to participate in the election. However, it has become clear that this approach only partially explains the data (Dowding 2005, 8).

An alternative strategy to ad hoc modifications is to integrate RCTs into a more general theory of action. Dual-mode theories provide a good starting point (see Chaiken & Trope 1999). These theories distinguish between different modes of action. In the first mode, actors act rationally as defined in RCTs. In the second mode, actors follow internalized norms rather than reacting to structural incentives of the public good characterizing the situation. For instance, there are recent attempts to integrate the theory of voting into a general and formal theory of frame selection (e.g., Esser 2001; Kroneberg et al. 2010). This theory is based on the idea that actors make decisions by considering the social situation within which the decision takes place. The actors define a given situation with specific incentives by activating a particular frame (see step 2 on Coleman's boat). Frames not only include information about what kind of situation the actor is embedded in but can also provide behavioral predispositions, for example, in the form of social norms for typical situations of social and political life. Behavior is still considered to be rational because, within the frame, it is goal-oriented. Additionally, RCTs can come into play when frames do not sufficiently guide the course of action and actors must actively decide how to behave. As such, RCTs turn into a special case of this more general theory.

Adopting the theory of frame selection to explain voting behavior has important implications. Given an electoral norm that exists in a society, the more internalized that electoral norm, the fewer voters take the costs of voting into account in their voting decision. Only when a voter has not internalized a norm will he actively consider the costs of voting and other aspects to calculate his expected benefits of voting. Kroneberg et al. (2010) argue that as long as it can be theoretically specified under which conditions rational action is to be expected, the integration of RCTs into a general theory of action should not be understood as an immunization strategy against empirical criticism. At the same time, the theory can indeed predict the voting participation of people who have internalized the electoral norm.

This discussion shows that analytical variants of RCTs face several challenges in explaining individual behavior. By including social preferences or norms conceptually into such analytical variants, they are gradually turned into empirical variants. We take this to be an indicator for the emergence of a partial consensus among political scientists that analytical variants of RCTs are limited in causally explaining human behavior. Despite those challenges, political scientists have reasons to argue for the usefulness of empirical variants to explain individual political behavior (Satz & Ferejohn 1994). The described modifications in the economic theory of voting have been justified on an ad hoc basis to reject criticism based upon empirical findings. Yet, RCTs seem to fulfill their explanatory potential in domains concerned with individual behavior only if their psychologically informed empirical variants are applied. Such variants in turn require an empirical analysis of actual preferences and restrictions to justify them.

5. EXPLAINING THE BEHAVIOR OF COLLECTIVE ACTORS AND THEIR CHALLENGES

We have seen that analytical variants of RCTs are confronted with challenges when used to explain human behavior; those variants rarely fulfill the explanatory demands raised by the mode of psychological explanations. The fact that analytical variants are often in conflict with how human agents actually behave implies that they are more likely to fail in their role of causally explaining individual behavior. However, given that different *explananda* require distinct modes of explanation that raise in turn different explanatory demands, RCTs need not always be used as a psychological theory in order to be considered useful in political science. Analytical variants of RCTs are typically considered successful in situations with strong structural incentives where individual choice does not play a role because in these cases, the ascribed preferences and beliefs do not play a causally relevant role. Additionally, the empirical inadequacy of the analytical variants might not be as problematic when used to explain the behavior of collective agents. In this case, they are also more likely to be useful.

The most plausible applications of analytical variants of RCTs in political science are in moderate externalist explanations of actions involving collective actors. In such explanations, the institutional, or more generally, social context plays a crucial role in bringing about behavior. In situations in which structural incentives sharply restrict the choice of available options, psychological mechanisms can be neglected. Examples are high-cost situations (Mensch 2000) or institutional contexts with intense evolutionary pressure where it has been argued that, in the long run, non-rational actors are driven out or focus on instrumental goods whose usefulness for all actors can be assumed (Zintl 2001). More generally, similar to Karl Popper's (1985) account of situational analysis, externalists argue that it is not the intentions but the context that must be sufficiently specified in order to causally explain behavioral patterns at the macrolevel. This is because not the motives but the structural features of the context modeled as situational restrictions that are assumed to direct an agent's behavior are the causally relevant factors. Consequences of behavior—mostly on the macrolevel—are explained by a change in external conditions of the situation in which this behavior is performed.

Providing an explanation in terms of externally given structural features avoids the problem of attributing actual preferences and beliefs to individual agents. In cases where an agent's choice does not play a primary role in bringing about the behavioral changes, scientists can "concentrate on the logic of the agent's situation and are spared the complexities of the psychology of the agent in that situation" (Latsis 1972, 211). For a satisfying representation of individual behavior in such explanations, it is sufficient that the principle of (expected) utility adequately describes the behavior observed, a move that is often justified by the assumption that actors behave *as if* they maximize their utility. A consequence of this strategy is that the scope of RCTs frequently acknowledged also by instrumentalists is limited to only those situations where behavioral changes can be attributed entirely to changes in the structural features characterizing the context.

Some political scientists justify as-if assumptions by means of an evolutionary argument (Riker 1995; Satz & Ferejohn 1994). Political actors survive in a competitive environment only if they have successfully asserted themselves in the past and will do so in the future. Otherwise, they would in the long run be excluded from the political arena and economic life (Riker 1995, 36). Going back to Coleman's boat (see Figure 4.1), this process would be specified in step 6. A number of transformational assumptions would have to be made about the competitive features of the environment to specify the aggregation process. Those assumptions would make sure that only those actors survive in the market that behave in line with RCTs.

To see an example, let us start with the observation that political parties stand in competition with other parties (Downs 1957a). In order to survive, they behave as if they represent the aims of their potential voters, which would be the rational thing to do; parties might or might not actually be motivated in that way. However, for explaining their behavior, it matters only that they behave as if they were intending to represent the interests of the voters. This is because only then could a party remain competitive alongside other political parties in terms of attracting voters and survive in the political market. Parties that do not behave in line with the principle of expected utility will remain niche parties and are negligible in the political process. In such cases, the strong institutional context allows the ascription of preferences and desires by means of bridge assumptions (step 2) without measuring them directly. Accordingly, the externalist explanations of voting behavior are less successful than those of political parties because voting behavior does not occur in a particularly competitive environment. More specifically, the individual voter does not compete strongly with other voters in terms of achieving her goals. Therefore, the model of externalist explanations is less plausible to explain voting behavior (Satz & Ferejohn 1994, 79; Riker 1995, 35).

The model of moderate externalist explanations avoids the measurement problems that psychological explanations face. By shifting the explanatory focus to the situation, they partially counter the accusations that RCTs is an inadequate psychological theory. Furthermore, the account enables RCTs to be detached from the reductionist doctrine of methodological individualism. Such a detachment, albeit not extensively practiced in political science, seems plausible here, since collective actors play an important role in political science. The externalist model can explain the behavior of actors, such as parties, governments, committees, or states, if we accept that it is the irreducible external structures, such as competition, a voting system, a political order, a legal system, or bureaucratic structures, that directly affect the behavior of those actors.

Following Satz and Ferejohn (1994), the difference in explanatory power of the two central building blocks of Downs's theory of democracy (party positioning and voting behavior) can be explained by differences in the context in which both kinds of behavior take place. They argue that strong structures evoke specific interests of the parties, which allows for an externalist explanation of party positions. Ascribed preferences for parties, such as, e.g., office-seeking and a specific policy to maximize votes, are not directly measured or observed. Instead, those preferences are fictitiously imputed and solely grounded in the parties' position in exogenously given social structures. They are not grounded in psychological factors of any individual party. In comparison, there is no analogous mechanism with a strong competitive pressure in the case of the voters.

What is puzzling, however, is why such as-if assumptions about preferences lead to successful RC explanations only in the case of party positioning under strong social structures. Indeed, an equally powerful explanation cannot be found for voting behavior and under weak social structures. Even if this observation seems natural for rational choice theorists, instrumentalists fail to give a convincing explanation for this observation. If all ascriptions of preferences are merely fictitious, there should be no differences in the explanatory or predictive power of both parts of Downs' theory. In each of the parts, we find significant effects of social structures on the agents' attitude formation (see step 2 in Coleman's boat). Yet, while in the case of party positioning, the strong structural incentives allow for ascribing preferences with the bridge assumptions to parties that are empirically supported, this is not true for voting behavior. Here, the structural setting of the political market does not allow for making bridge assumptions that capture the preferences and beliefs of the individual actors. Instead, social norms and conventions, as well as other social and psychological factors, can come into play and have to be considered in constructing empirically valid bridge assumptions. In such cases, however, the bridge assumptions in question cannot be ascribed theoretically, but must be empirically assessed.

Looking more closely, we see that the success of RC explanations in political science lies in the combination of causally effective structures and causally active preferences and beliefs. This does not mean that operating with as-if assumptions is useless. We have described external structures that make the use of analytical models reasonable. However, insofar as RCTs are explanatory, instrumentalists' interpretations are misguided. Even RCTs that operate with as-if assumptions have to be understood realistically in that theoretical assumptions about structural features that make specific attitude ascriptions plausible should be interpreted as empirical hypotheses about causally active factors.

A convinced instrumentalist in political science might object that he is not interested in explanations but only in predictions. Our argumentation, nevertheless, challenges the instrumentalist position. If RCTs are not a miracle machine that sometimes give correct predictions and sometimes do not, one must specify the conditions under which analytical variants of RCTs operating with as-if assumptions work. We argued that the usefulness of RCTs described above depends on the fact that influential structural factors in the situational setting allow the ascription of empirically plausible bridge assumptions without the need to survey them empirically. In other words, analytical variants of RCTs are successful in explanations as long as they take the same variables as causally active as realistic accounts of RCTs would do in those cases.

A further observation may help to specify the range in which analytical models can be successfully applied. The application of RCTs to collective actors shows an advantage for the use of analytical variants of RCTs in this domain. Since it appears plausible that we cannot ascribe cognitive processes to collective actors (see also Kincaid 2019), they are less prone to psychological anomalies of rational action or committed to social norms or habits. Instead, structural factors can indeed be expected to play a significant role in explaining collective actors' actions. One could argue in line with orthodox methodological individualism that the explanation is incomplete as long as explanations do not refer to the interactions of individuals in the collective body that bring out their actions. Only when the individual level is considered, a proper causal explanation of the action is given, and, here at the latest, psychological factors come back into play.

There are good reasons to reject this objective (see Tollefsen 2002; Pettit 2014). List and Pettit (2011), for example, argue that collective actors should be treated as actors similar to individual actors and that standards of rationality concerning the beliefs of collective actors must not be met at the level of the individual but the level of the collective actor. These ideas have not yet been systematically explored in theory formation in the social sciences (List & Spiekermann 2013). As such, it remains one of the central puzzles in the future development of RCTs also in political science.

6. THE ROLE OF RATIONAL CHOICE THEORIES IN HOW-POSSIBLY EXPLANATIONS

So far, we discussed the ways in which political scientists think that RCTs can be successfully used in providing causal explanations. This discussion presupposes that the epistemic virtue of explanatory power is a justified and a key criterion for appraising RCTs. We argued that whether different variants of RCTs are useful for explanations depends on the kind of *explananda* targeted and whether RCTs can meet the explanatory demands those *explananda* require. Explanatory power is a property that is generally attributed to theories and models. Yet, political scientists also use RCTs for other epistemic purposes. As such, it has been debated whether explanatory power should be the only criterion for assessing RCTs in political science.

Instead of fundamentally questioning the criterion of explanatory power to assess the usefulness of RCTs, we ask whether the current concept of causal explanation in political science is the most useful one. Large parts of political science rest upon the traditional deductive-nomological model of explanation (Clarke & Primo 2012), recently complemented by the idea that laws should be further justified by identifying the causal mechanisms underlying them (Hedström & Ylikoski 2010). The goal is to provide what has been called a how-actually explanation (Machamer et al. 2000). In political science, this amounts to, first, identifying an observable stable regularity and, second, substantiating it with the actual mechanism, i.e., identifying the real components, activities, and organizational features that in fact bring about this regularity and thereby function as its cause. Here, a structural similarity between a realist interpretation of Coleman's boat and the concept of a mechanistic explanation becomes apparent (see Hedström & Swedberg 1998). We propose in this last section that in light of our discussion, this concept of explanation is too thin to cover all of the main explanatory practices in political science.

Johnson (1996, 2010, 2015) as a pragmatist and a defender of RCTs questions explanatory power and, more generally, empirical performance as useful and as the only criteria for appraising RCTs in political science. He argues that a "naive falsificationism" underlying most critical assessments of RCTs misleadingly suggests that political science is solely concerned with empirical testing of hypotheses and that RCTs are solely used for this purpose. According to Johnson, such a narrow view of what political scientists do overlooks the usefulness of RCTs in other epistemic contexts that do not target the deduction and falsification of singular statements to offer explanations and predictions (Johnson 2010; see also Hay 2004). He furthermore points out that this view rests on a misunderstanding of what a causal explanation should amount to in political science.[16]

Johnson supports his position by providing an alternative view of what RCTs are, how political scientists should think of explanations, and what role RCTs plays in such explanations. According to Johnson, RCTs such as game theory are not scientific *theories* of political action or of any other political phenomenon. Instead, we should think of them more modestly as a "methodology" that provides a set of mathematical techniques for modeling human behavior and strategic interaction (Johnson 2010, 283). Rather than using RCTs only for the deduction of testable hypotheses, they are also used as tools for other epistemic purposes, such as conceptual exploration (Johnson 2010, 2014). Such alternative applications are not acknowledged in the dichotomy between realism and instrumentalism that dominates the debate about the usefulness of RCTs in political science. Political scientists should therefore abandon this dichotomy to move forward in the debate. A pragmatist position would allow rational choice theorists to do so. While pragmatists can be realists about theoretical entities and causal explanations as the aim of science, they can have an instrumentalist view of theories as tools to solve empirical *and* conceptual problems (Johnson 2010, 290).

Johnson's argument rests on the idea that RC models are only sometimes used for explanation; and even if they are, RCTs do not all engage in the same kind of explanatory enterprise. While, for example, Kenneth Arrow's (1951) social choice theory—an RC variant—is not engaged in the business of explanation at all, other RC models such as Olson's (1965) are explanatory but in ways that differ from the traditional deductive-nomological model of explanation that a naive falsificationist in political science commits to (Johnson 1996). According to Johnson, explanation in political science also involves the search for causal mechanisms. However, the usefulness of exploring such mechanisms does not depend on them being true or producing good predictions. Rather, the usefulness of the mechanism depends on the empirical and conceptual "suppleness" that it lends to higher-level theories in which it is integrated (Johnson 1996, 85). RCTs allow for specifying such causal mechanisms and thereby provide one way to make conceptually explicit under which conditions the phenomenon is reliably produced, "reliably" here meaning that the specified mechanism would not be necessary but sufficient to bring about the phenomenon. They thereby allow us to also expand the domain within which the operation of the mechanism can be expected.

What does such conceptual exploration amount to and how does it relate to causal explanation? Johnson illustrates how one goal of using RC models in political science is the "rationalization" of patterns of political behavior by showing how a pattern of observed political behavior is shown to result from the assumptions of RCTs in that model. The aim of such a modeling exercise is to specify particular causal mechanisms that could bring the behavior about; in that sense, it is explanatory. Such explanations can be given on the basis of RCTs because RCTs help establish a set of sufficient conditions for producing the *explanandum*. While essential for RC explanations, such conceptual exploration is not directly an empirical task. It explains behavioral patterns based on a well-specified mechanism. But only when the specified conditions actually obtain can we expect the mechanism to actually operate.

This view of RC explanations comes closest to what has been called how-possibly explanations (e.g., Grüne-Yanoff 2009, 2013). As opposed to how-actually explanations that identify the actual mechanism, how-possibly explanations aim at providing mechanisms that could possibly bring about the *explanandum* in question (Reutlinger et al. 2018). How-possibly explanations do not claim that the mechanisms identified are actually operating in the world. Moreover, as causal mechanisms are often not directly observable, we do not always know which mechanism is *actually* driving the phenomenon. As such, it has been debated whether how-possibly explanations can be understood as adequate causal-mechanistic explanations (e.g., Craver 2006). They can be understood as explanations insofar as they identify a potential mechanism that explains the phenomenon observed by showing one possible way of how the phenomenon could have emerged (Johnson 2010, 294).[17] As such, how-possibly explanations figure as heuristically useful in marking out the space of explanatory mechanisms that could in principle be operating (Craver 2006, 361).

The concept of how-possibly explanation is useful when thinking about the way in which analytical variants of RCTs can be explanatory, even if they rest upon assumptions that do not hold in the particular situation. It is a scientific practice in political science that belongs to the scientific process toward providing causal explanations. By providing how-possibly explanations, modelers are not committed to the ontological claim that the assumptions in their model are empirically true. Rather, one aim is to provide counterfactual explanations. As such, however, they do not call into question established generalizations or violate the rules of logic (Hands 2016, 38). Rather, based on the generalization of utility maximization, they elaborate on how the world would be like if, for example, all people would maximize only income and power. Such models thereby provide a reference point to assess the impact of social preferences, norms, conventions, and other variables that can then be included in empirical variants of RCTs. Acknowledging this explanatory practice in political science would help us to better understand the performance of RCTs in terms of the performance of analytical and empirical variants.[18] RC explanations in the moderate externalist mode and grounded in analytical variants could be understood as attempts to identify one set alongside other possible causal mechanisms that *could* bring about a phenomenon.

Johnson himself suggests that instead of thinking about RCTs as explanatory theories, we should think of them as constituting a research tradition in the sense of Larry Laudan. That way, RCTs would not be questioned for lacking explanatory power, nor would a categorical rejection of any theory that is part of this research tradition be useful. A theory within such a tradition can only be assessed in a comparative way with an alternative theory (Johnson 1996). According to proponents of RCTs, however, hardly any comparable alternatives exist (Kirchgässner 2008). Less theory-oriented approaches, such as historical institutionalism, which exclusively refer to historical case studies, or behaviorism, which only focuses on empirical observation, are largely rejected as serious alternatives (Bevir 2008, 53).

However, as a discipline, political science is also too diverse and too pluralistic to argue that RCTs are the only theoretical games in town. In areas such as voting research, for example, political scientists increasingly use theories from social psychology (e.g., Redlawsk et al. 2017), while in research on social mobility, sociological theories play a crucial role (e.g., Buechler 2016). Some social scientists have therefore not only rejected the organization of social science research around one universal theory of human behavior but also around research programs or research traditions (Hedström & Udehn 2009). They argue for a middle ground to keep a commitment to theory-based research and to the goal of providing explanations while not taking any of those theories to be universal.

The primary search for causal mechanisms instead of an inquiry into general laws has been a recent trend also in political science (e.g., Alexander & Bennett 2005, Bennett 2003; Tilly 2001). Apart from the fact that we could accommodate how-possibly explanations, another advantage of prioritizing the mechanistic approach is that it takes seriously the idea that causal explanation is the main goal in political science, while allowing for theories to be empirically valid only in some local context. The mechanistic program aims at research in political science that (1) clarifies individual-level causal mechanisms; (2) theoretically captures the actual aggregation process from individual to social phenomena and back to individual behavior as well as how such behavior is constrained; (3) formulates middle-range theories that combine agent- and structure-centered mechanisms; and (4) aims at understanding how such theories can be applied when actors, interests, identities, and political rules and institutions are fairly stable (see Bennett 2003).[19] The search for mechanisms can be systematically assigned to the individual steps of Coleman's boat. It is required that reliable hypotheses about the influence of structural variables on the preferences and beliefs of the actors are established, that the behavior of the actors is appropriately recorded at the microlevel, and that the aggregation process is adequately mapped.

We suggest that the mechanistic program provides a notion of explanation that is most useful for political science to improve causal explanations of robust empirical regularities, such as Duverger's law or the Lipset hypothesis, and use those, in turn, to further inform theorizing about the causal mechanisms sustaining them (Bennett 2003, Johnson 2006).[20] This program would help settle disagreement on what a good model of causal explanation in political science amounts to. As this disagreement is most apparent in the debate about the explanatory power of RCTs (Tilly 2001, 22), adopting a mechanistic model of explanation would help provide a more precise understanding of the different explanatory practices in which political scientists make use of RCTs. The kind of how-possibly explanations that models based on analytical variants of RCTs provide would further advance such a program in political science (see also Johnson 2006).

Despite such pragmatist justifications of using RCTs for how-possibly explanations in political science, there remains a set of deeper philosophical concerns when such explanations are taken to identify the actual mechanism. In this case, Johnson also has to concede that they require attributions of mental state variables. RC explanations must then deal with the question of how mental phenomena, such as reasons, can cause physical phenomena such as bodily movements, which is the so-called mind-body problem. Furthermore, Davidson (1963) has argued that the attribution of beliefs, preferences, and actions is only possible when two of those three variables are given: Beliefs and preferences are needed to see the difference between bodily movements and an action. Action and beliefs are needed to ascribe preferences and knowledge about actions, and preferences allow for the ascription of beliefs. If we take Davidson's position seriously, one consequence would be that the character of the principle of rationality would change fundamentally. It would no longer be a statement that needs to, or could even be, empirically verified. Rather, it would have to be presupposed to make intentions and action comprehensible in the first place. Whether both concerns would have serious implications for the use of RCTs in causal explanations of human behavior is an issue that needs to be discussed further. However, it is remarkable that they have so far been largely ignored in discussions about the uses and usefulness of RCTs in political science altogether.

7. CONCLUSION

Despite their broad application, the benefit of RCTs in offering causal explanations in political science is controversial. In this chapter, we suggest that the debate about the explanatory power of RCTs would benefit from carefully considering the different kinds of explanatory practices that political scientists engage in. First, we propose distinguishing between different *explananda* in political science to assess the explanatory usefulness of RCTs. We separated individual human behavior and the behavior of collective actors as well as the consequences resulting from their interaction. In the case of individual behavior, the explanatory burden lies directly on RCTs; their explanatory role is that of a psychological theory. In the case of the behavior of collective agents, RCTs do not have to carry the explanatory burden of a psychologically informed theory. Rather RCTs facilitate an explanation by helping to specify evolutionary mechanisms or restrictions guiding a collective agent's behavior. Distinguishing between them shows that, similar to an appraisal of other approaches in political science, the usefulness of RC explanations would benefit from a nuanced discussion that takes seriously the distinction also between different modes of explanation and the distinct explanatory demands they raise. To capture this nuance, we suggested that political science should move toward a broad concept of explanation that captures not only the explicit search for causal mechanisms but also acknowledge explanatory activities—such as forms of conceptual exploration and how-possibly explanations—that are conducive to identify actual mechanisms. Acknowledging those different explanatory activities in political science would benefit the debate about the usefulness of RCTs in providing explanations more generally.

ACKNOWLEDGMENTS

Parts of this paper are grounded in Herfeld (2017) and Marx and Tiefensee (2015). Johannes Marx's research was financially supported by the German Research Foundation (DFG) in the context of the project "Simulating Collective Agency" (MA 4716/4-1).

NOTES

1. The most important critical assessment of RC explanations in political science is by Green and Shapiro (1994, 1999). They argue that because of severe deficiencies in empirical research that is meant to support RC explanations of political phenomena, RCT's explanatory power remains at best unclear.

2. "Directly observable" refers to the measurement of motives via survey methods and interviews.

3. Note that the terminology of "analytical variant" is misleading in that the specification of the core concepts are—via the use of theory—ultimately also informed by the world. However, those specifications about the content of preferences and beliefs are not directly empirically assessed and are typically theoretically specified. For a detailed description of the characteristics of each variant see Opp (2009, 2011).

4. Other variants of RCT used in political science are game theory and social choice theory. For discussions see Arrow (1958), Johnson & Schrodt (1991), and Osborne (2004).

5. Note that transitivity does not say anything about the intensity of preferences.

6. The distinction is in part reflected in the ongoing debate in philosophy about the interpretation of preferences as either behavioral or mentalist (see, e.g., Angner 2018, Guala 2019).

7. Theories of decision-making under uncertainty are extensively used for normative questions, such as, for example, in Rawls' modeling of the decision situation in the original position and the function of the "veil of ignorance" (1971, 119).

8. There is a sophisticated discussion in the philosophical literature about this distinction and its role in the debate about RCT and a theory of action more generally (see, e.g., Ross 2005; Dennett 1991, 1987). While we are not able to go into the complexities of actual political science practices, here we are primarily concerned with the self-descriptions of political scientists.

9. There is a debate about what exactly structuralism as an explanatory model and structural causation amount to that we cannot engage with here. Little defines causal structural explanations in terms of two claims: First, that societies are complex systems embodying an infinite range of social structures; and, second, that key features of societies can be explained as the causal consequence of the particular details of these structures, whereby the causal powers of such social structures are taken to be embodied in particular causal mechanisms mediated by individual action (Little 1991, 103). For a discussion of the

difficulties of understanding structuralist explanations as causal explanations, see also Little (1991, ch. 5).

10. The ongoing philosophical discussion about whether mental states can also be attributed to collective actors is largely ignored in political science (see Pettit 2014).

11. Note that even if the utility function that we provide fit the observed behavior, the radical externalist would not use it to causally explain behavior because she denies the existence of mental states altogether.

12. While critical realists defend the view that supra-individual entities, including organizations and other institutions, have causal powers, Satz and Ferejohn seem to presuppose ontological individualism underlying the positions of radical and moderate externalism.

13. Coleman's boat has been formulated and interpreted in many different ways (see Ylikoski 2016). The central idea of this scheme goes back to McClelland. Coleman became familiar with this scheme through Siegwart Lindenberg (Raub & Voss 2017). We closely follow Lindenberg in our terminology and interpretation of the diagram. For example, Lindenberg introduced the concept of "bridge assumptions", which should not be confused with bridge principles famously introduced by the logical empiricists.

14. For an exposition and interpretation of Coleman's boat, see Ylikoski (2016).

15. Note that there is a debate about whether intentional explanations are causal explanations or whether they are in fact a counter model to causal explanations (see, e.g., von Wright 1971).

16. Johnson mainly discusses game theory. However, his arguments can be extended to other RCT as well.

17. The mechanism specified in the model can as such be understood as a sufficient but not necessary condition for the existence of the social phenomenon.

18. For a discussion of what makes models epistemically useful in giving how-possibly explanations, see Grüne-Yanoff and Verreault-Julien (forthcoming).

19. There is an ongoing debate about whether mechanism-based social explanations imply a commitment to methodological individualism and which has been argued against by, e.g., Van Bouwel (2019).

20. Duverger's law asserts that electoral systems characterized by plurality rule in single-member districts sustain two-party systems, and Lipset's hypothesis postulates a regularity between prosperity and the propensity to experience democracy (Johnson 2006, 240).

References

Anand, Paul, Prasanta K. Pattanaik, and Clemens Puppe (Eds.) (2009): *The Handbook of Rational and Social Choice: An Overview of New Foundations and Applications.* Oxford: Oxford University Press.

Andeweg, Rudy W., Lieven De Winter, and Patrick Dumont (Eds.) (2011): *Puzzles of Government Formation: Coalition Theory and Deviant Cases.* New York: Routledge.

Angner, Erik (2018): What Preferences Really Are. *Philosophy of Science*, 85 (4), pp. 660–681.

Arrow, Kenneth J. (1951): *Social Choice and Individual Values.* New Haven, CT: Yale University Press.

Arrow, Kenneth J. (1958): Utilities, Attitudes, Choices: A Review Note. *Econometrica*, 26 (1), pp. 1–23.

Bennett, Andrew (2003): *Beyond Hempel and Back to Hume: Causal Mechanisms and Causal Explanation*. Unpublished Paper presented at the American Political Science Association Annual Conference, Philadelphia, August 28, 2003.

Berlin, Isaiah (1999): Does Political Theory Still Exist? In Henry Hardy (Ed.): *Concepts and Categories: Philosophical Essays*, pp. 143–172. London: Pimlico.

Bevir, Mark (2008): Meta-Methodology: Clearing the Underbrush. In Janet M. Box-Steffensmeier, Henry E. Brady, and David Collier (Eds.): *The Oxford Handbook of Political Methodology*, pp. 48–70. New York: Oxford University Press.

Box-Steffensmeier, Janet M., Henry E. Brady, and David Collier (Eds.) (2008): *The Oxford Handbook of Political Methodology*. New York: Oxford University Press.

Brady, Henry E. (2008): Causation and Explanation in Social Science. In Janet M. Box-Steffensmeier, Henry E. Brady, and David Collier (Eds.): *The Oxford Handbook of Political Methodology*, pp. 217–270. New York: Oxford University Press.

Buechler, Steven M. (2016): *Understanding Social Movements: Theories from the Classical Era to the Present*. New York: Routledge.

Bueno de Mesquita, Bruce, Alastair Smith, Randolph M. Siverson, and James D. Morrow (2005): *The Logic of Political Survival*. Cambridge, MA: MIT Press.

Bunge, Mario (1995): The Poverty of Rational Choice Theory. In Ian C. Jarvie, and Nathaniel Laor (Eds.): *Critical Rationalism, Metaphysics and Science*, pp. 149–168. Dordrecht: Springer.

Chaiken, Shelly, and Yaacov Trope (Eds.) (1999): *Dual-Process Theories in Social Psychology*. New York: Guilford Press.

Clarke, Kevin A., and David M. Primo (2012): *A Model Discipline: Political Science and the Logic of Representations*. New York: Oxford University Press.

Coleman, James S. (1986): Social Theory, Social Research, and a Theory of Action. *American Journal of Sociology*, 91 (6), pp. 1309–1335.

Coleman, James S. (1990): *Foundations of Social Theory*. Cambridge, MA: Belknap Press of Harvard University Press.

Craver, Carl F. (2006): When Mechanistic Models Explain. *Synthese*, 153, pp. 355–376.

Davidson, Donald (1963): Actions, Reasons, and Causes. *The Journal of Philosophy*, 60 (23), pp. 685–700.

Dennett, Daniel C. (1991): *Consciousness Explained*. New York: Little, Brown and Company.

Dowding, Keith (2005): Is it Rational to Vote? Five Types of Answer and a Suggestion. *The British Journal of Politics and International Relations*, 7 (3), pp. 442–459.

Downs, Anthony (1957a): An Economic Theory of Political Action in a Democracy. *Journal of Political Economy*, 65(2), pp. 135–150.

Downs, Anthony (1957b): *An Economic Theory of Democracy*. New York: Harper.

Dryzek, John S., Bonnie Honig, and Anne Phillips (2006): Introduction. In John S. Dryzek, Bonnie Honig, and Anne Phillips (Eds.): *The Oxford Handbook of Political Theory*, pp. 3–41. Oxford: Oxford University Press.

Dryzek, John S., Bonnie Honig, and Anne Phillips (Eds.) (2006): *The Oxford Handbook of Political Theory*. Oxford: Oxford University Press.

Elster, Jon (1986): The Market and the Forum: Three Varieties of Political Theories. In Jon Elster, and Aanund Hylland (Eds.): *Foundations of Social Choice Theory*, pp. 103–132. Cambridge: Cambridge University Press.

Elster, Jon (1988): The Nature and Scope of Rational-Choice Explanation. In Edna Ullmann-Margalit (Ed.): *Science in Reflection. The Israel Colloquium: Studies in History, Philosophy, and Sociology of Science Volume 3*, pp. 51–65. Dordrecht: Springer.

Elster, Jon (2000): Review: Rational Choice History: A Case of Excessive Ambition. *American Political Science Review*, 94 (3), pp. 685–695.

Esser, Hartmut (2001): *Soziologie. Spezielle Grundlagen: Band 6: Sinn und Kultur*. Frankfurt a. M.: Campus.

Ferejohn, John A. and Morris P. Fiorina (1974): The Paradox of Not Voting: A Decision-Theoretic Analysis. *American Political Science Review*, 68 (2), pp. 525–536.

Friedman, Milton (2008/1953): The Methodology of Positive Economics. In Daniel M. Hausman (Ed.): *The Philosophy of Economics: An Anthology*, pp. 145–178. Cambridge: Cambridge University Press.

Gigerenzer, Gerd, Peter M. Todd, and ABC Research Group (1999): *Simple Heuristics that Make us Smart*. New York: Oxford University Press.

Green, Donald P. und Ian Shapiro (1994): *Pathologies of Rational Choice Theory: The Critique of Applications in Political Science*. New Haven, CT: Yale University Press.

Green, Donald P. und Ian Shapiro (1995): Pathologies Revisited: Reflections on our Critics. *Critical Review*, 9 (1/2), pp. 235–76.

Green, Donald P. und Ian Shapiro (1999): *Rational Choice: Eine Kritik am Beispiel von Anwendungen in der Politischen Wissenschaft*. München: Oldenburg Wissenschaftsverlag.

Grüne-Yanoff, Till (2009): Learning from Minimal Economic Models. *Erkenntnis*, 70 (1), pp. 81–99.

Grüne-Yanoff, Till (2013): Appraising Models Nonrepresentationally, *Philosophy of Science*, 80 (5), pp. 850–861.

Grüne-Yanoff, Till, and Philippe Verreault-Julien (forthcoming): How-Possibly Explanations in Economics: Anything Goes? [Preprint] URL: http://philsci-archive.pitt.edu/id/eprint/18423 (accessed 2020-12-05).

Guala, Francesco (2019): Preferences: Neither Behavioural nor Mental. *Economics & Philosophy*, 35 (3), pp. 383–401.

Hands, D. Wade (2016): Derivational Robustness, Credible Substitute Systems and Mathematical Economic Models: The Case of Stability Analysis in Walrasian General Equilibrium Theory. *European Journal for Philosophy of Science*, 6 (1), pp. 31–53.

Hardin, Russell (1976): Hollow Victory: The Minimum Winning Coalition. *The American Political Science Review*, 70 (4), pp. 1202–1214.

Hardin, Russell (1990): Book Review of "Beyond Optimizing: A Study of Rational Choice" by Michael Slote. *American Political Science Review*, 84 (3), pp. 977–978.

Hardin, Russell (1993): From Power to Order, from Hobbes to Hume. *Journal of Political Philosophy*, 1 (1), pp. 69–81.

Harrison, Glenn W., and J. Todd Swarthout (2016): Cumulative Prospect Theory in the Laboratory: A Reconsideration. No 2016-04, Experimental Economics Center Working Paper Series, Experimental Economics Center, Andrew Young School of Policy Studies, Georgia State University.

Hay, Colin (2004): Theory, Stylized Heuristic or Self-Fulfilling Prophecy? The Status of Rational Choice Theory in Public Administration. *Public Administration*, 82 (1), pp. 39–62.

Hechter, Michael, and Satoshi Kanazawa (1997): Sociological Rational Choice Theory. *Annual Review of Sociology*, 23, pp. 191–214.

Hedström, Peter, and Petri Ylikoski (2010): Causal Mechanisms in the Social Sciences. *Annual Review of Sociology*, 36 (1), pp. 49–67.

Hedström, Peter, and Lars Udehn (2009): Analytical Sociology and Theories of the Middle Range. In Peter Hedström, and Peter Bearman (Eds.): *The Oxford Handbook of Analytical Sociology*, pp. 25–47. Oxford: Oxford University Press.

Hedström, Peter (2005): *Dissecting the Social: On the Principles of Analytical Sociology.* Cambridge: Cambridge University Press.

Herfeld, Catherine (2017): Philosophie der Politikwissenschaft. In Simon Lohse, and Thomas Reydon (Eds.): *Grundriss Wissenschaftsphilosophie: Die Philosophien der Einzelwissenschaften*, pp. 615–650. Hamburg: Felix Meiner Verlag.

Herfeld, Catherine (2020): The Diversity of Rational Choice Theory: A Review Note. *Topoi*, 39 (2), pp. 329–347.

Herne, Kaisa, and Majia Setälä (2004): A Response to the Critique of Rational Choice Theory: Lakatos' and Laudan's Conceptions Applied. *Inquiry*, 47 (1), pp. 67–85.

Hoggett, Paul, and Simon Thompson (Eds.) (2012): *Politics and the Emotions: The Affective Turn in Contemporary Political Studies.* New York: Bloomsbury Publishing.

Johnson, James (1993): Is Talk Really Cheap? Prompting Conversation between Critical Theory and Rational Choice. *American Political Science Review*, 87 (1), pp. 74–86.

Johnson, James (1996): How Not to Criticize Rational Choice Theory: Pathologies of "Common Sense." *Philosophy of the Social Sciences*, 26 (1), pp. 77–91.

Johnson, James (2002): How Conceptual Problems Migrate: Rational Choice, Interpretation, and the Hazards of Pluralism. *Annual Review of Political Science*, 5, pp. 223–248.

Johnson, James (2006): Consequences of Positivism: A Pragmatist Assessment. *Comparative Political Studies*, 39 (2), pp. 224–252.

Johnson, James (2010): What Rationality Assumption? Or, How "Positive Political Theory" Rests on a Mistake. *Political Studies*, 58 (2), pp. 282–299.

Johnson, James (2014): Models Among the Political Theorists. *American Journal of Political Science*, 58 (3), pp. 547–560.

Johnson, James (2015): Simon Hug's Retrospective on Pathologies of Rational Choice Theory: A Dissent. *Swiss Political Science Review*, 21 (1), pp. 180–187.

Johnson, Paul E. and Philip A. Schrodt (1991): Analytic Theory and Methodology. In William Crotty (Ed.): *Political Science: Looking to the Future, Vol. I*, pp. 99–163. Evanston, Illinois: Northwestern University Press.

Kahneman, Daniel (2003): A Psychological Perspective on Economics. *American Economic Review*, 93 (2), pp. 162–168.

Kahneman, Daniel, and Amos Tversky (1979): Prospect Theory: An Analysis of Decision under Risk. *Econometrica*, 47 (2), pp. 263–291.

Kincaid, Harold (2019): Beyond Causalism and Acausalism. In Gunnar Schuman (Ed.): *Explanation in Action Theory and Historiography Causal and Teleological Approaches*, pp. 179–194. New York: Routledge.

Kirchgässner, Gebhard (2008): *Homo Oeconomicus: The Economic Model of Behaviour and Its Applications in Economics and Other Social Sciences.* New York: Springer Science & Business Media.

Klein, Dominik, Johannes Marx, and Kai Fischbach (2018): Agent-Based Modeling in Social Science, History, and Philosophy: An Introduction. *Historical Social Research*, 43 (1), pp. 7–27.

Klein, Dominik, Johannes Marx, and Simon Scheller (2020): Rationality in Context: On Inequality and the Epistemic Problems of Maximizing Expected Utility. *Synthese*, 197 (1), pp. 209–232.

Kogelmann, Brian, and Gerald Gaus (2017): Rational Choice Theory. In Adrian Blau (Ed.): *Methods in Analytical Political Theory*, pp. 217–242. Cambridge: Cambridge University Press.

Koremenos, Barbara, Charles Lipson, and Duncan Snidal (2001): The Rational Design of International Institutions. *International Organization*, 55 (4), pp. 761–799.

Kroneberg, Clemens, Meir Yaish, and Volker Stocké (2010): Norms and Rationality in Electoral Participation and in the Rescue of Jews in WWII: An Application of the Model of Frame Selection. *Rationality and Society*, 22 (1), pp. 3–36.

Latsis, Spiro J. (1972): Situational Determinism in Economics. *The British Journal for the Philosophy of Science*, 23 (3), pp. 207–245.

Lakatos, Imre (1980): *The Methodology of Scientific Research Programmes: Philosophical Papers Volume 1*. Cambridge: Cambridge University Press.

Lewis-Beck, Michael S., and Mary Stegmaier (2007): Economic Models of Voting. In Russel J. Dalton, and Hans-Dieter Klingemann (Eds.): *The Oxford Handbook of Political Behavior*, pp. 518–527. Oxford: Oxford University Press.

Lindenberg, Siegwart (1981): Erklärung als Modellbau: Zur soziologischen Nutzung von Nutzentheorien. In Werner Schulte (Ed.): *Soziologie in der Gesellschaft: Referate aus den Veranstaltungen der Sektionen der Deutschen Gesellschaft für Soziologie, der Ad-hoc-Gruppen und des Berufsverbandes Deutscher Soziologen beim 20. Deutschen Soziologentag in Bremen, 16. bis 19. September 1980*, pp. 20–35. Bremen: Deutsche Gesellschaft für Soziologie (DGS).

List, Christian, and Philip Pettit (2011): *Group Agency: The Possibility, Design, and Status of Corporate Agents*. Oxford: Oxford University Press.

List, Christian, and Kai Spiekermann (2013): Methodological Individualism and Holism in Political Science: A Reconciliation. *American Political Science Review*, 107 (4) pp. 629–643.

Little, Daniel (1991): *Varieties of Social Explanation: An Introduction to the Philosophy of Social Science*. Oxford: Westview Press.

Lovett, Frank (2006): Rational Choice Theory and Explanation. *Rationality and Society*, 18 (2), pp. 237–272.

MacDonald, Paul K. (2003): Useful Fiction or Miracle Maker: The Competing Epistemological Foundations of Rational Choice Theory. *American Political Science Review*, 97 (4), pp. 551–65.

Machamer, Peter K., Darden, Lindley, and Carl F. Craver (2000): Thinking about Mechanisms. *Philosophy of Science*, 67 (1), pp. 1–25.

Mansbridge, Jane J. (1995): Rational Choice Gains by Losing. *Political Psychology*, 16 (1), pp. 137–155.

Marx, Johannes, and Christine Tiefensee (2015): Rationalität und Normativität. *Zeitschrift für Politische Theorie*, 6 (1), pp. 19–37.

Mensch, Kirsten (2000): Niedrigkostensituationen, Hochkostensituationen und andere Situationstypen: Ihre Auswirkungen auf die Möglichkeit von Rational-Choice-Erklärungen. *KZfSS Kölner Zeitschrift für Soziologie und Sozialpsychologie*, 52 (2), pp. 246–263.

Monroe, Kristen R., and Kristen Hill Maher (1995): Psychology and Rational Actor Theory. *Political Psychology*, 16 (1), pp. 1–21.

Monroe, Kristen R. (1991): The Theory of Rational Action: What Is It? How Useful Is It for Political Science. In William Crotty (Ed.): *Political Science: Looking to the Future: The Theory and Practice of Political Science Volume 1*, pp. 77–93. Evanston, IL: Northwestern University Press.

Monroe, Kristen R. (1997): Review: Pathologies of Rational Choice Theory: A Critique of Applications in Political Science. *Political Theory*, 25 (2), pp. 289–95.

Moon, J. Donald (1991): Pluralism and Progress in the Study of Politics. In William Crotty (Ed.): *Political Science: Looking to the Future: The Theory and Practice of Political Science Volume 1*, pp. 45–56. Evanston, IL: Northwestern University Press.

Neal, Patrick (1988): Hobbes and Rational Choice Theory. *Western Political Quarterly*, 41 (4), pp. 635–652.

Olson, Mancur (1965): *The Logic of Collective Action: Public Goods and the Theory of Groups*. Cambridge, MA: Harvard University Press.

Olson, Mancur (1982): *Rise and Decline of Nations: Economic Growth, Stagflation, and Social Rigidities*. New Haven, CT: Yale University Press.

Opp, Karl-Dieter (2009): Das individualistische Erklärungsprogramm in der Soziologie: Entwicklung, Stand und Probleme [The Individualistic Research Program in Sociology: Development, Present State, and Problems]. *Zeitschrift für Soziologie*, 38 (1), pp. 26–47.

Opp, Karl-Dieter (2011) Modeling Micro-Macro Relationships: Problems and Solutions. *Journal of Mathematical Sociology*, 35 (1-3), pp. 209–234.

Opp, Karl-Dieter (2019): *The Rationality of Political Protest: A Comparative Analysis of Rational Choice Theory*. New York: Routledge.

Opp, Karl-Dieter (2020). Rational Choice Theory, the Model of Frame Selection and Other Dual-Process Theories: A Critical Comparison. In Vincent Buskens, Rense Corten, Rense, Chris Snijders (Eds.): *Advances in the Sociology of Trust and Cooperation: Theory, Experiments, and Field Studies*, pp. 41–74. Berlin: De Gruyter.

Osborne, Martin J. (2004): *An Introduction to Game Theory* (Vol. 3). New York: Oxford University Press.

Pettit, Philip (2014): Group Agents Are Not Expressive, Pragmatic or Theoretical Fictions. *Erkenntnis*, 79 (9), pp. 1641–1662.

Popper, Karl (1985): The Rationality Principle. In David Miller (ed.): *Popper Selections*, pp. 357–365. Princeton, NJ: Princeton University Press.

Raub, Werner, and Thomas Voss (2017): Micro-Macro Models in Sociology: Antecedents of Coleman's Diagram. In Ben Jann, and Wojtek Przepiorka (Eds.): *Social Dilemmas, Institutions and the Evolution of Cooperation. Festschrift for Andreas Diekmann*, pp. 11–36. Berlin: De Gruyter.

Rawls, John (1971): *A Theory of Justice*. Cambridge, MA: Harvard University Press.

Redlawsk, David P. and Douglas R. Pierce (2017): Emotions and Voting. In Kai Arzheimer, Jocelyn Evans, Michael S. Lewis-Beck (Eds.): *The SAGE Handbook of Electoral Behaviour*, pp. 406–432. Los Angeles: SAGE Reference.

Reutlinger, Alexander, Dominik Hangleiter, Stephan Hartmann (2018): Understanding (with) Toy Models. *British Journal for the Philosophy of Science*, 69 (4), pp. 1069–1099.

Riker, William H. (1962): *The Theory of Political Coalitions*. New Haven, CT: Yale University Press.

Riker, William H. (1995): The Political Psychology of Rational Choice Theory. *Political Psychology*, 16 (1), pp. 23–44.

Riker, William H., and P. C. Ordeshook (1968): A Theory of the Calculus of Voting. *American Political Science Review*, 62, pp. 25–42.

Ross, Don (2005): *Economic Theory and Cognitive Science: Microexplanation*, Cambridge: MIT Press.

Samuelson, Paul (1938): A Note on the Pure Theory of Consumer's Behaviour. *Economica*, 5 (17), 61–71

Satz, Debra, and John Ferejohn (1994): Rational Choice and Social Theory. *Journal of Philosophy*, 91 (2), pp. 71–87.

Samuelson, Larry (1987): A Test of the Revealed-preference Phenomenon in Congressional Elections. *Public Choice*, 54, pp. 141–169.

Schofield, Norman (1993): Political Competition and Multiparty Coalition Governments. *European Journal of Political Research*, 23 (1), pp. 1–33.

Sen, Amartya K. (2005): Why Exactly Is Commitment Important for Rationality?, *Economics and Philosophy*, 21, pp. 5–13.

Shapiro, Ian (2004): Problems, Methods, and Theories: What's Wrong with Political Science and What To Do About It. In Stephen K. White und J. Donald Moon (Eds.): *What is Political Theory?*, pp. 193–216. London: SAGE Publications.

Shepsle, Kenneth A. (1989): Studying Institutions: Some Lessons from the Rational Choice Approach. *Journal of Theoretical Politics*, 1 (2), pp. 131–147.

Simon, Herbert A. (1959): Theories of Decision-making in Economics and Behavioral Science. *American Economic Review*, 49 (3), pp. 253–283.

Snidal, Duncan (2002): Rational Choice and International Relations. In Walter Carlsnaes, Thomas Risse and Beth A. Simmons Beth (eds.): *Handbook of International Relations*, pp. 73–94. London: SAGE.

Strøm, Kaare (1997): Democracy, Accountability, and Coalition Bargaining: The 1996 Stein Rokkan Lecture. *European Journal of Political Research*, 31(1–2), pp. 47–62.

Tilly, Charles (2001): Mechanisms in Political Processes. *Annual Review of Political Science*, 4, pp. 21–41.

Tollefsen, Deborah P., (2002): Collective Intentionality and the Social Sciences. *Philosophy of the Social Sciences*, 32 (1), pp. 25–50.

Tsebelis, George (2002): *Veto Players: How Political Institutions Work*. Princeton: Princeton University Press.

Van Bouwel, Jeroen (2019): Do Mechanism-based Explanations Make a Case for Methodological Individualism? *Journal for General Philosophy of Science*, 50 (2), pp. 263–282.

Von Wright, Georg H. (1971): *Explanation and Understanding*. Ithaca, NY: Cornell University Press.

Watkins, John (2002): The Propositional Content of the Popper-Lakatos Rift. In George Kampis, Ladislav Kvasz, and Michael Stöltzner (Eds.): *Appraising Lakatos: Mathematics, Methodology, and the Man*, pp. 3–12 Dordrecht: Springer.

Weber, Max (1921/1980): Soziologische Grundbegriffe. In Max Weber (Ed.): *Wirtschaft und Gesellschaft: Grundriß der verstehenden Soziologie*, pp. 1–30. Tübingen: Mohr Siebeck.

White, Stephen K. and J. Donald Moon (eds.) (2004): *What is Political Theory?* London: SAGE Publications.

Ylikoski, Petri (2016): Thinking with the Coleman Boat, https://liu.diva-portal.org/smash/get/diva2:1048216/FULLTEXT02.pdf, (accessed on December 18, 2020).

Zaller, John, and Stanley Feldman (1992): A Simple Theory of the Survey Response: Answering Questions versus Revealing Preferences. *American Journal of Political Science*, 36 (3), pp. 579–616.

Zintl, Reinhard (2001): Rational Choice as a Tool in Political Science. *Associations*, 5, pp. 35–50.

Zuckert, Catherine H. (1995): On the 'Rationality' of Rational Choice. *Political Psychology*, 16 (1), pp. 179–198.

CHAPTER 5

STRATEGIC THEORY OF NORMS FOR EMPIRICAL APPLICATIONS IN POLITICAL SCIENCE AND POLITICAL ECONOMY

DON ROSS, WYNN C. STIRLING,
AND LUCA TUMMOLINI

1 INTRODUCTION

The study of social norms sprawls across all of the social sciences. Consequently, the concept lacks a unified conception, let alone a generally acknowledged formal theory. In this chapter we do not seek, grandiosely, to legislate across the various approaches that have been developed. However, we do aim to synthesize an account that can be applied generally, at the *social* scale of analysis, and can be applied to empirical evidence generated in the experimental laboratory and in field experiments.

More specifically, we provide new analysis on representing norms for application in political science, and in parts of economics that do not follow the recent trend among some behavioral economists to build models of the cognitive and motivational states of individuals taken, as it were, one at a time.[1] Sociologists, criminologists, and social psychologists may also find our theoretical construction useful. For purposes of our analysis, a norm is a feature of a social structure (Martin 2009), that is, an element of prevailing patterns in relationships among recurrently interacting people that constrains and motivates the behavior of at least some of them, which arises, persists for a finite time, and ends by decay or catastrophic collapse. Though a norm depends for its continuing existence on being behaviorally accommodated by a significant subset of agents embedded in a social structure, any given agent coexisting with a norm in her social environment may or may not cognitively recognize the norm in question, and may adapt her behavior to accommodate the norm to a varying degree over time, where the variance in question can range from unwavering commitment to complete neglect.

Prior to embarking on analysis, it may be helpful to indicate examples of norms in the sense we intend. Alongside legal injunctions and other explicit requirements, people in all large-scale human societies are also regulated by more informal social norms against, for instance, self-serving factual misrepresentation, self-interested and institutionally unauthorized coercion of people, and willfully selfish driving that impedes the efficiency of traffic flow. Norms of most interest to social scientists are often those on which there is variation among people who cohabit geographically and politically. Thus in most contemporary Western societies majorities behaviorally and cognitively support, but to varying degrees, a norm of nondiscrimination against LGBT people, but there are at the same time very substantial subcommunities in which such discrimination is normatively expected. Many norms are usually moralized, such as norms against gratuitous cruelty to animals, but many are not, such as localized norms around appropriate colors for painting houses. Social scientists are motivated to study norms, and to incorporate the concept of a norm into theoretical models, because the existence and relative strength of norms influences individual and coordinated behavior, affects the sharing and concealment of information, and drives the relative stability of formal and informal institutions. For political scientists, norms are arguably the most important determinants of the efficiency and durability of political orders, as elements of the causal vectors of core political actions like voting (Gerber & Rogers 2009), and contribute to explaining the varieties of political orders and their different patterns of loyalty, participation, and resistance (Mansbridge et al. 2006).

Though norms as we understand them here are features of social structures, they have ontological prerequisites at psychological and biological scales. Norms govern the cognition and behavior only of agents—e.g., people, probably some other intelligent social animals, corporations, political parties and lobbies, but not rocks or everyday electronic computers or corpses. Though our account will incorporate some principles of game theory that presuppose various explicit forms of consistency over time in agents, in general our framework assumes only minimal necessary criteria for agency: agents must manifest goal-governed behavior that can be modified by shifts in incentives.

The most important foundational sources for our project in the chapter are Bicchieri (2006, 2017), Kuran (1995), and Stirling (2012, 2016).

From Bicchieri we adapt a general philosophical conception of a norm, according to which a norm exists in a social structure when a significant networked subset of individuals (1) explicitly or implicitly (behaviorally) represent the norm as effective within the subset; and (2) prefer to conform their own behavior faithfully or partially to the norm in instances of social interaction where (2a) they expect that others in the subset (the extension of which may be uncertain) will govern their behavior in accordance with the norm, and (2b) believe that others think that such behavior is what members of the subset *should* do. Bicchieri does not interpret the "should" here as moral, on grounds that moralized preferences are distinguished by applying unconditionally, and therefore as not depending on agents' expectations about others. This implies a philosophically strong and somewhat tendentious conception of morality that will not play a role in our analysis.

From Kuran we take the insight, developed theoretically and based on empirical evidence, that prevailing norms may come to be widely disliked by participants in networks that the norms govern, but nevertheless survive for a time because behavior that would generate public knowledge of this general disenchantment is itself suppressed by the operation of the norm. Such norms are relatively fragile because the suppression of information is likely to leak. This is of special interest in political science, because norms with this characteristic are potential sources of political and social change that appears as sudden and surprising to both participants and observers. At the same time, Kuran's account, unlike most otherwise similar models developed by economists, recognizes that publicly expressed preferences for initially widely disfavored norms can feed back upon and modify individual preferences. Consequently, his account captures patterns whereby fragile norms that survive into a second generation can manufacture their own climate and become locked in.

From Stirling we apply conditional game theory (CGT). This is an extension of standard noncooperative game theory that incorporates strategic resolution of uncertainty on the part of agents about their own preferences, on the basis of conjecturing and observing evidence about the preferences of others. The explicit motivation for Stirling's theory is to allow game theorists to model the diffusion of social influence through networks as strategically endogenous rather than exogenous. We refer to CGT as an *extension* rather than a *refinement* of standard game theory because it does not narrow the set of standard noncooperative solution concepts by reference to any special model of rationality. The core elements of CGT are summarized in a technical appendix to the chapter (see https://cear. gsu.edu/wp-2020-19-strategic-theory-of-norms-for-empirical-applications-in-political-science-and-political-economy/).

The chapter is organized as follows. In Section 2 we locate Bicchieri's and Kuran's conceptions of norms in the wider landscape of concepts used in the social and behavioral sciences, particularly in economics. A main practical purpose of this critical review is to identify tension between Bicchieri's philosophical analysis of norms, which we broadly follow, and the explicit forms of utility functions by means of which researchers have operationalized the conditional nature of norm response for empirical application, particularly in the laboratory. We present Kuran's model of preference falsification dynamics as a natural complement to Bicchieri's analysis of norms that is particularly relevant to the interests of political scientists, and motivate our subsequent adaptation of the utility functional that Kuran proposes. In Section 3 we criticize experimental design procedures used by Bicchieri and her coauthors in their applications of her account of norms in the lab, and indicate an improved approach. The choice data to be elicited from such improved procedures imply demands and restrictions on the form of theory required for model identification. The example we use is a multiplayer Investment/Trust Game. In Section 4 we show how to represent the endogenous resolution of preference uncertainties in an Investment/Trust Game using CGT. In Section 5 we present simulations of two phenomena involving diffusion of normative influence in social networks discussed by both Bicchieri and Kuran. These illustrate the capacity of CGT to represent mechanisms of endogenous norm change, and serve as stylized examples of our procedure for rendering the general account of norms derived from Bicchieri and Kuran as an operational instrument for modeling empirical choice data and for identifying parameters in our enriched version of Kuran's utility model.

Thus the chapter yields the following as sources of value for empirical political scientists: a general philosophical conception of norms as elements of social structure; a high-level experimental method for eliciting attitudes to norms in the lab; a formal theory of norms to aid in writing down empirically identifiable models; and incorporation into the theory of a property of norms, relative fragility, that is fundamental to explaining and perhaps predicting political change.

2 MODELING SOCIAL NORMS: CATEGORICAL VERSUS CONDITIONAL PREFERENCES FOR CONFORMITY

In this section we critically set the theoretical perspectives on norms that we aim to refine and generalize, those of Bicchieri (2006, 2017) and Kuran (1995), in the context of wider literatures.

The construct of social norms figures in most the social sciences—from psychology to sociology, economics, and political science—but the lack of a unified, formal, and operational conception has so far limited its use for causal identification and explanation of empirical data. We endorse a widespread view that given game theory's well-developed resources for representing interactional statics and dynamics (Gintis 2014), it provides the most promising technical apparatus for filling this gap.

Since social norms exist insofar as they are complied with by some agents, early game-theoretic analyses of norms focused on explaining their characteristic stability. Starting with the seminal contribution of Schelling (1980), norms have been viewed as rules emerging from repeated or recurrent strategic interaction that are stable because they are *self-enforcing*. On this understanding, a necessary condition for something's being a norm is that it must be one among two or more equilibria of a game that is an empirically plausible model of the situation the norm purportedly regulates. More specifically, norms have been characterized as playing the role of equilibrium selection devices (Lewis 1969; Sugden 1986/2004; Binmore 1994, 1998, 2005) or of sources of shared information for a correlating equilibrium (Aumann 1987; Gintis 2014; Guala 2016). The stability of a norm critically relies on a shared system of mutual *empirical* expectations, first-order beliefs about the typical behavior of others.

Although her approach is rooted in this tradition, Bicchieri (2006) has argued that the equilibrium conception of social norms naturally fits conventions and other kinds of descriptive norms for which self-interest is enough to motivate conformity (e.g., driving on the left in Cape Town because that is what one expects others to do), but falls short of identifying what is peculiar to social norms proper: they often prescribe actions that go against the interests that agents would have independently of the social existence of the norm (e.g., in public I would scratch any part of my body that was itchy if such behavior weren't generally regarded as offensive). According to Bicchieri, social norms arise to regulate behavior in situations characterized both by an element of conflicting interests as well as some potential for general benefit.

Consider for instance the well explored "Investment" or "Trust" game first introduced by Berg, Dickhaut, and McCabe (1995). In the standard paradigm, an agent, "the Investor," decides what proportion of an endowment (if any) she will transfer to another agent, "the Trustee." This action is viewed as investing an amount of money in a project that will generate a surplus, typically simulated in the lab by the experimenter tripling its value. The Trustee decides what proportion of this account to transfer back to the Investor. If players in this game are narrowly self-interested, not risk-lovers, derive utility only over money, and all of this is common knowledge, then no money is transferred in the unique Nash equilibrium of the one-shot game. But players can achieve Pareto superior outcomes if a suitable social norm exists in their society. A norm, for instance, could prescribe that actions should contribute to equality of final monetary positions (an "Equality" norm), or to outcomes that reflect reciprocal proportionality of contributions (an "Equity" norm), or some other culturally specific norm conditioned on distinctive social roles such as "parent/child" or "venture capitalist/entrepreneur."

The key feature of Bicchieri's analysis is that an agent's conformity to whatever norm is established (whether it is Equality or Equity, in the case above) is not primarily driven exclusively by her private attitude toward it, but is instead influenced by how other people in her reference network are expected to behave and by what they believe about one another. In this view, conformity to a social norm is motivated by *conditional preferences*, i.e., an agent prefers to conform to a norm conditional on the fact that (1) she expects that most others will conform to it (*empirical* expectations or first-order beliefs), and (2) she expects that others believe she ought to conform (*normative* or in some literature *injunctive* expectations or second-order beliefs about the normative beliefs of others, that is, what others believe people *ought* to do). It is often added that she must expect sanctioning if she violates the norm, but arguably this is already built into the analysis if one takes a revealed-preference view of expectations, that is, that they must be behaviorally and publicly manifest in actions. Provided that these conditions are met, social norms operate by *transforming* a mixed-motive game like the trust game into a new game in which the interests of norm followers are aligned: norm followers will end up playing a coordination game among themselves where general norm compliance is an equilibrium.

Given the crucial explanatory role conditional preferences play in Bicchieri's framework, an adequate operationalization of her analysis must incorporate this concept. First we should distinguish it from two other senses of conditional preference that have featured in the economics literature.

In the first sense, an agent might be said to have a conditional "preference" for conformity in the norms-as-equilibria conception, because, after all, her reason to conform depends on her expectation about others doing their part in the equilibrium. Expecting different equilibrium behavior from others (and thus a different norm) would motivate a different choice. This "conditional" preference for a norm-compliant action actually springs from standard fixed and stable preferences defined over outcomes. As clarified by Lewis (1976), an agent can be said to prefer to conform to some rule rather than not, on condition that others conform as well, simply because the state of affairs in which both she and others conform to the rule is preferred to the state of affairs in which others conform but she does not.

A second variety of conditionality is that a preference to conform may depend on the value of an exogenous "state of nature." For example, I might prefer to join everyone at the most popular jazz club in town under normal conditions, but find a less well-frequented one if there is an epidemic going around. In this case my preference is state-dependent (Karni 1990; Hirschleifer & Riley 1992; Chambers & Quiggin 2000).

According to Bicchieri, however, neither of these ideas expresses the sense of conditionality that underwrites conformity to social norms. In her view, given the right conditions (the existence of appropriate empirical and normative expectations), social norms in fact *transform* analytically prior preferences into new ones. Thus, Bicchieri's conditional preferences are best described counterfactually (Lewis 1976, p. 117), that is, by reference to hypothetical knowledge of what an agent would prefer if her expectations about others' behavior and beliefs were different. In what follows we do not assume that this revisionary understanding of conditional preferences *competes with* modeling conditionality as state-dependence. Instead we aim to demonstrate that the revisionary conception is tractable in the formal language of game theory, and under some circumstances adds value as a tool for empirical analysis. Such value potentially includes avoiding the need to resort to a predefined context specification of what does and does not count as a genuinely exogenous "state of nature" (Andersen et al. 2008).

In order to formally capture how individual preferences are shaped by the existence of social norms, Bicchieri (2006, 52) initially proposed a model in which the utility function is a linear combination of a player's baseline material payoff and a norm-based component representing the maximum loss suffered by any norm-following player as result of a norm violation. Let $\mathbf{X} = \{X_1, \dots, X_n\}$ denote a set of n players; $A_i = \{x_{i1}, \dots, x_{iM_i}\}$ $i = 1, \dots, n$ denote their action sets; and $a = (a_1, \dots, a_n) \in \mathcal{A} = A_1 \times \cdots \times A_n$ the set of action profiles or outcomes. A norm for a player X_i is represented by a correspondence $\mathcal{N}_i$ from an agent's expectations about the other players' strategies to the strategy the agent *ought* to take, that is, $\mathcal{N}_i : \mathcal{L}_{-i} \to A_i$ with $\mathcal{L}_{-i} \subseteq A_{-i}$ where A_{-i} is $\mathcal{A}$ with A_i removed and a_{-i} is the set $(a_1, \dots, a_n)$ with a_1 removed. A strategy profile a is said to *violate* a norm when X_j does not follow the norm, that is, where $a_j \neq \mathcal{N}_j(a_{-j})$. Let π_i denote the hypothetical prenormative *or baseline* payoff function of player X_i. The norm-regulated utility function is given by:

$$u_i(a) = \pi_i(a) - k_i \max_{a_{-j} \in \mathcal{L}_{-j}} \max_{m \neq j} \left\{ \pi_m(a_{-j}, \mathcal{N}_j(a_{-j})) - \pi_m(a), 0 \right\} \tag{1}$$

where $k_i \geq 0$ is a parameter specifying X_i's sensitivity to the established norm. While the first maximum operator considers the possibility that a norm might apply to multiple players, the second one ranges over all the players except for the norm violator and specifies the maximum payoff deductions derived from all norm violations.

Although this model can be used to characterize an agent's preference for conformity under the assumption that the empirical and normative expectations conditions are satisfied, the fact that a specific pattern of empirical and normative expectations can *change* the baseline utility to promote conformity to a behavioral rule is left implicit and exogenous.

To partially overcome this limitation, Bicchieri and Sontuoso (2020) have proposed extending Bicchieri's framework to dynamic psychological games, a generalization of standard game theory that has been developed precisely to represent motivations rather than only patterns of observed choices (Battigalli & Dufwenberg 2009). As with the original Bicchieri model, the norm-based "psychological" utility of a player is conceived as a linear combination of her material payoff and a norm-based component. However, this latter component is now conceived as an anticipated negative emotion and is a function of a positive difference between the initially *expected* payoff to X_m and the payoff that X_m would get in case of a violation of the behavioral rule. Drawing on the Battigalli and Dufwenberg (2007) concept of *simple guilt*, Bicchieri and Sontuoso end up modeling norm compliance as an aversion to disappointing others' *empirical* expectations. Besides failing to actually take *normative* expectations into account (see Tummolini et al. 2013 and Andrighetto, Grieco and Tummolini 2015 for empirical evidence), approaches based on latent psychological motivation are more restrictive, and more challenging to try to observe empirically, than the more general social conception reflected in Bicchieri's own original analysis.

The Bicchieri and Sontuoso model resembles a small tradition of models by economists that analyze implications for equilibrium dynamics of the insertion of fixed (but varying across agents) preferences for conformity with others into individuals' utility functions. The seminal model in this literature is Bernheim (1994), and theoretical extensions are developed by Brock and Durlauf (2001) and Michaeli and Spiro (2015, 2017). This strand of theory has been experimentally applied by Andreoni and Bernheim (2009) and Andreoni, Nikiforakis, and Siegenthalier (2021). These authors all refer explicitly to equilibria they derive from hypothesizing psychological satisfaction or dissatisfaction associated with conformity, where the equilibria vary in efficiency. Agents *do* undergo preference shifts in the Bernheim-style models, but this is exogenously imposed rather than endogenously driven by specifically normative dynamics. Consequently, the focus in this tradition has tended to generalize in the direction of the "herding" literature (e.g., Banerjee 1992; Chamley 2004) that addresses informational dynamics in markets where agents infer asset values from observing others' choices. This has generated some experimental applications (e.g., Duffy & Lafky 2019) where, although the language of "norms" is featured, they are the object of inquiry only at such an abstract level that any peculiarly normative dynamics disappear from view. Financial asset markets, a prime domain of application for herding theory, are arguably a setting where, because all agents are expected to aim to maximize expected monetary returns, norms in our and Bicchieri's sense, that is, social structures that coordinate descriptive and normative expectations, play no role at all. Notably, Chamley's (2004) advanced textbook on herding includes no index entry for "norms."

In political science contexts, attention has frequently focused on cases where disagreements about norms are thought to be relevant to analyzing shifts in policies or coalitions. Norms in such contexts are typically assumed to be standing commitments by subsets of political actors to specific "ways of doing things," and not merely generalized preferences for conformity. Review of the literature and topics surveyed in Druckman et al. (2011) indicates the absence of an experimental literature in political science focused on norms per se, notwithstanding widespread use of Investment/Trust games (Wilson &

Eckel 2011). Such experiments are often used to furnish evidence of behavioral sensitivity to hypothesized social preferences, but descriptive and normative expectations are not distinguished from one another, let alone separately estimated so that their mutual alignment can be assessed.

Attention to norms is arguably crucial to integrating pioneering work by Kuran (1995) on the dynamics of public opinion, and political responses to these dynamics, with the experimental traditions from economics on which experimenters in political science often draw. Kuran concentrates on cases where what he calls agents' "intrinsic" utility (meaning utility that is independent of social context, e.g., utility derived from a policy's effect on an agent's financial portfolio value) drops out of analysis because agents' preferences and choices concerning social conformity cannot influence the policy choice. While not framing his analysis in terms of responses to norms per se, Kuran invites us to focus on causally effective networks of descriptive and normative expectations as social structures. Furthermore, Kuran considers, as we do, norms as drivers of endogenous preference changes at the level of individuals. Other similarly synthetic work by economists that begins to come to grips with social structures as causal mechanisms that influence preferences is Akerlof and Kranton (2010), who consider the complex and important web of relationships between norms and social identities. Here we leave identity as a topic to which the modeling techniques we go on to present might usefully be extended in the future.

In Kuran's basic model, agents face the recurrent problem of deciding whether, and under what social and political circumstances, to express their "true" private preferences or to instead express preferences that align with "public opinion," which Kuran identifies with modes of distributions of publicly expressed preferences. This *can* be a problem even when an agent's private preference aligns with public opinion because the agent might have incentives to appear to be uncommitted or rebellious. But the primary interest concerns cases of misalignment between private and publicly signaled preferences. Kuran argues, with a range of nonhypothetical examples, that it is a pervasive element of the human social and political predicament that people are regularly confronted with choosing trade-offs between their *expressive* utility, derived from exercising and demonstrating their autonomy and self-authenticity, and their *reputational* utility, which derives from the social rewards and sanctions associated with, respectively, conformity and dissent. By "reputation" Kuran refers not only to an agent's relative valuation by other agents, but to utility that parties to an interaction receive through coordinated expectations, which may be both descriptive and normative. Kuran also recognizes *intrinsic* utility, as characterized above. For example, a wealthy person might benefit from the abolition of capital gains tax independently of whether she thinks, from a detached point of view, that such abolition is good public policy, and also independently of any social rewards or sanctions that come her way from expressing an opinion that conforms with or diverges from those of others, or is expected by them. Kuran's main analysis sets intrinsic utility derived from outcomes as exogenously fixed, on grounds that in typical political contexts most agents' expressions of preferences have no special influence on what policy choice will in fact prevail. That is, the "client" to be served by Kuran's primary analysis is not a President or a celebrity activist. He focuses on cases where agents are norm-takers, not norm-makers.

Pervasive tension in real social and political life between expressive and reputational utility gives rise, as Kuran shows, to a range of recurrent patterns. It explains why people often conceal religious beliefs in secular settings, and why secularists disagree among themselves over whether public religious displays should be encouraged or restricted. It explains why there is controversy over whether members of disparaged minorities (e.g., LGBT people) should conceal their identities or give comfort and strength to their fellows by revealing their identities. It explains why politicians arrange anonymous leaks as trial balloons. It explains the very point of secret ballots, blind refereeing, and conducting elite political bargaining behind closed doors. In general, the *preference falsification* that responds to incentives associated with reputational utility blocks straightforward inference from the distribution of publicly expressed preferences to the distribution of true private preferences.

Again, Kuran is most interested in the social dynamical effects of preference falsification. In cases of bimodal public opinion, preference falsification can lead to polarization into extremist camps, if people who express moderate opinions find themselves sanctioned by both sides. People of only slightly less moderate views in either direction have rational incentive to deliver such sanctions, so as to grow the pressure mass of their own faction. In addition, preference falsification often promotes the phenomenon extensively studied in social psychology by Katz and Allport (1931) under the label of "pluralistic ignorance" (PI). PI is a major theme to which Bicchieri (2006, 2017) applies her analysis of norms when she turns to policy implications. It obtains when a behavioral pattern, regime, or policy that the majority of a population dislikes prevails because no one can observe that their private dispositions or opinions are widely shared. In the case of a norm, as discussed by Bicchieri (2017), PI arises when expectations supporting the norm are maintained and repeatedly confirmed by experience, despite widespread or even majority disapproval of the norm in question, because the extent of the disapproval is invisible or concealed. In Kuran's terms, concern for reputational utility can lead agents to sanction violators of norms that they themselves would secretly prefer to violate, or do in fact violate when they are out of public view. Kuran cites, as a familiar example, gay people in oppressively heteronormative environments engaging in demonstrative homophobia. This pattern can lead to unpredicted and sudden lurches in revealed public opinion. An example is the very rapid shift in public opinion in most developed countries in the late 1980s from viewing drunk driving as a reckless but often amusing misdemeanor to viewing it as a breach of social morality deserving criminal prosecution (Lerner 2011).

In the context of our interest in conditional preferences, a particularly interesting feature of public opinion dynamics discussed by Kuran is that preference falsification often leads to preference *revision*, as a person's expressed preferences over time become integrated into the social identity she continuously constructs for herself, and on which others with whom she interacts ground expectations about her actions. This has echoes of Aristotle's view that people become moral agents by becoming habituated to behaving morally. As Kuran stresses, however, this process can apply equally to morally destructive norms, for example the biologically interpreted racism that was socially diffused through most Western societies during the nineteenth century period of European and American global imperialism (Hanneford 1995), and for decades was normatively established in the largest part of these populations. This is the aspect of dynamic preference influence through networks that most directly corresponds to norm *origination*. Such diffusion and entrenchment typically involves little or no deliberative reflection on the part of most individuals, and in that sense is more accurately modeled as a social process than as a psychological one.

As noted, in Kuran's model agents vary in the weights attached to intrinsic, expressive, and reputational utility in composing their total utility functions. In large-n cases, as explained, intrinsic utility is strategically irrelevant, so we need only attend to variation in binary weightings between expressive and reputational utility. Kuran refers to agents who attach much higher weight to expressive than to reputational utility as "Activists." Such agents will tend not to falsify their preferences even when these preferences are socially unpopular and expression of them generates sanctions. They are, then, more likely to violate norms. Types of such Activists include ideologues, religious fundamentalists, moralists, and people whose identities are nonnegotiably associated with sectarian lifeways that cannot be concealed from others. Since Activists limit the extent to which public opinion hides the existence and distribution of falsified private preferences, their presence mitigates against PI, and makes dynamic social norm-reversal more likely. Bicchieri (2017) introduces essentially the same concept, though without Kuran's analytic structure, under the label of "Trendsetters." Below we will, for balanced attribution, call agents with such total-utility composition functions "Activists/Trendsetters."

When he models individual agents as "norm-takers," Kuran abstracts from dynamical interactions between norms as social structures and potential individual preference shifts in response to social influence. But he does not deny that there is such an aspect. Large-scale norms emerge from (and feed back upon) the formation of norms in smaller subnetworks. Such dynamics are important in the laboratory setting of a typical Investment/Trust game experiment. Subjects in such experiments may be expected to bring into the lab various normative expectations that have diffused through their large-scale cultural environments (Binmore 2007). But the setting is novel for most participants, and it is equally clear across the large literature on these experiments that when subjects play multiple rounds they frequently learn to coordinate on expectations that evolve over the course of play. Interesting though such evolution might often be to an experimenter, she might alternatively be mainly concerned to identify subjects' preplay descriptive and normative expectations by designing tasks that create conflict between available intrinsic utility and hypothesized norms: where subjects must be offered extra monetary incentive to do what is to their intrinsic advantage, this can reveal their beliefs about the existence and influence of a norm. Agents' influence over relevant intrinsic utility in small-n settings thus furnishes a methodological reason to turn to the laboratory even when the ultimate subject of interest, as in Kuran's work and in most contexts that preoccupy political scientists, is norm distribution at the large-n scale.

We also note that Kuran's basis for factoring out intrinsic utility and for assuming that agents are norm-takers in exemplary applications of his utility model are only expository idealizations. We can easily conjure examples of politically important situations in which norms are contested in smaller-scale settings where participants are not norm-takers and influence available intrinsic utility. Consider, for example, recent anxieties about the undermining of norms of professionalism, technocratic control, and responsiveness to scientific consensus in US government agencies under pressure from an antibureaucratic and antiexpert presidential administration. Some agencies are reported as having resisted this pressure much more successfully, or at least for longer, than others (Lewis 2018). It is unlikely that officials engaged in such struggles, with acute self-awareness, perceived themselves to be bereft of individual influence on the outcome, even when they were not optimistic about their capacity to successfully hold out indefinitely. We might expect that in this sort of setting, considerations of expressive and reputational utility exert strong influence along with the intrinsic utility called into play by individual influence. A great deal of attention in political science is devoted to smaller-scale institutional settings of this kind.

A natural general question to ask about such instances is: what are the characteristics of a network that makes its norms more or less fragile under competitive pressure from alternative or (as in the example above) subversive norms?

Progress toward an adequate formal and operational model mandates, then, the adoption of a new approach enabling the possibility for agents to endogenously modulate their preferences in response to discoveries about population-scale distributions of empirical and normative expectations, and not just to agents' prestanding preferences concerning possible actions of others with whom they individually happen to interact. We seek a model according to which agents do not just *express* norms through their choices of strategies and actions, but *recalibrate* their own preferences upon encountering norms as social structures. We follow a course of conservatism in one respect, however. We worried earlier about the degrees of freedom allowed in state-dependent utility models by the absence of a principled general ontology of exogenous states of nature. Furthermore, we follow Binmore (2010) in objecting that the social preference approach is unduly liberal in allowing any equilibria in games used as models to be rationalized by freely conjecturing specific and idiosyncratic arguments in utility functions based on unobservable psychological costs and benefits. There would be no obvious methodological gain to be expected from swapping degrees of freedom in state-dependent and social preference theories for abandonment of general constraints on specifications of utility functions and solution concepts. Therefore, in our analysis to follow, we adopt the following practices. First, we apply Kuran's version of norm-sensitive utility rather than Bicchieri's, on grounds that the former is more general. Second, we deploy an extension of game theory, conditional game theory (Stirling 2012, 2016) that does not *refine* standard solution concepts by imposing special restrictions on strategic rationality as in theoretical work by Kreps (1990) and Bicchieri (1993).

3 REQUIREMENTS FOR IDENTIFYING AND ESTIMATING MODELS OF NORMS IN EMPIRICAL DATA

The experimental literature on norms is extensive, and includes both laboratory and field experiments. No systematic cross-disciplinary survey as yet appears to exist, which arguably reflects the lack of conceptual unification to which we seek to make an incremental contribution. Attempting such a survey would be beyond the scope of the chapter, and tangential to its purpose, which is to provide a formal account of the strategic dynamics of norms that is consistent with the philosophical analysis provided by Bicchieri (2006, 2017), and can form the basis for estimating experimental data.

Part of the motivation for this challenge is that the modeling approach suggested by Bicchieri and her various coauthors for estimating their own experimental data, as reported and analyzed in Bicchieri and Xiao (2009), Xiao and Bicchieri (2010), Bicchieri and Chavez (2010), Bicchieri, Xiao, and Muldoon (2011), Bicchieri and Chavez (2013) and Bicchieri, Lindemans, and Jiang (2014), models social norm compliance as the optimization of a norm-based utility function in which, as discussed in Section 2, the losses of others figure as an explicit argument rather than allowing preferences for conformity to arise endogenously through strategic interactions. In consequence, analyses of the experiments consist in identifying specific behavioral frequencies and characteristics rather than estimating parameters of a theory of norms. Similarly, the authors of the rich vein of experimental evidence for the influence of experience of market-like institutions and transactions (along with adherence to Christianity or Islam) on normatively governed strategic behavior in small-scale societies (Henrich et al. 2004; Ensminger & Henrich 2014) assume that norms reflect individuals' social preferences, but offer no comments on whether norms are social structures that influence individual social preferences, or are simply emergent aggregate descriptions of the social preferences themselves.[2] Bicchieri (2006, 2017), at least, offers the basis of a theoretical specification of a social norm, but then does not bring it clearly to bear on analysis of her own (and coauthors') experimental observations. Our main aim in the chapter is to close this methodological gap.

Before we take up this task, we point to some limitations in the experimental methods used in the studies by Bicchieri and coauthors cited above. We concentrate on these studies both because they are motivated by the philosophical conception of norms we aim to develop, and because in one crucial respect they are improvements on methods generally used in experiments on norms that have been conducted by psychologists and political scientists. The respect in question is that Bicchieri and her coauthors appreciate the importance of eliciting both first-order empirical expectations of subjects about what other subjects *will* do in games, and their second-order normative beliefs about what players *should* do, using *salient incentives*. This is generally essential to valid inference in all behavioral experiments (Harrison 2014), but is particularly crucial in eliciting beliefs about social and personal values, where even subjects aiming to be sincere may be motivated by interest in self-signaling of virtue or in minimizing dissonance between social expectations and their self-conceptions (Bicchieri 2017). We indicate improvements in belief elicitation methods that are important for the sake of structural modeling using general theory. But where the experiments of Bicchieri and her coauthors are concerned, it is gratifying not to need to argue for introducing incentives in the first place.

Many experiments reported by Bicchieri are based on variants of the "Investment" or "Trust" game as discussed in Section 2. In the lab, subjects may play the game sequentially, or using the "strategy method" in which players simultaneously submit their decisions over discretized sets of transfers at every possible decision node for one or both roles. As noted previously, players can achieve Pareto efficient outcomes if they operate normative expectations, under one or another interpretation of "norm." The least determinative of such expectations is simply that non-zero levels of trust and reciprocity are expected, in which case the game is a pure coordination game. An influential literature using the framework of psychological game theory purports to test hypotheses that players' norm-based utility functions include some form of social preference for egalitarian outcomes or proportional reciprocity (Azar 2019), but do not elicit incentivized reports of subjects' beliefs about the extent to which they expect others to share such preferences. The form of interpretation of evidence we would need for consistency with Bicchieri's analysis of norms is that players might share consistent descriptive and normative expectations that, in a class of interactions that includes the Investment/Trust game setup, they use to regulate their behavior, and may normatively endorse, such as the "Equality" or "Equity" norms mentioned in Section 2. Investment/Trust games conducted in the laboratory can provide evidence of the existence of norms governing communities from which subjects are drawn just in case players' first- and second-order empirical and normative beliefs are elicited for comparison with their chosen strategies (Bicchieri 2017).

Below we describe procedures that can straightforwardly be applied to incentivize subjects' first-order descriptive beliefs about the frequency of a norm in a population with which they experimentally interact. By contrast, it is not possible to incentivize subjects' first-order normative beliefs, since in the absence of some currently unavailable (and perhaps in principle incoherent) neuropsychological test, there are no independent measures against which such reports could be compared. Both second-order descriptive and normative beliefs, on the other hand, can be incentivized by asking subjects to predict reports of other subjects and rewarding such predictions based on their accuracy. Bicchieri and her coauthors have generally followed this practice. Bicchieri, Xiao and Muldoon (2011) incentivized second-order descriptive beliefs but not second-order normative beliefs. Bicchieri and Xiao (2009), Xiao and Bicchieri (2010), and Bicchieri and Chavez (2010, 2013) incentivized both types of beliefs. These experiments have thus represented progress in the direction of best practice. However, the incentivization methods have all involved serious limitations with respect to the goal of identifying and estimating structural models of utility conditioned on beliefs about social structures.

A first, straightforward, limitation is that all of the experiments above used reward magnitudes for second-order belief elicitation that were arguably too small to be reliably payoff dominant. University student subjects were paid one US dollar for correct point predictions, and otherwise zero. Of course the way to overcome this limitation is simple and obvious.

A more interesting problem is that in all of the experiments above, what are elicited are only averages of subjects' point estimates of modal beliefs. This approach provides no basis for estimation of any individual subject's descriptive or normative expectations as explanatory factors for choices. In realistic settings, what the analyst who aims to predict normatively sensitive behavior needs to know are distributions of an individual agent's expectations in social contexts, and the relative *confidence* with which an individual agent expects that responses will be norm-governed, since, on Bicchieri's analysis, she will conform her own choices to norms only to the extent that she believes that those with whom she interacts will do so.

Methods for eliciting beliefs as degrees of confidence have been developed. For example, Harrison et al. (2017) ask each subject in an experiment to distribute tokens over a set of "bins" that range across the possible realization values of variables about which the experimenter wants to discover their beliefs. Subjects are rewarded according to a proper scoring rule, specifically the quadratic scoring rule (QSR), which maps probability mass functions onto payoffs distributed around the realized outcome (Matheson & Winkler 1976). Subjects using the interface presented in Harrison et al. (2017) need not learn to represent the rule explicitly. As they operate a slider that controls token allocations over the bins, they are shown money rewards they can expect if the realization corresponds to the center of the probability mass of the allocation they have tentatively selected. Experience in the laboratory is that subjects quickly learn to manipulate allocations fluidly.

This elicitation in itself is not sufficient for estimating subjects' confidence in their beliefs unless it is known that they are risk-neutral subjective expected utility maximizers. In the Trust game experiments of Bicchieri and coauthors, this is a maintained a priori assumption. However, although many people in laboratory experiments designed to elicit risk preferences through incentivized choices over pairs of lotteries do choose consistently with expected utility theory (EUT), Harrison and Ross (2016) report that majorities in most samples exhibit *rank dependence*. Rank-dependent utility theory (RDU; Quiggin 1982) describes a family of specifications of utility that nest EUT but allow for subjective decision weights on lottery outcomes, indicating that subjects display relative pessimism or optimism with respect to outcomes depending on their ranking of these outcomes from best to worst. Furthermore, most people, at least in risky decisions involving money, are moderately risk averse (Harrison & Rutström 2008).

A decision by a person to follow a norm, on Bicchieri's analysis, necessarily involves risk, since according to that analysis she will regard this decision as correct only if those with whom she interacts will do likewise, and that they will do so is typically an uncertain conjecture. Clearly, in the Investment/Trust game experimental setting both Investors and Trustees make risky choices, and the game would be of little interest otherwise. Thus there are two reasons for eliciting risk preferences: using the observed lottery choices to identify and estimate structural utility models (i.e., allowing for RDU) at the level of the individual, and incorporating these models in analysis, when investigating norms using Trust games. First, assuming as Bicchieri and coauthors do, that people are risk-neutral expected utility maximizers will typically involve maintaining a counterfactual, leading to incorrect characterizations and predictions (Chetty et al. 2020). Second, estimating a subject's rank-dependent adjustment and confidence in her beliefs, based on elicitation using the QSR of her priors on the distribution of probabilities of outcomes, depends on independent elicitation of her risk preferences. This is typically done using lottery-choice experiments (Harrison & Rutström 2008).

Much of the existing experimental literature on norms involves use of repeated games that are designed to allow for observation of learning by subjects, typically interpreted as learning about norms, over the course of play. This makes good sense where, as is typically the case, the laboratory design confronts subjects with what is expected to be a novel situation for them. In other cases, however, where the point of an experiment is to identify norms that players bring with them into the lab, one-shot designs are more appropriate. In these cases, the experimenter who lacks empirical access to convergence on equilibria over time might yet want to be able to estimate what *would* happen dynamically in the limit, particularly if she is interested in the welfare implications of the normative structures she finds, but expects, as Bicchieri (2017) emphasizes, that these should often take account of scope for norms to influence preferences through interactive learning. Following standard methodology, she might do this by simulating Bayesian learning over a hypothetical sequence of play. This might tell her about expected equilibria in beliefs and actions. However, it is not clear in advance of further analysis of the operationalization of the concept of a norm how she might simulate the endogenous evolution of norms themselves, unless norms are identified with individuals' beliefs. But it is precisely the advantage of Bicchieri's analysis that although agents' decisions over whether to follow norms are based on their individual expectations about others' actions (thus requiring that these be estimated in empirical applications), the norms themselves are functions of pre-existing *networks* of expectations. The analyst who aims to understand how a conjectured norm might lead agents to potentially improve their welfare by adapting their preferences to accommodate the norm needs a method that allows her to model hypotheses about effects of interaction on norm stability in a way that is sensitive to empirical data about her subjects' initial belief distributions and risk preferences.

What is needed, then, for adequate operationalization of Bicchieri's philosophical analysis of norms if the theory in question is to be used to specify intended models of laboratory data, is that it allow scope for (1) varying degrees of risk aversion, (2) rank-dependent utility, and (3) varying full distributions of subjective beliefs about probabilities of outcomes, but without (4) depending on empirical observation of learning in real time. Our theory construction below respects these desiderata.

4 Conditional Game Theory

4.1 Conditional Game Preference and Solution Concepts

In this section we explain the concept of conditionality as it is formally constructed by CGT. We will subsequently demonstrate the power of this construction to simultaneously express the idea of conditional preference we attributed to Bicchieri (2006, 2017), and identify prospective dynamic normative influence from observed choice data. The reader who would like to see more of the formal background theory is referred to the Appendix, (see https://cear.gsu.edu/wp-2020-19-strategic-theory-of-norms-for-empirical-applications-in-politi cal-science-and-political-economy/) and to Stirling (2012, 2016).

The essential components of a game are (a) a set of n agents, denoted $\mathbf{X} = \{X_1, \ldots, X_n\}$, each with its *action set*, denoted $\mathcal{A}_i\{x_{i1}, \ldots, x_{iM_i}\}$, $i = 1,\ldots,n$; (b) the set of *outcomes* as a function of the *action profiles*, denoted $\mathrm{a} = (a_1,\ldots,a_n) \in \mathcal{A} = \mathcal{A}_1 \times \cdots \times \mathcal{A}_n$; (c) a *preference concept* for each X_i that specifies X_i's metric by which the elements of A are evaluated; and (d) a *solution concept* that defines equilibria. Thus, a game analysis reconciles the fact that the consequence to each agent depends on the choices of all agents, but each agent has control only over their own actions. Under standard noncooperative game theory, each X_i has preferences specified by a utility function $u_i: \mathcal{A} \to \mathbb{R}$, and solutions are defined as strategically best responses—that is, actions drawn from A_i that maximize X_i's welfare under the expectation that others will do likewise (e.g., Nash equilibria, dominance).

The major difference between a standard noncooperative game and a conditional game involves the interpretation of the preference concept. Standard game theory defines preferences *categorically*, by specifying fixed, immutable, and unconditional utility for each player. This structure requires players to respond to the expected actions of all others as specified by a selected equilibrium. The key innovation of CGT is that it allows agents to modulate their preferences by responding locally to the social distribution of preferences, not just to the expected actions of others. In CGT, preferences are interpreted as hypothetical propositions, with the preferences of others as antecedents and actions of the reference agent as consequents. This structure exactly parallels the logical structure of Bayesian probability theory, namely, conditionalization—the process of determining the cumulative influence of acquired evidence. The best known application of Bayesian probability is as a device for modeling epistemological theories. The cumulative process of belief revision in response to updated evidence is expressed as a Bayesian network with vertices as random variables and edges as conditional probability mass functions that define the statistical relationships among the random variables. These conditional relationships are combined via the chain rule to generate a joint probability distribution that incorporates all of the interrelationships that exist among the random variables. Once defined, unconditional belief orderings for each random variable can be deduced by marginalization.

CGT appropriates the Bayesian network syntax to model a praxeological theory of preference and preference recalibration based on social influence. The general model defines a three-phase *meso-to-macro-to-micro* process comprising socialization, diffusion, and deduction, as illustrated in Figure 5.1. Socialization (the meso, or intermediate-level phase) is achieved by expressing preferences as *conditional utility mass functions* that modulate individual preferences as functions of the preferences of those who socially influence them. Diffusion (the macro, or global-level phase) is represented by modeling the social influence network with the syntax of a Bayesian network with agents as vertices and conditional payoffs as edges. As social influence diffuses through the network via these linkages, nascent social interrelationships emerge, thereby generating a *coordination function* that is isomorphic to a joint probability mass function. Deduction (the micro, or local-level phase) is then achieved by marginalization, yielding *individual coordinated payoff functions* that can be analyzed using standard game-theoretic solution concepts.

Diffusion is an iterative dynamic process of complex multidirectional and reciprocal mindshaping (Zawidzki 2013; Ross & Stirling 2020), where each agent responds to social influence exerted by her neighbors and, in turn exerts social influence on her neighbors, who again exert influence on her, and so forth. There are two possible ways for such iterative behavioral influence to play out. Under some circumstances it can result in nonterminating but repeating oscillations, in which case nothing gets resolved. But for a range of social situations modeled as games in the literature (Stirling 2016) diffusion results in convergence to unconditional or *steady-state* utilities for each player, where each player possesses

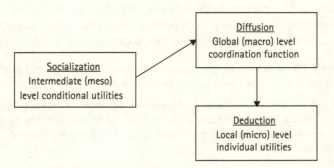

FIGURE 5.1. The socialization, diffusion, deduction process.

totally ordered preferences that form the basis for standard equilibrium analysis. Expressing diffusion with the probability syntax is restricted by two important conditions. First, we require that diffusion be *coherent*, that is, each agent must have "a seat at the table" in the sense that her utility function influences resolution. In other words, no agent may be subjugated (i.e., disenfranchised) by her neighbors. Of course, real human communities often oppress individuals and subcommunities. Our restriction is technical: in CGT, we would model such exclusion as a relationship between networks rather than as a relationship within a single network. Second, the process must *converge*, in that it results in unambiguous criteria that enable all agents to make coherent choices. Stirling (2012, 2016) establishes that both of these conditions can be satisfied if and only if the diffusion process complies with the probability axioms. Specifically, by requiring the conditional utilities to conform to the syntax of probability mass functions and combining them according to the rules of probability theory (e.g., conditionalization, the chain rule, Bayes's rule), we may invoke two fundamental theoretical results from probability theory: the Dutch book theorem and the Markov chain convergence theorem. A Dutch book is a gambling scenario that results in a sure loss, and the Dutch book theorem establishes that a sure loss is impossible if and only if the gambler's beliefs and behavior comply with the probability axioms. In our context, subjugation is isomorphic to a sure loss (Stirling 2016), and it follows that such a condition is impossible if and only if all agents' preferences and behavior comply with the probability axioms. Furthermore, by viewing the diffusion process as a Markov chain, the Markov convergence theorem can be applied to establish that each agent's preferences converge to a unique utility function that takes into account all of the social relationships that are generated by the conditional utilities.

4.2 The Investment/Trust Game

We will illustrate the application of CGT to the theory of norms by reference to the Investment/Trust game. As discussed, this game was originally introduced as a two-agent game between an Investor, who possesses an endowment ε and a Trustee who manages the investment. The Investor sends $\sigma\varepsilon$, with $0 < \sigma < 1$, to the Trustee and retains $(1 - \sigma)\varepsilon$. The standard model is that this investment is exogenously (e.g., by an experimenter playing the role of a market process or administrator) tripled in value to $3\sigma\varepsilon$, resulting in combined non-integrated wealth of the two players of $(1 + 2\sigma)\varepsilon/2$. The Trustee then returns a portion of her holdings to the Investor with the amount returned depending on the normative posture of the Trustee. For purposes of an illustrative example throughout the chapter, we consider two possible norms that might regulate the choices of players:

N_1: **Equality:** A fair return is one that equalizes the final (non-integrated) positions of the players. Under this norm, the payoff to both Investor and Trustee is $(1 + 2\sigma)\varepsilon/2$.

N_2: **Equity:** A fair return is one that is proportional to the share of the endowment that was invested. The Trustee returns the same fraction of the multiplied outcome to the Investor, that is, she returns $3\sigma^2\varepsilon$. Thus, the payoff to the Investor is $(1 - \sigma + 3\sigma^2)\varepsilon$ and the payoff to the Trustee is $3(\sigma - \sigma^2)\varepsilon$.

The hypothetical setting for our analysis of the Investment/Trust game throughout the paper will be a scenario in which there are two initial communities, where one community begins with prevailing expectations that the game is played under governance of the Equality norm, and the other community begins with prevailing expectations that the game is played under governance of the Equity norm. We will investigate various scenarios under which these communities might encounter one another, in the sense of an agent drawn from one community finding herself playing Investment—Trust against an agent drawn from the other community. This will allow us to examine patterns by which normative variation influences individuals' preferences, as revealed by probabilities of choices of actions. Because players also interact with members drawn from their original normative communities, each agent's preferences are subject to two channels of normative influence: direct influence from expectations concerning play against an agent governed by a "foreign" norm, and indirect influence of this exposure through its effect on the expected play of "domestic" game partners. Thus our setup will reflect Bicchieri's core idea that norms are networks of expectations on which preferences are conditional.

In standard versions of the Investment/Trust game in the literature, the Investor is free to transfer 0 to the Trustee. Because in this setting the Trustee can take no action that expresses her normative preferences, for simplicity and transparency of the mechanism of interest, we exclude such narrow self-interest from the set of available norms. In a laboratory setting this unrealistic restriction would need to be relaxed. We will assume throughout that players' choices are elicited by the "strategy method," that is, that they choose an action for every possible vector of actions by other players, under the assumption that a random process will allocate them to Investor and Trustee roles. Thus, where players coordinate on one of the two norms above, the expected monetary value I of the game is the mean of the return to the Investor and the Trustee conditional on the norm:

$$I_{N_1} = (1 + 2\sigma)\varepsilon / 2 \tag{2}$$

$$T_{N_1} = (1 + 2\sigma)\varepsilon / 2$$

and

$$I_{N_2} = (1 - \sigma + 3\sigma^2)\varepsilon \tag{3}$$

$$T_{N_2} = 3(\sigma - \sigma^2)\varepsilon$$

Consider a bilateral transaction between agents Z_i and Z_j. To begin with, suppose that $\mu(I) = I$. Let I_{N_j} be the utility Z_i receives from Z_j who abides by norm $N_j \in \mathcal{N} = \{N_1, N_2\} = \{\text{Equality}, \text{Equity}\}$, and let T_{N_i} be the utility that Z_i retains. By symmetry, Z_j receives I_{N_i} from Z_i and retains T_{N_j}. This situation may be represented by the network graph

$$Z_i \overset{\tilde{u}_{z_j|z_i}}{\underset{\tilde{u}_{z_i|z_j}}{\rightleftarrows}} Z_j \tag{4}$$

where $\tilde{u}_{z_j|z_i}$ and $\tilde{u}_{z_i|z_j}$ are conditional utilities that express the influence that they exert on each other.

We aim to model situations under which groups of agents governed by different norms encounter one another. Therefore, consider a six-agent graph showing the interconnection of two three-agent subnetworks, $\{X_1, X_2, X_3\}$ and $\{Y_1, Y_2, Y_3\}$, of the form

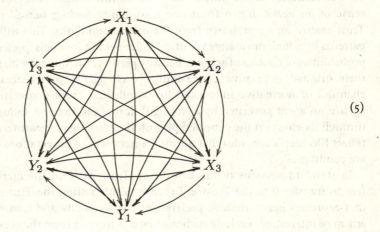

$$(5)$$

where agents $\{X_1, X_2, X_3\}$ begin with descriptive expectations that others play as per the Equality norm, and agents $\{Y_1, Y_2, Y_3\}$ begin with descriptive expectations that others play as per the Equity norm. In each conjectured play of the game, each agent chooses from the norm set $\mathcal{N}$, and defines her conditional payoff $Pz_i \,|\, z_j z_k z_l z_m z_n : \mathcal{N} \,|\, \mathcal{N}^5 \to \mathbb{R}$ with clock-wise indexing convention

$$Z_i \,|\, Z_j Z_k Z_l Z_m Z_n \in \{X_1 | X_2 X_3 Y_1 Y_2 Y_3, \; X_2 | X_3 Y_1 Y_2 Y_3 X_1, \; X_3 | Y_1 Y_2 Y_3 X_1 X_2,$$
$$Y_1 | Y_2 Y_3 X_1 X_2 X_3, \; Y_2 | Y_3 X_1 X_2 X_3 Y_1, \; Y_3 | X_1 X_2 X_3 Y_1 Y_2 \}. \tag{6}$$

Let N_{z_i} denote the norm conjecture for the conditioned agent (the agent on the left side of the conditioning symbol "$|$"), let $\mathbf{N}_{jklmn} = \{N_{z_j}, N_{z_k}, N_{z_l}, N_{z_m}, N_{z_n}\}$, denote the norm conjectures for the conditioning agents, and let $I_{N_{z_i}}$ and $T_{N_{z_i}}$ with $Z_i \in \{X_1, X_2, X_3, Y_1, Y_2, Y_3\}$ denoting the payoffs for the conditioning agents. The general form of the payoff function is

$$p_{z_i | z_j z_k z_l z_m z_n}(N_{z_i} | \mathbf{N}_{jklmn}) = I_{N_{z_j}} + I_{N_{z_k}} + I_{N_{z_l}} + I_{N_{z_m}} + I_{N_{z_n}} + 5 T_{N_{z_i}} \tag{7}$$

where the utilities are additive if each agent plays an Investment/Trust game with every other player and accumulates the results.

The values expressed by (7) are in monetary units, which must be transformed to conform to the syntax of probability theory. It is thus convenient to now discharge the assumption that $\mu(I) = I$, which we must do in any case to bring the modeling within the rubric of economic theory. We thus map these values to the unit interval via the linear transform

$$\hat{p}_{z_i|z_j z_k z_l z_m z_n}(N_{z_i}|\mathbf{N}_{jklmn}) = \frac{p_{z_i|z_j z_k z_l z_m z_n}(N_{z_i}|\mathbf{N}_{jklmn})}{p_{z_i|z_j z_k z_l z_m z_n}(N_{zi}|\mathbf{N}_{jklmn}) + p_{z_i|z_j z_k z_l z_m z_n}(\neg N_{z_i}|\mathbf{N}_{jklmn})}$$

(8)

$$\hat{p}_{z_i|z_j z_k z_l z_m z_n}(\neg N_{z_i}|\mathbf{N}_{jklmn}) = \frac{p_{z_i|z_j z_k z_l z_m z_n}(\neg N_{z_i}|\mathbf{N}_{jklmn})}{p_{z_i|z_j z_k z_l z_m z_n}(N_{z_i}|\mathbf{N}_{jklmn}) + p_{z_i|z_j z_k z_l z_m z_n}(\neg N_{z_i}|\mathbf{N}_{jklmn})},$$

where $\neg N_{z_i}$ is the alternative to N_{z_i}.

Standard Bayesian network theory applies only to acyclic (i.e. hierarchical) influence relationships, where influence propagates unidirectionally, and independently specified reciprocal relationships are prohibited (i.e. Bayes's rule must be satisfied). To represent normative influence through conditionalization, however, reciprocal relationships are indispensable, and the corresponding conditional payoffs must be independently specifiable. The concept of dynamic exchanges among individuals is fundamental to mindshaping as discussed by Zawidzki (2013), that is, the processes by which individuals engineer social environments through imitation, pedagogy, conformity to norms, and coordinated narrative self-constitution, in ways that influence others to modify their beliefs and preferences. To deal with networks of the form in (5), we must generalize beyond hierarchical network structures and accommodate networks with cycles. We begin by recognizing that it is not the concept of reciprocity that is prohibited by Bayes's rule. Rather it is *simultaneous* reciprocity that is problematic. But reciprocity of the type we are considering requires time-dependent exchanges. Consider the two-agent network (4). Z_j's preferences influence Z_i's preferences, which then influence Z_j's preferences, which again influence Z_i's preferences, and so on, ad infinitum. The critical question of interest is whether this sequence of exchanges oscillates indefinitely or converges to a unique limit where each agent is assigned an unconditional utility defined over her action set. The key mathematical tool for this investigation is the Markov chain convergence theorem. In its conventional probabilistic application, this theorem establishes necessary and sufficient conditions for the joint distribution of a set of time-evolving discrete random variables (termed a Markov chain) to achieve a stationary distribution. Because the syntactical structure of a conditional game satisfies the mathematical conditions for the application of the Markov chain convergence theorem, we can apply the theory to compute steady-state (i.e., stationary) utilities.[3]

Our task, therefore, is to model the dynamic relationship between the utility of the normative profiles of the agents as time evolves. This task is particularly challenging due to the complex interrelationships between agents as expressed by the graph displayed in (5). Fortunately, however, a graph of a network is *not* the network; it is only a representation of it, and graphical representations of a network are not unique. To be useful, however, two representations of a network must be *Markov equivalent*, meaning that the conditionalization properties of the two graphs are identical. In particular, we are interested in defining a Markov equivalent graph that converts a graph whose vertices are single agents and whose edges are multidirectional linkages [i.e., (5)] into a graph whose vertices comprise multiple agents and whose edges are unidirectional linkages. As is established in the Appendix (see https://cear.gsu.edu/wp-2020-19-strategic-theory-of-norms-for-empiri

cal-applications-in-political-science-and-political-economy/), such a Markov equivalent network is

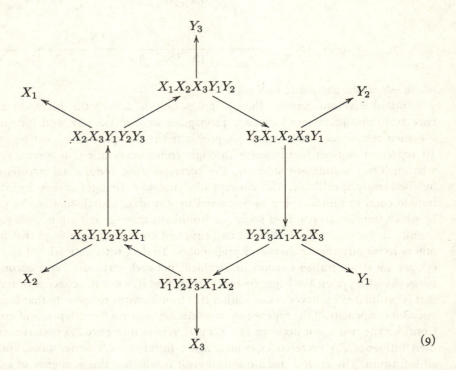

$$\tag{9}$$

where the edges linking five-agent subnetworks to five-agent subnetworks are transition matrices $T_{ijklm|jklmn}$, as defined in the Appendix (A.4), for

$$Z_i Z_j Z_k Z_l Z_m \mid Z_j Z_k Z_l Z_m Z_n \in \{X_1 X_2 X_3 Y_1 Y_2 \mid X_2 X_3 Y_1 Y_2 Y_3,\ X_2 X_3 Y_1 Y_2 Y_3 \mid$$
$$X_3 Y_1 Y_2 Y_3 X_1,\ X_3 Y_1 Y_2 Y_3 X_1 \mid Y_1 Y_2 Y_3 X_1 X_2,\ Y_1 Y_2 Y_3 X_1 X_2 \mid Y_2 Y_3 X_1 X_2 X_3,$$
$$Y_2 Y_3 X_1 X_2 X_3 \mid Y_3 X_1 X_2 X_3 Y_1,\ Y_3 X_1 X_2 X_3 Y_1 \mid X_1 X_2 X_3 Y_1 Y_2\},$$
$$\tag{10}$$

and where the entries in these matrices are composed of the conditional utilities $\hat{p}_{z_i|z_j z_k z_l z_m z_n}$. The Markov chain convergence theorem then establishes that the steady-state coordination functions for each five-agent subnetwork are the eigenvectors corresponding to the unique unity eigenvalues of the closed-loop transition matrices formed as

$$T_{ijklm} = T_{ijklm|jklmn} T_{jklmn|klmni} T_{klmni|lmnij} T_{lmnij|mnijk} T_{mnijk|nijkl} T_{nijkl|ijklm},$$
$$\tag{11}$$

yielding in matrix format $\bar{w}_{ijklm}, \bar{w}_{jklmn}, \bar{w}_{klmni}, \bar{w}_{lmnij}, \bar{w}_{mnijk}, \bar{w}_{nijkl}$ as defined by A.18 in the Appendix.[4] We emphasize that convergence is independent of the initial state.

The steady-state network is illustrated in (13), where the edges denoted by ⤳ are *dormant*—they still exist but are inactive once steady-state (i.e., convergence) is achieved. Finally, the individual coordinated utilities are obtained as

$$\bar{w}_i = T_{i|jklmn}\,\bar{w}_{jklmn} \tag{12}$$

where the transition matrices $T_{i|jklmn}$ are composed using the conditional utilities $\tilde{p}_{i|jklmn}$ as described in the Appendix (A.4).

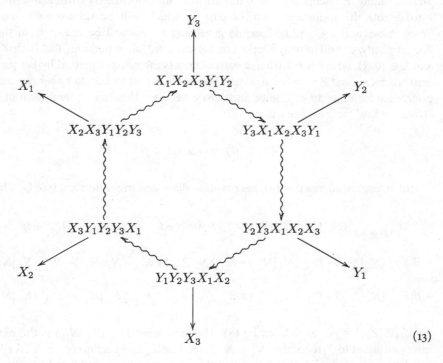

$$\tag{13}$$

We have now shown how to use the mechanism of conditionalization to represent influence on beliefs, which might in principle be normative beliefs, in the setting of the Investment/Trust game with two sets of competing norms we have simply stipulated as such. However, we have yet to introduce any machinery for representing normative expectations. Thus what has been developed so far has not yet reconstructed Bicchieri's analysis. Conditionalization as developed to this point operates only over potential utility gains from adjustments of descriptive expectations when the X_n and Y_n networks are combined. But if we can formally capture Kuran's cases of normative change, which depends on dynamics of expectations, then it follows that we will have shown that our formal operationalization of conditionality is isomorphic to Bicchieri's informal idea of it.

5 NORMATIVE DYNAMICS

5.1 Modeling Conflicting Norms in the Investment/Trust Game

As discussed above, Kuran (1995) models an agent's *total utility* from a transaction as being additively composed of her *intrinsic* utility I, her *reputational* utility R, and her *expressive* utility E. Adapting this framework to the Investment/Trust game, we will use I to denote the monetary value of payoffs, which will be transformed into utilities. From Subsection 4.3, agents' baseline governing norms will be drawn from the set $\mathcal{N}$. For simplicity, we will initially suppose that R and E are "all or nothing," that is, that $R \in \{0, 1\}$ and $E \in \{0, 1\}$, where R = 1 when a player chooses the action expected by her partner, and zero otherwise, and E = 1 when a player chooses the action mandated by her pre-conditioned preference for Equality or Equity, and zero otherwise. Then the general form of a player's "Kuran utility" for the game will be

$$\omega\big(I, R, E\big) = \omega(\alpha + I + \beta R + \delta E) \tag{14}$$

which, expressed as a conditional payoff as discussed in Section 4.2, (see (7)), becomes

$$\omega_{z_i|z_jz_kz_lz_mz_n}(N_{z_i}|N_{z_j},N_{z_k},N_{z_l},N_{z_m},N_{z_n}) = \alpha + I_{N_{z_j}} + I_{N_{z_k}} + I_{N_{z_l}} + I_{N_{z_m}} + I_{N_{z_n}} + 5T_{N_{z_i}}$$

$$+ \beta[R_{z_i|z_j}(N_{z_i}|N_{z_j}) + R_{z_i|z_k}(N_{z_i}|N_{z_k}) + R_{z_i|z_l}(N_{z_i}|N_{z_l}) + R_{z_i|z_m}(N_{z_i}|N_{z_m}) + R_{z_i|z_n}(N_{z_i}|N_{z_n})]$$

$$+ \delta[E_{z_i|z_j}(N_{z_i}|N_{z_j}) + E_{z_i|z_k}(N_{z_i}|N_{z_k}) + E_{z_i|z_l}(N_{z_i}|N_{z_l}) + E_{z_i|z_m}(N_{z_i}|N_{z_m}) + E_{z_i|z_n}(N_{z_i}|N_{z_n})] \tag{15}$$

for $Z_i | Z_j Z_k Z_l Z_m Z_n$ as defined by (6). The expression $R_{z_i|z_h}(N_{z_i}|N_{z_h})$ is the reputational utility awarded to Z_i for action $N_{z_i} \in \mathcal{N}$, given that Z_h takes action $N_{z_h} \in \mathcal{N}$, for $h \in \{j, k, l, m, n\}$. The parameter α is the player's baseline monetary assets, and β and δ are independent parameters that determine the shadow prices, in the currency of I, of R and E, respectively. The expression

$$I_{N_{z_i}} + I_{N_{z_k}} + I_{N_{z_l}} + I_{N_{z_m}} + I_{N_{z_n}} + 5T_{N_{z_i}} \tag{16}$$

is the intrinsic component,

$$\beta\Big[R_{z_i|z_j}\big(N_{z_i}|N_{z_j}\big) + R_{z_i|z_k}\big(N_{z_i}|N_{z_k}\big) + R_{z_i|z_l}\big(N_{z_i}|N_{z_l}\big) + R_{z_i|z_m}\big(N_{z_i}|N_{z_m}\big) + R_{z_i|z_n}\big(N_{z_i}|N_{z_n}\big) \Big] \tag{17}$$

is the reputational component, and

$$\delta\left[E_{z_i|z_j}\left(N_{z_i}|N_{z_j}\right)+E_{z_i|z_k}\left(N_{z_i}|N_{z_k}\right)+E_{z_i|z_l}\left(N_{z_i}|N_{z_l}\right)+E_{z_i|z_m}\left(N_{z_i}|N_{z_m}\right)+E_{z_i|z_n}\left(N_{z_i}|N_{z_n}\right)\right] \quad (18)$$

is the expressive component. We rescale these payoffs to the unit interval by the linear transform

$$\hat{\omega}_{z_i|z_jz_kz_lz_mz_n}\left(N_{z_i}|\mathbf{N}_{jklmn}\right)=\frac{\omega_{z_i|z_jz_kz_lz_mz_n}\left(N_{z_i}|\mathbf{N}_{jklmn}\right)}{\omega_{z_i|z_jz_kz_lz_mz_n}\left(N_{z_i}|\mathbf{N}_{jklmn}\right)+\omega_{z_i|z_jz_kz_lz_mz_n}\left(\neg N_{z_i}|\mathbf{N}_{jklmn}\right)}$$

$$\hat{\omega}_{z_i|z_jz_kz_lz_mz_n}\left(\neg N_{z_i}|\mathbf{N}_{jklmn}\right)=\frac{\omega_{z_i|z_jz_kz_lz_mz_n}\left(\neg N_{z_i}|\mathbf{N}_{jklmn}\right)}{\omega_{z_i|z_jz_kz_lz_mz_n}\left(N_{z_i}|\mathbf{N}_{jklmn}\right)+\omega_{z_i|z_jz_kz_lz_mz_n}\left(\neg N_{z_i}|\mathbf{N}_{jklmn}\right)}, \quad (19)$$

with $\mathbf{N}_{jklmn}=\{N_{z_j},N_{z_k},N_{z_l},N_{z_m},N_{z_n}\}$.

We pointed out in Section 3 that majorities of experimental participants exhibit moderate risk aversion and rank-dependent utility. Because part of the point of the simulations is to model our theory for laboratory application, we specify $\hat{\omega}_{z_i|z_jz_kz_lz_mz_n}$ in such a way as to allow for agents whose choices either respect expected utility theory (EUT), or violate EUT axioms only in ways consistent with rank-dependent utility theory (RDU), as per Quiggin (1982). (RDU formally nests EUT.) A specification of RDU that has proven particularly useful in estimation of data from risky choice experiments is due to Prelec (1998), which is conventionally used to map a set of probability mass functions into a set of probability weighting functions to account for risk aversion. In the conditional game context, we use its most general (2-parameter) form[*]

$$P(\omega)=\exp[-\eta(-\ln\omega)^\varphi]\quad \varphi>0,\eta>0 \quad (20)$$

We assume that all agents are risk averse across all payoff intervals (though to degrees that can vary across the agents) and, therefore, use a strictly concave Prelec operator to transform $\hat{\omega}_{z_i|z_jz_kz_lz_mz_n}$ into a utility weighting function. We may render the Prelec operator to be strictly concave for any given value of ϕ by setting

$$\eta=\exp\left[\ln\left(-\ln\omega_c\right)(1-\phi)\right] \quad (21)$$

where ω_c is value such that the Prelec operator crosses the diagonal at $\omega_c=0$. Thus, to ensure that the agents are risk averse, we transform them via

$$\bar{\omega}_{z_i|z_jz_kz_lz_mz_n}=P\left(\hat{\omega}_{z_i|z_jz_kz_lz_mz_n}\right)=\exp[-\eta\left(-\ln\hat{\omega}_{z_i|z_jz_kz_lz_mz_n}\right)^\varphi] \quad (22)$$

[*] To avoid singularities, the zero crossing is set at $\omega_c=0.0001$.

Although this nonlinear transform does not preserve the requirement to sum to unity, we may achieve this condition by applying the model developed by Quiggin (1982), yielding

$$
\tilde{\omega}_{z_i|z_jz_kz_lz_mz_n}\left(N_{z_i}|\mathbf{N}_{jklmn}\right) =
$$
$$
\left\{
\begin{array}{l}
\overline{\omega}_{z_i|z_jz_kz_lz_mz_n}\left(N_{z_i}|\mathbf{N}_{jklmn}\right) \text{ if } \overline{\omega}_{z_i|z_jz_kz_lz_mz_n}\left(N_{z_i}|\mathbf{N}_{jklmn}\right) \geq \overline{\omega}_{z_i|z_jz_kz_lz_mz_n}\left(\neg N_{z_i}|\mathbf{N}_{jklmn}\right) \\
1-\overline{\omega}_{z_i|z_jz_kz_lz_mz_n}\left(\neg N_{z_i}|\mathbf{N}_{jklmn}\right) \text{ if } \overline{\omega}_{z_i|z_jz_kz_lz_mz_n}\left(N_{z_i}|\mathbf{N}_{jklmn}\right) < \overline{\omega}_{z_i|z_jz_kz_lz_mz_n}\left(\neg N_{z_i}|\mathbf{N}_{jklmn}\right)
\end{array}
\right\}
$$

$$(23)$$

$$
\tilde{\omega}_{z_i|z_jz_kz_lz_mz_n}\left(N_{z_i}|\mathbf{N}_{jklmn}\right) =
$$
$$
\left\{
\begin{array}{l}
1-\overline{\omega}_{z_i|z_jz_kz_lz_mz_n}\left(N_{z_i}|\mathbf{N}_{jklmn}\right) \text{ if } \overline{\omega}_{z_i|z_jz_kz_lz_mz_n}\left(N_{z_i}|\mathbf{N}_{jklmn}\right) < \overline{\omega}_{z_i|z_jz_kz_lz_mz_n}\left(\neg N_{z_i}|\mathbf{N}_{jklmn}\right) \\
\overline{\omega}_{z_i|z_jz_kz_lz_mz_n}\left(\neg N_{z_i}|\mathbf{N}_{jklmn}\right) \text{ if } \overline{\omega}_{z_i|z_jz_kz_lz_mz_n}\left(N_{z_i}|\mathbf{N}_{jklmn}\right) \geq \overline{\omega}_{z_i|z_jz_kz_lz_mz_n}\left(\neg N_{z_i}|\mathbf{N}_{jklmn}\right)
\end{array}
\right\}.
$$

In the context of unconditional utility, subjective decision weights are understood as reflecting idiosyncratic *beliefs* about probabilities of outcomes based on their utility ranking. In the praxeological context modeled by CGT, it is most natural to interpret the weighting function as reflecting the idea that an agent might strategically adjust the preferences expressed by actual *or* conjectured choices to reflect uncertainty about the extent to which those with whom she interacts are guided by the norm she anticipates. Since CGT utilities comply with the probability syntax, we may define a utility weighting function as analogous to a probability weighting function by transforming conditional utilities as developed above to account for this praxeological uncertainty.

In the simulations to follow we will *not* exploit the full flexibility of utility representation offered by the 2-parameter Prelec function. This is because the point of the simulations is to demonstrate the capacity of conditionalization to serve as a mechanism for effecting the kinds of normative dynamics Kuran identifies. For this purpose it is preferable to minimize other sources of complexity, so, as stated, we restrict attention to utility functions that are concave throughout the interval space. For now, we simply make the point that the theory can accommodate the more complicated functions (e.g., S-shaped, inverse S, and others; see Wilcox 2015) that often provide best fits to laboratory choice data. In empirical applications, identification of the Kuran parameters would require the experimenter to empirically estimate risk preferences and subjective probability weightings. As argued in Section 3, this is something experimenters interested in norms are motivated to do anyway.

5.2 Conditional Game Simulations of Normative Behavior

The Investment/Trust game in the six-agent network introduced in Section 4.2 provides a context for testing CGT modeling of relative norm fragility with Kuran utilities using computer simulations. The network graph (5) comprises two subnetworks, each of which begins (i.e. prior to conditionalization) with a different governing norm in Bicchieri's sense. The subnetwork $\{X_1, X_2, X_3\}$ abides by norm N_1, Equality, and the subnetwork $\{Y_1, Y_2, Y_3\}$

abides by N_2, Equity. In the simulations, each agent chooses strategies that determine an action for each possible vector of others' strategies, on the assumption that they are equally likely to find themselves in the Investor role or the Trustee role. The endowment for each agent in the Investor role is specified as $\varepsilon = \$12$ and the fraction of the endowment that may be offered is capped at $\sigma = 2/3$. Under both the Equality and Equity norms it is a dominant strategy for the Investor to choose the maximum possible transfer. This generates the following monetary payoffs:

$$I_{N_1} = (1+2\sigma)\varepsilon/2 = \$14$$

$$T_{N_1} = (1+2\sigma)\varepsilon/2 = \$14, \tag{24}$$

And

$$I_{N_2} = (1-\sigma+3\sigma^2)\varepsilon = \$20$$

$$T_{N_2} = 3(\sigma-\sigma^2)\varepsilon = \$8 \tag{25}$$

We assume, as stated in Section 5.2, that the agents are risk averse, which corresponds to a strictly concave Prelec function that crosses the diagonal at $\omega = 0$. Our simulations are run with each agent assigned a Prelec function by randomly drawing ϕ from a uniform distribution over the interval $(1, 1.5)$. Figure 5.2(a) displays the realizations from the random draw of Prelec functions and Figure 5.2(b) displays the average Prelec function with parameters $(\overline{\phi}, \overline{\eta}) = (1.228, 0.6628)$. A representative agent's baseline utility is computed by considering intrinsic utility only, that is, with $\alpha = 10$ and $\beta = \delta = 0$, computed for the average Prelec parameters, yielding $\mu(I_{N_1}) = 0.525$ and $\mu(I_{N_2}) = 0.475$. Note that although expected monetary payoffs are the same for all players and under both norms, Equity involves higher variance, so, given the risk aversion built into $\tilde{\omega}$, $\mu(I_{N_1}) > \mu(I_{N_2})$.

We now demonstrate how application of CGT generates normative change for players with Kuran utility functions. We simulate three social scenarios. In each case, we depict two 3-agent "communities" distinguished from one another by prevalence in each of an

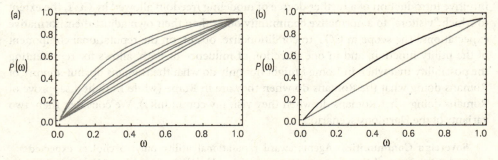

FIGURE 5.2. Prelec mapping functions: (a) random Prelec functions, (b) average Prelec function.

alternative norm regulating play in the Investment/Trust game. X agents begin by following the Equality norm and Y agents begin by following the Equity norm. We simulate encounters between the two communities, and apply conditionalization as the engine of their normative adjustments to one another.

Harmony is a baseline scenario for comparison with subsequent more interesting ones. Here all agents are content with their respective normative status quo positions, in the sense that they earn δ expressive utility when they play according to their community's preferred norm.

Pluralistic Ignorance is a scenario in which Y agents are satisfied with their community's norm, but X agents are preference falsifiers, privately dispreferring their community's norm, but each unaware that their dissenting attitude is shared by their compatriots. Thus X agents trade off expressive utility for reputational utility, and their choices will be sensitive to the relative magnitudes of β and δ.

Activist/Trendsetter names a scenario that replicates **Harmony** except that one agent, Y_3, is an Activist (Kuran) or Trendsetter (Bicchieri) who does not have reputational utility as an argument in her utility function, but always multiplies expressive utility by 2δ. This agent will thus play against the norm preferred by both her native community and herself only when δ is below some threshold in relation to I.

We summarize the relationship between theory and our simulation setup. First, in every simulation players conditionalize on intrinsic utility, meaning here that their risk preferences influence one another. Specifically, Equity-governed agents will be conditioned, on encountering Equality-governed agents, to increase their probability of playing according to the Equality norm because they expect their partner to favor lower variance, and will accordingly attach greater weight to this preference in their own play. Players do not conditionalize on expressive utility, except in the special case we construct for the third simulation of a network that includes an Activist/Trendsetter. The basic mechanism of normative influence is conditionalization on reputational utility.

5.3 Harmony

We simulate four subscenarios. The symmetry of the Harmony scenario facilitates the intuitive introduction of a further degree of modeling freedom allowed by CGT, the extent to which "visitors" to a normative community other than their own adjust their normative expectations. The scope in CGT to conditionalize, or not, on the reputational component of the utility function, and in one direction of influence or both, allows for representing the possibility that when in Rome I might not only do what the Romans do, but *approve* of Romans doing what the Romans do when they are in Rome (while I might disapprove of Romans doing what Romans do when they visit my community). We consider, then, two variants of the Harmony scenario:

> **Sovereign Communities:** Agents award reputational utility only to choices expected under the norm of their home community: $R_{X_i|X_j}(N_{X_i}|N_{X_j}) = 0$ and $R_{Y_i|X_j}(N_{Y_i}|N_{X_j}) = 0$ in (16) for all i, j.

Table 5.1 Harmony simulation results

	Sovereign Community		Cosmopolitan Community	
Utility	$\beta = 40$ $\delta = 4$	$\beta = 4$ $\delta = 40$	$\beta = 40$ $\delta = 4$	$\beta = 4$ $\delta = 40$
$\bar{w}_X$ (N1)	0.820	0.859	0.788	0.848
$\bar{w}_X$ (N2)	0.180	0.141	0.212	0.152
$\bar{w}_Y$ (N1)	0.239	0.182	0.720	0.195
$\bar{w}_Y$ (N2)	0.761	0.818	0.280	0.805

Cosmopolitan Communities: Agents award reputational utility when agents play as expected according to the norm that governs their community by members of a community governed by a different norm: $R_{X_i|X_i}(N_{X_i}|N_{X_j}) = 1$ and $R_{Y_i|X_j}(N_{Y_i}|N_{X_j}) = 1$ in (16) for all i, j.

In each subscenario, we simulate an instance of the two possible general inequalities between β and δ:

$\beta > \delta$: Reputational utility dominates expressive utility ($\beta = 40$, $\delta = 4$).
$\beta < \delta$: Expressive utility dominates reputational utility ($\beta = 4$, $\delta = 40$).

We show the results of the above simulations in Table 5.1. Because all players within each community have identical utility functions and expectations, the table shows outcomes for a representative agent from each community. These can be summarized as follows. First, comparison of Table 5.1 with the baseline numbers shows the obvious result that adding reputational utility and expressive utility as components of players' total utility increases the value to players in each community of playing according to their respective norms. More interestingly, when players conditionalize on reputational utility (that is, in the Cosmopolitan Communities subscenario) and the weight of reputational utility dominates the weight of expressive utility, followers of the less intrinsically valuable norm, Equity, earn higher expected utility from playing according to the foreign norm (Equality) when they visit members of the other community than they do by maintaining their home norm. Players whose native Equality norm earns higher expected intrinsic utility, on the other hand, prefer to trade off some of that gain in exchange for improved prospects when they meet Equity-governed counterparts under Cosmopolitan conditions. Mutual respect promotes normative pluralism.

5.4 Pluralistic Ignorance

We simulate a pluralistic ignorance scenario by assuming that X agents, privately disliking their community's Equality norm, can gain expressive utility only when they play according to the other community's norm. We investigate two subscenarios:

$\beta > \delta$: Reputational utility dominates expressive utility ($\beta = 40$, $\delta = 4$).
$\beta < \delta$: Expressive utility dominates reputational utility ($\beta = 4$, $\delta = 40$).

Table 5.2 Pluralistic Ignorance simulation results.

Utility	$\beta = 40$ $\delta = 4$	$\beta = 4$ $\delta = 40$
$\bar{w}_X(N1)$	0.402	0.189
$\bar{w}_X(N2)$	0.598	0.811
$\bar{w}_Y(N1)$	0.302	0.187
$\bar{w}_Y(N2)$	0.698	0.813

We simulate these subscenarios only for the "Cosmopolitan Communities" environment, because it is trivial that in a "Sovereign Communities" environment, preference falsifiers would simply swap reputational for expressive utility when they "go abroad," so conditionalization would have no effect independent of the arbitrarily chosen weighting parameters; any observed changes relative to the relevant comparison with the Harmony scenario would be entirely attributable to the interaction of risk aversion with the exogenously stipulated $\beta{:}\delta$ ratio.

Table 5.2 shows the results for each subscenario. The key result is that, consistently with the prediction of the theory, conditionalization flips the dominant probability mass of initial Equality play to Equity play among the preference falsifiers, notwithstanding the interaction of their risk aversion with Equity play's higher risk. This effect is about twice as large when expressive utility dominates reputational utility as in the opposite case.

Analysis of this case confirms that modeling captures the theoretical target of interest, and shows that norms that are privately unpopular are relatively fragile in encounters with norms that are privately supported, even when, as here, there is no mechanism by which players can update their priors from interactions in their home network and learn directly about their pluralistic ignorance.

5.5 Activist/Trendsetter

Both Bicchieri (2017) and Kuran (1995) express interest in modeling the impact on normative dynamics of agents who are unconcerned with reputational utility but derive utility directly from expressing their normative preferences, and who reward others whose choices reflect this preference by promoting their reputations. Bicchieri refers to such agents as "trendsetters," and Kuran calls them "activists." We introduce an Activist/Trendsetter agent into the simulation environment by revising the basic utility function of one agent, Y_3, who possesses an idiosyncratic utility function, adopted from (14), as follows:

$$\omega(I, E) = \omega(\alpha + I + \gamma E). \tag{26}$$

For convenience in the simulation we arbitrarily set $\gamma = 2\delta$. Y_3 supports the norm of her group, but consistently with the concept of activitism/trendsetting is unconcerned with reputational utility. This alteration by itself would not allow the Activist/Trendsetter to influence the utility functions of other agents because, in the austere informational conditions of the model, her pattern of play is not distinguishable from that of other Equity-governed agents. However, another aspect of activism as discussed by Kuran is that the Activist derives utility directly from converting agents who do not share her norm to adoption of her normative point of view. We represent this in the model by means of the following device. We allow the Activist to exert "missionary" influence by programming her to award reputational utility to any agent who plays according to her favored norm.

In all other respects, agents in this scenario are assigned the same utility structure as in the Harmony scenario.

By placing the Activist/Trendsetter in the community governed by a norm that mandates the behavior that earns riskier intrinsic utility, we ensure that any behavioral change we observe against the Harmony baseline must be driven by conditionalization on the nonmonetary payoffs. To investigate this possible effect we simulate the same environments (Cosmopolitan and Sovereign communities) as in the Harmony simulations. General inequalities between β and δ are tested for the same exogenous assignments as in the previous scenarios:

$\beta > \delta$: Reputational utility dominates expressive utility ($\beta = 40$, $\delta = 4$).
$\beta < \delta$: Expressive utility dominates reputational utility ($\beta = 4$, $\delta = 40$).

Table 5.3 displays the simulation results. Since the X community is homogenous, we show results for a representative X agent. To interpret this table we must compare it to the results of the Harmony case as displayed in Table 5.1. Upon comparing the utility values for the X agents, it is clear that under all conditions, the X-group agents in the Activist/Trendsetter scenario shift the probability mass associated with playing according to the Equality norm toward Equity. However, this shift is minimal when reputational utility dominates expressive utility. It is as if agents are drawn to adapt their

Table 5.3 Activist/Trendsetter simulation results.

Utility	Sovereign Community		Cosmopolitan Community	
	$\beta = 40$ $\delta = 4$	$\beta = 4$ $\delta = 40$	$\beta = 40$ $\delta = 4$	$\beta = 4$ $\delta = 40$
$\bar{w}_X$ (N1)	0.673	0.846	0.367	0.844
$\bar{w}_X$ (N2)	0.327	0.154	0.633	0.156
$\bar{w}_{Y_1}$ (N1)	0.679	0.188	0.309	0.187
$\bar{w}_{Y_1}$ (N2)	0.321	0.812	0.691	0.813
$\bar{w}_{Y_3}$ (N1)	0.322	0.119	0.323	0.119
$\bar{w}_{Y_3}$ (N2)	0.678	0.881	0.677	0.881

preferences more by the extra welfare they observe to be available from "ideological purity" than by the reputational advantages they gain from impressing the Activist. In addition, followers of the Equity norm are no longer drawn strongly toward efficiency gains from flipping to Equality-governed play when reputational utility dominates expressive utility in the Cosmopolitan subscenario. That this effect is not observed in the Sovereign subscenario shows it does not result mainly from direct influence of the activist agent on her own compatriots. It results rather from the increased incidence of initial Equality players who come to "think well of" Equity players as a result of the Activist agent's influence on them.

These scenarios serve as demonstrations of the capacity of CGT to represent and facilitate estimation of mechanisms of normative influence and diffusion. We have shown how three of Kuran's instances of normative change at the social level could be identified in possible choice data. The mechanism used to achieve this identification is conditionalization of preference mediated by both descriptive and normative expectations. Thus, we contend, we have operationalized Bicchieri's analysis of norms for potential use by empirical political scientists or economists presented with controlled observations of choice behavior.

6 CONCLUSION

A fully general theory of norms that can be applied to empirical data, and in particular to data generated by choice experiments, remains an outstanding goal that must consolidate the following contributions:

1. a satisfactory philosophical analysis of the concept of a norm;
2. a relatively general economic theory that links norms as social structures with incentives that motivate normatively regulated agents' choices in small-n scenarios where agents influence what Kuran calls "intrinsic utility" and cannot be modeled as norm-takers; and
3. a menu of standard experimental and econometric estimation procedures that are aligned with (1) and (2).

In this chapter, we have not focused on goal (1). Bicchieri's philosophical analysis may be overdemanding in requiring *fully* aligned expectations of descriptive and normative beliefs, but it is not clear how this criterion might best be relaxed without removing the teeth from its bite. However, we have proceeded on the assumption that Bicchieri's basic insight that norms are networks of expectations is correct, provided it is consistently given a genuinely social rather than an implicitly psychological interpretation as we urge in Section 2.

We believe that Kuran has provided a useful high-level economic model of norms for large-n scenarios in which agents are norm-takers and cannot influence their own utility except through their choice between falsifying and not falsifying their preferences, or adopting activist behavior. This model is obviously not general in failing to apply to small-n interactions. In addition it is defined only over low-information representations of utility functions as categorical preference orderings. In the chapter we have taken a step toward greater generality on the second dimension by incorporating risk attitudes and subjective probability weighting into the basic Kuran utility model. We did this not for its own sake but because of our primary interest in adopting Kuran's theory to the kinds of small-n interactions that occur in the experimental laboratory.

This goal reflects our aim to have, at the very least, shown social scientists some of what will be required theoretically and conceptually if norms are to become direct objects of experimental study in themselves. It is particularly political scientists who are the intended audience here, as some sociologists might view norms, even if not conceived as fundamentally psychological, as too grounded in intentional structure and attitudes to be good constructs for integration into their theoretical space. Perhaps in that case, however, our modeling apparatus of CGT may carry some appeal. Though CGT, like any extension of game theory, operates on utility, agency, and choice, it represents these concepts as fundamentally social, indeed as, effectively, distributions in populations of dispositions to be influenced in certain ways. In representing responses to social norms as strategic, it might also be said that we correct for tendencies in sociological models to treat normatively oppressed agents as purely passive in the face of power.

It seems difficult, from any disciplinary perspective, to imagine fully modeling political dynamics as independent of normative identities, normative commitments of varying degrees of flexibility, and energies marshaled for the exercise of normative influence. We hope in this chapter to have offered some tools for such modeling that political scientists will want to refine, adapt, and ultimately apply to data.

Summarizing the tools in question, probability theory is an ideal mechanism with which to model dynamics that are fundamentally driven by weights of relative influence. Merging probability theory with network theory through the structure of Bayesian networks serves as natural syntax for representing a mechanism by which normative influence diffuses throughout a community. Standard Bayesian network theory is restricted to acyclic networks, but CGT relaxes that restriction by incorporating recognition that a cycle can be modeled as an infinite time sequence of acyclic networks. Thus, a cyclic network can be modeled as a Markov chain, and the Markov chain convergence theorem establishes necessary and sufficient conditions for convergence. The usefulness of this theorem is further enhanced by the fact that the converged state can be derived from the closed-loop transition matrix without having to conduct or trace iterations in literal time. We do not deny that people generally learn about norms and their effects by encountering one another in sequences of interactions in real time, and updating their expectations on the basis of such experience. But it is frequently inconvenient or impossible to experimentally set up such dynamics for controlled observation. In such circumstances the experimenter may need a representation of dynamics in the limit to compare with those she observes in her lab. We will have succeeded in our main aim if, when that need arises, she finds value in the resources we have provided.

Notes

1. For extended discussion of the intended distinction within economics, see Ross (2014).
2. Henrich et al. (2004) at one point (p. 376) suggest that norms at least sometimes reflect institutionalized practice, but offer no comment on the dynamics of relationships between such institutions and individual preferences.
3. An important technical property for the application of the Markov chain convergence theorem is that the conditional utilities must satisfy the Markov property, which means that the conditional utility at a given time depends only on the state of the network at the immediately previous cycle.
4. Notice that it is not necessary to compute the limit as $t \to \infty$ in (A.18). Once the closed-loop transition matrices are defined, the steady-state vectors are immediately available upon the calculation of the relevant eigenvectors.

References

Akerlof, G. & Kranton, R. (2010). *Identity Economics*. Princeton University Press.

Andersen, S., Harrison, G., Lau, M., & Rutström, E.E. (2008). Lost in state space: Are preferences stable? *International Economic Review* 49: 1091–1112.

Andreoni, J. & Bernheim, B.D. (2009). Social image and the 50-50 norm: A theoretical and experimental analysis of audience effects. *Econometrica* 77: 1607–1636.

Andreoni, J., Nikiforakis, N., & Siegenthaler, S. (2021). Predicting social tipping and norm change in controlled experiments. *Proceedings of the National Academy of Sciences* 118(16), https://doi.org/10.1073/pnas.2014893118.

Andrighetto, G., Grieco, D., & Tummolini, L. (2015). Perceived legitimacy of normative expectations motivates compliance with social norms when nobody is watching. *Frontiers in Psychology* 6: 1413.

Aumann, R.J. (1987). Correlated equilibrium as an expression of Bayesian rationality. *Econometrica* 55(1): 1–18.

Azar, O.H. (2018). The influence of psychological game theory. *Journal of Economic Behavior & Organization* 167: 445–453.

Banerjee, A. (1992). A simple model of herd behavior. *Quarterly Journal of Economics* 107: 797–817.

Battigalli, P. & Dufwenberg, M. (2007). Guilt in games. *American Economic Review* 97(2): 170–176.

Battigalli, P. & Dufwenberg, M. (2009). Dynamic psychological games. *Journal of Economic Theory* 144(1): 1–35.

Berg, J., Dickhaut, J. & McCabe, K. (1995). Trust, reciprocity, and social history. *Games and Economic Behavior* 10: 122–142.

Bernheim, B.D. (1994). A theory of conformity. *Journal of Political Economy* 102: 841–877.

Bicchieri, C. (1993). *Rationality and Coordination*. Cambridge University Press.

Bicchieri, C. (2006). *The Grammar of Society: The Nature and Dynamics of Social Norms*. Cambridge University Press.

Bicchieri, C. (2017). *Norms in the Wild*. Cambridge University Press.

Bicchieri, C. & Chavez, A. (2010). Behaving as expected: Public information and fairness norms. *Journal of Behavioral Decision Making* 23: 161–178.

Bicchieri, C. & Chavez, A. (2013). Norm manipulation, norm evasion: Experimental evidence. *Economics and Philosophy* 29: 175–198.

Bicchieri, C., Lindemans, J., & Jiang, T. (2014). A structured approach to a diagnostic of collective practices. *Frontiers of Psychology* 5: 1418, doi: 10.3389/fpsyg.2014.01418.

Bicchieri, C., & Sontuoso, A. (2020). Game-theoretic accounts of social norms: The role of normative expectations. In C.M Capra, R. Croson, M. Rigdon, & T. Rosenblatt, eds., *Handbook of experimental game theory*, pp. 241–255. Edward Elgar.

Bicchieri, C. & Xiao, E. (2009). Do the right thing: But only if others do so. *Journal of Behavioral Decision Making* 22: 191–208.

Bicchieri, C., Xiao, E. & Muldoon, R. (2011). Trustworthiness is a social norm, but trusting is not. *Politics, Philosophy and Economics* 10: 170–187.

Binmore, K. (1994). *Game Theory and the Social Contract, Volume 1: Playing Fair.* MIT Press.

Binmore, K. (1998). *Game Theory and the Social Contract, Volume 2: Just Playing.* MIT Press.

Binmore, K. (2005). *Natural Justice.* Oxford University Press.

Binmore, K. (2007). *Does Game Theory Work? The Bargaining Challenge.* MIT Press.

Binmore, K. (2010). Social norms or social preferences? *Mind and Society* 2: 139–157.

Brock, W. & Durlauf, S. (2001). Discrete choices with social interactions. *Review of Economic Studies* 68: 235–260.

Chambers, R., & Quiggin, J. (2000). *Uncertainty, Production, Choice, and Agency: The State-Contingent Approach.* Cambridge University Press.

Chamley, C. (2004). *Rational Herds.* Cambridge University Press.

Chetty, R., Hofmeyr, A., Kincaid, H. & Monroe, B. (2021). The Trust game does not (only) measure trust: The risk-trust confound revisited. *Journal of Behavioral and Experimental Economics,* 90: 101520.

Druckman, J., Green, D., Kuklinski, J. & Lupia, A., eds., (2011). *Cambridge Handbook of Experimental Political Science.* Cambridge University Press.

Duffy, J. & Lafky, J. (2019). Social conformity under evolving private preferences. Working paper: https://www.socsci.uci.edu/ duffy/papers/LivingLie12132019.pdf.

Ensminger, J. & Henrich, J., eds. (2014). *Experimenting With Social Norms.* Russell Sage Foundation.

Gerber, A.S. & Rogers, T. (2009). Descriptive social norms and motivation to vote: Everybody's voting and so should you. *Journal of Politics* 71: 178–191.

Gintis, H. (2014). *The Bounds of Reason: Game Theory and the Unification of the Behavioral Sciences- Revised Edition.* Princeton University Press.

Guala, F. (2016). *Understanding Institutions: The Science and Philosophy of Living Together.* Princeton University Press.

Hanneford, I. (1995). *Race: The History of an Idea in the West.* Johns Hopkins University Press.

Harrison, G. (2014). Real choices and hypothetical choices. In S. Hess & A. Daly, eds., *Handbook of Choice Modelling*, pp. 236–254. Edward Elgar.

Harrison, G., Martínez-Correa, J., Swarthout, J.T. & Ulm, E. (2017). Scoring rules for subjective probability distributions. *Journal of Economic Behavior & Organization* 134: 430–448.

Harrison, G. & Ross, D. (2016). The psychology of human risk preferences and vulnerability to scaremongers: Experimental economic tools for hypothesis formulation and testing. *Journal of Cognition and Culture* 16: 383–414.

Harrison, G. & Rutström, E. (2008). Risk aversion in the laboratory. In J. Cox & G. Harrison, eds., *Risk Aversion in Experiments*, pp. 41–197. Emerald.

Henrich, J., Boyd, R., Bowles, S., Camerer, C., Fehr, E., & Gintis, H., eds. (2004). *Foundations of Human Sociality*. Oxford University Press.

Hirscheifer, J., & Riley, J. (1992). *The Analytics of Uncertainty and Information*. Cambridge University Press.

Karni, E. (1990). State-dependent preferences. In J. Eatwell, M. Milgate, & P. Newman, eds. *The New Palgrave: Utility and Probability*, pp. 242–247. Norton.

Katz, D. & Allport, F. (1931). *Student Attitudes*. Craftsman.

Kreps, D. (1990). *Game Theory and Economic Modelling*. Oxford University Press.

Kuran, T. (1995). *Private Truths, Public Lies: The Social Consequences of Preference Falsification*. Harvard University Press.

Lerner, B. (2011). *One For the Road: Drunk Driving Since 1900*. Johns Hopkins University Press.

Lewis, D. (1969). *Convention: A Philosophical Study*. Harvard University Press.

Lewis, D. (1976). Convention: Reply to Jamieson. *Canadian Journal of Philosophy* 6: 113–120.

Lewis, M. (2018). *The Fifth Risk*. Norton.

Mansbridge, J., Hartz-Karp, J., Amengual, M. & Gastil, J. (2006). Norms of deliberation: An inductive study. *Journal of Public Deliberation* 2: 7.

Martin, J.L. (2009). *Social Structures*. Princeton University Press.

Matheson, J.E. & Winkler, R.L. (1976). Scoring rules for continuous probability distributions. *Management Science* 22: 1087–1096.

Michaeli, M. & Spiro, D. (2015). Norm conformity across societies. *Journal of Public Economics* 132: 51–65.

Michaeli, M. & Spiro, D. (2017). From peer pressure to biased norms. *American Economic Journal: Microeconomics* 9: 152–216.

Prelec, D. (1998). The probability weighting function. *Econometrica* 60: 497–528.

Quiggin, J. (1982). A theory of anticipated utility. Journal of Economic Behavior and Organization 3: 323–343.

Ross, D. (2014). *Philosophy of Economics*. Palgrave Macmillan.

Ross, D. & Stirling, W.C. (2020). Economics, social neuroscience, and mindshaping. In J. Harbecke & C. Hermann-Pillath, eds., *The Brain and the Social–Methods and Philosophy of Integrating Neuroscience and Economics*, pp. 174–201. Routledge.

Schelling, T.C. (1980). *The Strategy of Conflict*. Harvard University Press.

Stirling, W.C. (2012). *Theory of Conditional Games*. Cambridge University Press.

Stirling, W.C. (2016). *Theory of Social Choice on Networks*. Cambridge University Press.

Sugden, B. (1986/2004). *The Economics of Rights, Co-operation and Welfare*. Palgrave Macmillan.

Tummolini, L., Andrighetto, G., Castelfranchi, C. & Conte, R. (2013). A convention or (tacit) agreement betwixt us: On reliance and its normative consequences. *Synthese* 190: 585–618.

Wilcox, N. (2015). Unusual estimates of probability weighting functions. *ESI Working Paper 15-10*. Retrieved from https://cear.gsu.edu/files/2019/09/WP_2019_05_Unusual-Estimates-of-Probability-Weighting-Functions_2019_0924.pdf.

Wilson, R. & Eckel, C. (2011). Trust and social exchange. In J. Druckman, D, Green, J. Kuklanski, & A, Lupia, eds., *Cambridge Handbook of Experimental Political Science*, pp. 243–257. Cambridge University Press.

Xiao, E. & Bicchieri, C. (2010). When equality trumps reciprocity. *Journal of Economic Psychology* 31: 456–470.

Zawidzki, T.W. (2013). *Mindshaping: A New Framework for Understanding Human Social Cognition*. MIT Press.

CHAPTER 6

....

EXPLAINING INSTITUTIONAL CHANGE

....

N. EMRAH AYDINONAT AND PETRI YLIKOSKI

1. INTRODUCTION

....

EXPLAINING institutional change,[1] particularly explaining gradual and endogenous change, has long been the Achilles heel of institutional analysis. All major approaches to institutions—historical institutionalism, sociological institutionalism, and rational-choice institutionalism (RCI)—seem to have problems with it. These problems are rooted in the way in which institutions are conceived:

> Despite many other differences, nearly all definitions of institutions treat them as relatively enduring features of political and social life (rules, norms, procedures) that structure behavior and that cannot be changed easily or instantaneously. The idea of persistence of some kind is virtually built into the very definition of an institution. (Mahoney & Thelen 2009, p. 4)

The inability to deal with institutional change is a serious challenge for *any* theory of institutions. Moreover, a theory that deals with institutional change only in an ad hoc manner or rules out conceivable, and possibly important, forms of institutional change cannot be fully satisfactory as a theory of institutions. Such a theory will have an explanatory handicap. Consider, for example, the distinction between exogenous and endogenous change. Since most institutional change is (and will be) a result of a combination of exogenous and endogenous factors, approaches that rule out some or all forms of endogenous change will have an explanatory disadvantage. Likewise, consider the distinction between discontinuous and incremental change. Although most theories of institutions see change as a discontinuous phenomenon and overlook incremental developments (Mahoney & Thelen 2009), it is also widely accepted that institutions change incrementally (e.g., North 1990). Leaving out the possibility of incremental change creates an explanatory shortcoming for theories of institutions; not only that such a theory cannot get the cases involving incremental change right, but it cannot shed light on the preconditions of abrupt changes it might be able to explain either. Our point is a theoretical one in that we are not claiming that endogenous or incremental sources of change are more important or more powerful, but that an acceptable theory should be able to deal with them both.

In this Chapter, we address the challenge of explaining institutional change and ask whether the much-criticized rational-choice perspective can contribute to the understanding of institutional change in political science. We aim to identify the methodological reasons why RCI assumes that institutional change is exogenous and discontinuous. We also ask whether it is possible to overcome these biases. More specifically, we will address the question of why RCI has difficulty conceiving endogenous change and why it has "a tendency to see change mostly in terms of dynamics unleashed by some exogenous shift or shock" (Streeck & Thelen 2005, p. 7). Our diagnosis of *the endogeneity blindness* of RCI will address the general limitations of this approach in explaining institutional change, but also reveal some of the ways in which it can contribute to the understanding of institutional change in political science.

The chapter will proceed as follows. In Section 2, we will begin by describing the core ideas of the rational-choice approach and showing how they give rise to endogeneity blindness. We will focus on Francesco Guala's (2016) *rules-in-equilibrium approach* (RE), which is a recent attempt to unify various RCI strands. Nevertheless, our points apply more generally. In Section 3, we will discuss three ways of incorporating endogenous change into RCI: Greif and Laitin's (2004) introduction of quasi-parameters, Jack Knight's (1992) bargaining approach, and Farrell and Héritier's (2003) account of endogenous change in the context of EU institutions. This discussion will help us identify some of the possible ways in which RCI can be extended to be more useful in understanding institutional change in political science. In Section 4, we will explore these pathways by opening up the black box of rule compliance a little bit further, discussing the basic reasons why institutional rules are indeterminate and how this gives rise to important sources of incremental institutional change. In Section 5, we conclude by briefly reflecting on what RCI theorizing would look like if it began to take endogenous change seriously. By giving up the simplifying assumptions underlying endogeneity blindness, game theory can still be a useful tool for analyzing institutional change in political science, but choosing this path has consequences for the generality of the models in RCI as well as for the style of its theorizing.

2. The Rules-in-Equilibrium Approach

There are two prominent ways in which RCI scholars have conceptualized institutions: institutions-as-rules (e.g., North 1990; Ostrom 2005) and institutions-as-equilibria (e.g., Lewis 1969; Schotter 1981; Calvert 1995; Greif 2006; see Greif & Kingston 2011 for a review).[2] The rules approach sees institutions as rules that govern individual behavior and create behavioral regularities. In this approach, institutions are considered as rules that help individuals solve societal problems or facilitate social interaction. The equilibrium approach, on the other hand, defines institutions as the equilibria of games that represent societal problems. It focuses on the motivations of individuals in choosing particular strategies to solve the coordination and cooperation problems that they face, rather than the rules that govern individual behavior. We will focus here on a recent attempt to unify

	L	R
L	1, 1	0, 0
R	0, 0	1, 1

FIGURE 6.1. A Symmetric Coordination Game

these approaches, called the rules-in-equilibrium approach (RE; Guala 2016). However, to understand RE, it is useful to start with the equilibrium approach.

The equilibrium approach begins with a representation of a societal problem in game form. The symmetric coordination game in Figure 6.1 is helpful in illustrating the main characteristics of this approach. In this game, each player has two options, L and R, which could, for example, represent the side of the road they choose to drive on. The payoff matrix shows that players benefit from coordination and thus they have an incentive to choose what the other player chooses. (L, L) and (R, R) are the Nash equilibria of the game, in which no player can benefit from unilaterally choosing another option. The Nash equilibria of this game are taken to represent alternative coordination conventions that are considered as basic institutions. Naturally, the coordination of two players cannot be conceived of as an institution. One can talk about an institution if a population of players somehow end up choosing the same option repeatedly, expecting everyone else to do the same to solve a recurrent coordination problem (Lewis 1969). For the equilibrium approach, the key characteristics of an institution are the following. First, there are multiple equilibria that represent alternative institutions. Second, the existence of an institution requires concordant mutual expectations (beliefs) by the members of the population (i.e., everyone expects—or, believes—that everyone else will act in a certain way). Third, the institution provides a solution to a recurrent societal problem. Fourth, once this solution emerges no one has an incentive to change her behavior.[3]

The equilibrium approach to institutions is said to provide the micro-foundations for institutions (Weingast 1996, p. 168). Its main strength over the rules approach is its ability to explain why people are motivated to follow the rules (Greif and Kingston 2011; Guala 2016).

> Although an equilibrium model is unable to tell us exactly how they have discovered these rules, it is able to explain why people continue to follow them even in spite of small deviations, and what must happen (how the incentives must change, how the beliefs must be manipulated) to make them stop following the rules. Thus the equilibrium model will support a functional explanation of the form: "the rules exist because they help people solve a coordination problem." (Guala 2016, p. 31)

The main shortcoming of the equilibrium approach is that it describes individual action "from an external point of view" and does not take into account the human "capacity to represent and to follow rules" that "may help converge on an equilibrium" (Guala 2016, p. 54). Guala (2016) follows other scholars (e.g., Aoki 2001, 2007; Greif 2006; Greif and Kingston 2011) in combining the main insights of the rules and equilibrium approaches. Basically, Guala's approach (RE) considers *institutions as rules in equilibrium*, where rules are considered as agents' representations of equilibria and the institution as an equilibrium of a coordination game.[4] In RE, "an institution may be considered as an equilibrium or as a rule of the game, depending on the perspective that one takes" (Guala 2016, p. 50). "From the point of view of an external observer" an institution corresponds to an equilibrium, but from the perspective of an agent an institutional rule "takes the form of a rule that dictates . . . what to do" in a given situation (Guala 2016, p. 50).

By combining the insights of the rules and equilibrium approaches, RE is able to overcome some of the difficulties faced by both accounts. Unlike the rules account, it can explain why people follow some rules and not others and, unlike the equilibrium account, it can take the agents' point of view into account. Nevertheless, because it makes heavy use of the equilibrium concept, it also inherits some of the problems of the equilibrium approach. First, it does not explain the origin of institutions. RE rather presumes that one of the multiple equilibria, that is, one of the alternative institutions, will be selected. Guala presumes that an external public signal such as a toss of a coin (a correlation device, Aumann 1974) announced by a third party (a "choreographer," Gintis 2009) can coordinate a player's behavior. Guala also assumes that the public signals will be in conditional form, such as "if in England, always drive on the left," and help individuals coordinate, but he does not explain where these public signals come from.

Second, like the equilibrium approach, RE is at its best in explaining the raison d'être and persistence of institutions *in general.* It shows that the institution at stake is a *solution* to a general societal problem (i.e., problems that individuals repeatedly face in their encounters with others) and once the solution is attained no one has an incentive to deviate from equilibrium behavior. For example, RE provides a raison d'être for money by pointing out that it solves a market coordination problem and can explain its persistence by showing that individuals have no incentive to deviate from the equilibrium behavior once the institution is in place.

Third, although RE does not explicitly try to explain institutional change, the way in which it conceptualizes institutions brings with it a certain way of thinking about change, since if institutions are persistent and self-enforcing structures that solve societal problems then institutional change must be due to external shocks.

> A self-enforcing institution is one in which each player's behavior is a best response. The inescapable conclusion is that changes in self-enforcing institutions must have an exogenous origin. (Greif & Laitin 2004, p. 633)

As RE relies heavily on equilibrium thinking it invites thinking about institutional change as a move from one persistent state to another, or from one equilibrium to another, or in terms of punctuated equilibria (Krasner 1984). Notice that this division between periods of endurance ("normal periods") and exceptional moments of change ("critical junctures") is set by a methodological bias rather than empirical facts about historical institutional change. Any explanation of change that can be developed within the RE must be developed on a "per need" basis, giving the explanations an ad hoc character. RE takes the self-enforcing nature of the resulting game-theoretical equilibrium as a defining feature of institutions, but it has no account of the stability of an institution over time.[5]

· How does RE end up with this peculiar way of analyzing institutions? The key factor is the goal of having a general theory that could account for a *type* of institution, rather than for a particular institution.[6] The *explanandum* is a highly stylized version of a "fully-formed" generic institution, rather than a concrete historical one. This sets RE aside from other approaches, like historical institutionalism, which has always focused on particular institutions. With the generic *explanandum*, all historical details are seen as contingent features of particular situations that are not of theoretical interest. They are just details that must be filled in when the theory is applied to particular cases. What matters is a theoretical how-possible explanation for a type of institution. This disregard for historical context is further strengthened when an *explanandum* is formulated in terms of the *existence* of the institution, rather than in terms of explaining its particular details. Naturally, with an abstract *explanandum* like this, there is much less change to be observed or to be explained. Thus, explaining change feels much less pressing.

Together with the methodological choices of the RE, its highly abstract *explanandum* shapes the characteristics of RE explanations. Although in principle the characteristics, social roles, and the history of particular agents might be represented by a combination of player types and payoffs, these matters are ignored in the analysis for the sake of generality. Similarly, the *agents are usually represented as homogenous*: everybody is assumed to have exactly the same capabilities, resources, beliefs, and incentives. This is not a formal denial of individual differences; they are just not considered theoretically interesting. Moreover, societal problems that are supposed to be the key to understanding institutions are *analyzed as if* they exist *in an institutional vacuum*. However, rational-choice models often presuppose, albeit implicitly, the working of certain generic institutions such as markets, property rights, the rule of law, etc.[7] Also, and more importantly for our purpose, they do not systematically take into account the role of extant institutions in determining institutional outcomes. This is not to say that the importance of existing institutions is denied; rather, in practice they are treated as historically variable contexts that can be ignored in developing a general theory. Finally, RE theorists *take rule compliance for granted*. While in principle it is acknowledged that rules can be ambiguous, indeterminate, and open to conflicting interpretation, in practice these issues are treated as random disturbances that do not have long-term consequences.

For RE, these *methodological choices and simplifications* are small sacrifices that allow the development of truly general theory. However, in explaining institutional change, as we just argued, these simplifications are far from harmless, making RE incapable of explaining endogenous change. Only by giving up these simplifications and the associated ideas about abstract *explananda* can RCI overcome its current shortcomings in explaining institutional change. The following sections will demonstrate this by showing how giving up these simplifications one by one increases the theory's ability to explain change.

3. Overcoming Endogeneity Blindness

We have seen that endogeneity blindness is a product of simplifying assumptions that are ultimately justified by the choice of a highly abstract *explanandum*. In what follows we will analyze the resources available to RCI to overcome its endogeneity blindness, based on attempts by some rational-choice theorists to incorporate endogenous change into their theories. We will argue that overcoming endogeneity blindness requires giving up the simplifying assumptions described above. By paying attention to the details ignored by mainstream RCI it is possible to increase its explanatory power with respect to real-world institutional phenomena.

We will start with a discussion of Greif and Laitin's (2004) prominent attempt to analyze endogenous change in terms of quasi-parameters. We will then briefly introduce Knight's (1992) bargaining approach that can increase the leverage of RCI. Finally, we will show how Farrell and Héritier (2003) employ the Knightian approach to develop an interesting model of endogenous change.[8]

3.1. Greif and Laitin: Quasi-Parameters

The basic idea of the Greif-Laitin approach is that an institution influences many things in the society, "such as wealth, identity, ability, knowledge, beliefs, residential distribution, and occupational specialization" (Greif & Laitin, 2004, p. 636) that could change or even undermine the institution in the long run. Normally, most things that institutions can influence are considered as exogenous parameters in the analysis. Greif and Laitin suggest considering them as endogenous when investigating institutional change. They call these parameters *quasi-parameters*, as their status as an exogenous parameter depends on the explanatory question asked. In the Greif-Laitin approach, an institution can cause a change in quasi-parameters, which can in turn either undermine or reinforce the equilibrium underlying that very institution. When more individuals in a wider range of situations find it best to adhere to the institutional rules—i.e., when the equilibrium is self-enforcing in a wider range of parameters—the institution is considered as *self-reinforcing* (Greif & Laitin, 2004, p. 634). When fewer individuals in fewer situations find the rules compelling, the institution is considered to be *self-undermining*. While Greif and Laitin work with the same idea of equilibrium as Guala, the idea of quasi-parameters allows them to conceive an institution as having consequences that have a "feedback effect" on itself, thus expanding or reducing the set of situations in which the institution is self-enforcing.

The idea of a quasi-parameter is ingenious. First, it allows one to see the difference between *game-theoretical equilibrium* as a representation of an institution and the *stability of the institution*. For comparison, consider RE. Although the RE approach distinguishes between the theoretical representation of the institution and the institution itself (Guala 2016), it does not operationalize this distinction. In RE analysis, equilibrium equals institutional stability or persistence. Greif and Laitin, on the other hand, identify the proper *explanandum* both for institutional persistence and change with the help of quasi-parameters. Second, in Greif and Laitin's framework, similar causal mechanisms could explain both stability and change. There is no longer a need to assume that stability and change require different kinds of explanation, as suggested by Guala. Finally, the Greif-Laitin approach allows for incremental change, or at least incremental build-up for a change, since the institutional change occurs "when the self-undermining process reaches a critical level such that past patterns of behavior are no longer self-enforcing" (Greif & Laitin, 2004, p. 634).

Despite these appealing features, the Greif-Laitin approach does not fully address the challenge of explaining endogenous change. It does describe, very abstractly, how endogenous change could happen, but it does not really go very far: the quasi-parameters are just placeholders for whatever indirect institutional consequences might influence the set of situations in which the institution is self-enforcing. The model itself does not provide any insight as to which parameters should be conceived as quasi-parameters *ex ante*. Quasi-parameters must be decided case by case, "based on empirical observations" (Greif & Laitin, 2004, p. 634). The introduction of quasi-parameters helps to save the idealizing assumptions of the game-theoretical approach while bringing in more flexibility for explaining particular cases of institutional change. The crucial question, however, is whether the model actually contributes to explanations of particular cases of institutional change. For example, in Greif and Laitin's (2004; Greif 2006) historical case studies, the formal models only seem to serve as non-essential parts of the explanatory narratives and they can be discarded without losing much of the explanatory insight as the real explanatory work is done by the context and historical details.

3.2. Knight: Institutions as Unintended Consequences of Conflict

Social scientific common sense suggests that power asymmetries between agents are important determinants of institutional change. While this insight often motivates empirical RCI analyses, it is not well reflected in theoretical work. As we have seen, the institutional analysis is done in an institutional vacuum without taking the extant institutions into account and assuming that the agents are homogenous. However, the influence of existing institutions on resource allocation and bargaining power is crucial for understanding why the institution has the rules it has.

In *Institutions and Social Conflict* (1992), Jack Knight presents a version of RCI that takes power asymmetries between agents as its analytical basis. While Knight does not offer new ideas about endogenous change, his approach introduces ideas that are useful for analyzing endogenous processes. He argues that understanding conflict over the expected benefits from alternative institutions provides a key to understanding institutions. His account shows how distributional consequences of institutions and conflict over institutional benefits can be integrated into an equilibrium approach to institutions.

According to Knight,

> the main goal of those who develop institutional rules is to gain strategic advantage vis-a-vis other actors, and therefore, the substantive content of those rules should generally reflect distributional concerns. (Knight 1992, p. 40).

Rather than assuming that institutions are efficient in facilitating coordination or cooperation, Knight suggests regarding them as by-products of substantive conflicts over distributional outcomes. This makes the power asymmetries between the agents analytically salient. The basic idea is that in a bargaining situation an individual who has more power (e.g., in terms of access to resources such as wealth or holding an influential institutional position) usually has an advantage over individuals who lack power because a lengthy bargaining process would be more costly and risky for the latter. Those who have resources can wait, while those who do not will feel pressure to settle the situation irrespective of the distributional consequences because they cannot afford to wait for a resolution or take the risk of failure.

In Knight's analysis, bargaining power acts as an equilibrium selection "device," selecting the equilibrium that favors the powerful. Note that the same considerations are also important for understanding institutional change: for example, if the formal institutional rules are ambiguous or in need of revision, the power asymmetries can determine the course of institutional change. In Knight's account, the preferences and resources of the powerful do not directly determine the content of the rules, but the focus on the asymmetries in power and the interests of the agents are important points of analytical focus.

Knight's approach is not formally in conflict with RE. While RE focuses on the common interests of the parties, Knight employs an analytical perspective that focuses on the heterogeneity of the agents and asymmetries of power. As Knight argues, the emphasis

> on the theoretical primacy of distribution does not deny the importance of gains from coordination or trade. The main point here is that such gains cannot serve as the basis for a social explanation; rather, these benefits are merely a by-product of the pursuit of individual gain. (Knight 1992, p. 38)

Those who have more resources would have more leverage and hence an ability to influence the distributional consequences of the resulting institution. Furthermore, as Knight recognizes that the resources available to the participants and the rules of the bargaining are products of already existing institutions, it is much easier to avoid the temptations of the state of nature theorizing.

One of the advantages of this approach is that it allows more powerful explanations in that it can provide more general theoretical explanations as well as more precise (Ylikoski & Kuorikoski 2010) explanations for particular cases. Rather than focusing on the explanation of the existence of an institution, it addresses details of the institution: why does it have the rules it has? The explanatory contrast is not the absence of an institution, but an institution with different characteristics such as rules and distributional consequences. This is an appealing feature when explaining some real-world institutions rather than wondering about the existence of institutions in general. Another advantage is the clear distinction between the sources of an institution—i.e., the struggles over how benefits are distributed—and its consequences (Farrell 2009, p. 18), which makes the approach much less prone to flirting with functionalism. Rather, it makes systematic theorizing in terms of social mechanisms more salient (Knight 1992; Hedström & Ylikoski 2010). Overall, the emphasis on the differential capacities of agents and the unintended consequences of institutions helps to connect game-theoretical theorizing with parallel research done by historical and sociological institutionalists.

Nevertheless, Knight (1992) does not provide a full toolset for analyzing endogenous change. A closer look shows that his approach makes it difficult to explain endogenous change because of the great emphasis on the endurance of institutions.[9] Moreover, Knight follows the common RCI practice of taking rule compliance for granted. As a result, he downplays the role and extent of institutional change. Nonetheless, Knight provides an important perspective change for RCI analysis of institutions and paves the way to models about endogenous change. An example of such a model is presented by Henry Farrell and Adrienne Héritier (Farrell and Héritier 2003, 2007; Héritier 2007), which we discuss next.

3.3. Farrell and Héritier

Farrell and Héritier (2003) add to Knight's approach the assumption that formal institutional rules are incomplete contracts. They reject the simplification that all institutional features are fixed once the institution is in place. Instead, they assume that the formal rules are subject to renegotiation in the course of their daily application. In particular, they assume that informal rules govern the application of the formal rules. In the context of EU institutions, they claim that Treaties established in EU Intergovernmental Conferences are incomplete contracts that leave room for *bargaining* among the main organizational actors within the EU legislative process: The European Parliament, the Council, and the Commission (Farrell & Héritier 2004). In the RCI analysis of Farrell and Héritier, these actors seek to maximize their own legislative competence by bargaining over how ambiguities in the treaty texts ought to be interpreted and applied to the legislative process. The basic idea is that bargaining over the appropriate interpretation of ambiguous formal institutional rules has distributional consequences and that informal institutions will influence this bargaining process.

A crucial element of this model is the distinction between agents who design the formal rules and other agents: those who are affected by the formal rules and those who are involved in the implementation of the formal rules. Not all agents can participate in the negotiation about the formal rules, but they may be involved in the implementation of the formal rules and influence their interpretation, and possibly, the future reformulations of the formal rules. For example, the EU member states have control of the treaty process, but the Parliament, the Council, and the Commission may take over when the treaties are implemented. This may involve the creation of informal institutions that structure actors' relations within the legislative process. These informal institutions may accommodate existing formal rules by specifying or complementing them, but they may also transform them in a way that shifts the institutional structure and its distributional consequences (Farrell & Héritier 2003, 2004, 2007; Héritier 2007).

Farrell and Héritier analyze the situation in RCI terms. The informal rules that guide the daily application of ambiguous formal rules are products of bargaining. Two main sources of bargaining power are the agent's formal institutional position (determined by extant institutional rules) and resource availability, which determine what time horizon the agent has and how sensitive it is to failure. These factors influence the ability of agents to shape the outcome of the negotiation and thus the informal rules governing the application of the formal rule. This constitutes the first phase of institutional change since the formal institutional rules might change as the informal institutions that guide their interpretation change.

Since the second phase consists of the interaction between informal and formal institutions, the informal rules *recursively* affect the next bargaining round in the revision of formal rules. The designing actors (such as EU member states) have to take into consideration the *de facto* rule change created and this will influence how formal rules are reformulated (e.g., how EU member states formulate the next intergovernmental treaty). More generally, if the designing agents find the results of the "interstitial" institutional change beneficial, they might formalize these *de facto* rules. In other situations, they might try to abolish the interstitially bargained informal rules or close the observed loopholes. However, this might not be possible when they disagree, and the results of the interstitial bargaining will remain. In any case, the *de facto* informal rules are something that designing agents have to take into account in negotiating the new formal rules. (Farrell & Héritier 2003, 2007; Héritier 2007; see also Jupille 2004 for an account of procedural politics that involves a similar idea about endogenous change.)

In the Farrell-Héritier model, institutional change is not only partly endogenous but also continuous. It is not analyzed in terms of off-and-on formal redesigns driven by independently given preferences, but a more continuous process of bargaining over informal practices that have feedback on future negotiations about the formal rules. The model is based on the idea of a feedback loop between the formal and informal rules that guide their application. Because of the heterogeneity of agents and the role of existing institutions, the institutional outcomes are under constant negotiation and never simply reflect the interests of the participants.

This ingenious model is enabled by giving up some typical RCI simplifications about institutions. First, the Farrell-Héritier model inherits all the benefits of Knight's approach. The institutions are analyzed from the beginning in terms of conflicts about distributional consequences rather than cozy coordination arrangements between equal parties. However, they go further and give up some other RCI simplifications. The second important move is to pay more attention to the differences between agents. Not only are there power differences between agents, but they also have different roles: not all agents participate in the negotiations about formal rules, but they might still influence the way they are applied. This makes formal game-theoretical modeling of the situation much harder in that we have not only the game of setting the rules, but also the game of interpreting the rules, and the interactions between the two. Furthermore, not only are there multiple interrelated games, but these games also have different players, at least in part.[10]

Third, the Farrell-Héritier model does not take rules and rule compliance for granted. The key assumption is that the agreement about formal rules does not uniquely determine how the rules are to be applied or implemented. This idea about "incomplete contracts" opens the door to a continuous process of negotiation about the application of the rules which can give rise to incremental institutional change. Although the Farrell-Héritier model operates with a crude distinction between formal and institutional rules, their model suggests that unpacking the black box of rule compliance makes it possible to open up room for new forms of institutional change. In the next section, we will open this box a little bit further to see how it affects RCI assumptions and how it may enable seeing new forms of endogenous change. To this end, we will highlight some further aspects of rule-following. This will show that paying more attention to how the institutions—and rules—work paves the way for more sophisticated accounts of institutional change (and stability).

4. TAKING RULE-FOLLOWING SERIOUSLY

Most RCI models assume homogeneous agents and focus on simple institutions, such as coordination conventions, in an institutional vacuum. Although these models are useful for certain explanatory tasks, they fall short of explaining institutional change. They also have limited use in analyzing the complex institutions that political scientists are interested in. In what follows, we will explore how RCI could be extended to be useful for explaining

Table 6.1 *RCI and its possible extensions for political science.* The table shows how RCI can be extended to be useful for understanding institutional change in political science (Extended RCI) by relaxing some of the typical assumptions in RCI.

	Typical RCI assumptions	Extended RCI
Agents	Homogenous	Heterogeneous
	No institutional/social roles	Diverse institutional/social roles
	No asymmetries in power (e.g., with respect to access to resources)	Power asymmetries, in terms of a. Resources b. Roles (rule makers vs. rule takers)
Institutional environment	No pre-existing institutions	Existing institutions and practices determine roles, power asymmetries, etc. a. Interaction between formal and informal rules/practices b. Conflict between rules
Rules	No ambiguity, no room for interpretation No bargaining over meaning Universal rule compliance	Ambiguous rules, open to interpretation Bargaining over meaning / interpretation No universal rule compliance

change in political institutions. So far, our discussion has shown that relaxing the typical RCI assumptions such as the homogeneity of agents, the absence of preexisting institutions, and unproblematic rule compliance enables a better understanding of institutional change. Following the path pioneered by Farrell and Héritier, let's discuss what taking into account power asymmetries, diverse institutional roles, rule ambiguity and rule compliance might mean for institutional theorizing (Table 6.1).

RCI models typically do not take into account the fact that the agents may have diverse institutional and social roles. The Farrell-Héritier model suggests that the differing roles of agents require more attention. Individuals may have roles as rule makers, rule enforcers, or only as rule takers (Mahoney & Thelen 2009). Some individuals might also take multiple roles. Once the importance and diversity of roles is accepted, attention to historical dynamics becomes more important because the roles of individuals, as well as the roles themselves, might change in time. Moreover, again as Farrell and Héritier suggest, because individuals in various roles might rank institutional outcomes differently it would not be possible to understand the bargaining processes that bring about institutional change if one ignores this. For example, many agents whose compliance is crucial for the institution are often "forced" into obeisance by the expectation of punishment or the current unfeasibility of more favorable institutional rules (Moe 2005). The "losers" will try to improve their situation when opportunities arise, and the "winners" will counter these moves to continue to utilize their position to their advantage (Pierson 2016). Looking at how individuals holding different positions bargain over institutional outcomes opens up the internal dynamics of the institution which are important for many kinds of endogenous change.

Second, the interaction between formal and informal rules requires more attention. Both formal and informal rules function against the background of a complex set of practices.

Focusing on the formal rules, one can easily see that the application of any formalized rule is built upon an implicit set of practices that are not part of the formalized rule itself. It should also be noted that calling these practices "informal rules" and acknowledging their importance is not sufficient to understand how they operate and interact (cf. Turner 1994). A proper analysis of how rules work *as a part of these practices* is essential for understanding institutional change because the change in these practices can change the meaning and consequences of the formal rules. Paying attention to how rules work also opens the possibility of analyzing the role of material technologies underlying institutions. This is going to be an increasingly important dimension of institutions in the future.

Third, the indeterminacy of institutional rules—the foundation for the idea of incomplete contracts in Farrell and Héritier's analysis—is another key element of institutional change. Taking this into account, however, will pose a challenge for the rational-choice design perspective. It is not realistic to assume that the agents who are setting the rules for an institution can fully anticipate all future scenarios where the rules would be put into use. There are at least two reasons for this. First, taking into account a huge number of imaginable future situations would be very costly and time-consuming. Second, there is no reason to assume that any agent can imagine all possible current and future scenarios where the rules might be put to use. Thus, even in the best circumstances, formal rules have to be considered as "incomplete contracts." There is also a strategic aspect of the ambiguity of the rules in that many formal rules are compromises that are *only possible because of the ambiguity or imprecision of the rules*. Removing ambiguity is often costly and time-consuming, and hence might not be possible or preferable. Moreover, for some agents, it could be strategically advantageous to leave the rules abstract and ambiguous as this might give them some advantage in later negotiations about their interpretation. As Thelen and Conran put it: "institution building is almost always a matter of political compromise. Institutions and rules are often left deeply ambiguous by the coalitions of (often conflicting) interests that preside over their founding" (2016, p. 57).

However, the indeterminacy and ambiguity of rules do not imply that we should set aside the basic insights of RCI. As Thelen and Conran observe: "institutions instantiate power, they are contested. Losers in one round do not necessarily disappear but rather survive and find ways not just to circumvent and subvert rules, but to occupy and redeploy institutions not of their own making" (2016, p. 57). The rational-choice perspective is useful in understanding this process, but only if the existence of an institution is regarded as a continuous process that involves ambiguities and negotiations between heterogeneous agents with diverse roles and interests. This implies that change and stability are two sides of the same coin, rather than things that require completely different explanations. The life of institutions does not consist of serene equilibriums that are sometimes disrupted by external shocks, but of an ongoing struggle with coalitional dynamics that are vulnerable to smaller and larger shifts.[11]

Fourth, the conflicts between rules of different institutions as well as rule conflicts within institutions can be important sources of institutional change. Rules may overlap and conflict with each other. As such conflict requires a resolution, some of these rules either need to be changed or given a new interpretation, at least with respect to their domain of application. Either way, these conflicts can be important sources of institutional change. The conflicts between institutions are especially interesting because they might expand the set of agents that have a stake in the institution and resources to influence it. This could also mean a change in the definition of the "social problem" that the institution addresses. This point about ambiguity and possible overlap of institutional boundaries is general since the institutional rules of any given society cannot be conceived as a coherent and fixed bundle of rules as envisioned by many RCI accounts. The real-world societies live with a hodgepodge of complex rules and institutions of various origins and purposes.[12] The conflicts between their rules are an important source of institutional change. However, the typical methodological practice of analyzing institutions in isolation—or even in a vacuum—makes it hard for RCI to recognize this source of endogenous change.

Finally, rule cognition—the way in which people learn and apply the rules—demands more attention. This is most clearly seen in the case of informal rules. As the agents learn the rules from a limited set of observed examples and even more limited cases of positive and negative feedback (sanctions), there is no guarantee that they will learn exactly the same rules and that they will interpret these rules in exactly the same way. While there might be a broad agreement about typical applications of a rule, agents' interpretations of the rule might diverge with respect to peripheral cases and novel situations. That is, diverse interpretations of a rule can co-exist. This variance in learned rules can be a source of future incremental changes in meaning, and hence a source of institutional change. This diversity might only become apparent with interpretative conflict among individuals or organizations. Biological speciation and the origins of languages and dialects are good models for thinking about change like this because small populations, local interactions, and variation-creating learning mechanisms can give rise to significant long-term change both within and between populations.[13] Change could in fact be a random-walk process that does not have uniform direction or generic explanation, but this does not imply that it cannot be explained. While highly abstract RE models cannot capture *institutional drift* like this, it is clear that these endogenous processes can still be analyzed in terms of causal mechanisms that incorporate some elements of RCI.[14]

Taken together, these observations point to a rich set of conceptual resources for analyzing endogenous change, and institutional change more generally. Although our discussion has been brief, we hope that it shows that one does not have to give up RCI completely to accommodate these sources of institutional change.

5. CONCLUSION

The starting point of this chapter was that any acceptable theory of institutions should be able to handle institutional change. We argued that RCI, particularly RE, suffers from *endogeneity blindness*, which is caused by the excessively abstract *explananda* and simplifying assumptions that accompany it. These assumptions lead to missed explanatory opportunities as they push endogenous change out of the reach of the theory. We have seen that RCI typically aims to provide generic explanations of the existence or persistence of an institution, rather than its attributes. It addresses highly stylized descriptions of types of institutions, rather than the historically variable attributes of particular institutions. The underlying belief is that addressing highly abstract *explananda* gives the theory generality, and thus explanatory power. However, the generality of this approach does not necessarily imply general explanatory power as there are very few real-world cases where the theory would apply directly, and it has given up the most important heuristic ideas that would help it adapt to concrete historical institutions. What in fact happens is that rational-choice theorists end up pursuing functionalist explanations that can *only* address the persistence or raison d'être of institutions. Highly limited *explananda* and incongruence with the causal mechanisms pursued by other social scientists limit the explanatory value of most RCI models.

Although it is customary in RCI to distinguish between explanations of the origins and stability of institutions (e.g., Greif 2006; Guala 2016), there is a sense in which this distinction is misleading. While the emergence of new institutions is quite rare, the change is a constant feature of most institutions. Hence, it needs to be understood. Furthermore, these three *explananda* (i.e., origin, stability, and change) are not completely independent. For example, the configuration of causes that gave rise to an institution need not be the same as one that sustains it, or drives its change, but the two processes might still have interesting common elements. Of course, while theories and models that address only a subset of institutional *explananda* are not useless, this should not prevent us from acknowledging their limitations. In our case, it must be acknowledged that systematically ignoring change-related explananda creates such limitations for a theory of institutions. It is a serious hindrance for a theoretical approach to rule endogenous change out on purely conceptual grounds or otherwise to make it invisible. Moreover, it is possible that the perceived stability of institutions in RCI is an optical illusion created by too abstract a perspective. If this is the case, RE would be even further from capturing how institutions really work.

Our discussion has focused mainly on endogenous change, but our main points apply more generally. Endogenous change is theoretically intriguing, but all institutional change demands attention. We do not claim that endogenous processes are the most important cause of institutional change. This is clearly an empirical question, and most interesting cases of change are probably combinations of both endogenous and exogenous processes (Koning 2016). The point is that it is difficult to justify the explanatory handicaps of a theory that rules out some possible forms of institutional change—especially on non-empirical grounds. Because understanding change is a key element of understanding how institutions stay in existence (or vanish), a general theory of institutions that ignores change is not credible.

Acknowledging the limitations of typical RCI models is also helpful in seeing how to move forward in analyzing the more complex institutions that interest political scientists. One of our main claims is that giving up some typical RCI methodological simplifications makes explanatory progress—understood as an ability to explain how real social institutions work—possible. These simplifications are mostly justified by abstract *explananda*. If they are replaced by more concrete *explananda* that political scientists and other social scientists address, the pathway we have sketched is fully open. RCI can still generate important insights about social institutions. Although RCI—no matter how it is interpreted—is never going to be sufficient for a comprehensive understanding of the workings of institutions, it can be a powerful part of the toolbox, as recent debates show (Mahoney & Thelen 2009; Hall 2009).[15]

It must be realized, however, that giving up the simplifications of RCI to gain an explanatory advantage in explaining institutional change has consequences for the style of theorizing. First, to explain change, institutions must be considered as historical individuals, rather than tokens of some abstract types. Institutions are not natural kinds (pace Guala

2016). There is general knowledge to be had about institutions, but it does not arise from starting with highly abstract *explananda*. General knowledge will not be about functionally defined institution types, but about social mechanisms that are parts of institutions (Aydinonat & Ylikoski 2018). This understanding is often the result of painstaking analysis of particular institutions. Thus, "history matters" (North 1990, p. vii). And history here means more than just initial conditions for a general model. An institution is a historically changing entity and we have to understand the dynamics of this change. When institutions are conceived this way, there is no reason to assume that explaining their stability or persistence has any explanatory priority. Explaining persistence is important, but so is accounting for the changes and origin.

Second, the historical nature of the study of institutions has consequences for the role of elaborate formal models. While they will remain useful for more limited purposes, their role is now less central. They are tools for understanding the "logics of situation" the agents encounter, not direct explanatory representations. This is not a completely new idea. For example, when Thomas Schelling was arguing that the highly idealized game-theoretical models that are typical in RCI should not be considered as "instant theory" that could be directly applied to real-world cases, but as a framework for analysis (Schelling 1984, p. 241),[16] he was making a similar point. What is needed is the development of ways to combine historically sensitive analysis of institutions with insights provided by the formal models. As we hope to have shown in this Chapter, it matters what you model: to fully understand how institutions work, we have to address their historical nature—how they originate, how they change, and how they end—not just some theoretically salient aspect of them.

Notes

1. What counts as institutional change is ambiguous. While it could mean a change in the rules (or other elements) of the institution, it could also mean changes in the consequences/functions of the institution. These two do not always match. Furthermore, even small changes in the institution could have dramatic long-term consequences, while sometimes large changes in the institution do not make much difference to the consequences of interest. Here, as elsewhere in the social sciences, the principle that the "size" of the causes and effects do not have to match applies. In any case, in this chapter, we will have to rely on an intuitive idea of institutional change.
2. RCI frequently distinguishes between organizations and institutions (e.g., North 1990; Khalil 1995). For example, North (1990) distinguishes between the players of the game (organizations) and rules of the game (institutions). Others in RCI consider organizations as institutional elements, rather than as institutions: "An institution is a system of rules, beliefs, norms, and organizations that together generate a regularity of (social) behavior" (Greif 2006, p. 30). Nevertheless, this distinction does not deny the institutionality of organizations; rather, it serves to direct the analytical focus on the rules that agents (including organizations) follow or on equilibria that represent alternative institutions.
3. On economics of conventions see Sugden (1986, Chp. 3) and Young (1996).
4. We are simplifying here. Guala employs the solution concept of correlated equilibria, which presumes the existence of a correlation device that facilitates coordination, and institutional rules take the form of conditional rules.

5. One could object to this claim by saying that evolutionary models such as Young's (1998) provide an account of the stability of institutions, but such models account for the stability of institutions at a very general level and are not helpful in explaining the temporal stability of particular institutions.

6. For a discussion of Guala's ideas about institution types and tokens, see Aydinonat & Ylikoski (2018).

7. See Field (1979, 1981) for a critique of rational choice models of institutions from this point of view.

8. Here, we are focusing on a few selected approaches that employ the rational choice framework. For a comparative review of theories of institutional change, see Kingston & Caballero (2009). For other overviews, see Aoki (2008) and Brousseau et al. (2011).

9. Knight is aware of the difficulty of explaining endogenous change, especially in the case of spontaneous change: "institutional change is not easily accomplished" (p. 145), "requires repeating the emergence process" and is "made even more difficult by the fact that unlike the case of initial emergence when expectations are not fixed on a particular rule, change requires persuading social actors to alter an expectation that is now fixed" (p. 147).

10. See Ross (2008) on how the "game determination" problem relates to the game theoretical accounts of conventions and convention formation.

11. There is a further dimension of rule-following that we will not discuss in detail in this chapter. A typical RE discussion only sees two possibilities: following the rule or not following it. In real social life, the agents usually have more options. Not following the rule can have multiple meanings: it might mean breaking the rule in a specific situation (while generally following the rule), or it might mean rejection, that is, rejecting its legitimacy as a policy. Sometimes there is also the third option of avoiding the rule. Finally, and most importantly, even following the rule might be guided by strategic employment of its ambiguity in a manner that an outsider might call biased.

12. There is surprisingly little discussion about the demarcation between individual institutions in the literature. It is easy to agree with North's (1990, p. 3) definition: "Institutions are the rules of the game in a society or, more formally, are the humanly devised constraints that shape human interaction," but this definition talks about a complete set of institutions rather than an individual institution. Philosophical debates in social ontology suffer from the same problem. From the ontological perspective, this issue might seem secondary, but it is a real issue when one is attempting to explain real world institutions.

13. These points have been taken seriously by credible cultural evolution theories (e.g., Boyd & Richerson 2005).

14. Acemoglu and Robinson have something similar in mind when they write: "In the same way that the genes of two isolated populations of organisms will drift apart slowly because of random mutations in the so-called process of evolutionary or genetic drift, two otherwise similar societies will also drift apart institutionally—albeit, again, slowly. Conflict over income and power, and indirectly over institutions, is a constant in all societies. This conflict often has a contingent outcome, even if the playing field over which it transpires is not level. The outcome of this conflict leads to institutional drift. But this is not necessarily a cumulative process" (2012, p. 431).

15. See Ylikoski and Aydinonat (2014) for our account of the epistemic import of highly idealized models. See Aydinonat (2008) for a discussion of the value and limits of highly idealized game-theoretical models of institutions.

16. See Aydinonat (2008, Ch. 8) for a more extensive discussion of these issues.

REFERENCES

Acemoglu, D. & J. Robinson (2012). Why Nations Fail: The origins of power, prosperity and poverty. London: Profile Books.

Aoki, M. (2001). *Toward a Comparative Institutional Analysis* (Vol. 1). Cambridge, MA: MIT Press.

Aoki, M. (2007). Endogenizing institutions and institutional changes. *Journal of Institutional Economics*, 3(1), 1. https://doi.org/10.1017/S1744137406000531.

Aoki, M. (2008). Analysing Institutional Change: Integrating Endogenous and Exogenous Views. In J. Kornai, L. Mátyás, & G. Roland (Eds.), Institutional Change and Economic Behaviour (pp. 113–133). London: Palgrave Macmillan UK. http://doi.org/10.1057/9780230583429_6.

Aumann, R. J. (1974). Subjectivity and correlation in randomized strategies. *Journal of Mathematical Economics*, 1(1), 67–96. https://doi.org/10.1016/0304-4068(74)90037-8.

Aydinonat, N. E. (2008). *The Invisible Hand in Economics: How Economists Explain Unintended Social Consequences*. London: Routledge.

Aydinonat, N. E., & Ylikoski, P. (2018). Three Conceptions of a Theory of Institutions. *Philosophy of the Social Sciences*, 48(6), 550–568. https://doi.org/10.1177/0048393118798619.

Boyd, R., & Richerson, P. (2005). *The Origin and Evolution of Cultures*. Oxford: Oxford University Press.

Brousseau, E., Garrouste, P., & Raynaud, E. (2011). Institutional changes: Alternative theories and consequences for institutional design. *Journal of Economic Behavior & Organization*, 79(1–2), 3–19. https://doi.org/10.1016/j.jebo.2011.01.024.

Calvert, R. R. (1995). Rational actors, equilibrium and social institutions. In J. Knight & I. Sened (Eds.), *Explaining Social Institutions* (pp. 57–94). Ann Arbor, MI: University of Michigan Press.

Farrell, H. (2009). *The Political Economy of Trust*. Cambridge: Cambridge University Press.

Farrell, H., & Héritier, A. (2003). Formal and informal institutions under codecision: Continuous constitution-building in Europe. *Governance*, 16(4), 577–600. https://doi.org/10.1111/1468-0491.00229.

Farrell, H., & Héritier, A. (2004). Interorganizational negotiation and intraorganizational power in shared decision making: Early agreements under codecision and their impact on the European Parliament and Council. *Comparative Political Studies*, 37(10), 1184–1212. https://doi.org/10.1177/0010414004269833.

Farrell, H., & Héritier, A. (2007). Codecision and institutional change. *West European Politics*, 30(2), 285–300. https://doi.org/10.1080/01402380701239723.

Field, A. J. (1979). On the explanation of rules using rational choice models. *Journal of Economic Issues*, 13(1), 49–72. https://doi.org/10.1080/00213624.1979.11503610.

Field, A. J. (1981). The problem with neoclassical institutional economics: A critique with special reference to the North/Thomas model of pre-1500 Europe. *Explorations in Economic History*, 18(2), 174–198. https://doi.org/10.1016/0014-4983(81)90025-5.

Gintis, Herbert. (2009). *The Bounds of Reason: Game Theory and the Unification of the Behavioral Sciences*. Princeton: Princeton University Press.

Greif, A. (2006). *Institutions and the Path to the Modern Economy: Lessons from Medieval Trade*. Cambridge: Cambridge University Press.

Greif, A., & Laitin, D. D. (2004). A theory of endogenous institutional change. *American Political Science Review*, 98(4), 633–652. https://doi.org/10.1017/S0003055404041395.

Greif, A., & Kingston, C. (2011). Institutions: Rules or equilibria? In A. Greif & C. Kingston (Eds.), *Political Economy of Institutions, Democracy and Voting* (pp. 13–43). Dordrecht: Springer. https://doi.org/10.1007/978-3-642-19519-8_2.

Guala, F. (2016). *Understanding Institutions: The Science and Philosophy of Living Together*. Princeton, NJ: Princeton University Press.

Hall, P. A. (2009). Historical Institutionalism in Rationalist and Sociological Perspective In J. Mahoney & K. Thelen (Eds.), Explaining Institutional Change (pp. 204–223). Cambridge: Cambridge University Press.

Hedström, P., & Ylikoski, P. (2010). Causal Mechanisms in the Social Sciences. *Annual Review of Sociology*, 36(1), 49–67. https://doi.org/10.1146/annurev.soc.012809.102632.

Héritier, A. (2007). *Explaining Institutional Change in Europe*. Oxford: Oxford University Press.

Jupille, J. (2004). *Procedural Politics*. Cambridge: Cambridge University Press.

Khalil, E. L. (1995). Organizations versus institutions. *Journal of Institutional and Theoretical Economics (JITE) / Zeitschrift für die gesamte Staatswissenschaft*, 151(3), 445–466.

Kingston, C., & Caballero, G. (2009). Comparing theories of institutional change. *Journal of Institutional Economics*, 5(2), 151–180. https://doi.org/10.1017/S1744137409001283.

Knight, J. (1992). Institutions and Social Conflict. Institutions and Social Conflict. Cambridge: Cambridge University Press. https://doi.org/10.1017/CBO9780511528170.

Koning, E. A. (2016). The three institutionalisms and institutional dynamics: Understanding endogenous and exogenous change. *Journal of Public Policy*, 36(4), 639–664. https://doi.org/10.1017/S0143814X15000240.

Krasner, S. D. (1984). Approaches to the state: Alternative conceptions and historical dynamics. *Comparative Politics* 16(2), 223–246. https://doi.org/10.2307/421608.

Lewis, D. (1969). *Convention*. Cambridge, MA: Harvard University Press.

Mahoney, J., & Thelen, K. (2009). A theory of gradual institutional change. In J. Mahoney & K. Thelen (Eds.), *Explaining Institutional Change* (pp. 1–37). Cambridge: Cambridge University Press. https://doi.org/10.1017/CBO9780511806414.003.

Moe, T. M. (2005). Power and Political Institutions. *Perspectives on Politics*, 3(2), 215–233.

North, D. C. (1990). *Institutions, Institutional Change and Economic Performance*. Cambridge: Cambridge University Press.

Ostrom, E. (2005). *Understanding Institutional Diversity*. Princeton, NJ: Princeton University Press.

Pierson, P. (2016). Power in Historical Institutionalism. In O. Fioretos, T. G. Falleti, & A. Sheingate (Eds.), *The Oxford Handbook of Historical Institutionalism* (pp. 124–141). Oxford: Oxford University Press. https://doi.org/10.1093/oxfordhb/9780199662814.013.7.

Ross, Don. (2008). Classical game theory, socialization and the rationalization of conventions. *Topoi*, 27(1–2), 57–72. http://doi.org/10.1007/s11245-008-9028-1.

Schelling, T. C. (1984). *Choice and Consequence*. Cambridge, MA: Harvard University Press.

Schotter, A. (1981). *The Economic Theory of Social Institutions*. Cambridge: Cambridge University Press.

Streeck, W., & Thelen, K. (2005). Introduction: Institutional Change in Advanced Political Economies. In W. Streeck & K. Thelen (Eds.), *Beyond Continuity: Institutional Change in Advanced Political Economies* (pp. 1–39). Oxford: Oxford University Press.

Sugden, R. (1986). *The economics of rights, co-operation and welfare*. Oxford: Basil Blackwell.

Turner, S. P. (1994). *The Social Theory of Practices*. Cambridge: Polity Press.

Weingast, B. R. (1996). Political Institutions: Rational Choice Perspectives. In R. E. Goodin & H.-D. Klingemann (Eds.), *A New Handbook of Political Science* (pp. 167–190). Oxford: Oxford University Press.

Weingast, B. R. (2002). Rational-Choice Institutionalism. In I. Katznelson & H. V. Milner (Eds.), *Political Science: The State of the Discipline* (pp. 660–692). New York: W.W. Norton & Company.

Ylikoski, P., & Aydinonat, N. E. (2014). Understanding with theoretical models. *Journal of Economic Methodology*, 21(1), 19–36. https://doi.org/10.1080/1350178X.2014.886470.

Ylikoski, P., & Kuorikoski, J. (2010). Dissecting explanatory power. *Philosophical Studies*, 148(2), 201–219. https://doi.org/10.1007/s11098-008-9324-z.

Young, H. P. (1996) Economics of convention. *Journal of Economic Perspectives*, 10(2): 105–122.

Young, H. P. (1998). *Individual Strategy and Social Structure: An Evolutionary Theory of Institutions*. Princeton, NJ: Princeton University Press.

CHAPTER 7

······

PUBLIC CHOICE VERSUS SOCIAL CHOICE AS THEORIES OF COLLECTIVE ACTION

······

JESÚS ZAMORA-BONILLA

1. INTRODUCTION

······

POLITICS is the art of collective decision-making in the presence of conflicting points of view. As such, politics exists as long, and as soon, as there is anything that requires a collective decision and such that some members of the collective would prefer different decisions about. In that sense, politics is surely much older than humans; for example, the "dance" of bees as a procedure to select a place where the hive will collect nectar can be seen as a "political process," even more a case of "deliberation" than one of "voting." If politics is usually seen as something essentially related to power (a notion perhaps not too relevant in the context of bee dancing), it is because political power is most often one fundamental mechanism in the determination of collective decisions. Of course, if we understand "political power" as just the capacity to make that the collective decision tends to favor the interests of some specific agent or group of agents, then it is trivial that politics has to do with power; but I prefer to understand power as a mere political instrument among others, rather than as something that belongs into the definition of politics. The "essence" of politics, what makes of something "political," consists hence in the fact that some decisions are necessarily collective, and that there is a conflict about what the decision should be. One ("authoritarian") traditional line of thought in the history of political philosophy is that this conflict can only be rationally resolved by means of the group (or "the collective") being organized in such a way that one single person is in power, as the chief, monarch, pharaoh, dictator, abbot, captain, or householder. The danger that this individual acts only in search of his own benefit instead of the "collective good" has prompted an alternative ("democratic") tradition that looks for mechanisms that favor the participation of a larger group of people in the political decision-making process. However, the problem of combining conflicting points of views into a single collective decision does not reduce to the choice between authoritarianism and democracy: even in the case of strongly authoritarian regimes, there are many cases in which conflicting interests have to be integrated or counterbalanced, even if they are not the "general" interests, but only the concerns of specific powerful groups or individuals. As a matter of fact, systematic logical reflection on "voting procedures," which is the topic of this chapter, started historically more as a set of remarks about the selection of leaders between a very small élite (e.g., the election of the pope by the cardinals, or that of the German emperor by the prince-electors), than as a meditation about the democratic assemblage of the "general will."

Conflict and collectiveness are, hence, the essential elements of politics. The former can simply be represented by the fact that different individuals (or just different, not necessarily individual, members of the group) have different *preferences* over the question the collective decision will be about. Collectiveness consists in the fact that the group has to take one decision, *the same one for all the members*, and cannot solve the conflict by just "letting each member act as he or she pleases" (well, in some cases this can be one collective decision among others: the collective decision of *not* deciding onto something in a collective way). In this sense, the existence of problems that have to be collectively solved is equivalent to the existence of what economists call "public goods," and hence it is interesting to start our discussion by briefly summarizing this central notion.

2. The Problem of Collective Goods

In economics, something is called a *public good* if it has the two following properties (see, e.g., Stiglitz 2000):

Nonexcludability: Once the good or service is provided, it is impossible to preclude anyone from benefiting from its provision, independently on whether she has paid for it or not (it is not necessarily "impossible" in the physical sense, but merely in the sense that the costs of excluding someone from the good are prohibitive).

Nonrivalry: Once the good or service is provided, the fact that one more person benefits from it does not diminish the wellbeing that is obtained by others.

Notice that being a public good is not, in economic theory, a *normative* property, in the sense that the theory does not assert, for example, that these goods "should" be publicly provided instead of left to the private market. What the theory provides is just a *description* of the factual properties of some goods, features that usually explain why, *as a matter of fact*, it is difficult, or even impossible, for those goods to be offered and bought through a private market, at least in quantities that the individuals interacting in that market would find satisfactory. In general, the most important feature that makes of something a public good is what economists call *joint consumption* (or, not meaning exactly the same, "joint offer"): the good is necessarily *one and the same* for everyone, in the strong sense that it is not only that you and I consume *equal* goods, but that there is *only one "unity"* of the good, and everyone consumes exactly that "unity." Sometimes this property is also referred to as *nondivisibility*. For example, all ships are guided by the same lighthouse while they are in the same area, all people in a country are protected by the same army and the same courts, all citizens are subject to the same law, etc. Law, in particular, is perhaps the prototypical example of a public good, and the object of the most important collective decisions at the state level.

The "economic" problem with nonprivate, nondivisible, or "collective" goods is, of course, that, contrarily to the case of private goods, the actual determination of their supply, demand or use cannot be left to the atomic decision of each individual consumer or firm, but has to be *collectively decided* in some way or another (even if the "way" consists in letting one dictator decide for all). Under what law is a community governed, for example, cannot be independently decided by each citizen, for that would be exactly the contrary of what it means *to be a law*. In order to decide which law to approve, where to place a lighthouse, or whether to declare the war, it is necessary that different individuals, with different opinions about those questions, organize in some way in order to reach a *unique* decision. There have been several approaches in the social sciences, and in economics in particular, trying to understand how this collective decisions are reached, or how they could be made in the "best" way. Here, I will concentrate on the two most important economic theoretic paradigms about collective choice, known, respectively, as *social choice theory* (SCT) and *public choice theory* (PCT), but other schools exist as well: for example, collective action theory, cooperative game theory, mechanism-design theory, or Elinor Ostrom's common goods theory.

One fascinating fact about this diversity of approaches, particularly if one is interested in the relationship between epistemic and ideological views within the social sciences, is that besides their often very different methodological and formal features of each one of these theories, they have tended to be pursued by scholars with characteristically different political leanings, and applied to specific economic, social or political problems deemed more important depending on those ideological affiliations. In this sense, we might say that SCT tends to be more "left-wing" and PCT more "right-wing," the former more concerned about problems of "social justice," and the latter more preoccupied by questions like government malfeasance or the inefficiency of public policies. Collective action theory, of which the pioneer was Mancur Olson (1965), has been more usually applied to problems like how to avoid free-riding in groups of interests, social movements or labor unions, rather than to "parliaments" or "governments" (which are the paradigmatic subjects of both SCT and PCT). Still "closer to the ground" institutions have usually been the object of Elinor Ostrom's studies (see Ostrom 1990), whereas mechanism-design and cooperative game theory have been typically applied to the engineering of sophisticated contracts and auctions in market-like contexts (see Hurwicz and Reiter 2007). As I have said, this chapter will concentrate on social choice and public choice theories, which are the most widely applied approaches, within political science, among the formal paradigms that have been developed in order to deal with the problem of collective decision-making. Both schools, however, share what we might call their prehistory, which would correspond to the slow and more or less casual development of the theoretical reflection about the most typical act of political decision: voting.

3. VOTING THEORY: A SHORT HISTORY

That collective decisions made through voting may lead to some weird consequences is something probably well known since the first time one tribe started to use some kind of voting in order to reach an agreement. We don't have many deep reflections on the topic from the otherwise prolific Greek philosophers of the Classical Age, though surely they encountered many cases in which voting procedures could be somehow improved: it seems that they tended to consider that the problems with voting were more an effect of the poor rationality of individual voters (as when the Athenian great jury condemned Socrates to death by more votes than had been cast to declare him guilty of impiety), than of the voting system itself. Some passing remarks about the possibility of manipulating the result of voting by modifying the number or the order in which the proposals are voted were made by the roman writer Pliny the Younger, but apparently with no hindsight about the possibility of experimenting with different voting rules. It was the process for the election of a new Pope in the Catholic Church what provided the opportunity for a deeper reflection on voting procedures, more than a millennium after Pliny: until the twelfth century, the fiction was kept that those elections, as well as the canons from the councils, were always approved by unanimity or near unanimity (acclamation or *compromissum*), but in 1179 Alexander III introduced the rule of two-thirds, a kind of qualified majority, surely backed by a thoughtful discussion among the nascent representatives of Scholastic philosophy, of which, unfortunately, no records exist.

It was the Spanish intellectual Ramon Llull (latinized as Raymundus Lullius), described by Martin Gardner as "one of the most inspired madmen who ever lived," who gained the honor of being the first author who elaborated something like a theoretical discussion about voting rules, in several texts from the end of the thirteenth century, including his Catalan book *Blanquerna*, the first novel written in a modern European language. In particular, Llull proposed a system in which there was a vote amongst each possible pair of candidates (if candidates are also electors, the two members of each pair are not allowed to vote), and the candidate winning most pairwise single contests is then elected (this is, of course, a procedure analogous to the traditional "league" tournaments in many sports). The candidate that would be elected under such a voting procedure will later became known as a "Condorcet winner." More than one century later, the churchman, philosopher and mathematician Nicholas Cusanus proposed a method equivalent to what will become known as "Borda count": each elector orders all the n candidates according to his or her preferences (these procedures were intended to be applied to the election of abbots and abbesses by the monks or nuns of the monastery), and numbers them from n to 1; the winner is the candidate that gets more points when these numbers are summed up.

After this brief flash of relatively primitive reflection on voting, nothing of interest was produced within the next three centuries, until a group of *philosophes*, very probably without any knowledge of those forerunners, started to study the topic in the eve of the democratic revolutions of the Enlightenment. The most important figures were the already mentioned Jean-Charles de Borda and the Marquis of Condorcet. It was Condorcet who, reflecting on the method of voting proposed by Borda, discover what became known as the "*Condorcet paradox*": the fact that pairwise comparisons among candidates can lead to cycles (candidate A beating candidate B, B beating C, and C beating A). This may happen not only with the Borda count, but with most other procedures, and entails that *collective preferences may not be transitive*, at least if derived from individual preferences by means of voting. Another severe problem soon discovered in these voting rules is that they might be subject to *manipulation*, not by the people with power to decide who are electors and candidates, but by the electors themselves, in the sense that there may be cases in which a voter has a higher chance of reaching a better result by voting in contradiction with his or her real preferences: for example, in a Lullian-Condorcet contest between candidates A and B, one elector may vote for B even if preferring A, if that makes C (the elector's favorite candidate) more likely the final winner; or, in a Cusan-Borda election, one voter may rank his second best candidate in the last position, if that makes the victory of his favorite candidate more probable. It was again a Spaniard mathematician, José Isidoro Morales, who discovered this fact, to which Borda replied that his method was only attempted for "honest electors."

Unfortunately, the Borda-Condorcet-Morales debate was mostly forgotten for almost another century, and some of their ideas had to be independently rediscovered in the 1870s by the mathematician Charles Dodgson (better known by his pseudonym Lewis Carroll), who also worked on proportional representation. Another Victorian Englishman (but based in Australia) who worked on electoral rules, this time with knowledge of the Enlightened precursors, was Edward Nanson. But, again, neither of their contributions had any repercussion on the political or theoretical development of electoral rules in their time, in spite of being an epoch of growing introduction of more or less democratic systems in many Western countries; to use the words of the author whose historical survey is my guide on this topic: "the record shows that these electoral systems were mostly adopted by politicians who perceived partisan advantages in them, and not because of any mathematical arguments."[1]

Non-transitivity and manipulability are two members of the triad of "classical paradoxes" that may affect voting rules. This triad was completed by the American mathematician Edward Huntington in a paper of 1938, where he showed that procedures like the Borda count violate what he called the *"principle of relevance"*: introducing a new alternative or candidate which is not the favorite one of any elector may affect the choice of the winner. This is, of course, the principle that soon was to be baptized as "independence from irrelevant alternatives." Just a few years after Huntington's discovery, our two big schools, social choice theory and public choice theory, emerged as full blown theoretical approaches to attack the problems of electoral systems.

4. SOCIAL CHOICE

The transformation of a bundle of more or less deep insights on a few voting procedures into something like a general logico-mathematical theory about the aggregation of individual preferences into a collective choice was the work of a single man, Kenneth Arrow, in his 1951 book *Social choice and individual values* (based on his PhD dissertation, that had been defended that same year). Arrow's idea was to consider the relation between individual and collective preferences as a general mathematical function, a concept for which he employed the term *social welfare function* (SWF) that had been introduced and developed in the preceding years by the economists Abram Bergson and Paul Samuelson. There is a fundamental difference between the Bergson-Samuelson notion and Arrow's: whereas for the former the SWF is a *numerical* utility function, that takes as its domain the set of numerical utility functions of each individual member of the relevant group, Arrow's idea was to define the social welfare function just on the basis of the individual *comparative* (or "qualitative") preferences, i.e., the *ranking* of alternatives as they are ordered by each individual, without assuming that some numerical values could represent the relative "intensity" of those preferences, and the same for the collective preferences. In a nutshell, an Arrovian "collective choice" is just a mathematical function that says which ordering of alternatives is collectively preferred given the orderings made by the individual members of the group. The term "choice" is justified because the top alternative in the ordering would be the collectively preferred one, if available, but, if it is not, then the ordering could be used to define, between each pair of available options, which one would be selected by the group. This limitation to purely qualitative or comparative preferences entails significant formal limitations, but is a reasonable answer to the problem of the "incomparability of individual preferences" that had plagued in the previous decades the discussions of the idea of a quantitative SWF. Another terminology that became popular in the next years, and perhaps a more intuitive one, was that of an *aggregation of preferences*.

Arrow proceeded then to reflect on the desirable properties a social welfare function should have. First of all, both the individual and the collective preferences must be *real* orderings, i.e., they should not lead to cycles, but obey the rule of transitivity (if A is preferred to B, and B to C, C must *not* be preferred to A). Next, the following is a small list of some other reasonable properties, either because of formal, or of ethical reasons:

(1) *Unrestricted domain*: the function should be defined for all possible sets of individual preferences (i.e., the group should not order the members to change their values just because they are incompatible with the way it aggregates them).

(2) *Nondictatorship*: the SWF should not identify a priori one member of the group in order to mimic his or her preference (this is compatible with the fact that *in some cases*, i.e., a posteriori, the preferences of the group coincide with those of one of his members).

(3) *Pareto efficiency*, or *unanimity*: if all individuals prefer A to B, the SWF should rank A over B.

(4) *Independence of irrelevant alternatives*, i.e., the Huntington's principle we have seen above: formally, the collective choice between options A and B should only depend on the individual preferences between A and B, not of the preferences over another alternative like C. This condition, which is perhaps less intuitive than the others, is justified because, if it is not fulfilled, then the person with the power to set the agenda could determine the collective choice between A and B just by adding or deleting an "irrelevant" option like C.

And then came the disturbing result with the power of a strict mathematical demonstration:

Arrow's impossibility theorem: there is no SWF simultaneously satisfying properties 1 to 4.

This theorem made it clear that the "problems" that other authors had identified in the voting rules previously mentioned are not faults of those particular procedures, but a general "defect" of all possible ways of aggregating individual preferences. Actually, Arrow's theorem was only the first one in a list of similarly negative results, of which I will mention three of the most important ones:[2]

Sen's paradox: there is no SWF that satisfies the Pareto principle (property 3) and "minimal liberalism" principle (i.e., the condition that, for each member of the group, there are at least two options A and B, such that, if the member prefers A, then the group also "prefers" A, or, in other words, the group "respects" the individual choice). This result was also known as "the impossibility of a Paretian liberal."

Gibbard-Satterthwaite theorem: there is no SWF that is non-dictatorial (property 2), allows the choice between more than two options, and is not strategically manipulable (i.e., some member of the group might modify the collective choice in his favor by misrepresenting his own preferences).

The discursive dilemma: this is a theorem that refers not to the aggregation of "preferences," but about the aggregation of "judgments," i.e., individual opinions about whether some propositions are true or false; contrarily to the case of a SWF, where the options over which the preferences are defined are different and incompatible "states of the world," a judgment aggregation function (JAF) is defined over sets of *sentences*, between which there can exist other logical connections besides logical incompatibility (i.e., some propositions may be con- sistent with others, or even logically entail others); the discursive dilemma or "doctrinal par- adox" asserts that *there is no JAF* that satisfies the following properties: *universal domain* (applicable to all possible sets of individual self-consistent judgments), *anonymity* (the out- come should not depend on which particular individuals believe what), *systematicity* (if the logical relations between a given set of propositions are the same ones than those between another set of sentences, and the individuals have analogous beliefs about the propositions in both sets, then the JAF must deliver analogous collective judgments) and *collective self- consistency* (i.e., the collective judgments must be internally coherent).

It would not be fair, however, to understand SCT as merely "the science of the *impossi- bility* of (rational) social choice," for these certainly negative results have served as a strong incentive to find out specific conditions under which some more "reasonable" collective outcomes can emerge, both in the logical and the ethical senses of "reasonable." We can remember that the title of Amartya Sen's 1998 Nobel Prize conference (Sen 1999) was "The possibility of social choice," where he argued in favor of both exploring more realistic procedural systems of collective choice, even combining the formal and the empirical re- search on their properties and distributional consequences, and studying SWF's capable of containing more information about the welfare of the different individuals, in line, for example, with John Harsanyi new utilitarianism. In particular, SCT has been extremely productive in discussing and elaborating sophisticated and applicable criteria of economic fairness (e.g., Fleurbaey and Maniquet 2011).

5. PUBLIC CHOICE

Social choice theory has kept since its Arrovian origins a strong tendency toward *axiomatic* analysis and *normative* concerns ("what aggregation or distribution procedures can guar- antee certain ethical properties like equality, rights, justice, etc.?"). In parallel, and since around the same time, a very different school started also to work on voting and other political processes, but with a more resolute view on the *positive* question of how political matters will go under certain procedures, and hence, more easily applicable to study the working of *real* political institutions. These people developed what was described as "an ec- onomic theory of politics": a set of mathematical *models* that studied the behavior of both the electors and the elected in a similar way as how microeconomics studies the behavior of consumer and firms in the market, i.e., under the assumption that they are agents that try to maximize a given utility function under economic and institutional constraints. These models have obviously the capacity to be contrasted with the empirical facts, in order to determine to what extent they represent them in a sufficiently accurate way. It was also called "the economic theory of nonmarket processes," "the rational choice theory of politics," or more simply, public choice theory. The two founding fathers of PCT were the Scottish Duncan Black and the American Anthony Downs; the former introduced in the late forties the mathematical analysis of voting with single-dimensional preferences (i.e., as if the values of each individual might be represented as preferences about what point of a straight line could be chosen; e.g., the size of the government budget, or a one-dimensional liberal-conservative scale), and proved that, if the utility function of each individual is concave (or, in other terms, "single-picked," with a maximum at some point of the line, and with diminishing utility as one goes further from that point in any direction), then simple majority voting reaches an equilibrium (there are no possible cycles), and this equilibrium coincides with the value that is optimal for the median voter (i.e., that individual whose optimum has equal number of other individuals' optima to the left and to the right); this is the famous *median voter theorem*, that allows one to predict that, in two-party political systems, or in many issues decided by a yes-no vote, there will be a tendency to the really existing options being extraordinarily similar (for, if one party goes a little bit to the right or to the left from the median voter's favorite option, the other can win by adopting some point between that option and the one defended by the first party). Downs (whose 1957 book, *An Economic Theory of Democracy*, was actually his PhD dissertation that had been supervised by no other than Kenneth Arrow) generalized this geometrical analysis to a number of other political issues, though probably with no previous knowledge of Black's contribution (Black 1958). Downs (and James Buchanan a few years before, though without employing that term) also introduced the concept of the *rational ignorant voter*, pointing to the fact that the much less direct connection between the action of the individual and the outcome obtained by her in the case of politics, as compared to the case of the market, creates an incentive for not collecting too much nor too accurate information about the available options, nor about their consequences. Actually, this concept created an important problem for the rational choice models of politics, known as *the paradox of voting*; for, if voting has a cost, however minimal, for the individual, and the probability of her individual vote being determinant in the result of the election, referendum, etc., is negligible, then it would be rational *not* to vote.

In the next decades, PCT models were developed for a big variety of political institutions: forms of government (division of powers, federalism vs. centralized government, unicameralism vs. bi- or multicameralism, democracy vs. autocracy, etc.), electoral systems (two-party vs. multiparty systems, voting rules, cabinet stability, etc.), economic policies (taxation, monetary policy, redistribution, size of government, etc.), and other aspects of political behavior (lobbying, logrolling, rent-seeking, bureaucracy, etc. . . .). In this sense, and even more taking into account its normative aspects that we shall consider in the next section, PCT is a much more systematic approach to politics than SCT. Nevertheless, as I mentioned at the beginning, the development of both theories have been driven to perhaps an undesirable extent by the ideological preferences of their practitioners, something that is probably more visible in the case of PCT: once economists started to see the political process not as a kind of "black box" governed from the heaven by a benevolent, omniscient, and almost invisible being, and included it as an aspect of economic behavior susceptible of being modeled as the rest of the economy (the "markets"), and populated by self-interested agents, the idea that the economic role of government was justified as the only possible way of solving the "failures of the market" also started to dim, and to go hand in hand with the idea that there also are "government failures," i.e., economic inefficiencies, or even noxious distributive outcomes, that are the result of the working of the political process. In particular, as stated in Mitchell (2001, p. 5):

> in politics, a less than unanimous choice is imposed on the losers by the winning plurality or majority. Accordingly, a citizen may vote for something, but if she is not on the winning side will not get what she voted for, while another voter may vote against some proposal or candidate and if on the losing side gets what is not wanted. Obviously, these results are at sharp variance with market experiences and outcomes. This basic insight was to provide the foundations of modern . . . public choice. More precisely, this insight led . . . public choice to be viewed as a pathology of politics or democracy. No matter how scientific or objective-sounding public choice may be there is always a theme of inefficiency lurking in the background. Just as welfare economics is a pathology of markets, so public choice is its equivalent in politics.

Perhaps because of the recognition of this common (as well as neither totally justified nor totally unjustified) identification of PCT with right-wing ideology, some of its most prominent scholars have attempted to establish a definition of "public choice" that covers every application of "economic" methods to the study of politics, and not only those explicitly based on the conceptualization of political activities as a kind of "marketplace" (i.e., those that see the politician exclusively as a mere "political entrepreneur," and the citizens are mere "consumers of public goods"). A good example is the author of the most important textbook on public choice, Mueller (2003), who includes in it all the basic content about SCT as if it were just a "natural part" of PCT, and who, in a more recent paper, writes that "I have asked several people why they shy away from using the term public choice to describe their research. The answers I have sometimes received are that 'public choice' has a right-wing connotation associated with it . . . People avoid the term 'public choice,' because of a kind of political correctness."[3]

6. CONSTITUTIONAL POLITICAL ECONOMY

Though probably it is not completely fair to distinguish SCT and PCT by saying that the former is concerned with the normative question of what *should* a group do (given the preferences of its members, and the neoclassical-economics style idea of "rationality"), and the latter with the positive question of what *will* they do (under the same assumptions), the truth is that much of the work done within each of the two schools fits rather well under this rather simplistic description. There is, however, an important exception, which is what has usually been referred to as the "normative branch" of PCT, and with which I shall finish this brief survey: *constitutional economics* or *constitutional political economy* (CPE). One way of understanding the peculiarity of this approach is by saying that, instead of having as its object (when analyzing political institutions) the problem of "what *should they* do?," or that of "what *will they* do?," CPE addresses a question more similar to "what *should we* do as a group?" Stated in a more customary way, CPE is devoted to the problem of the collective *choice of the rules*, rather than to the problem of collective *choices under given rules*. Or, still, CPE deals not about how a group will behave once they are playing some game, but about *what game* they will decide to play; it is *the theory of "the choice of the rules of the game."*

The foundation of CPE dates back to the publication of James Buchanan and Gordon Tullock's book *The Calculus of Consent* (1962), though clearly this work can be inscribed in the venerable tradition of contractarianism in political philosophy, and would perhaps be better understood as the starting of the application of economic theoretic tools to the idea of a "social contract." Basically, from neoclassical economic science Buchanan and Tullock select the idea of *free exchange* as the fundamental building block of the economic (and social) order, whereas from contractarianism they pick the notion of *rights and duties* as emerging from a free agreement among individuals. Hence, according to CPE the basic rules of a political body would emerge as the results of an exchange of liberties: each one renounces some freedom (and, therefore, creates a right in the other citizens), in exchange of others making a parallel cession (and, hence, the former being bestowed with some right himself). The question is, then, what exchange of rights and duties would be optimal *from the point of view of the individuals themselves*? (See Zamora-Bonilla (2007) for an application to judgment-aggregation-like cases).

In order to answer this question, Buchanan and Tullock offer an argument similar to what later would become more popular thanks to John Rawls' *A theory of justice* (1971), that of "the veil of ignorance." The main difference is that, in the case of the former, the argument is more "positive" than "normative," in the sense that it attempts to be an idealized *empirical* explanation of the actual adoption of constitutional rules by real constituencies (as a matter of fact, the book attempts to be a kind of "logical reconstruction" of the US Constitution), more than a philosophical speculation about the conceptual grounds of a universal idea of "justice." Buchanan and Tullock talk explicitly about a "veil of *uncertainty*," in the sense that what matters is not the absolute impartiality that would derive from an imaginary "original position" like that envisioned by Rawls (or from a Habermasian "ideal speech situation"), but the *relative* impartiality that derives from the fact that the real people choosing one norm (especially if the norm is expected to be in effect for a very long time) cannot predict with total certainty the circumstances under which they will really be in the future, once the norm has to be applied to them. Hence, contrarily to the Rawlsian case, the Buchanan and Tullock's constituents are not absolutely uncertain about which social or economic position they will have in the long term, for they know enough about it as to be able of making an educated guess (or, in economic idiom, of calculating their expected utility).

The best known example of Buchanan and Tullock's reasoning refers to the choice of a *special majority rule*: even knowing that all voting rules may lead to some problems, the constituents (i.e., the group of people that is trying to decide *under what rules* they will take in the future their collective decisions) will be conscious that choosing, for example, a "simple majority rule" (a proposal is approved if and only if it gets more votes in favor than votes against it) will have very different consequences than choosing a "unanimity rule" (a proposal is approved if and only if somebody votes for it and nobody votes against it). These consequences can be conceptualized as "expected costs"; in particular, there are *decision-making costs*, those derived from the difficulty of reaching an agreement under a given rule (these costs will be maximal under the unanimity rule); and there are also *external costs*, those derived from the fact that, if a collective decision can be taken without full unanimity, the "winners" may impose harder sacrifices to the "losers" than to themselves (unanimity, i.e., veto power, is a direct way of avoiding these "external costs," and hence these will be higher the less inclusive is the special majority rule that is selected). We can describe decision-making and external costs, as well as their sum (*total costs*), as three functions whose independent variable ranges from 0 to 1 (i.e., to 100%), so that, for a concrete special majority rule of k%, those costs are the expected (dis)utilities associated to establishing k as the threshold of votes a proposal has to obtain in order to become approved. The constitutional choice becomes, then, identical to *the choice the optimum k*, from the point of view of a set of people relatively uncertain about how this choice will affect their welfare in the future.

Buchanan and Tullock argue that an essential difference between the constitutional choice, on the one hand, and, on the other hand, the political decisions made *under* the constitutional norms (e.g., the votings made under a constitutionally chosen k-majority rule), is precisely that the constitutional rule would very probably (and certainly *should*) be chosen *by unanimity*: even if individual citizens don't happen to have the exact optimum k, they can "negotiate" and "compromise" some kind of intermediate rule, in order to make collective decisions possible. The constitutional rules are, hence, really "constitutional," in the sense that their unanimous approval is what "constitutes" the existence of the collective body that will act according to those rules. It is in this sense that we said that CPE is the "normative" branch of PCT: not because CPE is "purely normative," and "not empirical" (for it has also been applied to many cases of "positive" analysis of constitutional choices), but because it allows one to offer a normative (and contractarian) justification of the existing political norms of a given community, as norms that, though in their daily functioning can be the object of "instrumental" and "strategic" manipulation by means of specific groups, have nevertheless the legitimacy of having been accepted by all the people subjected to them. This argument, of course, can only be taken as a more or less reasonable approximation, for in the political reality it is extremely rare that constitutional norms have been unanimously accepted, even taking into account the people that, having voted perhaps for different constitutional norms (or not having voted at all, for example because the constitution was approved long before they were born), expresses their consent on those norms' legitimacy, and also taking into account that this legitimacy can be indirectly expressed, not by means of a real, democratic voting, but what political scientists often term "voting with the feet" (i.e., not choosing the norms of the country, but choosing the country, so to say; cf. Hirschman 1970). Be it as it may, CPE departs from the more traditional lines of PCT in that it does not reduce political interactions to the mere egotistic and isolated maximization of utility of the typical *homo oeconomicus* (in this case, the political entrepreneur and the voter-as-consumer), but, as it is clear in Buchanan's subsequent and influential book, *The Limits of Liberty*, it essentially understands the citizens that are embedded in the process of constitutional choice as subjects capable of reaching an agreement in order *to further social cooperation*:

> Constitutional political economy must be acknowledged to rest upon a precommitment to, or a faith in, man's cooperative potential. . . . But to do so, (men) must live by rules that they can also choose. (Buchanan, 2004, p. 66).

Another important aspect of CPE is that, contrarily to social choice, and more similarly to the public choice school from which it emerged, it has been thoroughly applied to empirical cases since the beginning (a big part of Buchanan and Tullock (1962) was a kind of "logical reconstruction" of the US bicameral system, for example). Proof of this is that the papers included in the most important journal of the field (named precisely CPE) are of an empirical character.[4]

ACKNOWLEDGMENTS

This chapter has benefited from Spanish Government's research projects FFI2017-89639-P ("Mechanisms in the sciences: from the biological to the social"), and RTI2018-097709-B-I00 ("Rationality and counterknowledge: the epistemology of fake news detection").

NOTES

1. McLean (2015, p. 28). I'm basically following this article for the main information contained in this section.
2. See Sen (1970), Gibbard (1973), Satterthwaite (1975), and List and Pettit (2002).
3. Mueller (2015, p. 386).
4. Just by way of example, the five papers included in the last published issue of that journal when this paper was written (March, 2020) contain some kind of empirical analysis or justification of the papers' claims, even when the topic of the paper is more "philosophical" (like Teague, Storr, and Fike 2020) or more "mathematical" (Huysmans and Crombez 2020).

REFERENCES

Arrow, K. J. (1951). *Social choice and individual values*. New Haven, CT: Yale University Press.
Black, D. (1958). *The theory of committees and elections*. Cambridge: Cambridge University Press.
Buchanan, J. (2004). "Constitutional political economy," in Ch. K. Rowley and F. Schneider (eds.), *The Encyclopedia of Public Choice, vol. I*. New York: Kluwer Academic Publishers, pp. 60–66.
Buchanan, J. M., and G. Tullock (1962). *The calculus of consent*. Ann Arbor, MI: University of Michigan Press.
Downs, A. (1957). *An economic theory of democracy*. New York: Harper & Row.
Fleurbaey, M., and F. Maniquet (2011). *A theory of fairness and social welfare*. Cambridge: Cambridge University Press.
Gibbard, A. (1973). "Manipulation of voting schemes: A general result," *Econometrica* 41: 587–602.
Hirschman, A. O. (1970). *Exit, voice, and loyalty*. Cambridge, MA: Harvard University Press.
Hurwicz, L., and S. Reiter (2007). *Designing economic mechanisms*. Cambridge: Cambridge University Press.

Huysmans, M., and Ch. Crombez (2020). "Making exit costly but efficient: the political economy of exit clauses and secession," *Constitutional Political Economy*, 31: 89–110.

List, C. and P. Pettit (2002). "Aggregating sets of judgments: an impossibility result," *Economics and Philosophy*, 18: 89–110.

McLean, I. (2015), "The strange history of social choice, and the contribution of the Public Choice Society to its fifth revival," *Public Choice*, 163: 153–165.

Mitchell, W. C. (2001). "The old and the new public choice: Chicago versus Virginia." in W. F. Shughart II and L. Razzolini (eds.), *The Elgar companion to public choice.* Cheltenham: Edward Elgar, pp. 3–32.

Mueller, D. C. (2003). *Public choice III.* Cambridge: Cambridge University Press.

Mueller, D. (2015). "Public choice, social choice, and political economy." *Public Choice*, 163: 379–387.

Olson, M. (1965). *The logic of collective action.* New Haven, CT: Yale University Press.

Ostrom, E. (1990). *Governing the commons: The evolution of institutions for collective action.* Cambridge: Cambridge University Press.

Rawls, J. A. (1971). *A theory of justice.* Cambridge, MA: Belknap Press.

Satterthwaite, M. A. (1975). "Strategy-proofness and arrow's conditions: Existence and correspondence theorems for voting procedures and social welfare functions," *Journal of Economic Theory* 10: 187–217.

Sen, A. K. (1970). "The impossibility of a Paretian liberal," *Journal of Political Economy* 78: 152–157.

Sen, A. K. (1999). The possibility of social choice. *American Economic Review.* 89(3): 349–378.

Stiglitz, J. (2000). *Economics of the public sector* (3rd ed.). New York: W. W. Norton & Company.

Teague, M.V., V.H. Storr, and R. Fike (2020), "Economic freedom and materialism: An empirical analysis," *Constitutional Political Economy*, 31: 1–44.

Zamora-Bonilla, J. (2007). "Optimal judgment aggregation," *Philosophy of Science*, 74(5):813–824.

CHAPTER 8

NINETEEN KINDS OF THEORIES ABOUT MECHANISMS THAT EVERY SOCIAL SCIENCE GRADUATE STUDENT SHOULD KNOW

ANDREW BENNETT AND BENJAMIN MISHKIN

INTRODUCTION

IN the last few decades philosophers of science, methodologists, and practicing researchers in the social, physical, and biological sciences have turned away from "covering law" explanations to focus on the role that causal mechanisms play in scientific explanation. This has generated useful and ongoing discussions on how best to define causal mechanisms and on the relationship between different research methods and the development and testing of theories about how causal mechanisms work. The present chapter builds upon these discussions but focuses on a pragmatic question: what theories about mechanisms do social scientists and social actors find most useful?

No single article can satisfactorily answer this question for every subfield and substantive issue area. Rather, this chapter briefly defines social causal mechanisms and identifies the *kind* of theories about such mechanisms that social actors and researchers find pragmatically useful. It focuses on what Robert Merton called "theories of the middle range," in contrast to both grand theoretical schools of thought and fine-grained theories on processes like brain chemistry. It then outlines a taxonomy of middle-range theories about social mechanisms that serves as a useful checklist to help researchers and social actors ensure that they do not leave out viable alternative explanations of the phenomena they are studying or trying to influence. The taxonomy includes within-agent, agent-agent, agent- structure, structure-agent, and structure-structure theories on ideas/identities, material power, and institutions. We have cited classic early discussions as well as recent literature reviews and empirical applications of each type of theory. One indication that social scientists do indeed find the kinds of theories discussed herein useful is that the sources in the bibliography have numerous citations—some have tens of thousands. Throughout, the discussion reflects the authors' biases and blind spots as political scientists in the international relations subfield, but the goal is to illustrate theories about mechanisms that apply across the social sciences, including economics, sociology, history, psychology, anthropology, and research on education, business, public policy, and public health.

DEFINING SOCIAL CAUSAL MECHANISMS

For many decades, philosophers of science followed David Hume in emphasizing what Hume called "constant conjunction," or what we would now call correlation, as the locus of causation, inference, and scientific explanation (Hume and Steinberg 2011). The twentieth century version of this approach, known as the "covering law" or "deductive-nomological" model and associated most closely with Carl Hempel and Paul Oppenheim, viewed "laws" as regularities that explain phenomena (Hempel and Oppenheim 1948). In this account, the existence and operation of laws was to be inferred inductively through statistical associations.

By the 1960s, however, this approach encountered major philosophical problems: it gave no warrant or explanation for laws themselves, and it could not distinguish causal from spurious correlations (Salmon 2006). This gave rise in the 1970s to what has been called the "critical realist" or "scientific realist" approach to causation and explanation (Bunge 1963; Bhaskar 1978; Archer 1995; Aronson, Harré, and Way 1999)

There are many theorists and variants of scientific realism, but generally they share three key commitments: "ontological realism (that there is a reality independent of the mind(s) that would wish to know it); epistemological relativism (that all beliefs are socially produced); and judgmental rationalism (that despite epistemological relativism, it is still possible, in principle, to choose between competing theories" (Wight 2006, 26). In this regard, scientific realists draw a strong distinction between theories and causal mechanisms: theories exist inside our heads and attempt to describe causal mechanisms and the processes through which they operate, and causal mechanisms are ontological entities with causal powers that exist in the world independent of the theories in our heads.[1] To the extent that the theories in our heads are accurate, they describe the mechanisms that generate outcomes and provide adequate explanations of those outcomes.

In this view, causal inference is strengthened not just by statistical inferences and experiments, but also by examining the events and processes that intervene between hypothesized causes and observed effects in particular cases. Our theories about mechanisms generate observable implications on what should be true if the posited mechanisms operate in the manner that we theorize. We can test these observable implications against the predictions of our theories even though we cannot directly observe mechanisms or causation.

While there are many debates about how to define causal mechanisms (Mahoney 2001, 578–580), one of us in an earlier work with Alexander George defined social causal mechanisms as "physical, social, or psychological processes through which agents with causal capacities operate, but only in specific contexts or conditions, to transfer energy, information, or matter to other entities," thereby changing the latter entities' "characteristics, capacities, or propensities in ways that persist until subsequent causal mechanisms act upon it" (George and Bennett 2005, 137).[2] Another common definition is that mechanisms are "entities and activities organized such that they are productive of regular changes from start or set-up to finish or termination conditions" (Machamer, Darden, and Craver 2000). David Waldner (2012) has usefully stressed that causal mechanisms embody some form of invariance—they cannot be "turned off" when the requisite conditions for their operation exist—and it is this invariance that gives theories about mechanisms the potential (to the extent that they are accurate) to provide satisfactory explanations.

Explaining outcomes by referencing causal mechanisms may seem similar to explaining them by invoking "laws," as both provide arguments that the observed outcomes were to have been expected under the circumstances. There is a critical difference, however: realist explanations are highly skeptical of "as if" assumptions, or the black-boxing of processes at lower units of analysis. Instead, they require that our theories about how the underlying mechanisms work must be consistent with the finest degree of detail that we can observe. For pragmatic reasons, social scientists might at times simplify theories with regard to fine-grained processes, but in so doing they recognize that more detailed and accurate theories about these processes provide more complete explanations. Scientific realism does not preclude the usefulness of macro level or systemic theories or explanations, and depending on the research question it may be useful to focus on macro level mechanisms. But this also requires the recognition that to the extent that individual actors do not in fact think or behave in the ways implied by a macro level theory's stated or implicit microfoundations, the macro level theory loses adequacy as an explanation of outcomes. In practice, in addition to developing both structural and agent-centered theories, most social scientists work at the meso level, that is, middle-range theories focused on interactions of agents and social structures, in settings where any invariance in the underlying causal mechanisms is contingent on the presence or absence of many other mechanisms, and therefore hard to infer.

MIDDLE-RANGE THEORIES VERSUS THEORETICAL ISMS AND THEORIES ON MICROMECHANISMS

The sociologist Robert Merton introduced the concept of "theories of the middle range," specifying them as follows (Merton 1968, 39):

> theories that lie between the minor but necessary working hypotheses that evolve in abundance during day-to-day research and the all-inclusive systematic efforts to develop a unified theory that will explain all the observed uniformities of social behavior, social organization, and social change. Middle-range theory . . . is intermediate to general theories of social systems which are too remote from particular classes of social behavior, organization, and change to account for what is observed and to those detailed orderly descriptions of particulars that are not generalized at all. Middle-range theory involves abstractions, of course, but they are close enough to observed data to be incorporated in propositions that permit empirical testing.

Social scientists have frequently noted that the concept of middle-range theory appears to be critically important but also ambiguous and hard to define any better than Merton did (Pawson 2000, 283). Yet the concept is also appealing and frequently invoked. For present purposes, we define middle-range social theories as realist theories about social mechanisms that operate neither at the highly abstract level of grand theories or paradigms, nor at highly specific levels such as biochemical physical processes in human brains.[3]

One of the challenges of defining middle range theory is that whatever is "too micro" to be considered middle range theory in a field of inquiry is largely a function of the social construction of professional research communities: we political scientists leave the neuronal level of detail to psychologists, neurologists, and microbiologists, and they typically leave the atoms and subatomic particles to the physicists. Some political scientists read and draw upon works in psychology but few if any of us produce research at the brain chemistry level of analysis. Meanwhile, theories about individual behavior that political scientists consider to be middle range—including theories about rational choice mechanisms, cognitive biases, and emotional reactions—may seem like grand theories to cognitive psychologists. Psychologists' theories about brain activity may in turn seem like grand theories to particle physicists. There are pragmatic reasons that fields of inquiry are (porously) bounded to enable specialized training, and that we hand off inquiry to other fields at higher and lower levels of analysis. Yet as noted above, a scientific realist approach suggests that for every field of inquiry, if the theories and findings at a more micro level of detail prove inconsistent with the middle range theories in use, those middle range theories need to be revised if they are to increase their explanatory power.

In between grand theoretical schools of thought and neuron level micromechanisms political scientists engage in middle range theorizing about how social mechanisms generate outcomes in various functional issue areas: the study of wars, regime types, elections, etc. Our conception of middle range theories on these phenomena includes not just individual mechanisms—Merton's own example was referent group theory and the attendant processes of feelings of relative deprivation—but also theories about combinations of mechanisms acting in specified and often recurrent scope conditions or contexts. Middle-range political science theories on ethnic and civil conflict, for example, often combine theories on relative deprivation mechanisms, framing and mobilization (Shesterinina 2016), structural opportunities (Fearon and Laitin 2003), credible commitments problems (Walter 1997), ethnic security dilemmas (Posen 1993), principal-agent relations (Salehyan 2009), lootable resources (Ross 2004), and bargaining indivisibilities (Goddard 2009).

Theories about specific individual mechanisms can contribute to the construction of "typological theories, or contingent generalizations on how different combinations of mechanisms interact in specified conditions" (George and Bennett 2005, 235). Typological theories can address, for example, the ways in which different types of agents—with different motivations, resources, information, networks, reputations, etc.—behave in different contextual mixes of institutions, normative structures, resource distributions, and so on. These theories, while themselves complicated, can model complex causal relationships, including nonlinear relations and higher-order interactions effects. Examples include typological theories on alliance burden sharing (Bennett, Lepgold, and Unger 1994), national unification (Ziblatt 2006), welfare capitalism (Esping-Andersen 1990), national political economies (Hall and Soskice 2001), and rebels' relations with their home states and host states (Bennett 2013).[4]

A Taxonomy of Theories about Social Mechanisms

Seven Kinds of Within-Agent Theories on Individual Behavior

Early discussions of critical realism (Harré and Madden 1975) had roots in psychology, and within-agent mechanisms lie behind all other kinds of agent-structure social mechanisms, as they involve basic processes through which individuals make sense of themselves and the world. This section outlines seven categories of theories about within-agent mechanisms of perception, choice and change that are common in the social sciences. It provides neither an exhaustive list of such theories nor a definitive statement of any one approach, and one could divide it into more sub-categories or lump several approaches together into fewer categories. It is meant to be pragmatically useful to researchers interested in learning more about these theories, to highlight some of the strengths, applications, and limits of each category of within-agent mechanisms, and to provide citations to sources that are good starting points into the literature on each.

1. *Rational Choice Theory*

One of the most widespread theoretical arguments in the social sciences is that individuals are largely rational actors seeking to make choices that influence outcomes in ways that maximize their preference-based utilities (Elster 1994). The appeal of rational choice theory is that it is simple and widely applicable, and it offers explanations for otherwise counter-intuitive social outcomes. In particular, rational choice theories have demonstrated how the rational individual pursuit of utility can lead to sub-optimal outcomes for society as a whole and even for each individual. Collective action theory, for example, explains why the temptation to free ride can lead to the under-provision of "public goods," or goods that are nonrival and nonexcludable (Olson 1965). The Prisoners' Dilemma, similarly, explains why in a single interaction, the logical choice of each player is to not cooperate with the other player, even though this leads to an outcome that is worse for both players than if they had somehow been able to enforce a mutual commitment to cooperate. In repeated play between the same players, however, cooperation can emerge through a tit-for-tat strategy that rewards the other player with cooperation or punishes them with defection depending on whether they cooperated or defected in the previous round (Axelrod and Hamilton 1981; Axelrod and Dion 1988) explore how the dynamics of this game depend on the number of players, the variability of the payoffs, and other factors). Another important game, Stag Hunt, highlights how providing transparency and lowering the costs of monitoring and enforcement can help achieve cooperation (Jervis 1978; Oye 1985).

Rational choice theories have thus made contributions toward understanding numerous substantive social and political issues, including voting behavior (Downs 1957; Fiorina 1981), public goods provision by nongovernmental groups (Ostrom 1990), strategic voting, electoral rules, political party behavior and decisions to run for office (Cox 1999), coalition government formation (Laver and Schofield 1998), agenda setting (Romer and Rosenthal 1978; 1979), and even the choice of which language to learn or to teach to one's children (Laitin 1993).[5] In the field of international relations, rational choice theories have clarified how actors' private information about their willingness and capabilities to go to war, together with strategic and tactical incentives to misrepresent that information, creates credible commitment problems that can contribute to the outbreak of wars, particularly during power transitions (Fearon 1995).

Notwithstanding its important contributions, rational choice theory has inherent limits regarding its two central concepts of "preferences" and "rationality," and it is problematic to apply the theory to collective behavior even if it provides insights into how individuals respond to the expected behavior of others.[6] Regarding preferences, a key distinction differentiates "thick" rational choice models, which make strong simplifying assumptions about actors' preferences, from "thin" rational choice models, which attempt to identify actors' preferences empirically and inductively and then explore how those preferences lead to the choices actors make within institutional, informational, resource, or other constraints (Hechter and Kanazawa 1997). Either approach has limits. Thick rational choice models aspire to claim universality, but to do so they require the oversimplified assumption that utility functions across cultures and time periods are reducible to something measurable and tangible like material wealth. Thin rational choice models, on the other hand, can incorporate nonmaterial and nonselfish interests, but they face various "revealed preference problems" in making inferences about what individuals actually prefer: individuals may have strategic reasons to mislead others about their actual preferences, preferences may change over time, people can be uncertain or incomplete about their own preferences, and there is the danger of tautology in inferring preferences from behavior and then using those same preferences to explain subsequent behavior.

With regard to the rationality assumption, some rational choice models make unrealistically strong assumptions about the ability or propensity of individuals to carry out mental procedures like multiple rounds of backward induction. Others adopt simpler notions of "instrumental rationality," but research in behavioral economics, discussed below, indicates that people often depart from even simple forms of rationality. Perhaps the simplest and most limited form of rationality is transitivity of preferences: if A is preferred to B, and B is preferred to C, then A should be preferred to C. Yet the "Arrow Theorem," outlined by the economist Kenneth Arrow, demonstrates that even if transitivity holds for individuals, it does not necessarily hold for decision-making groups unless one member of a group is allowed to have more influence over the group's choice than other members (Arrow 1950). This highlights the importance of understanding the institutional rules through which individual preferences are aggregated into collective choices, discussed below, which takes the locus of explanation beyond the within-agent level of analysis.

While most of the criticism of rational choice theory has focused on these issues of preferences and rationality, another key problem is that even when individuals are instrumentally rational and have the same preferences, they can vary widely in their expectations about which actions will lead to their preferred outcomes. Thus people who have the same preferences may make different choices because they have different beliefs about how the world works. For reasons similar to the challenges that make it hard to assess individuals' actual preferences, it is also difficult to assess their causal understandings of the world.

Despite these limitations, it is hard to get away from some form of assumption that individuals are purposive or goal-seeking, if not rational, and that large groups of people do on average respond in relatively predictable and rational ways to at least some simple and consistent systemic or institutional pressures and incentives (such as relative prices) over long periods of time. At the same time, the limits of rational choice theories have created room for additional middle range theories about within-agent mechanisms. Each of the next six theories on within-agent mechanisms discussed in turn below departs from at least one of the key assumptions of rational choice theory: theories about individual cognitive biases and information processing styles help get beyond strong assumptions about rationality; theories on emotions and those on personality types add insights about both nonrational processes of individual decision-making and the substance of preferences; and theories about the content of individuals' belief systems and about the evolution of individual preferences through life and career stages further fill out the missing or underdeveloped links in rational choice theories.

2. *Theories on Cognitive Heuristics and Biases*

The study of cognitive decision-making processes, and the finding that individuals are subject to many specific errors and biases in their everyday inferences in their personal and professional lives, has led "error and bias" theories to become one of the most prominent alternatives to rational choice explanations of individual behavior. Indeed, the study of cognitive shortcuts and biases has come to constitute the subfield of behavioral economics.[7] Herbert Simon's model of "bounded rationality" was an early contribution to this approach (Simon 1957), and Amos Tversky and Daniel Kahneman were important innovators in this area, carrying out experiments on how individuals make decisions in hypothetical scenarios involving different framing prompts and tradeoffs of risk and return (Kahneman, Slovic, and Tversky 1982). This work led to a large research program and a growing list of cognitive biases; we do not attempt a comprehensive accounting of every bias discussed in the literature, rather, we identify some of the most prominent examples and applications (Kahneman 2011; Caputo 2013).

Generally, research on cognitive biases has been framed around the concept of bounded rationality and its model of individuals as having limits to their time and ability to process fully all of the information that is potentially relevant to their behavioral choices. In this view, individuals are "naïve scientists"—scientists in the sense that they must engage in scientific kinds of inferences, such as sampling from the information available to them and then making causal inferences that inform their choices, and naïve in the sense that they employ fallible or potentially biased cognitive heuristics or shortcuts in making these inferences (Nisbett and Ross 1980). Important examples of such shortcuts and biases include the following: "anchoring," whereby initial information (such as an opening bid in negotiations) tends to anchor the range of expected values or base rates even if that initial information is of dubious quality; "availability bias," whereby information that is easily accessible is more likely to be weighed than information that is not; "vividness bias", whereby information that is visually and emotionally arresting or arousing has outsized influence; "representativeness bias," whereby individuals judge cases or information and population base rates relative to a case that they view as archetypical even if it is not representative of a population in a statistical sense; and "prospect theory bias," whereby individuals will put forth more effort or take greater risks to prevent a perceived loss than to achieve a perceived gain (Kahneman and Tversky 1979). Other important biases include the "fundamental attribution error," whereby individuals tend to place too much emphasis on variation in the internal psychological characteristics of other individuals in explaining the latter's behavior and too little emphasis on variations in the social context (E. D. Hall 2020); "confirmation bias", in which information consistent with a hypothesis is more likely to be sought, perceived, and recalled than information that is not consistent with that hypothesis (Oswald and Grosjean 2004); "hindsight bias", in which events that have taken place are seen in retrospect as having been, or having been judged, more probable than they were viewed in prospect (Guilbault et al. 2004); and "overconfidence bias" on the calibration of confidence intervals regarding knowledge and predictions (Alpert and Raiffa 1982; Fellner and Krügel 2012).

An important application of this work has been the design of policies and institutions in ways to offset biases and make it easier for individuals to make better decisions (Thaler and Sunstein 2008). More generally, scholars have sought to find ways to "de-bias" both individual and group assessments and predictions and improve predictive performance. Efforts have focused on changing both individual cognitive habits through training and on changing environmental factors, institutions, and procedures to reduce biases (Larrick 2004; Croskerry, Singhal, and Mamede 2013a; 2013b; Soll, Milkman, and Payne 2015). One research finding here is that groups trained in Bayesian inference and probability theory, and working together in teams to share judgments and information, perform better than individuals and simple algorithms in making predictions about political developments (Tetlock and Gardner 2015). Another line of research suggests that common cognitive shortcuts actually perform fairly well at common inferential tasks (Gigerenzer and Gaissmaier 2011).

3. *Information Processing and Cognitive Styles*

The degree to which individuals might have varying cognitive styles—something distinct from intelligence and from personality—has been a question for scholars since at least Charles Darwin, who argued that there were naturalists who tended to "lump" organisms together when classifying them and those who tended to "split" organisms into a panoply of species. Later, the philosopher Isaiah Berlin informally hypothesized that the Greek poet Archilochus' distinction between hedgehogs—who know one big thing—and foxes—who know many things—could be used to classify different styles of writers and intellectuals (Berlin and Ignatieff 2013). Since the 1940s, cognitive psychologists, applied psychologists, and neuroscientists have sought to make sense of the hypothesized existence of and variation in cognitive styles.

Psychological research on cognitive styles has tended to focus on the themes of basic cognitive skills such as perception (Witkin et al. 1954), classifying and organization (Gardner 1953; Pettigrew 1958), complexity in concept formation (Bieri 1955; Messick 1976), and holistic versus "step-by-step" problem-solving techniques (Pask 1972; Pask and Scott 1972). For example, Witkin et al. (1954) claimed to find field-independent (FI) and field-dependent (FD) thinkers. In a series of object orientation tasks, FI's tended to not rely on the field around the object to orient it in ambiguous situations, whereas the FD's tended to rely on clues from the field when determining how to orient the object. When connecting these results to personalities, they found that FI's had a more impersonal mode of social orientation, in comparison to FD's who did not tend to distance themselves psychologically or physically from other people as much. Other posited types included verbal versus visual imagery preference (Paivio 1971; Richardson 1977) and variation in expectations about the extent to which individuals believe their own actions will determine their life outcomes as opposed to a belief that external forces will determine their life chances (Rotter 1966).

This very boom in cognitive style research however eventually served to undermine psychologists' belief in the concept itself: the proliferation of apparent types and the degree to which many of them correlated among each other brought attention back to trying to unify the field. Several methodological difficulties also plagued the field (Kozhevnikov 2007). By the 1970s psychologists gave relatively less credence to the concept of cognitive styles. However, recent research has sought to revive the field. Kozhevnikov (2007) argues that a key new development is the hierarchical approach to understanding cognitive styles which sees cognitive styles as meta-cognitive regulators but which may intercede at different steps in the thinking process, from perception to overall use of mental energy (Nosal 1990). In addition, work in neuroscience has lent greater biological support to the notion that there are differences in how individuals' brains operate on a variety of cognitive tasks, implying the existence of biologically determined cognitive styles.[8]

Applied psychologists in several fields made perhaps more use of cognitive styles than cognitive psychologists themselves to explain variation in real world tasks and mental behaviors. In management studies, Agor developed a tripartite categorization of managers' cognitive profiles: analytical, who preferred to break problems down and frequently used quantitative approaches; intuitive, who relied on their feelings to solve problems and which they tended to solve therefore more holistically; and integrated, which used a mix of both strategies (Agor 1984; 1989). In psychotherapy, scholars proposed a variety of cognitive styles, such as optimistic-pessimistic, explanatory, anxiety prone, among others (Alloy et al. 1999; Haeffel et al. 2003; Uhlenhuth et al. 2002). Gregorc (1979; 1982) posited that there are two dimensions of learning styles: perception or the means through which people grasp information, which could be either abstract or concrete; and ordering information styles which could be either sequential or random. These two dimensions produce four types of learning styles. Entwistle et al. (1979) argued for four learning styles as well, albeit different ones: deep, surface, strategic, and apathetic. Dunn et al. (1989) composed the Learning Style Inventory, a 100-item questionnaire which asked students to report their learning preferences with respect to factors to such as their relative level of persistence, whether they liked to work with others or alone, whether they tended to be more analytical or holistic, and whether they tended to be more impulsive or reflective.

Political science has also used the concept of cognitive styles to understand the nature of ideology and ideological extremism (Tetlock 1984), to explain predictive ability (Tetlock 2017), and to explain how voters make decisions about which candidates to support (Lau, Kleinberg, and Ditonto 2018). Tetlock (1984) finds that ideological moderates had a more integratively complex cognitive style in which they took into account more competing social or moral values on a given issue than did ideological extremists on either side of the left-right divide. Those who valued two potentially competing values, such as freedom and equality, equally—moderate socialists—displayed the most integratively complex cognitive style, followed by moderate conservatives who were less committed to equality and therefore under less pressure to integrate their competing values. In other research, Tetlock (2017) builds from Berlin's hedgehog and fox theory to argue that foxes—who know many different things—were less likely to be ideological extremists, more likely to have integratively complex cognitive styles, and more likely to make accurate predictions. Finally, Lau et al. (2018), who in practice define cognitive style as decision-making style, identify five such styles in how voters make decisions about which candidate to support: Rational Choice, Confirmatory, Fast and Frugal, Heuristic-Based, and Going with Your Gut.

4. *Aging and Lifecycles*

A first understanding of age as a causal mechanism sees the effect of age as roughly in line with rational choice theories but tries to specify the particular incentives individuals might have at different points in their life. For example, research has found that individuals in middle age tend to care more about their work, family, and their responsibilities as these tend to dominate their time at this stage of their life (Angel and Stettersten 2012; Srivastava et al. 2003). In political science, Campbell finds that senior citizens, particularly low-income ones, become politically engaged to defend Social Security out of their own material self-interest to protect their retirement benefits (A. L. Campbell 2002). At the other end of the age gradient, polls show that individuals under the age of forty-five tend to support student loan forgiveness at higher rates than those above that age, potentially on account of the fact that younger voters might themselves still have more student debt than older voters who might have never incurred it on account of lower higher education rates, incurred less of it because of lower tuition rates, or have already paid them off by the time they reach their fifties (Stewart 2020). Work on different types of bureaucrats—zealot, statesmen, climber, conserver—implicitly assumes that the stage one is at in a career— either with a career ladder still to climb or with an institution one helms to conserve—will have a key effect on how one behaves within an organization (Downs 1964). When these stages take place empirically either in personal or professional lives and why the timing might have changed over time has been a focus of life course sociology and demography (K. U. Mayer 2009).

A second manifestation of age as a causal mechanism is generational or cohort effects whereby individuals who came of age together hold distinct beliefs or preferences on account of economic or cultural change during their lifetime, in particular during their formative years. In terms of social attitudes, scholars have found that, for example, baby boomers are distinctive from other cohorts in their support for civil rights of stigmatized groups and relatively liberal outlook (Davis 2004; Schwadel and Garneau 2014; Twenge, Carter, and Campbell 2015; Gonthier 2017). In an example from science studies, researchers have found important generational effects on productivity: contra the belief within fields such as physics that significant breakthroughs are overwhelmingly made by younger, more dynamic scholars, research has shown that this belief overinterprets a uniquely productive generation in the early part of the twentieth century that worked during the early years of the quantum revolution when theoretical work was highly innovative and prequantum work was uniquely obsolete, precluding the need to spend years mastering prior literature. Subsequent young physicists have not disproportionately made breakthrough discoveries (Jones and Weinberg 2011).

Explaining these generational effects leads to the third category of theories of aging: aging as a physiological or psychophysiological or neurological phenomenon. Several themes emerge from this literature: the relatively plasticity of young people in terms of adopting social attitudes (Campbell et al. 1960; Dinas 2013); the stability of attitudes once one becomes an adult (Alwin and Krosnick 1991); and differences in personality traits at different points in the life cycle, such as more openness to experience in younger individuals as compared to older individuals (Cornelis et al. 2009). However, other studies do point to data that show that older individuals are capable of changing their social attitudes, even if they never become as, for example, tolerant of historically stigmatized groups, as members of younger cohorts (Danigelis, Hardy, and Cutler 2007). One step below these findings a growing body of cognitive psychology and neuroscience is trying to better understand the cognitive changes that might underlie these phenomena. Of particular interest are differences in discounting (L. Green, Fry, and Myerson 1994; Read and Read 2004; Whelan and McHugh 2009) and goal setting (Löckenhoff 2011).

5. *Personality Types*

Individual personality traits or types is another key class of within-agent causal mechanisms prominent in the social sciences. Here we define personality as a system of an individual's parts, including motives, emotions, mental models, and sense of self, that is relatively enduring and that is expressed in that individual's behavior (this combines some elements of different definitions in (J. D. Mayer 2007). This definition overlaps to some degree with our discussion of emotions, which focuses on transient rather than enduring emotions, that on belief systems, which focuses on specific substantive beliefs, and that on cognitive style, which focuses on individuals' characteristic modes of thinking and problem-solving. It includes both "normal" personalities and personality disorders. Despite the American Psychiatric Association's norms against professional psychologists diagnosing leaders without having met them or obtained their consent, several have identified President Trump as having many of the characteristics of both narcissism and antisocial personality disorder as they are defined in the fifth edition of the Diagnostic and Statistical Manual of Mental Disorders (Lee 2017). Others have labeled the combination of these two disorders as "malignant narcissism" and used it to analyze foreign leaders (Kernberg 1989; Post 1993).

In political science, personality theories have been explored extensively as they relate to individuals' political ideologies, political party affiliations, and other objects of concern to political life. Adorno et al. (2019) famously looked at the so-called authoritarian personality as an explanation for the popular support of fascist, antidemocratic political regimes. Following this work, others extended the principle of looking at individual-level personality determinants of prejudice, extremist politics more generally (Eysenck 1954), open- versus closed-mindedness (Rokeach 1960) and variation in left-right political beliefs without focusing necessarily on extremists (McClosky 1958; Wilson 1973). Over time, psychologists developed the Big Five personality paradigm which built on and subsumed earlier measures of psychological traits (Goldberg 1992; 1993; McCrae and Costa Jr. 2005). The Big Five uses five categories of traits to measure an individual's personality: *openness to experience, conscientiousness, extraversion, agreeableness,* and *emotional stability/neuroticism,* frequently abbreviated as OCEAN. As one measure of the influence and widespread use of the Big

Five model of personality, a Google Scholar search for "Big Five" and "personality" returns over 40,000 citations just since 2017.

Federico (2022) argues that the core issues at the heart of research on the relationship between personality and political ideology have been variation in *epistemic concern*—the need for cognitive closure and certainty—and variation in *existential concerns*—the need for security and safety in the face of threat. When combined, these dimensions have yielded the "rigidity of the right" picture of the relationship between personality and political beliefs. In this picture, endorsers of conservative ideology tend to exhibit a rigidity in their personalities, defined as a desire for existential security from threats and epistemic security in the form of a relatively closed stance toward new ideas and a preference for cognitive closure and certainty. By contrast, holders of leftist views are relatively less troubled by the risks of threats from others and relatively more open to new ideas and comfortable with intellectual ambiguities and a lack of cognitive closure and certainty (Jost et al. 2003). In terms of the Big Five personality measures, those who score higher in conscientiousness tend toward right-wing political preferences and those who score higher on openness to experience lean toward left-wing political preferences (Carney et al. 2008; A. S. Gerber et al. 2010; Mondak et al. 2010).

Research has also sought to link personality with behavior beyond attitudes. Research has found that those scoring higher in extraversion tend to be more civically engaged in terms of attending and speaking at political meetings and volunteering for campaigns, but are not more likely to engage in less social political activities such as putting up yard signs or contributing to candidates for office (Mondak and Halperin 2008; A. Gerber et al. 2009). By contrast, *conscientiousness* has more ambiguous effects on participation in politics: whereas political activity might be framed as fulfilling one's civic duty, which would appeal to those high in conscientiousness, if political activity is seen as a luxury pursuit this would tend to decrease the chances that a highly conscientious person would choose to prioritize this over work or family (Mondak et al. 2010). Hanania (2017) finds that politicians themselves differ systematically from the general public on Big Five traits, specifically that (with some notable exceptions) they are more extraverted, agreeable, emotionally stable, and conscientious than average. In addition, Republican officeholders were found to score higher on conscientiousness—an orientation toward reliability and dependability and fulfilling one's duty—than Democratic officeholders, whereas Democratic officeholders scored higher on intellect and imagination and agreeableness.

Researchers have sought to provide a neuroscientific basis for differences in personality. Several scholars have identified a relationship between heightened physiological threat sensitivity and conservatism or rightist policy beliefs, such as opposition to foreign aid, gun control, and gay marriage (Oxley et al. 2008; Smith et al. 2011; Aarøe, Petersen, and Arceneaux 2017). These studies have not been without their critics. Bakker et al. (2020) find that conservatives and liberals have similar physiological responses to threatening stimuli. Crawford (2017) argues that findings of differing responses to threat on the part of conservatives and liberals depend on how one defines threat and conservatism. Other findings echo the need to draw a distinction between varieties of conservatism, especially social versus economic. Whereas in the sociopolitical realm conservatism seems to stem from a heightened threat sensitivity and thus low openness correlates with conservatism, in the economic realm conservatism—right-wing economic beliefs—seems to stem from a need for competitive dominance, which correlates more with measures of (non)-agreeable-ness or less prosocial behavior (Bakker 2017; Bardeen and Michel 2019).

Finally, scholars continue to work on better understanding the relationship between personality, beliefs, and one's environment to explain the significant variation in person-ality profiles and issue positions across cultures and even within cultures depending on individuals' exposure to cultural and elite cues (A. S. Gerber et al. 2010; Malka et al. 2014).

6. *Emotions and Behavior*

The study of emotions and behavior has generally evolved along two tracks. The first looks at the relatively stable mixes of emotional drives and needs that help define the kinds of personality types discussed above. The second track, and the focus of this section, involves the study of short term stimuli, including rhetoric, symbols, gestures or other contextual events or behavior by other individuals, and the ways in which short term physiological responses to these emotional stimuli shape behavior. We do not attempt a comprehensive review, rather we provide an overview and several important examples (for a recent review of both tracks, see Marcus 2000).

Early research on physiological or emotional arousal tended to view emotionally charged decision-making as leading to less rational or optimal choices. Research on crisis decision-making, for example, found that information processing during crises, which create both emotional pressures and time pressures, is marked by less tolerance for ambiguity, consid-eration of fewer options, and other decision-making shortcomings (Jervis, Lebow, and Stein 1985). Subsequent research found that subjects with physical damage to their brain regions governing emotions, but with otherwise undamaged faculties, performed extremely poorly on tasks involving tradeoffs of risks and rewards, exhibiting indecision and making outright irrational choices (Damasio 1994). This suggests that at least some degrees and forms of emotional investment are conducive to good decision-making.

More recent research has focused on a model involving two intertwined decision processes that coexist within each individual. The first, variously labeled the intuitive, ex-periential, or "system one" process, involves nearly instantaneous judgments, including the association of affective feelings with stimuli. The second, labeled the analytical, rational, or "system two" process, is slow, deliberative and calculating (Kahneman 2011; Slovic et al. 2002). The affective associations created by system one orient and frame the decision processes of system two. This can save time and usefully limit the demands on system two, but it can also introduce the kinds of biases discussed above. Intuitive affective associations are also vulnerable to deliberate manipulation of emotional cues by other actors (Slovic et al. 2002).

One empirical application of the role of emotions in decision-making concerns coercive diplomacy. The threat to use force if stated demands are not met can provoke feelings of fear, anger, and humiliation. Whether the actor targeted by the threat of force responds with fight, flight, or freeze depends on the symbols and language involved in the threat and the emotional associations these hold for that actor (Markwica 2018).

Another interesting and important finding is that emotional arousal may provide one an-swer to the puzzle of costly collective action. In the literature on voting, social movements, and violent mobilization, a recurring paradox is that individuals often undertake costly action for collective goods when the rational incentives would suggest that they should free ride. Experimental evidence suggests that a perceived threat to in-group identity, together with a perception of solidarity and efficacy, can lead individuals to undertake individually costly action on behalf of group security or other collective goals (Mackie, Devos, and Smith 2000; van Zomeren et al. 2004; Rydell et al. 2008).

Another finding related to emotional cues is that individuals are willing to undertake costly action to punish those whom they consider unfair. One of the most replicated experiments in social science is the "Ultimatum Game," in which one individual makes an offer to divide some amount of money and the recipient of the offer has the choice of either accepting or rejecting the proposed division. If they accept, the money is divided, and if they reject the offer neither gets any reward. Across many different replications in different cultural settings, experimentalists have found at least some willingness to punish offers considered too unequal (Forsythe et al. 1994; Nowak, Page, and Sigmund 2000; Henrich et al. 2004; Debove, Baumard, and André 2016).

7. Substantive Beliefs about Social Life

A final approach to understanding individual decision-making concerns specific substantive beliefs that individuals hold about how the world works. An early contribution here is Nathan Leites' (1950) concept of the "operational code" which is a generalized set of beliefs about political life. This construct included ideas about whether politics was inherently cooperative or conflictual, whether or not individuals could have much influence over outcomes, and operational ideas about connections between means and ends. Empirical applications include studies of leaders' beliefs and their effects on American foreign policy-making (Walker 1977; Saunders 2011) and the evolution of Soviet/Russian ideas and behavior regarding military intervention (Bennett 1999).

Substantive beliefs can also take the form of analogies shared by members of a generation who had shared experiences in their formative years. Khong (1992) argues that American leaders who had been shaped by the interwar period in international relations frequently used the analogies of appeasement of Hitler in 1938, the Korean War, and the French defeat at Dien Bien Phu to make sense for themselves of the situation they faced during the Vietnam War. These analogies thus served a specific cognitive sense-making function in addition to serving as effective rhetorical devices in intragovernmental and public debates. Shared generational experiences can also affect public opinion, as in the German public's aversion to inflation after the experience of hyperinflation in the 1920s (Hayo 1998), or the German and Japanese aversion to the use of force after World War II (Berger 1996).

In social psychology and American public opinion research, a rich tradition has explored the role that individuals' understanding of the causes of social problems, such as poverty, has on their policy preferences (Sabatier and Hunter 1989; Skitka et al. 2002). Sniderman et al. (1986) find that the effect of racial animus or conservative ideology overwhelmingly predicts beliefs about the causes of poverty - either to internal individual-level or external society-level forces - and not the other way around but that causal beliefs are part of the reasoning chain and help voters to solidify their beliefs. Weiner et al. (2011) argue that how an individual attributes another's poverty will shape their response to the person in need. In a more recent study, Suhay et al. (2020) similarly find that among wealthy Americans dispositional (as opposed to situational) beliefs about the causes of inequality corresponds to opposition to redistributionist policies more than the less wealthy (Jost, Federico, and Napier 2009).

Twelve Kinds of Theories about Social Mechanisms

While social scientists share an interest with psychologists in explaining individual behavior, our research often focuses on the social level of analysis as either the cause or the consequence of individual choices. To categorize theories at this level, we have developed a taxonomy of theories about social mechanisms that is organized along two dimensions. The first dimension draws on structuration theory (Giddens 1984) and social constructivism (Wendt 1992) to capture the four possible kinds of settings and mechanisms through which agents and structures interact: (1) direct agent-to-agent processes, including strategic interaction, direct mobilization, manipulation, coercion, persuasion, principal-agent monitoring and enforcement, emulation, socialization, shaming, honoring, and other mechanisms; (2) structure-to-agent mechanisms through which structures, including norms, material resources, and property rights enable and/or constrain agents; (3) agent-to-structure mechanisms that change, strengthen, or destroy social structures; and (4) structure-to-structure mechanisms that involve emergent properties and unintended changes in norms, material distributions, or institutions, including moral hazard, adverse selection, and demographic change.

The second dimension of this taxonomy embodies a categorization of three kinds of social mechanisms that is common across many fields although it goes by different names. Here, we have labeled these categories as mechanisms involving legitimacy (defined broadly to include norms, ideas, and the identities and social relations of actors), material power (to include distributions of economic, geographic, and military resources), and functional efficiency (including institutional rules and their associated transactions costs). The first of these, legitimacy, is sometimes discussed as involving the "logic of appropriateness," while the latter two, material power and functional efficiency, relate to the "logic of consequences"—of carrots, sticks, inducement, coercion, and transactions costs (March and Olsen 1984).

This tripartite categorization of kinds of mechanisms mirrors many explanatory schema in the social sciences. It draws directly upon James Mahoney's (Mahoney 2000) typology of sociological explanations of institutions, which includes those rooted in material power, efficiency, and legitimacy. Our taxonomy also overlaps with James Coleman's focus on links between micro and macro level processes, with the important difference that our approach includes macro-macro explanations and nonrational choice mechanisms (Coleman 1994).[9]

We have added illustrative examples of theories on mechanisms in each of the boxes in the taxonomy, outlined in Table 8.1, and an example of an empirical application of each.[10]

It is important to note two limitations of the taxonomy. First, it is not exhaustive—there are many more theories about mechanisms that could fit in each of the boxes, and one could argue for different, more numerous, or more finely differentiated rows or columns on kinds of mechanisms. Second, the categories are not as mutually exclusive as they ideally should be in such a taxonomy—some of the examples arguably involve or could fit into more than

Table 8.1 Taxonomy of Theories about Social Mechanisms

	Agent to Agent	Structure to Agent	Agent to Structure	Structure to Structure
Legitimacy	Emulation (DiMaggio and Powell 1983), Socialization (Grusec 2011), Shaming (Hafner-Burton 2008), Framing (Goffman 1974), Persuasion (Checkel 2001), Altercasting (Malici 2006), Exit, Voice, Loyalty (Hoffman 2008)	Culture (Katzenstein 1996), norms as enabler (Risse, Ropp, and Sikkink 1999)andconstraint (Tannenwald 1999)	Norm entrepreneur (Finnemore and Sikkink 1998), routinization/habit (Bourdieu 1977)	Unintended evolution of social norms (Ingiriis and Hoehne 2013)
Material Power	Hegemonic socialization (Ikenberry and Kupchan 1990), principal-agent theory (Miller 2005), manipulation of strategic interaction (Schelling 1960)	Resources as enabler and constraint (Jenkins 1983)	Revolution (Skocpol 1979), Destruction (Scheidel 2017)	Power transition theory (Gilpin 2008)
Functional Efficiency	Emulation (DiMaggio and Powell 1983), diffusion (Elkins and Simmons 2005), individual competition	Evolutionary selection (Currie et al. 2010)	Functional competition (Adam Smith), innovation (Solow 1957), markets, network externalities (Coase 1960), optimal institutional design (Koremenos, Lipson, and Snidal 2001)	Moral hazard (Pauly 1968), adverse selection (Akerlof 1970)

one category. Principal-agent relations, for example, involve agent-to-agent mechanisms but they also interact so intimately with institutional and normative structures that it is challenging theoretically and empirically to sort out the effects of each.

This taxonomy serves five purposes in research and theorizing about social life. First, it provides a checklist that scholars can use to make sure that they are not leaving out important potential explanations of the phenomena they are studying. Second, and related, researchers can develop increasingly comprehensive historical explanations of particular cases drawing on theories from any of the categories in the taxonomy. Third, scholars can drill down deeper into any one of the boxes in the taxonomy, refining or creating theories on the mechanisms in that category, or disaggregating theorized mechanisms into different subtypes. Fourth, researchers can refine the scope conditions of the theories in any of the categories, clarifying the conditions under which they are strongest and weakest and specifying more clearly the populations to which they apply. Finally, scholars can use the taxonomy to develop typological theories about how combinations of mechanisms interact in shaping outcomes for specified cases or populations.

Two particularly important kinds of interactions of mechanisms involve those across units and over time. Interactions across units can involve self-reinforcing dynamics whereby each additional unit's behavior increases the likelihood that other units will follow or emulate, such as races to the bottom (Drezner 2001), races to the top (Vogel 1997), tipping points (Gladwell 2002), information cascades (Lohmann 1994), and increasing returns to scale. Counteracting this can be limiting processes through which each additional unit makes it less likely that other units will imitate or follow. These include diminishing marginal returns and crowding effects.

The explanatory approaches of the columns in the typology also help explain stasis and change in institutions across time. Path dependence is a crucial example of this type of process. Under path dependence, institutions are formed in periods of contingency, often when one political group achieves some sort of dominance over another and then tries to lock in its advantage by designing or reforming an institution that enshrines its political leverage. This could happen either in the international system in the aftermath of wars (Jervis 1985; Ikenberry 2011); through the use of supranational organizations such as the EU during peacetime (Moravcsik 2000); after civil wars, or after realignment elections in domestic politics (Key 1955). While these institutions can lock in power advantages for a period of time, no victory is permanent and over time the institution might drift either from its designers' original intent or from a certain standard of functional efficiency (Hacker, Pierson, and Thelen 2015). In addition, exogenous shocks to the power, legitimacy, or efficiency can create an opening for a competing set of institutions.

CONCLUSION

The disciplinary incentives across the social sciences at times have motivated researchers toward "naming and claiming"—identifying "new" mechanisms and attaching memorable labels to gain attention and citations. Fields and subfields have also at times been consumed by disputes between structural and individual-level explanations, or arguments between rational choice models and their alternatives. These pursuits are not necessarily fruitless— isolating new mechanisms or submechanisms and contesting the different roles of agents versus structures in particular domains can be useful and productive. Our emphasis, however, has been on developing an inclusive if necessarily incomplete overview and taxonomy of the diverse set of theories about mechanisms that form a common explanatory repertoire across the social and policy sciences. Practically speaking, we hope that having a wider view of theories about causal mechanisms can facilitate more typological theorizing, a useful middle way between idiographic historical accounts and unrealistic monocausal explanations.

ACKNOWLEDGMENTS

Thanks to Daniel Little for suggestions on this paper.

NOTES

1. Of course this relationship is more complex in the social sciences than in the physical sciences due to the hermeneutic circle: each individual, and the theories in their head, are part of social realities, and participate in the social construction of those entities. Yet there are still social realities that exist largely separately from the theories of any one individual.

2. While scientists tend to talk in terms of mechanisms operating in scope conditions, scope conditions are also simply other entities and mechanisms that interact with the mechanism of interest, either to enable it, to prevent it from operating, or to change the way in which it operates and/or the nature, magnitude, or timing of the outcome it produces. We tend to foreground the mechanisms of interest in our research, and to background entities and mechanisms whose presence is common, but this speaks to the focus of our attention, not to the underlying causal processes generated by interacting mechanisms.

3. Ray Pawson draws a similar linkage between scientific realism and middle range theory, arguing that "the blueprint for a middle-range hypothesis is captured perfectly by [scientific] realism's basic explanatory strategy of positing how social regularities are constituted by the action of underlying generative mechanisms." Pawson (2000). p. 284.

4. For analysis of some of these examples and many other typological theories in political science, see Collier, LaPorte, and Seawright (2012).

5. For these and many other examples see Cox (1999).

6. For these and other critiques of rational choice theory, see D. P. Green and Shapiro (1994) and Elster (2000). Rational choice theories have also been critiqued for their assumption that individuals seek to optimize outcomes – Herbert Simon has argued, for example, that due to the transactions costs of gathering information, people tend to behave under "bounded rationality," and to "satisfice," or choose an action that is "good enough," rather than to optimize (Simon 1957). Adding information costs to utility functions, however, and acknowledging that the information needed to make a decision with high confidence is typically incomplete, is not inconsistent with individuals behaving rationally.

7. For a review of the history and development of behavioral economics, see Angner and Loewenstein (2012).

8. See Kozhevnikov (2007, pp. 475–477) for a review of these findings.

9. For a critique of Coleman that is aligned with our approach see Daniel Little blog post at https://understandingsociety.blogspot.com/2012/02/causal-pathways-through-colem ans-boat.html.

10. Daniel Little has provided a useful critique of an earlier version of the taxonomy in a blog post at https://undsoc.org/2014/07/06/mechanisms-thinking-in-international-relati ons-theory/. Little's blog cites Mikko Huotari's unpublished revisions on the earlier taxonomy, some of which we have added to the taxonomy here, including manipulation, altercasting, persuasion, authority, routinization of practice, destruction, markets, individual competition, and network externalities. Little himself gives a looser grouping of theories about mechanisms, organized around the subject matter or disciplines within which they emerged, in another blog post at https://understandingsociety.blogspot.com/ 2014/06/a-catalogue-of-social-mechanisms.html. Charles Tilly has written an analogous discussion of cognitive, environmental, and relational mechanisms (Tilly 2001).

REFERENCES

Aarøe, Lene, Michael Bang Petersen, and Kevin Arceneaux. 2017. "The Behavioral Immune System Shapes Political Intuitions: Why and How Individual Differences in Disgust Sensitivity Underlie Opposition to Immigration." *American Political Science Review* 111 (2): 277–294.

Adorno, Theodor, Else Frenkel-Brenswik, Daniel J. Levinson, and R. Nevitt Sanford. 2019. *The Authoritarian Personality*. Verso Books.

Agor, Weston H. 1984. *Intuitive Management: Integrating Left and Right Brain Management Skills*. Englewood Cliffs, N.J.: Prentice-Hall.

Agor, Weston H. 1989. *Intuition in Organizations: Leading and Managing Productively*. Newbury Park, CA: Sage Publications.

Akerlof, George A. 1970. "The Market for 'Lemons': Quality Uncertainty and the Market Mechanism." *The Quarterly Journal of Economics* 84 (3): 488–500.

Alloy, Lauren B., Lyn Y. Abramson, Wayne G. Whitehouse, Michael E. Hogan, Nancy A. Tashman, Dena L. Steinberg, Donna T. Rose, and Patricia Donovan. 1999. "Depressogenic Cognitive Styles: Predictive Validity, Information Processing and Personality Characteristics, and Developmental Origins." *Behaviour Research and Therapy* 37 (6): 503–531.

Alpert, Marc, and Howard Raiffa. 1982. "A Progress Report on the Training of Probability Assessors." In *Judgment under Uncertainty: Heuristics and Biases*, edited by Daniel Kahneman, Paul Slovic, and Amos Tversky, 294–305. Cambridge: Cambridge University Press.

Alwin, Duane F., and Jon A. Krosnick. 1991. "Aging, Cohorts, and the Stability of Sociopolitical Orientations Over the Life Span." *American Journal of Sociology* 97 (1): 169–195.

Angel, Jacqueline L., and Richard A. Stettersten. 2012. "The New Realities of Aging: Social and Economic Contexts." In *New Directions in Social Demography, Social Epidemiology, and the Sociology of Aging*, edited by Linda J. Waite and Thomas J. Plewes. The National Academies Collection: Reports Funded by National Institutes of Health. Washington, DC: National Academies Press. http://www.ncbi.nlm.nih.gov/books/NBK179089/.

Angner, Erik, and George Loewenstein. 2012. "Behavioral Economics." In *Philosophy of Economics*, edited by Uskali Mäki, 13:641–690. Handbook of the Philosophy of Science. Amsterdam: Elsevier.

Archer, Margaret S. 1995. *Realist Social Theory*. Cambridge: Cambridge University Press.

Aronson, Jerrold L., Rom Harré, and Eileen Cornell Way. 1999. "Realism Rescued: How Scientific Progress Is Possible." *The British Journal for the Philosophy of Science* 50 (1): 175–179.

Arrow, Kenneth J. 1950. "A Difficulty in the Concept of Social Welfare." *Journal of Political Economy* 58 (4): 328–346.

Axelrod, Robert, and Douglas Dion. 1988. "The Further Evolution of Cooperation." *Science* 242 (4884): 1385–1390.

Axelrod, Robert, and W. D. Hamilton. 1981. "The Evolution of Cooperation." *Science* 211 (4489): 1390–1396.

Bakker, Bert N. 2017. "Personality Traits, Income, and Economic Ideology." *Political Psychology* 38 (6): 1025–1041.

Bakker, Bert N., Gijs Schumacher, Claire Gothreau, and Kevin Arceneaux. 2020. "Conservatives and Liberals Have Similar Physiological Responses to Threats." *Nature Human Behaviour* 4 (6): 613–621.

Bardeen, Joseph R., and Jesse S. Michel. 2019. "Associations Among Dimensions of Political Ideology and Dark Tetrad Personality Features." *Journal of Social and Political Psychology* 7 (1): 290–309.

Bennett, Andrew. 1999. *Condemned to Repetition? The Rise, Fall, and Reprise of Soviet-Russian Military Interventionism, 1973-1996*. Cambridge, Mass: The MIT Press.

Bennett, Andrew. 2013. "Causal Mechanisms and Typological Theories in the Study of Civil Conflict." In *Transnational Dynamics of Civil War*, edited by Jeffrey T. Checkel, 205–230. Cambridge: Cambridge University Press.

Bennett, Andrew, Joseph Lepgold, and Danny Unger. 1994. "Burden-Sharing in the Persian Gulf War." *International Organization* 48 (1): 39–75.

Berger, Thomas U. 1996. "Norms, Identity, and National Security in Germany and Japan." In *The Culture of National Security*, edited by Peter J. Katzenstein, 317–356. New York: Columbia University Press.

Berlin, Isaiah, and Michael Ignatieff. 2013. *The Hedgehog and the Fox: An Essay on Tolstoy's View of History, Second Edition*, edited by Henry Hardy. 2nd edition. Princeton, NJ: Princeton University Press.

Bhaskar, Roy. 1978. *A Realist Theory of Science*. Atlantic Highlands, NJ: Humanities Press.

Bieri, James. 1955. "Cognitive Complexity-Simplicity and Predictive Behavior." *The Journal of Abnormal and Social Psychology* 51 (2): 263–268.

Bourdieu, Pierre. 1977. *Outline of a Theory of Practice*. Translated by Richard Nice. Cambridge Studies in Social and Cultural Anthropology. Cambridge: Cambridge University Press.

Bunge, Mario. 1963. *The Myth of Simplicity: Problems of Scientific Philosophy*. 1st edition. Englewood Cliffs, NJ: Prentice-Hall.

Campbell, Andrea Louise. 2002. "Self-Interest, Social Security, and the Distinctive Participation Patterns of Senior Citizens." *The American Political Science Review* 96 (3): 565–574.

Campbell, Angus, Philip E. Converse, Warren E. Miller, and Donald E. Stokes. 1960. *The American Voter*. Chicago: University of Chicago Press.

Caputo, Andrea. 2013. "A Literature Review of Cognitive Biases in Negotiation Processes." *International Journal of Conflict Management* 24 (4): 374–398.

Carney, Dana R., John T. Jost, Samuel D. Gosling, and Jeff Potter. 2008. "The Secret Lives of Liberals and Conservatives: Personality Profiles, Interaction Styles, and the Things They Leave Behind." *Political Psychology* 29 (6): 807–840.

Checkel, Jeffrey T. 2001. "Why Comply? Social Learning and European Identity Change." *International Organization* 55 (3): 553–588.

Coase, Ronald H. 1960. "The Problem of Social Cost." *Journal of Law and Economics* 3 (October): 1–44.

Coleman, James. 1994. *Foundations of Social Theory*. Cambridge, Mass: Belknap Press.

Collier, David, Jody LaPorte, and Jason Seawright. 2012. "Putting Typologies to Work: Concept Formation, Measurement, and Analytic Rigor." *Political Research Quarterly* 65 (1): 217–232.

Cornelis, Ilse, Alain Van Hiel, Arne Roets, and Malgorzata Kossowska. 2009. "Age Differences in Conservatism: Evidence on the Mediating Effects of Personality and Cognitive Style." *Journal of Personality* 77 (1): 51–88.

Cox, Gary W. 1999. "The Empirical Content of Rational Choice Theory: A Reply to Green and Shapiro." *Journal of Theoretical Politics* 11 (2): 147–169.

Crawford, Jarret T. 2017. "Are Conservatives More Sensitive to Threat than Liberals? It Depends on How We Define Threat and Conservatism." *Social Cognition* 35 (4): 354–373.

Croskerry, Pat, Geeta Singhal, and Sílvia Mamede. 2013a. "Cognitive Debiasing 1: Origins of Bias and Theory of Debiasing." *BMJ Quality & Safety* 22 Suppl 2 (October): ii58–ii64.

Croskerry, Pat, Geeta Singhal, and Sílvia Mamede. 2013b. "Cognitive Debiasing 2: Impediments to and Strategies for Change." *BMJ Quality & Safety* 22 (Suppl 2): ii65–ii72.

Currie, Thomas E., Simon J. Greenhill, Russell D. Gray, Toshikazu Hasegawa, and Ruth Mace. 2010. "Rise and Fall of Political Complexity in Island South-East Asia and the Pacific." *Nature* 467 (7317): 801–804.

Damasio, Antonio. 1994. *Descartes' Error: Emotion, Reason, and the Human Brain*. Putnam Publishing.

Danigelis, Nicholas L., Melissa Hardy, and Stephen J. Cutler. 2007. "Population Aging, Intracohort Aging, and Sociopolitical Attitudes." *American Sociological Review* 72 (5): 812–830.

Davis, James A. 2004. "Did Growing Up in the 1960s Leave a Permanent Mark on Attitudes and Values?: Evidence from the General Social Survey." *Public Opinion Quarterly* 68 (2): 161–183.

Debove, Stéphane, Nicolas Baumard, and Jean-Baptiste André. 2016. "Models of the Evolution of Fairness in the Ultimatum Game: A Review and Classification." *Evolution and Human Behavior* 37 (3): 245–254.

DiMaggio, Paul J., and Walter W. Powell. 1983. "The Iron Cage Revisited: Institutional Isomorphism and Collective Rationality in Organizational Fields." *American Sociological Review* 48 (2): 147–160.

Dinas, Elias. 2013. "Opening 'Openness to Change': Political Events and the Increased Sensitivity of Young Adults." *Political Research Quarterly* 66 (4): 868–882.

Downs, Anthony. 1957. *An Economic Theory of Democracy*. 1st edition. Boston: Harper and Row.

Downs, Anthony. 1964. "Inside Bureaucracy." RAND Corporation. https://www.rand.org/content/dam/rand/pubs/papers/2008/P2963.pdf.

Drezner, Daniel W. 2001. "Globalization and Policy Convergence." *International Studies Review* 3 (1): 53–78.

Dunn, R., K. Dunn, and G.E. Price. 1989. *Learning Styles Inventory*. Lawrence, KS: Price Systems.

Elkins, Zachary, and Beth Simmons. 2005. "On Waves, Clusters, and Diffusion: A Conceptual Framework." *The ANNALS of the American Academy of Political and Social Science* 598 (1): 33–51.

Elster, Jon. 1994. "The Nature and Scope of Rational-Choice Explanation." In *Readings in the Philosophy of Social Science*, edited by Michael Martin and Lee C. McIntyre, 311–322. Cambridge, MA: MIT Press.

Elster, Jon. 2000. "Rational Choice History: A Case of Excessive Ambition." *The American Political Science Review* 94 (3): 685–695.

Entwistle, Noel, Maureen Hanley, and Dai Hounsell. 1979. "Identifying Distinctive Approaches to Studying." *Higher Education* 8 (4): 365–380.

Esping-Andersen, Gøsta. 1990. *The Three Worlds of Welfare Capitalism*. Princeton, NJ: Princeton University Press.

Eysenck, Hans. 1954. *The Psychology of Politics*. New York: Praeger.

Fearon, James D. 1995. "Rationalist Explanations for War." *International Organization* 49 (3): 379–414.

Fearon, James D., and David D. Laitin. 2003. "Ethnicity, Insurgency, and Civil War." *American Political Science Review* 97 (1): 75–90.

Federico, Christopher M. 2022. "The Personality Basis of Political Preferences." In *Cambridge Handbook of Political Psychology*, edited by Danny Osborne and Chris G. Sibley, 68–88. Cambridge: Cambridge University Press.

Fellner, Gerlinde, and Sebastian Krügel. 2012. "Judgmental Overconfidence: Three Measures, One Bias?" *Journal of Economic Psychology* 33 (1): 142–154.

Finnemore, Martha, and Kathryn Sikkink. 1998. "International Norm Dynamics and Political Change." *International Organization* 52 (4): 887–917.

Fiorina, Morris P. 1981. *Retrospective Voting in American National Elections*. New Haven, CT: Yale University Press.

Forsythe, Robert, Joel L. Horowitz, N. E. Savin, and Martin Sefton. 1994. "Fairness in Simple Bargaining Experiments." *Games and Economic Behavior* 6 (3): 347–369.

Gardner, R. W. 1953. "Cognitive Styles in Categorizing Behavior." *Journal of Personality* 22 (2): 214–233.

George, Alexander L., and Andrew Bennett. 2005. *Case Studies and Theory Development in the Social Sciences*. BCSIA Studies in International Security. Cambridge, MA: MIT Press.

Gerber, Alan, Gregory Huber, Connor Raso, and Shang E. Ha. 2009. "Personality and Political Behavior." SSRN Scholarly Paper ID 1412829. Rochester, NY: Social Science Research Network.

Gerber, Alan S., Gregory A. Huber, David Dohert, Conor M. Dowling, and Shang E. Ha. 2010. "Personality and Political Attitudes: Relationships across Issue Domains and Political Contexts." *The American Political Science Review* 104 (1): 111–133.

Giddens, Anthony. 1984. *The Constitution of Society: Outline of the Theory of Structuration*. Illustrated edition. Cambridge: Polity Press.

Gigerenzer, Gerd, and Wolfgang Gaissmaier. 2011. "Heuristic Decision Making." *Annual Review of Psychology* 62 (1): 451–482.

Gilpin, Robert. 2008. *War and Change in World Politics*. Revised edition. Cambridge: Cambridge University Press.

Gladwell, Malcolm. 2002. *The Tipping Point: How Little Things Can Make a Big Difference*. Boston: Back Bay Books.

Goddard, Stacie E. 2009. *Indivisible Territory and the Politics of Legitimacy: Jerusalem and Northern Ireland*. Cambridge University Press.

Goffman, Erving. 1974. *Frame Analysis: An Essay on the Organization of Experience*. Frame Analysis: An Essay on the Organization of Experience. Cambridge, MA: Harvard University Press.

Goldberg, Lewis R. 1992. "The Development of Markers for the Big-Five Factor Structure." *Psychological Assessment* 4 (1): 26–42.

Goldberg, Lewis R. 1993. "The Structure of Phenotypic Personality Traits." *The American Psychologist* 48 (1): 26–34.

Gonthier, Frederic. 2017. "Baby Boomers Still in the Driver's Seat? How Generational Renewal Shapes the Dynamics of Tolerance for Income Inequality." *International Journal of Sociology* 47 (1): 26–42.

Green, Donald P., and Ian Shapiro. 1994. *Pathologies of Rational Choice Theory: A Critique of Applications in Political Science*. New Haven, CT: Yale University Press.

Green, Leonard, Astrid F. Fry, and Joel Myerson. 1994. "Discounting of Delayed Rewards: A Life-Span Comparison." *Psychological Science* 5 (1): 33–36.

Gregorc, A.F. 1979. "Learning/Teaching Styles: Potent Forces behind Them." *Educational Leadership* 36: 234–237.

Gregorc, A.F. 1982. *Gregorc Style Delineator*. Maynard, MA: Gabriel Systems.

Grusec, Joan E. 2011. "Socialization Processes in the Family: Social and Emotional Development." *Annual Review of Psychology* 62 (1): 243–269.

Guilbault, Rebecca L., Fred B. Bryant, Jennifer Howard Brockway, and Emil J. Posavac. 2004. "A Meta-Analysis of Research on Hindsight Bias." *Basic and Applied Social Psychology* 26 (2–3): 103–117.

Hacker, Jacob S., Paul Pierson, and Kathleen Thelen. 2015. "Drift and Conversion: Hidden Faces of Institutional Change." In *Advances in Comparative-Historical Analysis*, edited by James Mahoney and Kathleen Thelen, 180–208. Strategies for Social Inquiry. Cambridge: Cambridge University Press.

Haeffel, Gerald J., Lyn Y. Abramson, Zachary R. Voelz, Gerald I. Metalsky, Lisa Halberstadt, Benjamin M. Dykman, Patricia Donovan, Michael E. Hogan, Benjamin L. Hankin, and Lauren B. Alloy. 2003. "Cognitive Vulnerability to Depression and Lifetime History of Axis I Psychopathology: A Comparison of Negative Cognitive Styles (CSQ) and Dysfunctional Attitudes (DAS)." *Journal of Cognitive Psychotherapy* 17 (1): 3–22.

Hafner-Burton, Emilie M. 2008. "Sticks and Stones: Naming and Shaming the Human Rights Enforcement Problem." *International Organization* 62 (4): 689–716.

Hall, Elizabeth Dorrance. 2021. "Fundamental Attribution Error." In *The International Encyclopedia of Media Psychology*, 1–5, edited by Jan van den Bulck. Hoboken, NJ: Wiley-Blackwell

Hall, Peter A., and David Soskice, eds. 2001. *Varieties of Capitalism: The Institutional Foundations of Comparative Advantage*. Illustrated edition. Oxford: Oxford University Press.

Hanania, Richard. 2017. "The Personalities of Politicians: A Big Five Survey of American Legislators." *Personality and Individual Differences* 108 (April): 164–167.

Harré, Rom, and E.H. Madden. 1975. *Causal Powers: A Theory of Natural Necessity*. Oxford: B. Blackwell.

Hayo, Bernd. 1998. "Inflation Culture, Central Bank Independence and Price Stability." *European Journal of Political Economy* 14 (2): 241–263.

Hechter, Michael, and Satoshi Kanazawa. 1997. "Sociological Rational Choice Theory." *Annual Review of Sociology* 23 (1): 191–214.

Hempel, Carl G., and Paul Oppenheim. 1948. "Studies in the Logic of Explanation." *Philosophy of Science* 15 (2): 135–175.

Henrich, Joseph, Robert Boyd, Samuel Bowles, Colin Camerer, Ernst Fehr, and, Herbert Gintis (eds). 2004. *Foundations of Human Sociality: Economic Experiments and Ethnographic Evidence from Fifteen Small-Scale Societies*. Oxford University Press.

Hoffman, Frank G. 2008. "Dereliction of Duty Redux?: Post-Iraq American Civil-Military Relations." *Orbis* 52 (2): 217–235.

Hume, David, and Eric Steinberg. 2011. *An Enquiry Concerning Human Understanding*, 2nd Edition. Hackett Publishing Co.

Ikenberry, G. John. 2011. *Liberal Leviathan: The Origins, Crisis, and Transformation of the American World Order*. Princeton University Press. https://www.jstor.org/stable/j.ctt7rjt2.

Ikenberry, G. John, and Charles A. Kupchan. 1990. "Socialization and Hegemonic Power." *International Organization* 44 (03): 283–315.

Ingiriis, Mohamed H., and Markus V. Hoehne. 2013. "The Impact of Civil War and State Collapse on the Roles of Somali Women: A Blessing in Disguise." *Journal of Eastern African Studies* 7 (2): 314–333.

Jenkins, J. Craig. 1983. "Resource Mobilization Theory and the Study of Social Movements." *Annual Review of Sociology* 9 (1): 527–553.

Jervis, Robert. 1978. "Cooperation Under the Security Dilemma." *World Politics* 30 (2): 167–214.

Jervis, Robert. 1985. "From Balance to Concert: A Study of International Security Cooperation." *World Politics* 38 (1): 58–79.

Jervis, Robert, Richard Ned Lebow, and Janice Gross Stein. 1985. *Psychology and Deterrence.* Baltimore, MD: Johns Hopkins University Press.

Jones, Benjamin F., and Bruce A. Weinberg. 2011. "Age Dynamics in Scientific Creativity." *Proceedings of the National Academy of Sciences* 108 (47): 18910–18914.

Jost, John T., Christopher M. Federico, and Jaime L. Napier. 2009. "Political Ideology: Its Structure, Functions, and Elective Affinities." *Annual Review of Psychology* 60 (1): 307–337.

Jost, John T., Jack Glaser, Arie W. Kruglanski, and Frank J. Sulloway. 2003. "Political Conservatism as Motivated Social Cognition." *Psychological Bulletin* 129 (3): 339–375.

Kahneman, Daniel. 2011. *Thinking, Fast and Slow.* 1st edition. New York: Farrar, Straus and Giroux.

Kahneman, Daniel, Paul Slovic, and Amos Tversky, eds. 1982. *Judgment under Uncertainty: Heuristics and Biases.* Cambridge: Cambridge University Press.

Kahneman, Daniel, and Amos Tversky. 1979. "Prospect Theory: An Analysis of Decision under Risk." *Econometrica* 47 (2): 263–291.

Katzenstein, Peter J., ed. 1996. *The Culture of National Security.* New York: Columbia University Press.

Kernberg, Otto F. 1989. "An Ego Psychology Object Relations Theory of the Structure and Treatment of Pathologic Narcissism: An Overview." *Psychiatric Clinics of North America* 12 (3): 723–729.

Key, V. O. 1955. "A Theory of Critical Elections." *The Journal of Politics* 17 (1): 3–18.

Khong, Yuen Foong. 1992. *Analogies at War: Korea, Munich, Dien Bien Phu, and the Vietnam Decisions of 1965.* Princeton, NJ: Princeton University Press.

Koremenos, Barbara, Charles Lipson, and Duncan Snidal. 2001. "The Rational Design of International Institutions." *International Organization* 55 (4): 761–799.

Kozhevnikov, Maria. 2007. "Cognitive Styles in the Context of Modern Psychology: Toward an Integrated Framework of Cognitive Style." *Psychological Bulletin* 133 (3): 464–481.

Laitin, David D. 1993. "The Game Theory of Language Regimes." *International Political Science Review / Revue Internationale de Science Politique* 14 (3): 227–239.

Larrick, Richard P. 2004. "Debiasing." In *Blackwell Handbook of Judgment and Decision Making,* 316–337, edited by Derek Koehler and Nigel Harvey. Malden: Blackwell Publishing.

Lau, Richard R, Mona S Kleinberg, and Tessa M Ditonto. 2018. "Measuring Voter Decision Strategies in Political Behavior and Public Opinion Research." *Public Opinion Quarterly* 82 (S1): 911–936.

Laver, Michael, and Norman Schofield. 1998. *Multiparty Government: The Politics of Coalition in Europe.* Revised edition. Ann Arbor: University of Michigan Press.

Lee, Bandy X. 2017. *The Dangerous Case of Donald Trump.* New York: Thomas Dunne Books.

Leites, Nathan Constantin. 1950. *The Operational Code of the Politburo.* Santa Monica, CA: RAND Corporation.

Löckenhoff, Corinna E. 2011. "Age, Time, and Decision Making: From Processing Speed to Global Time Horizons." *Annals of the New York Academy of Sciences* 1235 (October): 44–56.

Lohmann, Susanne. 1994. "The Dynamics of Informational Cascades: The Monday Demonstrations in Leipzig, East Germany, 1989–91." *World Politics* 47 (1): 42–101.

Machamer, Peter, Lindley Darden, and Carl F. Craver. 2000. "Thinking about Mechanisms." *Philosophy of Science* 67 (1): 1–25.

Mackie, D. M., T. Devos, and E. R. Smith. 2000. "Intergroup Emotions: Explaining Offensive Action Tendencies in an Intergroup Context." *Journal of Personality and Social Psychology* 79 (4): 602–616.

Mahoney, James. 2000. "Path Dependence in Historical Sociology." *Theory and Society* 29 (4): 507–548.

Mahoney, James. 2001. "Beyond Correlational Analysis: Recent Innovations in Theory and Method." *Sociological Forum* 16 (3): 575–593.

Malici, Akan. 2006. "Reagan and Gorbachev: Altercasting at the End of the Cold War." In *Beliefs and Leadership in World Politics: Methods and Applications of Operational Code Analysis*, edited by Mark Schafer and Stephen G. Walker, 127–49. Advances in Foreign Policy Analysis. New York: Palgrave Macmillan.

Malka, Ariel, Christopher J. Soto, Michael Inzlicht, and Yphtach Lelkes. 2014. "Do Needs for Security and Certainty Predict Cultural and Economic Conservatism? A Cross-National Analysis." *Journal of Personality and Social Psychology* 106 (6): 1031–1051.

March, James G., and Johan P. Olsen. 1984. "The New Institutionalism: Organizational Factors in Political Life." *The American Political Science Review* 78 (3): 734–749.

Marcus, G. E. 2000. "Emotions in Politics." *Annual Review of Political Science* 3 (1): 221–250.

Markwica, Robin. 2018. *Emotional Choices: How the Logic of Affect Shapes Coercive Diplomacy.* Oxford University Press.

Mayer, John D. 2007. "Asserting the Definition of Personality." *P: The Online Newsletter for Personality Science* 1: 1–4.

Mayer, Karl Ulrich. 2009. "New Directions in Life Course Research." *Annual Review of Sociology* 35 (1): 413–433.

McClosky, Herbert. 1958. "Conservatism and Personality." *The American Political Science Review* 52 (1): 27–45.

McCrae, Robert R., and Paul T. Costa Jr. 2005. *Personality in Adulthood, Second Edition: A Five-Factor Theory Perspective.* Second edition. New York, NY: The Guilford Press.

Merton, Robert K. 1968. *Social Theory and Social Structure.* New York, NY: Free Press.

Messick, S. 1976. "Personality Consistencies in Cognition and Creativity." In *Individuality in Learning*, edited by S. Messick, 4–23. San Francisco: Jossey-Bass.

Miller, Gary J. 2005. "The Political Evolution of Principal-Agent Models." *Annual Review of Political Science* 8 (1): 203–225.

Mondak, Jeffery J., and Karen D. Halperin. 2008. "A Framework for the Study of Personality and Political Behaviour." *British Journal of Political Science* 38 (2): 335–362.

Mondak, Jeffery J., Matthew V. Hibbing, Damarys Canache, Mitchell A. Seligson, and Mary R. Anderson. 2010. "Personality and Civic Engagement: An Integrative Framework for the Study of Trait Effects on Political Behavior." *American Political Science Review* 104 (1): 85–110.

Moravcsik, Andrew. 2000. "The Origins of Human Rights Regimes: Democratic Delegation in Postwar Europe." *International Organization* 54 (2): 217–252.

Nisbett, Richard E., and Lee Ross. 1980. *Human Inference: Strategies and Shortcomings of Social Judgment.* Y First printing edition. Englewood Cliffs, NJ: Prentice-Hall.

Nosal, C.S. 1990. *Psychologiczne Modele Umysłu [Psychological Models of Mind].* Warsaw, Poland: PWN.

Nowak, Martin A., Karen M. Page, and Karl Sigmund. 2000. "Fairness Versus Reason in the Ultimatum Game." *Science* 289 (5485): 1773–1775.

Olson, Mancur. 1965. *The Logic of Collective Action; Public Goods and the Theory of Groups.* Harvard Economic Studies, v. 124. Cambridge, Mass: Harvard University Press.

Ostrom, Elinor. 1990. *Governing the Commons: The Evolution of Institutions for Collective Action.* 1st edition. Dallas, TX: Cambridge University Press.

Oswald, M.E., and S. Grosjean. 2004. "Confirmation Bias." In *Cognitive Illusions. A Handbook on Fallacies and Biases in Thinking, Judgement and Memory,* edited by R.F. Pohl, 79–96. Hove: Psychology Press.

Oxley, Douglas R., Kevin B. Smith, John R. Alford, Matthew V. Hibbing, Jennifer L. Miller, Mario Scalora, Peter K. Hatemi, and John R. Hibbing. 2008. "Political Attitudes Vary with Physiological Traits." *Science* 321 (5896): 1667–1670.

Oye, Kenneth A. 1985. "Explaining Cooperation under Anarchy: Hypotheses and Strategies." *World Politics* 38 (1): 1–24.

Paivio, Allan. 1971. *Imagery and Verbal Processes.* Holt, Rinehart and Winston.

Pask, G., and B. C. E. Scott. 1972. "Learning Strategies and Individual Competence." *International Journal of Man-Machine Studies* 4 (3): 217–253.

Pask, Gordon. 1972. "A Fresh Look at Cognition and the Individual." *International Journal of Man-Machine Studies* 4 (3): 211–216.

Pauly, Mark V. 1968. "The Economics of Moral Hazard: Comment." *The American Economic Review* 58 (3): 531–537.

Pawson, Ray. 2000. "Middle-Range Realism." *European Journal of Sociology / Archives Européennes de Sociologie / Europäisches Archiv Für Soziologie* 41 (2): 283–325.

Pettigrew, Thomas F. 1958. "The Measurement and Correlates of Category Width as a Cognitive Variable." *Journal of Personality* 26 (4): 532–544.

Posen, Barry R. 1993. "The Security Dilemma and Ethnic Conflict." *Survival* 35 (1): 27–47.

Post, Jerrold M. 1993. "Current Concepts of the Narcissistic Personality: Implications for Political Psychology." *Political Psychology* 14 (1): 99–121.

Read, Daniel, and N. L Read. 2004. "Time Discounting over the Lifespan." *Organizational Behavior and Human Decision Processes* 94 (1): 22–32.

Richardson, Alan. 1977. "Verbalizer-Visualizer: A Cognitive Style Dimension." *Journal of Mental Imagery* 1 (1): 109–125.

Risse, Thomas, Stephen C. Ropp, and Kathryn Sikkink, eds. 1999. *The Power of Human Rights: International Norms and Domestic Change.* Cambridge Studies in International Relations. Cambridge: Cambridge University Press.

Rokeach, Milton. 1960. *The Open and Closed Mind.* Oxford, England: Basic Books.

Romer, Thomas, and Howard Rosenthal. 1978. "Political Resource Allocation, Controlled Agendas, and the Status Quo." *Public Choice* 33 (4): 27–43.

Romer, Thomas, and Howard Rosenthal. 1979. "Bureaucrats Versus Voters: On the Political Economy of Resource Allocation by Direct Democracy." *The Quarterly Journal of Economics* 93 (4): 563–587.

Ross, Michael L. 2004. "What Do We Know about Natural Resources and Civil War?" *Journal of Peace Research* 41 (3): 337–356.

Rotter, Julian B. 1966. "Generalized Expectancies for Internal versus External Control of Reinforcement." *Psychological Monographs: General and Applied* 80 (1): 1–28.

Rydell, Robert J., Diane M. Mackie, Angela T. Maitner, Heather M. Claypool, Melissa J. Ryan, and Eliot R. Smith. 2008. "Arousal, Processing, and Risk Taking: Consequences of Intergroup Anger." *Personality and Social Psychology Bulletin* 34 (8): 1141–1152.

Sabatier, Paul A., and Susan Hunter. 1989. "The Incorporation of Causal Perceptions into Models of Elite Belief Systems." *Western Political Quarterly* 42 (3): 229–261.

Salehyan, Idean. 2009. *Rebels without Borders: Transnational Insurgencies in World Politics.* 1st ed. Cornell University Press. https://www.jstor.org/stable/10.7591/j.ctt7z6bx.

Salmon, Wesley C. 2006. *Four Decades of Scientific Explanation.* 1st edition. Pittsburgh, PA: University of Pittsburgh Press.

Saunders, Elizabeth N. 2011. *Leaders at War: How Presidents Shape Military Interventions.* Cornell Studies in Security Affairs. Ithaca, NY: Cornell University Press.

Scheidel, Walter. 2017. *The Great Leveler: Violence and the History of Inequality from the Stone Age to the Twenty-First Century.* Princeton, NJ: Princeton University Press.

Schelling, Thomas C. 1960. *The Strategy of Conflict.* Cambridge, MA: Harvard University Press.

Schwadel, Philip, and Christopher R. H. Garneau. 2014. "An Age–Period–Cohort Analysis of Political Tolerance in the United States." *The Sociological Quarterly* 55 (2): 421–452.

Shesterinina, Anastasia. 2016. "Collective Threat Framing and Mobilization in Civil War." *American Political Science Review* 110 (3): 411–427.

Simon, Herbert Alexander. 1957. *Models of Man: Social and Rational- Mathematical Essays on Rational Human Behavior in a Social Setting.* 1st edition. Wiley.

Skitka, Linda J., Elizabeth Mullen, Thomas Griffin, Susan Hutchinson, and Brian Chamberlin. 2002. "Dispositions, Scripts, or Motivated Correction? Understanding Ideological Differences in Explanations for Social Problems." *Journal of Personality and Social Psychology* 83 (2): 470–487.

Skocpol, Theda. 1979. *States and Social Revolutions: A Comparative Analysis of France, Russia, and China.* New York: Cambridge University Press.

Slovic, Paul, Melissa Finucane, Ellen Peters, and Donald G MacGregor. 2002. "Rational Actors or Rational Fools: Implications of the Affect Heuristic for Behavioral Economics." *The Journal of Socio-Economics* 31 (4): 329–342.

Smith, Kevin B., Douglas Oxley, Matthew V. Hibbing, John R. Alford, and John R. Hibbing. 2011. "Disgust Sensitivity and the Neurophysiology of Left-Right Political Orientations." *PLOS ONE* 6 (10): e25552.

Sniderman, Paul M., Michael G. Hagen, Philip E. Tetlock, and Henry E. Brady. 1986. "Reasoning Chains: Causal Models of Policy Reasoning in Mass Publics." *British Journal of Political Science* 16 (4): 405–430.

Soll, Jack B., Katherine L. Milkman, and John W. Payne. 2015. "A User's Guide to Debiasing." In *The Wiley Blackwell Handbook of Judgment and Decision Making*, edited by Gideon Keren and George Wu, 924–951. Malden, MA: Wiley-Blackwell. https://papers.ssrn.com/abstract=2455986.

Solow, Robert M. 1957. "Technical Change and the Aggregate Production Function." *The Review of Economics and Statistics* 39 (3): 312–320.

Srivastava, Sanjay, Oliver P. John, Samuel D. Gosling, and Jeff Potter. 2003. "Development of Personality in Early and Middle Adulthood: Set like Plaster or Persistent Change?" *Journal of Personality and Social Psychology* 84 (5): 1041–1053.

Stewart, Emily. 2020. "Americans Want to Cancel Student Loans — but Not All of Them." *Vox.* December 11, 2020. https://www.vox.com/policy-and-politics/2020/12/11/22167555/biden-student-loan-cancellation-poll.

Suhay, Elizabeth, Marko Klašnja, and Gonzalo Rivero. 2020. "Ideology of Affluence: Explanations for Inequality and Economic Policy Preferences among Rich Americans." *The Journal of Politics* 83 (1): 367–380.

Tannenwald, Nina. 1999. "The Nuclear Taboo: The United States and the Normative Basis of Nuclear NonUse." *International Organization* 53 (3): 433–468.

Tetlock, Philip E. 1984. "Cognitive Style and Political Belief Systems in the British House of Commons." *Journal of Personality and Social Psychology* 46 (2): 365–375.

Tetlock, Philip E. 2017. *Expert Political Judgment: How Good Is It? How Can We Know? - New Edition*. Princeton, NJ: Princeton University Press.

Tetlock, Philip E., and Dan Gardner. 2015. *Superforecasting: The Art and Science of Prediction*. Crown.

Thaler, Richard H., and Cass R. Sunstein. 2008. *Nudge: Improving Decisions About Health, Wealth, and Happiness*. New Haven, CT: Yale University Press.

Tilly, Charles. 2001. "Mechanisms in Political Processes." *Annual Review of Political Science* 4 (1): 21–41.

Twenge, Jean M., Nathan T. Carter, and W. Keith Campbell. 2015. "Time Period, Generational, and Age Differences in Tolerance for Controversial Beliefs and Lifestyles in the United States, 1972–2012." *Social Forces* 94 (1): 379–399.

Uhlenhuth, E. H., Vladan Starcevic, Teddy D. Warner, William Matuzas, Teresita McCarty, Brian Roberts, and Steven Jenkusky. 2002. "A General Anxiety-Prone Cognitive Style in Anxiety Disorders." *Journal of Affective Disorders* 70 (3): 241–249.

Vogel, David. 1997. *Trading Up: Consumer and Environmental Regulation in a Global Economy*. Cambridge, MA: Harvard University Press.

Waldner, David. 2012. "Process Tracing and Causal Mechanisms." In *The Oxford Handbook of Philosophy of Social Science*, edited by Harold Kincaid, 65–84. Oxford University Press.

Walker, Stephen G. 1977. "The Interface Between Beliefs and Behavior: Henry Kissinger's Operational Code and the Vietnam War." *Journal of Conflict Resolution* 21 (1): 129–168.

Walter, Barbara F. 1997. "The Critical Barrier to Civil War Settlement." *International Organization* 51 (03): 335–364.

Weiner, Bernard, Danny Osborne, and Udo Rudolph. 2011. "An Attributional Analysis of Reactions to Poverty: The Political Ideology of the Giver and the Perceived Morality of the Receiver." *Personality and Social Psychology Review: An Official Journal of the Society for Personality and Social Psychology, Inc* 15 (2): 199–213.

Wendt, Alexander. 1992. "Anarchy Is What States Make of It: The Social Construction of Power Politics." *International Organization* 46 (2): 391–425.

Whelan, Robert, and Louise A. McHugh. 2009. "Temporal Discounting of Hypothetical Monetary Rewards by Adolescents, Adults, and Older Adults." *The Psychological Record* 59 (2): 247–258.

Wight, Colin. 2006. "Realism, Science and Emancipation." In *Realism, Philosophy and Social Science*, edited by Kathryn Dean, 32. Palgrave-Macmillan.

Wilson, Glenn D. 1973. *The Psychology of Conservatism*. The Psychology of Conservatism. Oxford, England: Academic Press.

Witkin, H. A., H.B. Lewis, M Hertzman, K Machover, P. M. Bretnall, and S. Wapner. 1954. *Personality through Perception: An Experimental and Clinical Study*. 1St Edition. Harper & Brothers.

Ziblatt, Daniel. 2006. *Structuring the State: The Formation of Italy and Germany and the Puzzle of Federalism*. Princeton University Press.

Zomeren, Martijn van, Russell Spears, Agneta H. Fischer, and Colin Wayne Leach. 2004. "Put Your Money Where Your Mouth Is! Explaining Collective Action Tendencies through Group-Based Anger and Group Efficacy." *Journal of Personality and Social Psychology* 87 (5): 649–664.

PART 2

....

METHODS IN POLITICAL SCIENCE, DEBATES, AND RECONCILIATIONS

....

PART 2, *Methods in Political Science, Debates, and Reconciliations*, provides a critical assessment and systematic comparison of political science methods. Deploying philosophical tools, it scrutinizes issues concerning measurement and concept delineation, the alleged 'eternal' dichotomies between quantitative versus qualitative as well as positivist versus interpretivist methodologies, and the challenges faced by mixed methods. It also addresses specific philosophically interesting questions concerning qualitative comparative analysis, process tracing, Large-N Qualitative Analysis, lab experiments as well as randomized controlled trials in political science. The general thrust is that with the explosion of interesting methodological work in political science in recent decades, it is important to carefully analyze the strengths and weaknesses of the respective methods in light of what research questions one is addressing. Philosophy of science is well-equipped to help with this analysis, pointing at unacknowledged assumptions, lacunae, conceptual ambiguities, and so on as part of a more productive analysis of political science methods.

CHAPTER 9

CONCEPTUALIZING AND MEASURING DEMOCRACY

SHARON CRASNOW

1. INTRODUCTION

DEMOCRACY is one of the most extensively studied subjects in political science. Approaches to the topic are normative, empirical, and related to policy. Normative approaches generally fall under political theory, but also serve as a basis for both empirical and policy work. Empirical research on democracy covers a wide variety of topics. Examples include transitions to and reversions from democracy; the relationship between democracy and peace (the Democratic Peace literature); between democracy and economic development; and democracy and human rights. Policy questions address issues such as how to support emerging democracies or shore up those that appear to be in danger of reverting to authoritarianism. Policy debates are informed—to varying degrees—by both theory and empirical research.

Research on democracy has been altered by changes in understanding of what it is to study democracy—how and why it is to be studied. The optimistic framing of the progress of democracy captured in Samuel Huntington's description of the late twentieth century as the Third Wave of democracy (Huntington 1991)—the idea of a steady march to world democratization—has been replaced by a more tempered view in the twenty-first century. Although new democracies continue to emerge, there has also been a "backsliding" from democracy among polities previously thought to be stable democracies and an increasing number have reverted to outright authoritarian rule. The current status internationally might be better described as a "churning" with the net number of democracies stabilized; however, mere counting hides transitions, and troubling reversions. There is an apparent slowing or plateauing of what had at one time seemed to be a worldwide progression toward democratization (Mainwaring and Bizzarro 2019). Of particular concern have been those middle-income democracies that once appeared to be stable, such as Venezuela, Turkey, Philippines, Poland, and Hungary (Kaufman and Haggard 2019).

Analyses of the spread or decline of democracy are sensitive to the complexity and vagueness of the concept, suggesting that democracy can be thought of as coming in degrees or that the various components of democracy are not all equal—some matter more than others and both that and the relationships between them require closer scrutiny.

The contested nature of democracy and the resulting different understandings of what it is may influence both the political structure of nations and how they present themselves to the world. If, for example, democracy is identified solely or predominantly through elections, many states will be classified as democracies that might fail on other criteria, such as liberties. Larry Diamond (2002) has suggested, for example, that one of the reasons for the increase in hybrid or semiautocratic regimes—usually regimes that have some form of election but lacking freedoms—is that it is a result of identifying democracy with elections simpliciter. Nations that want the benefit of support from powerful and wealthy democratic states are motivated to adopt electoral practices that establish them as democracies under this broad characterization.

Research on democracy has also been shaped by current disciplinary trends in methodology. For empirical research in political science, this has meant the dominance of formal and statistical methods familiar to economics. These types of methods make use of quantitative techniques for the analysis of data and consequently give rise to the need for numerical values through which to do research on democracy and its components.

Such pressures give rise to the general question of how to measure democracy—questions about what democracy is and how to assign the values to democracy and its components. Attempts to measure result in indices of democracy—data sets that sort types of polities, rank them on a range between autocracy and democracy, or assign polities values based on the various indicators of democracy. Scholars have produced many such indices. Sometimes an index may be created for a specific research project, although it might have applications for others, or an index may be created specifically as a standalone exploration of democracy, with the hope that it will be widely used.

In this chapter I explore measuring democracy as a case of measurement in the social sciences. It might at first seem that something as abstract as democracy could not be measured, but the sorts of questions raised by transitions to and reversions from democracy, as well as other questions about the relationships among democracy, inequality, the economy, and a variety of other social phenomena are motivations for finding a means to do so.

Measures of social science concepts are contentious for a variety of reasons. The concepts that make their way into theory often make their appearance pretheoretically, that is, based in ordinary language. Measurement project for intelligence and well-being are examples. While democracy has a long theoretical history, its broadest understanding as "rule by the people" is also pretheoretic. As with intelligence and well-being, making the concept precise so that it is amenable to measurement often comes with perils. Such social science concepts frequently carry with them value presuppositions and implications, and decisions made in order to measure them will do so as well.

This chapter explores these concerns, looking closely at one recent approach—the Varieties of Democracy Project (V-Dem).[1] V-Dem is of interest because it directly tackles many issues generated by measurement in a particularly transparent way. Specifically, it considers in detail how to specify the concept to be measured and how to evaluate measures.

I begin with a brief consideration of what requirements need to be fulfilled in order to produce any measure. In this discussion I argue that democracy is a mixed concept—a concept that carries with it value presuppositions and implications (Alexandrova 2017). In Section 3 I describe key elements of V-Dem as an example. Section 4 tackles the question of evaluation and considers what it means to get the measure of democracy right making use of resources from measurement theory and other accounts of measurement in the social sciences. Evaluation is complicated by value aspects of the various different conceptions of democracy. I conclude with some thoughts on how to address the pitfalls and retain the benefits of measuring democracy.

2. MEASUREMENT

In order to organize the discussion, I use the account of measurement developed by Cartwright, Bradburn, and Fuller. They describe measurement as requiring three "steps": identification of the boundaries of concept to be measured (characterization), identification of a metric to which that concept will be matched (representation), and rules or procedures through which the matching is to be done (procedures; Cartwright, Bradburn, and Fuller 2017, 78).[2] For the first, specifying how the concept "democracy" is to be understood proves challenging. Democracies may be similar to each other in some sense—at the most general level democracy is rule by the people—but this sort of vague similarity does not offer either a core property or a common set of properties through which democracy can be identified precisely enough to allow for measurement. Cartwright, Bradburn, and Fuller suggest that such concepts, are "*Ballung*" concepts—cluster concepts or family resemblance-like concepts.[3] Such concepts have no specific core—"different clusterings of features among the congestion (*Ballung*) can matter for different uses" (Cartwright et al. 2017, 81). The boundaries of such a concept need to be delineated—we need to know what we are measuring. The way this is usually put is that the concept needs to be *specified*. But with *Ballung* concepts all possible specifications will inevitably leave out some of the understandings that the umbrella term covers. All measurement of democracy will thus have to be acknowledged as measurement under a particular understanding.

"Democracy" is sometimes referred to as a "latent concept" in contrast to a manifest concept. We do not directly observe democracy—it is abstract and complex—and so judgments about which countries are and are not democratic are made through the identification of attributes that democracies are thought to have, many of which are also abstract and complex. Decisions about which attributes to focus on—how to conceptualize democracy—are a first step toward measurement. But, ultimately, all attributes need to be identified through indicators (observables) that are understood to be related to higher level concepts in some designated way. Choices of which attributes to include (conceptualization), as well as what might count as indicators (operationalization), are both necessary for measurement.

Political scientists Adcock and Collier (2001) describe the process of defining a concept through indicators as the adoption of a "systematized concept." They call the abstract, latent, *Ballung* concept the "background concept." The specification of the systematized concept through indicators makes precise what aspects of the *Ballung* concept are relevant to the research being done and that specification also opens a path to measurement of the specified concept.

Many social science concepts are like democracy in this respect and some of these have also been candidates for measurement. "Well-being" is an example, recently discussed by Anna Alexandrova (Alexandrova 2017). The concept of "well-being" is interesting in other ways as well, some of which it shares with democracy. It incorporates normative presuppositions and consequently it is what Alexandrova calls a "mixed" concept—mixing the moral and the empirical (Alexandrova 2017, 80). Democracy is also a mixed concept, in the sense that it carries political/moral value assumptions and political/moral value implications; this means that different specifications may carry different values.[4]

Nonetheless, democracy differs from a concept like well-being in some ways that may be important. The background concept of well-being refers directly to human experience. Democracy does not and so the value elements are less directly attached to the concept. Both well-being and democracy are thought to be desirable but in different ways. Well-being is a property of individuals whereas democracy is a social property. Nonetheless, the value that is thought to accrue to democracy derives from benefits believed to come to individuals living under democracy—such as well-being.[5] It is partly on these grounds that I argue it is a mixed concept.

But also, ranking regimes as more or less democratic does not merely serve as a descriptive judgment of the features those democracies display since when regimes fall short they are judged negatively. We see this in the current discussion about the erosion of democracy. "Backsliding" is a metaphor with negative connotations of falling away from the summit or the goal. Minimally the notion that some polities are better democracies than others indicates the normative heft of the concept.

Some of the contested nature of democracy as well as its instability is produced by differences in values. For example, in thinking about suffrage as a component of democracy, deciding whether to treat suffrage as minimally inclusive of male adults or all adults is not a value-neutral decision and the empirical results that follow differ depending on which understanding is adopted (Paxton 2000). Given that universal suffrage is a component of democracy in many indices, the understanding of that component can shift the understanding of democracy. The Polity IV index measures democracy on a scale that runs from autocracy to democracy (−10 to +10) and these scores are derived from a variety of components. Suffrage does not appear explicitly as one of those components. The result is that neither the extension of the franchise to formerly enslaved male adults nor its later extension to women shows as an effect on the level of democracy (measured by the Polity IV score) in the United States.

The other two elements involved in measurement—identifying a metric and the rules for how the indicators are mapped onto that metric—further complicate measurement of democracy. Some indices have treated democracy dichotomously whereas others have treated it through a scalar measure—either ordinal or interval. There are still others that combine these approaches. For example, Freedom House has a scalar measure of civil and political liberties but a dichotomous measure of electoral democracy. While a dichotomous index might be all that is needed if one is counting democracies, it can fail to give information that would be relevant for the exploration of some phenomena, such as incremental changes in the level of democracy, backsliding, or investigating the *degree to which* being democratic might contribute to other characteristics of a polity—such as its economy. There are interesting questions about democracy that an ordinal metric could both generate and provide data for which could aid in understanding shifts in regimes.

Nonetheless in the history of the measurement of democracy there has been a debate about the viability of nondichotomous measures, centering around two issues. First, it has been argued that differences in types of democracy make comparisons across polities problematic. Second, there are concerns about assessing the correctness and consistency of such measures. These are concerns about validity and reliability—standards of evaluation for any measurement model.

Validity is judged by how well the measurement model captures the phenomenon—that is whether the measurement and the procedure through which it is carried out yield correct results. For democracy this would mean that the polities that are democratic and how democratic they are have been correctly identified. This would not seem to tell us very much however unless we know ex ante *which* polities are democratic to begin with. Similarly, measurement models that consistently produce correct results can also be considered reliable, but without being clear what counts as a correct result it is not obvious how to make such a judgment. The agreement of measures with each other would seem to fail as a test of reliability without there also being some agreed upon standard to which measures must conform. All measurement projects face this problem of circularity, but the problem is particularly vexing in the case of democracy given that it is abstract, contested, and complex.

Rules for mapping concepts onto metrics include both rules for operationalizing indicators—that is, coding rules—and rules for aggregation of those measures into middle and high-level measures. These include rules for weighting the various components that are constitutive of democracy. Such rules also carry with them normative assumptions and consequently have normative implications. Even if there is agreement about the components of democracy, there can be disagreement about the how to weight various sub-concepts and their indicators (and hence quantitative values) that are aggregated into higher level indices. Such disagreements correspond to different theoretical understandings of the core concept "democracy" indicating that systematizing the concept through the specification of components (and indicators) is only part of what goes into measurement. An example of one such difference in understanding might be about whether the components of democracy should be treated as jointly necessary for democracy or better understood on a family resemblance model. Different answers to this question result in different aggregation formulae. Another issue is which components it is necessary to include or how they might be weighted. For example, some might think that elections are necessary, but specific freedoms are not.

Measurement, metrics, and rules all suggest standardization. But a further complication is that the theoretical understanding of democracy can and has changed in response to the changing character of regimes. Relatively stable competitive authoritarian regimes—hybrid regimes—are a somewhat new phenomenon and they challenge some ways of thinking about democracy as they share some characteristics of democracies (elections, for example) while lacking others. They raise questions about what, if any, features are crucial to democracy. New regime types may call for revisiting the conceptualization of democracy (Levitsky and Way 2010).

An additional challenge for conceptualizing democracy results from the emergence of new democracies in cultural settings that differ from those of the democracies in the global North. Measures of democracy have been developed by scholars who primarily reside in the established democracies of that region. These measures rank democracies such as Sweden and the United States highly and it could be argued that the understanding of democracy in relation to these exemplars produces indices that emphasize characteristics of Western culture and so are biased against democracies in other parts of the world. Given that judgments about the level of democracy can have adverse effects on aid and other policy decisions, such bias can be consequential.

Around 2005 a group of political scientists began to work on a new approach to measuring democracy—the V-Dem project. By 2011 the first data sets were completed and the first iteration appeared. The project is currently ongoing with updates and expansions each year. As of 2019 there were nine versions of V-Dem—with v.9 covering data through 2018 and released in April 2019. V-Dem approaches measuring democracy somewhat differently than other indices have and in what follows, I use V-Dem's approach to shed light on the measurement of democracy.

3. THE V-DEM PROJECT

The V-Dem website provides the following description of the project[6]:

> Varieties of Democracy (V-Dem) is a new approach to conceptualizing and measuring de-
> mocracy. We provide a multidimensional and disaggregated dataset that reflects the com-
> plexity of the concept of democracy as a system of rule that goes beyond the simple presence
> of elections. The V-Dem project distinguishes between five high-level principles of de-
> mocracy: electoral, liberal, participatory, deliberative, and egalitarian, and collects data to
> measure these principles. (https://www.v-dem.net/en/about/)

There are several aspects of this description that are worth highlighting. First, the approach that V-Dem adopts differs from other indices both in terms of how democracy is conceptualized and in how they set out to measure it. As already noted, Polity IV measures on a continuum ranging from autocracy to democracy with scores determined through components that em-phasize the structural features of the state as indicators. Freedom House focuses on political rights and civil liberties and so might be thought of as looking at a component of democracy, although Freedom House also identifies electoral democracies through an index.[7] V-Dem is broader in its conceptualization of democracy identifying five principles corresponding to five conceptions of democracy that they identify through a literature review.

Second, the "complexity of the concept of democracy" is reflected through these prin-ciples. They are: electoral, liberal, participatory, deliberative, and egalitarian.[8] Each prin-ciple is distinguished in terms of "core values" formulated as questions about the extent to which a state has institutions that cohere with the principle and so qualify it as demo-cratic under that principle (Coppedge et al. 2017, 25). The principles can be thought of as properties of democracy (latent concepts) that are correlated with specific indicators (man-ifest concepts). Different theoretical traditions weight some principles as more important for democracy than others. The principles might also be thought of as different types of democracy or different weightings of its component parts. To do so is one way of handling the multiple meanings of the term.[9]

Other indices distinguish types of democracy, most commonly electoral and liberal democracy, but V-Dem differs in identifying a broader range of attributes and allowing for further disaggregation. Since some attributes of democracy may conflict with others, the approach provides a means of identifying and evaluating potential trade-offs, some-thing not so easily achieved through other measures (Coppedge et al. 2017). An example of such a tension is compulsory voting. While compulsory voting increases participation (often treated as a feature of electoral democracy), it limits freedom (liberal democracy). Compulsory voting is treated as a distinct variable (indicator) in V-Dem and coded sepa-rately so that it figures distinctly when aggregated to a higher-level index.

Third, V-Dem emphasizes the "multidimensional" and "disaggregated" nature of its indices, specifically noting that they measure democracy across dimensions other than its electoral dimension. "Dimensions" in this sense are properties that might manifest as different modes of the property and so may vary independently even though all versions reflect the property. For example, freedom may manifest as freedom of expression, freedom of movement, freedom of assembly, and so on. These freedoms are generally highly correlated but they need not be. Suffrage is another example of a dimension. Male and female suffrage can be identified independently and vary independently but suffrage can also be treated more generally, as universal suffrage.

The five principles that V-Dem works with are "properties [of the democracy] with normative connotations"—that is, each principle reflects the core values with which it might be associated and as such represents a different understanding of the core concept "democracy" (Coppedge et al. 2017, 42). Properties are general attributes or "conceptual building blocks" of the core concept "democracy" and so may be thought of as components of democracy.

While representing relationships between indicators, sub-components, and the core concept is a standard way of structuring coding in other indices, V-Dem is notable for both the degree of disaggregation of the various conceptual levels and the transparency with which it presents its interpretation of the relationships among them. Details of the structure are all readily accessible to researchers through the V-Dem website.

The V-Dem Methodology offers the following schema showing these relationships (Coppedge et al. 2019a, 12):

- Core concept (1)
- Democracy Indices (5)
- Democracy Components (5)
- Subcomponents, and related concepts (87)
- Indicators (493)

Democracy is the Core Concept. The five Democracy Indices each reflect properties associated with the five principles (Democracy Components)—five different conceptions of democracy. These components are typically lower-level indices that result from the aggregation of subcomponents that are in turn measured through discrete indicators.

Consider polyarchy (electoral democracy) as an example. Polyarchy is a particular version (systematized concept) of electoral democracy and is the understanding of electoral democracy that V-Dem uses. It is as expressed by the following aggregation formula:[10]

$$v2\_polyarchy = .5(v2x\_elecoff* \ v2xel\_frefair *v2x\_frassoc\_thick *v2x\_suffr * \ v2x\_free\_altinf)$$
$$+ .5(1/8 \ v2x\_elecoff + 1/4 \ v2xel\_frefair + 1/4 \ v2x\_frassoc\_thick + 1/8v2x\_suffr$$
$$+ 1/4 \ v2x\_free\_altinf)$$

Where $v2x\_freexp\_altinf$ = freedom of expression and alternative sources of information index (aggregate of media bias, print/broadcast media critical, print/broadcast media perspectives); $v2x\_frassoc\_thick$ = freedom of association index; $v2x\_suffr$ = share of the population with suffrage index; $v2el\_frefair$ = clean elections (free and fair) index; and $v2x\_elecoff$ = elected officials index.

There are several things worth noting about this aggregation formula. First, it reflects that V-Dem incorporates both the family resemblance conception of democracy (the components are multiplicative) and what they refer to as a classical definition in terms of necessary and sufficient conditions (the components are additive).[11] The formula represents this through "*" for multiplication and "+" the standard sign for addition. By giving half weight (.5) to each, V-Dem intends to indicate that they are equally plausible understandings of how the components contribute to democracy.

Second, polyarchy—a higher level index—is itself made up of components, each of which is constructed from multiple subcomponents. For example, *v2x_freexp_altinf* is an aggregate of:

- Government censorship effort
- Media harassment of journalists
- Media self-censorship
- Media bias
- Print/broadcast media perspectives
- Freedom of discussion for men
- Freedom of discussion for women
- Freedom of academic and cultural

Thus subcomponents may be either indicators or other indices. However, all values ultimately derive from indicator values.

Where do the values (quantities) for the indicators come from? V-Dem is innovative in its use of within-country experts to the extent that it is possible. While both Polity IV and Freedom House also use experts, these experts are not typically within-country.

Version 9 of the V-Dem codebook distinguishes five main types of indicators.[12] Type A variables, described as primarily factual, are coded by Project Managers and Research Assistants who are part of the V-Dem Project. Type B indicators are coded by Country Coordinators or Research Assistants. Type C indicators are those coded by Country Experts. Type D and E are values derived from non-V-Dem indices (Freedom House, for example). I focus on the use of country experts since their role is central to the project.[13]

Type C: Variables coded by Country Experts. A Country Expert is typically a scholar or professional with deep knowledge of a country and of a particular political institution. Furthermore, the expert is usually a citizen or resident of the country. Multiple experts (usually five or more) code each variable (Coppedge et al. 2019b, 27).

The values for the indicators are derived from country expert answers to questionnaires specific to each of the various components and subcomponents of democracy. Most questions are answered on a Likert scale and the value for the variable for the country is derived through aggregating the responses of the experts and using "methods inspired by the psychometric and educational testing literature" (Coppedge et al. 2019a, 31)— Bayesian factor analysis and IRT (Item Response Theory).[14] In this way the measurement model is able to produce a point estimate of the indicator value.

An example is the following question specific to government censorship effort, an indicator for the "freedom of expression" and "alternative sources of information" index, which is itself a subcomponent of the polyarchy index (see the aggregation formula).

Question: Does the government directly or indirectly attempt to censor the print or broadcast media? . . .

Responses:
    0: Attempts to censor are direct and routine.
    1: Attempts to censor are indirect but nevertheless routine.
    2: Attempts to censor are direct but limited to especially sensitive issues.
    3: Attempts to censor are indirect and limited to especially sensitive issues.
    4: The government rarely attempts to censor major media in any way, and when such exceptional attempts are discovered, the responsible officials are usually punished. (Coppedge et al. 2019b, 185)[15]

V-Dem takes polyarchy to be a core component of democracy and thus incorporates the polyarchy index in the aggregation formulae for other higher-level indices (liberal, participatory, deliberative, and egalitarian). This means that in addition to components that are unique to the liberal democracy index—for example, values from the *equality before the law and individual liberty index*—values from the polyarchy index are also part of the aggregation formula. Thus aggregation formulae for the other indices treat elections as a minimal requirement for democracy.[16] Again, V-Dem argues that this is consistent with the understanding of democracy in the theoretical literature: a basic level of democracy must be satisfied before other democratic components contribute to the level of democracy. Different views about whether anything else is needed for democracy, and if so what, reflect different understandings of democracy as captured by the five principles. A judgment about the quality or degree of the democracy presupposes that the baseline (polyarchy) has been met (Coppedge et al. 2017, 7). Additionally, for any of the higher-level indices cut-offs are established below which the polity is not considered to be democratic.

The complete V-Dem data set presents the five high level indices (corresponding to the five principles), other lower level indices from which the higher levels are constructed, and values for all indicators used to construct the indices.[17] Consequently the data set includes both aggregated and disaggregated data. In this way V-Dem provides a variety of resources—different levels of indices for all included countries which can be used in an "off the shelf" manner, as well as the disaggregated indicators from which these indices have been constructed. The disaggregation makes it possible for researchers to create alternative aggregation formulae to construct alternatives to those on offer. Additionally, because of the level of disaggregation, they can use any of the lower level values to explore relationships among the various components of democracy directly. For example, researchers may be interested in the effects of corruption quite apart from its particular role in any conception of democracy. V-Dem provides data on corruption that can be correlated with other outcomes or other components of democracy.

The level of disaggregation, as evidenced by the number of indicators, is unlike any other index. Polity IV codes six variables, the two primary Freedom House indices (Civil Liberties and Political Rights) code fifteen and ten, respectively.

The use of experts for the construction of indices is debated within the discipline. Questions have been raised about their objectivity and about intercoder reliability. Such worries are part of the motivation for a minimalist definition of democracy based solely on objective/factual criteria. Przeworki et al. (2000) proposed such a minimalist conception that understands democracy as the filling of offices through contested elections. "Offices" and "contested" are procedurally defined so as to eliminate subjective interpretation. This results in a dichotomous classification of regimes into democracies and dictatorships (referred to as *DD*). Cheibub, Gandhi, and Vreeland took this dichotomous classification and expanded it offering the following support for the approach: "The coding is clear and stark, so that precise information is conveyed by the coding of each observation, and the coding involves no subjectivity, so it is easily reproducible" (Cheibub, Gandhi, and Vreeland 2010, 71).[18]

There are at least two concerns about subjectivity. The first has to do with reliability—that is, the consistency of the coding. We see this as a concern raised by Cheibub et al. when they appeal to reproducibility. The second concern has to do with cultural biases that might result from who the experts are. As previously noted, the dominance of the global North has been flagged as potentially skewing the understanding of democracy. If experts from the global North are coding, it is possible that their views may fail to recognize as democratic emerging democracies located in other parts of the world.[19]

V-Dem explicitly addresses these two concerns—the first is answered through tests of intercoder reliability and the second through the use of within-country experts as coders.[20] V-Dem recruits a minimum of five experts (when possible) from the countries included in the data set. Information about how they are selected and how the consistency of coding and reliability are checked is spelled out in the V-Dem materials, but questions of subjectivity and bias bring us more generally to the question of evaluation of models of measurement for democracy—validity and reliability.

4. EVALUATION: EXPERTS, VALIDITY, AND RELIABILITY

Measurement models are evaluated in relation to their validity and reliability. Validity is a measure of accuracy. Does the measure correctly represent the phenomenon to be measured? Does it correctly identify those countries that are democratic, the way that they are democratic, or the degree to which they are democratic?

Measurement theory offers a variety of approaches for assessing validity.[21] One approach is to evaluate measurement models in terms of the laws that make use of the measures. If the measurement model gives values that support the laws—that is, the laws function correctly with these measures—that supports the validity of the model. Mathematical laws, such as those found in physics, are best suited to this approach. Social science—or more specifically for democracy, political science—is not a science in which laws figure prominently and so determining whether the measure is correct or accurate by reference to its nomic functionality does not appear to be an option. However, there is a similar way of thinking about how to evaluate measures by whether they are "sufficient for meeting the requirements of a specified application" (Tal 2011, 1085). Eran Tal refers to this as pragmatic measurement accuracy.

Another sense of validity is through direct comparison, such as, at one time, the Standard Meter in Paris. Tal refers to this as operational measurement accuracy. A third approach is comparative measurement accuracy—comparing measures from one model with measures produced by others. Do the different approaches produce the same (or very similar) results? If so, this increases confidence in measurement validity. Finally, another approach is to assess validity through reliability—the consistency of measures among measurers—intercoder reliability—and across contexts. It is this last alternative that V-Dem emphasizes, namely devoting considerable attention to intercoder reliability. Efforts in this regard include both trying to ensure intercoder consistency at the outset—through standardization of procedures and the choice of coders—but also through conducting a variety of reliability checks.

As discussed in the previous section, concerns arise about expert subjectivity and the possibility of bias for indices that rely on experts. V-Dem uses experts, but many other indices use experts as well. Freedom House uses in-house coders and a variety of experts from think tanks, academia, and the human rights community. Scores are discussed in a series of review meetings organized by region that include Freedom House staff and "expert advisers."[22] Polity began with one coder who relied on secondary (historical and journalistic) sources. More recent iterations (Polity IV, with Polity 5 in development) are currently coded using two teams of coders—one at the University of Maryland and one at the University of Colorado (Polity IV Project: Dataset Users' Manual v2018, 6).

V-Dem's 3000 experts respond to questionnaires containing questions that are linked to the indicators. These ultimately result in values for the high-level indices through aggregation formulae. The decision to use country experts addresses some of the concerns about subjectivity. Experts are mostly recruited from the countries in which they reside, with multiple experts coding each country (five per country whenever possible).[23] Choosing within-country experts is motivated in part by the desire to address the issue of potential bias, but also by a general belief that detailed case knowledge of the country will provide the best information about the indicators.

The majority of experts come from academia although some experts are employed by think tanks or are public servants. Experts respond to questions through an online interface. Bayesian factor analysis and IRT, techniques imported from psychometrics and educational testing, are used to calculate the values, as noted in the previous section. Questionnaires are made available in multiple languages in an effort to mitigate misunderstandings that might result from language barriers. Additionally, questions come with clarifications in order to minimize ambiguity. These are some steps taken to address anticipated barriers to reliability at the outset.

Information used to detect bias or unreliable coding comes from several sources. At least some country experts engage in bridge coding—coding the entire time series for their own and another country. Other experts engage in lateral coding—coding a specific attribute or set of attributes at some point in time across countries. Since the 2015/2016 update V-Dem has also used anchoring vignettes. These are imaginary cases for which the same set of questions are asked as for real cases. The vignettes are designed so as to require no specific country expertise and in this way they are intended to check for consistent understandings of key concepts.

Approaches to standards of validity are both theoretical and empirical and this is apparent in the way reliability of measures of democracy are determined. Checks on intercoder understanding of concepts are checks on familiarity with theory given that the five principles associated with the core concept "democracy" are all identified through theory. The construction of idealized anchoring vignettes as a way of judging intercoder reliability illustrates this point.[24] Vignettes do not include features of context but are crafted through theory. The idea is that when country experts complete a questionnaire for a vignette, a better understanding of how they are interpreting the Likert scale in relation to the questions posed to them will emerge and inconsistencies, if they exist, will be revealed. Anchoring vignettes serve this function even in the case of coders who cannot be assessed through bridge or lateral coding because they are not qualified to code cases with which they are unfamiliar.

Coder reliability has also been probed by gathering information about country experts through a postsurvey questionnaire. A number of variables that might affect reliability are considered, among them coder knowledge of relevant concepts. Coders who rate as having less knowledge appear to be less reliable. One indication of "less knowledge" is the way coders rank countries as democratic on a scale of 1 to 100 with higher scores being more democratic. Those who rate nondemocratic countries, such as North Korea, as democratic, or rate clearly democratic countries like Sweden as less than fully democratic are identified as having lower awareness of the concept of democracy. There is some indication that coders that do this are less reliable, although the evidence is inconclusive (Marquardt et al. 2018).

The use of North Korea and Sweden as exemplars of the two extremes in this way seems to treat them as standards, similar to that of the Standard Meter in Paris—Tal's operational accuracy. Intersubjectivity or intercoder reliability is thus constrained both theoretically and empirically—both by shared theory and by experts matching features of their own countries to extant exemplars.

Although measuring democracy is unlike measuring physical phenomena, such as mass or length, it is nonetheless measuring something empirically real. The connection between theory and the empirical is manifest in the political structures and institutions, actions of governments, and the activities of those who operate within such systems—all of which the indicators are intended to reflect. But because of both its theoretical and social (empirical) aspects—how theory is put into practice—the understanding of democracy is also in flux. Theory manifests differently in different contexts. This, in turn, affects how those theorizing democracy describe it and understand it and so, to some extent, democracy theory changes as democracies change.

Theoretical constraints on the concept of democracy are normative as well as descriptive—in part because it is a mixed concept (as characterized in Section 2). There may be many ways to enact democratic values, but some enactments ultimately stray too far from those values. At what point this happens is debated since democracy is contested, complex, and the boundaries of the correct application of the concept may shift. One notable difference is over the question of the extent to which freedoms (liberties and rights) must figure in democracy. As we have seen, minimalists have argued for elections (contested, free and fair elections) as all that is required for democracy. A counterargument is that without at least some freedoms (such as freedom of speech, assembly, and association) contested, free and fair elections are not possible. V-Dem comports with other indices (Polity IV for example) that show a divergence in values between electoral democracy and liberal democracy. The difference in values supports the idea that freedoms matter. Democracy may be malleable and plural—changing over time and in response to new regime types—but it is not infinitely malleable.

We can think this through with an example. Surveys indicate many Chinese perceive their form of government as democratic and additionally do not take elections to be a key element of democracy.[25] The understanding of democracy underlying these views is that a regime is democratic if it governs in way that is consistent with the well-being of the people (Lu and Shi 2015; Zhang and Meng 2018).[26] Lu and Shi argue that this understanding of democracy is the result of a deliberate policy of the Chinese Communist Party (CCP) in which Confucian and Leninist ideas already prevalent in the culture were used to inform an understanding of democracy that supports the current regime. In their view, the regime promotes a false conception of democracy for its own ends. Zhang and Meng have a similar take based on their survey of Chinese elites, but when interpreting their findings, they characterize the understanding they attribute to the Chinese as an alternative conception of democracy rather than a false one.

China ranks near the bottom on all five V-Dem indices of democracy (2019 V-Dem Annual Democracy Report), as it does on Polity IV and Freedom House indices as well. This ranking supports Lu and Shi's claim that this is a false view of democracy rather Zhang and Meng's attribution of an alternative interpretation is consistent with V-Dem's understanding. But it could be argued that this analysis also raises the question of cultural bias.

Marquardt et al. 2018 consider the question of the extent to which coders thought elections were important for democracy in their post survey.[27] They take this to be an indication of how well a coder understands the concept of democracy. This understanding would seem to back up Lu and Shi interpretation. An alternative that does not include elections is not accommodated by V-Dem's indices since they all include polyarchy. How should we think about the relationship between these measures and this different understanding of democracy?[28]

If democracy is understood as a mixed concept, the incorporation of particular cultural values should be expected. If these values are indeed cultural rather than universal, either cultural bias appears to be ineliminable or the concept of democracy is likely to be a concept defying measurement since its meaning cannot be stabilized.

The theoretical resources that describe and prescribe democracy are those of the Global North and indeed, the country experts who are academics are most likely to have been trained in that tradition. Consequently, it is not clear that worries about cultural domination in democracy studies could ever be fully addressed or even what it would be like to do so as long as the framework for discussion remains that of the Global North. It is not simply a matter of *who* is doing the coding or *where* they are from but what the norms for conceptualizing democracy within the profession are. The fundamental debate is not about what is the correct definition of democracy, but whether democracy as understood by the Global North is informed by values worth pursuing.

5. PRAGMATIC VALIDATION OF MEASURES

There is another way of thinking about how measures of democracy are constrained empirically—one that falls in line with pragmatic measurement accuracy.[29] If a measure of democracy is used to identify empirical regularities, such as, the robust empirical generalization that democracies do not go to war with each other (the Democratic Peace) or the correlation between economic development and democracy then this is a reason to think that the measure is sufficiently correct. The usefulness of the measure in providing evidence for such robust generalization is evidence of the measure's accuracy.

Some recent research on backsliding illustrates how this pragmatic validation might work. Consider the idea that there have been three waves of democracy and the related perception that the progress seen in the third wave is leveling out starting around 2000. Closer scrutiny of this "leveling out" indicates that it is the result of a combination of new democracies emerging while during the same period there has been backsliding in states previously thought to be stable democracies (Mainwaring and Bizzarro 2019). This idea has challenged the assumption of progress—an assumption also challenged by the emergence of stable autocracies (e.g., China) and hybrid regimes (e.g., Russia). Understanding phenomena such as backsliding, stable authoritarianism, and hybrid regimes could be aided through disaggregated measures such as V-Dem.

Haggard and Kaufman are engaged in a project that seeks to identify patterns (mechanisms) through which democracy is eroded. Through comparing middle-income countries (Hungary, Turkey, and Venezuela) that have experienced backsliding, they suggest a pattern beginning with social polarization and political strain, followed by changes in the constitutional balance of power, weakening horizontal checks on executive power, and eroding of political rights and civil liberties (Kaufman and Haggard 2019; Haggard and Kaufman 2021). The disaggregated approach of V-Dem is well-suited to investigating such patterns since the disaggregation allows for exploring relationships among various components of democracy that are identified as part of the hypothesized pattern. If the use of V-Dem facilitates a successful understanding of such patterns this in turn supports the validity of the measures used.

6. CONCLUSIONS

The measurement of democracy is itself a project that contributes to knowledge production. V-Dem's identification of 493 indicators of democracy brings a richer understanding of what is involved in the core concept. However, the proliferation of indicators also raises questions about how we should think of democracy and can even result in new problems. To what extent is each of these indicators independent of the others? To what extent are they redundant? Although not all indicators figure directly in the measuring of democracy, many do, and one cannot help but think that there is at least some redundancy and in which case the disaggregation is excessive.

There is another related worry stemming from understanding the concept of democracy as a mixed concept. Both the way in which democracy is conceptualized and the way the components are aggregated incorporate values and have value implications. The different conceptions of democracy associated with V-Dem's five principles (and similar differences captured in Polity IV and Freedom House indices) carry with them different moral/political values. The understanding of democracy as liberal democracy emphasizes freedoms in a way that understanding democracy as electoral democracy does not. Choices about which index to use in research reflect those political values. If democracy is a mixed concept, then it is not the inclusion of value assumptions that is the problem, since they are ineliminable, but the failure to be explicit about them may be problematic. If the value-laden components, subcomponent, indices, aggregation formulae, and measurement models are invisible or unexamined then, what Alexandrova refers to as the *imposition* of or *inattention* to values can occur (Alexandrova 2017). Values are imposed when the values incorporated into measures result in the judgments that affect people's lives without their input or explicit consideration and public deliberation about those values. Concerns about aid to nations based on how they are perceived to be democratic or how democratic they are perceived to be might fall under this heading. For the latter, we might, for example, give aid to a county because it is an electoral democracy if we were to use a minimalist understanding even though those elections might occur under circumstances where freedoms were severely curtailed.

Another worry is that when there is inattention on the part of researchers to the value component of a measure the effect of those values on the research may be invisible to them. Given that objectivity is so often associated with the use of numbers and that measures are often devised in aid of quantitative research, the likelihood of such inattention is high.

Alexandrova offers three rules as a way of mitigating imposition and inattention: (1) unearth the value presuppositions in constructs and measures; (2) check the value presupposition for controversy; and (3) consult the relevant parties (Alexandrova 2017, 99–104). All of these contribute to a transparency about the role of values. The normative literature in democracy is implicated in democracy measurement projects very clearly—democracy is a touchstone. But discussion and explicit identification of values are not always present in the presentation of indices. V-Dem comes closer than other indices—many of the deliberations around these issues appear in the V-Dem materials available on their website. But how the information that V-Dem makes available is used is up to researchers. The inclination may well be to take the data at face value and use the various indices as "off the shelf" ready-made resources. Researchers can easily avoid considering the role of values along the lines that Alexandrova's rules prescribe.

The "disappearance" or invisibility of assumptions in coding is a problem inherent in the measurement of many abstract social science concepts. The need to code such concepts is driven, at least in part, by the belief that the best tools for understanding the social world are quantitative tools. Such tools require a numerical representation of the phenomena and measurement projects aim to fill that need. This chapter outlines what goes into the process and in doing so suggests moments in the process that raise questions about the enterprise. There are epistemic gains to be made and research programs that make use of such measures have been under way for some time. This chapter has argued that one of the most promising approaches is the V-Dem project, in part because the project operates with a greater awareness of potential pitfalls and provides tool to answer at least some of the concerns measurement of democracy raises.

In addition to providing measures through which research on democracy can be conducted, these measurement projects also illustrate that seeking measures can contribute to knowledge production in a variety of other ways. Measurement projects can force the examination of concepts and when those concepts are mixed, as democracy is, it may, and should, inspire deliberation about the values those concepts carry with them.

NOTES

1. All discussion of V-Dem in this chapter is based on the 2019 version of V-Dem, version 9. On March 2022, version 12 of the V-Dem dataset was published online and the V-Dem project website has also been updated. However, the general analysis of this chapter remains relevant.

2. The account was presented in 2010 at The Workshop on Advancing Social Science Theory: The Importance of Common Metrics and is summarized in *National Research Council* 2011. The ideas are summarized in Cartwright and Runhardt 2014 and developed in Cartwright, Bradburn, and Fuller (2017). I rely primarily on the last of these.

3. The term *Ballung* is borrowed from Otto Neurath.

4. "Values" is used in two different senses throughout this chapter. The first sense is the quantitative value of the measures. Indicators are coded and so assigned values, when those values are aggregated to produce a measure of democracy, there is a resultant quantitative value that is the measure of democracy. The second sense is moral, political, social, or cultural values. When I first introduce this use I indicate it with these modifiers. Subsequently, I rely on context to disambiguate.

5. The normative component of democracy might be thought to also be justified through seemingly robust evidence that when asked people say that they would prefer to live in a democratic state. However, recent research suggests that interpreting responses in this way is not wholly reliable. Apparently people do not share a common conception of democracy (Ulbricht 2018).

6. The discussion of the project in this chapter is based primarily on version 9 of the project (2019). Version 10 was released in March of 2020. While there are changes in some of the indicators (additions and subtractions), coding of more countries, and some modifications to the measurement model, they do not affect the discussion of V-Dem in this chapter.

7. Interestingly the title of Freedom House's 2019 report is *Democracy in Retreat* (https://freedomhouse.org/report/freedom-world/freedom-world-2019/democracy-in-retreat).

8. Earlier versions of V-Dem also identified majoritarian and consensual principles of democracy. "Two principles—majoritarian and consensual—have proven impossible for us to operationalize and measure fully in a coherent and defensible way" (Coppedge et al. 2019a, 6).

9. Thus, we could distinguish electoral democracy, liberal democracy, participatory democracy, deliberative democracy, and egalitarian democracy. Alternatively, these could be thought of as aspects of democracy rather than distinct types.

10. This understanding of polyarchy is due to Robert Dahl (1971, 1989) and an understanding of electoral democracy widely accepted in the discipline.

11. * is used to indicate multiplication; the prefix *v2x_* indicates that this is a value in the V-Dem data set (either an indicator or a lower level index).The multiplicative half of the formula provides a way of representing the presence a non-zero value for any of the components (any member of the family) contributes to the overall value for electoral democracy. The additive half of the formula weights the components (1/4 or 1/8) but requires that they all be present for polyarchy (necessary and sufficient conditions). V-Dem methodology (Coppedge et al. 2019a, 8) gives very little justification for weighting each of these approaches as half the value, other than they see no reason to prefer one over the other. However, they do note that because there is so much overlap among the components (they frequently occur with each other) there is very little difference in the values derived through this formula and either a strictly multiplicative or additive formulae.

12. While these main groupings are the same as in previous versions, version 9 also gives more information about who is coding within these main groupings. For example, "(A*) **factual indicators** pre-coded by members of the V-Dem team and provided in

the surveys for Country Coordinators and Country Experts to indicate their confidence regarding the pre-coded data. **(A) factual indicators** coded by members of the V-Dem team" (Coppedge et al. 2019a, 16). These finer distinctions would seem to indicate an awareness that it matters who codes. Indeed, the reasons for seeking within country coders also reflects that awareness.

13. This is consistent with V-Dem's treatment of measurement. "Having discussed the process of data collection, we proceed to the task of measurement. Under this rubric, we include (a) the questionnaire, (b) our measurement model, (c) methods of identifying error in measurement, (d) studies of measurement error, and (e) methods of correcting error. In principle, the discussions are relevant for different types of data (A, B, and C in the V-Dem scheme) but most if not all of them are much more acute when it comes to expert-based coding of evaluative, non-factual yet critical indicators. Hence, most of the following focuses on the C-type indicators" (Coppedge et al. 2019a, 29).

14. Bayesian factor analysis and IRT provide a means of identifying outlier responses and producing a single value for an indicator from the expert responses.

15. All questions include clarification. For this question: "*Clarification:* Indirect forms of censorship might include politically motivated awarding of broadcast frequencies, withdrawal of financial support, influence over printing facilities and distribution networks, selected distribution of advertising, onerous registration requirements, prohibitive tariffs, and bribery. We are not concerned with censorship of non-political topics such as child pornography, statements offensive to a particular religion, or defamatory speech unless this sort of censorship is used as a pretext for censoring political speech." (Coppedge et al. 2019b, 185).

16. That is, it is a necessary condition for democracy. This is somewhat puzzling since it seems at odds with their general commitment to the idea that there is no reason to prefer an understanding of the core concept that takes democracy to have necessary conditions over an account that understands it as a family resemblance concept.

17. Other indices that have been constructed by using V-Dem lower level indices and indicators—for example, the women political empowerment index which is formed through an aggregation formula using the women's civil liberties index, women's civil society participation index, and women's political participation index.

18. While I will not address the issue here, it is worth noting that there is a debate in measurement theory about whether classification counts as measurement (see Tal 2017 for a discussion of this issue).

19. Freedom House mentions this concern noting that the conceptions of liberty that they use are internationally agreed upon and consistent with the Universal Declaration of Human Rights (https://freedomhouse.org/report/freedom-world-2012/methodology).

20. Polity IV's current manual now states that they do run some intercoder reliability checks.

21. See Seawright and Collier 2014 for a discussion of validity specific to political science. The approaches they describe overlap with those discussed in Tal 2011 and 2017. I have used Tal's terminology.

22. Freedom House website (https://freedomhouse.org/report/methodology-freedom-world-2018).

23. Countries for which five experts were not recruited are flagged and V-Dem recommends that point estimates not be used for these countries as they have been shown to be unreliable.

24. "Anchoring vignettes are descriptions of hypothetical cases that provide all the necessary information to answer a given question. Since there is no contextual information in the vignettes, they provide a great deal of information about how individual experts understand the scale itself" (Luhrmann et al. 2018, 10).

25. "When asked to evaluate the nature of the CCP regime, only 1.3% of the respondents believed that China was not a democracy; 18.2% thought China was a full democracy; and 59.7% regarded China as a democracy with minor or major problems" (Lu and Shi 2015, 30).

26. "We find that many Chinese officials understand democracy according to the Confucian tradition of *minben* and the CCP's political heritage of mass line, that officials should listen to the people and make benevolent policies for them" (Zhang and Meng 2018, 656).

27. "The indicator Low awareness represents experts who reported in a post-survey questionnaire that they do not consider electoral democracy important to the concept of democracy. Since electoral democracy underpins most definitions of democracy, experts who are not aware of this connection may be less reliable" (Marquardt et al. 2018, 5).

28. Cut-offs or thresholds for scores on components of democracy might be a way of addressing this problem, but the cut-offs would still need to be justified and so do so requires an argument.

29. I adapt Tal's notion of a pragmatic measure of accuracy here.

References

Adcock, Robert and David Collier. 2001. "Measurement Validity: A Shared Standard for Qualitative and Quantitative Research," *American Political Science Review* 95(3): 529–546.

Alexandrova, Anna. 2017. *A Philosophy for the Science of Well-Being.* Oxford: Oxford University Press.

Bradburn, Norman, Nancy Cartwright, and Jonathan Fuller. 2017. "A Theory of Measurement," in McClimans, L. (ed.), *Measurement in Medicine: Philosophical Essays on Assessment and Evaluation*, 73–88. London: Rowman & Littlefield International, Ltd.

Cartwright, Nancy and Rosa Runhardt. 2014. "Measurement," *Philosophy of Social Science: A New Introduction*, 265–287. Oxford: Oxford University Press.

Cheibub, J.A., Gandhi, J., Vreeland, J. R. 2010. "Democracy and Dictatorship Revisited," *Public Choice* 143: 67–101.

Coppedge, Michael, John Gerring, Staffan I. Lindberg, Svend-Erik Skaaning, and Jan Teorell. 2017. "V-Dem Comparisons and Contrasts with Other Measurement Projects," *Varieties of Democracy (V-Dem) Project.* https://www.v-dem.net/media/publications/v-dem_working_paper_2017_45.pdf

Coppedge, Michael, John Gerring, Carl Henrik Knutsen, Staffan I. Lindberg, Jan Teorell, Kyle L. Marquardt, Juraj Medzihorsky, Daniel Pemstein, Josefine Pernes, Johannes von Römer, Natalia Stepanova, Eitan Tzelgov, Yi-ting Wang, and Steven Wilson. 2019a. "V-Dem Methodology v9." *Varieties of Democracy (V-Dem) Project.* https://www.v-dem.net/media/filer_public/2b/e8/2be80341-348e-453e-b766-e74f314155d2/v-dem_methodology_v9.pdf.

Coppedge, Michael, John Gerring, Carl Henrik Knutsen, Staffan I. Lindberg, Jan Teorell, David Altman, Michael Bernhard, M. Steven Fish, Adam Glynn, Allen Hicken, Anna Lührmann, Kyle L. Marquardt, Kelly McMann, Pamela Paxton, Daniel Pemstein, Brigitte Seim, Rachel Sigman, Svend-Erik Skaaning, Jeffrey Staton, Agnes Cornell, Lisa Gastaldi, Haakon Gjerløw, Valeriya Mechkova, Johannes von Römer, Aksel Sundtröm, Eitan Tzelgov, Luca Uberti,

Yi-ting Wang, Tore Wig, and Daniel Ziblatt. 2019b. "V-Dem Codebook v9" *Varieties of Democracy (V-Dem) Project*. https://papers.ssrn.com/sol3/papers.cfm?abstract_id=3441060

Dahl, Robert. 1971. *Polyarchy: Participation and Opposition*. New Haven, CT: Yale University Press.

Diamond, Larry. 2002. "Thinking about Hybrid Regimes," *Journal of Democracy* 13(2), 21–35.

Freedom House, Methodology. 2012. https://freedomhouse.org/report/freedom-world-2012/methodology.

Haggard, Stephan and Robert R. Kaufman. 2021. *Backsliding: Democratic Regress in the Contemporary World*. Cambridge: Cambridge University Press.

Huntington, Samuel. 1991. *The Third Wave: Democratization in the Late Twentieth Century*. Oklahoma City: University of Oklahoma Press.

Kaufman, Robert and Stephan Haggard. 2019. "Democratic Decline in the United States: What Can We Learn from Middle-Income Backsliding?" *Perspectives in Politics* 17(2): 417 – 432. https://doi.org/10.1017/S1537592718003377.

Levitsky, Steven and Lucan A. Way. 2010. *Competitive Authoritarianism: Hybrid Regimes after the Cold War*. New York: Cambridge University Press.

Lu, J., Shi, T. 2015. "The Battle of Ideas and Discourses Before Democratic Transition: Different Democratic Conceptions in Authoritarian China," *International Political Science Review* 36(1): 20–41.

Luhrmann, Ann, Sirianne Dahlum, Staffan I. Lindberg, Laura Maxwell, Valerie Mechkova, Moa Olin, Shreeya Pillai, Constanza Sanhueza Petrarca, Rachel Sigman, Natalia Stepanova. 2018. *Democracy for All? V-Dem Annual Report 2018*. University of Gothenburg.

Mainwaring, Scott and Fernando Bizzarro. 2019. "The Fates of Third Wave Democracies," *Journal of Democracy* 30(1): 99–113.

Marquardt, K. L., Pemstein, D. Seim, B., Wang, Y. 2018. "What Makes Experts Reliable?" Working Paper Series 2018.68, Gothenburg: Varieties of Democracy Institute.

Paxton, P. 2000. "Women's Suffrage and the Measurement of Democracy: Problems of Operationalization," *Studies in Comparative International Development* 43, 92–111.

Polity IV Project: Dataset Users' Manual v2018. 2019. http://www.systemicpeace.org/inscr/p4manualv2018.pdf.

Przeworski, A., Alvarez, M. E., Cheibub, J. A., Limongi, F. 2000. *Democracy and Development: Political Institutions and Well-being in the World, 1950–1990*. Cambridge: Cambridge University Press.

Seawright, Jason and David Collier. 2014. "Rival Strategies of Validation: Tools for Evaluating Measures of Democracy," *Comparative Political Studies* 47(1): 111–138.

Tal, Eran. 2011. "How Accurate is the Standard Second?" *Philosophy of Science* 78: 1082–1096.

Ulbricht, Tom. 2018. "Perceptions and Conceptions of Democracy: Applying Thick Concepts of Democracy to Reassess Desires for Democracy," *Comparative Political Studies* 51(11): 1387–1440.

V-Dem. Varieties of Democracy. https://www.v-dem.net/.

Zhang, K., Meng, T. 2018. "Political Elites in Deliberative Democracy: Beliefs and Behaviors of Chinese Officials," *Japanese Journal of Political Science* 19(4): 643–662.

CHAPTER 10

....

QUALITATIVE RESEARCH IN POLITICAL SCIENCE

....

JULIE ZAHLE

1. INTRODUCTION

....

IN political science, qualitative research has been on the rise roughly since the mid-1990s (Bennett and Elman 2006:455). This means that even though quantitative research is still the dominant approach and has been so from around the early 1960s, qualitative research has at least come to occupy a more central role in political science (see, e.g., Vromen 2018:237ff; Johnson et al. 2008:49ff).

In this paper, I provide a twofold characterization of the current state of qualitative research in political science. Further, I briefly consider how political science and other social sciences compare in terms of qualitative research. The first part of the characterization is a presentation of three prominent methods, namely qualitative comparative analysis (QCA), process tracing, and the ethnographic method. In political science, research involving these methods is widely regarded as exemplary instances of qualitative research. In Sections 2–4, I discuss the methods in turn while focusing in particular on how they work in practice. The second part of the characterization is an examination of what is taken, in political science, to be distinctive of qualitative research in general. As there are diverse conceptions to this effect, I outline four influential ones. Moreover, I show that the conceptions do not agree on the classification of QCA, process tracing and the ethnographic method as forms of qualitative research. In this fashion, the discussion brings out that though the use of the methods is commonly taken to instantiate qualitative research, there is no consensus on this matter in political science. Lastly, I put this twofold characterization into perspective in Section 6. Here, I briefly discuss how the state of qualitative research in political science compares to that in other social sciences. I wrap up in Section 7.

Before embarking on this task, one comment is in order. Many discussions of qualitative research in political science take as their starting point or consider Gary King, Robert O. Keohane, and Sidney Verba's *Designing Social Inquiry: Scientific Inference in Qualitative Research* from 1994 (see, e.g., Mahoney 2010; Koivu and Damman 2015). In the book, King, Keohane and Verba maintain that qualitative research should be improved by bringing it more in line with the tenets of quantitative research. The book became highly influential and sparked an intense debate (see, e.g., Brady and Collier 2004, 2010). Due to lack of space, and since the approach has already been extensively discussed, I do not consider it in the following.

2. QUALITATIVE COMPARATIVE ANALYSIS

QCA is a method of data analysis that involves the comparison of data about a (typically limited) number of cases with the aim of identifying causal relations. Charles Ragin is the originator of the method, which he laid out in *The Comparative Method: Moving beyond Qualitative and Quantitative Strategies* from 1987 (Ragin 2014[1987]). Today, the method is often called crisp-set qualitative comparative analysis (csQCA) in order to distinguish it from later versions of the method such as fuzzy-set QCA (see Ragin 2000) and multivalue QCA (see, e.g., Cronqvist and Berg-Schlosser 2009). In the following, I focus exclusively on crisp-set QCA and so I simply refer to it as QCA. Until recently at least, it has been the most widely used version of QCA (Marx et al. 2014:126, Ryan 2018:283).

In *The Comparative Method*, Ragin states that QCA bridges, and goes beyond, the divide between qualitative and quantitative research (Ragin 2014[1987]: xix). In political science discussions, however, QCA is widely described as a qualitative approach: to use the method is to conduct qualitative research (see, e.g., Bennett and Elman 2006:455; Mahoney 2010:133; Koivu and Damman 2015; Blatter et al. 2016). For now, I set aside the status of QCA as a form of qualitative research; I examine this issue at length in Section 5. Instead, I focus on presenting the method, its basic assumptions, and some criticisms of it.

QCA is a method for the identification of causal relations so a good place to start is by explicating its conception of causation. To this end, it is instructive to consider John Mackie's notion of an INUS condition. According to it, a cause is an INUS condition, that is, "an *insufficient* but *necessary* part of a condition which is itself *unnecessary* but *sufficient* for the result" (Mackie 1993:34). Or, to put these points in slightly more colloquial terms, a cause does not, on its own, bring about some effect; it is only when it teams up with other causes, that an effect is produced. Moreover, a cause is a nonredundant part of such a combination of causes: without it, the rest of the combination fails to produce the effect. Finally, the combination, which a given cause is part of, is not alone in being able to bring about some effect: other combinations of causes may do so too.

Mackie's formulation succinctly captures the view of causation that informs QCA (see, e.g., Mahoney and Goertz 2006:232, Thiem 2017:422). Its proponents maintain that the successful application of QCA results in the identification of causal relations in the sense of representations of how different combinations of causes, with all the features listed by Mackie, bring about some effect or outcome. In particular, they often highlight that QCA is able to accommodate two of the features stated by Mackie. One is that a cause combines with other causes to produce an effect: causation is conjunctural. The other is that multiple different combinations of causes may produce a given type of outcome, that is, causation is equifinal. QCA-proponents put these two points together by saying that QCA is compatible with multiple conjunctural causation (see, e.g., Berg-Schlosser et al. 2009:8).

This clarified, how does QCA purport to identify causal relations? What should a researcher who employs the method do? One prominent answer is outlined in a widely used textbook edited by Benoît Rihoux and Ragin (2009).[1]

In preparation of the application of QCA, a researcher defines the outcome she is going to explain (the outcome variable) and selects a (typically small or intermediate) number of relevantly similar cases, some in which the outcome occurred and some in which it didn't occur (Berg-Schlosser and De Meur 2009). Further, she settles on the conditions (explanatory variables) to look into, that is, the likely causes of the outcome to examine. Lastly, she generates data about each of the cases using various data generating methods like the collection and reading of documents, interviewing, surveys, and participant observation.

The researcher is now in a position to build a dichotomous data table (Rihoux and De Meur 2009:39ff). To this end, she dichotomizes her data, that is, codes her variables so that they have either the value "1" (indicating the presence of a condition or outcome) or "0" (indicating its absence). The resulting data are then displayed in a dichotomous data table where each row corresponds to a case and each column to a variable.

QCA is a computer-aided method and the first stage in its application consists in the computer software transforming the dichotomous data table into a truth table (Rihoux and De Meur 2009:44ff). The latter displays each of the *actual* and *possible* combinations of conditions associated with a positive outcome (the outcome occurred) and each of those associated with a negative outcome (the outcome didn't occur). That is, the truth table lists both observed configurations and unobserved ones—ones not found in any of the examined cases and called logical remainders. The truth table also shows if a combination of conditions is associated with a positive outcome in some cases and a negative one in others. Here, the researcher has to make adjustments so that the contradictory configurations, as they are called, disappear.

Next, the computer software uses Boolean minimization algorithms to perform its key operation: it minimizes, and hence expresses in the shortest possible way, the different observed configurations of conditions associated with a positive and negative outcome respectively (Rihoux and De Meur 2009:56). The software also performs minimizations that include logical remainders. By including logical remainders as simplifying assumptions, the software is typically able to generate expressions that are even more parsimonious. In both cases, the upshot of the minimizations are referred to as minimal or solution formulas. Proponents of QCA contend that minimal formulas may typically be given a causal interpretation: a formula represents how different configurations of conditions *caused* the same type of outcome.

Following the application of QCA, the researcher may in different ways employ and elaborate on her findings. For instance, the researcher may return to her cases and use the identified causal relations as a basis for further study of the cases (a point to which I return in the next section), or she may consider to what extent her findings generalize to other cases (Rihoux and Lobe 2009:235ff).

In order to illustrate the method, the example presented in Rihoux and Ragin's textbook may be slightly modified (Rihoux and Ragin 2009). The example draws on a study of why some European democracies survived in the period between World War I and World War II, whereas others perished (Rihoux and De Meur 2009). Its simplified—and hence fictionalized—version goes as follows: the researcher first selected 18 European countries as her cases and decided to focus on five explanatory variables, namely level of wealth, industrialization, education, urbanization, and governmental stability. Then she generated her data. On this basis, she produced a dichotomous data table with rows corresponding to each of the eighteen countries and with columns corresponding to each of the conditions and the outcome. In this connection, she dichotomized her data such that "1" represented a high level of wealth, industrialization, etc. and "0" a low level of wealth, industrialization, etc. Also, she used "1" to denote the survival of a democracy, and "0" to represent its demise. Next, the software produced a truth table, which listed each of the actual and possible configurations of conditions associated with the survival of democracy, and each of the actual and possible combinations of conditions associated with the collapse of democracy. She continued by making the computer software perform minimizations of the observed combinations associated with the survival and demise of democracy respectively, and she repeated this procedure with added logical remainders. On this basis, the researcher offered a causal interpretation of her formulas. For instance, she contended that one of them (generated without logical remainders) showed that, among the countries she studied, the survival of democracy was caused either by a high level of wealth, education, industrialization, and governmental stability; or by a high level of wealth, education, and governmental stability, and a low level of urbanization (Rihoux and De Meur 2009:57).

The method of QCA has been criticized on different grounds. One type of complaints focuses on the limitations of the method. For instance, Steel states that one weakness of QCA is that it can only be used to analyze a small number of possible causes (Steel 2011:292). As soon as many conditions are considered, the number of actual and possible combinations of the conditions becomes too large to handle. Another line of objections has it that the method fails to deliver on its promise: the minimal formulas (sometimes) fail to represent causal relations. For example, Baumgartner points out that according to Mackie's INUS conception of causation, causes make a difference to their effect. Since QCA relies on this conception, he argues, minimal formulas must be maximally parsimonious, that is, not contain any conditions, whose elimination makes no difference to the occurrence of the outcome (Baumgartner 2014). Otherwise, the formulas fail to represent causal relations. Yet, he contends, in order to obtain such maximally parsimonious minimal formulas, researchers have to make simplifying assumptions that are untenable in that they posit empirically impossible configurations.

3. PROCESS TRACING

The method of process tracing is, broadly speaking, a method of data analysis: it consists in the analysis of generated data, and sometimes also prospective data, about a single case with the aim of identifying the mechanisms that link two events as cause and effect.

George Alexander introduced the notion of process tracing into political science in the late 1970s (Bennett and Checkel 2014:5). Yet the method did not gain prevalence until after the publication of his and Andrew Bennett's "Case Studies and Theory Development in the Social Sciences" in 2005. Today, process tracing is regarded as an important form of qualitative research (see, e.g., Collier 2011; Mahoney 2012; Waldner 2012). In this section, I offer a brief introduction to the method, its underlying assumptions, and some objections to it. I leave a discussion of how its use exemplifies qualitative research to Section 5.

The notion of mechanisms is central to process tracing. Proponents of the method maintain that mechanisms connect a cause to its effect. More precisely, they hold that two events are linked as cause and effect via continuous and contiguous causal processes (causal chains of events), while identifying these processes with mechanisms (see George and Bennett 2005:140). In discussions of process tracing, the idea of mechanisms is further elaborated in diverse ways (see, e.g., Beach and Pedersen 2019:29ff). Here is for example George and Bennett's widely cited definition: mechanisms are "ultimately unobservable physical, social, or psychological processes through which agents with causal capacities operate, but only in specific contexts or conditions, to transfer energy, information, or matter to other entities. In so doing, the causal agent changes the affected entity's characteristics, capacities, or propensities in ways that persist until subsequent mechanisms act upon it" (George and Bennett 2005:137). Simplifying, the gist of this formulation is that mechanisms are processes involving entities that, under the right circumstances, pass on energy, information, or matter to other entities. However specified, advocates of the method maintain that mechanisms may be traced by pointing to data that are indicative of their occurrence. That is, researchers should use process tracing. It is a method of data analysis broadly speaking in that it involves the scrutiny of generated data *and* sometimes also the specification of the data to be generated about a single case. I now describe in more detail how the method works drawing mainly on Bennett and Checkel (2014).

A researcher begins by selecting the outcome her study is going to explain and a case in which the outcome occurs. Sometimes, she has a theory that posits a cause of the outcome and she is able, perhaps drawing on the theory, to formulate hypotheses about the mechanisms that linked the posited cause and outcome in the case. In this situation, the researcher engages in theory testing process tracing which is the most discussed variety of the method. Thus, she begins by specifying the observable implications of her hypothesized mechanisms, that is, the types of data she may expect to generate if her hypotheses are correct and if she is granted access to relevant people, documents, and the like. In addition, she contemplates possible alternative causes, posits mechanisms that might link them to the outcome, and specifies some of their observable implications. Lastly, she considers the probative value of the different types of prospective data, that is, how much they will each lend support to her mechanism hypotheses.[2] The point of this exercise is that she makes sure to look for types of data with high probative value and, more generally, for enough data to properly test her mechanism hypotheses.

Against this backdrop, the researcher generates her data about the case looking for the different types of data she should expect to find if the hypothesized mechanisms are correct. To this end, she typically uses different methods of data generation such as semi- and unstructured interviewing, the collection and reading of documents, participant observation, and surveys. She then interprets her data (do they exemplify her prespecified data types?). And, she assesses to what extent the data lend support to her hypothesized mechanisms and hence to her favorite theory about the cause of the outcome, and to what extent the data refute alternative mechanism hypotheses and posited causes.

There is also a second variety of process tracing. At the beginning of a study, when a researcher has selected the outcome to be explained and the case she is going to examine, she may also find herself in the situation of having at most a highly tentative idea about what the cause of the outcome was and no hypotheses about connecting mechanisms. In this case, she engages in theory building process tracing. Here, she proceeds directly to generate data about the case while aiming for data she thinks might be indicative of the mechanisms and the cause. She then analyzes her data and, on that basis, comes up with hypotheses about the mechanisms and the cause of the outcome. Moreover, she examines whether the data lend support to alternative posits of causes and linking mechanisms.

Often, a researcher uses both theory testing and theory building process tracing in a single study (Bennett and Checkel 2014:17). For instance, at the beginning of her study, she may not have any hypotheses about mechanisms. Accordingly, she generates data and then comes up with mechanism hypotheses on their basis. She may then set out to test these hypotheses by specifying some of their further observable implications (i.e., types of data different from those that led her to posit the mechanisms), and so on (Bennett and Checkel 2014:8).

Nina Tannenwald's study of why the US has not deployed nuclear weapons after World War II is often discussed as an example of well-conducted process tracing (Tannenwald 1999, 2007; for its discussion, see, e.g., Beach and Pedersen 2019; Bennett 2014; Collier 2011). Tannenwald examined her research question in relation to four different cases (Tannenwald 1999). I briefly consider one of these, namely the Korean War case. She started out postulating that, during this war, the American decision-makers decided against the use of nuclear weapons because of a norm against their use. Among other things, she then hypothesized that the norm (the cause) influenced the decision-makers' deliberations about whether or not to use nuclear weapons (the linking process) and that these deliberations resulted in their decision not to deploy the nuclear weapons (the outcome). More precisely, she proposed, the norm constrained the decision-making process either through having been internalized by the decision-makers or by being perceived by them as "an exogenously given constraint" on their decision-making (Tannenwald 1999:440). Tannenwald continued by specifying two observable implications: if the norm had these constraining effects, there should be data indicating that some decision-makers explicitly argued against the use of nuclear weapons on normative grounds and that others (those in favor of using the weapons) openly complained about the norm. In addition, Tannenwald considered possible alternative causes of the nonuse of nuclear weapons and specified the observable implications of their accompanying mechanisms. This done, Tannenwald generated her data: she collected documents and conducted interviews. Her data lent support to her claim that the norm against nuclear weapon use did indeed influence the decision-makers' choice not to employ them in the Korean War.

It may be noted that process tracing may be combined with QCA in the sense that the methods may be employed in succession. For example, a researcher who has conducted a qualitative comparative analysis may return to some of her cases and carry out process tracing in order to identify the mechanisms that link the cause-effect relations she discovered by way of QCA. Or a researcher may, by way of process tracing, establish that two events in a case are causally related while subsequently engaging in research using QCA to determine whether a similar cause-effect relation occurs in other cases as well.

The method of process tracing has been criticized on the ground that, contrary to what its proponents hold, its employment does not, on its own, make it possible to establish that two events are related as cause and effect. For instance, Daniel Steel argues that it is not enough, by way of process tracing, to point to data indicating that the hypothesized mechanisms operated in a case (Steel 2008:186). The reason is that the data, on their own, fail to establish that the chain of events, occurring between the putative cause and effect, was a *causal* chain of events. To show that the intervening processes are causal, it is necessary to point to causal generalizations about the linking events yet "it is difficult to see how causal generalizations could be learned without some type of inference from statistical data" (Steel 2008:186). Coming from a different angle, Sharon Crasnow criticizes process tracing of the theory-testing variety on the ground that it focuses exclusively on how data may confirm (or refute) hypothesized mechanisms (Crasnow 2017:7). This overlooks the importance of providing a narrative about the case under study. Thus, she states, process tracing should be reconceived as involving the creation of "a narrative through a hypothesized causal mechanism" since this facilitates reflection on both alternative mechanism hypotheses, and the connection between the data and the explanation of the case.

4. THE ETHNOGRAPHIC METHOD

The ethnographic method is a method of data generation that involves the use of participant observation, possibly in combination with methods like semi- and unstructured interviewing and the collection and reading of documents, with the aim of generating data about multiple aspects of the ways of life under study.

Richard Fenno's "Home Style" from 1978 and James C. Scott's "Weapons of the Weak" from 1985 are two early and classic works in political ethnography (Fenno 2003[1978]; Scott 1985; for their discussions, see, e.g., Schatz 2009b:4 and Kapiszewski et al. 2015:240–241). At the time of their publication, the ethnographic method played a very peripheral role in political science and this situation has continued until recently. However, in 2009, the edited volume "Political Ethnography: What Immersion Contributes to the Study of Power" appeared (Schatz 2009a). It both reflected, and further stimulated, a growing interest in the ethnographic method among political scientists (see, e.g., Wedeen 2010:259 and Schwartz-Shea and Majic 2017:97–98).

Ethnographic research is taken to exemplify qualitative research in political science (see, e.g., Schatz 2009b; Bevir and Blakely 2018:90). In the next section, I take a closer look at its status as a qualitative form of research. Here, I explicate the method and briefly consider some criticisms of it. I begin by outlining how a researcher should proceed when carrying out participant observation (the key method in ethnographic research), and conducting semi- and unstructured interviewing (two methods that commonly accompany its use). I base the exposition on Zahle (2018, 2021) and Halperin and Heath (2012:287ff).

Before a researcher engages in ethnographic research, she decides on a research question and selects the specific setting (or possibly settings) in which to conduct her study. Typically, she settles on an open question, i.e., one to which she has no prefixed possible answer. This means that she will first generate her data and then, on their basis, come up with an answer to her research question. Moreover, the researcher usually regards her research question as preliminary: she expects to render it more precise, to modify it in other ways, or even to substitute it with a different research question after she has commenced to generate her data. Alternatively, and much less commonly, the researcher formulates a hypothesis in response to her research question before she starts to generate her data, which are then used to test the hypothesis. In any case, she does not make any detailed plans as to what data to generate, but decides this, on a running basis, in the field. In this respect, the research design accompanying the employment of the ethnographic method is a flexible or adaptive one.

When carrying out participant observation, the ethnographer participates in the research participants' ways of life in their usual surroundings. The researcher may participate to different degrees. For instance, she may participate in the weak sense of merely staying in the background, or in the stronger sense of interacting with the research participants, or in the even stronger sense of also engaging in their activities. While participating, the researcher observes, i.e., notes, what goes on. Subsequently, she describes this in her field notes in as much detail as possible and in terms that comes as close as possible to the research participants' perspectives. The ethnographer proceeds in this manner over an extended period of time that allows her to immerse herself in the ways of life she studies.

When conducting semi- or unstructured interviews, the ethnographer poses questions to an interviewee who, in her replies, is permitted or encouraged to digress, to expand on her views, to exemplify her points, to introduce her own concerns, and the like. In semistructured interviewing, the researcher has a list of questions that she goes through. She may pose them in whatever order seems natural during the interview just as she may add questions. In unstructured interviewing, the researcher has at most a list of topics that she wants to cover. She does not introduce these in any prefixed order and formulates her questions as she goes along. As a result, the interaction comes close to an ordinary conversation. In both cases, the interview is typically conducted in a setting familiar to the research participant who is interviewed at length on one or several occasions. After an interview, the researcher describes the interview in her interview notes.

Commonly, the researcher begins to analyze her data when data generation is still ongoing. After she leaves the field, she then continues this task in a more intensive manner and ends by writing an account of her findings.

By way of illustration of the method, consider Richard Fenno's famous ethnographic study, "Home Style" (Fenno 2003[1978]). The focus of Fenno's study was how American politicians (members of the House of Representatives) perceived their constituencies and how these perceptions influenced their behavior (Fenno 2003[1978]:xxviii). Fenno generated the main bulk of his data by way of participant observation and interviewing carried out in the politicians' home districts (Fenno 2003[1978]:251). More precisely, he spent time with eighteen politicians (three to eleven days with each), while they engaged in various activities in their home districts. In addition, he conducted follow-up interviews with eleven of the politicians in Washington. Before he set out to generate his data, he did not formulate any hypotheses in response to his research questions and he didn't make any detailed plans as to what data to generate. Thus, in reflecting on his approach, Fenno describes how his visits to the districts "were totally open-ended and exploratory. I tried to observe and inquire into anything and everything these members did. I worried about whatever they worried about. Rather than assume that I already knew what was interesting, I remained prepared to find interesting questions emerging in the course of the experience. The same with data. The research method was largely one of soaking and poking—or just hanging around" (Fenno 2003[1978]:xxviii). As soon as he had begun to generate data, he also notes, he started to analyze them and the latter eventually led to the findings presented in "Home Style" (Fenno 2003[1978]:283).

The application of the ethnographic method is commonly associated with a commitment to interpretivism. The latter maintains that the social sciences should mainly provide

interpretations of the meaningful aspects of social reality while motivating this contention by reference to various ontological claims about social reality. Interpretivists spell out
this theoretical position in various ways. For instance, Blakely and Bevir make it clear that
interpretations, or interpretive explanations as they call them, may assume various forms
(Bevir and Blakely 2018:21ff). Among other things, interpretive explanations may account
for an individual's beliefs or actions by showing how these fit into her wider web of beliefs
and by providing a narrative of what preceded and followed the beliefs or actions (Bevir
and Blakely 2018:21–25). Also, interpretive explanations may explain individuals' beliefs by
reference to the social background that gave rise to them or, conversely, show how changes
in individuals' beliefs prompted alterations in the social background (Bevir and Blakely
2018:29).

These reflections bring into view that ethnographic data, which focus on the research
participants' perspectives and on multiple aspects of their ways of life, are well suited to serve
as basis for interpretative explanations. Hence, it is no surprise that there is a long tradition for combining ethnographic research with interpretivism. At the same time, though, it
should be stressed that ethnographic data may also ground noninterpretivist accounts: they
may be used for other purposes than offering interpretations and without making the ontological assumptions characteristic of interpretivism (see, e.g., Bevir and Blakely 2018:92ff;
Kubik 2009; Schatz 2009b; and Wedeen 2010). For instance, the method may be combined
with the theoretical position of functionalism (as, say, the famous anthropologist Bronislaw
Malinowski did) or with the position of structural-functionalism (as exemplified by another well-known anthropologist, Edward Evans-Pritchard) (see Kubik 2009).

Just as ethnographic research is compatible with different theoretical positions, it may
also go together with different methods of data analysis. For the present purposes, this point
may be illustrated in relation to QCA and process tracing. Ethnographic data may be used
as basis for a qualitative comparative analysis (possibly in combination with other types of
data). All it requires is that the ethnographic data are dichotomized so that they may be
inserted into a dichotomized data table (see, e.g., Rihoux and Lobe 2009). Likewise, a researcher engaged in process tracing may decide to use the ethnographic method to generate
some, or all, of the data needed to test or build her hypotheses about mechanisms (see, e.g.,
Kapiszewski et al. 2015:249–250).

The most common objection to the ethnographic method is that it tends to generate data
of questionable quality. For example, Johnson et al. report two such criticisms (Johnson
et al. 2008:254). One states that reactivity may occur, that is, the researcher may influence
the research participants' behavior, and by implication, the data she generates. The other
notes that the researcher's observations, and by implication her data, may be biased: she
may pay attention to some aspects of the ways of life she studies and not to others even
though the disregarded aspects are equally, if not more, relevant to the focus of her study.
The implication is that since reactivity and bias frequently transpire, the researcher tends
to end up with low-quality data. As it stands, this line of reasoning is not convincing because it fails to consider that an ethnographer may in various ways address the issues of
reactivity and bias. For instance, she may try to minimize reactivity and/or she may try
to determine how she influenced the research participants such that she may take this
into account when interpreting her data. Accordingly, the more interesting version of the
criticisms maintains that whatever measures the researcher takes, her data are likely to be
of poor quality.

5. CONCEPTIONS OF QUALITATIVE RESEARCH IN POLITICAL SCIENCE

In the previous sections, I have characterized qualitative research in political science through an examination of three methods whose use is widely held to exemplify qualitative research. I now approach the characterization of qualitative research in political science from a different angle, namely through considering what is taken to be distinctive of qualitative research in general. A quick glance at political science discussions shows that there is no agreement on this matter. Accordingly, I look at four influential conceptions of qualitative research that are currently defended in political science. Moreover, I explore how these conceptions apply to QCA, process tracing, and the ethnographic method. This will both add some more content to the conceptions and pick up on an issue left hanging in the foregoing presentation of the methods, namely their status as qualitative forms of research. In other words, why, if at all, does research that relies on these methods amount to qualitative research? To anticipate, I show that the conceptions disagree on the classification of research that employs these methods as qualitative. In this fashion, the discussion brings into view that even though research based on the methods is often regarded as qualitative, there is no consensus on this point.

In political science discussions, qualitative research is often identified with research that generates and analyzes qualitative data, which are said to have certain distinctive features in common.

John Gerring's definition of qualitative research exemplifies this line of approach (Gerring 2017). Gerring states that qualitative data are noncomparable data, that is, bits and pieces of data that address different aspects of a research question and that are drawn from different populations (Gerring 2017:18–19). Accordingly, the data may not be displayed in a matrix (rectangular) data set where the rows indicate cases and the columns variables. Both these features, Gerring explains, differentiate qualitative from quantitative data: the latter are defined by being comparative and as such they may be arrayed in a matrix rectangular data set (Gerring 2017:18). Gerring goes on to observe that methods of data generation are qualitative to the extent that they generate qualitative data. Similarly, the discussion suggests, methods of data analysis are qualitative to the extent that they involve the analysis of qualitative data.

Gerring's definition may now be applied to QCA, process tracing, and the ethnographic method. QCA is not concerned with the analysis of noncomparative data. That is, though a researcher may generate noncomparative data about her cases, she must turn these into comparative data that she inserts in a dichotomized data table—a matrix rectangular data set—before they may be analyzed by way of QCA. Thus, QCA does not count as a qualitative method of data analysis (see Gerring 2017:18). It is a different matter with process tracing. In process tracing, Gerring maintains, diverse types of data are always used for the purposes of establishing that two events are related as cause and effect (Gerring 2006:173). That is, "multiple types of evidence are employed for the verification of a single inference – bits and pieces of evidence that embody different units of analysis (they are each drawn from unique populations). Individual observations [bits of data] are therefore noncomparable" (Gerring 2006:173). This being the case, process tracing is a qualitative method of data analysis.

Lastly, turn to the ethnographic method. For the sake of simplicity, I shall henceforth take it that the method only comprises participant observation in combination with semi- and unstructured interviewing and/or the collection and reading of documents.[3] Thus conceived, the method is a straightforward qualitative method of data generation: participant observation and its supplementary methods produce data (field, interview, and document notes) that are noncomparable in that they pertain to multiple different aspects of the research question (see Gerring 2006:19). It is worth noting that these data may subsequently be transformed into comparable ones. This point does not undermine the claim that the data "originally" generated by the methods are noncomparative ones.

Peregrine Schwartz-Shea and Dvora Yanow's definition is another example of a conception that identifies qualitative research with the generation and analysis of qualitative data (Schwartz-Shea and Yanow 2002). They identify qualitative data with data that are word-based and hence they specify qualitative methods of data generation as ones that produce word-based accounts, and qualitative methods of data analysis as ones that examine word-based accounts (Schwartz-Shea and Yanow 2002:460–461). In comparison, they imply, quantitative data are numerical and the methods that produce or analyze such data are quantitative.

Relative to this conception, QCA is not a qualitative method of data analysis since it does not analyze word-based data but works on numerical data, viz. variables that take the value of "1" or "0." Regarding process tracing, it may be used to analyze both word-based and numerical data. For instance, a process tracing analysis may draw both on word-based data generated by way of semistructured interviewing and the collection and reading of documents, and on numerical survey-data. Hence, process tracing is not a qualitative method or its status as a qualitative method varies depending on the extent to which it is applied to word-based data. As to the ethnographic method, Schwartz-Shea and Yanow state that participant observation, semi- and unstructured interviewing, and the collection and reading of documents generate word-based accounts (Schwartz-Shea and Yanow 2002:460). Accordingly, the ethnographic method counts as a qualitative method.

Another family of conceptions of qualitative research identifies it with studies that have certain broader features or basic orientations, as Goertz and Mahoney put it, in common (Goertz and Mahoney 2012:2). Goertz and Mahoney's own conception exemplifies this sort of position (Goertz and Mahoney 2012; Mahoney and Goertz 2006). Their characterization is confined to stating what is distinctive of qualitative studies whose prime concern is causal analysis (Mahoney and Goertz 2006:228–229). Such studies, they contend, have most or all of the following features (Mahoney and Goertz 2006:230–245). Explanations are offered that: (1) list the causes of outcomes in particular cases; (2) conceive of causation in terms of necessary and sufficient causes; (3) specify how a combination of causes brought about some outcome(s); (4) point out how different (combinations of) causes may bring about some outcome; and (5) generalize only to a limited number of cases, if at all. Further, (6) the researcher begins by selecting cases in which the outcome to be explained occurred; (7) pieces of evidence (data) are not assigned equal probative value; (8) all cases are not necessarily regarded as being equally important; (9) an account as to why a particular case fails to be covered by the researcher's causal model is sought; and (10) much time and effort is spent defining the central concepts.

In their discussion, Mahoney and Goertz make it clear that they regard studies, which employ QCA or process tracing, as key instances of qualitative research (see, e.g., Goertz and Mahoney 2012:7 and 9). For lack of space, I limit myself to drawing attention to a few of the obvious ways in which QCA and process tracing studies fit Mahoney and Goertz' characterization. Accordingly, it may be noted that in QCA studies, explanations of outcomes in particular cases are offered, causation is conceived of in terms of necessary and sufficient causes just as the method is compatible with multiple conjunctural causation (point 3 and 4). As to process tracing studies, they likewise point to causes of outcomes in particular cases, the researcher begins by selecting a case in which the outcome to be explained occurred, and pieces of evidence (data) are not assigned equal probative value.

What about studies which employ the ethnographic method? Mahoney and Goertz' characterization does not say anything about such studies. That is, the ethnographic method may well be employed to generate data that form the basis for causal analysis (their focus), but from the perspective of assessing whether research is qualitative, its application is irrelevant. In this sense, ethnographic research falls outside the scope of their conception.

Another example of this sort of conception of qualitative research is presented by David Collier, Henry Brady, and Jason Seawright (Collier, Brady, and Seawright 2010). They contend that studies with the following features exemplify qualitative research. The studies: (1) primarily involve data that are organized at a nominal level of measurement (i.e., the categories in the scale of measurement are not ranked); (2) concentrate on relatively few cases (roughly less than ten or twenty cases); (3) do not involve any, or only few, statistical tests to establish their end results; and (4) involve detailed knowledge about the cases (Collier, Brady, and Seawright 2010:155). Collier et al. stress that studies may, of course, have only some of these features. In that case, the studies may still be classified as being to some extent qualitative depending on how many of the features they possess.

Equipped with this characterization, consider once more studies that involve the three methods. In a QCA study, data are organized at a nominal scale of measurement: in a dichotomous data table, "1" indicates the presence of a possible cause, "0" is absence (Ragin 2014[1989]:86).[4] Further, no statistical tests are used. At the same time, proponents of QCA typically recommend that a researcher gains detailed knowledge about her cases, but they also recognize that the more cases a researcher studies, the more difficult it becomes to acquire in-depth knowledge about all of them (see Rihoux and Lobe 2009). Further, though some QCA studies focus on less than ten or twenty cases, most studies today consider a larger number of cases (see, e.g., Arel-Bundock 2019:4–5). These latter two points show that QCA studies often fail to count as instances of full-blown qualitative research. In process tracing studies, nominal scale data are primarily used in that heterogeneous bits and pieces of data are used to test or build hypotheses about the linking mechanisms. Further, the studies focus on a single or few cases, their end results are not established using statistical tests, and they involve detailed knowledge about the cases under study. Thus, process tracing studies exemplify qualitative research. Lastly, in ethnographic research, the employment of participant observation, semi- and unstructured interviewing, and the collection and reading of documents primarily result in nominal scale data about a single or a few cases. The data are not suited for statistical tests just as their use gives rise to detailed knowledge about the case or cases. Hence, ethnographic studies are qualitative too.

This concludes the examination of different positions in political science as to what is distinctive of qualitative research. The discussion brought out that the different conceptions of qualitative research do not agree on whether or not the use of QCA, process tracing, and the ethnographic method exemplifies qualitative research.

6. PUTTING QUALITATIVE RESEARCH IN POLITICAL SCIENCE IN PERSPECTIVE

So far I have offered a twofold characterization of qualitative research in political science. I now briefly compare the current state of qualitative research in political science with that in other social sciences. It goes without saying that I will be painting with the big brush.

In political science, there is a marked focus on qualitative research whose goal is to identify causal relations (see Cooper at al. 2012:12). Considering QCA and process tracing as forms of qualitative research, they illustrate this point: they are both methods that purport to uncover causal relations. In other social sciences, there is not a similar concern. Qualitative researchers in, say, cultural anthropology and sociology, do not to the same extent aim for causal findings and explicitly discuss the use of qualitative research for this purpose. In fact, taking this point even further, Glaser et al. contend that in most other social sciences, there is even "a widespread tendency on the part of qualitative researchers today to reject causal analysis as unnecessary, undesirable, and/or impossible" (Cooper at al. 2012:13).

Further, and relatedly, discussions in political science have particularly revolved around qualitative data analysis. Again, counting QCA and process tracing as qualitative forms of research, they are representative of this trend as they are methods of data analysis. By comparison, issues relating to qualitative data generation have received much less attention. The situation is the exact opposite in many other social sciences. Here, qualitative forms of data generation (rather than data analysis) are, and have traditionally been, the main preoccupation. For instance, Alan Bryman's widely used textbook on "Social Research Methods" exemplifies this observation: five chapters are dedicated to different methods of qualitative data generation, whereas one chapter discusses qualitative data analysis and one offers an introduction to qualitative data analysis software (Bryman 2012).

Moreover, among the three methods discussed in this paper, the ethnographic method is the approach most widely used outside political science. There is a long tradition for its employment particularly in cultural anthropology and sociology where the methods were originally developed (Halperin and Heath 2012:287). QCA and process tracing are also applied outside political science, yet they are not to the same extent, it seems, presented as *qualitative* forms of research. Or better perhaps, they tend not to figure in standard textbooks on qualitative research aimed at students outside political science. This, though, may also have to do with the fact that they are more recently developed methods.

Finally, political science is not alone in displaying diverse conceptions of qualitative research. In other sciences, there are similar discussions to this effect. Among the four conceptions considered, it is the identification of qualitative research with methods that generate and analyze word-based data that is most commonly encountered in other social sciences.

7.   CONCLUSION

In this paper, I have characterized qualitative research in political science. First, I presented the methods of QCA, process tracing, and ethnography that are regarded as central methods in qualitative research. Next, I discussed four different conceptions of qualitative research in political science, while showing that they disagree on the classification of the three methods as forms of qualitative research. Thus, it appeared, even though research based on the three methods is often regarded as qualitative, there is no consensus on this matter in political science. Lastly, I compared the state of qualitative research in political science to that in other social sciences.

For a while now, the notion of qualitative research has been disputed (and as part of this its distinction from quantitative research). By way of ending, it is worth stressing that this does not render the present focus on qualitative research potentially problematic. The label of qualitative research continues to be widely used in political science and hence it is perfectly reasonable to discuss methods which use is taken to exemplify qualitative research in political science, as well as different conceptions of qualitative research within this field. Doing so, of course, is not the same as showing that the notion of qualitative research should remain in use because it usefully groups together certain forms of research. A discussion along these lines is the topic of another paper.[5]

NOTES

1. In the presentation of the method, I also say a few words about the steps preceding and following the application of the method. Proponents of QCA typically stress the importance of these additional steps while referring to the *method* of QCA in combination with these steps as the QCA *approach*.
2. In this process, it is commonly recommended to rely on Van Evera's widely cited distinction between four different ways, or extents to which, data may provide support for hypotheses (Van Evera 1997:30–32, see also the discussion of his distinction in, e.g., Collier 2011; Mahoney 2012).
3. This is a simplification since ethnographic research may also involve the employment of participant observation in combination with other data generation methods. Which ones is a matter of dispute.
4. Here, and in the following discussion of this conception, I assume that the data analyzed or generated by the method under consideration are the data primarily involved in a study.
5. I would like to thank Harold Kincaid and Jeroen Van Bouwel for their very helpful comments. Also thanks to Michael Baumgartner for all his useful suggestions.

REFERENCES

Arel-Bundock, V. (2019, online first). "The Double Bind of Qualitative Comparative Analysis," *Sociological Methods & Research*. doi:10.1177/0049124119882460.

Baumgartner, M. (2014). "Parsimony and Causality," *Quality & quantity*, 49(2): 839–856.

Beach, D., and Pedersen, R. B. (2019). *Process Tracing Methods*. Ann Arbor, MI: University of Michigan Press.

Bennett, A. (2014). "Appendix: Disciplining our Conjectures. Systematizing Process Tracing with Bayesian Analysis," in *Process Tracing*, Andrew Bennett and Jeffrey T. Checkel (eds.). West Nyack: Cambridge University Press, pp. 276–298.

Bennett, A. and Checkel, J. (2014). "Process Tracing: From Philosophical Roots to Best Practices," in *Process Tracing*, Andrew Bennett and Jeffrey T. Checkel (eds.). West Nyack: Cambridge University Press, pp. 3–37.

Bennett, A. and Elman, C. (2006). "Qualitative Research: Recent Developments in Case Study Methods," *Annual Review of Political Science* 9: 455–476.

Berg-Schlosser, D. and De Meur, G. (2009). "Comparative Research Design: Case And Variable Selection," in *Configurational Comparative Methods: Qualitative Comparative Analysis (QCA) and Related Techniques*, B. Rihoux and C.C. Ragin (Eds.). Thousand Oaks: SAGE Publications, pp. 19–32.

Berg-Schlosser, D. De Meur, G., Rihoux, B. and Ragin, C.C. (2009). "Qualitative Comparative Analysis as an Approach," in *Configurational Comparative Methods: Qualitative Comparative Analysis (QCA) and Related Techniques*, B. Rihoux and C.C. Ragin (Eds.). Thousand Oaks: SAGE Publications, pp. 1–17.

Bevir, M. and Blakely, J. (2018). *Interpretive Social Science. An Anti-Naturalist Approach*. Oxford: Oxford University Press.

Blatter. J.K, Haverland, M., and Hulst, M.v., eds. (2016). *Qualitative Research in Political Science*. Vol. II. London: SAGE Publications.

Brady, H.E. and Collier, D. eds. (2004). *Rethinking Social Inquiry: Diverse Tools, Shared Standards*. Lanham: Rowman and Littlefield.

Brady, H. E. and Collier, D. eds. (2010). *Rethinking Social Inquiry: Diverse Tools, Shared Standards*. 2nd edition. Lanham: Rowman and Littlefield.

Bryman, A. (2012). *Social Research Methods*, 4th edition. Oxford: Oxford University Press.

Collier, D. (2011). "Understanding Process Tracing," *Political Science and Politics*, vol. 44(4): 823–830.

Collier, D., Brady, H.E., and Seawright, J. (2010). "Sources of Leverage in Causal Inference: Toward an Alternative View of Methodology," in *Rethinking Social Inquiry: Diverse Tools, Shared Standards*, Henry E. Brady and David Collier (eds.), 2nd edition. Lanham: Rowman and Littlefield Publishers, pp. 141–173.

Cooper, B., Glaesser, J., Gomm, R., Hammersley, M. (2012). *Challenging the Qualitative-Quantitative Divide. Explorations in Case-Focused Causal Analysis*. London: Continuum.

Crasnow, S. (2017). "Process Tracing in Political Science: What's the Story?" *Studies in History and Philosophy of Science*, 62: 6–13.

Cronqvist, L. and Berg-Schlosser, D. (2009). "Multi-Value QCA (mvQCA)," in *Configurational Comparative Methods: Qualitative Comparative Analysis (QCA) and Related Techniques*, B. Rihoux and C.C. Ragin (Eds.). Thousand Oaks, CA: SAGE Publications, pp. 69–86.

Fenno, R.F. (2003[1978]). *Home Style: House Members in Their Districts*. New York: Longman.

George, A.L. and Bennett, A. (2005). *Case Studies and Theory Development in the Social Sciences*. Cambridge, MA: MIT Press.

Gerring, J. (2006). *Case Study Research: Principles and Practices*. Cambridge: Cambridge University Press.

Gerring, J. (2017). "Qualitative Methods," *Annual Review of Political Science* 20: 15–36.

Goertz, G. and Mahoney, J. (2012). *A Tale of Two Cultures: Qualitative and Quantitative Research in the Social Sciences*. Princeton, NJ: Princeton University Press.

Halperin, S. and Heath, O. (2012). *Political Research: Methods and Practical Skills*. Oxford: Oxford University Press.

Johnson, J. B., Reynolds, H. T. and Mycoff, J. D. (2008). *Political Science Research Methods*. 6th edition. Washington DC: CQ Press.

Kapiszewski, D., Maclean, L. M., and Read, B. L. (2015). *Field Research in Political Science: Practices and Principles*. Cambridge: Cambridge University Press.

King, G., Keohane, R. O., and Verba, S. (1994). *Designing Social Inquiry: Scientific Inference in Qualitative Research*. Princeton, NJ: Princeton University Press.

Koivu. K. L. and Damman, E. K. (2015). "Qualitative variations: the sources of divergent qualitative methodological approaches," *Quality and Quantity* 49(6): 2617–2632.

Kubik, J. (2009). "Ethnography of Politics: Foundations, Applications, Prospects," in *Political Ethnography: What Immersion Contributes to the Study of Power*, E. Schatz (Ed.). Chicago: Chicago University Press, pp. 25–52.

Mackie, J.L. (1993). "Causes and Conditions," in *Causation*, Ernest Sosa and Michael Tooley (Eds.). Oxford: Oxford University Press, pp. 33–55.

Mahoney, J. (2010). "After KKV: The New Methodology of Qualitative Research," *World Politics*, 62(1): 120–147.

Mahoney, J. (2012). "The Logic of Process Tracing Tests in the Social Sciences," *Sociological Methods and Research* 41(4): 570–597.

Mahoney, J. & Goertz, G. (2006). "A Tale of Two Cultures: Contrasting Quantitative and Qualitative Research," *Political Analysis* 14(3): 227–249.

Marx, A., Rihoux, B. and Ragin, C. (2014). "The origin, development, and application of Qualitative Comparative Analysis: the first 25 years," *European Political Science Review* 6(1): 115–142.

Ragin, C. C. (2014[1987]). *The Comparative Method. Moving Beyond Qualitative and Quantitative*. Berkeley: University of California Press.

Ragin, C. C. (2000). *Fuzzy-Set Social Science*. Chicago: University of Chicago Press.

Rihoux, B. and De Meur, G. (2009). "Crisp-Set Qualitative Comparative Analysis (csQCA)," in *Configurational Comparative Methods: Qualitative Comparative Analysis (QCA) and Related Techniques*, B. Rihoux and C.C. Ragin (Eds.). Thousand Oaks, CA: SAGE Publications, pp. 33–68.

Rihoux, B., and Ragin, C. eds. (2009). *Configurational Comparative Methods: Qualitative Comparative Analysis (QCA) and Related Techniques*. Thousand Oaks, CA: Sage Publications.

Rihoux, B. and Lobe, B. (2009). "The Case for Qualitative Comparative Analysis (QCA): Adding Leverage for Thick Cross-Case Comparison," in *The SAGE Handbook of Case-Based Methods*, D. Byrne and C.C. Ragin (Eds.). London: SAGE Publications, pp. 222–242.

Ryan, M. (2018). "The Comparative Method," in *Theory and Methods in Political Science*, 4th edition, V. Lowndes, D. Marsh, and G. Stoker (eds.). London: Palgrave, pp. 271–289.

Schatz, E. eds. (2009a). *Political Ethnography: What Immersion Contributes to the Study of Power*. Chicago: Chicago University Press.

Schatz, E. (2009b). "Ethnographic Immersion and the Study of Politics," in *Political Ethnography: What Immersion Contributes to the Study of Power*, E. Schatz (Ed.). Chicago: Chicago University Press, pp. 1–22.

Schwartz-Shea, P. and Majic, S. (2017). "Ethnography and Participant Observation: Political Science Research in this 'Late Methodological Moment'," *PS: Political Science and Politics* 50(1): 97–102.

Schwartz-Shea, P. and Yanow, D. (2002). "'Reading' 'Methods' 'Texts': How Research Methods Texts Construct Political Science," *Political Research Quarterly* 55(2): 457–486.

Scott, J.C. (1985). *Weapons of the Weak: Everyday Forms of Peasant Resistance.* New Haven, CT: Yale University Press.

Steel, D. P. (2008). *Across the Boundaries. Extrapolation in Biology and Social Science.* Oxford: Oxford University Press.

Steel, D. (2011). "Causality, Causal Models, and Social Mechanisms," in *The Sage Handbook of Social Sciences*, Ian C. Jarvie and Jesús Zamora-Bonilla (Eds.). London: Sage Publications, pp. 288–304.

Tannenwald, N. (1999). "The Nuclear Taboo: The United States and the Normative Basis of Nuclear Non-Use," *International Organization*, 53(3): 433–468.

Tannenwald, N. (2007). *The Nuclear Taboo.* Cambridge: Cambridge University Press.

Thiem, A. (2017). "Conducting Configurational Comparative Research With Qualitative Comparative Analysis: A Hand-On Tutorial for Applied Evaluation Scholars and Practitioners," *American Journal of Evaluation*, 38(3): 420–433.

Van Evera, S. (1997). *Guide to Methods for Students of Political Science.* Ithaca, NY: Cornell University Press.

Vromen, A. (2018). "Qualitative Methods," in *Theory and Methods in Political Science*, V. Lowndes, D. Marsh, and Gerry Stoker (Eds.). 4th Edition. London: Palgrave, pp. 237–253.

Waldner, D. (2012). "Process Tracing and Causal Mechanisms," in *The Oxford Handbook of Philosophy of Social Science*, Harold Kincaid (Ed.). Oxford: Oxford University Press, pp. 65–84.

Wedeen, L. (2010). "Reflections on Ethnographic Work in Political Science," *Annual Review of Political Science* 13, 255–272.

Zahle, J. (2018). "Values and Data Collection in Social Research," *Philosophy of Science* 85(1), 144–163.

Zahle, J. (2021). "Objective Data Sets in Qualitative Research," *Synthese* 199, 101–117.

CHAPTER 11

....

INTERPRETIVISM VERSUS POSITIVISM IN AN AGE OF CAUSAL INFERENCE

....

JANET LAWLER AND DAVID WALDNER

INTRODUCTION

....

CONTEMPORARY debates between interpretivists and positivists continue a long tradition of disputes over how to study human beings and social reality dating back to the *Methodenstreit* of the late nineteenth century. In this chapter, we revisit the debate in light of recent methodological developments within empirical Political Science and related disciplines. We believe that these developments constitute a sufficiently important departure from philosophical positivism that the old debate between positivism and interpretivism needs revisiting.

We harbor no illusions that we can somehow resolve this old debate. We start from the position, however, that many interpretivists express their antipathy to an outdated form of positivism, one that would be largely unfamiliar to the average empirical political scientist today. At minimum, updating this view of positivism—a view that is sufficiently obsolete that we recommend jettisoning the term positivism in favor of "inferentialism"—will give interpretivists a corrected version of what they define themselves against. Furthermore, we suggest later in this essay that to some extent, inferentialists already interpret and interpretivists already infer causal relationships, yet each transgresses these boundaries in ways that may not be fully satisfactory: the two sides can, perhaps mutually inform one another. Most ambitiously, then, we hope that replacing an outdated positivism with inferentialism will create some space for inferentialists and interpretivists to collaborate and we conclude the chapter with discussion of a joint project around which collaboration should be encouraged.

To prefigure our argument and to encourage enemies in this dispute to suspend, temporarily, their mutual suspicions, we offer the following metaphor: the much-heralded murder mystery (Fox, 2018 gives the philosophical background). Contained in the question, "why did the victim die," are two distinct but related questions. The first question is somewhat pedestrian but no less essential to answer: what caused the victim to cease living? This

is a causal question, the domain of the inferentialist, and while the answer is not necessarily startling, it does take the form of a particular type of narrative, a causal chain: a
gaping wound in the chest led to excessive bleeding, depriving the brain of oxygen and
thus its ability to continue functioning. The second question is that of meaning: why would
someone wish to kill this person? This is a question for the interpretivist, as it involves an
actor, agency, and meaning—perhaps meaning that draws heavily on cultural context and
intersubjective understandings and hence requires intensive interpretation. Just as with the
causal-mechanical answer, this answer entails a narrative, albeit one that is more glamorous
and dramatic, more steeped in an understanding of the events, the *dramatis personae*, and
the context in which they were constituted and acted. Unraveling the·mystery inextricably
draws on both perspectives, the nerdy forensic experts and the dashing detectives, working
in concert, not contest. We expect no less from our efforts to understand social reality.

We concede, of course, that "positivist" political science and interpretivism are both large
and heterogeneous fields. Some political scientists still adhere, implicitly if not explicitly, to
mid-twentieth century positivism, searching for universal laws (e.g., democracies do not
fight one another) by estimating multivariate regression models (Goertz 2012). But we consider this approach to be increasingly outdated, and the position we call "inferentialism"
best represents what is taught in leading graduate programs and what informs a great deal
of work in the leading journals. Similarly, interpretivism is not a monolithic bloc: some
interpretivists are oriented to normative theory, while others emphasize open-ended
free-will and the potential for interpretivist scholarship to be "world-making," not just
third-person description and explanation. We believe, however, that there is an emergent
strand within interpretivism that is oriented toward explanation, if not explicitly causal
explanation; and we argue that there are grounds for collaboration between this strand of
interpretivism and causal inferentialism.

FROM POSITIVISM TO CAUSAL INFERENTIALISM

Weighty tomes have been written about the history of positivism: to make the topic more
tractable, we draw on a recent statement of positivism and its contrasts to antinaturalism
that focuses specifically on trends in the study of politics. Mark Bevir and Jason Blakey
(2018) argue that naturalism rests fundamentally on the late nineteenth century belief in the
unity of science: nothing, in principle divides the study of natural objects from the study of
humans, and the latter is best served by emulating the methods and models of the natural
sciences, especially physics. From this starting point, they claim that three assumptions
combine to constitute naturalism: (1) the assumption that human beliefs and actions are
identifiable as brute facts, stripped of meaning and hence analogous to classical mechanics,
or the study of physical bodies in motion; (2) the assumption that scientific explanation
seeks general causal laws, as exemplified by the logical positivism of Carl Hempel; and
(3) the goal of scientific knowledge is prediction.

Some of this depiction still rings true; much does not. We think it worthwhile to highlight what has changed. Late nineteenth century believers in the unity of science would
also have been inclined to agree with the eminent physicist, Ernst Mach, who believed that
scientific knowledge required an exclusive reliance on sensory information and thus the

ruthless elimination of any references to unobserved and unobservable entities, proceeding only through the logical and mathematical analysis of empirical data. This utter disdain for the unobservable, which smacked of mysticism and metaphysics, led Mach to famously dismiss emerging atomistic theories on the grounds that one cannot observe such entities directly. Equally striking was Bertrand Russell's claim (1927) that "The law of causality, I believe, like much that passes muster among philosophers, is a relic of a bygone age, surviving, like the monarchy, only because it is erroneously supposed to do no harm."

Some of these ideas were retained by Hempel, the logical positivists of his time, and the earlier generations of political scientists who took their philosophical cues from them. While Hempel's famous essay on the deductive-nomological model occasionally used the term "cause," his entire enterprise was premised on a reductive notion of causation, such that "cause" meant nothing more than "regularly occurring." Hempel's deductive-nomological model itself never used the term cause: it conjoined one or more well-confirmed universal generalizations of the form "if A then B," a set of particular existential statements that events of type A had occurred, and then a purely logical deduction that because A is invariably followed by B, then the observation of A-type events is sufficient to explain the occurrence of B-type events. One implication of this model of explanation is that explanation and prediction are symmetrical and hence essentially equivalent; while explanations would require statements that A-type events had occurred and were followed by B-type events, predictions would require the claim that were A-type events to occur, they would invariably be followed by B-type events.

There is no doubt that midcentury political scientists were deeply influenced by Hempel, sought to model political science on physics, and frequently adopted a naturalist, overly formalistic, and ahistorical perspective. This was the heyday of behaviorism, systems theorizing, and the obsessive search for general laws in an effort to mimic the physical sciences. One of us was force-fed Hempel and A. J. Ayer as a political science undergraduate in the early 1980s (but fortunately the more *au courant* graduate teaching assistants assigned readings by Thomas Kuhn, Paul Feyerabend, and Imre Lakatos). And no doubt one can still find lingering traces of this approach in the fifteenth edition of undergraduate textbooks first published in 1968.

Hempel's influence, however, has waned considerably over the past four decades. One source of that decline has been the relentless critical assault waged by philosophers of causation and explanation, led by Wesley Salmon's (1989) detailed and widely accepted critique of Hempel's "epistemic" conception of explanations; for contemporary philosophers of causation, Hempel's distillation of logical positivism appears to be a relic of the past deserving no more than passing reference (Illari and Russo 2014).

Empirical social sciences have also broken from the Hempelian tradition, if only implicitly. The deductive-nomological model of explanation is no longer the philosophical model taught to most first-year graduate students in a political science department in the twenty-first century. Let's date the transition from the Hempelian tradition to the causal inference approach, roughly, to 1994, with the publication of a canonical text, *Designing Social Inquiry*, by the Harvard political scientists Gary King, Robert Keohane, and Sidney Verba. Consider how these influential authors (1994, 8) define the goal of scientific research: not, as in the third assumption of Bevir and Blakely, in terms of prediction and control, and not in terms of universal covering laws, but rather in terms of *inference*:

The goal is inference . . . attempting to infer beyond the immediate data to something further that is not directly observed. That something may involve descriptive inference—using
observations from the world to learn about other unobserved facts. Or that something may
involve causal inference—learning about causal effects from the data itself. The domain of
inference can be restricted in space and time—voting behavior in American elections since
1960, social movements in Eastern Europe since 1989—or it can be extensive—human behavior since the invention of agriculture.

The goal of scientific research as explicitly stated here is neither explanation, nor prediction and control, but rather *inference*, especially causal inference; and inference neither
requires universality nor necessarily aspires to the status of a universal law: note how the
quoted sentences explicitly acknowledge that causal inferences may be spatially and temporally local, not global. Building on earlier work by Jerzey Neyman (1934), Donald Rubin
(1974), and Paul Holland (1986), political scientists, sociologists, economists, statisticians,
epidemiologists, philosophers, and others have produced a large and highly influential
literature constituting what we are calling "causal inferentialism" over the past two or three
decades (Angrist and Krueger 2001; Angrist and Pischke 2009; Dunning 2012; Gerber and
Green, 2012; Hernán and Robins 2020; Imbens and Rubin, 2015; Morgan and Winship 2015;
Pearl 2000; Rosenbaum 2017; Woodward 2005).

Long gone are the days when political scientists would gather reams of data in search of
correlations from multivariate models, correlations that can be called "causal" if one believes
the model "controls" for all the confounding variables. Research designs like this are called
"selection on observables" and are seen as methodologically less credible because when
working with observational data, one never knows that the selection of control variables is
adequate; indeed, there is an extensive literature on how the improper selection of control
variables (variables to be adjusted for in a multivariate model) can introduce various forms
of bias, including collider bias and post-treatment bias (Dunning 2012; Elwert and Winship
2014; Acharya, Blackwell, and Sen 2016; Keele, Stevenson, and Elwert 2020; Montgomery,
Nyhan and Torres 2018; Seawright 2019). We can still find research claiming to "discover"
general laws based exclusively on multivariate regression models (Goertz 2012 summarizes
this literature); but anybody who believes that contemporary political science as a discipline
is motivated exclusively by a search for correlations that can claim the status of objective
universal law is simply working with an outdated understanding of the field.

The emphasis today is on the design of research that allows for causal identification, or the
unbiased estimation of a causal effect. Estimating unbiased causal effects is notoriously difficult. Causal effects are defined as the difference in outcomes for a single unit under treatment
and under control—i.e., under two states of the world that cannot be observed simultaneously. Since each unit can be observed under only one of the two treatment assignments, the
simple calculation of a causal effect involves inferences about counterfactuals, or missing
data, a condition known as the "fundamental problem of causal inference" (Holland 1986).
Within the social sciences, causal inference is deeply challenging precisely because political
actors are endowed with consciousness and intentions and they exercise agency: put in the
dry technical language of causal inference, units can select their own treatment status based
on other characteristics or intentions that influence their outcomes; hence a major source
of concern is bias induced by nonrandom assignment to treatment status (Dunning 2008,
236). A central component of graduate training in most leading programs involves the study

of research designs satisfying strict technical criteria such that observations of units under control represent an unbiased estimate of the counterfactual outcomes of units assigned to treatment, had those same units been assigned to control.

The emphasis on research design and causal identification marks an enormous divide between positivism of the nineteenth and mid-twentieth century and contemporary practices; rooting contemporary political science in Hempel's theory of explanation is thus utterly mistaken. Most basically, causal claims do not require any statement of a general law; to be valid, causal claims require only a research design such that observations of units under control can be taken as the counterfactual outcome for units under treatment, a condition generally known as "ignorability" or "exchangeability." Second, design-based causal inferences do not acquire the status of general law. As research on causal identification makes very clear, many well-defined and identified causal effects are local causal effects: literally, LATE, or local average treatment effect that applies only to a subset of all units in a study that is itself restricted in time and space. This restriction on the scope of a causal effect follows directly from the nature of the design. For example, in a regression discontinuity design, researchers look for circumstances in which eligibility is determined by the score on some measure—a test score, for example—such that people who are eligible for some treatment like a college scholarship may differ by only a point or two from people who are ineligible, i.e., assigned to control. The idea is that people who score well above the threshold are probably very different from people who score very low beyond the threshold. But people who differ by only a point or two in the immediate vicinity of the threshold are probably very similar to one another, such that we can think of assignment as essentially haphazard. The estimated causal effect applies only within the narrow band within which assignment to treatment is plausibly understood as random. There is literally nothing universal about it.

In effect, a great deal of contemporary scholarship has self-consciously traded generality for causal identification. It is thus ironic to criticize contemporary political science for its persistent adherence to Hempel, who famously prioritized general and noncausal laws. If anything, the more biting criticism would be that contemporary political science overemphasizes small-scale, nongeneralizable, and often undertheorized knowledge (Deaton 2014; Deaton and Cartwright 2018).

Therefore, we can reject Bevir and Blakely's second and third assumptions about the nature of naturalist political science: standard scientific practice in contemporary political science does not give priority to either general laws or predictions. One can find work that claims generality; one can find work that makes predictions. But one cannot responsibly claim that these works represent the field as a whole and thus demonstrate its continued fealty to late nineteenth through mid-twentieth century positivism.

What about the first naturalist assumption: that human beliefs and actions are identifiable as brute facts, with behavior understood in terms of classical mechanics, as bodies moving through space? Clifford Geertz (1973, 6), drawing on Gilbert Ryle, famously discussed different interpretations of a single physical act: the rapid contraction of the right eyelid. It could be interpreted as an involuntary and hence unintended twitch or it could be interpreted as a "conspiratorial signal to a friend," or a wink. Physically, the movements are identical; it is only an interpretation of a cultural context that converts a physical movement into a wink. Frederic Schaffer (1998, 88) updates this example with a discussion of voting behavior: Does placing a ballot into a box mean that the person has voted? Only, Schaffer rightly insists, if the person intended to register a preference. A janitor sweeping up unused ballots and discarding them in an empty box would not be voting. And once the question of intentions has been posed, Schaffer continues, interpretation may be an open-ended process: once we have established that somebody intended to vote, we can then ask about the voter's intentions in supporting one candidate over another, and so on.

We think most contemporary political scientists would agree with Schaffer's point about intentions; we feel quite certain that virtually no contemporary political scientist would claim that human behavior can be modeled on classical mechanics as the movement of a physical object through time and space. Perhaps the best way to put our position is to observe that in a variety of ways, contemporary political scientists recognize that their observations are not "objective brute facts," but rather that in many ways their observations are mediated by the instruments they use. In that sense, many contemporary political scientists would at least implicitly agree with the claim that our observations of the world are "theory-laden," in the sense that they are influenced by the frameworks and techniques we use to study the world. We consider four areas in which contemporary political science has self-consciously reflected upon how its own theories and instruments mediate what researchers observe: laboratory experiments, conceptual and operationalization schemes, survey research, and rational-choice models.

Consider first the experiment, or the randomly controlled trial, the methodological gold standard of causal inference, because the combination of random assignment to treatment status and experimenter control over the manipulation of the treatment minimize many threats to the validity of the causal inference. Yet experimenters are well aware that the design of the experiment itself matters greatly, and that many effects observed in experimental studies are artifacts of design that might not be observed in nonexperimental settings. One problem emerges from the high level of control experimenters exercise over the manipulation of the treatment, which implies that subjects' experience of a treatment within a laboratory setting will be quite dissimilar from how subjects would experience the treatment in question in a "natural" setting. Experimental observations, in other words, are produced by the interaction of the experimental intervention with the intentions and subjective experiences of experimental subjects. This concern is expressed as a preference for experimental designs that embody the property of "mundane realism," or designs that minimize the obtrusiveness of interventions and maximize the extent to which experimental settings are more representative of the settings of ordinary life (Iyengar 2011). A second concern is that subjects who are aware of the experimental setting may respond differently, perhaps by seeking to meet perceived experimenter expectations.

Finally, to be valid, inferences based on experimental data must satisfy SUTVA, the "stable unit value treatment assumption," an assumption about noninterference between units such that the outcome observed in one unit is unaffected by the treatment assignment of another unit. SUTVA can be violated, for example, when human subjects learn of their treatment status and *intentionally* alter their behavior based on that knowledge. Compensatory rivalry occurs, for example, when subjects in the control group decide that they can do just as well as the subjects in the treatment group who are perceived as being treated more favorably, while resentful demoralization occurs when those not receiving the perceived favorable treatment become demoralized as a result (Brady 2008, 265). Establishing SUTVA, therefore, requires interpretation of subjects' intentional behavior. .

In all these ways, and others too numerous to discuss here, inferentialists working with experimental data are aware that their observations can be influenced by the instruments they use and that the proper assessment of an experiment may require the interpretation of subjects' intentions.

Concept formation and measurement are critical to any empirical science: here too, we find contemporary political scientists evincing much greater self-consciousness that their theoretical and methodological choices influence their observations. Suppose we claim that country X is a democracy: Can that observation be considered a "brute, objective fact?" The standard approach (Adcock and Collier 2001, 531) depicts conceptualization and measurement as a series of tasks, each of which involves deliberate choice: from a background concept that may contain multiple connotations, derive an explicit definition for use by a particular community of scholars, develop one or more indicators of the underlying latent and unobservable concept, and then apply the concepts to individual cases and record the score. For any given conceptualization and operationalization scheme, errors can be introduced at every stage; for any given background concept, more than one conceptualization and operationalization scheme can be formulated, and units may be scored differently in different schemes. Our "observations," then, are products of the conceptualization and operationalization scheme that is selected, on the one hand, and the degree of measurement error, on the other.

Given the multiplicity of conceptualization and operationalization schemes, how do we choose between them? A long-standing debate, for example, is whether democracy should be operationalized as a dichotomous variable (democracy versus non-democracy) or as a graded variable (more or less democratic), a choice that affects substantive findings about the causes or consequences of democracy (Elkins 2000). As Michael Coppedge (1999) has observed, moreover, alternative conceptualizations can often be arrayed on a thin-to-thick continuum, along which "thicker" concepts are inherently multi-dimensional and so cannot be reduced to a single indicator without sacrificing conceptual validity. To those who have thought long and hard about this problem of rival conceptual schemes, there is simply no effort to argue that observations are brute, objective facts. Rather, leading scholars recommend a more pragmatic approach in which, according to Collier and Adcock (1999, 539),

> specific methodological choices are often best understood and justified in light of the theoretical framework, analytic goals, and context of research involved in any particular study. As theory, goals, and context evolve, choices about concepts likewise may evolve.

Thus, rather than an implicit or explicit claim about concepts that faithfully represent an objective world existing prior to our conceptual scheme for apprehending it, major statements of concept formation explicitly recognize that what we observe depends upon our theories, the conceptual schemes believed to best correspond to them, and the concept-dependent observations that result. We do not deny that some empirical research—perhaps much of it—only minimally reflects upon these conceptual decisions; we deny, however, any claim that the discipline self-consciously and deliberately adopts the view that observations are observer-independent.

Survey research was at the core of the behavioral revolution and remains one of the most important methodological instruments of empirical research in political science. Conventionally, survey research was understood in a reductionist and mechanistic

framework: individuals possess fixed preferences on a given issue and reveal them faithfully to interviewers. Belief that survey research yielded objectively true data about public
opinion seems, in retrospect, naïve, and has long given fodder to interpretivist critiques
that positivism is reductionist, essentialist, and ignores the contingency and the social
situatedness of agents and their beliefs.

To some extent, at least, survey research has made amends. One core assumption today is
that individuals do not possess fully formed preferences waiting to be revealed, they possess
a series of incomplete attitudes and beliefs that are partially independent and perhaps inconsistent with one another (Zaller 1992). Revealed attitudes, then, may not correspond to
any "true" beliefs and attitudes because these do not exist. In a further development, public
opinion researchers have theorized that responses arise from the social nature of the interaction in the survey, a phenomenon exacerbated when surveys probe attitudes toward
socially sensitive topics. Under some circumstances, according to Adam Berinsky (1999,
1210), "the opinion constructed by the respondent is not necessarily the same as the opinion
expressed by that respondent . . . It is plausible that under circumstances where respondents
fear they might be "censured" or socially shunned for their attitudes—either by society or
the interviewer—they might shade those attitudes when reporting them to the interviewer."
Thus, the response "I don't know" might be interpreted as "I do not wish to reveal this to
you." One response by researchers has been to develop a literature on effects on survey
responses due to the race of the interviewer (Davis 1997), the gender of the interviewer
(Kane and Macaulay 1993), and the religiosity of the interviewer (Blaydes and Gillum 2013).
Thus, responses must be *interpreted* along two dimensions: their construction from partial
beliefs held by respondents that are then filtered through—reconstructed during—the social interaction with the interviewer, when both respondent and interviewer share social
knowledge about socially desirable responses.

Finally, consider rational-choice models. Claims about *homo economicus* are the antithesis of an interpretivist philosophy, as they substitute an abstract universalism for any form
of particularistic, context-dependent description of human behavior. Dating back at least
to Hobbes' *Leviathan*, this reductionist view of human action has often and self-consciously
drawn on mechanistic models derived from physics. The axiomatic-rationalist approach to
politics can be particularly vexing when combined with a positivist emphasis on prediction; in the famous—but we would argue obsolete—statement of Milton Friedman (1953),
our substantive assumptions about human behavior can be utterly false but still acceptable
if they allow us to make correct predictions. If such instrumental rationalism is the norm,
then any effort to build bridges between inferentialism and interpretivism would be futile.

But we believe that interpretivist interpretations of dogmatic rational-choice models and
of models more generally may need to be updated. First, causal inferentialism does not require any claims about rational actors: indeed, while laboratory experiments testing models
based on standard micro-economic reasoning are quite common, inferentialism is not
wedded to this approach. Some experimental studies do not test any background theory,
others test theories that are at odds with the tenets of rational-choice theory. Second, contemporary political science exists in a state of multiple models and multiple interpretations
of models that are hard to reconcile with either Hobbes' mechanistic model or Friedman's
"truth-be-damned" prediction model. Kevin Clarke and David Primo expressly reject the
mid-twentieth century "received view" that scientific theories are statements about the

world that we can evaluate as true or false. In contrast to this older view, they interpret models (2012, 12) as objects, and "to ask whether an object is true or false is to make a category mistake." One implication of this view, they continue, is that models cannot be tested definitively by data, as in the received view; rather, models are confronted by *data models* that are themselves (14) "partial, have limited accuracy, and are purpose-relative." In a similar vein, Scott Page (2018) proposes the "many-model" approach that acknowledges the multiplicity of nonrivalrous models that must be combined into an ensemble to make sense of complex phenomena. The two dozen models he discusses, moreover, can be interpreted in one of three ways: as an *embodiment* approach to models, which stresses realism, as the *analogy* approach, which seeks to capture the essence of a causal process, and as an *alternative reality* approach that considers interesting counterfactual possibilities.

To acknowledge the multiplicity of models is to acknowledge, at least tacitly, that our models are contingent human constructions and that the world they reveal to us is, at least partially, constituted by our constructions. As Peter Ordeshook (1986, 52) wrote about formal decision models, the approach does not ignore "the sociological or communal determinants of preference and choice. Exactly the opposite is true...Utility functions are simply abstract representations, and the *a's, o's, x's,* and *y's* that express them await interpretation." Thus, even if contemporary rational-choice theorists believe in the singular truth of their models, they are reluctant to say so publicly. Nolan McCarty and Adam Meirowitz preface their advanced textbook on game theory in political science by noting (2007, 6) that while assumptions of rationality and intentionality are subjects of a lively debate, "we omit the debate between *Homo economicus* and *Homo sociologicus* and jump immediately into the classical model of rational choice." Meanwhile, the growing field of behavioral game theory is based on the premise that individual decision-making in strategic contexts is affected by the actor's "cultural and historical background, their feelings and psychological attitudes and their ethical values...Human players play games in a human way." (Innocenti and Sbriglia 2008, 1–2, cited in Williams 2012, 14).

This more relaxed and permissive view of models creates an opportunity to consider a more central role for an explicit interpretivism in the development and application of models. Rational-choice models treat behavior as intentional and purposive, or oriented towards some goal, even as they acknowledge the lack of complete correspondence between models and actual behavior. As Max Weber observed (1947), instrumental rationality is only one of the four main types of social action, albeit one that was increasingly predominant in rationalizing Western cultures. Weber recommended taking instrumental rationality as a baseline model of behavior and adding other types of social action insofar as actual behavior deviates from predictions. James Farr (1985, 1088) updates Weber's methodology with a model of "situational analysis" whose central component is the "problem-situation in which an actor finds himself or herself, defines his or her problems, and tries out tentative solutions." These situations are constituted by concepts, ideas, and theories and they are thus all intentional phenomena; describing these situations and hence properly interpreting them is, according to Farr, "the fundamental task of political science." Once we recognize that all models—either variants of rational-choice models or other types of models—are representations, based on thinner or thicker descriptions of actor's intentions and purposes, the possibility of a middle ground between inferentialism and interpretivism becomes visible, if perhaps still hazy and in the distance.

It is not our contention that contemporary political scientists are proto interpretivists; the references to interpretivism we have made here are conclusions drawn by particular scholars with reference to particular domains of research. Our contention is that contemporary political science has moved to a new methodological position that is large inconsistent with positivism, and that this methodological transition has coincided with the explicit acknowledgment, in many areas, that causal inference has an ineluctably interpretivist component. Political scientists may engage with interpretivism more tacitly than explicitly and their interpretive efforts may at times fall short of the standards set by interpretivists. But the potential for enhanced collaboration between inferentialists and interpretivists definitely exists and should be encouraged, not dismissed. Whether a cooperative project is feasible or valuable depends partially on whether interpretivists are prepared to devalue, at least partially, the antagonistic justification of their approach.

INTERPRETIVISM: ANTI-WHAT?

The idea of the "thick description" is usually how students first encounter interpretivism as a method. The thick description is the thorough, explicit and specific, detailed articulation of concepts for the aim of understanding human behavior and action embedded in a culture (Geertz, 1973). It opens up a broad focus of the interpretive method—to gather meaning from holistic observation rather than mere observation. This mere observation is contained in the implication of a "thin" description, only discrete pieces of a person are harvested as stand-ins for the whole in order to generalize or predict, a positivist notion. Interpretivism begins with a philosophy which undergirds these principles, rooted in continental philosophies of science, which critiques the use and method of science in modernity. As it began to define itself methodologically, interpretivism came to justify itself as a route to avoiding the ills these critiques represented, becoming antipositivist, antifoundationalist, and antinaturalist. It is on the grounds of these philosophical oppositions for which many scholars have invoked and still justify the use of the interpretive method.

There are some indications, however, that contemporary interpretivism as understood by political scientists has begun to move beyond its oppositional stance as an antijustification. Scholars writing on the methodology have begun to make the explanatory goals of interpretivism far more explicit than previous practitioners of the method had. By making explicit the theoretical and methodological tools to create explanatory interpretive claims, this recent turn can justify interpretivism on its own terms, perhaps implying a more relaxed attitude toward its traditional antithesis, positivism.

Philosophically, interpretivism wishes to push against what has been traditionally conceived as empty empiricism. In opposition to the positivist, naturalist, foundationalist, scientific notions of persons as atomistic, obviously divisible, and unembedded, the interpretivist considers the person as indivisible, rooted in relationships, belief systems, language, and tradition. The vocabulary of interpretivism leans on superior "richness" to the philosophies it defines itself against. Vocabulary like "webs," "fabric," and "lived-in" point out its opposition to singular points, uncontextualized observations, and the laboratory as a space and concept. Meanwhile other phrases like, "inspire creativity," "sense of play," and "imagine with" refer to the unique toolkit available to the interpretivist who, when understanding the world their subject and their actions occupy, can treat phenomena just as richly as a text. This pairing of treatment from text to social phenomena has its roots in other philosophies of social science, especially political theory.

The philosophy of interpretivism can trace its lineage to the early formation of the continental school of political theory, notably Hegel, Heidegger, Gadamer, and Habermas. Gadamer (1975) especially provides interpretivism with a forerunner of reflexivity, as he understands the researcher's unique prejudices to inform rather than hinder the close observations of history, persons, meanings, and symbol, a clear contrast to the positivist belief in brute and objective facts.[1] Through Gadamer's reading of Heidegger, interpretivism transmutes its basic epistemological assumption, namely, that discovery and inquiry rely on uncovering both the phenomena and how the phenomena are understood within a nonstatic environment, an ecosystem, a lifeworld (Habermas 1984). The concept of lifeworld includes not only mutual recognitions but, for Habermas, also a linguistic environment, making uses of language a helpful interpretive subject in order to derive meaning. The interpretivist philosophical tradition, then, entails a methodological commitment that privileges the close reading, the deep commitment to understanding a phenomenon within its interconnected environment of meaning and contexts. The philosophy that Habermas and Gadamer represent is a holistic empiricism, where no single event is divisible from the greater embeddedness of the broader social and cultural fabric. This often makes empirical, explanatory, and predictive work seem suspect to interpretivists, as it threatens to dismember the holism that interpretivists wish above all else to maintain.

This philosophical underpinning has methodological implications for interpretivist studies of politics (Schwartz-Shea and Yanow 2012). Interpretivism employs close, contextual studies of persons, cultures, events, uses of language, human action and belief and motive, in order to develop a narrative or a web of meaning. Doing this interpretivist work means using some unique skill on behalf of the researcher whether it be interviews, observational field work, ethnography, historiography, or comparison (see, especially, Yanow 2006a; Wedeen 2003; Schatz 2013; and Ding 2020). Interpretivists strive to understand human action empathetically through observation and conversation, phenomenologically, linguistically, and reflexively (Schwandt 2000). The choice to use the interpretive method is often justified via the critique of positivism or an appeal to the philosophical obligations to reflexivity or capturing the distinctiveness of the narrative, comparison, or culture of the subjects. As such interpretivism also employs analysis methods which depend deeply on the researcher themselves including semiotic and hermeneutical analysis.

In fact, the role of the researcher is essential to the particular reflexivity which interpretivism employs. The researcher is expected to analyze their own experiences, emotions, and connections to their subjects as the act of studying entails the researcher embedding themselves into that same web (Yanow 2006b; Soss 2006). The justification for the use of interpretivism then becomes a critique of objective positivistic methodologies, which demand an unattainable position presuming the researcher can separate meaningful facts from their own values absolutely and accurately (Yanow 2006b; Wedeen 2002). This reflexivity has been referred to as "bespoke," implying the work is specifically tailored to the subject but also distinctively produced with the characteristics of the researcher (Boswell, Corbett, and Rhodes, 2019). This distinctive work is not only unique to the researcher but also the time during which the research (and the researcher as an evolving person themselves) took place (Bevir and Blakely 2018, 82–83). Reproducibility, then, is unattainable, even for the researcher themselves, but not necessarily warranted for the larger interpretive goal, common in part to all such scholars, to paint a picture, weave a narrative of human action and agency.

Despite this shared philosophical and methodological background, there are diverse understandings of what kinds of claims interpretivism can ultimately make, especially in regard to the possibility of making generalizable or explanatory claims. The more idiographic practitioners of interpretivism tend to see the extent and quality of the method as nonexplanatory and particularistic, seeking to provide no more than rich descriptions and detailed concept formation (Denzin 1983). This variety of interpretivism views ethnography, or situated interpretive study, as a method to describe particular groups, actors within those groups, and the meanings they create for themselves through reperforming memories and interpreting language (Denzin 2001). Many of the landmark interpretive empirical works have taken this general tack, with the motivating justification of true understanding through an antipositivist methodology.

And yet, as we look more closely at many of these works, we find that even as they eschew causal analysis, we can identify implicit causal explanations. For example, in his 1980 book, *Negara*, Clifford Geertz provides a descriptive, close reading of the text he composes from the historical ceremonies, rituals, and spectacles organized by the state. In this fascinating text, Geertz claims that the state constitutes itself, not as kingship or quasigovernment, but as the theater itself. Theatrical rites of the temple directly executed the work of the state, especially the allocation and management of water. These are interpretive claims, marked by their goal to provide new empirical evidence which, by being interpretively uncovered can also provide a useful meaning to those empirics. It is his interpretation of what events constitute theater that shape our understanding of the history of the region.

Yet Geertz goes beyond the microscale and the close reading of the text in two ways. First, he creates a model of the theater-state, extrapolating a more general account from his interpretive, micro-historical account. In this paradigmatic model, power is theater:

> On the basis of the Balinese material, one can construct, therefore, a model of the negara as a distinct variety of political order, a model which can then be used generally to extend our understanding of the developmental history of Indic Indonesia. . . . Such a model is itself abstract. Although it is constructed out of empirical data, it is applied experimentally, not deductively, to the interpretation of other empirical data. It is thus a conceptual entity. . . . it is a guide, a sort of sociological blueprint" (9–10).

With this model firmly in hand, Geertz then ventures into making causal claims, at least implicitly—indeed, he does not shy away from standard mechanistic metaphors of causation. Spectacle and theater, he avers, are the "motor" that instantiate power and the material structure that it underpins. The prosperity and perceived material wealth of the region was not informed by the king but rather by the ceremonies, both political and religious, originating from actors operating beneath the king (129). Geertz, then, is not only interpreting power as theater, but he is also arguing that theater and spectacle are the causal foundations of the political and material order; counterfactually, absent spectacle, the political order collapses.

Lisa Wedeen's *Ambiguities of Domination* (1999) builds on her extensive field work and reflexive interpretive methods to understand the cult of personality surrounding the Syrian

President Hafiz Assad. Wedeen reads two types of texts, one in which Syrian citizens partic-ipate in a set of ritualistic displays of loyalty and another in which they commit small acts of rebellion against the message of the personality cult. In one memorable narrative thread, she recounts the story of a Syrian officer, M, who interprets his own dreams as acts of rebel-lion and whose story Wedeen interprets within interlocking frames of meaning, including a colonial legacy, gender and identity, totalitarianism, family-country bonds, and others (1999, 67). She carefully identifies each thread which comprise the tapestry of meaning re-lated by the story:

> M, after all, chooses not to boycott the ritual but to engage it rebelliously on its own terms. His country, he implies, has sold itself to a corrupt military . . . Helpless to prevent his mother-country from selling her body to the officer, M nevertheless can and does watch it. His self-announced voyeurism suggests his awareness of his own complicity. (Wedeen 1999, 70)

Yet Wedeen also interprets the cult of personality in a narrower causal framework. The puzzle she threads through her work concerns why Syria lived under Assad's power for so long, despite the personal rebellions and individual disillusionment. It is not simply that the cult's propaganda indoctrinates citizens, as the story of M attests. Rather, the ambiguities of the cult create division inside the citizen and between citizens, ultimately preventing citizens from engaging in collective action to effect change. The cult of person-ality, then, is the cause of long-term stability despite widespread citizen dissatisfaction and disillusionment.

Frederic Schaffer (1998) uses an interpretive analysis of language in Senegal, tracing the linguistic and cultural development of democracy, or *demokaraasi*. Schaffer's linguistic analysis is a tool to illuminate the difficulties of understanding democracy across cultures. Senegalese citizens, in Schaffer's reading of their text, ascribe a particular meaning to the term democracy that would be foreign to a Western political sensibility that sees democracy as an instrument for producing accountable governments. In Senegal, participating in de-mocracy is a community-building exercise and a means to obtain goods and services for a particular community, not an opportunity to rescind the fiduciary bond with representative government: democracy means something very different in a very different cultural setting. Without knowing the specific historical and ethnic understandings of this communal pro-cess, a scholar who simply observes that Senegal is a democracy would fail to understand the nature of democratic practices there.

Although Schaffer (1998) denies that his linguistic analysis implies any causal claims about voting behavior (114), this implication is hard to ignore, however. Along with material dep-rivation, Senegal's historical-cultural context motivates and makes reasonable a linguistic understanding of *demokaraasi* as community-based reciprocity and hence paves the way for a political system based on the unequal and vertical ties of a party-based clientelist system. And Schaffer is willing to consider this as a more general claim: "If the case of Senegal is at all generalizable, it can be concluded that ballot casting in other African societies may not in fact be a way for voters to hold elected officials accountable" (115). This may be true; but it too suggests a connection between material deprivation, a historical-cultural context, and the generation of meaning and meaning-motivated behavior. Democracy may mean something different in different contexts, but this claim does not obviate the possibility of causal claims about those contexts, the values they motivate, and the behavior they induce. Schaffer may abjure this conclusion; like many interpretivists do for their bespoke work, he dissuades the use of cross-cultural, large-scale observational analysis, favoring the detailed interpretation of particular institutions in particular cultural contexts. But perhaps the implicit causal claim will become more palatable when it has been severed from positivism, as we have suggested here.

In *Secularism & Revivialism* in Turkey, Andrew Davison (1998) begins with a standard interpretivist justification of method, antithetical to mistaken positivist norms of objectivity and attentive to historical context. Through his hermeneutical linguistic analysis, he explains, at the meta-empirical level, "how certain policies, practices, and institutional relations are what they are *because of*, not despite, a conceptual tension between separation and control in their very conception" (175, emphasis added). As his main text, Davison interprets the writings of the Turkish poet, sociologist, and political activist Ziya Gokalp, who came to prominence after the 1908 Young Turk movement reinstated constitutionalism in the Ottoman Empire and whose work was very influential in the development of Turkish secular nationalism under Kemal Ataturk. Davison's work makes traditional interpretivist claims, leaning heavily on close textual readings and hermeneutical analysis to produce purely descriptive claims.

Yet once again, once we divorce ourselves from positivist notions of universal covering laws, it is not difficult to discern a set of latent causal claims. The power of the state looms large: as the state elite adopted secularizing reforms, they helped to create and define the very meaning of secularism in Turkey, but also helped to create and define its ideological opposite, traditional religious resurgence movement. Depending on how the state pushed secular values, the traditionalist concepts accordingly changed. Davison thus provides an informal causal model in which the secular political ideology of the state explains a host of Turkish cultural and political institutions. From a positivist perspective, these might not qualify as a causal explanation: there is no covering law, for example. Yet, as we have argued, contemporary political science does not require a covering law to make a causal claim; from the viewpoint of causal inferentialism, Davison makes a plausible causal claim about local institutions.

Because interpretivism is often employed, the conclusions of interpretive work usually provide a meaning to events, symbols, languages, actions, histories, etc., where there previously had not been, or provides an adjudication of contesting interpretive meanings. The conclusions of interpretivism for deep understanding and contextualization provide a background and foreground for objects of interest which the researcher argues were lacking before to the detriment of understanding the phenomena. However, interpretivists have, we have shown, always implicitly advocated causal explanation, and recently this movement toward explanation has become much more explicit.

Indeed, recent writings on interpretivism, while maintaining a commitment to the project of meaning-making, contextualizing, unpacking implications, and normative analysis and critique, have begun to develop possible models to provide more general explanations. These models include efforts to draw correspondence between intensive description and general explanations (Davison 1998, 75; Geertz 1980, 134–135), explanatory narratives (Bevir and Blakely 2018, 9), and plausible conjectures (Boswell, Corbett, and Rhodes 2019, 29-30). Effectively, these three models share the inferentialist goal of explaining the world without the positivist downfalls which interpretivists perceive as inherent to causal inference. Interpretivists using these models seek to recapture "explanation" by supplanting causal accounts with their own ontological and epistemological philosophy. In doing so, they create an interpretivist vocabulary for causal explanations identified from the interpretivist lens. For instance, intensive descriptions lead to generally applicable explanations in a limited, contextual way, not generalizable causal laws. Explanatory narratives, rather than causal pathways, bring a history and context along with the explanation. As for plausible conjectures, Boswell, Corbett, and Rhodes contend, citing Boudon (1993), that they "are to interpretive research what generalisations [sic] are to naturalist research. They are general statements that are plausible because they rest on good reasons, and the reasons are good because they are inferred from relevant information" (29).

Indicatively, interpretivist methodology is moving across a threshold, with the traditional empirical method of interpretation on one side and philosophically laden causal explanations on the other. While the earlier, idiographic mode sought to represent phenomena through interpretation and thick description, these more recent approaches identify a novel project: to explain actions, beliefs and events within their interconnected environment which includes the researcher. To repeat our point: this explanatory project requires no covering laws—but neither does causal inferentialism.

These three models of interpretivist explanation—thick description, explanatory narratives, and plausible conjectures—differ from one another in important ways, yet they also converge in interesting ways: they all focus on human actors, their beliefs, as well as individual actions, which can allow the researcher to arrive at recurring reasons for their actions—the motivation for their actions as they and the interpreter understand these reasons. This is not dissimilar from the general contours of mechanistic causation which also seeks to identify a recurring reason why actors might act, which can include notions of agency, embedded consciousness and self-articulated intentions; we return to this issue in the essay's final section. As Boswell, Corbett, and Rhodes (2019, 24–25) summarize,

> the interpretive approach is about explanation, not understanding. The natural and interpretive sciences use different concepts of causation, and the interpretive version of explanation differs from that often found among political scientists. Narratives are the way the interpretive approach explains actions and practices.

This enunciation of interpretivism, then, wishes to understand causation distinctively from positivist notions of causality. It seeks explanations that are unique, contextualized deeply into both the limited temporal and spatial world, but also unique to the researcher's own frame of mind. These explanations can be mechanistic, divulging how actions and beliefs interplay to yield an intended and perceived effect. Interpreting the mechanism of actions and practices requires understanding actors, knowing the bounds and abilities of their agency and intentions within that snapshot of discovery. As we argue in the next section, we can find some common ground between this approach and causal inferentialism.

However, it is very possible common ground will not be wanted or accepted, as the shared goal, yet antinomous justifications of interpretivist research presume an abject incommensurability to the methodological philosophies of interpretivism and inferentialism. Following Wittgenstein, it is possible the interpretivists and inferentialists are engaging in separate language games, and following Kuhn, these languages of discovery and methodological philosophy are simply incommensurable without any translation between them. So, we understand that the commonality we present may not be taken up by some in both traditions.

A last question: as interpretivists move toward more explicitly explanatory work, what criteria will be used to evaluate explanations? Are all explanations equally valid? Here too we find evolving standards. Given the nature of interpretive work, as highly personally participatory on behalf of the researcher's interactive experience, as well as the nonabsolute nature of interpretation lending meaning the ability to change over time and person, interpretivists are noting a need for a community of critique among scholars of similar phenomena (Davison 1998, 62–63). For example, some interpretivists advocate for a quasi-adversarial academic environment which fosters criticism and correction of interpretivist work (see Lincoln 1995; Boswell, Corbett, and Rhodes 2019). The logic is clear. If a scholar leaves out critical detail from an interpretation which another member of that particular scholarly community has access to, the narrative picture will only be thickened by their correspondence. The communal creation of standards of interpretation can only develop through accepting methodological fallibility and encouraging discourse around it. Boswell, Corbett, and Rhodes (2019) call this "intersubjective objectivity," which allows them to re-define objectivity as a commitment to this environment of critique and general intellectual honesty providing there is an environment which can foster this benevolent adversarial practice (34). Not only does this mentality around interpretivism foster more interpretive scholarship but also the necessity for more interpretive scholars to enter the field.

SEARCHING FOR THE ELUSIVE MIDDLE GROUND: COMBINING EXPLANATION AND UNDERSTANDING

To this point, we have argued that the epistemological center of gravity in political science does not resemble the outdated model held by antipositivists. Most strikingly, the movement over the past quarter-century toward causal identification has thoroughly displaced the mid-twentieth century alliance between political science and logical positivism. Carl Hempel's deductive-nomological model, which itself only reluctantly employed any notion of causation, is an ancient relic. Research taking identification as its guiding spirit worries about correctly estimating local causal effects, an endeavor that forces researchers to worry about causal heterogeneity and raises high barriers to external validity, or the generalization of findings from one study to additional units, treatments, outcomes, and settings. If there is a critique to be made about the identification revolution, it is that it has entailed a relatively atheoretical narrowing of scope, not a universalizing project.

We have also given some reason to believe that contemporary political science cannot be accused of treating data as objective brute facts. The self-conscious choices involved in concept formation, measurement, survey formats, experimental design, and the selection and interpretation of models all attest to this more reflexive understanding of the nature of observations and the relationship of observations to theory. In some instances, this means that contemporary political sciences are aware that "facts" are theory-laden and instrument-specific; in other instances, it means that contemporary political scientists are aware that "facts" require interpretation. Inferentialists have not explicitly adopted any element of interpretivist theory; rather, elements of contemporary practice may make contemporary inferentialists more open to interpretivist methods and insights than an older generation of positivists would have been.

Across the epistemological divide, contemporary interpretivism has moved far more explicitly into the field of desiring nuanced, contextual, reflexively oriented, and narrow explanations. It seeks to derive these explanations from a legacy of producing thick description and privileging holistic understanding, webs of meaning, and tapestries of belief. These more recent philosophical and methodological shifts allow interpretivists to call for generalizable and cross-contextual explanations, which can inform larger patterns of politics (Boswell, Corbett, and Rhodes 2019, 41–42). Rather than implying the explanatory power of detail-driven, immersive, interpretive work, such as linguistic analytic work (see Pouliot 2016) and ethnographies (see Simmons and Smith 2017), interpretivism now seeks to make these explanations explicit through deriving new vocabularies and elucidations of what an explanation can be beyond the positivist lens. Interpretivism, though still setting itself against naturalism and the specter of positivism, also seeks to accomplish the kind of claims, goals, and more general statements which inferentialists often privilege.

At minimum, then, we have updated beliefs about the nature of the terrain that divides inferentialists and interpretivists; the last question to consider is whether we have created fertile ground for at least tentative cooperation. Perhaps inferentialists and interpretivists can teach each other how to interpret and infer better; and perhaps these can even collaborate on shared projects.

We would like to suggest that the most suitable domain for potential cooperation is research into causal mechanisms. For strict inferentialists, there is nothing beyond the identification of causal effects; for strict interpretivists, the very idea of causation may violate fundamental epistemological and ontological assumptions. Yet many inferentialists care about mechanisms as explanatory devices, and at least some interpretivists appear to care about causation; perhaps thinking about causal mechanisms, then, will enlarge the grounds for potential collaboration. The greatest opportunity for cooperation exists, we argue, insofar as we share two beliefs: (1) that the identification of causal mechanisms is a distinct and valuable project beyond pure causal identification or thick description, and (2) that we conceive of mechanisms as existing at the intersection of explanation and understanding.

In the causal inference literature, mechanisms are often treated as equivalent to intervening variables, or mediators in graph-theoretical approaches. Alternatively, some scholars equate mechanisms to an entire causal system that transmits some input from beginning to end along a chain of causal relationships; in the graph-theoretical approach, an entire directed acyclic graph may be referred to as a mechanism for bringing about a causal effect. Pragmatically, these definitions of mechanism would not advance our goal of promoting collaboration between inferentialists and interpretivists. Epistemologically, the approach also provides little value. If the idea—and the promise—of mechanisms was to move beyond correlations between X and Y, then adding an intervening variable, $X \rightarrow M \rightarrow Y$, where M denotes the mediator in a directed acyclic graph, accomplishes little; it disaggregates the XY correlation into separate XM and MY correlations. True, such disaggregation can be useful for other reasons, including causal identification along a "frontdoor path," but it offers little in terms of the conceptually deeper understanding of causation associated with mechanisms in the philosophical literature.

We propose an interpretation of mechanisms as elements of a defined causal system that cannot be manipulated. In any given system, we can (in principle, at least) intervene on a variable to set it to a new value, but we cannot intervene directly on a mechanism within that system. We conceive of mechanisms as the latent elements of a causal system represented by the arrows connecting two nodes by a causal relationship in the graph-theoretical perspective (Waldner 2012, 2019). Following Machamer, Darden, and Craver (2000, 3), we conceive of mechanisms as "entities and activities that are productive of regular changes." Entities engage in activities, while activities produce either continuity or change with regularity because they are constrained by the properties of the entity. Following Petri Ylikoski (2012; see also Wendt 1999), we distinguish causation between events from the constitution of an entity via the relation of its properties. Thus, mechanisms are entities that act in specified ways as constrained by their constitutive structure; given that structure, mechanisms act invariably. It is this constitutive nature of mechanisms that gives them the capacity to propagate or transmit causal influence from one variable (or event) to another.

If causal explanation (in contrast to causal identification) requires mechanisms, and mechanisms require detailed descriptive knowledge of constitutive properties, then, as Peter Manicas (2006, 15) put it, explanation presupposes understanding. This pairing of explanation and understanding potentially undermines the traditional antinomy between explanation and understanding. The constitutive explanation, a hallmark of contemporary interpretivism, becomes a necessarily justifiable method in its own right rather than a justification premised on a superannuated antinaturalism.

Interpretivists might object, at this point, that we have smuggled an outdated notion of natural kinds into the study of human affairs, a notion that many believe is inappropriate even in the natural sciences where, as John Dupré argues (1993, 18), "there are countless legitimate, objectively grounded ways of classifying objects in the world. And these may often cross-classify one another in indefinitely complex ways." Yet consider the proximity of Dupré's claim to Page's proposition that understanding a complex world requires an ensemble of nonrivalrous models. We do not need, in other words, the idea of natural kinds to make our point about mechanisms; we do not need to attribute any singular and universal attributes to human beings. We need only to identify particular attributes in particular causal systems. The only abstract and universal claim that we make—the source of invariance in our understanding of causal mechanisms—is that humans have causal powers because (1) they have the properties of consciousness, intentionality, and agency, and (2) because they are embedded in particular contexts based on particular systems of cultural signification by which human beings understand themselves in relation to others and act accordingly, with their actions constituting potential causal powers.

From this open-ended perspective, interpretivists could read a rationalist causal mechanism as just one among many potential interpretations of the context, its meaning, and the induced action. For example, Clifford Geertz (1973, 430) can simultaneously interpret the Balinese cock fight through the lens of particularistic cultural constitution in which the main wagers follow a culturally prescribed form *and* describe side betting between odds-givers and odds-takers as "a pronounced mini-max saddle," a concept drawn from some of the earliest work on noncooperative, two-person game theory.

Interpretivists who insist on thick description, then, need not abjure a rationalist interpretation on a priori grounds; they need only insist that a particular interpretation, drawn from a large set of possible interpretations, be contextually superior to others given a history of evidence gathering and a theory of instruments by which we gather evidence. Inferentialists, who place their greatest priority on the design of research and causal identification, need not insist on a particular model of human action as the proper interpretation of a causal mechanism. Nothing in this account is incompatible with interpretivist sensibilities and philosophies, on one side, or with inferentialist research designs, on the other. Assigning each approach to its proper domain—inferentialists acting as forensic experts and interpretivists as detectives describing motives—can be mutually informative and leave us all in an epistemologically superior position. Much still divides inferentialism and interpretivism, but these divisions need not necessarily impede a satisfactory division of labor.

ACKNOWLEDGMENTS

The authors wish to acknowledge Izza Din, James Mahoney, Sayres Rudy, and Jennifer Rubenstein for their generous comments on earlier drafts.

NOTES

1. However, following Chapter 25 in this very volume, this construction of the original positivist commitment to "brute facts" could be misplaced as well.

REFERENCES

Adcock, Robert, and David Collier. 2001. "Measurement Validity: A Shared Standard for Qualitative and Quantitative research." *American Political Science Review*, 95(3): 529–546.

Acharya, Avidit, Matthew Blackwell, and Maya Sen. 2016. "Explaining Causal Findings Without Bias: Detecting and Assessing Direct Effects." *American Political Science Review*, 110(3): 512–529.

Angrist, Joshua D., and Alan B. Krueger. 2001. "Instrumental Variables and the Search for Identification: From Supply and Demand to Natural Experiments." *Journal of Economic Perspectives*, 15(4): 69–85.

Angrist, Joshua D., and Jörn-Steffen Pischke. 2009. *Mostly Harmless Econometrics: An Empiricist's Companion*. Princeton University Press.

Berinsky, Adam J. 1999. "The Two Faces of Public Opinion." *American Journal of Political Science*, 43(4): 1209–1230.

Bevir, Mark, and Jason Blakely. 2018. *Interpretive Social Science: An Anti-Naturalist Approach*. Oxford University Press.

Blaydes, Lisa, and Rachel M. Gillum. 2013. "Religiosity-of-Interviewer Effects: Assessing the Impact of Veiled Enumerators on Survey Response in Egypt." *Politics and Religion*, 6(3): 459–482.

Boudon, Raymond. 1993. "Towards a Synthetic Theory of Rationality." *International Studies in the Philosophy of Science*, 7: 5–19.

Boswell, John, Jack Corbett, J., and R. A. W. Rhodes. 2019. *The Art and Craft of Comparison*. Cambridge University Press.

Brady, Henry. 2008. "Causation and Explanation in Social Science." In *The Oxford Handbook of Political Methodology*, edited by Janet Box-Steffensmeier, Henry Brady, and David Collier. Oxford University Press, 217–270.

Clarke, Kevin, and David Primo. 2012. *A Model Discipline: Political Science and the Logic of Representations*. Oxford University Press.

Collier, David, and Robert Adcock. 1999. "Democracy and Dichotomies: A Pragmatic Approach to Choices About Concepts." *Annual Review of Political Science*, 2: 537–565

Coppedge, Michael. 1999. "Thickening Thin Concepts and Theories: Combining Large N and Small in Comparative Politics." *Comparative Politics*, 31(4): 465–476.

Davis, Darren W. 1997. "The Direction of Race of Interviewer Effects Among African-Americans: Donning the Black Mask." *American Journal of Political Science*, 41(1): 309–322.

Davison, Andrew. 1998. *Secularism and Revivalism in Turkey: A Hermeneutic Reconsideration*. Yale University Press.

Deaton, Angus. 2014. "Instruments, Randomization, and Learning about Development." In *Field Experiments and Their Critics: Essays on the Uses and Abuses of Experimentation in the Social Sciences*, edited by Dawn Langan Teele. Yale University Press, 141–184.

Deaton, Angus and Nancy Cartwright. 2018. "Understanding and Misunderstanding Randomized Controlled Trials." *Social Science & Medicine*, 210: 2–21.

Denzin, Norman. 1983. "Interpretive Interactionism." In *Beyond Method: Strategies for Social Research*, edited by Gareth Morgan. Sage Publications, 129–146.

Denzin, Norman K. 2001. *Interpretive Interactionism* 2nd ed. Sage Publications.

Ding, Iza. 2020. "Performative Governance." *World Politics*, 72(4): 1–32.

Dunning, Thad. 2008. *Natural Experiments in the Social Sciences: A Design-Based Approach*. Cambridge University Press.

Dupré, John. 1995. *The Disorder of Things: The Metaphysical Foundations of the Disunity of Science*. Harvard University Press.

Elkins, Zachary. 2000. "Gradations of Democracy? Empirical Tests of Alternative Conceptualizations." *American Journal of Political Science*, 44(2): 287–94.

Elwert, Felix, and Christopher Winship. 2014. "Endogenous Selection Bias: The problem of Conditioning on a Collider Variable." *Annual Review of Sociology*, 40: 31–53.

Farr, James. 1985. "Situational Analysis: Explanation in Political Science." *The Journal of Politics*, 47(4): 1085–1107.

Fox, Margalit. 2018. *Conan Doyle for the Defense: The True Story of a Sensational British Murder, a Quest for Justice, and the World's Most Famous Detective Writer*. Random House.

Friedman, Milton. 1953. *Essays in Positive Economics*. The University of Chicago Press.

Gadamer, Hans-Georg. 1975. *Truth and Method*. Seabury Press.

Geertz, Clifford. 1973. *The Interpretation of Cultures*. Basic Books.

Geertz, Clifford. 1980. *Negara: The Theater-State in Nineteenth Century Bali*. Princeton University Press.

Goertz, Gary. 2012. "Descriptive-Causal Generalizations: 'Empirical Laws' in the Social Sciences?" In *The Oxford Handbook of Philosophy of Social Science*, edited by Harold Kincaid. Oxford University Press, 85–108.

Gerber, Alan S., and Donald P. Green, D. 2012. *Field Experiments: Design, Analysis, and Interpretation*. W. W. Norton & Company.

Habermas, Jürgen. 1984. *The Theory of Communicative Action*, Vol. II. Beacon Press.

Hernán, Miguel, and James Robins. 2020. *Causal Inference: What If?* Chapman and Hall.

Holland, Paul W. 1986. "Statistics and Causal Inference." *Journal of the American Statistical Association*, 81(396): 945–960.

Illari, Phyllis, and Federica Russo. 2014. *Causality: Philosophical Theory Meets Scientific Practice.* Oxford University Press.

Imbens, Guido W., and Donald B. Rubin. 2015. *Causal Inference for Statistics, Social, and Biomedical Sciences: An Introduction.* Cambridge University Press.

Innocenti, Alessandro, and Patrizia Sbriglia. 2008. *Games, Rationality, and Behaviour: Essays on Behavioural Game Theory and Experiments.* Palgrave Macmillan.

Iyengar, Shanto. "Laboratory Experiments in Political Science." In *Cambridge Handbook of Experimental Political Science*, edited by James N. Druckman, Donald P. Green, James H. Kuklinksi, and Arthur Lupia. Cambridge University Press, 73–88.

Kane, Emily, and Laura Macaulay. 1993. "Interviewer Gender and Gender Attitudes." *Public Opinion Quarterly*, 57(1): 1–28.

Keele, Luke, Randolph T. Stevenson, and Felix Elwert. 2020. "The Causal Interpretation of Estimated Associations in Regression Models." *Political Science Research and Methods*, 8(1): 1–13.

King, Gary, Robert O. Keohane, and Sidney Verba. 1994. *Designing Social Inquiry: Scientific Inference in Qualitative Research.* Princeton University Press.

Lincoln, Yvonna. S. 1995. "Emerging Criteria for Quality in Qualitative and Interpretive Research." *Qualitative Inquiry*, 1(3): 275–289.

Machamer, Peter, Lindley Darden, and Carl F. Craver. 2000. "Thinking about Mechanisms." *Philosophy of Science* 67(1): 1–25.

Manicas, Peter. 2006. *A Realist Philosophy of Social Science.* Cambridge University Press.

McCarty, Nolan, and Adam Meirowitz. 2007. *Political Game Theory.* Cambridge University Press.

Montgomery, Jacob. M., Brendan Nyhan, B., and Michelle Torres. 2018. "How Conditioning on Posttreatment Variables Can Ruin Your Experiment and What to Do About It." *American Journal of Political Science*, 62(3): 760–775.

Morgan, Stephen L., and Christopher Winship. 2015. *Counterfactuals and Causal Inference: Methods and Principles for Social Research*, 2nd ed. Cambridge University Press.

Neyman, Jerzy. 1934. "On the Two Different Aspects of the Representation Model: The Method of Stratified Sampling and the Method of Purposive Selection." *Journal of the Royal Statistical Society*, 97(4): 558–625.

Ordeshook, Peter C. 1986. *Game Theory and Political Theory: An Introduction.* Cambridge University Press.

Page, Scott. 2018. *The Model Thinker: What You Need to Know to Make Data Work for You.* Basic Books.

Pearl, Judea. 2000. *Causality: Models, Reasoning, and Inference.* Cambridge University Press.

Pouliot, Vincent. 2016. *International pecking orders: The politics and practice of multilateral diplomacy.* Cambridge University Press.

Rosenbaum, Paul R. 2017. *Observation & Experiment: An Introduction to Causal Inference.* Harvard University Press.

Rubin, Donald. 1974. "Estimating Causal Effects of Treatments in Randomized and Nonrandomized Studies." *Journal of Educational Psychology* 55(5): 688–701.

Salmon, Wesley C. 1989. *Four Decades of Scientific Explanation.* University of Minnesota Press.

Schaffer, Frederic. C. 1998. *Democracy in Translation: Understanding Politics in an Unfamiliar Culture.* Cornell University Press.

Schatz, Edward. (Ed.). 2013. *Political ethnography: What Immersion Contributes to the Study of Power*. University of Chicago Press.

Schwandt, Thomas. A. 2000. "Three Epistemological Stances for Qualitative Inquiry: Interpretivism, Hermeneutics, and Social Constructionism. In *Handbook of Qualitative Research* 2nd ed., edited by Norman K. Denzin and Yvonna S. Lincoln. Sage Publications, 189–214.

Schwartz-Shea, Peregrine, and Dvora Yanow. 2012. *Interpretive Research Design: Concepts and Processes*. Routledge.

Seawright, Jason. 2019. "Statistical Analysis of Democratization: A Constructive Critique." *Democratization*, 26(1): 21–39.

Simmons, Erica. S., and Nicholas Rush Smith. 2017. Comparison with an Ethnographic Sensibility. *PS: Political Science & Politics*, 50(1): 126–130.

Soss, Joe. 2006. "Talking Our Way to Meaningful Explanations: A Practice-Centered View of Interviewing for Interpretive Research." In *Interpretation and Method: Empirical Research Methods and the Interpretive Turn*, edited by Dvora Yanow and Peregrine Schwartz-Shea. M. E. Sharpe, 127–149.

Waldner, David. 2012. "Process Tracing and Causal Mechanisms." In *The Oxford Handbook of Philosophy of Social Science*, edited by Harold Kincaid. Oxford University Press, 65–84.

Waldner, David. 2019. "Causal Mechanisms and Qualitative Causal Inference in the Social Sciences." In *Contemporary Philosophy and Social Science: An Interdisciplinary Dialogue*, edited by Michiru Nagatsu and Attilia Ruzzene. Bloomsbury Academic, 275–300.

Wedeen, Lisa. 1999. *Ambiguities of Domination: Politics, Rhetoric, and Symbols in Contemporary Syria*. The University of Chicago Press.

Wedeen, Lisa. 2002. "Conceptualizing Culture: Possibilities for Political Science." *American Political Science Review* 96(4): 713–728.

Wedeen, Lisa. 2003. "Seeing Like a Citizen, Acting Like a State: Exemplary Events in United Yemen." *Comparative Studies in Society and History*, 45(4): 680–713.

Wendt, Alexander. 1999. *Social Theory of International Politics*. Cambridge University Press.

Williams, Kenneth C. 2012. *Game Theory: A Behavioral Approach*. Oxford University Press.

Woodward, James. 2005. *Making Things Happen: A Theory of Causal Explanation*. Oxford University Press.

Yanow, Dvora. 2006a. "Thinking Interpretively: Philosophical Presuppositions and the Human Sciences." In *Interpretation and Method: Empirical Research Methods and the Interpretive Turn*, edited by Dvora Yanow and Peregrine Schwartz-Shea. M. E. Sharpe, 5–26.

Yanow, Dvora. 2006b. "Neither Rigorous nor Objective? Interrogating Criteria for Knowledge Claims." In *Interpretation and Method: Empirical Research Methods and the Interpretive Turn*, edited by Dvora Yanow and Peregrine Schwartz-Shea. M. E. Sharpe, 97–119.

Ylikoski, Petri. 2012. "Micro, Macro, and Mechanisms." In *The Oxford Handbook of the Philosophy of Social Science*, edited by Harold Kincaid. Oxford University Press, 21–45.

Zaller, John R. 1992. *The Nature and Origins of Mass Opinion*. Cambridge University Press.

CHAPTER 12

··

QUALITATIVE COMPARATIVE ANALYSIS (QCA)
A Pluralistic Approach to Causal Inference

··

FEDERICA RUSSO AND BENOÎT RIHOUX

1. POLITICAL SCIENCE AND QCA

··

IN this section we briefly position QCA as an approach to studying problems in the diverse political science subfields. We recall the origins of QCA since the influential work of Charles Ragin (1987) and we sketch its more recent developments highlighting how it is currently used in empirical research settings (see, e.g., Marx, Rihoux, and Ragin 2014; Rihoux 2020).

Political science, as the term suggests, studies the "political" sphere; it is concerned with issues of governance, political activities, and/or theories, or political behavior. The discipline is itself diverse, in that it has numerous sub-fields, such as political economy, international relations, policy analysis, public management, comparative politics, electoral studies, etc. It is beyond the scope of this chapter to provide a consensus definition about "political science"; instead, qualifications such as the one given by Dowding (2015) will be a useful starting point for us:

> What do we understand by the term "political science"? As in the nature of the analysis of this book, I do not think there is much worth in defining it a length. Politics can be understood narrowly or broadly—as concerned only with matters of the state or polity or as expressed in virtually any sets of human interaction. (p. 243)

Interestingly, this characterization of political science arrives at the very end of the book, where methods and approaches in the field are presented in what we may call a "pluralistic" spirit. Supposedly, there isn't one method to be preferred over another, because the objects of investigations within the realm of what we call "political science" may be very different. Political science studies many objects—this may reflect a more general characteristic of the social sciences, whose internal and external boundaries have been shifting and are likely to shift again as time passes by (see, e.g., Gulbenkian Commission on the Restructuring of the Social Sciences 1996; Montuschi 2003). In political science, for instance, areas such as "electoral studies" or "comparative politics" are also labeled "electoral sociology" and "comparative political sociology," respectively, showing gradual permeability of the borders of political science and of sociology.

These boundaries not only concern what, narrowly or broadly, defines a discipline (for instance, what makes sociology different from psychology, or anthropology from sociology), but also the methods of the social sciences, and of political science for the matter. In this sense, political science is no different from other social sciences that collectively show high variability and variety in the methods and, one may dare say, high permeability in borrowing new methods from other fields (see, e.g., Blanchard, Rihoux, and Álamos-Concha 2017; Rihoux, Kittel, and Moses 2008).

While we generally endorse a pluralistic stance in political science methodology and in the sciences more generally, the specific kind of pluralism that we will be concerned with in this chapter has to do with the de facto existence of different methodologies—quantitative and qualitative ones—in political science and with the attempts to combine them or to go beyond them in approaches such as qualitative comparative analysis (QCA) and mixed methods research (MMR; see, e.g., Blanchard, Rihoux, and Álamos-Concha 2017; Gerring 2017; Pierce 2008). In particular, we shall be concerned with the former approach, and we will systematically discuss its methodological and epistemological underpinning in view of "combining" or "integrating" methods. We will return later to the issue of properly defining qualitative and quantitative approaches, but it will suffice to mention at this stage that, in this chapter, we will not be concerned with the deep constructivist, interpretivist qualitative approaches typical of certain ethnographic research; instead, our interest in qualitative approaches is restricted to "realist" qualitative approaches, namely those approaches that may take on board some elements of "postpositivism." Labels and conventions used in philosophy (of science) and in social science methodology vary somehow but, simply put, these approaches take it that qualitative studies do have a grip on reality—not everything is a matter of interpretation and of construction—and that qualitative studies can, under certain conditions, uncover causal relationships in the patterns of the social world (see, e.g., Orne and Bell 2015, chap. 1).

The chapter is organized as follows. In Section 2, we introduce QCA as is used in political science, paying particular attention to the comparison of cases and to its core methodology. In Section 3, we discuss whether, and to what extent, QCA bridges the gap between qualitative and quantitative methodologies. In so doing, we discuss QCA as a "mixed-method" approach, which we hope positively contributes to the foundations of QCA. In Section 4, we ask whether, and to what extent, can QCA shed light on causal questions and contribute to causal explanation. To do so, we assess QCA in relation to another prominent and relatively recent approach in political science, namely, the process-tracing approach. While the possibility of drawing causal conclusions from QCA studies has been addressed, we hope to provide further elements at the theoretical and applied level about the conditions under which QCA studies license causal inferences. In Section 5, we conclude the chapter with a general reflection on what it means to integrate or combine approaches, and whether QCA achieves that. We argue that the positive payoff of combining methods as is done in QCA is to obtain a richer epistemic access to the phenomenon under investigation. To explain what that means, we adopt Ruphy's "foliated pluralism." With foliated pluralism, we aim to provide solid foundations to the practice of QCA, in which both qualitative and quantitative methods are used, and in which questions about "why" and "how" are addressed again adopting a plurality of methods.

2. QUALITATIVE COMPARATIVE ANALYSIS

Within the realm of the plurality of methods used in political science, we examine in this chapter one method specifically, namely, QCA. QCA is a methodology for systematically analyzing and comparing cases. Its pioneering theorizer is Charles Ragin, who has been developing the approach since the mid-1980s. QCA has been taken up by a number of scholars in different fields (see, e.g., Rihoux et al. 2013; Rihoux and Marx 2013). A growing QCA community has developed across different disciplines, notably across political science and management research, producing a wealth of publications on the subject, as well as organizing training and research events (see compasss.org for numerous resources). The early developments of QCA in the late 1980s and early 1990s aimed at offering analytical tools in political science (and especially comparative politics) and historical sociology. Therefore, QCA was initially designed as a "macro-comparative" approach, in which the comparison is made at the level of societies, economies, states, etc. (see, e.g., Berg-Schlosser and Cronqvist 2005; Rihoux and Ragin 2009, chap. 1). As will become clear throughout the discussion, QCA is in fact a bundle of methods and can even be conceived of as a combination of methods.

Two characteristics of QCA are worth highlighting, before proceeding with presenting the approach in greater detail. First, the emphasis on "comparison" and second (and relatedly) the emphasis on "cases." We follow Ragin here in characterizing the social sciences as being *comparative* in nature. Ragin (1987), to be sure, thinks this is especially true of qualitative, case-oriented, and historical approaches, but an argument can be made that a comparative, or contrastive, or variational epistemology is also at the core of quantitative methods (see Russo 2009). While it is widely acknowledged that the social sciences are pluralist in their methods (see also later Section 4), according to Russo (2009), the existence of a common rationale, namely a variational epistemology, is what binds qualitative and quantitative approaches together qua *scientific* methods.

As we shall see later, it was Ragin's starting point to keep the richness of qualitative and case-oriented approaches but scaling up so as to compare *several* cases using some kind of formal tool. This comparative aspect unfolds at different levels of abstraction—notably that of variables rather than specific cases—and is essential to be able to make inferences, notably, causal inferences (see Russo 2009). So why do we compare? We attempt here an answer, which remains speculative at this stage, and that hopefully motivates the interest in considering QCA as a legitimate candidate to go beyond the qualitative-quantitative divide. We need to compare for a very basic epistemological reason: without (empirical) comparison we cannot build knowledge.

This leads us to the second characteristic of QCA, the emphasis on "cases." We start with single cases, but to properly understand each case, and to build *general* knowledge from the cases, we need to compare. This is no breaking news, as Ragin also notices that a comparative method has its roots in the work of a most eminent methodologist, namely John Stuart Mill. QCA has its epistemological roots in the Millian Methods of Agreement and of Difference, which, coincidentally, are based on the rationale of variation (Russo 2009). QCA is thus part of a broader, and well-established, social scientific tradition, the core of which is precisely the analysis of cases, also called "case study approach" (see, e.g., Gerring

2011) and that, as Gerring (2006, chap. 1) had already noticed, is also widespread in other areas beyond political science, from anthropology to education, from medicine to business.

QCA was initially developed as an alternative to the standard quantitative, statistics-oriented methods of the social sciences, those in which the whole research question boils down to quantifying the net-effect of variables. The problem, or the dissatisfaction, with this approach is that the richness of working with (historical) cases, in a qualitative way, is lost in the dryness of numbers (an argument that, in the ears of History and Philosophy of Science [HPS] scholars, echoes those of historian Theodor Porter 1996). At the same time, the possibility of analyzing *several* cases, as is done in standard quantitative and statistical approaches, is also lost when working in standard qualitative, case-based approaches.

The problem seems to be rather well-known to social science methodologists, trapped in the typical dichotomy, as discussed by Wood and Welch (2010): either we subscribe to a methodology—the quantitative one—that is objective and positivist in character, or we subscribe to a methodology—the qualitative one—that is subjective, interpretivist, and phenomenological. In this context, positivism refers to views about the role of the observer (who should be independent), of human interests (that should not be relevant), or of explanation (meant to be primarily causal)—all in sharp contraposition to the subjective, interpretivist, and phenomenological character of qualitative research. This, however, can be seen a false dichotomy, for at least two reasons. On the one hand, there are, currently, at least two different "qualitative" spheres in social sciences: a case-oriented one that is also willing to discuss "causes," "effects," "variables," "data sets," "coding," "measurement," etc., and that believes we can attempt to apprehend empirically the "real world"—adopting different empirical stances depending on the author: typically, scholars in this camp are called "realist" or "critical realist," but also sometimes "(post)-positivist," versus an interpretivist camp that rejects both this "too positivist" case-oriented approach and the quantitative (statistical, formal) approach (see, e.g., Blanchard, Rihoux, and Álamos-Concha 2017). On the other hand, QCA presents itself, in fact, both as a case-oriented *and* variable-oriented methodology (what Ragin coined a "synthetic strategy" in his early writings), one in which we can deal in particular with small and intermediate-N designs. Incidentally, QCA is sometimes said to be particularly useful when N is not too big or too small, i.e., in intermediate-N situations—but this is not a core definitional feature of QCA, as it can also be used in larger-N research (Fiss, Sharapov, and Cronqvist 2013; Ragin and Fiss 2017).

How to study cases is addressed by Ragin and Amoroso (2019, part. 2), who discuss three methodological approaches—the qualitative, comparative, and quantitative ones—highlighting the specific goals and assets of each. In a case-based approach, the choice will be between analyzing many cases in order to be able to identify general patterns and analyzing fewer cases in order to go in more depth in each of them. Or, to echo Ragin and Amoroso (2019, 119), the question is about a "trade-off between the *number of cases* and the *number of the features of cases* social researchers typically can study and then represent." Simply put, according to Ragin and Amoroso, qualitative approaches are good to find commonalities, and to clarify the categories and concepts involved; comparative research is good to identifying complex patterns that involve both similarities and differences between cases; quantitative approaches, finally are best suited to find covariations of features by analyzing many cases. As we read Ragin and Amoroso, there is no strict hierarchy between these approaches, and in fact *all* are routinely employed in social science research, whether in political science or elsewhere. We embrace this pluralistic attitude too, and we hope to further contribute to the reflection on what it means to combine or integrate methods throughout the chapter.

Let us examine more in detail what QCA amounts to. The core of QCA is grounded in the use of set theory and of Boolean algebra to systematically compare a given group (population, subpopulation or purposive sample) of cases that display a contrasted outcome (equivalent to the "dependent variable" in quantitative research). From the description of a given number of cases, each one of which is operationalized as a "configuration" (values on a certain number of conditions and on an outcome), we derive propositions to describe salient characteristics of the cases, which can be analyzed via, e.g., truth tables (tables of configurations). Boolean logics is then exploited to systematically reduce complexity. Ultimately, QCA is most frequently used as a tool to evaluate specific hypotheses (between respective conditions and the outcome), formulated in terms of necessity and sufficiency, driving the comparison across cases.

With QCA, we can combine strengths of both the qualitative and quantitative approach, and use the method for a number of purposes, e.g., summarize data that describe a number of cases, check the analytical coherence of a given set of cases, evaluate existing theories by testing them against a number of cases, and even explore new data and assess new ideas in political science.

Ragin (2014, chap. 8) illustrates how his Boolean-based approach proves useful in a variety of research situations. In that chapter, he runs crisp-set QCA (csQCA, i.e., dichotomizing both the outcome and the conditions) past the classic analysis of Rokkan (1970) on nation building in Western Europe, then on a study of ethnic political mobilization, and finally on an analysis of juvenile courts in the United States. These examples are meant to demonstrate how a Boolean approach proves useful in a range of research areas, using individual or aggregate data. The application of QCA, in a particular study, requires the identification (1) of a specific outcome-driven research question (typically in the form of "which core combinations of conditions will produce the outcome?") and (2) of the outcome and of possible "causal" conditions, stemming from theory but also potentially from case-based knowledge. We leave "causal" in scare quotes for the time being because we address the question of how QCA allows drawing causal conclusions later in Section 4. The examples discussed by Ragin in that chapter use categorical data, of relatively easy analysis, but QCA has been extended beyond categorical data, via fuzzy sets techniques that have been developed and are increasingly used (see, e.g., Ragin 2008; Schneider and Wagemann (2012).

According to Rihoux, Álamos-Concha, and Lobe (2021), it is in the very nature of QCA to combine it with other methods. They present QCA as part of a mixed or multi-method design, in which one can choose from several options, including (non-limitative list):

1) A thorough single case analysis, followed by QCA;
2) A QCA, followed by one or more in-depth cases;
3) A QCA, followed by or concurrent with statistical study.

A typical QCA protocol, as presented in Rihoux (2020), consists of (i) a "pre-QCA" stage, in which the researcher gathers knowledge of the case(s), builds a model, and prepares data; (ii) a QCA stage proper, in which QCA techniques are applied; and (iii) a "post-QCA" stage in which the researchers provides an interpretation, based on cases and/or theory.

In the second stage, or QCA-proper, there isn't one single technique, but QCA is to be considered as a *bundle* of techniques. Rihoux and Ragin (2009) define QCA as an "umbrella term" to capture the use of Boolean or crisp sets, multi-value sets, and fuzzy sets, as well as diverse extensions such as two-step QCA, that can integrate different types of conditions (Schneider 2019), or temporal QCA, that can include the time dimension (Caren and Panofsky 2005). The characterization of QCA as essentially plural in their methods or technique immediately poses the question of how different methods or techniques can co-exist. Notably, Rihoux, Álamos-Concha, and Lobe (2021) introduce an aspect of QCA that will interest us here in quite some detail, namely QCA as *mixed* method approach, which we examine next.

3. QCA and Mixed Methods Research

In this section we discuss QCA in relation to its peculiar status in between or across qualitative and quantitative methods. While, for Ragin, QCA had to take the best of both the qualitative and quantitative worlds, we stress here how, methodologically, QCA can be combined with qualitative and quantitative methods, or can itself be considered as a combination of qualitative and quantitative methods. This allows us to use QCA to address a fundamental, overarching methodological question in the social sciences: the reasons traditionally offered to prefer qualitative over quantitative methods (or vice versa), and to develop "mixed methods" (i.e., MMR) that are on the rise. We therefore differ from Ragin's narrative. He was ambitioning to create a *sui generis*, or a sort of "third way" methodology, whereas our narrative is that there are some deep "contact points" between QCA and both qualitative and quantitative methods—and that therefore QCA lends itself naturally to MMR (and is itself a MMR approach, as discussed above).

The status of qualitative and quantitative methodologies, as well as any approach in between or beyond these two, is matter of controversy. Social science methodology is in fact replete with questions concerning the difference between quantitative and qualitative methods, giving rise to very different research schools and teaching programs. A historical reconstruction of how the social sciences came to form such a divide is beyond the scope of this chapter, and in a sense orthogonal to the arguments made here. It suffices to mention that both quantitative and quantitative methods are routed in the development of different social science methods, some even tracing back to the nineteenth century. For a thorough historical perspective on research methods we direct the reader to Alastalo (2008) and to the rich literature mentioned there.

As a matter of fact, there is no coded, standard, or universally agreed definition of what counts as a quantitative or qualitative method. Generally speaking, quantitative methods analyze large enough populations or large enough samples, while qualitative methods focus on small, targeted groups. Quantitative methods analyze large enough data sets, while data collected in qualitative studies are usually fewer. Quantitative methods use formal, statistical approaches for data analyses and data is typically collected via surveys or interviews or from other sources such as health or municipality registries. In qualitative studies, data comes from interviews, but also from participatory observation, or focus groups; the collected data can then be analyzed using techniques such as discourse analysis but can also use statistical analyses. A number of contributions offer ways to map existing available methods, as is done for instance in methodology textbooks for pedagogical purposes, or to emphasize innovation in research methods and techniques. Against this background, Blanchard, Rihoux, and Álamos-Concha (2017) adopt a bottom-up approach to mapping methods. There, the mapping is based on a survey on how methods are taught in different courses and curricula and reveals, among other things, that while a divide between qualitative and quantitative methods still exists, what these precisely amount to has not reached consensus yet. This, in a sense, is good news, as it creates a space to discuss the possible combination or integration of methods outside the constraints of the straitjacket of rigid definitions.

The practical operations of a QCA protocol can actually be linked to both qualitative and quantitative (or case-oriented and variable-oriented, as labeled by Ragin) operations. For instance, each one of the "configurations" contained in the QCA truth table (table of configurations) actually constitute a summary of a sort of a case narrative, from a more holistic, case-based perspective. Conversely, when coding the data for the QCA analyses, one clearly adopts an analytic perspective, using distinct properties, i.e., variables (some "condition" variables and an "outcome" variable)—as is usually done in statistical analysis. The profound difference with statistics, though, is that QCA treatment is configuration-oriented, i.e., it always includes the full configurations in the minimization procedure—in other words, it never considers the contribution of individual conditions separately from other conditions, and therefore QCA conditions fundamentally do not constitute "independent" variables.

To repeat, in this chapter, we endorse a pluralistic stance about methods. For us this means that there is no intrinsic or essential criterion to place methods in rigid hierarchies. We reject therefore the view that quantitative methods are inherently superior to qualitative methods, just because they are formal, mathematized, or even taking advantage of automatized algorithmic analysis (incidentally, QCA is at the same time "qualitative," "formalized," and "mathematized"). Instead, quantitative and quantitative studies can be both well conducted and rigorous—it depends on *how* they are conducted, not on the mode of data analysis per se (see, e.g., Cardano 2009; Montuschi 2004). To be sure, the question of the presumed objectivity of quantitative methods is relevant not only in social science contexts, but widely across the sciences. A notable example is the debate about evidence in the biomedical sciences, where the status of randomized controlled trials (RCTs) as gold standard for causal inference has been long challenged and more pluralistic approaches have been advocated instead (see, e.g., Anjum, Copeland, and Rocca 2020; Cartwright and Hardie 2012; Clarke, Ghiara, and Russo 2019; Parkkinen et al. 2018).

In the social sciences, the idea that the qualitative-quantitative distinction was hindering rather than fostering progress has been recognized already for some time, and MMR has presented itself as the way forward, using *both* qualitative and quantitative methods (for an overview of MMR see, e.g., Timans, Wouters, and Heilbron 2019). Even if rather implicitly, methodological pluralism is adopted in *Mixed Methods Research*. MMR is a methodological approach in which, simply put, both qualitative and quantitative methods are used, without establishing a (principled) priority or superiority of one over the other. There is no predefined way in which qualitative and qualitative methods are used, and it is actually in the intentions of MMR researchers that each approach brings advantages and helps solving problems the other may fall short of (for the various approaches represented within MMR, see Hesse-Biber and Johnson 2015). However, quite frequently one method holds a de facto more central position—see, e.g., Leech and Onwuegbuzie (2009).

In the MMR literature, the discussion is also whether it is a new paradigm. Ghiara (2020) specifically evaluates these claims with respect to the original claims made by the historian of science Kuhn about what it means for a scientific field to work within a period of "normal science" framework and when the community reaches to point of moving into a new paradigm (see also Teddlie and Tashakkori 2009, chap. 5). While the notion of "paradigm" has been criticized for its vague character and for the multiple definitions in Kuhn's work, Ghiara argues that, by choosing a specific definition of paradigm, it can be positively argued that MMR is a new paradigm. Most importantly, Ghiara specifies the conditions under which we can claim that two or more paradigms are mixed in a single study—an issue that we shall further examine in Section 5.

Notwithstanding the question whether MMR is properly a new paradigm, another issue concerning MMR is that it can be defined in many possible ways. Here, we find it useful to adopt Creswell's approach (2015), according to which MMR is primarily and foremost a *methodology*. This means that the whole MMR perspective has to be seen through the lenses of data collection and data analysis, for the purpose of answering a specific research question or set of research questions. As Creswell notices, advocating the use of both qualitative and quantitative approaches is not an "anything goes" strategy about research methods. MMR can be described precisely and rigorously, starting from the type of design that is intended. Creswell distinguishes two main types of MMR: (1) a convergent design, and (2) an explanatory sequential design. Convergent design means that one gathers both quantitative and qualitative data and tries to integrate the results that follow from separate analyses of them (an updated version of the classical logic of "triangulation"). Explanatory sequential methods take various forms. One starts with a quantitative analysis, and subsequently a qualitative phase is performed in order to validate and further interpret the results of the quantitative phase. Another starts with a qualitative phase, which is supplemented later with a quantitative analysis—and there are multiple other variants with more than two main phases. What is clear is that MMR is not a random juxtaposition of qualitative and quantitative methods. Instead, the specific use made of them has to be justified with respect to the research question(s) and the objective(s) of the study—this is to be further examined in Section 5.

MMR is of interest here because it sets out to go beyond the "qualitative-quantitative" divide, or to integrate qualitative-quantitative methods. As MMR appears to be rather liberal as to what "quantitative" or "qualitative" methods exactly refer to, the question then arises whether QCA, especially in the formulation of Rihoux, Álamos-Concha, and Lobe (2021), is an instantiation of MMR. In fact, QCA can in itself, inherently, be seen as a "mixed methods" research approach (Berg-Schlosser 2012). Indeed, QCA rests in essence on five cornerstones:

(1) the integration of case-based and other forms of substantive knowledge,
(2) the allowance for causal complexity,
(3) the resort to the incremental and context-informed elimination of (causal) conditions,
(4) the focus on (quasi-)set-theoretic relations, and
(5) the implementation of case-oriented counterfactual analysis.

It is thus fed by several methods and traditions, both on the "qualitative" (case-oriented) and on the "quantitative" (mathematical, albeit nonstatistical) sides. QCA is about case-based evidence, but also about mathematical formalization in the research process (Rihoux, Álamos-Concha, and Lobe 2021). The strength of QCA with respect to other methodologies is that, by codifying a (flexible) way of using more methods and approaches in a single study, gives a very concrete meaning to "methodological pluralism." Earlier in the chapter, we said we would endorse this stance, and here we start giving concrete indications of what it means—in practice—to be pluralists. Saying that qualitative and quantitative approaches each have value and carry epistemic virtues is not apologetic, and must be accompanied with an account of what these values and virtues are. This, in turn, helps us provide a justification for the choice of the sequence in which methods are used, and within each method, for the specific choices made. There are multiple ways in which QCA can be sequenced with qualitative and quantitative methods. Probably one of the richest example is the work of Berg-Schlosser (2012) that includes several iterations between QCA and statistical analyses, in a multistage MMR also comprising some case studies.

In sum, the long-standing debate between qualitative and quantitative methods is certainly not exhausted and resolved here. Yet, QCA takes a pragmatic rather than an ideological or principled approach to the issue: it is not a question of siding with one or another, but take the *best of both worlds*, depending on the research question at stake—and in fact it is possible to exploit QCA in a rather more "qualitative" way (more case-oriented, smaller- or intermediate-n design) or in a more "quantitative" way (more variable-oriented, larger-n design) (on this point, see Thomann and Maggetti 2017). In our view, this pragmatic attitude is the first step to move beyond the "qualitative-quantitative divide"; it still remains to be discussed what this "best of both worlds" means—a task that we further undertake later in Section 5.

4. QCA and the Quest for Why- and How-Questions

In this section we build on the previous discussion of QCA, as a combination of qualitative and quantitative methods, and zoom into another "philosophy of science" question, namely how to address why- and how-questions. We first explain why causality and mechanisms remain central in political science and, for the matter, more generally in social science, and in the sciences even more broadly. Second, we highlight connections with existing methods in political science, notably process tracing, and with existing debates in philosophy of science, notably the philosophy of mechanisms. In this way, we aim to contribute to QCA methodology, and especially to detailing the way in which QCA can be used for causal inference and explanation.

The quest for explanation and, specifically, for *causal* explanation, is widespread across the sciences. We want to know *why* some event happened, and *how* it happened. We also want to know why some *type* of event may have happened, and how it may have happened. For instance, we may want to understand the why and how of Arab Spring, or the why and how of similar uprising phenomena. In the jargon of the philosophy of explanation, explaining how the Arab Spring could happen is to provide an "how-actually" explanation;

instead, explaining how other similar phenomena, maybe using the explanatory model of the Arab Spring, amounts to proving a "how-possibly" explanation (see, e.g., Bokulich's contribution in Magnani and Bertolotti 2017). In some cases, providing explanations of one of these types amounts to finding the causes (tracing the etiology), and/or to showing the mechanisms that bring these phenomena about, and/or to pointing to the function an institution, event, or other has in the social domain.

The question arises whether QCA can assist us with this business of providing etiological explanations and/or explanatory mechanisms and, if so, in which way. Rihoux (2017) mentions five uses of QCA, some of which are about "minimizing complexity." The QCA machinery, explains Rihoux, is geared toward reducing the full configuration of the characteristics of the analyzed cases to more parsimonious ones. This is intended to test theories using empirical data (the cases), and more specifically testing a causal hypothesis that links conditions of the cases to an outcome. This way of simplifying helps with causal inference for two reasons. First, it forces the researcher to express the causal hypothesis in a very clear way—using the logic of necessity and sufficiency. Second, by specifying the links between the conditions of the cases and the outcome, we can carry out a better cross-case comparison. However, Rihoux (2017, 389) also expresses a cautious warning:

> the QCA results (the parsimonious solutions) do not by themselves establish 'causal' mechanisms linking the conditions and the outcome; this requires case-based and theory-based interpretation by the researcher.

What do these "case-based" and "theory-based" interpretations amount to? The issue is addressed by, e.g., Schneider and Wagemann (2012). According to Schneider and Wagemann, QCA is an adequate methodology when the research hypothesis is that the phenomenon at hand can be explained using a "special kind of causal complexity" (76). This, they argue, is independent of the number of cases analyzed. The causal complexity they have in mind is captured by the so-called "INUS" and "SUIN" conditions. They build on the framework elaborated by Mahoney, Kimball, and Koivu (2009) that is supposed to elucidate the meaning of "cause" in the context of historical explanations in the social sciences. The broader context, to be sure, is an analysis of causation in terms of necessary and sufficient conditions. An individual cause, in their approach, can be (1) necessary but not sufficient, (2) sufficient but not necessary, (3) an "INUS," or (4) a "SUIN." Such analysis helps establishing the sequence of events and the role of salient factors in the explanation. According to Mahoney, Kimball, and Koivu (2009) this kind of analysis is not in competition or contraposition with other approaches, but the adequacy rather depends on the goals and the questions of the study at hand; this, to be sure, is a form of "causal pluralism" very much in line with the one advocated by Illari and Russo (2014).

To return to QCA and causal inference, the most relevant types of causes are INUS and SUIN. INUS stands for "Insufficient but Necessary Part of condition that is itself Unnecessary but Sufficient"; put simply, this means that, for instance, an electric circuit is necessary to initiate fire, but insufficient because it always needs presence of oxygen for that. INUS conditions have been theorized by Mackie as early as (1965/1990), and widely used in epidemiology (Rothman 1976; Rothman and Greenland 2005; Rothman, Greenland, and Lash 2008) and also in social science (Mahoney 2008). SUIN stands for "Sufficient, but Unnecessary parts of a factor that is Insufficient but Necessary for the result" (Mahoney,

Kimball, and Koivu 2009, 126); put simply, this means that, for instance, if our theory postulates that nondemocracy is necessary for war, we need to consider that nondemocracy is itself a bundle of conditions, and these will be SUIN-causes of war.

Set-theoretic methods such as QCA are rather well-equipped to analyze INUS and SUIN (while quantitative methods fare rather poorly in this respect). INUS and SUIN point to three general features of causal complexity:

(1) Equifinality: This is to emphasize that there exist alternatives to sufficient conditions to produce an outcome.
(2) Conjunctural: This is to emphasize that conditions, to produce an effect, need to act in combination.
(3) Asymmetry: This is to emphasize that in complex INUS and SUIN settings, their necessary part is inherently asymmetric.

Using QCA, we can test hypotheses against empirical data, for instance to check whether *different conjunctions of factors* (named "conditions" in QCA) may lead to the same outcome for different groups of cases. This is something that standard statistical methods are ill equipped to test. For instance, one type of statistical models, the potential outcome model, rest on the assumption that there is but *one* cause (the treatment). Other types of statistical method, for instance multiple regression, will instead return a different kind of information, notably about the average effect of variables in large populations (on this point, see also Mahoney, Kimball, and Koivu 2009). While statistical methods are valuable, the methodology of QCA has its own specificity, especially when the question at stake is the *comparison* of cases.

Up to now, QCA methodology is geared toward generating evidence *that* some INUS or SUIN configuration leads to the sought outcome. There isn't as yet any indication that QCA can *also* generate evidence of *why* and *how* a given INUS or SUIN configuration brings a given outcome about. For the time being, we don't need to draw a sharp distinction between "why" and "how," that are typically associated with, respectively, the quest for an etiological explanation and for a mechanistic explanation—both are broadly causal endeavors. This broad causal endeavor is addressed by Schneider and Wagemann (2012), when they present two-step approaches in QCA. In the first step, the researcher constructs a truth table that minimizes the complexity from the cases. This is meant to get a grip on "remote" factors (namely, factors that are "far away" from the outcome to be explained), or on background context in which a given process happens or given actors operate. In the second step, the researcher constructs different truth tables "for each outcome enabling context" (254). This is meant to get a grip on "proximate" factors, namely, factors that are "close by" the outcome and that, in the context of the previously identified remote factors, produce the outcome. For instance, in explaining the Arab Spring, remote factors include the more structural long-term social, economic, and political situation characterized by oppressive regimes, violation of human rights, and poverty; proximate factors are instead the very "close by" conditions that made it happen, for instance the uprising in Tunisia happened after a series of conflicts in the previous three years.

It is worth noting that Schneider significantly updates this two-step methodology in his (2019) contribution. In particular, step one is here reconceptualized as the identification of *necessary* conditions for the outcome to occur. These necessary conditions amount to emphasizing that "(a) that they are causally more distant than proximate factors and (b) that these conditions alone are not supposed to already fully explain the occurrence of the outcome" (Schneider 2019, 1114). While Schneider emphasizes, in this two-step protocol, the necessary and sufficient components of the first and second step respectively, we wish here to emphasize that step two is concerned with sufficient *paths*. We emphasize "paths" because, while the approach of Schneider and Wagemann (2012) and of Schneider (2019) can help shedding light on "why" an outcome occur, the reference to "paths" hints to the unravelling the "how" part too. In our view, unraveling the causal mechanisms is done by analyzing the different possible configurations (also as part of "within-case" analysis or of "two typical cases" analysis). This, we submit, may be the missing link between QCA and how- and why-questions.

While until about ten years ago there was virtually no discussion of how- and why-questions within QCA-proper, the subject is now gaining attention. Why-questions have somehow been addressed in the literature, but, admittedly, QCA literature does not develop much further how mechanisms can be unraveled, that is, how QCA can provide answers to how-questions. To further contribute to this debate, we take the following route: comparing QCA with another widely used methodology in political science, namely process tracing.

Process tracing is a qualitative approach to analyze cases (see, e.g., Beach and Pedersen 2013, 2016; Collier 2011; Hall 2008, among others). It is meant to provide evidence for causal claims, this evidence being observational and generated in qualitative studies. The exact meaning of "process tracing" is not univocal. Crasnow (2012) points out that, in the first theorization of the method, process tracing referred to decision processes of given agents and that lead to a certain outcome, which traces back to the work of George and McKeown (1985). Later on, the term started being used to *any* process, not just agent's decisions, and the goal is to identify the chain of events that lead to a certain outcome (Van Evera 1997). It is now customary to take the term to refer to processes in general, and for which we seek evidence in our observations. Specifically, according to Crasnow's reconstruction of process-tracing methodology, we reason about single cases using general causal hypotheses. The precise way in which this reasoning happen may vary, but what is key is the systematic examinations of factors, especially in "within-case analysis," which consists of careful and detailed descriptions of trajectories of change in phenomena, and to the sequence of relevant variables used in such descriptions. Ruzzene (2014) points out that Little (1991, 1998) sees process tracing as a way of collecting, analyzing, and organizing historical evidence, including information about social, historical, economic, political context, etc. This point is also made by George and Bennett (1997): process tracing is analogous to the practice of colligation in history.

If these characterizations of process tracing are broadly correct, one may then see it as *complementary* to QCA. Following Schneider and Rohlfing (2013) we suggest that process tracing (PT) can help the "post-QCA" phase, to analyze the causal mechanisms involved (for typical cases) and to improve on existing theory (for deviant cases). In concrete terms: one may handpick typical cases based on the QCA solution, and open up, via PT, the "black box" of the actual causal mechanisms "on the ground" that link some core QCA conditions and the outcome. For deviant cases, one may for instance, via PT, uncover a hidden (or not hypothesized) causal mechanism at play between some QCA conditions that unexpectedly popped up in the QCA solutions.

While process tracing typically evokes notions of "path" and of "process," in which the sequence of events and/or factors in time seem to be key, the relation between processes and mechanisms remains contentious. In the philosophy of mechanisms, there have been attempts to distinguish processes from mechanisms proper, and one argument is that with mechanisms we can answer why- and how-questions, as mechanisms provide information about the *organization* of the variables or entities involved. Here, as it has already happened in the literature, parallel debates started to exist, and it would be important to build more systematic bridges between the vast and complex literature on mechanisms in the philosophy of (social) science (see relevant chapters in, e.g., Glennan and Illari (2017); Illari and Russo (2014); and Illari, Russo, and Williamson (2011)). This literature seems to have developed on a track parallel to the influential work of Beach and Pedersen (2019), that indeed attempts to link process tracing to mechanisms—or rather it defines process tracing precisely as a tool to study causal mechanisms in case-based research.

In order to fill the gap between these parallel literatures, it would be worth exploring the prospects of adopting the definition of "minimal mechanism" as given by Glennan and Illari (2017, chap. 1):

> A mechanism for a phenomenon consists of entities (or parts) whose activities and interactions are organized so as to be responsible for the phenomenon.

We lack space to run a systematic examination of the notion of "minimal mechanism" in the context of QCA and process tracing, but we can nonetheless give some indications of why we think it is the right way to go.

First, this definition is "minimal" in the sense that it abstracts from specific features mechanisms may have in fields as diverse as biology, physics, sociology, or even information security, and for this reason is meant to be widely applicable across scientific practices. Second, this definition emphasizes the importance or organization but is liberal about whether "part-hole" or "sequential" organizations is most appropriate—which in fact may depend on the context. Third, while it sticks to "entities" and "interactions," these may be studied and described with different methodologies (e.g., qualitative or quantitative) and using different vocabularies (e.g. statistical or natural language) depending on the case at hand.

Equipped with "minimal mechanisms" we would then detail how, in one of the phases of typical QCA analysis, process tracing can provide not just the sequence, but also the *organization* (synchronic or diachronic) of the variables, factors, events, or agents involved. Arguably, it is the specification of the organization of the components of the mechanism that does most of the explaining and it does so by complementing the phase of QCA-proper, in which we minimize complexity using one of the available techniques. In other words, combining QCA and process tracing requires: (i) having a broader notion of "process," which can be captured by "minimal mechanism," and (ii) complementing the QCA-proper step with a description of the entities and of their interactions (that is the organization mentioned in the definition of "minimal mechanism").

We hope to have provided some evidence that QCA, as bundle of techniques and a theoretical framework in constant evolution, has the potential, especially when appropriately complemented with process tracing, to answer why- and how-questions in a deep and meaningful way. This also requires that a certain understanding of mechanisms is adopted.

At the end of this section, we are again confronting ourselves with a question about integration or combination of approaches within QCA: first, the combination of qualitative and quantitative methods, and now of set-theoretic and process-tracing approaches. This leads us to posing the question of integration—or combination—in a rather more systematic way, and it is the object of the next, and final, section of the chapter.

5. WHAT DOES IT MEAN TO INTEGRATE METHODS?

In this section we go deeper in the discussion of QCA as a possible MMR method: what does it mean to integrate or combine methods? Using the debates on "integration and pluralism" in philosophy of science, we reflect on what it means to integrate methods (here, qualitative and quantitative methods) and what implications this may have for the daily practice of social science research.

There is a fast-growing philosophical literature on integration in science that also connects to questions about (methodological) pluralism and the unity of science. The literature has already been around for a solid two to three decades and is becoming increasingly sophisticated and complex. We first try to recap what this literature is about and then explain why this is relevant to the discussion of QCA.

There is a sense in which philosophical discussions about integration and pluralism stem from much older debates about the unity of science. In fact, "unity of science" was one objective of the Vienna Circle (Neurath 1973). In her book *Scientific Pluralism Reconsidered*, Ruphy (2016) reconstructs in an original way the aims of the project of the Vienna Circle and, specifically, its formulation in terms of the "linguistic unity" of science. Ruphy explains that how to cash out this unity was far less consensual among Vienna Circle members than is usually thought. In particular, the Carnapian project was to reduce all scientific statements to a basic set of statements (the protocol statements) which, in turn, would express properties and motions of physical entities. In other words, the linguistic project of the unity of science boils down to the possibility of expressing disciplinary knowledge (other than physics) in the language of physics. This narrow form of physicalism however differs from Neurath's, whose view was broader in scope in that it allowed protocol sentences to include the name of the observer or verbs such as "perceive" or "observe." According to Ruphy, Neurath's version of physicalism was also accompanied by an anti-foundationalist stance, that is to say protocol statements could be revised or abandoned as needed—this is the meaning of the famous metaphor of the boat, whose pieces are replaced while sailing. Another difference between Carnap and Neurath concerned the question whether linguistic unity ought to be accompanied with a nomic unity—something Carnap would support, but not Neurath. But one should not be mistaken about the motivation behind such project: the goal was not the reduction to physics per se, but the *possibility of integrating different kinds of theoretical knowledge for practical purposes*—this is a first meaning of "unity." Furthermore, Ruphy carefully explains that linguistic unity does not imply ontological unity, namely the unity at the level of the nature of the things studied by different sciences—this is a second meaning of "unity." The Carnapian project allows for the existence of different kind of things the sciences studies, and the project aimed at finding a unique framework for expressing such knowledge. As is well known, that objective was never met.

At the same time, however, there is a third meaning of unity that philosophers have been trying to establishing, that is at the level of *method*, and this is what most interests us. The question is whether what unifies science is having *one* method, which had been answered in the positive by Popperian falsificationism or by Hempelian hypothetico-deductivism, in that they provide *one* logic of justification. The latest attempt to formulate a unified methodological account is Bayesianism, but is beyond the scope of our discussion whether it is a hype or hope (and, for the record, Ruphy expresses some concerns in this respect). The methodological question of unity can also be posed in more nuanced terms, namely as a set of general canons, which led philosophers of science to provide *general* accounts of scientific method. Inevitably, notices Ruphy by echoing Nickles (1987), this also led to a philosophy of science much detached from the actual practice of science because these canons are supposed (or hoped) to be independent of the objects of study. But this is clearly at variance with the real practice of the sciences, where methods are indeed very much dependent on the object of study. QCA is no exception in this respect; in fact, as we explained in Section 2, methods of QCA are tailored to the analysis and comparison of specific types of cases.

For a long time, unity of science hasn't been on top of philosophers' agenda, but the topic has been revived in recent times. This time, however, it was to emphasize *dis*unity, rather than unity, of science (see, e.g., Dupré 1996; Cartwright 1999). The question posed in Dupré's contribution was to justify a form of anti-reductionism that was not dependent on the temporal and local contingency of not being able to reduce one theory to another. His view is that there isn't one way to classifying things. Things may belong to different "kinds," and so his position is at once realist and pluralist—what he himself dubbed "promiscuous realism." In sum, the disunity of Dupré is about what exists and how to classify it. The disunity discussed by Cartwright has a more methodological flavor, although ultimately it is about metaphysics too: her "dappled" world refers to the fact that the world rarely displays ordered features to be studied by (reductionist) approaches. We need to acknowledge a *plurality* of possible approaches to study a world that is all *but* ordered. This is a consequence of another famous position of Cartwright's, namely that scientific laws are not universal but rather ceteris paribus. In the last couple of decades, besides the question of disunity as posed in the work of Dupré and of Cartwright, there has been another facet to it. The plurality may concern the way in which we *represent* a phenomenon, or in other words whether we can offer several scientific accounts of it. The issue is addressed in the influential volume edited by Kellert, Longino, and Waters (2006). Specific accounts, for instance Longino's (2013) or Giere's (2006), differ as to the way they cash out, epistemologically, the relation between these representations and the world, but the main gist is preserved: there exists a plurality of ways in which a same phenomenon can be studied or represented, often corresponding to different disciplinary perspectives, and there is no a priori reason for one such account to dominate others—this last variant of pluralism is of potential interest to us, as we shall see later.

Ruphy takes us from the problem of unity to the one of disunity of science, as both being concerned, albeit in different ways, with questions of pluralism about methods. But the philosophical debate is also heading in another direction. The observation that science is not one thing, that there exist a variety of objects, methods, perspectives, epistemologies, values, etc., led the philosophical community to investigate how these pluralities are often combined or integrated. This is how the literature on "integration" came into being. It is also worth noting that, quite often, discussions about integration became de facto discussions of interdisciplinarity and of interdisciplinary practices. This is because the kind of integration that has been under the spotlight of philosophers concerns collaborations between scientists from different disciplinary backgrounds, for instance integrating methods developed in physics to study economic phenomena (see, among others, Kellert, Longino, and Waters 2006; Longino 2013; MacLeod and Nagatsu 2018; MacLeod et al. 2019). And because of this emphasis on multiple *disciplinary* perspectives to be integrated, the discussion turned into a question about the meaning of interdisciplinarity. For instance, Grüne-Yanoff (2016) takes interdisciplinarity to mean increased cohesion of concepts and of practices. Yet, he does not think that disciplines "fuse" into each other.

Against this rich background, QCA constitutes an interesting episode of a scientific practice in which many of the aspects of the debates just mentioned converge. Whether and how to integrate qualitative and quantitative methods into "Mixed Methods," and whether and how QCA is an instance of MMR seems to be partly about a quest for *unity* of science, while acknowledging *dis*unity: the social sciences *do* belong to the realm of science, even when they use qualitative methods, so the sciences are, in a sense, unified by broad methodological and epistemological principles and by pervasive questions about values (see Schurz (2013)). Furthermore, in combining quantitative, qualitative, and QCA-proper approaches, we also touch upon questions of integration of different models, theoretical frameworks, and disciplinary perspectives—all points at the core of the "integration" debate.

Yet, while we are clearly in the middle of this tornado of concepts—(dis)unity, integration, pluralism, etc.—we suggest trying to step out and pose the question in different terms. Most probably our entry point, in the midst of the pluralism-integration debate, won't be unique, but we hope it clarifies the stakes for QCA and possible open up a different research path more generally for the (social) sciences.

Our specific problem may be presented in the following terms. Within one field (broadly construed as "social science methodology"), there exist different methods—qualitative, quantitative, and also QCA, as part of them. These led, traditionally, to quite distinct ways of doing social science research and have been associated with different "schools of thought," etc. (see also the discussion on qualitative vs. quantitative methods earlier in the chapter). But, as explained in the previous sections, there are also attempts to integrate or combine methods. MMR is paradigmatic in this respect, not only because it is part of its very built-in definition to "mix" methods as different as qualitative and quantitative ones, but also because it is a core foundational debate what exactly this mixing, or integration amounts to. Some argue that integration is of paramount importance, as it is in fact the real feature of the "best" MMR; some others defend a more modest perspective: MMR is about specific way of sequencing/combining methods, but these are not really "integrated." To remain within the MMR domain, in the literature the following distinctions are also made:

- "mixed methods design," namely combining/sequencing methods stemming from different paradigms/epistemologies (typically, quantitative and quantitative); and
- "multimethod design," namely combining/sequencing methods stemming from the same paradigm/epistemology.

There is a sense in which QCA and process tracing fall under the second category—multimethod designs—because their core feature is to be case-oriented, and to study cases via multiple methodologies are part of the research design.

With this clarification in mind let us now ask: *What happens, in practice, when multiple methods are part of the design, and what does this "combination" mean?* In practice, the combination of multiple methods happens at the level of research design and execution. This is partly discussed in Section 3, and is clearly part of core debates within QCA (the discussion of two steps methods is a case in point). What is at stake here are questions about choices about when to use which method. This leads us to ask a more fundamental question, namely, *Why combine methods in the first place?* What is at stake here is the kind of *epistemic access* that each of the employed methods gives us, and what kind of epistemic access does the *combination* of methods give us.

Admittedly, this a most crucial epistemological question, also related to the substantiation of the "best of both worlds" mentioned earlier in Section 3. We have no pretention to exhaust it here, but more modestly we hope to open a space that needs further discussion. On the one hand, quantitative methods give us epistemic access to "macroscopic" aspects of a phenomenon—this is what statistical relations between variables (e.g., correlations) represent: a description of how variables are related, at the *macro* level. On the other hand, qualitative methods give us epistemic access to the microscopic aspects of phenomenon. For instance, we can get detailed insight on *why* variables are related in such and such way. Such descriptions at the *micro* level come detailed studies of practices, behaviors, choices, etc. QCA, by its own design, is able to schematize and simplify complex setting of different factors. This can give us insights on direction of flow of causal relations, or on the logical structure of the reconstruction of phenomenon. This is a very coarse-grained distinction, quite easy to invalidate. For instance, historical sociology of social movements is, strictly speaking, a qualitative approach, but aims at providing macroscopic aspects of phenomena. In our mind, however, this case does not invalidate our argument, but lends further support to our pluralistic attitude: a rigid categorization into quantitative vs. qualitative methods is detrimental rather than beneficial, precisely because it obscures the *interesting* differences between methods and only creates rigid camps. While each of these methods comes with specific ways to gain epistemic access to the phenomenon under investigation, how to combine them remains an open question, and rightly so. In fact, the specific combination depends on the research question, on what is already known/available, on what data may be easier or more difficult collect, etc. This represent a very common mix of principled, pragmatic, methodological considerations. And, admittedly, there is no magic recipe to use.

At this point it is useful to return to the literature on pluralism, and especially to the version developed by Ruphy, namely, "foliated pluralism," which is an extension of Hacking's *style of reasoning*. Hacking builds on the account of Crombie (1994), who had identified six traditions of scientific thinking in Western science, and adds another one: (1) method of postulation (e.g., Greek maths), (2) experiments, (3) hypothetical construction of analogical models, (4) comparison and taxonomic reasoning, (5) statistics and probability, (6) historical derivation of genetic development, (7) lab practices to isolate and purify phenomena (something more specific than method (2)). The point is not to give a precise definition of "style" or of any of these styles. Also, these styles do not sharply correspond to crystalized methods, often they are used in combination, and their use through history and across disciplines invariably had ups and downs. Hacking puts forward four theses about styles of reasoning. First, what is key is what these styles allow us to achieve: introduce new objects of study, new laws, new explanations, etc. Second, styles determine which kinds of proposition are good candidates for being true or false, not what is true or false. Third, each style has its own way of getting "stabilized" *qua* style. Fourth, each style is somehow grounded in our cognitive capacities.

Hacking's styles of reasoning are clearly a pluralistic reconstruction of scientific practice, one that well explains, descriptively, the existence of the various traditions in social science methodology (and elsewhere). But to get an answer to our question about epistemic access, we need to appeal, specifically, to Ruphy's refinement of Hacking, namely her *foliated pluralism*.

According to Ruphy, when using another style of reasoning, it is not that we simply add a new entity, but we *enrich* the ontological space of scientific objects, in that "the use in scientific practice of different styles of reasoning widen and diversify the classes of propositions that can be true or false" (Ruphy 2016, 31). Thus, statistical analyses can add statistical properties, QCA-proper can add the identification of specific factors to be considered, qualitative analysis can add to the description of group dynamics, cultural aspects, or other. Our epistemic access is mediated by these different methods, and once we gain such access, the ontological space to describe, define, analyze, the object of study is enriched because we can look at it from different angles and perspectives, not just "add" new entities to the basket. We follow Ruphy in saying that this process of "ontological enrichment" is open-ended; at no point of the process we can claim to have attained a final, or complete, description of the object.

The main characteristics of Ruphy's foliated pluralism are the following:

- Transdisciplinarity: a style of reasoning does not belong to one discipline or domain only. (This is clearly true of QCA, as explained in Section 2.)
- Nonexclusiveness and synchronicity: several styles of reasoning can be combined at any given moment or in any given study. (This also happens in QCA, as there isn't one fixed protocol to establish the sequence of methods being used.)
- Cumulativeness: the use of multiple styles of reasoning leads to enlarging the basket of styles, rather than superseding anyone of them. (This is also a key characteristic of QCA that, in its MMR variant, precisely aims at using multiple styles in one study.)

We can make sense of the practice of QCA adopting her foliated pluralism, and in this way, we can give more solid foundations to QCA as a practice that is, by design, pluralistic and eclectic, and in need for a deeper justification for why it is a valuable methodological approach.

In sum, political science has a rich methodological tradition, to which QCA adds. Its addition is not simply in terms of providing the latest cutting-edge method, or a tolerant way to let different methods exist. Instead, a proper philosophical reflection of the foundations of QCA helps us make progress with fundamental questions about pluralism and integration in political science, and in the social sciences more generally. The specific point in which, we think, we make progress is in being able to articulate why a pluralistic methodology can achieve more than any methodology in isolation. The reason is not that the more the merrier, but that more methods, being instances of specific styles of reasoning, grant us epistemic access to a given phenomenon from different angles and perspectives, thus making the ontological (as well epistemological and methodological) space of scientific objects much richer.

ACKNOWLEDGMENTS

We are deeply grateful to the editors of this volume for the opportunity to cowrite about QCA, MMR, mechanisms, and methodological pluralism. The chapter has been long in the making, also because of the delays due to the pandemic; the patience and flexibility of the editors has been invaluable during these difficult times. We also received very helpful feedback and insightful comments from both the editors and an external reviewer, which all helped us make the chapter clearer and more usable to philosophers and methodologists. Any errors or inaccuracies remain, of course, ours.

REFERENCES

Alastalo, Marja. 2008. "The History of Social Research Methods." In *The SAGE Handbook of Social Research Methods*, by Pertti Alasuutari, Leonard Bickman, and Julia Brannen, 26–41. London: SAGE Publications Ltd. https://doi.org/10.4135/9781446212165.n3.

Anjum, Rani Lill, Samantha Copeland, and Elena Rocca. 2020. "Medical Scientists and Philosophers Worldwide Appeal to *EBM* to Expand the Notion of 'Evidence.'" *BMJ Evidence-Based Medicine* 25 (1): 6–8. https://doi.org/10.1136/bmjebm-2018-111092.

Beach, Derek, and Rasmus Pedersen. 2019. *Process-Tracing Methods: Foundations and Guidelines*. Ann Arbor, MI: University of Michigan Press. https://doi.org/10.3998/mpub.10072208.

Beach, Derek, and Rasmus Brun Pedersen. 2013. *Process-Tracing Methods: Foundations and Guidelines*. Ann Arbor: University of Michigan Press.

Beach, Derek, and Rasmus Brun Pedersen. 2016. *Causal Case Study Methods: Foundations and Guidelines for Comparing, Matching and Tracing*. Ann Arbor: University of Michigan Press.

Berg-Schlosser, Dirk. 2012. *Mixed Methods in Comparative Politics: Principles and Applications*. Basingstoke: Palgrave Macmillan.

Berg-Schlosser, Dirk, and Lasse Cronqvist. 2005. "Macro-Quantitative vs. Macro-Qualitative Methods in the Social Sciences — An Example from Empirical Democratic Theory Employing New Software." *Historical Social Research / Historische Sozialforschung* 30 (4 [114]): 154–175. www.jstor.org/stable/20762081.

Blanchard, Philippe, Benoît Rihoux, and Priscilla Álamos-Concha. 2017. "Comprehensively Mapping Political Science Methods: An Instructors' Survey." *International Journal of Social Research Methodology* 20 (2): 209–224. https://doi.org/10.1080/13645579.2015.1129128.

Cardano, Mario. 2009. *Ethnography and Reflexivity: Notes on the Construction of Objectivity in Ethnographic Research*. Torino: Dipartimento di scienze sociali Università degli studi di Torino.

Caren, Neal, and Aaron Panofsky. 2005. "TQCA: A Technique for Adding Temporality to Qualitative Comparative Analysis." *Sociological Methods & Research* 34 (2): 147–172. https://doi.org/10.1177/0049124105277197.

Cartwright, Nancy. 1999. *The Dappled World: A Study of the Boundaries of Science*. Cambridge: Cambridge University Press.

Cartwright, Nancy, and Jeremy Hardie. 2012. *Evidence-Based Policy: A Practical Guide to Doing It Better*. Oxford: Oxford University Press.

Clarke, Brendan, Virginia Ghiara, and Federica Russo. 2019. "Time to Care: Why the Humanities and the Social Sciences Belong in the Science of Health." *BMJ Open* 9 (8): e030286. https://doi.org/10.1136/bmjopen-2019-030286.

Collier, David. 2011. "Understanding Process Tracing." *PS: Political Science & Politics* 44 (04): 823–830. https://doi.org/10.1017/S1049096511001429.

Crasnow, Sharon. 2012. "The Role of Case Study Research in Political Science: Evidence for Causal Claims." *Philosophy of Science* 79 (5): 655–666. https://doi.org/10.1086/667869.

Creswell, John W. 2015. *A Concise Introduction to Mixed Methods Research*. Los Angeles: SAGE.

Crombie, A. C. 1994. *Styles of Scientific Thinking in the European Tradition: The History of Argument and Explanation Especially in the Mathematical and Biomedical Sciences and Arts*. London: Duckworth.

Dowding, Keith M. 2015. *The Philosophy and Methods of Political Science*. London: New York, NY: Palgrave Macmillan.

Dupré, John. 1996. *The Disorder of Things: Metaphysical Foundations of the Disunity of Science*. 3. printing. Cambridge, Massachusetts: Harvard University Press.

Fiss, Peer C., Dmitry Sharapov, and Lasse Cronqvist. 2013. "Opposites Attract? Opportunities and Challenges for Integrating Large-N QCA and Econometric Analysis." *Political Research Quarterly* 66 (1): 191–198. www.jstor.org/stable/23563602.

George, Alexander L., and Andrew Bennett. 1997. *Process Tracing in Case Study Research*. New York: MacArthur Foundation Workshop on Case Study Method.

George, Alexander L., and Timothy McKeown. 1985. "Case Studies and Theories of Organizational Decision Making." In *Advances in Information Processing in Organizations*, edited by Robert Coulam and Richard Smith. Vol. 2, 43–68. Greenwich: JAI Press.

Gerring, John. 2006. *Case Study Research: Principles and Practices*. Leiden: Cambridge University Press. http://public.ebookcentral.proquest.com/choice/publicfullrecord.aspx?p=288451.

Gerring, John. 2011. *The Case Study*. Oxford University Press. https://doi.org/10.1093/oxfordhb/9780199604456.013.0051.

Gerring, John. 2017. "Qualitative Methods." *Annual Review of Political Science* 20 (1): 15–36. https://doi.org/10.1146/annurev-polisci-092415-024158.

Ghiara, Virginia. 2020. "Disambiguating the Role of Paradigms in Mixed Methods Research." *Journal of Mixed Methods Research* 14 (1): 11–25. https://doi.org/10.1177/1558689818819928.

Giere, Ronald N. 2006. *Scientific Perspectivism*. Chicago: University of Chicago Press. http://chicago.universitypressscholarship.com/view/10.7208/chicago/9780226292144.001.0001/upso-9780226292120.

Glennan, Stuart, and Phyllis McKay Illari, eds. 2017. *The Routledge Handbook of Mechanisms and Mechanical Philosophy*. Routledge Handbooks in Philosophy. London: Routledge, Taylor & Francis Group.

Grüne-Yanoff, Till. 2016. "Interdisciplinary Success without Integration." *European Journal for Philosophy of Science* 6 (3): 343–360. https://doi.org/10.1007/s13194-016-0139-z.

Gulbenkian Commission on the Restructuring of the Social Sciences, ed. 1996. *Open the Social Sciences: Report of the Gulbenkian Commission on the Restructuring of the Social Sciences*. Mestizo Spaces (Espaces Métisses). Stanford, CA: Stanford University Press.

Hall, Peter A. 2008. "Systematic Process Analysis: When and How to Use It." *European Political Science* 7 (3): 304–317. https://doi.org/10.1057/palgrave.eps.2210130.

Hesse-Biber, Sharlene Nagy, and Burke Johnson, eds. 2015. *The Oxford Handbook of Multimethod and Mixed Methods Research Inquiry*. Oxford Library of Psychology. Oxford; New York: Oxford University Press.

Illari, Phyllis McKay, and Federica Russo. 2014. *Causality: Philosophical Theory Meets Scientific Practice*. First edition. Oxford, United Kingdom: Oxford University Press.

Illari, Phyllis McKay, Federica Russo, and Jon Williamson, eds. 2011. *Causality in the Sciences*. Oxford: Oxford University Press.

Kellert, Stephen H., Helen E. Longino, and C. Kenneth Waters, eds. 2006. *Scientific Pluralism*. Minnesota Studies in the Philosophy of Science, v. 19. Minneapolis, MN: University of Minnesota Press.

Leech, Nancy L., and Anthony J. Onwuegbuzie. 2009. "A Typology of Mixed Methods Research Designs." *Quality & Quantity* 43 (2): 265–275. https://doi.org/10.1007/s11 135-007-9105-3.

Little, Daniel. 1991. *Varieties of Social Explanation: An Introduction to the Philosophy of Social Science*. Boulder: Westview Press.

Little, Daniel. 1998. *Microfoundations, Method, and Causation: On the Philosophy of the Social Sciences*. Science and Technology Studies. New Brunswick, NJ: Transaction Publishers.

Longino, Helen E. 2013. *Studying Human Behavior: How Scientists Investigate Aggression and Sexuality*. Chicago: The University of Chicago Press.

Mackie, John L. 1990. *The Cement of the Universe: A Study of Causation.* 5. Dr. Clarendon Library of Logic and Philosophy. Oxford: Clarendon Press.

MacLeod, Miles, Martina Merz, Uskali Mäki, and Michiru Nagatsu. 2019. "Investigating Interdisciplinary Practice: Methodological Challenges (Introduction)." *Perspectives on Science* 27 (4): 545–552. https://doi.org/10.1162/posc_e_00315.

MacLeod, Miles, and Michiru Nagatsu. 2018. "What Does Interdisciplinarity Look like in Practice: Mapping Interdisciplinarity and Its Limits in the Environmental Sciences." *Studies in History and Philosophy of Science Part A* 67 (February): 74–84. https://doi.org/10.1016/j.shpsa.2018.01.001.

Magnani, Lorenzo, and Tommaso Bertolotti, eds. 2017. *Springer Handbook of Model-Based Science*. Springer Handbooks. Cham: Springer International Publishing. https://doi.org/10.1007/978-3-319-30526-4.

Mahoney, James. 2008. "Toward a Unified Theory of Causality." *Comparative Political Studies* 41 (4–5): 412–436. https://doi.org/10.1177/0010414007313115.

Mahoney, James, Erin Kimball, and Kendra L. Koivu. 2009. "The Logic of Historical Explanation in the Social Sciences." *Comparative Political Studies* 42 (1): 114–146. https://doi.org/10.1177/0010414008325433.

Marx, Axel, Benoît Rihoux, and Charles Ragin. 2014. "The Origins, Development, and Application of Qualitative Comparative Analysis: The First 25 Years." *European Political Science Review* 6 (1): 115–142. https://doi.org/10.1017/S1755773912000318.

Montuschi, Eleonora. 2003. *The Objects of Social Science*. London; New York: Continuum.

Montuschi, Eleonora. 2004. "Rethinking Objectivity in Social Science." *Social Epistemology* 18 (2–3): 109–122. https://doi.org/10.1080/0269172042000249246.

Neurath, Otto. 1973. "Wissenschaftliche Weltauffassung: Der Wiener Kreis." In *Empiricism and Sociology*, by Otto Neurath, edited by Marie Neurath and Robert S. Cohen, 299–318. Dordrecht: Springer Netherlands. https://doi.org/10.1007/978-94-010-2525-6_9.

Nickles, Thomas. 1987. "From Natural Philosophy to Metaphilosophy of Science." In *Kelvin's Baltimore Lectures and Modern Theoretical Physics*, edited by P. Achinstein and R. Kagon, 507–541. Cambridge, MA: MIT Press.

Orne, Jason, and Michael M. Bell. 2015. *An Invitation to Qualitative Fieldwork: A Multilogical Approach*. New York: Routledge.

Parkkinen, V-P, C. Wallmann, M. Wilde, B. Clarke, P. Illari, M. P. Kelly, C. Norell, F. Russo, B. Shaw, and J. Williamson. 2018. *Evaluating Evidence of Mechanisms in Medicine. Principles and Procedures*. New York: Springer Berlin Heidelberg.

Pierce, Roger. 2008. *Research Methods in Politics*. London: SAGE Publications Ltd. https://doi.org/10.4135/9780857024589.

Porter, Theodore M. 1996. *Trust in Numbers: The Pursuit of Objectivity in Science and Public Life*. History and Philosophy of Science. Princeton, NJ: Princeton University Press.

Ragin, Charles C. 1987. *The Comparative Method: Moving beyond Qualitative and Quantitative Strategies*. Berkeley, CA: University of California Press.

Ragin, Charles C. 2008. *Redesigning Social Inquiry: Fuzzy Sets and Beyond*. Chicago: University of Chicago Press.

Ragin, Charles C. 2014. *The Comparative Method: Moving beyond Qualitative and Quantitative Strategies*. Oakland: University of California Press.

Ragin, Charles C., and Lisa M. Amoroso. 2019. *Constructing Social Research: The Unity and Diversity of Method*. Third edition. Los Angeles: SAGE.

Ragin, Charles C., and Peer C. Fiss. 2017. *Intersectional Inequality: Race, Class, Test Scores, and Poverty*. Chicago; London: The University of Chicago Press.

Rihoux, Benoît. 2017. "Configurational Comparative Methods (QCA and Fuzzy Sets): Complex Causation in Cross-Case Analysis." In *Handbook on Methods and Applications in Political Science*, 383–399. Edward Elgar.

Rihoux, Benoît. 2020. "Qualitative Comparative Analysis (QCA): Discovering Core Combinations of Conditions in Political Decision Making." In *Oxford Encyclopedia of Political Decision Making*, edited by D. Redlawsk, 1–34. Oxford: Oxford University Press.

Rihoux, Benoît, Priscilla Álamos-Concha, Damien Bol, Axel Marx, and Ilona Rezsöhazy. 2013. "From Niche to Mainstream Method? A Comprehensive Mapping of QCA Applications in Journal Articles from 1984 to 2011." *Political Research Quarterly* 66 (1): 175–184. www.jstor.org/stable/23563600.

Rihoux, Benoît, Priscilla Álamos-Concha, and Bojana Lobe. 2021. "Qualitative Comparative Analysis (QCA): An integrative approach suited for diverse Mixed Methods and Multimethod research strategies." In *Routledge Reviewer's Guide to Mixed Methods Analysis*, edited by Tony Onwuegbuzie and Burke Johnson, 185–197. London: Routledge.

Rihoux, Benoît, Bernhard Kittel, and Jonathon W. Moses. 2008. "Political Science Methodology: Opening Windows across Europe... and the Atlantic." *PS: Political Science and Politics* 41 (1): 255–258. www.jstor.org/stable/20452157.

Rihoux, Benoît, and Axel Marx. 2013. "QCA, 25 Years after 'The Comparative Method': Mapping, Challenges, and Innovations—Mini-Symposium." *Political Research Quarterly* 66 (1): 167–235. https://doi.org/10.1177/1065912912468269.

Rihoux, Benoît, and Charles C. Ragin, eds. 2009. *Configurational Comparative Methods: Qualitative Comparative Analysis (QCA) and Related Techniques*. Applied Social Research Methods Series 51. Thousand Oaks, CA: Sage.

Rokkan, Stein. 1970. *Citizens, Elections, Parties*. New York: McKay.

Rothman, Kenneth J. 1976. "Causes." *American Journal of Epidemiology* 104 (6): 587–592.

Rothman, Kenneth J., and Sander Greenland. 2005. "Causation and Causal Inference in Epidemiology." *American Journal of Public Health* 95 (S1): S144–S150.

Rothman, Kenneth J., Sander Greenland, and Timothy L. Lash. 2008. *Modern Epidemiology*. Philadelphia, PA: Wolters Kluwer/Lippincott Williams and Wilkins.

Ruphy, Stéphanie. 2016. *Scientific Pluralism Reconsidered: A New Approach to the (Dis)Unity of Science*. Pittsburgh, PA: University of Pittsburgh Press.

Russo, Federica. 2009. *Causality and Causal Modelling in the Social Sciences. Measuring Variations*. Methodos Series. New York: Springer.

Ruzzene, Attilia. 2014. "Process Tracing as an Effective Epistemic Complement." *Topoi* 33 (2): 361–372. https://doi.org/10.1007/s11245-013-9195-6.

Schneider, Carsten Q. 2019. "Two-Step QCA Revisited: The Necessity of Context Conditions." *Quality & Quantity* 53 (3): 1109–1126. https://doi.org/10.1007/s11135-018-0805-7.

Schneider, Carsten Q., and Ingo Rohlfing. 2013. "Combining QCA and Process Tracing in Set-Theoretic Multi-Method Research." *Sociological Methods & Research* 42 (4): 559–597. https://doi.org/10.1177/0049124113481341.

Schneider, Carsten Q, and Claudius Wagemann. 2012. *Set-Theoretic Methods for the Social Sciences: A Guide to Qualitative Comparative Analysis* (Strategies for Social Inquiry). Cambridge: Cambridge University Press. doi:10.1017/CBO9781139004244.

Schurz, Gerhard. 2013. *Philosophy of Science: A Unified Approach*. New York, NY: Routledge.

Teddlie, Charles, and Abbas Tashakkori. 2009. *Foundations of Mixed Methods Research: Integrating Quantitative and Qualitative Approaches in the Social and Behavioral Sciences*. Los Angeles: SAGE.

Thomann, Eva, and Martino Maggetti. 2017. "Designing Research With Qualitative Comparative Analysis (QCA): Approaches, Challenges, and Tools." *Sociological Methods & Research* 49 (2): 356–386. https://doi.org/10.1177/0049124117729700.

Timans, Rob, Paul Wouters, and Johan Heilbron. 2019. "Mixed Methods Research: What It Is and What It Could Be." *Theory and Society* 48 (2): 193–216. https://doi.org/10.1007/s11186-019-09345-5.

Van Evera, Stephen. 1997. *Guide to Methods for Students of Political Science*. Ithaca, NY: Cornell University Press.

Wood, Michael, and Christine Welch. 2010. "Are "Qualitative" and "Quantitative" Useful Terms for Describing Research?" *Methodological Innovations Online* 5 (1): 56–71. https://doi.org/10.4256/mio.2010.0010.

CHAPTER 13

....

MIXED-METHODS RESEARCH AND VARIETY OF EVIDENCE IN POLITICAL SCIENCE

....

JAAKKO KUORIKOSKI AND CATERINA MARCHIONNI

1. INTRODUCTION

....

SINCE the publication of King, Keohane, and Verba's seminal and controversial methodological tract in 1994, political scientists have been prolific in formulating conceptual frameworks for mixed-methods research. This is not surprising, given that most questions vexing political scientists are straightforwardly causal. Does democracy promote peace? How do different voting systems affect the composition of governments and the platforms on which parties run? What are the conditions for a successful revolution? Although political science is not a monolithic discipline, and scholars focusing on international relations face different epistemic challenges compared to those faced by, say, voting theorists, for many of these questions the sample sizes are necessarily small, and it is impossible to conduct field experiments. Consequently, political scientists have had to seek rigorous procedures for combining different kinds of data and methods of analysis in their quest to resolve the fundamental problems of causal inference.

The shared ambition of mixed-methods research is that the different methods contribute in a mutually supporting and complementing way, so that the resulting research achieves more than the sum of its methodological parts. William Whewell called (something like) this principle the *consilience of inductions,* and in contemporary philosophy of science, it is referred to as the *variety-of-evidence thesis.* Although the thesis is in many ways intuitively appealing and may even seem to be a truism (e.g., Hempel 1966, 34), its epistemological rationale remains contested: *why* is it, exactly, that a *variety* of evidence should increase the *reliability* of a result?

Greater variety of evidence obviously entails more evidence, but for the thesis to be interesting and to underwrite the appeal of mixed-methods research, there should be something inherently valuable in the variety itself, or at least, in something reliably associated with it. Yet, as political scientist Creswell (2015, 60) writes, "Unfortunately, the question of the value-added of mixed methods is still under scrutiny by many individuals in the research community." This sentiment is shared by some philosophers of science (see, for example, Cartwright 1991; Hudson 2013; Stegenga 2009).

As long as the epistemic rationale for a variety of evidence remains unclear, so does the value of mixed-methods research. Why would using multiple unreliable methods make more epistemic sense than simply choosing the best single method for the job? Moreover, different research traditions often presuppose radically different ontologies and epistemic standards, which raises questions about their commensurability. According to Beach (2020, 163), given that alternative frameworks for mixed-methods research are based on different and often implicit epistemological and ontological assumptions, "scholars interested in using multi-method designs in the study of comparative politics will receive very different guidance in different accounts, making it into almost an 'everything goes' situation."

A related concern is that the commensuration of different methods that mixed-methods research requires ends up robbing them of precisely those characteristics that make each one successful in the first place. This, the argument goes, renders mixed-methods research a suboptimal compromise of poorly fitting and neutered versions of individually sound methodologies (Beach and Kaas 2020). Finally, there is skepticism concerning the practicality of mixing methods: it may drive researchers to do many things poorly instead of doing one thing well.

In this chapter we survey the landscape of mixed-methods frameworks in political science in light of the literature in the philosophy of science on the variety-of-evidence thesis. Our aim is to shed light on the epistemology of mixed-methods research. The discussion on mixed methods in political science is also an interesting test case for the methodological relevance of philosophy of science. Whereas most methodological disputes in science trade on decades-old philosophical *isms*, methodologists in political science have been eager to mine contemporary philosophical discussions on evidence, mechanisms and causality for arguments and insights.

Finally, a note on scope. The institutionalization of mixed-methods research as a specific research strategy ("third paradigm"), with its own dedicated journals, is a broader trend encompassing most social sciences. To keep the material manageable, however, our focus in this chapter will be on frameworks originally developed or extensively discussed by political science scholars.

2. THE MANY FACES OF EVIDENTIAL VARIETY

Combining evidence of different kinds can have both heuristic and confirmatory value. Statistical analysis can guide the selection of cases for in-depth analysis and case studies can provide hypotheses for more quantitative or experimental designs. Nobody would wish to question this heuristic role of mixing methods. Moreover, few would deny that it is, in general, better to have more evidence than less, or that it is better to have a more comprehensive empirical picture of a phenomenon of interest. However, is there a special epistemic added value in combining evidence of *different kinds,* as the variety-of-evidence thesis claims? Under what conditions does this added value outweigh the epistemic and practical costs of mixed-methods research?

In addressing this question, we need to be clear about the kind of variety that is presupposed in the variety-of-evidence thesis. One obvious way of thinking about different kinds of evidence is in terms of different kinds of data produced with different methods. With data we refer to the concrete public records produced by measurement and experiment (Hacking 1992; Woodward 2000), which become evidence only when they are taken to be reasons for believing or not believing a hypothesis. Data is *of* or *from* something, whereas evidence is always evidence *for* something, such as for the existence of a phenomenon or for the possession of certain features, or for a theoretical hypothesis about (the causes of) that phenomenon (Leonelli 2015; Longino 1979). It should therefore not be taken for granted that different methods produce evidence that is different in some epistemically relevant sense. Conversely, in some cases the same kind of method can generate evidence that is relevantly different.

To see why this is the case we will distinguish three ways in which different kinds of evidence can support each other. First, *evidential triangulation* refers to the use of *diverse and independent evidence* to shore up a claim about a single phenomenon such as a causal effect; second, *evidential integration* refers to the integration of evidence for *distinct* claims about the same phenomenon or system; third, *evidential security* refers to the use of one kind of (second-order) evidence to increase the reliability of another kind of (first-order) evidence. Even though difference in methods of data production is, in principle, neither necessary nor sufficient to ensure that the evidence is varied in any of the three relevant senses, in practice and under suitable conditions, different methods may produce evidence that is independent (as in triangulation), that supports distinct kinds of causal claims (as in integration), and that occurs at different points in the hierarchy of evidence in support of a claim (as in security).

We will discuss each rationale for evidential variety in more detail below, but to grasp the intuition behind this tripartite distinction and the associated meanings of variety, it is useful to draw an analogy with different ways of combining the testimony of witnesses at a trial. We could think of triangulation as when two independent witnesses each testify to having seen the suspect at the crime scene; of integration when two experts testify on different aspects of the case, one being a ballistics expert testifying about the way the gun was fired and the other being a criminal psychologist testifying about the suspect's motives; and of security when an expert testifies that the eye witnesses were in a position to see the suspect clearly enough.[1] The exact interrelations between these epistemic rationales remain an open philosophical question and we do not take a stance on whether some of them are more fundamental than others.[2]

All these interpretations are present in the literature on social-science methodology. For example, historically the rationale of mixed-methods research has been traced back to triangulation (Johnson, Onwuegbuzie, and Turner, 2007). According to Plano Clark and Ivankova (2016), "Mixed methods is the process of integrating quantitative and qualitative research to more completely address a study's purpose or research questions," suggesting that the purpose of mixed-methods research is captured by our concept of integration. In contrast, Beach and Kaas (2020, 214) write that, "The promise of multimethod research is that different methods can compensate for each other's relative weaknesses, enabling more robust inferences to be made about the world"—a way of characterizing multimethod research that seems to invoke either triangulation or security.

In fact, in many instances of diverse evidence it may be debatable under which, if any, of these categories the specific instance falls, which is why we propose our typology as representing ideal types. Nevertheless, we take them to have enough intuitive salience to illuminate the different epistemic rationales of the mixed-methods frameworks surveyed in Section 3.

2.1 Triangulation

We use the term *evidential triangulation* to refer to the use of diverse and independent evidence to shore up claims about a single phenomenon (such as a causal effect) or a theory. Despite its intuitive appeal, the provision of a cogent argument for its epistemic added value has proven surprisingly hard. Its feasibility has also been questioned: the suspicion is that the incompatible background assumptions and ontologies underlying different methods render any claims about shared theories or hypotheses impossible, and even meaningless.

The most straightforward model for multimethod triangulation in philosophy of science has been the measurement of a single quantity by different means or instruments. One possible (and frequently proposed) epistemic rationale explaining why the concordant readings of the different instruments provide better evidence for the value of the quantity than the measurements taken separately is that it would be an inexplicable coincidence— a miracle—that the measurements matched if they did not latch onto the one and the same property in the world. The paradigmatic example is the multiple determination of Avogadro's number as an argument for the reality of molecules. This no-miracle argument has been found problematic, however. It is also questionable whether this example is a clean case of triangulation in the above sense in that the concordance of the independent measurements is taken as evidence for something else, namely, the reality of molecules.

The next step forward from this problematic no-miracle argument is to suggest that the added value of triangulation derives from the fact that the different methods have *independent* characteristic errors and biases. According to this *robustness argument*, triangulation increases reliability because it diminishes the possibility of the result being an artifact of any particular error or bias. An important upshot of the robustness argument is that what is epistemically important is not variety per se, but the *independence* of the different sources of evidence. How exactly this independence should be understood is up for debate. Kuorikoski and Marchionni (2016), for example, argue that it should be understood in straightforward causal terms: inferences from data to phenomena concern the reliability of the causal processes used to generate the data, and the appropriate independence of different methods should be understood accordingly.

There have also been a number of attempts to provide a formal explication of the increased confirmation provided by independent means of determination—and a good number of counterexamples. Among these, Heesen et al. (2019) show that the majority verdict of a set of independent but noisy methods is more likely to be correct than the result of a randomly picked method, and that this probability increases with the number of methods. Stegenga and Menon (2017) and Claveau and Grenier (2019) present numerous examples using Bayes nets to model different kinds of inferences from multiple noisy but independent signals arising from a common source. At least in Bayesian terms, however, it seems that even in the ideal situation, the epistemic value added of evidential variety arising from independent signals is, at best, rather modest (Stegenga and Menon 2017), and fails altogether in a surprisingly large range of epistemic scenarios (Claveau and Greiner 2019).

As an alternative to inductive Bayesian reconstructions, Jonah Schupbach (2018) proposed explicating the epistemic value of robustness and the variety of evidence in terms of *eliminative* explanatory inference. In his framework, evidence is diverse insofar as it is able to eliminate different competing potential explanations of the result, thus variety is not tied to a probabilistic independence condition as in Bayesian reconstructions. In addition, diversity is relative to a given hypothesis and to its potential alternatives. Not all diverse pieces of evidence can rule out a relevant competing explanation of the result, however. Hence, there is still need for an account of what in the evidence or in its mode of production makes it so that a certain piece of evidence is "explanatorily relevant" with respect to the result.

2.2 Integration

Evidential integration refers to the use of diverse evidence to build a more complete picture of a phenomenon in such a way that the epistemic whole is better supported by the totality of evidence than the sum of the individual hypotheses. When the goal of mixed methods is integrative, the relevant notion of diversity pertains to evidence produced for distinct but inferentially related claims. The distinctive feature of integration is that such support is achieved by knowing more about the system of interest. Thus, unlike the case of triangulation, it is not a question of the methods producing evidence through causally independent processes: what matters is what the evidence is about.

In general, integration brings together different lines of evidence that need not be produced with different methods but are all about different aspects of the same system or theory (e.g., Lloyd 2009). Here we need not pursue the general question of the epistemic added value of integration given that mixed-methods frameworks focus exclusively on causal claims, as do we.

The Russo-Williamson thesis puts forward an influential argument for combining evidence of different kinds in mixed-method research, which comes close to our notion of integration. It states that evidence for *both* "difference-making" (in terms of experimental or statistical data) as well as for the mechanism linking the cause to its effect ("mechanistic evidence") is necessary (and jointly sufficient) for establishing causal claims (Russo and Williamson 2007).

The methodological discussion in political science tends to equate mechanistic evidence with different kinds of observational and archival data used in "process tracing" ("causal process observations"), which together with causal-background assumptions support case-specific token causal claims. The parallel between kinds of methods (statistical vs. "process tracing"), conceptions of causality, and kinds of evidence makes this idea seemingly suitable for application in the context of combining small-n and big-N studies, thereby vindicating methodological pluralism—differences in methods, concepts of causality and kinds of evidence are seamlessly run together. The problem is that as the authors of the Russo-Williamson thesis themselves acknowledge in later work (e.g., Clarke, Brendan et al.

2014), there is no straightforward relation between methods, causal concepts, and kinds of evidence.

First, variety of evidence can be produced with a single (kind of) method (see Marchionni and Reijula 2019). For example, both evidence about the average causal effect of an intervention and evidence about the mechanism through which the intervention works can be obtained by running a randomized experiment: whereas in the former the intervention is randomized, in the latter some downward component of the postulated mechanism is randomized. Of course, there is a sense in which evidence about the average causal effect and evidence about the mechanism are not different in kind (they are both experimental), but that is not the relevant notion of diversity for integration.

There is nevertheless something importantly correct about the thesis: the existence of a mechanism, supported by "causal process observations," is in itself evidence that an observed association between variables can be taken as evidence for the population-level causal effect. Acknowledging this, however, is compatible with holding that evidence for the existence of a mechanism is not always necessary to infer the existence of a causal relation from statistical evidence. Nor does it commit us to any form of causal pluralism in terms of different kinds of data or "levels of application" requiring different concepts of causation. In fact, a monist (difference-making) view of causality is perfectly capable of capturing the different evidential roles of case-based evidence of mechanisms and observational population-level evidence of association (Marchionni and Reijula 2019). Simply having a detailed historical account of a series of events does not enable one "to "see causation," and insisting that case studies employ a different concept of causality amounts to ignoring, not solving, the fundamental problem of causal inference.

This brings us to our last point. Given the importance attributed to *mechanistic* evidence in support of causal claims, it is surprising that most of the discussion about mixed methods is framed in terms of methods and the associated units of analysis (large-N studies of populations vs. intensive case studies of units) rather than levels of mechanisms. Observations of lower-level mechanisms obtained from case studies do not support causal generalizations by conceptual fiat; it is mainly because (and hence when) they are based on more reliable causal-background assumptions or the causal properties of the parts are less context-sensitive than the population-level causal relation (Steel 2006). As we argue below, however, none of the mixed-methods frameworks really codify such basic principles of causal inference in any detail: the added value of case studies is conceptualized either in terms of a more reliable way of ascertaining that the causal relation of interest obtains in the particular case, or as a heuristic source of hypotheses about mediating or interacting factors.

2.3 Security

The third type of epistemic rationale for combining evidence of different kinds is security (Staley 2004; Zahle 2019), in which second-order evidence (produced using a different method) speaks in favor of the first-order evidence for the primary claim.[3] Here is how Kent Staley (2004, 469) defines first-order and second-order evidence:

> If some fact E constitutes first-order evidence with respect to a hypothesis H, then it provides some reason to believe (or indicates) that H is the case. IF a fact E is second-order evidence with respect to a hypothesis H, then it provides some reason to believe (or indicates) that some distinct fact E' is first-order evidence with respect to H. (Staley 2004, 469).

Security, like triangulation, requires some degree of independence (if the results of two different tests are subject to the same bias or error, one cannot be evidence for the reliability of the other), but unlike triangulation the evidence is not evidence for the same causal claim.[4] As with integration, relevant variety has to do with the content of the evidence—what it is about—rather than with how it is produced. Unlike integration, however, second-order evidence is about another piece of evidence, not about the system or phenomenon of interest. The second-order evidence in the witness analogy proposed above is the expert witness who testifies that the eye witness was in a position to see the suspect clearly, whereas the first-order evidence is the testimony of the eye witness herself.

Although security is a common rationale in mixed-methods designs in practice—focus groups are routinely used to support inferences from survey results, for example—the possibility of mixing methods for this purpose has been largely ignored in the methodological literature in political science as well as in the philosophy of social science. An exception is Zahle (2019)'s discussion of the use of multiple methods in case-study research. She argues that participant observations and qualitative interviews can be used to increase mutual security insofar as they produce complementary data, and that the same idea can be applied to mixed-method research. We agree. Yet, none of the frameworks surveyed below explicitly discuss how the different methods could be used to estimate the internal validity of the results of the other methods. Many questions therefore remain open. What methods produce data that are complementary? How is the evidence to be combined to generate the epistemic added value? Can available frameworks for mixed-method research be used to increase security? In addressing these questions we discuss each framework in detail.

3. MIXED-METHODS FRAMEWORKS IN POLITICAL SCIENCE

Armed with the distinctions made above, we now review three mixed-methods frameworks: nested analysis, set-theoretic multimethod research, and Bayesian approaches. Our review is not merely descriptive: we also consider whether the proposed methodology aligns well with the expected epistemic value of mixing methods.

3.1 Nested analysis

Nested analysis is a heuristic procedure used for combining observational quantitative studies (regression analysis) with case studies carried out *within the sample* used in the quantitative study (Lieberman 2005). Hence, nesting refers primarily to the relationship between population- and unit-level analyses, not to the relationship between the macro-level effect and its micro-level mechanism, although the two distinctions are obviously interrelated.

Nested analysis begins with a regression analysis on the putative cause and effect of interest (large-N analysis, abbreviated as LNA). If these preliminary results are compatible with the initial causal hypothesis, cases are selected from the sample to further *test* the causal model in question (*model testing strategy*). These cases should be picked close to the regression line, because the function of the cases is to test whether the causal mechanism hypothesized in the theoretical model really mediates the cause and the effect (small-n analysis, abbreviated as SNA).

Suppose we were interested in the possible causal relationship between a given institutional form and policy outcomes (Lieberman 2005). Our initial statistical study would test the association within a set of otherwise comparable countries, given some set of control variables. If such an association were found, we would conduct a more in-depth inquiry into countries in which either the institutional form and the hypothesized outcomes were both present or both were absent, the aim being to look for traces of "the patterns of organization the institutional form supposedly influences" and which, in turn, influence the policy outcome. Such case studies could utilize a variety of different, mostly preexisting data (such as archival data and existing research and news), with quantitative data and methods in a supporting role.

If the cases provide corroborating evidence for the existence of the hypothesized mechanism, the analysis ends there. If they fail to fit the initial hypothesis, the analyst must make a further judgment on whether the particular case(s) were simply idiosyncratic, and if so pick new ones, or whether the studies really revealed a theoretical flaw in the original hypothesis, which would then prompt a new large-N study based on the clues that the cases provide. If the initial regression results do not support the original causal hypothesis, the case studies should be used to build new causal models (*model building strategy*). For this purpose, the cases should be picked from both on and off the regression line, guided by prior theoretical expectations about where theoretically revealing cases might be found. If the examined cases suggest a new coherent causal model, then this should be tested in a new large-N statistical study.

LNA and SNA differ not only in terms of the methods through which inferences are reached (statistical inference versus qualitative comparisons and process tracing), but also in terms of the claim that is inferred (population-level average causal effect vs. within-case claims about causal mechanisms).

According to Lieberman (2005), nested analysis is designed to make the most of the comparative advantages of large- and small-N methods. The evidential value of small-N studies is not automatically increased by having more cases. In fact, the number of case studies should be carefully considered to ensure an adequate level of depth and detail in each one. The cases should be chosen, and the studies designed, to answer questions that the large-N statistical study leaves open (such as the direction of causation). Prior statistical studies could guide the design of case studies to look for (traces of) possible causes of observed differences between data points or between the specific case and what one would expect given the population on average. Case studies may also force the researcher to be more specific about the concepts, constructs, and models at play.

Although LNA and SNA provide first-order evidence for distinct claims, the ultimate aim of nested analysis is "to make inferences about the unit of analysis that is shared between the two types of analysis" (Lieberman 2005, 440): the population-level average causal effect. Our interest in Lieberman's toy example presented above is in the causal relationship between institutional form and policy outcome on the population level, not the way in which such a relationship plays out in the small set of countries on which SNA has been conducted. The main rationale for mixing is therefore integrative: a primary claim is supported by first-order evidence as well as by evidence for a distinct but related secondary claim (about the working of the mechanism in one or more instances). The framework itself is silent about the principles of such mechanism-based causal inference, however. As the stated goal is to test the general population-level causal connection, the framework could be strengthened by explicitly including such principles.

3.2 Set-Theoretic Multimethod Research

Whereas nested analysis prioritizes the population-level (average) causal effect as the primary hypothesis of interest, the ultimate focus of *Set-Theoretic Multimethod Research* is on token case-specific causal claims. Instead of statistical and case studies, set-theoretic research combines in-depth case studies with small-N comparative studies (Rohlfing and Schneider 2018). Instead of standard regression analysis, the comparative small-N methodology used is qualitative causal analysis (QCA), which is a simple tabulation procedure for inferring combinations of necessary and sufficient conditions for the effect.

Despite the rather ostentatious label, set-theoretic MMR and QCA have little to do with set theory proper. The talk about sets and "set-relations" is mainly motivated by the observation that when the populations are small and all observable outcomes are likely to be affected by multiple factors, correlations between any two factors are unlikely to be very informative of causal relevance. In a "crisp-set" QCA, we are interested in one dichotomous effect variable, which has a number of potential dichotomous causal conditions, and a smallish population of cases (likely from preexisting empirical case-based research) with varying combinations of conditions and values of the effect. In contrast to multiple regression, the QCA procedure goes as follows: (1) A raw data table is produced in which for each case there is a combination of conditions and an outcome (both taking either the value of 0 or 1); (2) an algorithm ("truth table analysis") is used to produce a truth table displaying the data as a list of different combinations of some conditions and an outcome (called configurations); and (3) Boolean minimization is applied to the table so as to detect "causal regularities" in the data (presumably this set of conditions causes this outcome).

In the "fuzzy set" version the conditions are no longer binary as the units have degrees of membership of particular sets (e.g., a country could be 0.75 degrees democratic). This allows for the formulation of quantitative measures of causal sufficiency, necessity, and relevance (based on strong causal background assumptions).

What makes this a framework for multimethod research is that the QCA is supplemented with process tracing oriented case studies. The epistemic roles of QCA and process tracing are dependent on the order in which they are implemented. In the process tracing-first design, the focus of the case studies should be on typical cases, in which process tracing is supposed to reveal the causally important factors and the mechanisms between them. After this, the role of the QCA is mainly to estimate the generalizability of these causal mechanisms.

In a QCA-first design, the comparative study aims at identifying the set(s) of causally sufficient conditions for the effect of interest, and the role of the case studies is to uncover the mechanism for this effect. Another role for QCA is to uncover previously unconsidered factors in cases in which the causal factors identified in the QCA fail to bring about the outcome. Thus, QCA also guides case selection in the process tracing phase.

Set-theoretic MMR thus aims primarily to shore up evidence for case-specific token causal claims. This is not surprising, in that the whole set-theoretic enterprise is framed as an alternative to "correlational thinking" and associated quantitative population-level causal concepts such as the average causal effect. Yet even its proponents admit that QCA does not *directly* contribute to within-case inferences. Its role in both MMR designs discussed above is limited to suggesting new candidate factors for further process tracing or evaluating the generality of already uncovered mechanisms. Hence, insofar as MMR exemplifies the variety of evidence thesis, it does so as a framework for integration.

3.3 Bayesian approaches

As the questions of mixing methods and the value of variety of evidence are obviously rather general, why not use the most general formal framework for inductive reasoning to regiment mixed-methods research? Humphreys and Jacobs (2015), for example, do this by applying a comprehensive Bayesian analysis to mixed-methods research in political science. Whereas nested analysis and set-theoretic MMR provide heuristic recipes for conducting mixed methods, the Bayesian integration of quantitative and qualitative data (BIQQ) provides a broad framework for drawing epistemic conclusions about a whole class of evidential relationships between statistical and case-study evidence.

At the core of the BIQQ framework is a straightforward application of Bayes' rule (in particular, the specification of an appropriate likelihood function): How likely would it be to observe a given set of quantitative and qualitative observations if a particular causal proposition were true, compared to the likelihood of observing them if the alternatives were true? Whereas the previous two frameworks prioritize one type of causal inference, BIQQ facilitates the integration of evidence for different kinds of (causal) claims—on both the population- and the case-level—as well as for beliefs about mediating mechanisms. Moreover, unlike in the other frameworks, there is no particular set of methods to be combined, making BIQQ, at least in principle, applicable to any combination of quantitative and qualitative methods.

BIQQ treats case-based evidence produced via process tracing as a noisy signal (a clue) of a causal relationship, and the clue probabilities, in turn, are treated as parameters estimable from the data. Observing a clue will now shift the posterior probability for both the belief that a specific causal relationship obtains in the particular case and the probative value of the clue. The baseline probability model therefore has three sets of parameters: the population distribution of causal types; the probabilities with which types are assigned to treatment; the probabilities with which clues are associated with types. It can be extended to include multiple, nonbinary, and interconnected clues per case. Case selection is taken as random in the baseline model, but this assumption may also be relaxed.

Given that BIQQ as such does not provide a practical recipe for mixing similar-to-nested analysis and set-theoretic MMR, and that as a Bayesian framework, quantitative results are sensitive to essentially arbitrary priors, what inferential added value can it offer to the researcher in practice? Humphreys and Jacobs provide two case examples of existing research (drivers of electoral-system choice and the relationship between natural resources and civil war), as well as a set of simulations to demonstrate that the framework allows for drawing interesting and systematic epistemic conclusions. These conclusions rest on the assumption that the signals from the correlational data and the case-specific clues are independent.

First, formal modeling highlights the extent to which the comparative inferential leverage of case studies vs. correlational data depends on the case-selection method. Furthermore, the results from designs in which clue data are not collected for all cases depend substantially on which cases are selected for process tracing.

Second, whereas nested analysis and set-theoretic MMR set rules for case selection based on the initial statistical results or the inferential goal of the research project, BIQQ also models the way in which the optimal case-selection strategy depends on the probative value of clues and the causal heterogeneity in the population, as well as on the prior uncertainty related to both of these aspects. For example, on the assumption that the population is heterogeneous, receiving evidence about the causal effect in a single case naturally has a lower impact on the estimate of the average causal effect (ACE).

Third, when the target of the inference is the ACE, even cases with highly informative cues affect this posterior only relatively little. The implication is that highly evocative case studies may bias estimates *if* the ultimate goal is the ACE. Here, BIQQ seems directly to question at least part of the rationale of nested analysis, for example. We hypothesize that this contentious result follows from BIQQ's exclusively formalizing the logic of triangulation: case-specific clues provide independent evidence that the case in question is of a particular causal kind, and this is then added as an independent signal to the correlational evidence for ACE. It could be argued that, at least when used in this way, BIQQ does not fully capture the evidential contribution of case-specific mechanistic evidence in terms of integration. In making quantitative and case-based evidence comparable in terms of clues, the framework necessarily loses information and thus does not fully exploit the value that knowledge of the mechanism could add to case-based research.[5] Although BIQQ is in many ways the most versatile and informative of the frameworks reviewed here, it could be amended by including more explicit principles for linking mechanism-based reasoning and causal generalization, such as recent proposals based on graphical methods. For example, rules for conditioning on the values of mediating and interacting variables (mechanistic and contextual knowledge), analogous to those for removing bias in transporting an estimate of ACE from one population to another (e.g., Pearl and Bareinboim 2014), would add an element of integration to the triangulating logic of BIQQ.

4. WHITHER INTERPRETATION?

The mixed-methods frameworks discussed above conceptualize the evidential value of case studies in terms of process tracing. To a great extent, the literature defending and refining the process-tracing method is a reaction to the view that the evidential import of case-based research on causal questions is inferior to that of large-N quantitative studies, but also to the methodologically anti-naturalist self-understanding of many scholars engaged in qualitative research. Thus, one of the main drivers of this literature has been to bridge the gulf between "interpretivist" and "positivist" paradigms in social research.

The focus on the process-tracing features of case-based research that characterize mixed-methods frameworks would seem to imply that an important element of the case-study method, namely its distinctly interpretive, hermeneutic aspects, is left out. The idea would be that interpretative methods such as different forms of textual analysis, unstructured interviews, focus groups and ethnographic field work aimed at "thick descriptions" cannot be combined with process-tracing methods aimed at unpacking causal mechanisms, let alone with statistical methods. Beach and Kaas (2020), for example, argue that purely interpretive process-tracing methods differ radically in their ontological and epistemological assumptions, making them fundamentally incommensurable. Does this mean, in fact, that developments in mixed-methods research herald a return to the paradigm wars of the 1980s and 1990s?

We do not think so. It is true that interpretive methods do not always address questions about causal mechanisms, but they can be used to generate evidence that is relevant to hypotheses about social mechanisms. This is so not only because knowledge of the meaning of a practice for the people involved is an important source of information about causal mechanisms, but also because evidence generated by interpretive methods can be subjected to the same standards as any other evidence (Kincaid 1996; Little 1991).

What remains to be established is the scope of the evidential contribution of interpretative methods. Do they contribute to mixed-method research only via their contribution to within-case process tracing? Or can they contribute to mixed-method research on their own? It is quite clear that understanding the meaning-making practices of the individuals involved can help in tracing the mechanism within one case (integration). In addition, as Zahle (2019) argues, different qualitative within-case methods, such as interviews and participant observation, can increase their mutual internal validity (security). Interpretive methods can (and often should) be combined with more quantitative methods such as experiments and surveys. In these combinations, again, interpretive methods can be employed to gather information about the mechanism (when experimenting on social norms, for example, it is of utmost importance to understand whether the norm was there to begin with or had been created by the experiment) or to increase security. In place of proclamations of ontological disunity and epistemological incommensurability, the way forward is the formulation of procedures for interpretive studies to add to the variety of evidence in mixed-methods research as interpretive methods. For example, it is easy to envisage how the role of interpretive methods for updating the clue probabilities could be given a more explicit and thorough treatment in BIQQ.

5. CONCLUSIONS

We have distinguished different ways in which combining evidence of different kinds can have epistemic value. We also argue that worries about incommensurability need not arise once kinds of evidence and kinds of causal concepts have been decoupled. This should be welcome news for political science: rather than being a symptom of immaturity, the methodological plurality of the discipline could be harnessed in productive ways to increase the reliability of causal inferences.

Do current frameworks for mixed-methods research succeed to fully exploit the epistemic added value of a variety of evidence? Insofar as the different frameworks are suited to doing different things with different combinations of methods, the answer is positive. As we have shown, whereas nested analysis offers guidelines on how to combine small and large-N studies to confirm population-level causal claims, MMR combines different kinds of small-n-studies to shore up token-level causal claims. Both exemplify the logic of integration. The Bayesian framework is the most flexible of the three, allowing, in principle, the combining of any kind of study for different purposes. However, it does not offer the kind of recipe for construing mixed-method studies as the other frameworks do.

At the same time, however, all the frameworks reviewed above bracket out explicit considerations of the internal validity of inferences based on individual methods. This is understandable in that they are about mixing methods, not about methodology in its totality, but they have consequently missed key aspects of variety of evidence. First, treating individual methods as black boxes prevents discussion of the ways in which different methods can shed light on each other's assumptions. Thus, the frameworks offer little explicit guidance on how to use a variety of evidence to increase the *security* of causal inferences. Second, whereas the methodological literature on statistical causal inference is now massive, there are no widely agreed rules covering mechanism-based causal inference, meaning that the frameworks lack informative guidelines on the substantial integration of knowledge of mechanisms and of associations. A third aspect that deserves more attention than it has received thus far concerns the independent contribution that interpretive methods could make to mixed-methods research. Even aside from claims of outright incommensurability, there is still relatively little in the way of explicit guidelines on how such methods can assist case-based causal inference in assessing the reliability of observed traces of causal processes, for example.

NOTES

1. In all cases, the evidence could be produced within the same mixed method study, or across different studies such as when a new experimental design provides evidence that is relevant to an already established claim. Zahle (2019) proposes the same tripartite distinction between kinds of qualitative evidence produced within the same case study.
2. Staley (2004), for example, introduced the concept of security as a non-inductivist explication of the epistemic value of certain kinds of robustness reasoning, many of which we would classify under triangulation.
3. Like Zahle's (2019), our concept of security is also inspired by Staley (2004).
4. Staley (2004) proposes to understand triangulation as a special case of security. Hence, his discussion involves tests yielding the same result. Whether or not triangulation is a special case of security is not something we want to argue here one way or the other. For our purposes, it is sufficient to separate security from triangulation so that in security two tests do not give the same result, but rather results that are related so that one (second-order) constitutes evidence for the correctness of the other (first-order).

5. We do not mean that "the fundamental ontological assumptions" of case-based method are thereby taken less seriously (cf. Beach and Kaas 2020). This is just a claim about what kinds of things you can do with mechanistic information.

REFERENCES

Beach, Derek. 2020. "Multi-method research in the social sciences: A review of recent frameworks and a way forward." *Government and Opposition* 55 (1): 163–182.

Beach, Derek, and Jonas Gejl Kaas. 2020. "The great divides: Incommensurability, the impossibility of mixed-methodology, and what to do about it." *International Studies Review* 22 (2): 214–235.

Cartwright, Nancy. 1991. "Replicability, reproducibility, and robustness: Comments on Collins." *History of Political Economy* 23: 143–155.

Plano Clark, Vicki L., and Nataliya V. Ivankova. 2016. *Mixed Methods Research: A Guide to the Field*. Los Angeles: SAGE Publications Ltd.

Clarke, Brendan, Donald Gillies, Phyllis Illari, Federica Russo, and Jon Williamson. 2014. "Mechanisms and the evidence hierarchy." *Topoi* 33 (2): 339–360.

Claveau, François, and Olivier Grenier. 2019. "The variety-of-evidence thesis: A Bayesian exploration of its surprising failures." *Synthese* 196 (8): 3001–3028.

Creswell, John W. 2015. "Revisiting mixed methods and advancing scientific practices." in Hesse-Biber and Johnson (eds.) *The Oxford Handbook of Multimethod and Mixed Methods Research Inquiry*. New York: Oxford University Press, 57–71.

Hacking, Ian. 1992. "The self-vindication of the laboratory sciences." In Andrew Pickering (ed.), *Science as Practice and Culture*. Chicago: University of Chicago Press: 29–64.

Heesen, Remco, Liam Kofi Bright, and Andrew Zucker. 2019. "Vindicating methodological triangulation." *Synthese* 196 (8): 3067–3081.

Hempel, Carl. 1966. *Philosophy of Natural Science*. New York: Prentice Hall.

Hudson, Robert. 2013. *Seeing Things: The Philosophy of Reliable Observation*. Oxford: Oxford University Press.

Humphreys, Macartan, and Alan M. Jacobs. 2015. "Mixing methods: A Bayesian approach." *The American Political Science Review* 109 (4): 653–673.

Johnson, R. Burke, Anthony J. Onwuegbuzie, and Lisa A. Turner. 2007. "Toward a definition of mixed methods research." *Journal of Mixed Methods Research* 1 (2): 112–133.

Kincaid, Harold. 1996. *Philosophical Foundations of the Social Sciences: Analyzing Controversies in Social Research*. Cambridge: Cambridge University Press.

King, Gary, Robert O. Keohane, and Sidney Verba. 1994. *Designing Social Inquiry: Scientific Inference in Qualitative Research*. Princeton, NJ: Princeton University Press.

Kuorikoski, Jaakko, and Caterina Marchionni. 2016. "Evidential diversity and the triangulation of phenomena." *Philosophy of Science* 83 (2): 227–247.

Leonelli, Sabina. 2015. "What counts as scientific data? A relational framework." *Philosophy of Science* 82 (5): S810–S821.

Lieberman, Evan S. 2005. "Nested analysis as a mixed-method strategy for comparative research." *American Political Science Review* 99 (3): 435–452.

Little, Daniel. 1991. *Varieties of Social Explanation*. Boulder, CO: Westview Press.

Lloyd, Elisabeth A. 2009. "Varieties of support and confirmation of climate models." In *Aristotelian Society Supplementary Volume* 83 (1): 213–232.

Longino, Helen E. 1979 "Evidence and hypothesis: An analysis of evidential relations." *Philosophy of Science* 46 (1): 35–56.

Marchionni, Caterina, and Samuli Reijula. 2019. "What is mechanistic evidence, and why do we need it for evidence-based policy?" *Studies in History and Philosophy of Science Part A* 73: 54–63.

Pearl, Judea and Elias Bareinboim. 2014. "External validity: From do-calculus to transportability across populations." *Statistical Science* 29 (4): 579–595.

Rohlfing, Ingo, and Carsten Q. Schneider. 2018. "A unifying framework for causal analysis in set-theoretic multimethod research." *Sociological Methods & Research* 47 (1): 37–63.

Russo, Federica, and Jon Williamson. 2007. "Interpreting causality in the health sciences." *International Studies in the Philosophy of Science* 21 (2): 157–170.

Schupbach, Jonah N. 2018. "Robustness analysis as explanatory reasoning." *The British Journal for the Philosophy of Science* 69 (1): 275–300.

Staley, Kent W. 2004. "Robust evidence and secure evidence claims." *Philosophy of Science* 71: 467–488.

Steel, Daniel. 2006. "Methodological individualism, explanation, and invariance." *Philosophy of the Social Sciences* 36 (4): 440–463.

Stegenga, Jacob. 2009. "Robustness, discordance, and relevance." *Philosophy of Science* 76: 650–661.

Stegenga, Jacob, and Tarun Menon. 2017. "Robustness and independent evidence." *Philosophy of Science* 84 (3): 414–435.

Woodward, Jim. 2000. "Data, Phenomena, and Reliability." *Philosophy of Science* 67: S163–S179.

Zahle, Julie. 2019. "Data, epistemic values, and multiple methods in case study research." *Studies in History and Philosophy of Science Part A* 78: 32–39.

CHAPTER 14

GENERALIZATION, CASE STUDIES, AND WITHIN-CASE CAUSAL INFERENCE
Large-N Qualitative Analysis (LNQA)

GARY GOERTZ AND STEPHAN HAGGARD

Singular causal claims are primary. This is true in two senses. First, they are a necessary ingredient in the methods we use to establish generic causal claims. Even the methods that test causal laws by looking for regularities will not work unless some singular causal information is filled in first. Second, the regularities themselves play a secondary role in establishing a causal law. They are just evidence—and only one kind of evidence at that—that certain kinds of singular causal fact have happened.

Nancy Cartwright

The particular and productive character of mechanisms in fact implies that we should think of causation as fundamentally a singular and intrinsic relation between events, rather than as something mediated by laws or universals.

Stuart Glennan

INTRODUCTION

PHILOSOPHERS of social science and causation have a long tradition of distinguishing between type versus token causal inference. Types are abstract and general; tokens are concrete particulars. As illustrated in the epigraphs to this chapter, we think that all causal regularities or generalizations ultimately rest on the effects that operate in individual cases. If an experiment shows that there is a significant average treatment effect, that must mean that there are individual cases in which the treatment influenced the outcome for that case. Although cast in probabilistic terms, the average treatment effect is ultimately a kind of summing up of individual level causal influences. If there was no causal effect at the case level, there could be no treatment effect at the population level.

In this chapter we pursue the notion that type causation is a generalization of token causal inference. In the social sciences, serious interest in the role of token causal inference received little methodological attention until qualitative and multimethod research took off in political science and sociology over the course of the 1990s. Process tracing and counterfactuals have been focal points in that literature. Process tracing explores the mechanism by which X produced or caused Y in an individual case. Similarly, counterfactual analysis focuses on the determinants of outcomes in individual cases by posing and then confirming or dismissing alternative explanations. This is typically counterfactual dependence *with mechanisms*.[1] We focus on what in the causal mechanism literature is often known at the "trigger" that is the initial factor in a causal mechanism.[2] The logic here is of sufficient conditions: the initial factor is sufficient to set the causal mechanism in motion. In this chapter we leave the causal mechanism in general as a black box and focus on the generalizability of the mechanism.

A central contention of this chapter is that both experiments and case studies face the problem of external validity or, what we prefer, the problem of generalization. How generalizable is the randomized experiment or case study? Experimentalists in political science have started to tackle this problem. The Metaketa project has repeated experiments across different countries to see how generalizable findings are (Dunning et al. 2019). We are seeing a similar effort to think about generalization from case studies as well. A recent example is Kaplan's excellent book on civil society organizations in civil war (2017). It starts with what we call a causal mechanism case study. The remainder of the book is preoccupied with how generalizable that mechanism is in Columbia as well as in other settings such as Syria and Afghanistan. Ziblatt's (2017) analysis of the role of conservative parties in European democratization rests on an extensive causal mechanism case study of the UK as well as a comparison with Germany. In his last chapter, however, he provides additional case studies on other European countries and briefer discussions of transitions in Latin America, the Middle East, and Asia.

A new research practice has emerged in recent years both among multi-method and qualitative researchers: to multiply the number of qualitative case studies in order to strengthen causal inference that we call Large-N Qualitative Analysis (LNQA). Early examples of the work took a particular form: they sought to challenge prominent statistical or game-theoretical findings by showing that postulated causal relationships did not in fact hold when subjected to closer scrutiny via within-case causal inference; among the targets of this work were prominent accounts on inequality and democratization (Haggard and Kaufman 2016), democratization and war (Narang and Nelson 2009), the effect of audience costs on conflict (Trachtenberg 2012), and the role that rebel victory plays in civil war settlements (Wallensteen 2015; see Goertz 2017, chapter 7 for a discussion). However, the approach has subsequently expanded to define a wider research methodology aimed not only at disconfirming existing analysis but supporting multimethod and in-depth case study work as well.

LNQA is clearly most conducive to the analysis of rare events, or those in which the N is small, such as famines, wars and civil wars, regime changes or the acquisition of nuclear weapons. The approach sometimes starts with statistical analysis, and thus takes a multimethod approach. Other examples, such as the work by Kaplan just cited, start with a single in-depth case study and then augments it with others. But the core of the approach is the use of a (relatively) large number of individual case studies, and even a whole population, in order to strengthen causal inference and generalizability.

To date, these practices have not been justified by reference to methodological works or even by methodological discussions (see however Haggard and Kaufman 2016; Goertz 2017). In the spirit of what Goertz calls "methodological ethnography," this chapter outlines this approach and seeks to ground it theoretically. Based on practice both among experimentalists and those using case studies we argue that the logic of generalization at work is what we will call "absolute generalization" versus the statistical logic of comparison and relative generalization. Causal inference is strengthened via multiple within-case causal inferences rather than comparisons between control and treatment groups or other comparative approaches.

Toward the end of the chapter we explore some concrete examples of this methodology in action. We provide an extended discussion of two prominent books that have effectively employed the research methodology that we outline here. One is an international relations example, Sechser and Fuhrmann's *Nuclear weapons and coercive diplomacy*, the other is from comparative politics, Ziblatt's *Conservative parties and the birth of democracy*. They illustrate virtually all of the key features of LNQA.

Our analysis of case studies and generalization links very naturally to the philosophical literature on causal mechanisms. As we move through the methodological issues in a political science context we connect with familiar authors and works in the causal mechanism literature in philosophy. For example, our emphasis on within-case causal inference and generalization fits quite naturally with the requirement that causal explanation involve the analysis of mechanisms. As we shall see, "regularities"—be they observational or experimental—require more detailed analysis of mechanisms within cases.

GENERALIZATION AND (EXTERNAL VALIDITY, EXTRAPOLATION, REGULARITIES, TRANSPORTABILITY, ANALYTIC GENERALIZATION, ETC.)

The concepts of external validity, along with its partner internal validity, were introduced into the methodological literature in the classic Campbell and Stanley volume. Campbell and Stanley (1963) define external validity in terms of "generalizability: To what populations, settings, treatment variables, and measurement variables can [an] effect be generalized?"

As Shadish, Cook, and Campbell note, "Although internal validity may be the sine qua non of experiments, most researchers use experiments to make *generalizable* causal inferences" (2002, 18–20). However, experiments are generally seen as weak on external validity, in part because sample populations in lab experiments are not seen as representative (Druckman and Kam 2011; Bardsley et al. 2010). However, the problem goes deeper and extends to field experiments as well. What is to assure that an experiment in one setting will necessarily yield the same result in a different one where context is fundamentally different?

In her discussion of external validity, McDermott provides the standard solution: "external validity results primarily from replication of particular experiments across diverse populations and different settings, using a variety of methods and measures" (McDermott 2011, 34). Literature reviews and meta-analysis attempt syntheses of these findings, and implicitly reach judgments of the extent to which diverse experimental findings should be considered robust. Recently, a major research project—the Metaketa project—has attempted to test some core propositions in political science through highly structured replications. While meta-analysis and replication have gotten more sophisticated, however, there is surprisingly little guidance on how such replications might produce higher or lower levels of generalization.

In their very nice review of the experimental literature on behavioral economics Bardsley et al. call these experiments aimed at increasing external validity "exhibits." They define the exhibit as "a replicable experimental design that reliably produces some interesting result" (Bardsley et al. 2010, epub 409).

Among experimenters in political science the term "transportability" seems to have gained in popularity. We prefer the term generalization because external validity has other dimensions as well, such as how realistic the lab experiment might be. We think it is also the preferred language of those who do case studies: the question most often posed to such studies is exactly their generalizability.

For experimentalists, the definition of generalizability then becomes something like:

> The extent to which the same treatment $X = 1$ produces a similarly significant average treatment effect $Y = 1$ un der some scope conditions S.

Our working definition of generalization in the case study context, by contrast, underlines the importance of token causal inference to the process of achieving external validity:

> The same causal mechanism produces the same outcome based on valid within-case causal analysis in all or a high percentage of cases within some scope conditions S.

In the causal mechanism literature in philosophy this is the "regularity" condition that typically appears in conceptualizations of causal mechanisms.

In short, experiments and case studies have problems of generalizability. To be sure, these problems are subtly different. Experiments generate findings in the form of an average treatment effect, which may or may not extend to other settings. Within-case causal inference offers an explanation for a particular case but the mechanisms may or may not yield the same outcome in a different setting. When well done, however, both have high degrees of internal validity. But case studies are not alone in being vulnerable to the question of generalizability; experiments face this challenge too.

ABSOLUTE GENERALIZATIONS

A core claim of this chapter is one about methodological ethnography. Scholars doing large-N qualitative analysis, working either with the entire population of relevant cases or a relatively large sample of them (roughly ten-plus case studies), often perform what we call in this section absolute tests. A claim is made about a causal relationship or the operation of a causal mechanism in law-like, sufficient-condition, or even necessary-and-sufficient condition, form: if X then Y. Conversely, a number of prominent disconfirmatory studies have tested law-like statements, showing that they in fact fail the sufficient or necessary-and-sufficient condition test when mechanisms are examined more carefully. Yet these practices are rarely if ever justified methodologically or with reference to a corresponding methodological literature. In this and the following section we take up the logic of absolute and relative generalizations, starting with a basic reduced-form example of the former, and then introducing relative as well as absolute tests and the crucial role of causal mechanisms in the method.

Table 14.1 presents our basic set up in a 2×2 table. A distinctive feature of the approach is both its consideration of the distribution of cases and the particular emphasis it places on the $X = 1$ column. $X = 1$ means the treatment has been given in an experimental context or that X has occurred in an observational setting. Two outcomes are then possible: the treatment has an effect (the (1,1) cell) or it doesn't (the (1,0) cell). We call the (1,1) cell the causal mechanism cell, as consideration of cases from the cell are designed to test for the operation of the postulated causal mechanism. As we shall see below, the $X = 0$ column plays a role when we deal with equifinality, but not in the basic generalization of the causal mechanism.

Many multimethod and qualitative books in recent years include a core case study that illustrates the basic theory. In multimethod books these will sometimes follow the statistical analysis; in qualitative books they are more likely to lead and are often intensive, multi-chapter analyses. These cases inevitably come from the (1,1) cell; they are designed not just to illustrate but to test for the effect of the postulated causal mechanism in the nominally conforming cases.

In purely qualitative books, these central causal mechanism case studies generate the question about generalization which then occupies the latter part of the book. However, just looking at the (1,1) cell ignores the situation where the causal mechanism may not be working, which is critical to the generalizability question. This is the (1,0) cell of Table 14.1, and we return to it in more detail below.

An example from Levy and Thompson illustrates the basics of the generalization logic and the utility of focusing on the $X = 1$ column with a classic hypothesis from realism in international politics. Levy and Thompson test one of the most influential theories in the history of international relations, balance of power theory. As they note in another article "The proposition that near-hegemonic concentrations of power in the system nearly always trigger a counter-balancing coalition of the other great powers has long been regarded as

Table 14.1 Basic setup

	$X = 0$	$X = 1$
$Y = 1$	Equifinality	Causal mechanism
$Y = 0$		Falsification

an 'iron law' by balance of power theorists" (Levy and Thompson 2010). This "iron law" is a generalization in the terms of this chapter, a type-level causal claim, and one that is made in strong law-like or sufficient-condition form. A core version of the balance of power hypothesis involves balancing against hegemons: *if* there is a hegemon *then* other states will form an alliance to balance it. The short version of the hypothesis is "if hegemon, then balancing."

The logic of "if treatment then outcome" suggests where we need to go to see how generalizable a causal mechanism case study might be. The "if" defines what we call an absolute generalization: if $X = 1$ then the outcome $Y = 1$ occurs.

Table 14.2 shows balancing 55 percent of the time if there is a hegemon. If the iron law with respect to balancing held, then the probability of balancing would be near 1.0, which is the common-sense meaning of an "iron law." So this proposition is rejected because .55 is not near 1.0.[3]

If this were an experimental test, we would be asking whether the hegemon "treatment" were adequate to generate a statistically significant population-level effect or an average treatment effect. The comparative generalization test compares the percentages in the $X = 1$ versus the $X = 0$ column. This then generates well-known 2×2 statistics of association as well as average treatment effects.

In the relative test in Table 14.2 this becomes the bar of 30 percent in the nonhegemon column. This is of course why it is a relative test; it is the comparison of the percentages in the two columns as opposed to the absolute percentage in one column. Thus hegemonic balancing passes the relative test, i.e., significant χ^2. But note that it does not pass the absolute test; the generalization is in fact quite weak. The χ^2 test, like most tests of two-way tables—is comparing percentages across columns, i.e., 30 percent is significantly different from 55 percent. But Levy and Thompson are not posing the question in relative terms; they are postulating a law-like regularity. Literature on scientific laws, e.g., Armstrong (1983) almost inevitably discusses them in terms of how many Y's are also an X an absolute as opposed to comparative framing. The famous democratic peace example is posed as follows: joint democracy triggers a mechanism (or mechanisms) for not-war 100 percent of the time. The hegemonic balancing hypothesis has the form of a sufficient condition: *if* hegemon *then* balancing.

Despite its failure to meet the conditions of an absolute test, does it nonetheless constitute a modestly important generalization? And can we draw a judgment to that effect without relying on statistical, comparative analyses? Those interested in necessary conditions or qualitative comparative analysis (QCA) have thought about this question, and about standards for absolute generalizations, in this case a sufficient condition generalization.

Table 14.2 Relative versus absolute generalizations: balance of power theory

	Nonhegemon	Hegemon
Balancing	.30	.55
No Balancing	.70	.45

$\chi^2 = 28$, $p = .000$, $N = 445$
Source: Levy and Thompson 2005, table 2.

Within QCA there are some common standards, e.g., like p values, for saying there is significant support for a sufficient condition hypothesis. These tend to have a minimum bar of around 75–80 percent (often higher for necessary conditions; see Schneider and Wagemann 2012). Within QCA this constitutes the criterion for passing the sufficient condition test. Since the balancing hypothesis is a sufficient condition one, percentages above this or some other stipulated bar constitute passing the test. We call it an absolute test because *it only uses information in the $X = 1$ column.*

This example illustrates two key points. First, generalization from case studies is typically framed in terms of absolute not relative generalizations. Second, the absolute and relative criteria for judging generalization do not have to agree because they are *different* criteria. It is possible to have comparative effects that are significant and to also see strong absolute effects. However, two other outcomes are also possible. First, it is possible to have a clear a high absolute bar and still conclude that the relative evidence is weak. Conversely, the relative test might appear strong but there are too many falsifying cases (i.e., (1,0) cases) to satisfy an absolute criterion.

The hegemony example is a hypothesis that does not pass the absolute test; the generalization is weak. One might wonder whether this is "too hard" a test, and it could be in the social sciences if such tests were virtually impossible to pass. However the democratic peace examples suggests this is not the case; we see significant research programs in political science around generalizations of this sort. Below we consider a prominent book by Ziblatt in some detail and pursue this question. The basic hypotheses is "if strong conservative party before mass democratization then stable democracy." Ziblatt does not do an explicit test such as those presented in our tables, and it is not clear exactly what population is fulfilling the "if" which defines $X = 1$ column, i.e., the scope conditions. Nonetheless, it appears from his discussion that the proposition would pass the absolute test for both pre-war European democratic experiences and a sample of post-war cases. Ziblatt discusses a number cases in varying degrees of detail but mentions no clear falsifying example.

Until this point, causal mechanisms and within-case causal inference have not made an appearance. Whether we are performing an absolute or relative test we are still looking at patterns across data and are not looking at causal inferences within any of the given cases. However, the set-up is critical because it tells us where to go to do the within-case causal inference. Again, this is the critical role of the $X = 1$ column in defining the population for generalization and thus for case selection.

RELATIVE TESTS AND WITHIN-CASE CAUSAL INFERENCE

We shall treat the notion of a token cause to be roughly equivalent to within-case causal inference, which means making causal claims about individual cases. The modern philosophical literature on token causal inference, starting with Anscombe (1971) and Lewis (1973), rests basically on the possibility of doing counterfactuals as a way of generating causal inference in individual cases. However, as Holland has famously discussed, this is "impossible":

> *Fundamental Problem of Causal Inference.* It is impossible to *observe* the value of Y_t (i) and Y_c (i) on the same unit and, therefore, it is impossible to *observe* the effect of t on i. (Holland 1986, 947)

> The important point is that the statistical solution replaces the impossible-to-observe causal effect of t on a specific unit with the possible-to-estimate *average* causal effect of t over a population of units. (Holland 1986, 947)

One natural consequence of this statement of the problem of inference is that it is "impossible" to do within-case causal inference because one cannot construct a real counterfactual case for the comparison. As Holland notes, the best we can do is to compare control groups with treatment groups, hopefully with randomization of treatments, and to derive average treatment effects in populations. Causal inference is based on cross-case comparisons.[4]

The literature on process tracing and causal process observation, which adopts a mechanism approach to causation, rejects these assumptions. Rather, it assumes that token causal inference is possible. Overwhelming evidence from our everyday lives as well as natural science supports this claim. We assume that individual events can be explained "internally" without reference to population patterns. An example is the space shuttle Challenger explosion. Scientists devoted tremendous energy into why this single event happened, and in less than three years another Space Shuttle Discovery lifted off with a crew of five from Kennedy Space Center. Clearly, the teams investigating the initial failure believed it was possible to find the cause of the singular event that led to the explosion and confident they could prevent it from recurring.

Glennan makes this point in his discussion of the new mechanical philosophy, which is closely related to the move toward within-case causal inference. Based on the distribution of conforming and non-conforming cases in a statistical analysis such as Table 14.2, we only have what he calls "a bare causal explanation": "Bare causal explanations show what depends upon what without showing why or how this dependence obtains. The causal claims required are established, broadly speaking, by observational and experimental methods like Mill's methods of agreement and difference or controlled experiments. Ontologically speaking, causal dependencies require the existence of mechanisms, but bare causal explanations are silent on what those mechanisms are" (Glennan 2017, 224).

He then discusses at some length an example from the history of medicine where Semmelweis linked the failure to wash hands and instruments to sepsis in Vienna hospitals: "Semmelweis sought to explain the epidemic of puerperal (or childbed) fever among mothers giving birth at the Vienna General Hospital during the 1840s. His first observation was that the division of the hospital to which the women were admitted appeared to be causally relevant, since the death rate from puerperal fever for women in the First Division was three to four times that of women admitted to the Second Division (6.8–11.4% versus 2.0–2.7%)" (Glennan 2017, 224). These statistics imply basically something like Table 14.2.

In his specific example, Clara—a mother with puerperal fever contracted in the non-hygienic division of the hospital—clearly belongs in the (1,1) causal mechanism cell. She is definitely in the treatment group and perhaps even receives more specifically the treatment of unwashed hands and instruments. As Glennan notes this does not necessarily mean that she got the disease via those treatments:

> Let us start with the single case. Suppose Clara contracted puerperal fever (call this event e). What caused her to contract it? A first explanation might simply be that Clara contracted puerperal fever because she delivered her baby in the First Division (call this c). If the claim that c caused e is true, that is, if there exists a mechanism by which c contributes to the production e, then that claim provides a bare causal explanation of e. Note that the mere fact that there is a higher incidence of puerperal fever in the First Division is not sufficient to guarantee there is such a mechanism, because it might be the case that that mechanism did not depend upon Clara's being in the First Division. (Glennan 2017, 225)

The kicker comes in the final statement that he makes in discussing this example: "I would argue that until this generalization is attached to particular cases, there is no explanation" (Glennan 2017, 225).

The within-case causal inferences for cell (1,1) cases are important because, as in Table 14.2, correlation is not causation, neither in observational nor experimental research: it is always an *inference* more or less well founded. In an experimental setting those individual cases in the (1,1) cell all count as evidence for the impact of the treatment. This is exactly the point Cartwright is making in her epigraph to this chapter. The average treatment effect must be built upon individual cases where the treatment caused the outcome at least in part.

The within-case causal analysis is thus an examination of cases in the (1,1) cell to ascertain whether the postulated causal mechanism is active; within-case causal inference as used here implies a focus on causal mechanisms.

With that framing, we can now turn to some examples from the increasing body of mixed-method and qualitative research that seeks to strengthen causal inference and generalization by conducting within-case causal inference on a large number of cases. We start with the famous theory of Acemoglu and Robinson that inequality affects the likelihood of democratization. We draw on the multi-method analysis of Haggard and Kaufman (2016), which supplements statistical analysis with consideration of causal mechanisms in individual cases to see how this methodology plays out in one important substantive domain. We also use the case to again underline the difference between absolute and relative tests.

Acemoglu and Johnson's theory is presented in formal terms, through a series of game theoretic models. They do not explicitly state their core arguments in absolute terms, but game theoretic models typically generate necessary and sufficient conditions claims and their models do show crisp equilibria that should rule out certain transition paths. However, their claims about inequality and how transitions occur can be put in probabilistic terms. First, they argue that transitions to democratic rule are more likely at moderate levels of inequality than in highly unequal or highly equal countries; at high levels of inequality, elites will resist the attendant distributional outcomes; at low levels of inequality, demands for redistribution via regime change are muted. As stated, however, levels of inequality constitute only a permissive condition for democratization. Acemoglu and Robinson also argue that inequality is ultimately related to democratization via the mechanism of mass mobilization; it is through mass mobilization or the exercise of what Acemoglu and Robinson call "de facto power," that authoritarian rulers are ultimately dislodged. In the absence of such pressure, why would autocrats forego the advantages of incumbency?

We can now replicate the analysis on hegemony and balancing by taken data from Haggard and Kaufman (2016) on inequality and regime change, but now framing their findings both absolute and relative terms and adding in within-case causal analysis of the theory linking inequality and regime change via mass mobilization. This exercise is given in Table 14.3.[5] Again, both claims derived from the Acemoglu and Robinson model are subject to scrutiny here: those having to do with the greater likelihood of transitions in medium-inequality countries; and that they should occur via mass mobilization.

The absolute hypotheses would be that if there is medium-levels of inequality then there is democratization through the mechanism of mass mobilization. The relative hypotheses would be that they are more likely to occur in moderately unequal authoritarian regimes and via the mechanism of mass mobilization, ceteris paribus. Note that "relative" means relative to other paths to the outcome, and thus implicitly raises the issue of equifinality or other paths to the outcome.

Table 14.3 gives the same basic analysis as Table 14.2 above for the hegemony and balancing hypothesis. Now can begin to consider a stipulated causal mechanism. If a country is democratic for the entire inequality period, it is deleted; we are only considering the population of authoritarian regimes, seeing the conditions under which they might transition. We use the terciles of the inequality data for all authoritarian governments to constitute the inequality categories. Given that inequality changes quite slowly we have treated each country as one observation; we consider each of the three inequality categories as a "treatment." If a country never changes inequality category and never has a transition, it counts as one observation of $Y = 0$. If there is a transition, then that constitutes a positive value on Y for the whole inequality period. If a country's level of inequality changes to another category (tercile), however, that constitutes a new treatment. It is thus possible that a given country constitutes one observation if its inequality category does not change or potentially three or four observations if it changes inequality categories. Thus the number of years per observation, i.e., country-inequality category, can vary significantly depending on how long the country stays within a given inequality category. However, the number of years in each inequality category overall is based on equal treatment: because we use the terciles of authoritarian regime years, the basic categories have basically the same number of years.

The $X = 1$ column focuses on the core Acemoglu and Robinson inequality hypothesis in its absolute form. The $X = 0$ as well as the $X = 2$ columns present the incidence of

Table 14.3 Inequality and democratization: absolute test

	Low inequality $X = 0$	Medium inequality $X = 1$	High inequality $X = 2$
Democratization	19	21	29
No Democratization	34	41	29
Absolute test	.35	.34	.50
Total	53	62	58

$\chi^2 = 3.8$, $p = .15$, $N = 173$
Source: Haggard and Kaufman 2016, inequality data Solt 2020

transitions which do not occur at intermediate levels of inequality. As with the hegemony example above the key thing is the percentage of democratizing cases in the $X = 1$ column. The medium inequality column does not pass the absolute test, with the proportion of cases being about one-third. For the relative test the χ^2 statistic for the table is not significant either indicating that the proportions for the other columns are not radically different. It is higher for the high inequality category, but there is no difference between the low inequality category and the medium at all.

The game theory model in the book might be read to make an absolute claim regarding the high and low inequality columns: there should be no transitions in these situations. This would be an absolute test with probability of 0.0. One can do a probabilistic test of these absolute hypotheses saying that if the probability is less than, say, .25 (symmetric to the .75 used for the QCA sufficiency bar), then it passes the absolute test for these columns. As is clear from the table these columns do not pass this absolute test.

However the mere incidence of cases across different levels of inequality does not test for the presence of the stipulated causal mechanism, namely, mass mobilization. The theory rests on the presumption—quite reasonable—that such transitions are not simply granted from above, but ultimately reflect the exercise of "de facto power" on the part of mass publics; in Przeworski's (2009) terms, democracy is "conquered" not "granted." The (1,1) cell for Acemoglu and Robinson (2006) is thus ultimately not only a cell in which there is an intermediate level of inequality and a transition, but one in which there is an intermediate level of inequality and in which the transition occurs through mass mobilization. Using the usual symbols for tracing a causal mechanism, this can be indicated as $X \rightarrow M \rightarrow Y$ where X is moderate inequality and M is mobilization.

The within-case question is therefore whether the observed cases in the (1,1) cell were caused by inequality via mobilization; answering this question requires consideration of each observation individually, in short, token causal inference analysis. This could be done via process tracing, counterfactuals, or other within-case causal inference strategies; Haggard and Kaufman do it through construction of a qualitative data set that interrogates each case for the presence or absence of mass mobilization.

When using the within-case generalization strategy several things can happen. The first is that the cases in the (1,1) cell were generated via the mechanism of mobilization. These token analyses support the basic theory. But it could also be that an examination of the (1,1) cases reveals that moderate inequality leads to democratization but not via their proposed mechanism. We shall deal with this important issue in the next section, where we note that mobilization may appear as a mechanism in the $X = 0$ column as well as the $X = 2$ column. This could support the mobilization mechanism, but not the connection between democratization and a particular level of inequality and mass mobilization.

The causal mechanism test for generalization generally involves the simultaneous analysis of both X as well as the mechanism, M. In Table 14.4 we include those cases in the (1,1) cell that were generated by mobilization. We also include those in the other columns that were also generated by mass mobilization. In parentheses we have included the original Ns from Table 14.3.

While Table 14.4 looks like a regular two-way table it is fundamentally different from Table 14.3 above. To emphasize this we have put the number of cases in which democratization occurs via mobilization in boldface. We do this to stress that these are counts of token, within-case causal inferences: the number of cases that exhibit the postulated mechanism.

Table 14.4 Inequality, mobilization, democratization: token causal inference and causal mechanism tests

	Low inequality $X = 0$	Medium inequality $X = 1$	High inequality $X = 2$
Democratization via mobilization	13(19)	8(21)	14(29)
No Democratization	34	41	29

Source: From Haggard and Kaufman 2016, using Gini coefficient as measure of inequality.
$\chi2 = 1.96, p = .38, N = 65$
Note: Total transitions cases from Table 14.3 in parentheses.

Unlike Table 14.3, which might be used to make a causal inference, *Table 14.4 is a summary of token causal inferences.* The boldface numbers would be like summarizing the results of a number of experiments. The question then becomes does this summary of token causal inferences permit us to make a type causal inference about moderate inequality operating through the mechanism of mass mobilization?

Table 14.3 looks at the basic hypothesis with the mechanism still black boxed: $(X = 1) \rightarrow (Y = 1)$. This happened 21 times. We now include the mobilization mechanism into the mix. This is asking if in these 21 cases we saw this: $(X = 1) \rightarrow (M = 1) \rightarrow (Y = 1)$, where $M = 1$ means that the mobilization mechanism was part of the reason why Y occurred. Generating these counts requires process tracing and even counterfactual dependence Analysis, in short, token causal inference with respect to each case.

If we include mobilization token causal inferences into the mix, the data in Table 14.4 fails to show support either for the reduced-form inequality hypothesis nor for the mobilization mechanism. In other words, Table 14.4 shows that of the 21 $(X = 1) \rightarrow (Y = 1)$ cases only 8 had $(X = 1) \rightarrow (M = 1) \rightarrow (Y = 1)$. Only 38 percent of the transitions in the medium-inequality category come via their postulated causal mechanism. Hence some other mechanism generated the outcome in the other 13 cases.

It is also worth noting that the percentage of mobilization mechanism cases is higher in the high inequality category than it is in the middle category. If one did a χ^2 statistic just comparing the middle category to extreme inequality separately the χ^2 statistic begins to look quite significant, but not in the direction that Acemoglu and Robinson suggest; more transitions are likely to take place via mass mobilization in the high-inequality cases, even though they were not expected to take place there at all! This suggests that mass mobilization may play a role in some democratic transitions, but again, that inequality does not appear to play a significant causal role.

We have framed our discussion of hegemonic balancing in terms of strong regularities with percentages of .75 greater. One can go in the other direction and ask the skeptics question about whether there is any evidence at all for the hypothesis in question. This is basically asking if the regularity is in fact near zero. So in the hegemonic balancing example one might claim that .55 is some evidence in favor of the theory even though it does not form an iron law.

In their statistical analysis of Acemoglu and Robinson Haggard and Kaufman basically rejected their hypothesis. So their conclusion based on the econometric model is that that there is no relationship between medium levels of inequality and democratization. But as we have seen once one has started to do within-case causal inference on individual cases that can change conclusions.

As we noted above, 8/21=38 percent of cases of medium inequality showed support for the hypothesis. So while it is not a strong regularity it is significantly greater than zero at the same time. So based on within-case causal inference analysis there is modest support for the hypothesis. This again is perhaps quite different than rejecting the hypothesis altogether based on the statistical analysis.

The analysis opens doors onto other lines of research. Following the logic of LNQA, we might investigate in much more detail the eight cases that support their mechanism. These are the confirming cases and it could be worth exploring how the details of these eight match the details and discussion of their mechanism. Haggard and Kaufman ultimately use the information they collect on so-called "distributive conflict transitions" to theorize about other causal factors that might influence this class of transitions; we return to this feature of the approach in more detail below.

Nonetheless, the findings are damning: Haggard and Kaufman—using a combination of statistical and within-case causal analysis—find at best modest support for the Acemoglu and Robinson theory, neither with respect to their claims about inequality nor their claims about the role of mass mobilization. How damning depends the extent to which Acemoglu and Robinson were claiming to providing *the* mechanism for democratization or *a* mechanism, i.e., 8/21 for the Acemoglu and Robinson mechanism and 13/21 for some other unspecified mechanism. There is certainly evidence for the latter but not the former, but note that their claim is now reduced to one of identifying *a* causal path that sometimes occurs, but not with overwhelming frequency.

To summarize, the LNQA methodology involves investigation of absolute tests to see if there is any prima facie evidence for a strong generalization. However, it can also be used to support relative generalizations, particularly in mixed method designs with complementary statistical analysis. The next move, however, is crucial: within-case causal inference to see if the hypothesized mechanisms are present or not in the cases. The absolute test focuses on X while the causal mechanism tests focus on the M. As can be seen, these are related but separate analyses; a reduced form finding may or may not be supported when we turn to evidence of the presence of the mechanism.

EQUIFINALITY AND MULTIPLE PATHWAYS
TO THE OUTCOME

Our analysis above only focused on the connection between a particular theoretical hunch linking moderate inequality, mass mobilization, and democratization. However, it is critical to understand how multiple causal paths can lead to the same outcome. How does the ever-present possibility of equifinality figure into the methodology?[6] Note that mass mobilization was seen to operate in less than half of the cases across all levels of inequality, implying that some other causal mechanism or mechanisms were at work in the democratization process. For example, a number of scholars have argued that international pressure is another cause of democratization.

The question of equifinality arises when there are cases in the $X = 0$ and $Y = 1$ cell. That means something other than X is causing Y. In general most scholars do not claim there is only one path to the outcome; in various ways they assume equifinality. For example, international relations scholars would probably find it objectionable to claim that hegemony is the only circumstance under which balancing could occur. Similarly, it would be odd to claim that democratization only occurs in moderately unequal countries—and through mass mobilization—when there are plenty of instances where this is manifestly is not the case. That is exactly what Table 14.3 shows.

In the discussion of balancing against hegemony, it is quite clear that the basic hypothesis was in fact posed as an absolute one. However, it might be the case that the argument is rather a relative one. In the democracy case, moderately unequal authoritarian countries are more likely to democratize than very equal or unequal countries. If posed in these terms, the hypothesis demands a relative test. Haggard and Kaufman provide an extensive set of relative tests using standard statistical techniques, such as standard panel designs and fixed and random effects models. These tests reject the relationship between inequality and democratization in this relative form as well.

The question here is how causal mechanism and token analysis might fit into a comparative, relative test? We have already suggested an answer: that while their particular theory linking moderate inequality to democratization through mass mobilization is rejected, it is the case that mass mobilization is the causal mechanism at work in over half of all transitions. Haggard and Kaufman go on to argue that mass mobilization may not be due not to inequality but to the robustness of social organization: mass mobilization is more likely where unions and other civil society organizations are present. In effect, Haggard and Kaufman also use the distribution of cases not simply to cast doubt on the Acemoglu and Robinson model, but also to identify alternative causal pathways to democracy: from social organization, through mass mobilization to democracy.

Let's call this additional path Z, perhaps international pressure, social organization or some other mechanism. So now instead of a two-way table we would have a three-dimensional table with the third dimension being the alternative path to Y. This is in fact what Haggard and Kaufman do: they theorize that there are two causal pathways to democracy, one involving mass mobilization and the other not. They then go on to explore some of the underlying causal factors at work in cases not characterized by pressure from below, including international pressures and the calculations of incumbent elites.

Opening another theoretical front necessarily raises questions of overdetermination. Overdetermination means there are cases where $X = 1$ and $Z = 1$ are producing $Y = 1$. The key point is that a particular case might lie on two or more pathways or have two mechanisms present at the same time. This can be thought of as $(X = 1 \text{ OR } Z = 1) \rightarrow Y$. Equifinality can also occur at the mechanism level: $(X = 1) \rightarrow (M_1 \text{ OR } M_2) \rightarrow Y$. One sees this frequently in quantitative articles where the author proposes multiple mechanisms that can explain the significant effect of X on Y.

As discussed in all the process tracing literature, a key role of this methodology is to evaluate and adjudicate between competing explanations at the level of the individual case. This can be at X–Z level or the M level. That is exactly the problem here. If possible it would be useful to determine the extent to which one pathway is really the dominant explanation or the other. Of course one might conclude that there is a mixed mechanism involving them both.

These overdetermined cases would be thrown out of statistical analyses because they are not informative. But within-case causal analysis allows the researcher to take a more nuanced approach. For example, within case causal analysis could conclude that the other factor was present (say international pressure), but had no causal influence over the outcome. For example, Schenoni and his colleagues (2019) looking at the resolution of territorial conflicts in Latin America argue that they result from the conjunction of militarization of the territorial dispute, regime change toward democracy, and international mediation. A possible critique is that they have omitted a core explanatory factor in the form of US hegemony. US hegemony is a Z variable in addition to their three X variables. In a series of within-case analyses they argue that this was not the case for the individual settlements that they study: US actions were not a cause of territorial conflict resolution. In the case of Haggard and Kaufman treatment of democratization, moderate inequality might be present, but within-case analyses argue that it had no causal impact on the outcome via the causal mechanisms stipulated by Acemoglu and Robinson; it was the other path—e.g., international pressure—which had causal effect. The key point is that moderate inequality can led to democratization via M_1, the Acemoglu and Robinson mechanism, or via the M_2 via alternative mechanism.

As this short discussion stresses, the approach outlined here leads quite naturally to discussion of equifinality in a way that standard statistical tests do not. Balancing may be causally related to rising hegemons, but not only. Similarly, democracy maybe caused by mass mobilization, but not only. Considerations of equifinality lead the researcher to think about how to theorize alternative pathways and to establish the scope conditions under which one or another pathway emerges. To deal with issues of equifinality empirically also requires within-case causal analysis to disentangle the impact of confounders, which are in fact alternative pathways to Y.

The key point is that equifinality occurs both at the X--Z level as well as at the mechanism level. Within case analysis is essential to disentangling causal inference when there is potential overdetermination both at the X--Z level as well as at the M level.

CASE SELECTION STRATEGIES WHEN THERE ARE TOO MANY CASES FOR INTENSIVE WITHIN-CASE INFERENCE

Absolutely core to the within-case generalization strategy is establishing a list of cases where one should see the mechanism in action. This is the critical role of the *if* discussed above. Case selection establishes the universe of cases where one should see the mechanism in action based on the triggering conditions or whatever the scope of the mechanism might be. As practiced, a common feature of LNQA is the focus on rare events: the panel, typically a country-year panel—may include thousands of cells, but instances of the outcome are relatively rare. It might seem that the study of rare events would—virtually by definition—constitute an area of niche concern. In fact, nearly the opposite is the case. Many phenomena that are central to the disciplines of economics, political science and sociology are in fact rare events. In economics, examples include financial crises, episodes of unusually high growth, famines, or—rarer still—the emergence of international financial centers. In political science, transitions to and from democratic rule have been relatively infrequent, to which one could add coups, civil wars and—again, rarer still—social revolutions. International relations is similarly preoccupied with events that are fairly uncommon, most notably wars, but also phenomenon such as the acquisition of nuclear weapons or—again, rarer still—the rise or decline of hegemonic powers and possible reactions to those power shifts.

The precise definition of a rare event is of course relatively elastic, and practical considerations necessarily come into play. For example, the number of social revolutions in world history is relatively small, arguably less than ten. Considering such events permits much more complex causal arguments. Other events might be more common; for example, Haggard and Kaufman consider 78 discrete transitions, but focusing in on the presence or absence of a very particular causal mechanism. In the examples we discuss below, the number of cases considered falls in the 10–30 range. Ziblatt similarly looks at democratic transitions, making the claim initially around the European experience but then cautiously reaching beyond Europe in concluding chapters. Sechser and Fuhrmann consider an even smaller population of coercive nuclear threats. When the total number of cases in the $X = 1$ column is relatively small it becomes possible to examine them all in some detail via within-case causal inference. Sechser and Fuhrmann illustrate this very nicely by having a whole chapter devoted to the $(1,0)$ cases and another chapter devoted to all the $(1,1)$ cases. In a slightly different set up Ziblatt does more or less the same thing.

If one moves to phenomena in which the $X = 1$ cases are large, replicating within-case causal inference across all cases becomes impractical. There are two related approaches for addressing this problem, and they can be outlined by considering the democratic peace literature. The democratic peace illustrates a setting where the $X = 1$ column has many cases, all democratic dyads, and the outcome variable not-war (or peace), i.e., $Y = 1$, is quite common. This means virtually by definition that democracy will pass the absolute test as described above. In this relatively common scenario both in the $X = 0$ and $X = 1$ columns you have very high percentages. That means both $X = 1$ and $X = 0$ pass the absolute test. In the QCA framework this would raise the question of potentially trivial sufficient conditions. After passing the absolute test one would move to the trivialness test which involves the other column (see any QCA textbook for procedures for dealing with this issue, e.g., Schneider and Wagemann 2012).

Another way to deal with these cases is to use the same basic logic with the $Y = 1$ row instead of the $X = 1$ column, where $Y = 1$ is no war. This makes it a necessary condition test, but by definition one with relatively few cases because Y, war, itself is rare. If $Y = 1$ is common then by definition $Y = 0$ (war in the democratic peace) is rare and the visibility of falsifying examples, i.e., $(1,0)$ cell cases, goes up dramatically up. This can be seen in the democratic peace literature where there was a tremendous amount of attention given, by critics in particular, to potential falsifying cases of democracies fighting each other (e.g., Ray 1993).

When there are "a lot" of cases in the $(1,1)$ as well as the falsifying $(1,0)$ cell, making repeated within-case causal inference impractical, one could randomly select among the population of these relevant cases. Fearon and Laitin (2008) have argued for random case selection for case studies. There are few who have found their argument convincing. When they describe random selection it is among all of the cases in the 2×2 table. This has meant choosing cases that are not directly relevant to the causal mechanism because they are not in the $X=1$ column or the causal mechanism $(1,1)$ cell; $(0, 0)$ cases are particularly unhelpful in this regard and indeed virtually useless. However, if one restricts the analysis to say, the causal mechanism cell, then random selection makes much more sense. One is randomly selecting among all the cases which are used to support the causal generalization in the experiment or statistical analysis. If they are found to comport with the hypothesis, it would increase confidence in it.

In short, although LNQA has emerged largely to address rare events, it is possible that the method could be extended to larger populations. If there are too many cases to examine individually in the $X=1$ column or in the causal mechanism cell we think the first good response is to think about randomly selecting cases for intensive within-case analysis cases from the causal mechanism or (1,1) cell. Of course, this too is subject to practical constraints, but nevertheless is a very good starting point.

LARGE-N QUALITATIVE ANALYSIS: SOME EXAMPLES

In this section we give two more extended examples of LNQA in practice. Our purposes are several. First, from the standpoint of our anthropological approach to the method, they show how wide-ranging the applications of this approach have been, showing up in fields as diverse as the study of nuclear weapons and historical analyses of democratization. In addition to reiterating our analysis of the method, these cases also show how it is used both in a multi-method context and where the central approach is rooted in case studies, in this case an historical analysis of democratization in the UK and Germany.

Sechser and Fuhrmann (2017): Nuclear Weapons and Coercive Diplomacy

Sechser and Furhmann provide an example of a multimethod approach to LNQA. In the first half of the book, they undertake a large-N statistical analysis. They report on detailed statistical tests of the effect of possessing nuclear weapons on two outcomes: whether nuclear states make more effective compellent threats; and whether they achieve better outcomes in territorial disputes. Their statistical tests fail to find a nuclear advantage.

We ignore these chapters, however, and focus on the two main case study chapters which form at least half of the volume and which are structured along the lines we have outlined here. These chapters are self-consciously addressed to questions of the postulated causal mechanisms behind their "nuclear skepticism" argument, including particular questions about the credibility of nuclear threats and possible backlash effects of using them. They carefully delimit the scope of cases to those in which countries attempted nuclear coercion. They explicitly adopt the LNQA method we have outlined: "[W]e delve deeply into history's most serious coercive nuclear crises. Coercive nuclear threats are rare: nuclear weapons have been invoked to achieve coercive goals less than two dozen times since 1945. We study each of these episodes, drawing on declassified documents when possible" (Sechser and Fuhrmann 2017, 20).

Thus the $X = 1$ cases are those of attempted nuclear coercion and brinksmanship. The outcome is whether the state was able to coerce the target into changing its behavior. It should be emphasized that their theory explains nuclear coercion threat failure. This makes failure the $Y = 1$ cases (we do this to remain consistent with what we have done throughout this chapter). It then makes complete sense that their first case study chapter involves the causal mechanism cases where a coercive threat was made but failed. The next chapter by contrast takes up potentially falsifying cases: cases where the threat was made and appeared to succeed, making it the $(1, 0)$ set of cases (threat, but success instead of failure). They use this chapter to show that—following detailed within-case causal inference—these nominally falsifying cases may not be falsifying after all.

Their justification for the approach fits the large-N qualitative analysis that we have outlined: "The purpose of quantitative analysis was to identify general trends—not to explain any single case. Even if the quantitative analysis suggests that our argument is generally correct, nuclear skepticism theory may fail to explain some cases. Why does this matter? The unexplained cases—often referred to as outliers—may be particularly salient" (p. 130). Put differently, Sechser and Fuhrmann underline that we do not simply want relative comparisons; we want convincing explanations of cases that are deemed important on substantive grounds.

They pay particular attention to case selection, and seek to consider the entire universe of cases in which states attempt nuclear coercion. They identify 13 cases that are clear examples and another six "borderline" cases; the two groups are pooled. These include the (1,1) cases which confirm their theory of nuclear coercion failure: "In this chapter, we discuss nine nuclear coercion failures. These are cases in which countries openly brandished nuclear weapons but still failed to achieve their coercive objectives" (p. 132). Case studies of these failure cases show the operation of the causal mechanisms postulated in their theory of coercion failure, such as the fact that the threats were not credible and were resisted by presumably weaker parties.

In the next chapter—appropriately called "Think Again: Reassessing Nuclear Victories," they turn to the $(1, 0)$ cases: "cases in which nuclear blackmail seemingly worked" (p. 173). In these cases, causal mechanism analysis becomes central: the cases are designed to see if the mechanism proposed by nuclear coercion theorists really explains the outcome (i.e., that nuclear coercion "worked"). They could have probed for some conditional factors suggested by their theory that might have operated in these success cases, thus establishing scope conditions on their skepticism. But their within-case causal analysis concludes regarding the $(1, 0)$ cases that

> in each instance, at least one of three factors mitigates the conclusion that a nuclear threat resulted in a coercive victory. First, factors other than nuclear weapons often played a significant role in states' decisions to back down. Second, on close inspection, some crisis outcomes were not truly "victories" for the coercer. Third, when nuclear weapons have helped countries in crises, they have aided in deterrence rather than coercion. (p. 174)

By looking at the cases closely they in effect also identify measurement error. When they say that these were not cases of coercion success that means that that instead of being $Y = 0$ cases they are in fact $Y = 1$ cases in which nuclear coercion failed. Hence they are removed from the falsifying cases population. A related critique is that the outcome is not successful co-ercion but rather successful deterrence. This is more nuanced, but is arguing again that when Y is coercion success one should not count deterrence success as its equivalent. The treatment (attempted nuclear coercion) might produce other positive outcomes, but that is not what is being tested; the test is of the hypothesis that nuclear weapons can compel, not deter.

If one includes the clear 13 failure cases in the previous chapter, the absolute test will score at best 10 of 23 cases (44 percent). Once one takes mismeasurement into account, however, Sechser and Fuhrmann claim that not a single one of the apparently successful cases in fact constitutes a success. Their within-case analysis brings the total down from a potential 10 to zero. In other words, they find no clear-cut case of nuclear coercion success. This illustrates the potentially dramatic impact of doing causal mechanism, within-case causal analysis; purported causal mechanisms were found not to operate when interrogating the cases.

They end their book with this further reflection on the way generalizations can get drawn: "It is worth noting that the cases that provide the strongest support for the nuclear coercionist view—including the Cuban missile crisis—happened in the early days of the Cold War. . . . There is scant evidence that nuclear blackmail has worked since the collapse of the Soviet Union. The nuclear crises of the last quarter-century illustrate the coercive limits, rather than the virtues, of nuclear weapons." They are clearly thinking about how generalizable their findings are over time. They think that they are generalizable, but not in the way that "coercionists" would think: it is hard to find *any* success case in the last 30 years of international politics, a strong law-like statement.

Ziblatt (2017): Conservative Parties and the Birth of Democracy

Ziblatt's influential, prize-winning book on the role of conservative parties and democratization is an example of a study that is built from the start around intensive examination of two cases, and then broadened out to consider other cases using the LNQA generalization strategy.

Ziblatt is interested in the role of conservative parties as countries move from authoritarian regimes to democracy. He argues that democracy was not the result of underlying structural factors, such as socioeconomic change, nor class pressures, whether from the middle or working classes. Rather he argues that democracy depended on how successfully conservative political parties were able to recast themselves to adapt to electoral pressure while holding off authoritarian tendencies in their own right wings. His two core case studies occupy most of the book and include the UK, where the conservative party recast itself, and Germany which saw failures in that regard. UK is discussed in chapters 3–5, Germany appears in chapters 6–9.

In the final chapter (appropriately titled "How Countries Democratize: Europe and Beyond"), he considers generalization case studies. The generalization goal of the final chapter is stated clearly in the introduction:

> Strictly speaking this book's argument has made sense of political developments within
> Britain and Germany between the middle of the nineteenth and the middle of the

twentieth centuries. But a second purpose, as promised in the introduction, was that the interpretation of these specific historical experiences has general implications for how to think about the enduring impact of old-regime forces on democratization in other places and times. Is our understanding of the world in fact deepened when we widen our scope beyond the main cases we have studied? What more general implications can we draw? (Ziblatt 2017, 334–335)

In that final chapter he outlines the scope of these potential generalization case studies for Europe: "Table 10.1 provides a list of the major parties of the electoral right after 1918, noting which electoral right party had the greatest number of votes in the first postwar democratic elections, a score for the fragmentation of the right camp of parties in this period, and whether or not democracy survived the interwar years" (p. 336). He then proceeds to choose from these for case studies lasting a few pages. Then he considers the Latin American cases. Here the analysis is very short and arguably more superficial; however the purpose—as in Haggard and Kaufman—is focused: to test for the operation of the favored causal mechanism related to conservative parties.

For the European cases, he chooses causal mechanism cases for further generalization (aka "on-line" cases) from the (1,1) cell:

> We begin by analyzing two "well-predicted" cases that appear to fit the framework: one where the right was relatively cohesive and democracy survived (Sweden), and one where it remained organizationally fractious and democracy ultimately collapsed (Spain).

That is, for his generalization case studies he starts by choosing a case that is close to UK—Sweden—and one that is seen as similar to Germany, Spain. The Sweden case study takes up four pages, while the Spanish one eight.

Ziblatt then moves to consider non-European cases. He summarizes the patterns briefly: "In the four countries where conservative political parties emerged *before* mass suffrage—Chile, Colombia, Costa Rica, and Uruguay—democratization even if predominately oligarchic at first, was on average more stable than in the rest of the region. By contrast, in the remaining twelve countries—Argentina, Brazil, Ecuador, Peru, and so on—where no conservative political party existed until *after* mass democratization, democracy was, on average, less durable" (Ziblatt 2017, 358–359). He then proceeds to spend a couple of pages on Argentina as the Latin American example. He then spends one paragraph on some Asian cases like South Korea and Taiwan and then two paragraphs on the Arab Spring, in each case testing for the presence of absence of conservative parties and the presence or absence of the outcome, democratization.

This example illustrates nicely that the case studies need not be treated equally. The amount of space devoted to each case study can be skewed as long as adequate information is provided to reach a reasonable conclusion with respect to the presence or absence of the postulated causal mechanism. The book is framed around two core causal mechanism case studies, followed by a series of generalization case studies that are unequal in length but nonetheless focused on the core causal relationship. In each generalization case study, the purpose is to focus on the postulated causal mechanism and see if it works in that case; generalization is enhanced by effectively "summing" these well-explained cases.

CONCLUSION

In this chapter we explore a research paradigm involving within-case causal inference and a strategy using case studies to support generalization claims about causal mechanisms. The most distinctive feature of the approach are two. The first is the effort to use a large number of cases, and ideally the entire population of the $X = 1$ cases (for sufficient conditions claims) or $Y = 1$ cases (for necessary conditions claims). The second is the systematic use of within-case causal inference as opposed to experimental designs—in which treatment is contrasted with control—or cross-case observational designs, such as those deployed in many studies in comparative politics and international relations.

This research design typically takes advantage of the fact that there are often relatively few cases in the causal mechanism cell. Going back to Ziblatt the universe for half of the book is mass democratization in Europe after 1918 and he is thus able to consider the causal effect of his chosen theory involving the timing of the emergence of conservative parties and their relative strength. Similarly with Sechser and Fuhrmann, the panels they use for their statistical analysis have as many as 6,500 observations in some models. But the number of cases in which nuclear states unambiguously made coercive nuclear threats is not more than a couple dozen. This makes the design described here a plausible alternative (for Ziblatt) or complement (for Sechser and Fuhrmann) to standard statistical analysis.

One might argue that absolute tests with just one variable are very unrealistic, particularly with a relatively high bar of 75 percent. A widely held intuition is that it is unlikely that many factors will pass this sort of law-like test; note that it is much stronger than claims that a given causal variable has at least a statistically significant effect on a population when potential confounds are either randomized away or controlled for. Not surprisingly, some of the early examples of this work were aimed at taking down expansive law-like claims with respect to a diverse array of outcomes, from the role of economic interests in the design of electoral systems to the role of audience costs in war.

A natural response is to say there must be other factors that are important in producing the outcome, and that one causal variable is not likely adequate to generate convincing explanation. QCA deals with this by focusing on interaction terms: it is only when there is an interaction of three or four causal factors that the outcome is very likely to occur and will pass the absolute test. Yet we think it can in fact be useful to identify necessary or sufficient conditions relationships between causal factors and outcomes. Moreover, the logic of absolute tests is the same whether the hypothesis rests on the operation of one variable or the interaction of four or five. And that logic is quite different from an average treatment effect logic.

As we have noted, this design has become quite standard practice in both case study–only books in recent years as well as those engaged in mixed-methods approaches. But the practice has yet to appear in the methodological literature (again, see Goertz 2017, chapter 7). In almost all cases authors just "do it." The fact that it seems not to have provoked any backlash on the part of reviewers, commissioning editors, or others seems to indicate that the logic has some resonance.

We have sought to extract some of the main features of this approach and link them to wider discussions about generalization in philosophy and the social sciences. First, and most obviously, it is best suited to analysis of rare events, which in fact figure quite prominently in the political science canon. Second, it rests on focused tests of postulated causal mechanisms; theory matters. And finally, it requires use of within-case causal inference techniques, including process-tracing predominantly but potentially within-case counterfactuals as well.

We can see several ways in which this work might be pushed forward. One interesting link is to discussions in the Bayesian tradition about what amount of case work might be adequate to reach closure. Dion (1998) nicely showed that in a Bayesian framework five or six consistent case studies can easily lead to 90 percent posterior confidence starting with a uniform prior. Clear theorizing in this area might reduce the demands of this approach with respect to the conduct of detailed cases studies and thus strengthen its appeal.

More work might also be done on a version of generalization which can be called extrapolation. Using the classic Shadish, Cook and Campbell (2002) units, treatment, outcomes, and settings (UTOS) framework we can ask to what extent when we move along some dimension of UTOS the same results apply. For example, the quest for external validity and generalization in experimental work has been about doing the experiment or treatment on new units. Extrapolation could be about changing the treatments gradually in some direction within populations of case studies as well.

Often a strong generalization that is empirically founded naturally leads to questions about extrapolation. The democratic peace is a well-founded empirical generalization. This should, but does not seem to have, lead to a question about how generalizable it is to less democratic countries. So as we extrapolate from democratic towards authoritarian how far does the democratic peace generalize and extrapolate? We think that this is a clear next step in the analysis of generalization and external validity.

This methodology also has potential applications for experiments and other "well specified" designs as well as large-N statistical analyses: matching, difference-in-difference, instrumental variables or regression discontinuity designs. Currently the solution for the generalization problem for experiments or quasi-experimental designs is just to do more of them. We know of almost nothing that systematically tries to analyze what constitutes successful generalization criteria; we can see room for parallel work looking at how experiments on a given issue aggregate across the $X=1$ column. The critical cell is the causal mechanism $(1,1)$ cell. One could easily take a random sample of the $(1,1)$ cases in an experimental or quasi-experimental design to see if the causal mechanism is in fact present. This would represent an independent check on the statistical or experimental results.

We have barely begun to systematically analyze the crucial decisions and the crucial options in case study–generalization methodologies and in LNQA in particular. But our analysis suggests that there are a wide array of topics opened up by this research strategy that require more sustained analysis.

ACKNOWLEDGMENTS

Thanks to Sharon Crasnow, Harold Kincaid, and Julian Reiss for comments on an earlier draft, and Terence Teo for help with the data analysis of democratization and inequality. Goertz thanks James Copestake and the University of Bath for providing a wonderful environment for writing this chapter. Thanks to the participants in the *Handbook* workshop at Washington State University as well for valuable feedback.

NOTES

1. There is not agreement at all in the process tracing literature about counterfactuals. Some are opposed, some in favor.

2. We shall not deal with the more complex situation where there may be multiple factors, e.g., interactions, at the beginning of the chain.

3. In the philosophical literature on causal mechanisms one often reads about the initial conditions or a trigger which sets the causal mechanism in motion, for example: "Mechanisms are entities and activities organized such that they are productive of regular changes from start or set-up to finish or termination conditions." (Machamer et al. 2000, 3; displayed definition). The key point is that there is some initial triggering condition which then generates the mechanism. This always has logical form *if* triggering condition *then* mechanism *then* outcome. The "regular changes" means a generally reliable causal mechanism.

4. An increasing popular approach to within-case causal inference is to create a "synthetic" counterfactual case based on the combination of real cases and then compare that case with the actual one. Abadie et al. (2015) construct a counterfactual Germany to explore the impact of German unification on economic growth. This counterfactual Germany is amalgam of "similar" countries such as France, Canada, etc.

5. Inequality data are the Gini market data from Solt 2020. Transitions based on Haggard and Kaufman 2016. Division into the three inequality categories is based on the terciles of the Gini inequality data for authoritarian regimes, 1980–2008, the terciles are divided at less than 42.6, and greater than 47.6. In the polity data we consider all −66, −77, and −88 observations as authoritarian.

6. As discussed in some detail in Goertz and Mahoney (2012), equifinality is just assumed in many contexts. For example, it lies at the core of the INUS model. A non-INUS model is one like $Y = X_1$ AND X_2, where X_i are individually necessary and jointly sufficient for Y, there is only one path to Y. Why it is central in qualitative methods in general, and QCA in particular, is the idea that the number of mechanisms generating the outcome is limited to a few like in QCA and not a huge number like in general statistical models.

REFERENCES

Abadie, A., et al. 2015. Comparative politics and the synthetic control method. *American Journal of Political Science* 59:495–510.

Acemoglu, D., and J. Robinson. 2006. *Economic origins of dictatorship and democracy.* Cambridge: Cambridge University Press.

Anscombe, G. 1971. *Causality and determination.* Cambridge: Cambridge University Press.

Armstrong, D. 1983. *What is a law of nature?* Cambridge: Cambridge University Press.

Bardsley, N., et al. 2010. *Experimental economics: Rethinking the rules.* Princeton, NJ: Princeton University Press.

Campbell, D., and J. Stanley. 1963. *Experimental and quasi-experimental designs for research.* Chicago: Rand McNally.

Dion, D. 1998. Evidence and inference in the comparative case study. *Comparative Politics* 30:127–145.

Druckman, J., and C. Kam. 2011. Students as experimental participants a defense of the "narrow data base". In J. Druckman et al. (eds.) *Cambridge handbook of experimental political science*, pp. 41–57. Cambridge: Cambridge University Press.

Dunning, T., et al. (eds.). 2019. *Information, accountability, and cumulative learning.* Cambridge: Cambridge University Press.

Fearon, J., and D. Laitin. 2008. Integrating qualitative and quantitative methods. In J. Box-Steffensmier, H. Brady, and D. Collier (eds.) *The Oxford handbook of political methodology*, pp. 757–776. Oxford: Oxford University Press.

Glennan, S. 2017. *The new mechanical philosophy.* Oxford: Oxford University Press.

Goertz, G. 2017 *Multimethod research, causal mechanisms, and case studies: an integrated approach.* Princeton, NJ: Princeton University Press.

Goertz, G., and J. Mahoney. 2012. *A tale of two cultures: Qualitative and quantitative research in the social sciences.* Princeton, NJ: Princeton University Press.

Haggard, S., and R. Kaufman. 2016. *Dictators and democrats: Masses, elites, and regime change.* Princeton, NJ: Princeton University Press.

Holland, P. 1986. Statistics and causal inference (with discussion). *Journal of the American Statistical Association* 81:945–960.

Kaplan, O. 2017. *Resisting war: How communities protect themselves.* Cambridge: Cambridge University Press.

Levy, J., and W. Thompson. 2005. Hegemonic threats and great power balancing in Europe, 1495–1999. *Security Studies* 14:1–30.

Levy, J., and W. Thompson. 2010. Balancing at sea: Do states ally against the leading global power? *International Security* 35:7–43.

Lewis, D. 1973. *Counterfactuals.* Cambridge, MA: Harvard University Press.

Machamer, P., et al. 2000. Thinking about mechanisms. *Philosophy of Science* 67:1–25.

McDermott, R. 2011. Internal and external validity. In J. Druckman et al. (eds.) *Cambridge handbook of experimental political science*, pp. 27–40. Cambridge: Cambridge University Press.

Narang, V., and R. Nelson. 2009. Who are these belligerent democratizers? Reassessing the impact of democratization on war. *International Organization* 63:357–379.

Przeworski, A. 2009. Conquered or granted? A history of suffrage extensions. *British Journal of Political Science*, 39:291–321.

Ray, J. 1993. Wars between democracies: Rare or nonexistent? *International Interactions* 18:251–276.

Ripsman, N. 2016. *Peacemaking from above, peace from below: Ending conflict between regional rivals.* Ithaca, NY: Cornell University Press.

Schenoni, L. et al. 2019. Settling resistant disputes: The territorial boundary peace in Latin America. Manuscript. University of Notre Dame.

Schneider, C., and C. Wagemann. 2012. *Set-theoretic methods for the social sciences: A guide to qualitative comparative analysis.* Cambridge: Cambridge University Press.

Sechser, T., and M. Fuhrmann. 2017. *Nuclear weapons and coercive diplomacy.* Cambridge: Cambridge University Press.

Shadish, W., T. Cook, and D. Campbell. 2002. *Experimental and quasi-experimental designs for general causal inference.* Boston: Houghton Mifflin.

Solt, F. 2020. Measuring income inequality across countries and over time: The standardized world income inequality database. *Social Science Quarterly* 101:1183–1199.

Trachtenberg, M. 2012. Audience costs: An historical analysis. *Security Studies* 21:3–42.

Wallensteen, P. 2015. *Quality peace: Peacebuilding, victory and world order.* Oxford: Oxford University Press.

Ziblatt, D. 2017. *Conservative parties and the birth of democracy.* Cambridge: Cambridge University Press.

CHAPTER 15

••

PROCESS TRACING
Defining the Undefinable?

••

CHRISTOPHER CLARKE

1. INTRODUCTION

PROCESS tracing is a tool that political scientists use to hunt the causes of political phenomena. Indeed "process tracing is perhaps the tool of causal inference that first comes to mind when one thinks of qualitative methodology in political science" (Mahoney 2010, 123). It "represents the empirical core of many, if not most, case studies" (Rohlfing 2012, 150). Exemplars include classic works such as Skocpol (1979) on the French, Russian, and Chinese revolutions, Tannenwald (1999) on the taboo against using nuclear weapons during the Cold War, and Wood (2003) on the civil war in El Salvador, among many other lauded studies of elections, government policy making, international relations, and the like. What's more, it's claimed that process tracing can measure actual causal effects, in contrast to quantitative methods that supposedly can only measure probabilistic "averages" of these causal effects (Mahoney and Goertz 2006; Crasnow 2012). So, it is no surprise that political methodologists have started to pay process tracing a lot of attention.

This chapter seeks a precise definition of process tracing. The main reason to seek such a definition goes back to King, Keohane, and Verba (1994), the manifesto which sparked one of the central methodological debates within political science: what are the aims, limits and logic of the methods of political science? in particular, how do quantitative methods differ from qualitative methods in this regard? As methodologists have come to see process tracing as one of the central methods in the qualitative toolkit, much of this "post-KKV" debate has begun to focus on process tracing.

As I see it, a methodologically useful definition of process tracing should start with some exemplars of process tracing in the political science literature, and it should work out what most of these exemplars have in common, epistemically speaking. What is the common rationale that warrants the conclusions that each process tracing study draws? What epistemic problems and epistemic benefits does this rationale give rise to? How is this rationale distinct from the rationale that lies behind other studies that draw causal conclusions, quantitative studies in particular? If you define process tracing too broadly, thus grouping together studies that have different epistemic problems and epistemic benefits, then you risk mis-identifying those problems and benefits. If you define process tracing too narrowly, then you miss an opportunity to understand the epistemic problems and benefits of those studies that you've excluded from your definition.

Finding a useful definition will also help alleviate the concern that process tracing is an "ad hoc" method (Gerring 2006, 178), one that is "carried out informally and without a high level of transparency" and that "lacks systematization of technique and explicitness in execution" (Mahoney 2015, 201). As Beach and Pedersen (2016, 302) put it: "process-tracing has become a buzzword in recent years, but until recently there has been little agreement about what we actually are tracing or how to conduct this tracing properly."[1]

Here's how I will proceed. My proposed definition of process tracing contains four criteria. As I explain in Section 2, everyone agrees that

> (Criterion One) For a study to count as process tracing, it must identify the presence or absence of intermediate causal links between some factor and an outcome of interest.

In this sense, process tracing is the search for a chain of causes that led to an outcome of interest. Section 2 then explains how some methodologists place a further limit on what counts as process tracing:

> (Criterion Two) For a study to count as process tracing, it must describe each of these intermediate links in terms of entities engaging in regular, well-understood activities.

Section 3 then examines the idea that, although process tracing identifies intermediate links in a causal chain, this is not the ultimate aim of a process tracing study; instead it is merely a means of pursuing the following ultimate aim:

> (Criterion Three—Version A) For a study to count as process tracing, its ultimate aim must be just to test the hypothesis that the starting factor in the chain was a cause of the final outcome. Indeed, it must pursue this ultimate aim via a particular argumentative structure, one that I try to describe in Section 3.

Section 4 contrasts this view of the ultimate aim of process tracing with an alternative:

> (Criterion Three—Version B) For a study to count as process tracing, its ultimate aim must be the identification/description of the intermediate links in a causal chain.

That is to say, the description of these intermediate links is not a means to some further end, such as testing the hypothesis that first factor in the chain was a cause of the final factor. In Section 4, I show that whether a process tracing study is a success or as a failure can depend on whether version A or version B of Criterion Three is the correct view of the ultimate aim of the process tracing study in question.

Section 5 then examines the suggestion that what distinguishes process tracing from quantitative methods is in part the fact that quantitative methods use "rectangular" data sets. I argue that the use of rectangular data sets is a superficial symptom of a more fundamental difference between process tracing and quantitative methods. Namely,

> (Criterion Four) A study does not count as a process tracing study if it requires (Version A) any of the start–end causal relationships it measures, or (Version B) any of the intermediate causal relationships it measures, to be "unit homogeneous" across a largish population of cases.

In addition to criteria such as these, some methodologists explicitly offer (or implicitly hint at) the following limits on what counts as process tracing:

(F1) A study does not count as a process tracing study if it relies on numerical data.

(F2) A study does not count as a process tracing study if it relies on evidence from cases other than the single case under examination.

(F3) A study does not count as a process tracing study if it needs the probability distribution of some variable to take a particular form.

(F4) A study does not count as a process tracing study if it uses statistical methods.

(F5) A study does not count as a process tracing study if its results can be generalized.

Section 6 will argue that these suggested criteria *F1–F5* are incorrect: the limits they place on what counts as process tracing are unhelpfully restrictive. Section 7 then examines another three putative criteria:

(E1) For a study to count as process tracing, it must only use causal process observations, that is, diagnostic evidence to uncover the mechanism under examination.

(E2) For a study to count as process tracing, it must only use pattern matching.

(E3) Process tracing can use a very wide variety of evidence.

I argue that criteria *E1–E3* are empty: they do not place any substantive limits on what counts as process tracing. So we are left with Criterion One Two Three and Four as the primary ways of defining process tracing.

This raises a problem for process tracing version *B*—process tracing as an end in itself. This is because standard techniques of causal inference, such as regression, require unit homogeneity (King, Keohane, and Verba 1994, 91–94). So Criterion Four Version *B* rules out using standard causal inference techniques to study these intermediate causal relationships. So it is currently unclear how process tracing version *B* proposes to establish these intermediate causal links. To repeat, criteria *E1–E3* are empty: they do not describe how process tracing establishes intermediate causal links. (In contrast, process tracing for the ultimate aim of testing start–end hypotheses can appeal to any techniques it likes to establish intermediate causal links, including standard quantitative techniques.) Therefore I offer my four criteria as a helpful starting point from which one might build an account of process tracing version *B*, process tracing as an end it itself. If I am right, the methodological literature has only begun to answer the question: How do process tracers trace these intermediate links in causal chains?

2. PROCESS TRACING AS IDENTIFYING INTERMEDIATE LINKS

The first defining feature of process tracing, everyone agrees, is that process tracers search for (and try to make explicit) the mechanism that helped produce a given outcome in a given case or cases. What, for example, was the mechanism that prevented the Soviet Union from sending the Red Army to crush the pro-democracy movements in Poland and East Germany in 1989? What was the mechanism that caused El Salvadorian elites to compromise with the insurgents at the end of the civil war in 1992? What was the mechanism whereby new European Union states were integrated such that they came to share the norms of the other member states?

Of course, methodologists disagree about what it means to describe the mechanism that caused a given outcome (Hedstrom and Ylikoski 2010). Among methodologists interested in process tracing, however, there is at least agreement on one point. Namely, to describe a mechanism one must at very least describe a chain of causes that ends in the outcome in question: A caused B, B caused C, C caused D, and D caused E.[2] For example, Wood describes the following causal chain: (A) insurgents in El Salvador took over plantations in the 1980s. This caused (B) the El Salvadorian economy to rely less on primary commodities. This caused (C) the El Salvadorian elite's preferences to become more democratic. This caused (D) the elite and the insurgents to begin to bargain. And this caused (E) a transition toward democracy. Thus process tracing searches for the chain of causes that led, in the case under examination, to the outcome one is interested in:

> (Criterion One) For a study to count as process tracing, it must identify the presence or absence of intermediate causal links between some factor A and an outcome of interest E.

To this requirement, some methodologists would add that to describe a mechanism, one must also describe this causal chain in such a way that each link in the chain is described as an "entity" engaging in a regular and well-understood "activity." For example, the most profitable way for capital owners to produce primary commodities is to repress their workers, one might think; but to produce other commodities and services repression is less effective. If true, this fact helps one understand the causal link between B (the shift away from primary commodities) and C (elite preferences for democracy). This link arises, one might argue, because this new economic structure B constrained the opportunities available to capital owners; they are no longer able to make a profit by repressing their workers. And the idea of an economic structure constraining or expanding an individual's opportunities is a well-understood activity. What's more, all or most individuals adhere to the norms of belief–desire psychology, one might think, and so this activity that operates across individuals in a more or less regular fashion. Therefore, to describe the link between B and C in these terms is to describe it as an entity engaged in a regular and well-understood activity. And this is required if one wants to truly be describing the mechanisms that links A with E, say many methodologists.[3] Thus some methodologists would add to our definition of process tracing:

> (Criterion Two) For a study to count as process tracing, it must describe each of these intermediate links in terms of entities engaging in regular, well-understood activities.

Some theorists would elaborate on this point and say that, in political science, the best understood and most regular activities are those in which goal-oriented agents make decisions in light of the opportunities available to them.[4] For example, an individual member of the elite decides to bargain with the insurgents because that is the best way for this individual to maximize the return on the capital she owns. Or at least, one might say, the best understood (macro) activities are those activities for which one knows how the activity in question arises out of goal-oriented agents interacting with each other. Take for example a drought making it more difficult for farmers to grow coffee and thus causing a rise in its price. This is an entity of sorts (a drought) engaging in an activity (driving up the price of coffee). Standard microeconomic theory makes some assumptions about how consumers and firms interact with each other in market contexts, and about consumers' preferences for coffee and tea and other goods; and from these assumptions it deductively proves that the price of coffee will rise. And, insofar as this story is more or less true, then, this activity is well-understood, one might think. (A comparison: a Bunsen burner increases the pressure of a gas in a sealed container. One might think that this activity is only well-understood once one knows how this activity arises from the fact that a gas is just billions of individual particles moving in accordance with Newton's laws of motion.)

So we have one uncontroversial criterion (Criterion One) and one somewhat more controversial criterion (Criterion Two) for what counts as process tracing. At very least, process-tracing looks for the presence or absence of intermediate causal links between some factor A and an outcome of interest E.

3. THE LOGIC OF TESTING START–END HYPOTHESES

Methodologists use lots of suggestive metaphors to describe what process tracers do. Process tracers "break down" or "dis-aggregate" causes (Gerring 2006). They trace causes "forward" and "backward" in time (Bennett 2010). Their method "focuses" on the "intervening steps" in a causal chain (Bennett 2010). But it is surprisingly rare for methodologists to make precise the specific logic behind process tracing. And this is notwithstanding the fact that process tracers often point to Bayesianism as the general epistemological framework within which process tracing is to be understood (more on this point in due course).

However, at times, some methodologists seem to suggest the following as the specific logic behind process tracing:

> (Criterion Three—Preliminary Version) For a study to count as process tracing, it must ulti- mately aim to support the hypothesis that the starting factor in the chain A was a cause of the final outcome E. And the means by which it pursues this ultimate aim must be the following argumentative structure.
>
> Premises: A caused B. B caused C. C caused D. D caused E.
>
> Conclusion: A caused E

This criterion views process tracing as the study of intermediate causal links in order to *support a start–end hypothesis*, in this case the hypothesis that A caused E. Waldner (2012) is the most explicit in identifying the logical structure of this reasoning, which he calls the logic of "concatenation."

> To claim the existence of a causal chain is to claim that given entities and mechanisms, one event constrained future events such that a subsequent event was bound to happen, or at least that an earlier event substantially shifted the probability distribution governing the subse- quent event, making sequelae far more probable. . . . Process tracing accounts, for this reason,

tend to make deterministic causal claims that, given a set of initial and scope conditions, an outcome was bound to occur. (Waldner 2012, 69)

Some other methodologists hint at this logical structure too:[5]

For example, when analyzing World War I, it seems plausible to believe that Austria's decision to initiate war with Serbia was necessary for the general war. In turn, Austria's decision may have required the assassination of Ferdinand, such that this assassination may also have been necessary for the general war. (Mahoney 2015, 213)

If one can theorize a full sequence of steps, one should also test for the presence of each step because otherwise parts of the argument remain untested. In set-relational terms, this means that each step is a necessary component and they are jointly sufficient for inferring that the purported cause indeed is a cause. (Rohlfing 2012, 152)

Process-tracing study provides stronger evidence of the existence of a causal process(es) linking C and O because evidence is provided for each part of the causal process. (Beach and Pedersen 2016, 176)

In process-tracing, if we can collect confirmatory evidence of each part of a mechanism that we can trust, we can make a relatively strong inference that C is causally related to O through a causal mechanism. (Beach and Pedersen 2016, 273)

By tracing an explicit mechanism, we would be more justified in making the claim that C is linked to O through a causal mechanism. (Beach and Pedersen 2016, 83)

It's worth noting in passing that there is disagreement among the methodologists quoted here as to the nature of the causes being traced here. As you can see, some treat causes as in some sense necessary for their effects; others treat causes as in some sense sufficient for their effects.

I will now show that at least one exemplary process tracing study fails Criterion Three, in its preliminary form given above. This study is not a study of intermediate causal links to support a start–end hypothesis. The exemplary study I have in mind is Brady (2010)'s analysis of the 2000 presidential election in the United States. In this election, the national media reported at 8 pm EST that the polls in Florida had closed. But this report was false: ten counties in Florida's western Panhandle are in the Central time zone (CST) not the Eastern Time zone (EST). As a result, the polls in these ten counties remained open until 9 pm EST. What's more, at 8:48pm EST the national media reported that Al Gore had won Florida, even though polls in these ten counties were open for another twelve minutes. In these two respects, the media's call was premature. Did this premature media call cause would-be voters in these ten staunchly pro-Bush counties not to vote?

Lott (2005) uses a standard quantitative technique (differences-in-differences regression) to estimate that, if the media had not prematurely called the Florida election, Bush's victory over Al Gore in Florida would have been 7,500 to 37,500 votes greater than it actually was. Against this, Brady uses process tracing to dispute Lott's conclusions. Brady calculates that (F) there were 379,000 would-be voters in the Florida panhandle. That is to say, people who intended to vote in the election. Since the media declared a Gore victory twelve minutes before the close of the polls, Brady focuses his attention on late would-be voters: people who hadn't yet voted by the last twelve minutes of the polls being open, but who intended to do so. Drawing on evidence that in 1996 Florida voters didn't vote in disproportionately large numbers in the last hour, and assuming that 1996 and 2000 are similar in this respect, Brady infers from (F) that (G) there were at most 4,200 would-be late voters in 2000.[6] Drawing on general evidence about media reach, Brady infers from (G) that (H) at most 840 would-be late voters heard the media call. And drawing on evidence about the support for Bush in the Florida panhandle, he infers from (H) that (I) at most 560 would-be late Bush-voters heard the media call. And drawing on general evidence about voters' responses to premature media calls, he infers from (I) that (J) at most 56 would-be Bush-voters decided not to vote because of the media call. Even assuming that no would-be Gore-voters decided not to vote because of the media call, it follows that (K) if the media hadn't called the election prematurely, Bush's victory would at most have been 56 votes greater. Quite a different estimate from Lott's estimate of 7,500 to 37,500![7] This is a quick but (I think) faithful reconstruction of Brady's process tracing argument.[8]

What is the logical structure of Brady's process-tracing argument? On a first glance, one might be tempted to say the following: F caused G, and G caused H, and H caused I, and I caused J. So Brady's argument is clearly a study of intermediate causal links to support a start–end hypothesis, one in which the causal chain runs F to G to H to I to J. But a second look shows that this interpretation is incorrect.[9] To see this, note that an inference to support a start–end hypothesis using a causal chain running from F to J is an argument for the conclusion that F caused J. Applied to this case, the conclusion would be: the fact that there were 379,000 would-be voters in the panhandle caused the fact that at most fifty-six would-be Bush-voters decided not to vote because of the media call. But this is not Brady's conclusion. Brady's conclusion is instead J itself: at most fifty-six would-be Bush-voters decided not to vote because of the media call.[10] And so the structure of Brady's argument— despite appearances—is not a study of intermediate causal links to support a start–end hypothesis on the causal chain running from F to J.

Instead, the logic of Brady's argument is different. Here's how I see it. For any would-be voter we can ask whether the following conditions hold: (1) did the early media call A cause (B) this would-be voter to hear the media call? and (2) did hearing the media call B cause (C) this would-be voter not to vote, rather than voting for Bush? The evidence that Brady provides suggests that of the 379,000 would-be voters, at most 1/5 heard the media call, and so 1/5 satisfy condition one. It also suggests that at most 1/90 intended to vote late (rather than vote early or vote via absentee ballot) of which 2/3 intended to vote for Bush, and of which 1/10 would be put-off by an early call, so at most 1/1350 satisfy condition two. So at most 1/6750 would-be voters satisfy both condition one and condition two. That is to say, at most fifty-six people. However, one might claim that A can only cause C via a causal chain running through B. The only way in which the media call could influence a given voter's behavior is through that voter actually hearing the media call. It follows that the number of people for which A (the media call) caused C (that individual to refrain from voting for Bush) is at most fifty-six people. That's the logic of Brady's argument as I see it. (Interestingly, on my reconstruction, there is only one intermediate link in the chain being analyzed, rather than three or four as appears on a first glance. The inferential complexity instead arises because Brady needs to piece together lots of assumptions about population frequencies— $1/90 \times 2/3 \times 1/10$—in order to infer that at most 1/1350 would-be voters satisfy condition two.)

Note that, as I've reconstructed it, at no point does Brady's argument support a start–end hypothesis. Yes, it's true that—for any individual for whom A caused B and for whom B caused C—one might infer that A caused C. But this extra inference is entirely dispensable to Brady's overall argument. Instead the key move in Brady's argument has an altogether different structure. It's a study of intermediate causal links in order to *undermine a start-end hypothesis*:

Premise: *A* caused *C* only if *A* caused *B*, and only if *B* caused *C*.

Premise: *A* did not cause *B* (or *B* did not cause *C*).

Conclusion: *A* did not cause *C*.

Taking stock, I've identified two types of argumentative structure that are the basis of some process tracing studies: studying intermediate links to support a start–end hypothesis and studying intermediate links to undermine a start–end hypothesis.

I now want to clarify these two argumentative structures by responding to the following sort of worry. Most methodologists agree that the general epistemological framework in which process tracing should be understood is Bayesian epistemology (Humphreys and Jacobs 2015; Fairfield and Charman 2017): a causal hypothesis is tested by the observations that one expects to make, if that hypothesis is true. But my two forms of studying intermediate links don't seem to do that. They are presented as arguments in a premise–conclusion form, rather than as a probability function, which is the main currency of Bayesian epistemology. It's therefore unclear how they fit into the Bayesian framework. That's the concern.

(Readers unfamiliar with the Bayesian epistemological framework might consult Howson and Urbach ([1989] 2006) to understand the notation and underlying ideas in this section. Note that Bayesian epistemology differs from Bayesian statistics. Bayesian epistemology is a fully general epistemological framework capable of handling hypotheses of any type, causal hypotheses for example; Bayesian statistics is a more narrow and less philosophical. It's a set of tools for estimating the parameters of probability distributions.)

To address this important concern, I will now reformulate these two types of argumentative structure to bring out what is common to both, and to show how they fit within the Bayesian epistemological framework. To begin, let e denote the evidence uncovered by a given study in political science. And let h denote the start–end causal hypothesis that the study ultimately aims to test: A caused C. And consider the following two intermediate hypotheses: h_{AB} is the hypothesis that A caused B; and h_{BC} is the hypothesis that B caused C.

Now, for any given study one can ask: does the evidence e that it uncovers bear on start–end hypothesis h only by first bearing on these intermediate hypotheses? The intuitive idea here is that if one were to become certain of the truth or falsity of h_{AB}, and similarly of h_{BC}, then e would have no further bearing upon h. Suppose, for example, one were to learn of a given individual that h_{AB} the early media call caused her to hear the early media call, and h_{BC} hearing the early media call did indeed cause her not to vote, rather than voting for Bush. In this case, the evidence e' that two-thirds of the voters in the panhandle are pro-Bush becomes irrelevant for evaluating h, the hypothesis that the media call caused this voter not to vote (rather than voting for Bush). And the same goes for all the other evidence e collected in Brady's study. Put in terms of probabilities, the currency of the Bayesian framework: $P(h \mid h_{AB}h_{BC}) = P(h \mid h_{AB}h_{BC}e)$, and $P(h \mid \neg h_{AB}h_{BC}) = P(h \mid \neg h_{AB}h_{BC}e)$, and $P(h \mid h_{AB}\neg h_{BC}) = P(h \mid h_{AB}\neg h_{BC}e)$, and $P(h \mid \neg h_{AB}\neg h_{BC}) = P(h \mid \neg h_{AB}\neg h_{BC}e)$.

What's more, one can usually split the overall evidence e that a study uncovers into two or more parts. For example, one part of Brady's evidence was e_1 his general evidence about media listening rates; and a distinct part of Brady's evidence was his evidence e_2 about the support for Bush in the panhandle. Thus for each intermediate hypothesis one can ask: Is there part e' of the overall evidence e that bears on this intermediate hypothesis alone? In the Brady study, for example, evidence e_1 bore on h_{AB} but not on h_{BC}. That is to say, his general evidence about media listening rates bore on the hypothesis that the early media call caused a given individual to hear the media call; but it did not bear on the hypothesis that a given individual hearing the media call would cause her not to vote for Bush. In terms of probabilities: $P(h_{AB} | e_1) \neq P(h_{AB})$ but $P(h_{BC} | e_1) = P(h_{BC})$. Similarly, evidence e_2 bore on h_{BC} but not on h_{AB}. That is to say, Brady's evidence about the support for Bush in the panhandle bore on the hypothesis that a given individual hearing the media call would cause her not to vote for Bush; but it did not bear on the hypothesis that the early media call caused given individual to hear the media call. In terms of probabilities: $P(h_{BC} | e_2) \neq P(h_{BC})$ but $P(h_{AB} | e_2) = P(h_{AB})$.

This now puts me in a position to define the method of identifying intermediate causal links for testing start-end hypotheses:

> (Criterion Three—Version A) For a study to count as process tracing, it must ultimately aim to test the hypothesis that the starting factor in the chain was a cause of the final outcome. And the means by which it pursues this ultimate aim must be the following logical structure.
> (I)   The overall evidence e bears on hypothesis h only by first bearing on the intermediate hypotheses.
> (II) For each intermediate hypothesis, there is a piece of evidence e' that bears on this intermediate hypothesis alone.[11]

In the Brady example that I've just analyzed, I considered the start–end hypothesis h that A caused C and the intermediate hypothesis h_{AB} that A caused B and the intermediate hypothesis h_{BC} that B caused C. That is to say, I considered a single causal chain with only one intermediate link. But Criterion Three encompasses more complicated examples. One might consider the start–end hypothesis h that A caused E and the intermediate hypothesis h_{AB} that A caused B, and h_{BE} that B caused E. And one might, in addition, consider the intermediate hypothesis h_{AC} that A caused C, and h_{CD} that C caused D and h_{DE} that D caused E. In this more complicated setup, one is examining two causal chains that might run from A to E. The first has one intermediate link B, and the second has two intermediate links, C and D.

I conclude that many process tracing studies conform to the logic given in Criterion Three (Version A), namely identifying intermediate causal links for the ultimate aim of testing start–end hypotheses.

4. Identifying Intermediates as an End in Itself?

In this section, I want to examine an alternative idea, the idea that process tracing does not ultimately aim to test start–end hypotheses. Instead:

> (Criterion Three—Version B) For a study to count as process tracing, its ultimate aim must be the identification / description of the intermediate links in a causal chain.

In other words, the previous section dealt with the identification of intermediate links for the ultimate end of testing start–end hypotheses; and this section will deal with identifying intermediate links as an ultimate aim in itself. (Of course, there are also other aims to which one might put a process tracing study in addition to these two aims. But these two aims seem to me to be primary. For example, the aim of making effective policy is parasitic on these two aims, I'd suggest: for any given policy objective, to gain the knowledge required for effective policy interventions is just to gain the causal knowledge of a start–end relationship or an intermediate relationship that the policymaker can exploit.)

Why might testing one or more intermediate hypotheses be valuable for its own sake? One answer is that, although the knowledge that A causes E provides some understanding of why E occurred, this understanding is limited. In contrast, if one knows that A caused E via one causal chain that runs through B, and also via a second causal chain that runs through C and D, one has a deeper understanding of why E occurred—especially if the links in this causal chain are described in terms of entities engaged in well-understood activities (see Section 2).

To make the distinction between these two aims more vivid, imagine a scenario in which a method other than process tracing is able to establish that A caused E, to a high degree of certainty. Imagine, for example, that instrumental variables regression suggests that (A) the existence of institutions that guarantee private property rights causes (E) long run economic growth (Acemoglu, Johnson, and Robinson 2005). Let's also imagine that the assumptions needed for this technique to be reliable are known to be true. In this case, this instrumental variables regression puts us in a position to know the start-end hypothesis that private property rights A cause growth E. Is it still worth tracing the process between A and E? If you answer "no" then your ultimate aim is just to test the start–end hypothesis that A caused E. But if you answer "yes" then you take the identification of the intermediate causal links between A and E to be an ultimate end in itself.

Of course, there is no reason why one cannot adopt both of these two aims together as the ultimate aim of a single process tracing study. Nevertheless, it is important to analyze these aims separately, I will now argue. The reason I think one needs to analyze these two aims separately is that testing a start–end hypotheses (via identifying intermediate links) is often more difficult than testing one or more intermediate hypotheses themselves. I will give three examples of this.

Example one. Consider the hypothesis that A the rise of Nazism in the 1930s was a cause of E the formation of the state of Israel in 1948. Suppose that one tests the following intermediate hypotheses: (1) the rise of Nazism A caused B the genocide of Jews in Europe in the 1940s as well as their persecution in the 1930s; (2) B was a cause of C Jewish refugees fleeing to Mandatory Palestine from 1933–47; and (3) C was a cause of E the formation of Israel. Let's also assume the difference-making view of causation: to say that C was a cause of E is to say that C made a positive difference to E, which is to say that if C had not occurred, then E would not have occurred either. Suppose that one then discovers evidence that Israel would have been formed at any rate, even without the Jewish refugees who fled to Palestine 1933–1947. On this basis one concludes that (3) is false: C was not a cause of E. In this case, I think, this discovery has deepened one's understanding of why the state of Israel was formed, in that one has ruled out one of the plausible causes of this outcome.[12] However, this discovery has not done much to test the start–end hypothesis that A was a cause of E, I suggest. After all, there are lots of other plausible causal chains that link A to E. For example: the rise of

Nazism A caused B^* the war between the British Empire and Nazi Germany, which caused C^* damage to Britain's economy, which caused D^* Britain's inability to govern Palestine in the 1940s, which was a cause of E the formation of Israel in 1948. In sum, the study of intermediate links succeeds in rejecting the intermediate hypothesis that C caused E—and it thereby increases our understanding of the outcome E—but it fails to test the start–end hypothesis that A caused E. Judged by one ultimate aim it's a somewhat successful analysis; judged by the other ultimate aim it's mostly unsuccessful.

Example two. Recall the World War I example from Section 3. Suppose one fails to find evidence for or against the hypothesis that A the assassination of Franz Ferdinand caused B Austria to start a war with Serbia. But suppose one finds strong evidence that B Austria's starting a war with Serbia caused E the general war. In this case, one has almost completely failed to test the start–end hypothesis that A the assassination of Franz Ferdinand caused E the general war. Nevertheless, one has increased one's understanding of why the general war occurred: it's because Austria started a war with Serbia. In this case, the study of intermediate links succeeds in establishing the intermediate hypothesis that B caused E—and it thereby increases our understanding of the outcome E—but again it fails to test the start–end hypothesis that A caused E. Judged by one ultimate aim it's a somewhat successful analysis; judged by the other ultimate aim it's mostly unsuccessful.

Example three. Repurposing an example from Hitchcock (2001), suppose that one discovers that A high investment in the railroads in the 1890s in the United States caused B low investment in canals and roads in the 1890s. And suppose that one also discovers that B low investment in canals and roads caused E transport costs to be high. This analysis succeeds in the aim of testing these intermediate hypotheses. (And it seems to me that, by that same token, it deepens one's understanding of why US transport costs are high.) However, one might think that this analysis of intermediate links, as it stands, fails to test the start–end hypothesis that A caused E. For example, one might think that causation is just difference making; and one might think that railroad investment A made a difference to transport costs E via a positive route and a negative route. The positive route is this: railroad investment A made a positive difference to D railroad efficiency, which itself made a positive difference to E transport costs. The negative route is this: railroad investment A made a negative difference to B canal and road investment, which itself made a positive difference to E transport costs. Therefore, one might think, whether A railroad investment made a positive or negative or no difference to E transport costs will be determined by the relative strength of these positive and negative routes. And—let's imagine—this relative strength is something that we have yet to examine. So the analysis of intermediate links succeeds in establishing several intermediate hypotheses—and it thereby increases our understanding of the outcome E—but again it doesn't go far in testing the start–end hypothesis that A caused E. Judged by one ultimate aim it's a totally successful analysis; judged by the other ultimate aim it's mostly unsuccessful. (Of course, some people reject the view of causation as difference making. And for some of these alternative views, causation is transitive: if A caused B and if B caused E then it's impossible for A not to have also caused E.)

On the basis of these three examples—this third example especially—I conclude that one can often test one or more intermediate hypotheses (and thereby deepen one's understanding of the final outcome) while also falling short of testing a start–end hypothesis. It follows from this that there is no such thing as a good or bad study of intermediate causal links. Rather there are good and bad studies relative to the ultimate aim of testing start-end hypotheses, and relative to the ultimate aim of testing intermediate hypotheses alone. It follows from this that we need two sets of methodological guidelines for analyzing intermediate links in a causal chain: one for those political scientists who aim only to test a start-end hypothesis, and another for those who aim only to test some intermediate hypotheses. (Political scientists who pursue both aims in a single study will need to follow both sets of guidelines. They will need to trade-off these aims against each other if and when the guidelines conflict with each other.) For this reason, it's important for methodologists to draw a distinction between these two ultimate aims for which one might study intermediate links.

Unhappily, the literature does not yet draw a sharp distinction between these two ultimate aims.[13] For example, Beach and Pedersen (2016) distinguish between "explaining outcome" process tracing on the one hand and "theory building" and "theory testing" process tracing on the other. But this distinction—it is crucial to note—is nothing like my distinction between studying intermediate links as an ultimate end in itself versus as a means that serves the ultimate aim of testing start–end hypotheses. As far as I understand Beach and Pedersen, "explaining outcome" process tracing means process tracing that reconstructs a very long and detailed causal chain. As a result, this precise causal chain will be idiosyncratic to the case in question and will not be found in other cases—even though any individual link in the chain may be found is some other cases. So Beach and Pedersen's distinction has to do with whether a causal chain exhibits uniformity across cases. It has nothing to do with the distinction between ultimately aiming to test a start–end hypothesis versus ultimately aiming to test one or more intermediate hypotheses.

Even though the literature does not sharply draw this distinction, there are some hints as to which aim various methodologists have in mind when they talk about process tracing. On the one hand, Section 3 has already cited methodologists who seem to endorse testing start–end hypotheses as the ultimate aim of process tracing. On the other hand, Checkel (2013) thinks that one important aim of process tracing is to test the hypothesis that A caused B caused E against the rival hypothesis that A caused D caused E. This is clearly testing intermediate hypotheses as an ultimate end itself, not for the ultimate aim of testing the start–end hypothesis that A caused E. Similarly, Hall (2003) states that an important aim of process tracing is to increase the "explanatory power" of one's theory by establishing that A caused B caused E, so this sounds again like testing intermediate hypotheses as an end it itself (deepening understanding); see also Bennett and Checkel (2015).

In fact, some methodologists seem to take process tracing as having both these ultimate aims, even though they don't highlight these aims as distinct, or explore the implications of this distinction.[14] Contrast the citations of Beach and Pedersen in Section 3 with

> when embarking on a study of the mechanisms linking a cause and outcome, we often already possess cross-case knowledge about patterns of difference-making between the two factors. *The* reason we then trace mechanisms using in-depth case studies is to investigate the "how actually" question, shedding more light on whether there is evidence of a mechanism and thereby also informing us how a cause contributes to co-produce an outcome. (Beach and Pedersen 2016, 41, emphasis mine)

5. RECTANGULAR DATA SETS
AND COMPARABILITY

This section will examine the suggestion that the type of evidence used in process tracing studies differs from that used in quantitative studies: unlike process tracing, quantitative studies uses "comparable" data arranged into a "rectangular" data sets. I will argue that the best way of understanding this suggestion is that process tracing, unlike quantitative methods, does not rely on an assumption of "unit homogeneity."

Process tracing studies are often said to draw upon qualitative evidence, which is to be contrasted with quantitative evidence. One obvious way of making this idea more precise is to offer the following criterion:

> (F1) A study does not count as a process tracing study if it relies on numerical data, data of the form "the number of Xs is . . . " or "the proportion of Xs that were Ys is."

A moment's thought shows that this criterion is too restrictive. Exemplary instances of process tracing often rely on numerical data (Brady 2010; Gerring 2006). For example, Wood (2003) uses as evidence the percentage of farmland in El Salvador that was put to various purposes, the number of people killed at various stages of the civil war, and the proportion of town majors that resigned during the war.

Instead of criterion *F1*, a more promising suggestion is that process tracing studies handle numerical evidence differently from standard quantitative methods:

> Because each [numerical] observation is quite different from the rest, they do not collectively constitute a sample. Each observation is sampled from a different population. This means that each [numerical] observation is qualitatively different. It is thus the non-comparability of adjacent observations, not the nature of individual observations, that differentiates the process-tracing method from standard research designs. (Gerring 2006, 179)

What does Gerring mean when he suggests that quantitative studies use data sets in which the data is comparable? A common way of interpreting this suggestion is as the suggestion that quantitative studies use rectangular data sets: each data set is constituted by a number of cases (the rows of the data set) and by a number of variables (the columns of the data set) and for each case one observes the value of each of those variables (the cells of the data set); see Waldner (2012), Collier, Brady, and Seawright (2010), and Rohlfing (2012) for discussion.

But this suggestion cannot be quite right. To see this, consider the phenomenon of missing data. Quantitative studies that use many cases and many variables are often unable to observe the values of some of the cells in the rectangular data set, so their data set deviates from this rectangular ideal. But, according to the current suggestion, the more that a study's data set deviates from this rectangular ideal, the more methodologically similar that study is to process tracing studies, and the less similar it is to standard quantitative studies. But that can't be right, everyone would agree: quantitative studies with missing data are most fruitfully thought of as a sophisticated form of quantitative study, not as something that approaches a qualitative or process tracing method. This illustrates, I suggest, that the use of rectangular data sets by quantitative methods is, in fact, a superficial symptom of a deeper and more interesting epistemic distinction between quantitative studies and process tracing studies.

What might this deeper distinction be? Let's examine the logic of quantitative studies in more detail. Take for example a political scientist who is interested in the extent to which natural resource wealth R and ethnic diversity D contributed to the duration Y of the civil war in El Salvador, for example. Let r^a denote El Salvador's actual resource wealth (2 billion dollars say) and let d^a denote El Salvador's actual ethnic diversity (10 percent say) and let y^a denote the actual duration of the civil war in El Salvador (14 years).

Contrast this actual scenario A with a hypothetical scenario B in which El Salvador's resource wealth is instead r^b (1 billion dollars say) although its ethnic diversity r^b is the same as r^a (10 percent). Let y^b denote what the duration of the civil war in El Salvador would have been, if El Salvador had instead been in this hypothetical scenario B. Most quantitative methodologists agree that $y^a - y^b$ denotes the causal contribution that resource wealth being r^a (2 billion) rather than r^b (1 billion) made to the duration of the civil war in El Salvador. But how to measure $y^a - y^b$?

Consider any hypothetical scenario s you like, in which resources r^s are anything you like, and in which diversity d^s is anything you like. So y^s denotes what the duration of the civil war in El Salvador would have been if El Salvador had instead been in scenario s. Accordingly $E(Y^s)$ denotes the propensity of the civil war in El Salvador to endure in this scenario s. Metaphorically speaking, if one were to repeat history over and over again a large number of times, each time ensuring that El Salvadorian resources were r^s and diversity were d^s, but allowing other variables to vary, $E(Y^s)$ denotes the average duration of the civil war in El Salvador, averaged across these metaphorical repeats of history.

Now, to estimate causal contribution $y^a - y^b$, quantitative political scientists proceed by thinking about a larger population of cases—for example, all civil wars since 1945. And they assume that in each of these cases the propensity of the civil war in question to endure is a function of resource wealth and ethnic diversity. For example they might assume that, for each civil war post 1945, $E(Y^s) = \beta_1 r^s + \beta_2 d^s$ is true for any hypothetical scenario s. (Here β_1 and β_2 are unknown coefficients that are assumed to be the same for each scenario s and for each civil war post 1945.)

With this key assumption in place, it follows that $E(Y^a - Y^b) = \beta_1(r^a - r^b) = \beta_1(2-1) = \beta_1$. This fact allows one to proceed as follows. First, one collects data on R resource wealth, D ethnic diversity and Y civil war duration, from many civil wars since 1945. Second, one uses standard statistical techniques to measure the values of β_1 and β_2 that "fit" this data set best, or "explain" this data set best. Third, since $E(Y^a - Y^b) = \beta_1$, we can now use our estimate of β_1 as an (unbiased) estimate of $y^a - y^b$, the causal contribution that resource wealth being r^a (2 billion) rather than r^b (1 million) made to the duration of the war in El Salvador. This is the econometric approach to causal inference in a nutshell.

Note that our key assumption entails that there is a single mathematical function that describes the propensity of each civil war post 1945 to endure, for any hypothetical scenario s; for example, the function $E(Y^s) = 3r^s + 2d^s$. That is to say, all the civil wars post 1945 exhibit "unit homogeneity," it is assumed (King, Keohane, and Verba 1994, 91–94). To be clear, unit homogeneity does not say that the actual causal contribution $y^a - y^b$ of an extra billion dollars is the same for El Salvador as it is for Northern Ireland, say. This is because the above mathematical function is a description of a probabilistic average $E(Y^s)$, not of the hypothetical outcome y^s itself. Indeed, unit homogeneity itself does not even require that that the average contribution $E(Y^a - Y^b)$ is the same for El Salvador as it is for Northern Ireland. To see this, note that the mathematical function that satisfies unit homogeneity might be more complicated than the one I gave as an example. It might be $E(Y^s) = (3 + d^s)r^s$ for instance—in which case, those civil wars with greater ethnic diversity would be wars in which 1 billion extra resource wealth makes a greater causal contribution (on average) to the war's duration. To be clear, unit homogeneity is simply the assumption that there is a single mathematical function—and a single specification of the values of the coefficients in the function—that describes the propensity of each civil war post 1945 to endure.

This knowledge of unit homogeneity, across some largish population of cases, is absolutely essential to the reliability of the econometric method (King, Keohane, and Verba 1994). (Of course, there is no need to assume unit homogeneity across all cases: if the US Civil War isn't in one's data set, for example, or in the population of civil wars that one wants to study, then there is no need to assume that the above mathematical function describes the propensity of the US Civil War to endure.)

Taking stock, these reflections suggest another essential feature of process tracing. If you take the ultimate aim of process tracing to be to identify the start–end causal relationship between factor A and factor E, then:

> (Criterion Four—Version A) A study does not count as process tracing if it requires unit homogeneity for the starting factor A and the outcome E, that is, the existence of a largish population of cases for which there is a single mathematical function that describes the propensities governing E, given variation in A and some other variables.

In contrast, if you take the ultimate aim of process tracing to be to identify intermediate relationships in a causal chain, the suggestion is:

> (Criterion Four—Version B) A study does not count as process tracing if it requires unit homogeneity for any of the intermediate links in the chain, that is, the existence of a largish population of cases for which there is a single mathematical function that describes the propensities governing factor D, for example, given variation in C and some other variables.

To understand the difference between these two versions of Criterion Four, imagine a researcher who does the following. She examines a sample of 20 civil wars post 1990, and uses econometric methods to show that C caused D for civil wars post 1990; she next uses another sample of 20 civil wars in Central America, and uses econometric methods to show that D caused E for civil wars in Central America. On this basis, she argues that C caused E in civil wars in Central America post 1990. In this case, she has not assumed that the relationship between C to E is homogeneous across a largish population of cases, because there are only a handful of cases that are Central American civil wars post 1990. So this researcher has not violated version A of Criterion Four, although she has violated version B.

Criterion Four also distinguishes process tracing from those quantitative techniques—developed in psychology and imported into political science—that are labeled interchangeably as "mediation analysis" or "path analysis" or "structural equation modeling" (Mackinnon 2007; Tarka 2018).[15] Criterion Four also distinguishes process tracing from more recent quantitative innovations in political science that build on these older mediation-analysis techniques (Imai, Keele, and Tingley 2010; Imai et al. 2011). These techniques are all forms analyzing intermediate links in causal chains, but they do not count as process tracing, according to Criterion Four.

6. UNHELPFUL RESTRICTIONS ON PROCESS TRACING

Why have I not suggested the following additional criterion? one might ask. Namely: a study does not count as process tracing study if it needs any feature of the case in question to resemble any other case. This criterion seems to me unhelpfully restrictive. For example, many process tracers make assumptions that the agents they are studying behave in familiar ways. A process tracer might assume that agents will usually tend to hide information that casts them in a good light but be reluctant to volunteer information that casts them in a bad light. As a result a process tracer might credit negative confessions from her informants more strongly than she does positive boasting. But the process tracer's warrant for doing this is that she knows that the informants she is talking to is in this respect similar to most of the other people the process tracer has come to know in life. Therefore, I suggest, it is far too restrictive to debar process tracing from relying on any form of resemblance between her case and other cases.[16] (In contrast, Criterion Four debars process tracing from relying on a particular form of resemblance, namely unit homogeneity, but this leaves open the possibility that process tracing studies might rely on other forms of resemblance.)

For precisely the same reason, I reject the following criterion: (F2) a study does not count as a process tracing study if it relies on evidence from other cases. After all, my process tracer in the above example is relying on evidence about other people (people not within her case) to support her conclusions. (Sometimes criterion F2 is endorsed more or less explicitly: process tracing is the use of "observational within-case empirical material left by the workings of a causal mechanism within an actual case to make inferences about the existence of a mechanism in a case" (Beach 2017). Other times criterion F2 is heavily hinted at.[17])

Why have I not suggested the following additional criterion? one might ask. Namely: (F3) a study does not count as a process tracing study if it needs the probability distribution of some variable to take a particular form. Again, this criterion seems to me unhelpfully restrictive. As I've already noted, some process tracers like to use proportions as evidence—for example, the proportion of women who fought in the militias in El Salvador. But often to measure these proportions one will have to draw sample from a wider population: there are simply too many members of the militia to count them all. But the moment one seeks to use this sample to measure the proportion in a wider population, one will need to make probabilistic assumptions about one's sampling method, if only implicitly and informally.

This also highlights why I think is not strictly true that process tracing cannot use statistical methods, as criterion F4 says. This is contrary to what Mahoney (2004) and George and Mckeown (1985) claim. For example, Wood's study would still be an exemplary process tracing study, even if she had used formal statistical methods to establish the proportion of women who fought in the militias.

Why have I not suggested the following additional criterion? Namely, (F5) a study does not count as a process tracing study if its results can be generalized. *F5* is false because it says that (having used process tracing to establish the causes of a given civil war) one is never licensed to use this as evidence that the same causes are operating in another civil war. Whether or not one is licensed to extrapolate from one civil war to a second one depends primarily on one's knowledge of how similar these wars are, not on the methods one used to study the first war. Indeed, many process tracers explicitly say that process tracing often tries to generalize or extrapolate. As Hall (2003, 395) puts it, process tracing "is an effort to elaborate and assess the validity of theories capable of explaining a broad class of events or outcomes. It seeks generalizations that are both more simple and more portable than those at which historians typically aim." "As regards the ambition to go beyond the single case, this involves attempts to identify which mechanisms are systematic and non-systematic in the specific case study" (Beach and Pedersen 2016, 310).

In sum, *F1* to *F5* place unhelpful restrictions on what can count as a process tracing study.

7. The Elusive Nature of Process Tracing

Recall Criterion Four Version *B*: process tracing studies do not test intermediate causal hypotheses by methods that assume unit homogeneity, for example by standard quantitative methods. This immediately raises the question: if an intermediate causal hypothesis is not to be tested via standard quantitative methods, then how else is it to be tested?

To explore this issue, this section will examine some further criteria for what counts as process tracing. I will dismiss these putative criteria as empty: they do not offer any substantive, additional constraints over and above Criteria One to Four.

The first putative criterion I have in mind is: (E1) a study only counts as a process tracing study if relies solely on "causal process observations" (Brady 2010). But what are causal process observations supposed to be, one might ask? A promising preliminary clarification is to interpret criterion *E1* as follows: (E1*) a study only counts as a process tracing study if it uses "diagnostic evidence" to uncover the mechanism under examination. This criterion is offered by Collier (2011a) and Collier (2011b) among others. But what might it mean to say of some evidence that it is "diagnostic evidence" for some hypothesis? On one reading, all evidence for a given hypothesis is diagnostic evidence. In this case *E1* just becomes Criterion One and Criterion Two, the idea that process tracing uncovers mechanisms. On another reading, evidence counts as diagnostic evidence for an hypothesis about a given case whenever the evidence itself is a fact about the very same case. For example, the fact that Sophie's skin is yellow is diagnostic evidence that she has liver failure. In contrast, the fact that 90 percent of people with yellow skin have liver failure is evidence that Sophie has liver failure; but it is not diagnostic evidence, one might say, because it is a fact about other people, not about Sophie herself. (This seems to be the view of Beach (2017).) On this reading of the meaning of "diagnostic evidence," however, *E1* just becomes the criterion *F2* that I rejected in the last section.

Another interpretation of criterion *E1* is to re-express it as follows: (E2) a study only counts as a process tracing study if it uses pattern matching. See Mahoney (1999), Mahoney (2004), Bennett and Elman (2006), and Beach (2017) and Goertz and Mahoney (2012) for agreement.

Pattern matching is the process of taking an hypothesis—for example the hypothesis that Sophie has liver failure—and asking how well it can "account for" the patterns one sees in the data? How well can it account for the fact that Sophie has yellow skin, for example?

The problem is that according to most philosophies of scientific inference *all* scientific inference is pattern matching. Hypothetico-deductivism says that all scientific inference is pattern matching, where "accounts for the patterns in the data" is read as "the hypothesis entails the pattern as a matter of deductive logic." Falsificationism is just hypothetico-deductivism with the caveat that hypotheses are never supported by the data, only falsified. Inference to the best explanation says that all scientific inference is pattern matching, where "accounts for the patterns in the data" is read as "the hypothesis, if it were true, would explain the patterns in the data" (Lipton 1991). Bayesian epistemology says that all scientific inference is pattern matching, where "accounts for the patterns in the data" is read as "the scientist in question has a high degree of confidence that these patterns will be occur, supposing that the hypothesis is true" (Howson and Urbach [1989] 2006).

So $E2$ does not put any restriction on what counts as process tracing. It fails to tell us what is distinctive about process tracing as a method of causal inference. (The only philosophy of scientific inference that seems difficult to fit with the pattern matching idea is the frequentist philosophy of statistical inference. So my best guess at interpreting $E2$ is as a roundabout way of endorsing $F4$: a study does not count as a process tracing study if it uses statistical methods. Or perhaps it's a roundabout way of endorsing the more defensible version of $F1$, namely my Criterion Four.)

The third and final putative criterion I have in mind is the following: ($E3$) process tracing can use a very wide variety of evidence. For example, Bennett and Elman (2007, 183) says that process tracing uses "a wide variety of sources (often including archived documents, contemporary news accounts, secondary histories, biographies or memoirs, and interviews) with due attention to the potential motivated and informational biases of each source." Fairfield and Charman (2017, 368) adds that it often uses "information about timing and sequencing, actors' goals and intentions, and other aspects of causal mechanisms, as obtained from a wide range of sources including interviews, archives, media records, and secondary literature." All this is certainly true, but notice that it does not place any restrictions on what counts as process tracing. There is not a single study for which $E3$ suggests that that study doesn't count as process tracing. Instead, $E3$ is a kind of meta-criterion, which says that the criteria that we place on what counts as process tracing should not be too restrictive. In particular, the criteria we place on process tracing should allow process tracers to draw upon a wide variety of evidence. So, as a criterion for defining process tracing, $E3$ is entirely non-restrictive.

Taking stock, I've argued in this section that criteria $E1$–$E3$ are empty: they do not place any substantive constraints on what counts as process tracing, additional to Criteria One to Four.

8. CONCLUSION

I conclude that Criteria One to Four are the primary ways of defining process tracing that are suggested by the present methodological literature. Note that I offered two versions of these criteria. Version *A* is *process tracing for the ultimate aim of testing a start–end hypothesis*. For a study to count as this type of process tracing:

> It must identify the presence or absence of intermediate causal links between some factor *A* and an outcome of interest *E*.
>
> And, perhaps, it must describe each of these intermediate links in terms of entities engaging in regular, well-understood activities.
>
> It must ultimately aim to test the hypothesis that the starting factor in the chain was a cause of the final outcome. And the means by which it pursues this ultimate aim must be the following logical structure: (I) the overall evidence *e* bears on hypothesis *h* only by first bearing on the intermediate hypotheses; (II) for each intermediate hypothesis, there is a piece of evidence *e'* that bears on this intermediate hypothesis alone.
>
> It must not require unit homogeneity for the starting factor *A* and the outcome *E*, that is, the existence of a largish population of cases for which there is a single mathematical function that describes the propensities governing *E*, given variation in *A* and some other variables.

Version *B* is *process tracing as an ultimate end in itself*. For a study to count as this type of process tracing:

> It must identify the presence or absence of intermediate causal links between some factor *A* and an outcome of interest *E*.
>
> And, perhaps, it must describe each of these intermediate links in terms of entities engaging in regular, well-understood activities.
>
> Its ultimate aim must be this identification / description of the intermediate links in a causal chain.
>
> It must not require unit homogeneity for any of these intermediate links in the chain, that is, the existence of a largish population of cases for which there is a single mathematical function that describes the propensities governing factor *D*, for example, given variation in *C* and some other variables.

As it stands, process tracing as an ultimate end in itself is under-theorized. Given what I argued in Section 7, the methodological literature has barely begun to answer the question: if an intermediate causal hypothesis is not to be tested via methods that assume unit homogeneity, then how else is it to be tested? See Runhardt (2015) for a similar worry. Some methodologists seemed to answer this question by claiming that intermediate hypotheses could be directly observed to be true (Brady 2010). But I think it's fair to say that most methodologists now reject this claim (Beck 2006; Crasnow 2012).

How then to proceed? In my view, what we urgently need is a taxonomy of various different ways in which process tracers are supposedly able to test intermediate causal hypotheses without relying on unit homogeneity. This taxonomy would allow us to evaluate process tracers' claims that process tracing is good at eliminating rival causal hypotheses, that process tracing is not an inherently micro enterprise, and that process tracing really is its own method, distinct from quantitative methods.

Acknowledgments

This work has received funding from the European Research Council under the European Union Horizon 2020 Research and Innovation Programme, under grant agreement no 715530.

Thank you Jeroen van Bouwel, Harold Kincaid, and one anonymous referees for your constructive comments on the manuscript. And thanks to an audience at the University of Kent for discussion of these ideas.

NOTES

1. See Bennett and Checkel (2015) and Checkel (2013) for agreement.
2. See Gerring (2006) and Checkel (2008) and indeed most of the citations in his chapter.
3. Citations to e.g. Beach and Pedersen (2016) who agree, and those who disagree.
4. This suggest seems to be strongly implied in Evangelista (2015), Waldner (2012), Bennett (2008), and George and Mckeown (1985).
5. See for example Mahoney (1999), Mahoney (2004), Rohlfing (2012), Bennett (2010), Mahoney (2015), Collier (2011b), and perhaps also Humphreys and Jacobs (2015), and Gerring (2006).
6. Brady provides a second argument for the figure of 4,200, an argument that is more dubious in my view. This argument simply assumes that would-be voters did not intend to vote in disproportionately high numbers in the last hour. But the warrant for this assumption is highly questionable.
7. However, Brady is clearly focusing only on the second premature call (the 8:48 pm report that Gore had won). But Lott seems to focus on the two premature calls together (including the 8 pm report that the polls had closed).
8. Brady talks about "voters" rather than "would-be" voters as I do. But it seems to me that for Brady's argument to work he needs to be talking about would-be voters. So to make Brady's argument sound, one needs to tinker with the figures that Brady gives. For example, I suspect that Brady's figure of 379,000 is a report of the number of actual votes cast rather than an estimate of the number of would-be voters.
9. One might also dispute that some of these links in the chain are truly causal—the link between H and I to take just one example. But I will not explore this point further.
10. Or K itself.
11. Condition II is necessary, I suggest, because many studies that test hypothesis h but don't intuitively do so "via" testing h_{CD} and h_{DE} will nevertheless satisfy condition I, I suggest. At any rate, for broad agreement with my suggestion here, see Beach and Pedersen (2016) and Gerring (2006). Note also that Criterion Three does not require that one can partition the evidence e into evidence e_{AB} that bears on h_{AB} alone, and into evidence e_{BC} that bears on h_{BC} alone, with no evidence left over. Take for example a scenario in which one's evidence breaks down into three parts: e_A is evidence about the observed values of variable A, e_B is evidence about the observed values of variable B, and e_C is evidence about the observed values of variable C. Imagine further that e_A and e_B (but not e_C) bear on the intermediate hypothesis h_{AB} that A caused B; while e_B and e_C (but not e_A) bear on the intermediate hypothesis h_{BC} that B caused C. Therefore, e_A bears on h_{AB} alone, and e_C bears on h_{BC} alone, and so this case satisfies Criterion Three, even though e_B bears on both h_{AB} and on h_{BC} (Thank you Harold Kincaid for pointing this out to me.)
12. Philosophers often talk about understanding-why as causal knowledge. But I see no reason why this knowledge need be knowledge of the presence of a cause, rather than knowledge of the absence of a cause.

13. Waldner (2012) gestures toward this distinction but does not clarify it or study its implications. Beach (2017) and Bennett and Checkel (2015) mention these two aims, but do not draw attention to the distinction or study its implications.
14. See Beach (2017) and Bennett and Checkel (2015) for further examples.
15. This is not to be confused with structural equation modelling within economics. SEM in economics tend to be based on systems of simultaneous equations, and tend not to model latent (unobserved) variables other than of course the error term.
16. See Crasnow (2012) for a distinct argument to a similar conclusion.
17. See Bennett and Elman (2006) and Beach and Pedersen (2016) and Mahoney (2010) and Humphreys and Jacobs (2015) for just some examples.

REFERENCES

Acemoglu, Daron, Simon Johnson, and James A. Robinson. 2005. "Institutions as a Fundamental Cause of Long-Run Growth." In *Handbook of Economic Growth*, edited by Philippe Aghion and Steven N. Durlauf, IA, 385–472. Amsterdam: North Holland.

Beach, Derek. 2017. "Process-Tracing Methods in Social Science." https://doi.org/10.1093/acref ore/9780190228637.013.176.

Beach, Derek, and Rasmus Pedersen. 2016. *Causal Case Study Methods: Foundations and Guidelines for Comparing, Matching, and Tracing*. Ann Arbor, MI: University of Michigan Press. https://doi.org/10.3998/mpub.6576809.

Beck, Nathaniel. 2006. "Is Causal-Process Observation an Oxymoron?" *Political Analysis* 14: 347–352. https://doi.org/10.1093/pan/mpj015.

Bennett, Andrew. 2008. "The Mother of All "Isms": Organizing Political Science Around Causal Mechanisms." In *Revitalizing Causality: Realism about Causality in Philosophy nd Social Science*, edited by Ruth Groff, 205–219. London: Routledge.

Bennett, Andrew. 2010. "Process Tracing and Casual Inference." In *Rethinking Social Inquiry: Diverse Tools, Shared Standards*, edited by Henry E. Brady and David Collier, 2nd ed., 207–220. Lanham, MD: Rowman; Littlefield.

Bennett, Andrew, and Jeffrey T. Checkel. 2015. "Process Tracing: From Philosophical Roots to Best Practices." In *Process Tracing: From Metaphor to Analytic Tool*, edited by Andrew Bennett and Jeffrey T. Checkel, 3–38. Cambridge: Cambridge University Press.

Bennett, Andrew, and Colin Elman. 2006. "Qualitative Research: Recent Developments in Case Study Methods." *Annual Review of Political Science* 9: 455–476. https://doi.org/10.1146/annurev.polisci.8.082103.104918.

Bennett, Andrew, and Colin Elman. 2007. "Case Study Methods in the International Relations Subfield." *Comparative Political Studies* 40: 170–195.

Brady, Henry E. 2010. "Data-Set Observations Versus Causal-Process Observations: The 2000 US Presidential Election." In *Rethinking Social Inquiry: Diverse Tools, Shared Standards*, edited by Henry E. Brady and David Collier, 2nd ed., 237–242. Lanham, MD: Rowman; Littlefield.

Checkel, Jeffrey T. 2008. "Process Tracing." In *Qualitative Methods in International Relations: A Pluralist Guide*, edited by Audie Klotz and Deepa Prakash, 114–130. New York: Palgrave Macmillan.

Checkel, Jeffrey T. 2013. "Transnational Dynamics of Civil War." In *Transnational Dynamics of Civil War*, edited by Jeffrey T. Checkel, 3–30. Cambridge: Cambridge University Press.

Collier, David. 2011a. "Teaching Process Tracing: Examples and Exercises." http://ssrn.com/abstract=1944646.

Collier, David. 2011b. "Understanding Process Tracing." *Ps: Political Science and Politics* 44: 823–830. https://doi.org/10.1017/s1049096511001429.

Collier, David, Henry E. Brady, and Jason Seawright. 2010. "Sources of Leverage in Casual Interference: Toward an Alternative View of Methodology." In *Rethinking Social Inquiry: Diverse Tools, Shared Standards*, edited by Henry E. Brady and David Collier, 2nd ed., 161–200. Lanham MD: Rowman; Littlefield.

Crasnow, Sharon. 2012. "The Role of Case Study Research in Political Science: Evidence for Causal Claims." *Philosophy of Science* 79: 655–666. https://doi.org/10.1086/667869.

Evangelista, Matthew. 2015. "Explaining the Cold War's End: Process Tracing All the Way down?" In *Process Tracing: From Metaphor to Analytic Tool*, edited by Andrew Bennett and Jeffrey T. Checkel, 153–185. Cambridge: Cambridge University Press.

Fairfield, Tasha, and Andrew E. Charman. 2017. "Explicit Bayesian Analysis for Process Tracing: Guidelines, Opportunities, and Caveats." *Political Analysis* 25: 363–380. https://doi.org/10.1017/pan.2017.14.

George, Alexander, and Timothy J. Mckeown. 1985. "Case Studies and Theories of Organizational Decision Making." In *Advances in Information Processing in Organizations*, edited by Robert F. Coulam and Richard A. Smith, 2: 21–58. Greenwich, CT: JAI Press.

Gerring, John. 2006. *Case Study Research: Principles and Practices*. Cambridge: Cambridge University Press.

Goertz, Gary, and James Mahoney. 2012. *A Tale of Two Cultures: Qualitative and Quantitative Research in the Social Sciences*. Princeton, NJ: Princeton University Press.

Hall, Peter A. 2003. "Aligning Ontology and Methodology in Comparative Politics." In *Comparative Historical Analysis in the Social Sciences*, edited by James Mahoney and Dietrich Rueschemeyer, 373–406. Cambridge: Cambridge University Press.

Hedstrom, Peter, and Petri Ylikoski. 2010. "Causal Mechanisms in the Social Sciences." *Annual Review of Sociology* 36: 49–67. https://doi.org/10.1146/annurev.soc.012809.102632.

Hitchcock, Christopher. 2001. "A Tale of Two Effects." *Philosophical Review* 110: 361–396.

Howson, Colin, and Peter Urbach. (1989) 2006. *Scientific Reasoning: The Bayesian Approach*. 3rd ed. La Salle, IL: Open Court.

Humphreys, Macartan, and Alan M. Jacobs. 2015. "Mixing Methods: A Bayesian Approach." *American Political Science Review* 109: 653–673. https://doi.org/10.1017/s0003055415000453.

Imai, Kosuke, Luke Keele, and Dustin Tingley. 2010. "A General Approach to Causal Mediation Analysis." *Psychological Methods* 15: 309–334. https://doi.org/10.1037/a0020761.

Imai, Kosuke, Luke Keele, Dustin Tingley, and Teppei Yamamoto. 2011. "Unpacking the Black Box of Causality: Learning About Causal Mechanisms from Experimental and Observational Studies." *American Political Science Review* 105: 765–789. https://doi.org/10.1017/s0003055411000414.

King, Gary, Robert O. Keohane, and Sidney Verba. 1994. *Designing Social Inquiry: Scientific Inference in Qualitative Research*. Princeton, NJ: Princeton University Press.

Lipton, Peter. 1991. *Inference to the Best Explanation*. London: Routledge.

Lott, John R. 2005. "The Impact of Early Media Election Calls on Republican Voting Rates in Florida's Western Panhandle Counties in 2000." *Public Choice* 123: 349–361. https://doi.org/10.1007/s11127-005-7166-1.

Mackinnon, David P. 2007. *Introduction to Statistical Mediation Analysis*. New York: Routledge.

Mahoney, James. 1999. "Nominal, Ordinal, and Narrative Appraisal in Macrocausal Analysis." *American Journal of Sociology* 104: 1154–1196. https://doi.org/10.1086/210139.

Mahoney, James. 2004. "Comparative–Historical Methodology." *Annual Review of Sociology* 30: 81–101.

Mahoney, James. 2010. "After KKV: The New Methodology of Qualitative Research." *World Politics* 62: 120–147. https://doi.org/10.1017/s0043887109990220.

Mahoney, James. 2015. "Process Tracing and Historical Explanation." *Security Studies* 24: 200–218. https://doi.org/10.1080/09636412.2015.1036610.

Mahoney, James, and Gary Goertz. 2006. "A Tale of Two Cultures: Contrasting Quantitative and Qualitative Research." *Political Analysis* 14: 227–249. https://doi.org/10.1093/pan/mpj017.

Rohlfing, Ingo. 2012. *Case Studies and Causal Inference*. London: Palgrave Macmillan. https://doi.org/10.1057/9781137271327.

Runhardt, Rosa W. 2015. "Evidence for Causal Mechanisms in Social Science: Recommendations from Woodward's Manipulability Theory of Causation." *Philosophy of Science* 82: 1296–1307. https://doi.org/10.1086/683679.

Skocpol, Theda. 1979. *States and Social Revolutions: A Comparative Analysis of France, Russia, and China*. Cambridge: Cambridge University Press.

Tannenwald, Nina. 1999. "The Nuclear Taboo: The United States and the Normative Basis of Nuclear Non-Use." *International Organization* 53: 433–468. https://doi.org/10.1162/002081899550959.

Tarka, Piotr. 2018. "An Overview of Structural Equation Modeling: Its Beginnings, Historical Development, Usefulness and Controversies in the Social Sciences." *Quality and Quantity: International Journal of Methodology* 52: 313–354. https://doi.org/10.1007/s11135-017-0469-8.

Waldner, David. 2012. "Process Tracing and Causal Mechanisms." In *The Oxford Handbook of Philosophy of Social Science*, edited by Harold Kincaid, 65–84. Oxford: Oxford University Press.

Wood, Elisabeth Jean. 2003. *Insurgent Collective Action and Civil War in El Salvador*. Cambridge: Cambridge University Press.

CHAPTER 16

....

PROCESS TRACING
Causation and Levels of Analysis

....

KEITH DOWDING

INTRODUCTION

ALEXANDER George (1979) introduced the term "process tracing" into political science from cognitive psychology. Methodologically it has developed in various directions (see, for example, Bennett and Checkel 2015a). In its broadest sense, process tracing is systematic qualitative analysis using various sources of information in order to narrate a sequence of events leading to some outcome of interest.[1] In a narrower sense, it involves specific recommendations for how to go about detailed case studies, within-case, and historical analysis in a systematic and theorized manner for methodologically disciplined research. Process tracing is now widely used for qualitative case-study research in political science and international relations, and has accumulated a large and fruitful literature on qualitative historical and case-study methods (George and Bennett 2005; Bennett and Checkel 2015b). When using process tracing in empirical work, two approaches are recommended. One is inductive, and largely directed at explaining how a given outcome came about—such accounts can be theory generating (George and Bennett 2005; Bennett 2008). The other is usually described as deductive and is thought to be theory testing. Either can also be used to generate claims or hypotheses about turning points, decisive moments, and critical junctures in history. What is expected of excellent qualitative research is not in dispute; process tracing is largely about proclaiming such qualitative research as scientific endeavor. Faced with the theory-testing claims of quantitative research, qualitative researchers have argued not only that their methods can also test theories and discover causation, but are indeed superior.

I do not examine in this chapter the various recommendations of process tracing for qualitative researchers (see Collier 2011 or Beach and Pedersen 2016 for detailed discussions), though I will briefly discuss some techniques in Section 2. Rather, I will concentrate upon some of the philosophical claims made on its behalf with regard to causal analysis and theory testing. This discussion ought to affect what qualitative researchers aim to achieve, but will not change the practical techniques recommended by process-tracing experts.

The issues I cover in this chapter include causality and causal mechanisms, theory testing, generalizations versus mechanisms, distal and proximate causation, and the appropriate level of analysis.

1. Systematic Qualitative Methodology

Case studies provide detailed analyses of the course of events. They naturally form a narrative, and every narrative takes on a causal form in the sense that it drives toward a conclusion. In any narrative what we choose to report will be based upon what we think is important in that case study; and what we think important is bound to include what we think causes, in some sense, the outcomes that make that case study of interest. Process tracing is an attempt to systematize a narrative in order to provide stronger evidence of the important causal features.

Underlying the defense of process tracing is an account of the explanation of social outcomes in terms of causal mechanisms usually seen in opposition to generalizations that are often the focus of high-n studies. It is clear, however, that while invariant (or law-like) generalizations or laws can perform explanatory roles, empirical generalizations are the outcomes that need to be explained. Explanation using mechanisms is not in conflict with the search for empirical generalizations. Quite the opposite: we should expect mechanisms to explain the empirical generalizations we find, and even to explain those examples that do not fit the generalization. I have argued elsewhere that empirical generalizations are produced by mechanisms which themselves are underlain by invariant generalizations (Dowding 2016; see also Waldner 2012). Nevertheless, an important element of social explanation is understanding the mechanisms that lead to types of outcomes. I have also argued elsewhere that single case studies cannot test—as "testing" is normally understood—theories seen as either generalizations or mechanisms (although, of course, they can provide evidence that goes into a broader set of evidence that constitutes a test as ordinarily understood). Even "crucial case studies" fail to establish that theories are false. What they can do is provide evidence as to whether a given mechanism applies to a specific case and fill in some of the details of that mechanism as it applies to that case (Dowding 2020).

Some have argued that process tracing has an ontology and understanding of causation different from those employed by scholars who operate with high-n studies (Beach and Pedersen 2016, for example). If so, that would be unfortunate if social science is to be one science rather than forever a set of competing paradigms. Here I defend process tracing as a systematic way of examining causal mechanisms, making direct analogies with the understanding of causation in experimental and high-n statistical approaches, to explore both its strengths and weaknesses. To understand those strengths and weaknesses, we need to see that low-n qualitative work and high-n quantitative work are directed at different sorts of research questions posed at different levels of generality. The latter is directed at uncovering the ultimate or structural causes of *types*; the former aims to explain the proximate or historical causes of *tokens*.[2] A type is a class of objects composed of tokens and a token is an example of a type. In either case we can model the mechanism that is thought to be the causally important explanation.

Process tracing is generally tied to testing hypotheses derived from theories. The recommendation is that a clear theory of some process is proposed and evidence collected to defend that theory, often in comparison with rival explanations. The single case can be used as a test of the theory, but is often used as a paradigm example of the proposed mechanism being operant in other examples. Researchers look for causal inferences from the evidence collected about a single case. Producing evidence for or against any hypothesis will involve claims about the counterfactuals that enable us to make the causal inferences.

Process tracing seems to be defined by the four tests specified in Van Evera (1997), developed by writers such Bennett (2010), Collier (2011) and Waldner (2012), with a further completeness test suggested in Waldner (2015). The tests are classified according to whether passing them provides necessary and/or sufficient conditions for accepting the causal inference. Collier (2011) gives the most complete and simple explanation of Van Evera's four tests, using the Sherlock Holmes story *Silver Blaise* to illustrate them. As Collier and many others point out, though, in real examples it is much harder to specify simply what form evidence actually takes in terms of the tests.

Briefly, the tests are as follows. *Straw in the wind* tests are neither distinctive nor precise and do not supply strong evidence for or against competing hypotheses; they merely provide evidence that is consistent with a hypothesis. *Hoop* tests use evidence that is precise, but not distinctive.[3] Failing a hoop test means a given hypothesis is wrong, so they are used to exclude potential explanations, but do not provide strong evidence for a given hypothesis. A standard example is the ability of a murder suspect to provide an alibi. If the suspect has an alibi, then the test is failed; having no alibi means they are still suspect but does not confirm guilt. *Smoking gun* tests provide evidence distinctive to the case and thus support the hypothesis; however, failing the test does not really undermine the explanation. A suspect having a smoking gun in their possession following a shooting seems strong evidence they are guilty; but not having the gun does not prove they are not guilty. *Doubly decisive* tests provide evidence that is precise and distinctive to the case—supplying direct evidence for a given claim—and thus can either support or undermine alternative explanations. Cabinet minutes, for example, provide very strong evidence of what a government thinks it was doing, and sometimes why, with some controversial measure.

These tests all seem rather clear when we have simple examples. However, the social sciences offer few real examples where the tests are so clearly laid out. Bennett (2008) uses two examples, the Fashoda crisis and Heinz Goemans's (2000) research on Germany and the end of World War I. But even his careful article does not precisely lay out the arguments of the research at issue in terms of the four tests. The precise relationship between the evidence he discusses and the four tests is left to the reader to work out. While the process-tracing tests are an interesting justification for the sorts of evidence that we use when making inferences in case-study research, in practical terms, qualitative researchers narrate their arguments presenting the evidence they see fitting their findings. Indeed Van Evera (1997, p. 32) suggests his four tests are the types of evidence we usually work with in historical analysis, but does not argue that we need to use them systematically. Later writers have suggested that qualitative researchers need to think more systematically about the nature of their evidence and establish it in the context of the four tests in order to argue their case.

We can add to the four tests Waldner's (2015) "completeness standard". The completeness standard says process tracing gives a causal explanation when it can provide (a) a causal graph whose nodes are jointly sufficient for some outcome and (b) an event-history map establishing a correspondence between the nodes and the events, together with (c) a theory about the causal mechanisms, in which (d) rival explanations are discounted by failing (a)–(c). Waldner's completeness standard is a very demanding test, which probably over-formalizes the nature of descriptive narrative history.

Some have represented the nature of additional qualitative evidence in Bayesian terms (Bennett 2008, 2015; Beach and Pedersen 2016, pp. 83–99; Humphreys and Jacobs 2015). The general idea of the Bayesian representation of process tracing is that sometimes thick, highly granular description provides more confidence in updating our prior beliefs about some causal process than simply adding an extra example to some high-n regression. That is correct. However, without some systematic method of measuring the difference that different types of evidence provide, the Bayesian justification is simply a metaphorical way of defending process tracing (Fairfield and Charman 2017, 2019; Gerring 2017). It does not offer a way of actually quantifying case-study evidence in probabilistic terms.

2. Mechanisms and Causation

Process tracers have emphasized that their approach looks for evidence of mechanisms, initially proposing it as an alternative form of explanation to the search for generalizations (George and Bennet 2005). At times the advantages of process tracing have been highlighted by its ability to find intervening variables between some causal factor C and some outcome E. The general idea seems to be that the precise details of the mechanism (or process) is contained in these intervening variables. Now, of course, if some factor C always results in E, then C can be said to cause E. The fact that there might be several routes from C to E does not impugn the causal claim unless the causal claim is backed by different theories (or mechanisms). Showing in a given example that one rather than another route was present shows only that one mechanism was present in this case rather than another. Process tracing examines which of several different mechanisms operate in any given case. A single case study can only show which mechanism operates in that case; one would have to study every extant case to see whether that mechanism is always the causal process. One cannot test across rival mechanisms with one case study; one can only see which mechanism is present for the case under study (Dowding 2020).

It is this type of analysis that leads some process tracers to claim that qualitative methods operate with a different ontology and understanding of causation from quantitative ones. Beach and Pedersen (2016) suggest that process tracers are interested in "actual causation" rather than counterfactual accounts of causation. What they seem to mean is that process tracers are interested in the actual conditions of a particular case, rather than the conditions that cause outcomes of that type. In my terms, they track proximate causes of tokens rather than structural (or ultimate) causes of types. Beach and Pedersen (2016) also suggest that process tracers are interested in the arrows in diagrams of causation (c → e), rather than the cause (C), which is what quantitative writers are concerned with.[4] George and Bennett (2005) had likewise suggested process tracers are interested in the detailed stages between some purported cause and outcome. I have termed this "bump-bump" causation (Dowding 2016). There are often many bumps between the outcome and the initial causes—the fourth car in line hits the third, which hits the second, which hits the first. But, if we want to know why the first car is damaged, it is the speed of the fourth that is relevant, even though the damage to the first is mediated by that caused to all the others. It is true we might well be interested in the intervening cars and how they acted and were damaged (especially if one of them was ours). However, this is not a rival account of causation, nor does it impugn any claim about the initial cause. It just adds more detail to a specific case.

George and Bennett suggest the same initial conditions and final outcome can have different processes between them, and social science is interested in that process. We are indeed often interested in the details. "Process" here is taken to mean "mechanism"—and I have been using that term in that way in the two paragraphs above. And what process tracers claim is that different mechanisms can lead to the same outcome. They are surely right. However, there is some ambiguity in the term "mechanism" here. George and Bennett (2005) mean by "mechanism" the different details of the story, using the idea of equifinality as many different paths to the same outcome. So different processes (mechanisms) can lead to the same outcome. However, equifinality is usually thought of as system predictability—a system whose behavior is predictable from more than one preceding system (or starting point). That predictability is seen in terms of one mechanism—natural selection, for example. The mechanism is the structural conditions that lead to the same type of outcome. Hereafter, I will use the term "process" for description of the proximate causes of token outcomes, and "mechanism" for what structures those processes to the type outcome.[5]

All we need to understand by this ambiguity over the term "mechanism" is that if we are interested in high-granularity accounts of a token case, then our research questions are different from those who are attempting to explain types of outcome. Proximate token explanation is not the same as structural type explanation. They are not necessarily rival. Case studies can tell us the details of different processes, and might tell us whether one purported type mechanism or another operates in a given case, but they cannot test whether or not either mechanism describes any case at all.

I have not formally defined what a mechanism is. There are numerous competing definitions (for a review, see Hedstrom and Ylikoski 2010 or Beach and Pedersen 2016). We can think of a model as something that describes a mechanism. Woodward (2003) provides the most complete account of this, summarized here by Hedstrom and Ylikoski (2010, table 1, p. 51):

> A model of a mechanism (a) describes an organized or structured set of parts or components, where (b) the behavior of each component is described by a generalization that is invariant under interventions, and where (c) the generalizations governing each component are also independently changeable, and where (d) the representation allows us to see how, by virtue of (a), (b), and (c), the overall output of the mechanism will vary under manipulation of the input to each component and changes in the components themselves

Invariant generalizations underlie the counterfactual effects of manipulation. But an important aspect of a mechanism or a process is that it is composed of entities and activities—the latter being the things that entities do (Craver 2006, p. 371). We can define activities, at least in part, by the manipulability of the variables—that is, we can alter the value of one variable in the description of the mechanism by manipulating another (Woodward 2003; Pearl 2009). Process tracing tries to systematically study a given historical process in order to identify the important aspects or variables in a process, to allow us to isolate the important components that lead to some social outcome. However, we must bear in mind that we can have different intervening variables—different processes—across different systems, that are still processes of the same mechanism at higher level of generality.

History is a narrative. What we choose to include in the narrative is, generally speaking, what we think important for the narrative structure. There might be asides that include interesting facts or snippets of information. There might be elements where we make normative comments on the action or, especially in books, set up background conditions for another part of the story. Generally speaking, however, what we think is important for the narrative structure is what we think is important in the causal story for the outcome that we are narrating. One problem with having a hypothesis about a particular case is that it creates "the honest detective's problem" (Dowding 2017a). Once the prime suspect has been identified, it is efficient for the police to look for evidence that would convict that suspect. That means evidence that might convict someone else is less likely to be discovered. This is a form of bias in all case-study research. Examining rival hypotheses can help mitigate this bias—we examine two suspects—though there is still the danger that as one becomes frontrunner, evidence in its favor is emphasized.

Causation is much discussed, and here is not the place to discuss different accounts of causation in any detail. A very general account of causation, and that which most historians seem to have in mind, is a "but for" account. "But for" accounts are elucidated in detail in various forms of necessary and sufficient conditions, such as INUS (insufficient but nonredundant components of unnecessary but sufficient condition; Mackie 1974) or NESS tests (necessary element of a sufficient set of conditions; Wright 1985, 1988). Described at some level of granularity, no INUS condition is either individually necessary or individually sufficient for an outcome, but each is a non-redundant element of the sufficient set for that outcome. Any set of conditions sufficient for an outcome is composed of either necessary or INUS conditions. A NESS test looks for the necessary element of a sufficient set of conditions for the outcome. Both of these characterizations focus upon each element of a cause. When we analyze any outcome, however, we do not treat all these INUS or NESS conditions equally. Some we background, and some we concentrate on, for our explanation, as the cause. In a historical narrative, the choices we make in terms of what we background and what we foreground determine what we consider to be the important causal story in the process that we are addressing.

3. ANALOGY WITH EXPERIMENTS

If we do not accept that process tracing requires a different notion of causation, we can discuss it in direct relation to those approaches which provide the cleanest way of making causal inferences. That is, experiments where we can manipulate the variables—in experimental terminology, provide interventions—to directly measure causal effects.[6]

We know that for any outcome what happened earlier was sufficient for that outcome to occur. However, many of those conditions were not necessary for the outcome we are studying. Some are necessary for that outcome, but also necessary for other outcomes that we wish to distinguish from the outcome we are studying. Elections are necessary for any party to win an election, but we are not interested in "the election being called" for why the Labor Party rather than the Liberal Party wins a given election; rather, we are interested in the conditions that led to that victory. To be sure, choosing the date might sometimes be important (if they had called it earlier the governing party might not have lost, for example). However, the fact of elections, while necessary, is irrelevant to our consideration of who wins. We thus ignore necessary conditions that are of too high a level of generality for the outcome as denoted, as well as those not necessary for our outcome. Social science then concentrates upon the important elements of those that are necessary for the outcome specified by our research question. In other words, our specific research question denotes both the factors that are important to the explanation we offer and, importantly, the level of analysis.

Process tracing is not an alternative to high-n studies because a case study cannot answer the sorts of questions addressed by high-n quantitative analysis, addressed at explaining types of phenomena (Dowding 2016). Case studies can only examine whether a given mechanism applies to that case or trace the proximate elements (the specific process) in the type mechanism (Dowding 2020). But process tracing offers superior explanations of token phenomena, as it answers questions that address that phenomenon in much more detail. However, even at the finest-grained level of explanation, we still need to choose the important elements that enter our proffered explanation of an event or institution.

But how do we choose the "important elements"? We can think about them in terms of the stability of the elements that enter into the explanation. Some elements will be more robust or stable across changing context than others, and we tend to be interested in these. First, we ignore background circumstances—that is, those conditions not explicitly represented in the c–e relationship we are studying. In experimental conditions, for example, c is the intervention and e the outcome we observe, and the experimental setup can be considered as the background circumstances held constant during the experiment. Outside of the laboratory, we have no sharp distinction between the background conditions and the intervention. However, for any analysis we have to make some assumptions about what we are considering background conditions and what we are thinking of as the causes (interventions) that create the outcomes we observe. Sometimes debates in social science revolve around whether a researcher has made the right choices here. Such debates might concern the correct level of analysis for a specific outcome or the stability of the background itself.

The correct level of analysis is concerned with whether or not we are attempting to explain some general phenomenon—the type—or whether we are examining the precise process in a given (token) example. Tokens are examples of a given type; importantly, though, not only will all tokens *not* share all of their features with each other, there need be *no* feature that is distinctive of a type that is common to all token examples (Wetzel 2009; Dowding 2016). The fact that we can demonstrate for a particular case study that some key decisions made by some agents were important to the precise outcomes of that case does not mean that more general claims made about cases of that type are not true of the type including that token example. Claims about the type which are foregrounded (seen as the important causal features) might be only background conditions of the token when considered in detail. Descriptions of tokens are much more detailed, of a higher granularity, than of types. And it is the detail we are interested in that distinguishes our case study example from others of that type.

After all, predictions can be about types or tokens. A prediction about a token item will give us our expectations about what we will see *in that case*. It will establish the probability of what we expect to see in that case. But if there are many cases, then it will tell us what we expect in each of those cases and, if it is probabilistic, the distribution of expected outcomes over those cases. We might examine a token in order to see what we can learn about the type, and how it transfers to other tokens within that type. The claim made about highly detailed studies of such tokens is that this evidence is of higher quality and should be given more weight in our considerations. However, it might have more weight in consideration of the proximate cause of that particular example, but it does not follow that it is true of the type, unless it can be shown that all members of the type share the same feature with that case study. Keeping in mind the level of the analysis, and how evidence bears in higher levels (less granular descriptions of types), can allow us to see that some claims in social science are not incompatible as they are sometimes thought to be.

Reflecting on the stability of the background conditions, consider again interventions in the laboratory. We often make the distinction between the internal and the external validity of an experimental setup. An experiment is said to be internally invalid if a poor experimental arrangement impugns causal inference. External validity concerns the generalizability of findings. Given that an experiment is internally valid, how far do the results apply more broadly outside the experimental setting? A given internally valid experimental result is externally invalid at least where (1) the outcome is unstable with any slight change in the background conditions of the experiment and/or (2) when those conditions rarely hold precisely outside the laboratory. With any given case study, the precise conditions only apply to the case itself, so the second condition is not important for claims made about the proximate causes in that particular case (unless, of course, claims are extended from that case to other cases of that type). However, the first condition, the stability of the outcome regardless of varying background conditions, is important to any claim about the specific causal claims of that case.

The importance of any causal claim, C, varies with the stability of E, with regard to changes in the background conditions. The narrower the set of changes in the background conditions and the degree of their contingency will condition E's stability. Thus, when we are making causal claims in a case study, we are claiming that we have identified a cause c, where the counterfactual dependence of e on c is stable within a range of background circumstances that differ from the specific circumstances of c. Often when debate rages over a claim to have identified some c, the critics are pointing out that c's relationship to e is unstable with regard to some other factors c^*, c^{**}, and c^{***} they have identified. Without wanting to dismiss such debates, we can point out that they address the importance of the c's *relative to one another*. They are not questioning the causal implication of C with regard to E; rather, they are querying the detail of c's importance in this case. And that importance can be represented by claims about the stability of the background conditions. After all, saying that a given background condition only needs to vary slightly in order to reach a different outcome is to make the claim that it is an important causal condition. This means, slightly paradoxically, that a given causal claim for a specific case study might not have external validity for the very case that is being studied.[7]

Now the C factors we are interested in when considering a given case are ones that concern the proximate causes of an event. General theories, including those couched in the form of mechanisms, concern the ultimate or structural causes of outcomes. They concern what cause outcomes of this type, in the knowledge that the precise working through of the mechanism might have varying proximate causes. That is what is entailed by the idea of equifinality. Equifinality suggests that, for a given causal process, from different initial conditions, the same type of outcome will occur (Bertalanffy 1968). The precise elements—the bump-bump causal process—will vary across different token examples of the type, but the structure of the mechanism ensures that the same type of outcomes will accrue. Of course, at finer-grained description, that same type of outcome will have different characteristics—that is, different processes—but at the coarser description they are of the same type. Critics of a specific case study are often interested in the differences at the finer level of description, and for that reason they are interested in the proximate, bump-bump, causal process. But even here, however, we are still interested in the stability of the background conditions when we are describing what is important in proximate causal process. We have to pick out what we think are the important elements in our historical description; we do not describe everything.

So historical process tracing is an explanation given at the token level to provide a proximate causal explanation of a given case. The mechanics of process tracing as a methodology are Van Evera's four tests, designed to demonstrate how strong our causal inferences are, given the evidence we procure. They are designed to explain the unique case we are studying and to highlight these stability issues. However, we also need to see that uniqueness can mean different things with regard to any case study. For example, some people claim that all human events are unique and hence we cannot explain them as we do natural phenomena. If by that they mean that every social outcome has its own proximate (bump-bump) causal process, they are right: each such event is individuated differently. But then, so is every individuated event in natural processes. All events can be uniquely individuated by space–time coordinates (Fetzer 1975; Tucker 1998, p. 62). So, if they mean that this trivial truth about individuation entails that we can give no structural (or ultimate) causal story of types of which this example is a token, they are simply wrong. They are confusing claims made at different levels of analysis. However, they might mean that human events are unique in a stronger sense. For some events the claim might be that there are no actual individuated events of that type other than the one under consideration.

What does uniqueness in this sense mean? And what does it entail for our explanatory claims? If a case study is of a "unique" event in this second sense, then the proximate explanation will also be unique. No other actual events are like this one. However, it is does not follow that there is no structural explanation of the type of event of which this token constitutes an example. We can still consider such unique events to be tokens of a given class, where the other tokens in the class are not actual. Here the class would be given in terms of the stability of the background conditions to the specific C that is being investigated with regard to the purported explanation of E.

Of course, we might be claiming that the important element of some outcome E is that that specific outcome is highly unlikely and only came about because of the convergence of an (actually) unique set of precursors. If we could play that event over and over again, the actual outcome would rarely come about. Imagine repeating a specific scenario time and again in some computer simulation, especially where we do not fully understand the process or mechanism going on because of the complexity of the model. (Not "fully understand" here means we cannot mathematically model it at the granularity required to produce stable predictions.) Some of the interactions in the model at the limits of appropriate granularity are probabilistic, such that the same outcome will not occur if the model was played time and again. At best, we can give some probability distributions over given outcomes. Having done so, we find that the actual outcome is highly unlikely—say it comes about only 1/10,000 runs. All we can say is that this outcome is highly unlikely. What we might claim, following a very detailed examination of the case, is that specific, highly risky decisions, made by specific actors, led to the outcome.

Social scientists generally try to provide type-level explanations that are highly likely. They look for empirical generalizations and they theorize mechanisms to explain those generalizations. One form of historical explanation is to look for the unlikely. Some historians are specifically interested in individuals who make a difference—in Napoleon, Churchill, Stalin. These people might be special and therefore important in any causal story. Indeed, it seems that strong leaders are often those who take risks early in their careers, often against the interests of their core supporters (Dowding 2017b, ch. 8). The very fact that early on they took risky decisions that cemented their positions demonstrates the unlikeliness of the process described. The counterfactual question often takes such individuals out of the picture and asks how history would otherwise be. Those who see history as determined by social and economic structures tend to think history would not be so different without these characters; others, especially those interested in the details, believe such individuals are key elements in historical change. Historians tend to be interested in detail—high granularity of the token—while social scientists tend to be interested in the general form—low granularity of the type. These are two different forms of analysis, asking different questions, and both are important in their own right.

One danger of detailed story telling that defends some general mechanism at play is that we end up telling "just so stories" (Evangelista 2015, loc 3917). What is the problem with "just so stories"? Stephen Jay Gould's criticism was applied to evolutionary thinking where we find some characteristic of a creature and tell some story about how that characteristic confers some evolutionary advantage or is some holdover from some previous fitness advantage. Gould suggests that there might be "spandrels" that never served any purpose, but also never detracted enough from the animal's fitness to be eliminated (Gould and Lewontin 1979; Gould 1997). In that sense, a "just so story" is simply another name for a hypothesis—but one that cannot be adequately tested. The tests of process tracing are intended to enable us to make judgments about hypotheses, and to suggest where we might look for evidence. The problem with unique events such as "the end of the Cold War," is that hypotheses about which particular contributing events are necessary and jointly sufficient for the outcome cannot be directly tested. We cannot run the ending of the Cold War again. The four process-tracing tests, along with Waldner's (2015) "completeness standard," are there to see which mechanism seems to best fit the narrative.

4. CRITICAL JUNCTURES

The idea of critical junctures is not, strictly speaking, part of the methodology of process tracing. To some extent, it is part of a theoretical tradition associated with historical institutionalism that argues that societies take on their different forms because of path-dependencies given specific decisions or historical moments. Critical junctures mark the change from one institutional form to another. They are usually thought to involve major institutional changes, which are distinct from what went before and result in an enduring legacy. They are relevant to this discussion because a critical juncture is, by definition, an important causal factor in some broader claim about the nature of what we see as an important outcome. A great deal of literature is concerned with defining precisely what is meant by a critical juncture (for example, Soiffer 2012; Collier and Munck 2017; Stark 2018). How do we distinguish the critical juncture from other aspects of the history? delineate it from other events? separate antecedent conditions from the juncture itself? and how do we bound the concept?

In fact, I do not think we need worry too much about these elements at all. Any distinction between the antecedent conditions and the critical juncture itself, or discussion of how long was the critical juncture between the former institutional arrangements and the new ones, are simply verbal disputes over coding decisions. To be sure, some changes—for example, constitutional amendments—can be given precise dates and forms, though their impact on society might be less susceptible to precision. However, most critical junctures have fluid boundaries. It is rare that any critical juncture would be recognized by those living through it. Interest in critical junctures, and enduring debates over claims about them, usually derive from the way in which they are used to defend theoretical claims about types of mechanisms. Criticisms are usually at lower levels of granularity concerning the precise details of the purported mechanism and nature of the specific critical juncture in different societies. The theoretical claims are made at high generality, the critics concentrating upon details. Or the claim is that a specific episode, identified as a critical juncture leaving an enduring legacy, is not the full story and in fact change was slower and more incremental. Questions of determinacy and contingency are often involved in these disputes. Here the issue is the underlying theoretical basis of historical institutionalism, where path-dependency suggests determined outcomes, but incremental rather than single-event junctures indicate that the changes are more contingent than path-dependency suggests.

All of these issues can be seen in terms of the stability of the background conditions relative to the foregrounded explanation. There is really little point in trying to carefully define what constitutes a critical juncture, what makes something incremental rather than a radical change, or whether the process really was determined from some point in time or was more contingent. As long as we are aware of the relevant levels of analysis and use our evidence to suggest, for any given narrative, what should be foregrounded in terms of the stability of the background conditions, we can keep in mind the general claims being made. Far too often, competing theories or narratives are pitted against each other, when they are not rival at all.

5. CONCLUSION

Process tracing is designed to make qualitative historical description more systematic and better able to make secure causal claims. Historical narrative necessarily involves making causal linkages, but the four tests of process tracing are designed to make researchers carefully consider the nature of the evidence they offer. We can represent this in a Bayesian framework; but without actually measuring our probabilistic inferences, that framework is simply justificatory and not methodological. Process tracing is designed to examine the process of changes. It should not be confused with the idea of type-level mechanism—though, of course, the process can be a token example of such a mechanism. I suggest the term "process" be used to describe the detailed examination of token cases, and "mechanism" be reserved for the type-level low-granularity description.

There is no need to think of process tracing as using a rival account of causation to that of high-n statistical analysis. The decision to forefront some aspects of the causal process as "causes" and others as background conditions can be made in terms of the stability of the outcomes to changes in those foregrounded and those backgrounded. We can draw an analogy with the internal validity and external validity of experiments. Researchers should not waste too much time defining what aspects of their study are critical junctures or how incremental processes really are. Many of these debates are really about whether the correct decisions have been made to foreground some aspects of the narrative and what level of granularity we think appropriate to the research question being addressed.

Process tracing is a valuable methodology for the social sciences, but has attracted too much attention to ontological and epistemological questions over its explanatory status. These issues can be more easily seen in terms of the type–token distinction and of the historical-proximate or structural-ultimate nature of the explanations offered in different accounts. Different answers to similar questions are not necessarily rival once it is realized that those questions are addressed to different levels of analysis and thus require answers appropriate to that level.

Notes

1. I use the term "outcome" or sometimes "E" (for effect) in a broad sense to stand for some event or institution.
2. I use "structural" and "ultimate" interchangeably. In Dowding (2016) I adopted the term "ultimate" from biology, as "structural" can have rather different meanings in social science, and I thought "ultimate" came with less verbal baggage. Then about the time my book came out I read Kitcher (2003, ch. 4, loc 2213), who recommends to biologists that they ought to use the term "structural" rather than "ultimate," since that latter term seems to downgrade the worth of "proximate explanation" or what he prefers to call "historical explanation"! What really matters is the distinction, not how we label it.
3. Van Evera (1997, p. 31) uses the term "certain" rather than precise, but means by that "unequivocal forecast." I prefer "precise," since "certain" could be taken to mean 'determined'. He also uses the term 'unique' where I use "distinctive." He says "A *unique* prediction is a forecast not made by other known theories. The more unique the prediction, the stronger the test" (Van Evera 1997, p. 31). I prefer to use the term "distinctive" since below, with regard to case studies, I discuss the nature of uniqueness in a rather different sense.
4. I'm using lower case "c" and "e" for tokens and upper case "C" and "E" for type here.
5. The dictionary definitions of process and mechanism are very similar. According to the Oxford English Dictionary, the most common use of "process" is "A continuous and regular action or succession of actions occurring or performed in a definite manner, and having a particular result or outcome; a sustained operation or series of operations," whilst a mechanism is "a system of mutually adapted parts working together in a machine or in a manner analogous to that of a machine."

6. Gerring and McDermott (2007) draw analogies between case studies and experiments, but in a much more general manner than I do here.
7. The originator of the internal/external validity distinction of experiments, Donald Campbell (in Campbell and Stanley 1963), later regretted making the distinction in the manner he did as he felt it takes on too much importance in many discussions of causal inference from experimental results (Campbell 1986); this is my version of the reason. We make assumptions about the stability of backgrounds, both in the experimental setup and in application. My slightly paradoxical way of setting up the issue brings that out.

References

Beach, Derek, and Rasmus Brun Pedersen. 2016. *Causal Case Study Methods: Foundations and Guidelines for Comparing, Matching, and Tracing.* Ann Abor, MI: University of Michigan Press.

Bennett, Andrew. 2008. "Process Tracing: A Bayesian Perspective." In *The Oxford Handbook of Political Methodology*, edited by Janet M. Box-Steffensmeier, Henry E. Brady, and David Collier, 1–23. Oxford: Oxford University Press.

Bennett, Andrew. 2010. "Process Tracing and Causal Inference." In *Rethinking Social Inquiry: Diverse Tools, Shared Standards*, edited by Henry E. Brady and David Collier, 2nd ed., 207–219. New York: Oxford University Press.

Bennett, Andrew. 2015. "Appendix: Disciplining Our Conjectures: Systematizing Process Tracing with Bayesian Analysis." In *Process Tracing: From Metaphor to Analytic Tool*, in Andrew Bennett and Jeffrey T. Checkel (eds.), 276–298. Cambridge: Cambridge University Press.

Bennett, Andrew, and Jeffrey T. Checkel. 2015a. "Process Tracing: From Philosophical Roots to Best Practices." In *Process Tracing: From Metaphor to Analytic Tool*, Andrew Bennett and Jeffrey T. Checkel (eds), 3–37. Cambridge: Cambridge University Press.

Bennett, Andrew, and Jeffrey T. Checkel. 2015b. *Process Tracing: From Metaphor to Analytic Tool*. Cambridge: Cambridge University Press.

Bertalanffy, Ludwig von. 1968. *General Systems Theory: Foundations, Development, Applications*. New York: George Braziller.

Campbell, D. T. 1986. "Relabelling Internal and External Validity for Applied Social Scientists." In *Advances in Quasi-Experimental Design and Analysis*, W. M. K. Trochim (ed), 67–77. San Francisco, CA: Jossey-Bass.

Campbell, Donald T., and Julian C. Stanley. 1963. *Experimental and Quasi-Experimental Designs for Research*. Boston, MA: Houghton Mifflin.

Collier, David. 2011. "Understanding Process Tracing." *PS: Political Science and Politics* 44 (4): 823–830.

Collier, David, and Gerardo L. Munck. 2017. "Building Blocks and Methodological Challenges: A Framework for Studying Critical Junctures." *Qualitative and Multi-Method Research* 15 (1): 2–9.

Craver, Carl F. 2006. "When Mechanistic Models Explain." *Synthese* 154: 355–376.

Dowding, Keith. 2016. *The Philosophy and Methods of Political Science*. London: Palgrave.

Dowding, Keith. 2017a. *Power, Luck and Freedom: Collected Essays*. Manchester: Manchester University Press.

Dowding, Keith. 2017b. "So Much to Say: Response to Commentators." *Political Studies Review* 15: 217–230.

Dowding, Keith. 2020. "Can a Case-Study Test a Theory? Types and Tokens in Social Explanation." In *Handbook of Methods for Comparative Policy Analysis*, B. Guy Peters and Guillaume Fontaine (eds), 48–64. Aldershot: Edward Elgar.

Evangelista, Matthew. 2015. "Explaining the Cold War's End: Process Tracing All the Way Down?" In *Process Tracing: From Metaphor to Analytic Tool*, in Andrew Bennett and Jeffrey T. Checkel (eds), 153–185. Cambridge: Cambridge University Press.

Fairfield, Tasha, and Andrew E. Charman. 2017. "Explicit Bayesian Analysis for Process Tracing: Guidelines, Opportunities, and Caveats." *Political Analysis* 25 (3): 363–380.

Fairfield, Tasha, and Andrew E. Charman 2019. "A Dialogue with the Data: The Bayesian Foundations of Iterative Research in Qualitative Social Science." *Perspectives on Politics* 17 (1): 154–167.

Fetzer, James H. 1975. "On the Historical Explanation of Unique Events." *Theory and Decision* 6 (1): 87–97.

George, Alexander L. 1979. "Case Studies and Theory Development: The Method of Structured, Focused Comparison." In *Diplomacy: New Approaches in History, Theory and Policy*, edited by Paul Gordon Lauren, 43–68. New York: Free Press.

George, Alexander L., and Andrew Bennett. 2005. *Case Studies and Theory Development in the Social Sciences*. Cambridge, MA: MIT Press.

Gerring, John. 2017. "Qualitative Methods." *Annual Reviews of Political Science* 20: 15–36.

Gerring, John, and Rose McDermott. 2007. "An Experimental Template for Case Study Research." *American Journal of Political Science* 51 (3): 688–701.

Goemans, Heinz. 2000. *War and Punishment: The Causes of War Termination and the First World War*. Princeton, NJ: Princeton University Press.

Gould, Stephen Jay. 1997. "The Exaptive Excellence of Spandrels as a Term and a Prototype." *Proceedings of the National Academy of Sciences USA* 94: 10750–10755.

Gould, Stephen Jay, and Richard C. Lewontin. 1979. "The Spandrels of San Marco and the Panglossian Paradigm: A Critique of the Adaptationist Programme." *Proceedings of the Royal Society London* 205 (1161): 581–598.

Hedstrom, Peter, and Petri Ylikoski. 2010. "Causal Mechanisms in the Social Sciences." *Annual Review of Sociology* 36: 49–67.

Humphreys, Macartan, and Alan M. Jacobs. 2015. "Mixing Methods: A Bayesian Approach." *American Political Science Review* 109 (4): 653–673.

Kitcher, Philip. 2003. *In Mendel's Mirror: Philosophical Reflections on Biology*. Oxford: Oxford University Press.

Mackie, John L. 1974. *The Cement of the Universe: A Study in Causation*. Oxford: Clarendon Press.

Pearl, Judea. 2009. *Causality: Models, Reasoning and Inference*. 2nd edition. Cambridge: Cambridge University Press.

Soiffer, Hillel David. 2012. "The Causal Logic of Critical Junctures." *Comparative Political Studies* 45 (12): 1572–1598.

Stark, Alistair. 2018. "New Institutionalism, Critical Junctures and Post-Crisis Policy Reform." *Australian Journal of Political Science* 53 (1): 24–39.

Tucker, Aviezer. 1998. "Unique Events: The Underdetermination of Explanation." *Erkenntnis* 48: 59–80.

Van Evera, Stephen. 1997. *Guide to Methods for Students of Political Science*. Ithaca, NY: Cornell University Press.

Waldner, David. 2012. "Process Tracing and Causal Mechanisms." In *Oxford Handbook of the Philosophy of Social Science*, Harold Kincaid (eds), 65–84. Oxford: Oxford University Press.

Waldner, David. 2015. "What Makes Process Tracing Good? Causal Mechanisms, Causal Inference, and the Completeness Standard in Comparative Politics." In *Process Tracing: From Metaphor to Analytic Tool*, in Andrew Bennett and Jeffrey T. Checkel (eds), 126–152. Cambridge: Cambridge University Press.

Wetzel, Linda. 2009. *Types and Tokens: On Abstract Objects*. Cambridge: Cambridge University Press.

Woodward, James. 2003. *Making Things Happen: A Theory of Causal Explanation*. Oxford: Oxford University Press.

Wright, Richard. 1985. "Causation in Tort Law." *California Law Review* 73: 1735–1828.

Wright, Richard. 1988. "Causation, Responsibility, Risk, Probability, Naked Statistics, and Proof: Pruning the Bramble Bush by Clarifying the Concepts." *Iowa Law Review* 73: 1001–1077.

....

CHAPTER 17

RANDOMIZED INTERVENTIONS IN POLITICAL SCIENCE
Are the Critics Right?

....

PETER JOHN

RANDOMIZED interventions—often called randomized controlled trials (RCTs) or just trials—have become the research tool of choice for many political scientists, appearing frequently in the subfields of political behavior (de Rooij, Green, and Gerber 2009), the political economy of development (Humphreys and Weinstein 2009), and elites (Grose 2014), as well as becoming more common in other areas of the discipline (Druckman et al. 2006; Morton and Williams 2010; Druckman et al. 2011; Gerber and Green 2012; John 2017). This rapid increase in attention to randomized controlled trials since the late-1990s parallels their development in other parts of the social sciences, such as policy evaluation and applied economics (Glennerster and Takavarasha 2013), largely because scholars have rediscovered the unique advantage of this method. By ruling out the influence of both observed and unobserved factors determining an outcome other than the variable of interest, RCTs have given researchers a high degree of leverage to make causal claims for the impact of interventions.

Along with the enthusiasm, however, have emerged critical assessments (Heckman 1991; Heckman and Smith 1995; Cartwright 2007; Deaton 2010; G. W. Harrison 2011; Cartwright and Hardie 2012; G. W. Harrison 2013; Deaton and Cartwright 2018), echoing an older critique from realist epistemology (Pawson and Tilley 1997). These skeptical views largely come from outside political science (for an exception, see the debate in Teele 2014), either from the philosophy of science or from those who work in economics and evaluation fields. The critics home in on the limits to the method, questioning the knowledge claims of trials and their assumption of superiority in internal validity as well as making the more familiar attack on external validity. There is also a concern that RCTs restrict hypotheses to those that are testable, which limits the range of admissible policies or processes that can be investigated and so only advances knowledge for very particular kinds of activity, which leaves unanswered some very important questions, such as whether democracies go to war with each other or the impact of changing an electoral system. The result could be the biasing of the field of political science as a whole. On top of these concerns is a worry about the ethics of doing trials. Critics highlight the need to respect human autonomy as RCTs can harm people whose manipulation is needed in the research process (Desposato 2015). These are philosophical criticisms as well as practical ones about the use of the method. The aim of this chapter is to explore and assess such issues while at the same reviewing the extensive commentary on randomized controlled trials.

The chapter presents the argument that, in spite of asking good questions and raising many relevant points that political scientists should definitely consider when they use trials, many of the criticisms directed against trials go too far or are misplaced. The points made by critics are more about the limits to knowledge in the social sciences in general rather than concern trials in particular. While the criticisms rightly prune the excesses of the claims of the enthusiast and triumphalist—sometimes called the *randomista*—this position is not typical of the users of trials in political science, who are usually researchers working in critical communities of other skeptical scholars. The practical use of the trials is much more like an extension of normal science than a complete transformation of research methods.

The structure of this essay is as follows: Section 1 is on the background, describing what trials are and introducing the statistical framework that explains their claim to causal inference; Section 2 describes some examples of important trials in political science and how this method has gathered pace in recent years; Section 3 sets out the empirical critique and seeks to respond to it; Section 4 discusses and responds to the normative critique; and the conclusion sums up the current state of the debate about trials.

1. What Are Experiments?

Experiments occur when human beings manipulate the world to understand causal relationships.[1] They are a common means by which scientists acquire knowledge. The secret is to have precise control over the different elements of interventions and to measure carefully what happens during experiments. It is this degree of control over the external world that is the big attraction of experiments, which explains why researchers from outside the natural sciences seek to emulate the method. By intervening as well as observing experiments unlock knowledge in ways that cannot be fully achieved by observation alone.

In the social sciences, the researcher or policy-maker looks for or creates some random or chance variation that ensures that the difference in outcomes is only associated with an intervention or policy compared to the status quo. In what is called natural experiments, accidental differences between populations or areas that have been created by government or by nature, such as the impact of boundaries or cut-offs for eligibility in a policy program, may be thought of as if they were random (see Dunning 2012). Sometimes randomness happens directly, such as in a government decision or institutional rule that can be evaluated like an experiment, for example when the US government used a lottery to select conscripts to fight in the Vietnam war, which allowed for tests of the impact of military service on political behavior and attitudes (Erikson and Stoker 2011). More often, researchers and policymakers create the random variation themselves. This method is sometimes called artificial randomization, but it is more commonly known as randomized controlled trials or RCTs, whereby individuals or communities or other units are randomly allocated to two or more groups. In this procedure, one or more groups get an intervention while another group, the control, does not. A comparison can be made between the outcomes in these groups to see if the intervention (also commonly called the treatment) made an impact (a placebo may also be used instead of or in addition to the control group). If there are at least two comparison groups where one group receives an intervention while another does not—or gets a different intervention—and if assignment to these groups is random, then it is possible to make an inference that the difference in outcomes between the groups—other than random variation—has only been caused by the intervention.

This kind of method is sometimes known as field experiments, which are done in the community at large or within organizations (Harrison and List 2004). They may be contrasted with laboratory experiments done in controlled settings (excepting the hybrid form called "lab in the field" where laboratory experiments are done in the field). The field element is aimed to create real world constraints and opportunities from the intervention and is often thought to contrast favorably with the lack of full realism of the lab though field experiments can suffer from artificiality too (see Heckman and Smith 1995). There are four main stages to field trials. First, is the selection of the sample, which involves finding the relevant population from which researchers can answer their research questions. Second, researchers or policymakers randomize the units of the sample—for instance people—into groups. Third, the policy, program, or intervention is applied to one group, leaving the other group alone or just with a normal service or state of affairs, or with another program. Fourth, and finally, outcomes are measured after interventions take place (which can also be done at the start to compare change over time). In this outline, the design is quite simple, which is one of the attractions of doing trials.

Of course, trials can get complicated very quickly, not least in their design. It is possible to have many intervention groups that allow for multiple or several comparisons. Normally randomization takes place across people or other units at the start of a trial, but trials can have several stages with further randomizations that create new intervention groups or randomize the same people into different groups over time. Further, there are different kinds of randomization, such as when people or units are sorted into pairs and one person or unit out of each pair is picked randomly. Nonetheless, even with these variations, the idea of comparing outcomes across randomly allocated groups remains recognizable even in the most complex designs.

One of the most attractive features of trials is that they can offer a clear test of a hypothesis, usually resulting in either a clear yes or no to research questions. They also can quantify the impact of the intervention in measures of effect size or percentage-point changes, which can be very useful in policy evaluation where costs and benefits of interventions need to be assessed. Moreover, if enough high-quality trials are done, it is possible to conclude that the findings can be generalized across places and time periods. It is this claim to answer questions about causation that is the main appeal of trials and explains why they have become so popular in recent years.

It might sound surprising that the social sciences, which started using advanced statistical methods in earnest from the 1940s, should still want better leverage on causal questions. It is very hard to make causal inferences in social research, even when there is a very strong theory about the determinants of a particular outcome and good measurements of what might cause it. This weakness occurs because it is not possible to rule out with certainty factors other than the hypothesized one that caused the outcome of interest or to confirm the direction of causation in a correlation. In social science, as it has been practiced over the last fifty years or so, it is common to observe the simultaneous occurrence of an influencing and influenced variable and to measure its association. Take the example of canvassing a household by speaking to them face-to-face to persuade them to vote in an upcoming election—what is called a Get Out the Vote (GOTV) campaign (Green and Gerber 2019). The research question is whether canvassing causes members of the household to turn out to vote. There are various methods that could be used to test such a proposition. If there were data from a survey available that measured whether the respondents could recall having voted and having being canvassed, it would be possible to correlate or associate the two measures. It may be the case that the political parties keep records of which people they have canvassed that can be tied to the publicly available electoral registers. It is very likely there is a positive relationship. However, it is not possible to rule out other factors that may cause people to turn out to vote are also correlated with being canvassed. The correlation between the two is just that and does not represent a causal relationship from canvassing to turnout.

Researchers who analyze observational data have been aware of the problem of establishing causation for a long time. They have developed a number of strategies to overcome it through the application of advanced statistical models, such as using panel regression models where units vary over time and where within unit heterogeneity can be controlled for in fixed-effects statistical models. Yet it may still be possible that the researcher misses an alternative explanation, making the causal inference hard to support even when time-varying measures have been used as controls. It is often said that the relationship is confounded or that there are confounders in play, that is, factors associated with both the intervention and the outcome are being evaluated. The researcher can only guess what they are and cannot effectively control for them as they are unobserved.

For evaluation questions, another problem is that the outcomes for individuals or units will vary over time in any case. They might get worse or better in ways that follow a natural cycle, such as finding a job, becoming healthier, or the opposite. In this case, all the program or intervention picks up is what would have happened anyway. There needs to be a counterfactual, which is the state of affairs that would have occurred in absence of the program. In all these circumstances, it is important to have a method that rules out determinants of an outcome other than the intervention. Randomization generates the counterfactual of what would have happened without the intervention, such as between canvassed and noncanvassed individuals or households as in the GOTV example.

Even though trials can yield causal inferences, they can only do so if implemented correctly, in particular an experiment should be delivered in a way that respects its assumptions. The starting point for an experiment is that it is not possible in any one individual to observe both the intervention or manipulation and thus the counterfactual. It is better to speak of "potential outcomes" that represent the outcomes for an individual had they received the treatment or control respectively. Because the counterfactual is not directly observed, it is necessary to build in assumptions when working out what causes the difference in outcomes between people or units that are in the treatment and control group (Rubin 1974). It is possible to work through these assumptions to show how a randomized controlled trial can give a true estimate of the effect of the treatment (for a summary, see Gerber and Green 2012, 21–44). This formulation is what is referred to as causal inference or Rubin's causal model (RCM) or the Neyman–Rubin causal model.

The key assumptions are excludability—that the randomly assigned units only get the treatment and the control units do not—and noninterference—that that randomly assigned units do not affect each other (sometimes called the Stable Unit Treatment Value Assumption, or SUTVA). By remembering these assumptions, the researcher knows that trial designs need to have certain features, in particular that random allocation should be respected throughout the implementation process.

2. The Use of Trials in Political Science

The use of field experiments to evaluate research questions took hold in the 1920s in the work of Fisher (e.g. Fisher 1926), which found expression is his famous book, *The Design of Experiments* (Fisher 1935). Linked to their popularity in studies of agriculture, public policy, social policy and of course health, a number of experiments were carried out by political scientists at this time, such as Gosnell's GOTV experiments (Gosnell 1926, 1927). As Morton and Williams (2010, 6) point out, there are a number of other early experiments, such as Lund's manipulation of arguments in a political debate (Lund 1925). Hartmann's (1936) compared the emotional effects of leaflets in the 1935 election, which was done in the field. In the post-1945 period, there continued an interest in experiments with those from a background in psychology, such as Iyengar and Kinder's (1987) experiments testing for media influence, and a number of voting studies (e.g. Adams and Smith 1980).

In spite of these examples and the massive expansion of the use of trials in medical and health sciences, it was not until the late 1990s that they were fully rediscovered by political scientists (Druckman et al. 2006). The current interest in field experiments was stimulated by the landmark study conducted at Yale University by Gerber and Green (2000), which launched a large number of experimental studies of voter turnout (Green and Gerber 2015), encouraging the diffusion of trials into other areas in political science. Topics include radio broadcasts, campaign spending, positive and negative campaign messages, television campaign advertisements, and internet advertisements (for a full review of these fields and more background on the history, see John 2017).

3. The Empirical Critique

The critical approach to the use of trials in the social sciences is based on a careful examination their claims for superiority in establishing causation. A key distinction is between internal validity and external validity. Trials are supposed to be good at the former, but tend not to be so good at the latter. This is not a controversial position to take, but critics of trials seek to limit very strongly the external validity claims while at the same time setting out the very special conditions under which trials can also be internally valid. Few critics reject trials altogether, but they want to limit use of the method to answering only a few research questions.

A good starting place is the strong critique of RCTs made by Pawson and Tilly (1997). These two authors come from the policy evaluation world in the UK, and are well known in social policy and policy analysis circles; but most political scientists have probably not heard of them. Their arguments are of interest for this discussion because they home in on the philosophy of science, which tends not to be discussed by political scientists, possibly because the relative lack of attention to these questions within the discipline as a whole (which this volume hopes to correct). In their account of realist evaluation, Pawson and Tilly are probably the strongest critics of trials highlighting "its weakness at *science*" (1997, 30, their emphasis). They argue that trialists have not acknowledged the difference between secessionist and generative accounts of causation. The former is about ascertaining causes from the prevalence of factors prior to the cause; the latter is closer to experiments in the natural sciences whereby causation is ascertained by understanding the mechanisms involved. The latter is consistent with a realist account of knowledge gathering that might depend on many sources and exploring the complex relationship between context, mechanism, and outcomes, which are uncertain. Because trials are usually one-offs or carry out a limited number of tests, they tend not to take account of these complex relationships. There is as a result a lack of certainty in showing consistency of findings over time and place, which leads to the overclaiming from trials.

Pawson and Tilly are careful not to adopt a radically different epistemology from that commonly assumed with trials. As realists, they keep close to the way in which trialists actually design and draw inferences, whereby knowledge gathering in the social sciences is understood as limited and partial, gradually cumulating findings rather than having massive breakthroughs (see Campaner and Galavotti 2012). Rarely is one trial a game changer; more often it would lead to follow-up trials that might try out the intervention on different populations. Evidence cumulates gradually and where the finding from the first trial might even be qualified in subsequent research. In public policy, such as education practice, this is common and policymakers would need several trials to adopt a policy, ideally a meta-analysis whereby the contexts are taken account. In political science, the incentive to repeat trials so as to create enough experiments for a meta-analysis is low because of the lack of interest from funders in replicating results; but the replication movement is growing in political science and some areas such as GOTV now have enough studies to allow for reviews and meta-analyses (e.g. Green, McGrath, and Aronow 2013). Rather than Pawson and Tilly's position undermining trials, it shows how increases in knowledge are usually incremental whatever method is used.

It is also possible to use the data from experiments to understand the contextual factors more strongly, which is another way to deal with Pawson and Tilley's critique. This is about the impact of the treatment on different groups within the experiment, what is called to the analysis of subgroups in experiments or heterogeneous treatment effects. Although subgroup or heterogeneous effects are not inferred from random variation so are limited in extent to which a causal inference can be made from analyzing them (and also suffer from small samples size of the sample groups so lack the statistical power of the full experiment), further experiments can be carried out on these subgroups if the results are promising. In general, seeing experiments as part of a process of research rather than offering authoritative one-off adjudication of problems places them close to other methods in social science. Researchers can replicate results, see if they transfer to different jurisdictions, whether they work on subgroups, and whether treatments that convey a more precise causal mechanism can help say why an intervention works or not.

Other objections made by Pawson and Tilly rest on a set of familiar constraints usually acknowledged by experimenters, such as sample selection for the population who enter experiments, which is a familiar problem in most lines of research, such as survey research which relies on selecting participants to be representative of the general population, but for which there is ever-declining response rates; or the more general problem of selecting case study areas to carry out the research where getting agreement and consent means that a limited selection of places and people come forward. In spite of having the same problems of external validity and self-selection, Pawson and Tilly are quite happy to praise case studies for their supposed realist advantages. The more general point is that all methods in social sciences, whether panel regression, case studies, or trials, are limited in the extent to which they offer external validity, but this does not stop knowledge being advanced provided researchers are careful about claiming what they have found. Given that most methods have problems of external validity, the fact that RCTs are good at internal validity does give them superiority as many other methods are weak in both internal and external validity. The claim for RCTs to be the gold standard rests on their relative not absolute advantages. RCTs are not a ruling and all-conquering methodology. Rather than being pessimistic like Pawson and Tilly, it is possible to use the points they make to defend trials. The problem is more about the strong claims that have been made by the advocates of trials, which are bound to be dashed, rather than the practice of them as carried out by most researchers.

If Pawson and Tilly's attack rests on a stereotyped account of trials, understandable because the strong advocacy of randomization as the gold standard in their field of policy evaluation, the next line of criticism is stronger because critics examine the assumptions behind trials and suggest they are only fulfilled when certain conditions in place, which is also another limit on the external validity of trials. Some of this appears in the work of Heckman and Deaton, but the most extended treatment is by Cartwright in various collaborations including Deaton (Cartwright 2007; Cartwright and Hardie 2012; Deaton and Cartwright 2018). The argument is based on the sample selection point made by Pawson and Tilly, but also the idea that trials (outside medicine) are stylized events, only happening in certain circumstances which are limited whereby practitioners create special conditions to allow a trial to take place so it can fulfill its assumptions (see above). This means it is very hard to make inferences from outside the trial unless there is a similar population and set of procedures of the original trial.

This problem is not unusual in political science or policy studies in that the acts of researchers, in particular gathering data, can lead to distortions, such from the Hawthorne effect. As with other methods, researcher impacts can be anticipated and limited. For example, the placebo is one way to understand these effects whereby some subjects get an intervention but with a different causal mechanism than the main treatment. There is also the issue of how the findings from trials might change over time. They might suffer from the problem of novelty as when the intervention is new subjects will respond positively; but over time they can become routine as people get used to experiments being done on them and anticipate the experiments. In trials with policymakers, the implementers may change their behavior as well as subjects, as the trials may be implemented less faithfully and where administrative systems are not so tuned up to the delivery the trial as they are at the start. Partly as a result, there is a tendency for treatment effects to fade over time (Olfson and Marcus 2013). Techniques that can guard against the impact of subjects and interveners are not so easy to implement in political science. It seems to be often quite hard to assure blinding of the subjects as trials are done in the field. Sometimes participants need to be informed they are in a trial; and when not, they often can guess they are in one.

In general, the prevalence of null or even backfire results for trials would seem to caution against the fear of overclaiming (Karlan and Appel 2016), which is at the core of the critics' worry. Trials often show that things that appear to work with some methods actually do not work when tested with trials.

Cartwright also argues that the best kind of RCT work is deductive, that is strong on theory and occur when the test is a clincher (Cartwright 2011, 377), which narrows the selection of effective RCTs to a limited range, whereas other methods are more inductive so more encompassing. But this characterization by Cartwright may not be true. Some RCTs are deductive—that is led by theory—many other are more pragmatic and can be done with little theory as knowledge cumulates. This again shows how similar trials are to other methods. In fact, the common approach today is to combine methods, in particular to do RCTs alongside qualitative research (e.g. Bennett et al. 2019), and to have observational research happening at the same time as experiments (White 2013; Drabble and O'Cathain 2015).

4. The Ethical Critique

There is a similar argument about the comparison between RCTs and other methods when considering ethical issues. The discussion is about the use of research to extract information from human subjects, rather than the use of a policy tool, such as randomization in the policy process, although the two are connected because randomization by policymakers is an important way to gather evidence for researchers and often there is a government randomization then research carried on alongside this. For political scientists, these government trials are less common than for economists and policy research, so most research is carried out by the researchers acting alone or in partnership with another body, such as a political party or lobby group.

Ethics are, of course, essential in the conduct of all research with human subjects: this consideration comes from a respect for the autonomy of persons who are the subjects of research. Subjects should not be manipulated or harmed or feel humiliated by research or encouraged to breach their own ethical principles. Consent is another principle of research for this reason. Experiments seem to be scary for these reasons in that manipulation can be an essential part of process and some experiments only work if the subjects do not know what is happening. Randomization can convey a sense of loss of opportunity and disappointment from those in the control group. Fortunately, rather than showing experiments to be massively different from other methods, they are similar in that a balancing of considerations can be carried out, and which is built into the ethical review of procedures. Debriefing or informing after the event is usually enough to deal with the issue of informed consent if it is not possible to do it when the intervention is received, and occasionally researchers may have to inform and brief beforehand even if it damages the experiment. These considerations are usually considered during the formal review of ethics by university committees.

Ethical principles apply formally in that research councils and universities require official approval based on these rules. Researchers must get their projects approved by an Institutional Review Board (IRB) or ethics committee, which is a part of a university's governance structure. Some public bodies have their own review boards, such as the National Health Service in the UK. Other public bodies have recently set up their own procedures for review. The researcher has to abide by stated principles or else the research cannot be undertaken. It is possible to apply for ethical approval at different institutions if there is a research team from more than one university. It is frowned upon to "shop" around for ethical approval across institutions when there are different partners involved. In the UK, it is usually the principal applicants of research grants who seek approval from their institutions, and then the participants in other universities have to send the documentation showing ethical approval to the ethics committees in their institutions for confirmation, which is a useful compromise and gets around the problem of too many ethical approvals happening at the same time. Answering the questions for an ethics committee or board can be helpful in checking whether the people will be harmed, whether it is acceptable to use deception, and whether it is possible not to inform the participants. The text boxes in ethics forms force the researcher to write about the rationale of their project and to respond to particular concerns.

The temptation is that once the decision to do a piece of research has been made, ethical procedures are considered instrumentally so the researcher simply aims to get approval and provides suitable text that will jump through the hoops. Not that instrumentality is necessarily bad, as many ethics committee members know about this motivation and have the skills to assess the application text critically (many committees being composed of "poacher-turned-gamekeeper" researchers). It is better to think through the appropriateness issue early on as initial decision choices can be influenced by ethical thinking, which in fact can make it easier to get approval later on.

Ethical practices should also apply informally in the sense that researchers hold to a set of principles that come from their training and values, which they seek to apply to their study. Most social scientists have strong beliefs about the value of research: it should contribute to the good of society and to individual wellbeing, and not be gained in ways that harm people. The advantage of the more informal principles is that they can be applied day-to-day. Ethics committees and IRBs can have a limited remit and can lack experience with social science projects. It is possible to obtain formal ethical approval but not think very ethically when doing the research. Both formal approval and informal understandings should complement each other: they should be based on an active consideration of all the principles involved. For a more thorough treatment of ethics of field experiments, see Desposato (2015).

CONCLUSION

This chapter has reviewed the use of RCTs in political science, which have grown in popularity in recent years. The approach is to see this development in largely positive terms, the rediscovery of a method that had got neglected in the past in favor of the analysis of observational data, such as time series and surveys. RCTs allow political scientists to answer some very specific research questions, such as the impact of canvassing on voter turnout, which are very hard to achieve with other strategies of enquiry. The use of trials in political science has largely proceeded without massive criticism and resistance from the profession, but this is not a typical reaction in the academy. In this light, the chapter has highlighted critical work from the philosophy of science, applied economics, and from the study of policy evaluation, which has focused on the limits to knowledge acquisition from trials, which is in contrast to the common assumption that RCTs are the gold standard of research and that doing more of them is a costless benefit. The key criticism is that the RCTs rely on a set of narrow assumptions that limit the extent to which researchers can generalize from them. Making inferences to other populations from these findings might be limited and partial. There are also aspects of trials that limit external validity: the selection of areas and populations that are not representative. Trials may implement procedures in order to deliver the intervention and its measurement that make the findings of limited generalization. In addition, RCTs come with ethical limitations, which restricts where they are done and to whom.

As a response to these criticisms, it is possible to argue that RCTs are not greatly different from other methods in the social sciences. In particular, the contrast between internal and external validity is a common problem that most researchers face, with methods tending to focus on improving the former, which is where they have control over the data collection process, and paying less attention to the latter. Researchers who use case studies and interviews, or time series data, rely on the discussion of findings and assessing the contribution to the debate to make claims about external validity, which can often be contested by reviewers and critics. Trials are no different in this respect, and actually have some advantages in better purchase on internal validity while being no worse at making claims for external validity than other methods that rely in sampling in targeted areas. The conclusion to draw is that all researchers should think of ways to improve external validity (Pearl and Bareinboim 2014; Bareinboim and Pearl 2016). Ethics also covers all kinds of research, such as interviews and case studies, making the use of experiments not so problematic after all, and where most objections can be handled in special procedures as guaranteed by subject review or ethics committees. The conclusion to draw is that researchers should be careful with all methods, but they also should not discredit them with too much skepticism. These both positive and negative provisos apply to observational and experimental research methods in equal measure.

NOTES

1. Sections 1, 2, and 4 draw on John (2017).

REFERENCES

Adams, William C. and Dennis J. Smith. 1980. Effects of Telephone Canvassing on Turnout and Preferences: A Field Experiment. *The Public Opinion Quarterly* 44 (3): 389–395.

Bareinboim, Elias, and Judea Pearl. 2016. Causal Inference and the Data-Fusion Problem. *Proceedings of the National Academy of Sciences* 113 (27): 7345–7352.

Bennett, Judith, Pam Hanley, Ian Abrahams, Louise Elliott, and Maria Turkenburg-van Diepen. 2019. Mixed Methods, Mixed Outcomes? Combining an RCT and Case Studies to Research the Impact of a Training Programme for Primary School Science Teachers. *International Journal of Science Education* 41 (4): 490–509.

Campaner, Raffaella, and Maria Carla Galavotti. 2012. Evidence and the Assessment of Causal Relations in the Health Sciences. *International Studies in the Philosophy of Science* 26 (1): 27–45.

Cartwright, Nancy. 2007. Are RCTs the Gold Standard? *BioSocieties* 2 (1): 11–20.

Cartwright, Nancy. 2011. A Philosopher's View of the Long Road from RCTs to Effectiveness. *The Lancet* 377 (9775): 1400–1401.

Cartwright, Nancy, and Jeremy Hardie. 2012. *Evidence-Based Policy: A Practical Guide to Doing It Better.* Oxford: Oxford University Press.

Deaton, Angus. 2010. Instruments, Randomization, and Learning about Development. *Journal of Economic Literature* 48 (2): 424–455.

Deaton, Angus, and Nancy Cartwright. 2018. Understanding and Misunderstanding Randomized Controlled Trials. *Social Science & Medicine*, Randomized Controlled Trials and Evidence-based Policy: A Multidisciplinary Dialogue, 210 (August): 2–21.

Desposato, Scott, ed. 2015. *Ethics and Experiments.* 1st edition. New York, NY: Routledge.

Drabble, Sarah J., and Alicia O'Cathain. 2015. Moving From Randomized Controlled Trials to Mixed Methods Intervention Evaluations. In *The Oxford Handbook of Multimethod and Mixed Methods Research Inquiry*, edited by Sharlene Nagy Hesse-Biber and R. Burke Johnson. Oxford: Oxford University Press.

Druckman, James N., Donald P. Green, James H. Kuklinski, and Arthur Lupia. 2006. The Growth and Development of Experimental Research in Political Science. *American Political Science Review* 100 (4): 627–635.

Druckman, James N., Donald P. Green, James H. Kuklinski, and Arthur Lupia. 2011. *Cambridge Handbook of Experimental Political Science.* Cambridge: Cambridge University Press.

Dunning, Thad. 2012. *Natural Experiments in the Social Sciences: A Design-Based Approach.* Cambridge: Cambridge University Press.

Fisher, Ronald Aylmer. 1926. The Arrangement of Field Experiments. In *Breakthroughs in Statistics: Methodology and Distribution*, edited by Samuel Kotz and Norman L. Johnson, 82–91. Springer Series in Statistics. New York, NY: Springer New York.

Fisher, Ronald Aylmer. 1935. *The Design of Experiments.* Edinburgh: Oliver and Boyd.

Gerber, Alan S., and Donald P. Green. 2000. The Effects of Canvassing, Telephone Calls, and Direct Mail on Voter Turnout: A Field Experiment. *American Political Science Review* 94: 653.

Gerber, Alan S., and Donald P. Green. 2012. *Field Experiments: Design, Analysis, and Interpretation.* New York: W. W. Norton.

Glennerster, Rachel, and Kudzai Takavarasha. 2013. *Running Randomized Evaluations: A Practical Guide.* Princeton, NJ: Princeton University Press.

Gosnell, Harold F. 1926. An Experiment in the Stimulation of Voting. *American Political Science Review* 20 (4): 869–874.

Gosnell, Harold Foote. 1927. *Getting out the Vote: An Experiment in the Stimulation of Voting.* 4. Chicago: Greenwood Publishing Group.

Green, Donald P., and Alan S. Gerber. 2015. *Get Out the Vote: How to Increase Voter Turnout.* Washington, DC: Brookings Institution Press.

Green, Donald P., and Alan S. Gerber. 2019. *Get Out the Vote.* 4th Revised edition. Washington, DC: Brookings Institution Press.

Green, Donald P., Mary C. McGrath, and Peter M. Aronow. 2013. Field Experiments and the Study of Voter Turnout. *Journal of Elections, Public Opinion and Parties* 23 (1): 27–48.

Grose, Christian R. 2014. Field Experimental Work on Political Institutions. *Annual Review of Political Science* 17: 355–370.

Harrison, G. W. 2011. Randomisation and Its Discontents. *Journal of African Economies* 20 (4): 626–652.

Harrison, G. W. 2013. Field Experiments and Methodological Intolerance. *Journal of Economic Methodology* 20 (2): 103–117.

Harrison, Glenn W., and John A. List. 2004. Field Experiments. *Journal of Economic Literature* 42 (4): 1009–1055.

Hartmann, G. W. 1936. A Field Experiment on the Comparative Effectiveness of "Emotional" and "Rational" Political Leaflets in Determining Election Results. *The Journal of Abnormal and Social Psychology* 31 (1): 99–114.

Heckman, James J. 1991. Randomization and Social Policy Evaluation. Working Paper 107. Cambridge: National Bureau of Economic Research.

Heckman, James J., and Jeffrey A. Smith. 1995. Assessing the Case for Social Experiments. *Journal of Economic Perspectives* 9 (2): 85–110.

Humphreys, Macartan, and Jeremy M. Weinstein. 2009. Field Experiments and the Political Economy of Development. *Annual Review of Political Science* 12: 367–378.

Iyengar, Shanto, and Donald R. Kinder. 1987. *News That Matters: Television and American Opinion*. Chicago: University of Chicago Press.

John, Peter. 2017. *Field Experiments in Political Science and Public Policy: Practical Lessons in Design and Delivery*. New York: Taylor & Francis.

Karlan, Dean, and Jacob Appel. 2016. *Failing in the Field: What We Can Learn When Field Research Goes Wrong*. Princeton, NJ: Princeton University Press.

Lund, Frederick Hansen. 1925. The Psychology of Belief: A Study of Its Emotional, and Volitional Determinants. *The Journal of Abnormal and Social Psychology* 20 (2): 174–196.

Morton, Rebecca B., and Kenneth C. Williams. 2010. *Experimental Political Science and the Study of Causality: From Nature to the Lab*. Cambridge: Cambridge University Press.

Olfson, Mark, and Steven C. Marcus. 2013. Decline In Placebo-Controlled Trial Results Suggests New Directions For Comparative Effectiveness Research. *Health Affairs* 32 (6): 1116–1125.

Pawson, Ray, and Nick Tilley. 1997. *Realistic Evaluation*. 1st edition. London: Thousand Oaks, CA: SAGE Publications Ltd.

Pearl, Judea, and Elias Bareinboim. 2014. External Validity: From Do-Calculus to Transportability across Populations. *Statistical Science*, 29 (4): 579–595.

Rooij, Eline A. de, Donald P. Green, and Alan S. Gerber. 2009. Field Experiments on Political Behavior and Collective Action. *Annual Review of Political Science* 12 (1): 389–395.

Rubin, Donald B. 1974. Estimating Causal Effects of Treatments in Randomized and Nonrandomized Studies. *Journal of Educational Psychology* 66 (5): 688.

Teele, Dawn Langan. 2014. *Field Experiments and Their Critics: Essays on the Uses and Abuses of Experimentation in the Social Sciences*. Yale University Press.

White, Howard. 2013. The Use of Mixed Methods in Randomized Control Trials. *New Directions for Evaluation* 2013 (138): 61–73.

CHAPTER 18

....

LAB EXPERIMENTS IN POLITICAL SCIENCE THROUGH THE LENS OF EXPERIMENTAL ECONOMICS

....

ANDRE HOFMEYR AND HAROLD KINCAID

1. INTRODUCTION

....

EXPERIMENTS are becoming an increasingly popular tool in the political scientist's toolkit, but they are still often viewed with skepticism by (some) researchers in the field. This is partly because experiments are a relatively new addition to the methodological canon of political science, but also because there is a diverse set of empirical approaches that are classified as experiments. We clarify that diversity in this introduction and explain which elements of experimental political science we focus on and why.

Kittel and Morton [2012, p. 3–7] argue that there are three broad categories of experiments in political science: laboratory, survey, and field experiments. The boundaries delineating these different experiments can be fluid, e.g., a lab-in-the-field experiment, but they ultimately stem from different intellectual traditions. Specifically, lab experiments are the dominant approach in political economy, whereas field experiments are more popular in political psychology, studies of political behavior, and international relations. Finally, survey experiments are most often used in political sociology and studies of political communication.

The differences between these experimental approaches are also often couched in terms of internal and external validity, where lab experiments supposedly score high with respect to internal validity, while field and survey experiments score high in terms of external validity. Friedman and Sunder [1994, p. 5] argue that internal validity hinges on whether experiments, and the data derived from them, promote correct causal inferences. Clearly to draw meaningful inferences, theory is essential for guiding the experimental design, determining what information is worth collecting, and analyzing the resulting data. Thus, internal validity is determined by features of the experimental design, the degree to which theory informs the design, the extent of experimental control, and the statistical tools used to analyze experimental data.

Lab experiments tend to have a high degree of internal validity, e.g., construct and causal validity in the language of Morton and Williams [2010], because the experimentalist has maximal control over features of the experimental environment, institution, and incentives. By contrast, lab experiments are often criticized for lacking external validity: the extent to which results generalize to the population and/or environment of interest. Given that lab experiments typically use student samples and highly stylized, abstract framing, skeptics often question the extent to which results in the lab can, and do, generalize.

Field and survey experiments are often lauded for their external validity, two components of which are statistical validity and ecological validity [Morton and Williams 2010], because they can potentially recruit large, representative samples of the population of interest, and often occur in relatively natural environments. However, it is a false dichotomy to claim that lab experiments are high in internal validity, whereas field and survey experiments are high in external validity, because internal validity is a necessary condition for external validity. As McDermott [2011, p. 28] puts it,

> Internal validity comes first, both sequentially and practically. Without first establishing internal validity, it remains unclear what process should be explored in the real world. An experimenter has to know that the conclusions result from the manipulations imposed before trying to extrapolate those findings into other contexts. External validity follows, as replications across time and populations seek to delineate the extent to which these conclusions can generalize.

Thus, while field and survey experiments may be more representative of a population of interest, inferences drawn from them will be fatuous if they lack internal validity. The lessons learned about what tools and procedures work in the lab have played a crucial role in the development and refinement of institutions used in the field, with advances in mechanism design and auction theory being exemplars of the value of rigorous lab testing prior to field implementation (see Chen and Ledyard [2010] and Kagel and Levin [2010], respectively, for reviews) and in developing well-designed field experiments themselves.

The debate over the prospects for external validity of lab experiments continues, but it is likewise a debate over the generalizability of field experiments such as randomized controlled trials (RCTs).[1] We will not consider these issues directly in this chapter, placing our focus on the internal validity of lab experiments.

There is a common misconception in both economics and political science that equates experiments with some form of randomization. To be sure, randomization plays an important role in some experiments, but the defining characteristic of an experiment is that a researcher, or some other authority, such as a government agency or "nature," has *control* over the conditions under which behavior is observed. This misconceived adherence to the notion that randomization defines experiments is most readily seen in the literature on field experiments in political science. For example, Gerber [2011, p. 115], in a chapter on field experiments in the *Cambridge Handbook of Experimental Political Science*, argues that, "In social science experiments, units of observation are randomly assigned to groups, and treatment effects are measured by comparing outcomes across groups." In addition, Gerber [2011] and Gerber and Green [2012] appear to regard field experiments as synonymous with RCTs; the same can be said of Duflo [2006] and Banerjee and Duflo [2009] in the economics literature. The taxonomy of experiments proposed by Harrison and List [2004] makes it clear that experiments in general, and field experiments in particular, need not involve randomization to define them as such. Moreover, Harrison [2013] strongly rejects equating field experiments with RCTs for several reasons, not least because it appears to promote methodological intolerance. Thus, for the purposes of this chapter, we define experiments in terms of control over the conditions under which behavior is observed, and not by reference to randomization.

Figure 18.1 shows the distribution of 100 articles published in the *Journal of Experimental Political Science* (*JEPS*), from its inaugural issue in 2014 until the final issue (Volume 6, Issue 3) of 2019, broken down by the type of experiment (if any) that was run: Natural, Field, Survey, Online, Lab (Economics), Lab-in-the-Field, Lab (Psychology), and Methods. We explain the distinction between the psychology and economic traditions of lab experiments below.

Online experiments, run through internet services such as Amazon's MTurk, have become increasingly popular in experimental economics and experimental political science over the last few years. While these online experiments are typically inspired by lab experiments in either the economic or psychology traditions (in fact, of the five studies identified as online experiments, two were in the economic tradition and three were in the psychology tradition), the loss of control when one moves from the lab to the internet supports a separate category for these experiments. Lab-in-the-field experiments, or artefactual field experiments in the terminology of Harrison and List [2004], are, as the name suggests, lab experiments run with subject pools recruited in the field rather than students. The four

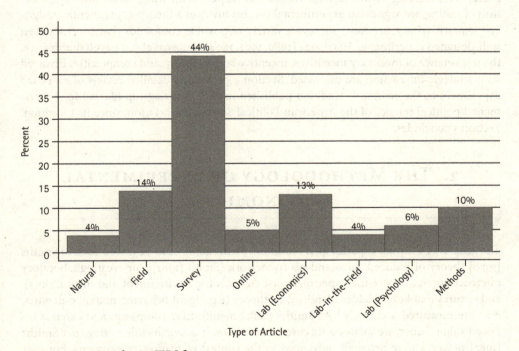

FIGURE 18.1. Articles in *JEPS* from 2014–2019

lab-in-the-field experiments we identified are experiments in the economic tradition, but given the lack of control when one moves from the lab to the field, even with a lab-in-the-field experiment, we classify them separately from conventional lab experiments in the economic tradition. Articles focusing either on experimental or statistical methods as opposed to the discussion and analysis of an actual experimental study are listed as Methods papers. Finally, natural experiments involve using naturally occurring events to achieve control through randomization.

We specifically classified lab experiments as either experiments in the economic tradition or the psychology tradition because, as Dickson [2011] explains, experiments in these two traditions differ along three primary dimensions: the level of stylization, the kinds of incentives offered, and the use of deception. Economic experiments tend to occur in highly stylized, "context free" environments whereas psychology experiments focus more on descriptive realism. Economic experiments pay subjects for the choices they make in the experiment while psychology experiments usually give subjects flat rate show-up fees or course credit for participation. Finally, deception is common in psychology experiments, but is taboo in economics, to the extent that experiments using deception will not be published in economic journals (Hertwig and Ortmann [2001]). Given our focus on lab experiments in political science through the lens of experimental economics, we devote our attention to lab experiments in the economic tradition, while acknowledging that experiments in the psychology tradition play a prominent role in experimental political science.[2]

The chapter proceeds as follows. Section 2 discusses the methodology of experimental economics and provides a framework for assessing the current state of lab experiments (in the economic tradition) in political science.[3] Specifically, we outline Smith's [1982] precepts for creating a controlled microeconomic experiment. Then, taking note of the holism of testing, we argue that experimental success involves a theory-experimental design-econometric trinity. Section 3 surveys a variety of possible confounds that confront even well-designed experiments. Harrison's [1989, 1992, 1994] concerns about payoff dominance, the importance of monetary incentives, incentive compatibility, and complexities involved with strategic interaction are discussed. Section 4 provides a detailed review of every lab experiment in the economic tradition published in *JEPS*, the flagship journal for experimental political science of the American Political Science Association, since its inception. Section 5 concludes.

2. THE METHODOLOGY OF EXPERIMENTAL ECONOMICS

The genesis of a formal experimental economic methodology can be traced back to Smith's [1976] theory of induced value and his framework (Smith [1982]) for creating laboratory microeconomies, where the experimentalist controls the environment and institution(s), and ensures that key variables identified by theory (e.g., agent behavior, market outcomes, etc.) are measured accurately.[4] As Smith's [1982] manifesto encompasses and extends induced value theory, we focus on its core tenets below. It is worthwhile noting that Smith's [1982] precepts were originally advanced in the context of market experiments, but they nevertheless provide crucial guidelines, if not rules, for the conduct of decision-theoretic and game-theoretic experiments too.

A laboratory microeconomy consists of an *environment* that specifies the set of economic agents, the list of commodities, and the characteristics of each agent, e.g., the agent's utility function and endowment. Within this environment, economic agents interact[5] through an *institution* that defines the rules that govern communication, and the exchange or transformation of commodities that ultimately determine each agent's outcome(s). This laboratory microeconomy is designed to allow the experimental economist to observe agent behavior, the outcomes that result from this behavior, and the performance of the *system*, i.e., the combination of the environment and institution, in achieving some objective, e.g., a Nash equilibrium strategy profile or Pareto optimal allocation. For such observation to be possible and judicious, control over elements of the system and measurement of relevant variables is required.

Control over elements of the system means to hold these elements fixed at some level, or to vary them across experiments, or within the same experiment at different points in time. To measure variables one needs to record the *messages* transmitted by agents through the choices they make in the experiment, and the outcomes resulting from these messages, with a view to understanding agent behavior and evaluating the performance of the system, respectively. Smith [1982] argues that to achieve these goals, a lab experiment has to satisfy a set of *precepts*: nonsatiation, salience, dominance, and privacy. Lab experiments are used for a number of purposes (see, for example, Roth [1995]) such as testing hypotheses derived from theory (or some other source), generating data to inform theory, testing institutions prior to field implementation, and as a measurement tool to elicit and compare preferences. Smith [1982] argues that these four precepts suffice to achieve internal validity in the type of experiments listed above, but if one wants to generalize lab results to a broader population outside the lab then *parallelism* must hold too. This is really just Smith's version of the standard concept of external validity.

Nonsatiation simply requires that experimental subjects prefer more of the reward medium to less, and do not become satiated. This is why money is typically used as the reward medium in economic experiments, because nonsatiation does not necessarily hold with primary rewards such as food.

Salience means that subjects know how the microeconomy's institution translates the messages they transmit, together with the messages of other agents in market experiments or game-theoretic experiments, into the rewards they receive. Thus, for salience to hold, subjects must understand how the institution induces value on messages, the rules that transform messages into experimental outcomes, and the mapping between outcomes and the (monetary) rewards that subjects ultimately receive. Importantly, not all rewards are salient: a fixed show-up fee for participation is not salient because it is not linked to the messages, viz., choices, that subjects send in the experiment.

Dominance is used to guard against satiation and requires that the reward structure induced by the institution dominates any subjective costs or benefits associated with the choices that subjects make in an experiment. For example, making a choice can be costly because subjects may have to perform, sometimes complex, calculations to determine how their choices, and those of other agents, combine to determine rewards. If these costs are not negligible and the rewards for incurring them low, subjects may become satiated and optimally decide not to engage with the experiment, implying dominance does not hold.

Alternatively, subjects may assign "game value"[6] to the choices they make in an experiment, which may either promote or undermine dominance depending on the direction of these effects. We return to the concept of dominance below in the context of the payoff-dominance critique.

Finally, privacy means that subjects only receive information on their own payoffs and not those of other subjects. This precept was advanced in the context of market experiments with the explicit aim to prevent interpersonal utility considerations that may hinder the experimenter's ability to induce value on abstract market commodities and outcomes. In market experiments it is important that buyers attempt to maximize consumer surplus and sellers seek to maximize producer surplus, so that a competitive equilibrium can, in principle, be attained. But if, say, buyers care about the profits of sellers then they may make choices that undermine the value that an experimenter intends to induce in the laboratory market. In game-theoretic experiments, by contrast, privacy is often unnecessary or unwarranted if the particular game under study assumes complete and consistent information about agents' payoffs. Thus, of all of Smith's [1982] precepts for creating a controlled microeconomic experiment, privacy is the most experiment-specific, and will not be wanted for many experiments in political science.

Nonsatiation, salience, dominance, and privacy are sufficient conditions for a *controlled* microeconomic experiment. As Smith [1982, p. 935] argues, "Precepts 1-4 permit us to study laboratory microeconomic environments in which real economic agents exchange real messages through real property right institutions that yield outcomes redeemable in real money." As mentioned above, though, if one is concerned with the generalizability of results, the parallelism precept must hold too.

Parallelism refers to the transferability of results from the lab to the world outside the lab, and is an assertion that behavioral patterns and the performance of institutions in the lab, will transfer to other settings when similar *ceteris paribus* conditions hold. This precept is easily the most contentious because whether these ceteris paribus conditions hold, or the extent to which they do, is open to question.[7] In arguing that results should transfer from the lab to the field, Smith sounds the call for experimentalists to take robust lab results and test them in the field, while ultimately putting the burden of proof on the skeptic who must explain why the field is so different to the lab that one would not expect lab results to generalize.

In actual lab experiments, Smith's precepts only ever hold to a certain degree. The precepts themselves have to be implemented using whatever theory we can bring to the table and they have to be tied to experimental results with the relevant statistics. This combination is a crucial methodological feature of experimental economics, called the theory-experimental design-econometric[8] trinity (Harrison et al. [2018]). As early as Smith [1982], experimental economists have emphasized the interplay of these three components of the research endeavor. Specifically, Smith [1982, p. 924] stresses that it is, "equally important that experimentalists take seriously the collective professional task of integrating theory, experimental design, and observation." More recently, Harrison, Lau and Rutström [2015] argue that a firm grasp of theory is essential in experimental economics because it informs experimental design and analysis. Furthermore, analysis itself should be constrained by, and interpreted jointly with, theoretical considerations, prior empirical work, complementary data, econometric methodology, and intended applications.[9] As Harrison, Lau, and Rutström [2015, p. 313] argue, "In short, one *cannot divorce the job of the theorist from the job of the econometrician*" (emphasis in original).

To understand the importance of the trinity, consider the role that risk preferences play in many strategic interactions (Harrison and Rutström [2008]). For example, in the ultimatum game, the proposer cannot be certain what amount the responder will accept, implying that attitudes to risk are likely to influence the proposed split. Similarly, in the trust game, the decision of whether to send money, and also, how much to send, is inherently risky because there is no guarantee that any of it will be returned. Consequently, to draw valid inferences from behavior in these experiments, it is crucial to elicit the risk preferences (and subjective beliefs) of subjects so that these can be incorporated in statistical analyses;[10] see Chetty et al. [2021] for evidence that trust games without independent measures of risk are not solely measuring trust. For example, without information on risk attitudes one could attribute an observed difference in amounts sent in the trust game to gender, when different risk attitudes across genders is actually driving the result.

In the context of experimental political science, the trinity implies that the ideal is to have an intimate theoretical knowledge of different models and their implications for choice behavior.[11] This knowledge should then be used to design experiments to elicit data that are amenable to rigorous statistical analysis. And the results from these statistical models must be interpreted jointly with the theory and experimental design that motivated their development.[12] While there are some wonderful examples of the interplay of theory, experimental design, and statistical analysis in experimental political science, our review in the next section will ask if this is the exception or the norm.[13]

The theory-experimental design-econometric trinity illustrates a universal situation for any investigative endeavor: what is known in the philosophy of science literature as the Duhem-Quine problem (Stanford [2017]). The Duhem-Quine problem arises because scientific hypotheses are tested only by combining them with further auxiliary assumptions about the experimental setup or needed statistical assumptions and methods; predictions are forthcoming only when the hypothesis H is combined with some set of auxiliary hypotheses $A_{1,\ldots,n}$. As the problem is typically put, it is only H and A jointly that entail what should be observed, so when the predicted evidence E is not observed but instead rather $\neg E$, then it is indeterminate where the blame lies: is it with H or A? This is the classic Duhem-Quine problem. While the problem is usually put in terms of failed predictions, there is no reason it must be, because the potential problem is perfectly general. If H and A entail E and E is indeed observed, it is still logically unclear how credit should be assigned, if at all: are H and A equally supported? To put the problem in Bayesian terms, we always have to evaluate any given experiment in terms of our confidence in the theory used in designing the experiment, the statistics used in tying hypotheses to data, and all the background assumptions involved in running experiments themselves, which for experimental economics are summarized by Smith's [1982] tenets.

Historically, the Duhem-Quine problem has been used to motivate a variety of "fuzzy holisms" (Wilson [2006]): holisms that draw relativist, postmodernist conclusions, starting with Kuhn [1962] and followed by various social constructivist views of science. While the move from simple positivist conceptions of evidence and confirmation was salutary, the pendulum swung too far. The holism of testing pointed to in the Duhem-Quine problem does not have such radical implications. It is crucial not to confuse the fact that testing is holistic with the much stronger conclusion that only wholes composed of theory, statistics, and experimental designs are jointly tested without ever being able to isolate anything specific shown by the evidence.

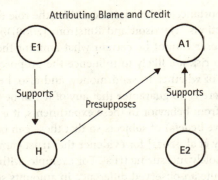

Attributing Blame and Credit

Note: E₁ and E₂ are Independent

FIGURE 18.2. The Holism of Testing and Simultaneous Isolation of Blame and Credit

Consider the situation in Figure 18.2, which shows that evidence can provide information for, or against, specific hypotheses. Specifically, testing H with evidence E_1 relies on auxiliary assumption A_1. So testing is holistic. However, if we have evidence E_2 that does not depend on either H or E_1, then if E_2 supports A_1, we have no vicious circle of justification. This point has been made in multiple convincing ways over a number of years (Dorling [1979]; Howson and Urbach [2005]). Unfortunately, this straightforward point often goes ignored.

One reason such answers may not convince is that, of course, E_2 in Figure 18.2 is itself probably only evidence for A_1, given some further auxiliary A_2. Are we off to an endless chase? Every self-conscious experimenter is aware of possible confounds not yet ruled out. This awareness leads Bardsley et al. [2009], a set of highly-respected experimental economists, to advocate a step back from the specifics of empirical testing and to look instead at the characteristics of research programs or traditions in the fashion of Lakatos [1978] to judge the scientific credibility of experimental social science.

While a complete overview of their argument is beyond the scope of this chapter, we draw attention to their discussion of testing game theory [Bardsley et al. 2009, p. 114–128], because game theory is one of the modern, theoretical foundations of political science, most lab experiments in political science involve strategic interaction, viz., games, and it illustrates their approach to the Duhem-Quine problem.

Bardsley et al. [2009] draw the distinction between the *statement* and *analysis* of a formal game. The statement of a game incorporates all of its essential structural features (e.g., the number of players, the order of moves in the game, the actions available to the players, etc.) along with a specification of players' preferences over outcomes induced by actions taken in the game. The structural features of the game constitute the *game form* and preferences over outcomes, viz., *payoffs*, complete the statement of the *abstract* game. The game theorist then analyses the abstract game by adopting a solution concept, e.g., dominance, to predict *equilibrium* outcomes.

Now suppose that an experimentalist wants to test a game-theoretic prediction in the lab, e.g., do committee decisions under majority rule converge to the core of the noncooperative game without side payments (Fiorina and Plott [1978]). To do so, the experimentalist must instantiate the core elements of the abstract game in the lab: human subjects take the place of theoretical agents, monetary payments substitute for payoffs, etc. By instantiating the theoretical elements in this way, the experimentalist transforms the abstract game into an *implemented* game. Assuming the implemented game incorporates the essential features of the abstract game, game-theoretic solution concepts can be tested in the lab by checking the correspondence between predictions and actual subject behavior. Thus, any test of a game-theoretic prediction is a joint test of the solution concept itself and the various assumptions that are used to instantiate the abstract game in the lab. These assumptions are typically referred to as *bridging principles* because they provide the bridge between theory and experiment. And it is the veracity of these bridging principles that affect the interpretation of hypothesis tests.

In relation to tests of game theory, one of the crucial bridges is between payoffs in the abstract game, that, as a matter of theory, capture everything of importance to the agent, and monetary rewards in the implemented game. Experimentalists typically adopt the *standard payoff bridging principle*: subjects' monetary rewards in an experiment are surrogates for their payoffs in the abstract game. Thus, any test of a game-theoretic prediction is really a joint test of the solution concept, the standard bridge, and every other auxiliary assumption, e.g., the subjects understood the instructions, used to link the abstract game to the implemented game.

Ignoring these other auxiliary assumptions for the moment, the question turns to the validity of the standard payoff bridging principle in experimental tests of game theory. A voluminous experimental literature on other-regarding preferences[14] casts doubt on the assumption that monetary rewards are appropriate proxies for everything that matters to the abstract theoretical agents of game theory. Specifically, to the extent that human subjects are motivated by non-pecuniary "rewards" (e.g., altruism, spite, envy, etc.), the standard bridge used to instantiate abstract games in the lab is not appropriate. Thus, if subject behavior does not conform to the predictions of a particular solution concept this does not necessarily imply failure of the solution concept itself, it may simply mean that the experimentalist has failed to implement the intended abstract game. As Binmore [2007b, p. 12] adroitly puts it, "Critics who think that human beings are basically altruistic therefore go astray when they accuse game theorists of using the wrong analysis of the Prisoners' Dilemma. They ought to be accusing us of having correctly analysed the wrong game."

In the face of the holism of testing, Bardsley et al. [2009], adopting a quasi-Lakatosian philosophy of science perspective (Lakatos [1978]), provide an approach for untying this Gordian knot. They argue that for game theory to be used empirically, bridging principles have to be adopted to transform abstract theory into applied theory. In addition, rather than an exclusive, Popperian focus on single hypothesis tests, the validity of game-theoretic predictions, whether in the lab or the "real" world, should be assessed over time from the perspective of a particular research program as a whole. The ultimate yardstick for success of a research program is whether it delivers both theoretical and empirical progress, while temporarily insulating certain assumptions that can be referred to as the program's "hard core," from the possibility of refutation.

Adopting this approach, Bardsley et al. [2009] identify two distinct game-theoretic experimental research programs that differ in the assumptions they accord a hard core status. In the *preference refinement* program, particular solution concepts form part of the hard core, but researchers allow assumptions about payoffs to vary. By contrast, the *applied game theory* program accords payoffs a privileged status, thereby adopting the standard payoff bridging principle, while assessing, refining, and extending solution concepts to better explain empirical data. Fehr and Schmidt's [1999] research on social preferences is an example of the former, whereas McKelvey and Palfrey's [1992, 1995, 1998] development of quantal response equilibrium is an example of the latter.[15]

Bardsley et al. [2009] argue that the two programs in game theory have Lakatosian hard cores and that the research programs those hard cores ground are *progressive*: they have led to a variety of results constituting scientific progress. In this way game theory can be seen as scientifically successful despite the apparently insolvable Duhem-Quine problem.

We think there is value in identifying research traditions in science in general and in experimental social science in particular. Our review in this chapter of experimental political science will ask whether these two programs of experimental research in economics are also prevalent in experimental political science. Experimental political scientists, like all scientists, want theoretical and methodological approaches that show them what to do next, raise fruitful questions, produce new results, organize a research community, and so on. It is not unreasonable to ask to what extent various traditions in experimental political science have these virtues.

However, we think more can and must be said. If we just stop with evaluating "research programs" as "progressive" or "degenerative," we end up once again with the fuzzy holism of Wilson [2006]. Fuzzy holism is bad largely because it is lazy: it does not do the hard work of identifying the essential and differential theoretical and experimental components that make for successful experiments and compelling experimental arguments. Defending untenable assumptions as the hard core that is progressive in some vague sense makes it easy to conduct experiments that ignore possible confounds.[16] And, it very easily produces a somewhat self-serving global skepticism in the face of hard experimental work to be done.

As much as we admire them, we think Bardsley et al. [2009] sometimes fall into this trap. They say, "But can we ever be *sure* that subjects understand an experimental design . . . ?" (emphasis in original) [p. 103] and "it is always logically possible to adjust some auxiliary hypotheses in ways that allow any target hypothesis to stand or fall" [p. 110]. However, if the standards for knowledge are a Cartesian certainty that rules out all logically conceivable sources of error, then this Lakatosian defense of experimental practice is just sophomoric skepticism.[17]

We outline above ways in which there can be compelling tests of specific hypotheses. We think that such tests are possible in experimental economics and experimental political science. The important task is to identify what realistically possible confounding factors, given our most confidence-inspiring and checkable background knowledge, might get in our way and then go about trying to eliminate them. The next section outlines a series of these possible complications as they have arisen in experimental economic practice.

3. Threats to Inference in Experimental Economics

There are now some well-known, if not always fully acknowledged, threats to typical inference in experimental economics. This section outlines them because they are also serious threats to inference in experimental political science. We discuss in turn problems with payoff dominance, hypothetical incentives, incentive incompatibility, and some issues raised by strategic interaction.

3.1 The Payoff-Dominance Critique

Harrison [1989, 1992, 1994] presents a wide-ranging critique of experimental economic practice by questioning the extent to which dominance actually holds in typical laboratory microeconomies. The crux of his argument is that for dominance to be achieved, rewards linked to the null hypothesis under study must be "perceptibly and motivationally greater" than rewards associated with the alternative hypothesis [Harrison 1992, p. 1426]. To flesh out this idea, assume that message m_o is consistent with the null hypothesis, e.g., behavior converges to a Nash equilibrium, and message m_a is consistent with the alternative hypothesis, e.g., behavior converges to a non-Nash strategy profile. For dominance to hold, the rewards linked to these messages, v_o and v_a respectively, must be such that $v_o > v_a + \delta$, where δ represents the subjective decision-making costs of sending message m_o as opposed to m_a. Put simply, for dominance to hold, an agent must be sufficiently incentivized to make an optimal decision, taking into account the costs of doing so, rather than simply making a near-optimal decision with lower attendant costs.

The left panel of Figure 18.3 represents this idea for two experimental designs, A and B. The payoff functions for these experiments, represented by the gray and black parabolas, are drawn so that the same message m_o is associated with same reward v_o. By contrast, the message m_a yields very different rewards in experiment A and B: v_a^A and v_a^B, respectively. Given the subjective decision-making cost δ represented in the figure, experiment B satisfies dominance ($v_o - \delta > v_a^B$) but experiment A does not ($v_o - \delta < v_a^A$). Thus, experiment A is subject to the *payoff-dominance critique*.[18]

More generally, Harrison argues that there will typically be a whole set of messages $\bar{m}$ that are sufficiently close to m_o, and for which dominance does not hold: $v_o(m_o) \leq v(\bar{m}) + \delta$. On the other hand, there exists a set of messages $\hat{m}$ for which dominance does hold: $v_o(m_o) > v(\hat{m}) + \delta$. In such instances, as represented in the right panel of Figure 18.3, no messages in the set $\bar{m}$ satisfy dominance but messages in the set $\hat{m}$ do satisfy dominance. The

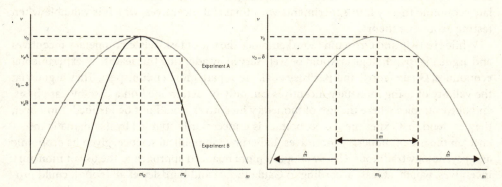

FIGURE 18.3. The Payoff-Dominance Critique

implication is that experiments should be designed to minimize the set $\bar{m}$ and maximize the set $\hat{m}$. Moreover, if an experiment is designed to test theoretical predictions, e.g., behavior converges to a Nash equilibrium, one can only claim that the theory is rejected if the messages supporting the alternative hypothesis, e.g., subjects adopt non-Nash strategy profiles, fall in the set $\hat{m}$.

Harrison [1989, 1992, 1994] reviews economic experiments on auctions, prospect theory, the endowment effect, the observed disparity between elicited willingness to pay and willingness to accept, predatory pricing, and tests of expected utility theory and Bayes rule, and concludes that in many of these experiments the costs of deviating from optimal behavior are negligible whereas the required cognitive effort to achieve optimality is high, implying a failure of payoff dominance and weak tests of theory.[19] Given that lab experiments in political science are often designed to test theory, or, more generally, hypotheses derived from theory or elsewhere, whether dominance holds will be one of the key metrics used to evaluate the current state of experimental political science. In other words, it is an important possible confound that successful experiments must address.

3.2 Task-Related Monetary Incentives

As mentioned earlier, another defining characteristic of experimental economics, unlike experimental psychology, is the use of task-related monetary incentives. For example, Camerer and Hogarth [1999] find that every experimental study published in the *American Economic Review* (a Top-Five economics journal) between 1970 and 1997 used task-related incentives. By contrast, Hertwig and Ortmann [2001] find that only 26% of articles published in the *Journal of Behavioral Decision Making* (a major outlet for experimental research in psychology) between 1988 and 1997 used task-related incentives.[20]

Hertwig and Ortmann [2001] argue that the use of monetary incentives in economics is typically justified on the following grounds: (1) monetary rewards are more attractive to participants and easier to implement than other, nonmonetary rewards; (2) monetary rewards satisfy Smith's precept of nonsatiation more readily and reliably than nonmonetary rewards; (3) there is a general presumption that monetary incentives tend to reduce the variability of subject performance; and (4) it is straightforward to translate economic theory into experiments with financial incentives, which is valuable when testing economic theory.

While Hertwig and Ortmann [2001] embrace the use of task-related monetary incentives and argue that psychologists would be well-served by adopting this feature of experimental economics, Guala [2005] and Bardsley et al. [2009] are more circumspect. They argue that the validity of using monetary incentives can only be determined on a case-by-case basis, and cite examples where the use of monetary incentives would not be justified. Moreover, they contend that experimental economics is unnecessarily stymied by its dogmatic insistence on the use of monetary incentives. Experimental political science, given its economic and psychology traditions, clearly adopts a more nuanced approach to the use of monetary incentives, which, at least according to Gaula [2005] and Bardsley et al. [2009], could provide important lessons for experimental economics.[21]

3.3 Incentive Compatibility

A closely related issue to the use of monetary incentives in experimental economics is the focus on adopting payment mechanisms that are *incentive compatible*. The issues here can be quite complex. We work through the details, but some readers may want to skim this section or return later.

Loosely, incentive compatibility means that subjects are incentivized to give truthful responses to the decision problems the experimentalist presents them with under the controlled conditions of the lab. Importantly, paying subjects for their responses is no guarantee of incentive compatibility. For example, suppose an experimentalist wants to elicit the risk preferences of subjects by presenting them with a choice between two simple lotteries, where a simple lottery is just a probability distribution over outcomes. Suppose further that the one lottery is objectively riskier than the other, i.e., the "risky" lottery is a mean-preserving spread of the "safe" lottery. Finally, suppose the experimentalist employs a payment mechanism that only pays out subjects who attain the highest reward in the task. This payment mechanism is not incentive compatible because subjects will be incentivized to select the risky lottery regardless of their true, underlying risk preferences, because the risky lottery, unlike the safe lottery, includes the highest reward in the task.

Given its importance in experimental economics, there is a well-established literature focusing on theoretical and experimental investigations of the incentive compatibility of different payment mechanisms. For example, Holt [1986] shows that the widely used random lottery incentive mechanism (RLIM), which randomly selects one of a subject's choices in an experiment for payment[22], is only theoretically incentive compatible if people satisfy the reduction of compound lotteries (ROCL) axiom *and* the independence axiom of expected utility theory. To understand this, consider an experiment where there is un-certainty about the payment a subject will receive from a particular choice, due to, say, the presence of objective risk, e.g., a choice between lotteries, or uncertainty engendered by the strategy choices of the subject's partner in a game. If subjects make a number of these choices and RLIM is used to randomly select one of them for payment, then RLIM induces a compound lottery, i.e., a lottery whose prizes are other lotteries, over experimental payments. If subjects satisfy ROCL then, when making a particular choice in the task, they will reduce the compound lottery induced by all of their other choices, to a simple lottery over outcomes. If, in addition, they satisfy the independence axiom, then each choice they make in the experiment will be independent of the reduced compound lottery induced by their other choices, thereby incentivizing them to treat each choice as if it is the only choice in the experiment. Thus, when ROCL and independence hold, RLIM is incentive com-patible because subjects maximize their experimental earnings by honestly reporting their preferences.

As RLIM is only theoretically incentive compatible under ROCL and independence, the question turns to whether people actually satisfy these axioms when making choices in experiments. A large body of literature, reviewed by Starmer [2000], suggests that people often violate the independence axiom in experiments on choice under risk, implying that RLIM is not robustly or universally incentive compatible. This has prompted many experimentalists to stress the importance of empirical or behavioral incentive compatibility instead, which focuses on which incentive mechanisms (appear to) "work" in practice. For example, Bardsley et al. [2009, p. 264–285]) argue that even if subjects do not satisfy ROCL and independence in an experiment employing RLIM, they may still treat each choice as if it is made in *isolation*,[23] thereby rendering the payment mechanism empirically incentive compatible.

Early tests of the behavioral incentive compatibility of RLIM provide mixed results (Starmer and Sugden [1991], Beattie and Loomes [1997], and Cubitt, Starmer and Sugden [1998]). These studies adopted experimental designs where some participants had to make a single choice between two lotteries in a pair, while others had to make a set of lottery pair choices, one of which was then randomly selected for payment. The logic of this approach is that a single choice between two lotteries must be incentive compatible (assuming, of course, that nonsatiation, salience, and dominance hold), but a single choice, embedded in a set of choices, only provides incentives to respond truthfully if subjects isolate (or satisfy ROCL and independence). Thus, if the choices of subjects who only face a single lottery pair differ to the choices other subjects make for this same pair, when it is combined with other lottery pairs in an experiment, then RLIM clearly distorts preferences and therefore lacks incentive compatibility. Starmer and Sugden [1991, p. 976] refer to this as a *contamination effect*: choices in an experiment employing RLIM are contaminated by the presence of other choices.

Starmer and Sugden [1991] find that RLIM does not distort choices in one of their comparisons ($p = 0.14$), but that it does distort choices in another comparison ($p = 0.051$). Similarly, Beattie and Loomes [1997] find no evidence that RLIM distorts choices in three of their comparisons, but do find that choices differ in a fourth comparison involving a compound lottery. With a more consistent set of experimental results, Cubitt, Starmer, and Sugden [1998, p. 130] conclude that the RLIM "system does appear to be unbiased when applied to choices among simple prospects."

Notwithstanding these early experimental results, recent investigations of RLIM cast more doubt on its incentive compatibility. For example, Cox, Sadiraj, and Schmidt [2014] find that choices differ when subjects are presented with a single choice between two lotteries, and when this pair is combined with another asymmetrically dominated lottery pair in an experiment employing RLIM. Similarly, Harrison and Swarthout [2014] find that estimates of the probability weighting function from a rank-dependent utility model of choice under risk differ both quantitatively and qualitatively depending on whether subjects make a single choice, or thirty choices, one of which is then selected for payment by RLIM.

In an attempt to organize these different findings on the validity of RLIM, and broaden the investigation of incentive compatibility generally, Cox, Sadiraj, and Schmidt (CSS) [2015] conduct a theoretical and experimental analysis of a range of different payment mechanisms, using a single choice in an experiment, what they refer to as the one task (OT) payment mechanism, as the benchmark for incentive compatibility. Their stated aim is to determine "whether different payment mechanisms elicit different data in otherwise identical experimental treatments and, if so, whether these mechanism effects have significant implications for conclusions drawn from the data" [CSS, p. 216]. RLIM[24] and *pay-all* are the most commonly used mechanisms in experimental economics (Azrieli,

Chambers, and Healy [2018]), so we limit the discussion below to these two payment protocols.

As the name suggests, the pay-all mechanism sequentially pays out subjects for every choice they make in an experiment.[25] Thus, subjects are rewarded for each choice prior to making their next choice. CSS [p. 223] show that pay-all is not theoretically incentive compatible for theories where terminal wealth is the argument of the utility function. Thus, pay-all is not incentive compatible for the canonical formulation of expected utility theory defined over terminal wealth, because wealth effects may distort behavior over the course of the experiment: subjects make choices different to what they would have made under the OT mechanism.[26] However, pay-all is incentive compatible for models defined over income as opposed to wealth, and if subjects treat each choice as independent of every other choice in an experiment. In fact, if subjects subscribe to this isolation hypothesis then all payment mechanisms will elicit the same data.

Another potential issue with pay-all is that it is susceptible to portfolio effects, which occur when subjects diversify their experimental choice "portfolio" to reduce the risk that they face. For example, whereas a subject may prefer option A to Option B if this choice is made in isolation, the subject may prefer the portfolio consisting of {A, B} to the portfolio {A, A} if the choice can be made twice. Thus, when faced with more than one payoff-relevant choice, subjects can diversify their choice portfolio and, hence, reduce their risk.

CSS [p. 229–236] combine different payment mechanisms with a simple lottery choice experiment on a between-subjects basis, and find robust evidence against the isolation hypothesis. Specifically, different payment mechanisms elicit demonstrably different risk preferences.[27] However, using the OT mechanism as the incentive-compatibility gold standard, they find that the pay-all mechanism does *not* distort risk preferences, whereas the RLIM mechanism does. This result is interesting because pay-all is widely believed to induce wealth and portfolio effects, or what Azrieli, Chambers, and Healy [2018] refer to as "complementarities at the top," and yet the risk preferences elicited with this mechanism are not biased. RLIM, on the other hand, which is not susceptible to wealth effects, clearly produces a contamination effect in choices between lotteries, at least in the CSS data.

The empirical analysis of CSS is limited purely to experiments involving lottery choices, but they provide a wide-ranging discussion of the impact of different payment mechanisms in other types of experiments, e.g., experiments involving strategic interaction. In experiments that typically involve multiple rounds with the same partner(s), such as voluntary contribution experiments or voting experiments, CSS advise against using RLIM due to the potential for contamination effects. In addition, they strongly advise against using RLIM to randomly select *more than* one choice for payment, because this combines the potential for contamination effects with portfolio effects. Instead, researchers should use pay-all in the examples above and only analyze the last period of play or, alternatively, explicitly model the wealth effects, portfolio effects, and repeated-game effects inherent in the strategic interaction in their analyses. Finally, CSS argue in favor of the OT mechanism wherever possible, acknowledging that sometimes it may be worthwhile to use an impure form of OT where subjects make a number of hypothetical decisions first before making the one decision that determines their earnings.

Azrieli, Chambers, and Healy (ACH) [2018, 2020] also investigate the incentive compatibility of payment mechanisms, and reach some different conclusions to CSS. A key insight of the ACH approach is the distinction between the set of choice objects X in an experiment, and the set of payment objects $P(X)$. Whereas subjects choose from X they receive payments in $P(X)$, so incentive compatibility depends on subjects' preferences over $P(X)$. Experiments are typically designed to elicit information on preferences over X without, as ACH show, considering whether these preferences map to $P(X)$. Consequently, it is often difficult to evaluate whether incentive compatibility actually holds in a given experiment. Thus, ACH derive conditions for preferences over $P(X)$ to ensure incentive compatibility.

Glossing over the technical details, ACH show that when subjects take part in multiple games with different partners and receive no feedback between periods, RLIM is incentive compatible. By contrast, if subjects play games against the same opponent over multiple periods, this is clearly a repeated game, implying that each choice is not independent, and it is not incentive compatible to use RLIM. Similarly, when subjects receive feedback between decisions this can undermine incentive compatibility if subjects' choices affect the feedback they receive. For example, subjects may test particular strategies against earlier partners to gather information and devise optimal strategies to use against later partners. In cases like these, the games should be analyzed as one large strategic interaction, thereby making RLIM inappropriate. One way to circumvent this problem is to employ the *strategy method*, which elicits every possible response to a subject's strategies, and then feedback all of this information to the subject between periods. This approach removes the subject's incentive to experiment with strategies earlier in the game because she automatically receives information on every possible contingency. Consequently, it is appropriate in this case to view each choice as independent and employ RLIM.[28]

ACH show that the pay-all mechanism is only incentive compatible if a "no complementarities at the top" (NCaT) condition holds for preferences over $P(X)$. Put simply, NCaT requires that if we form a bundle of a subject's preferred options from every decision, then this bundle must be preferred to every other possible bundle. This can be a hard property to satisfy, or know whether it is satisfied, in practice, leading ACH to argue against use of the pay-all mechanism in favor of RLIM. Specifically, ACH [2020, p. 1] state that, "the only broadly-applicable incentive compatible system . . . is to pay subjects for one randomly-selected decision."

Clearly, providing evidence for incentive compatibility *can* be a complex affair and certainly illustrates the holism of testing. However, there has been continual progress in understanding what those tests require, and progress in implementing them. To return to our philosophy of science theme, the complications resulting from the holism of testing are real but not insurmountable.

3.4 Strategic Interaction

Since the majority of lab experiments in political science involve strategic interaction, as opposed to individual decision making, it is worthwhile to discuss some issues specific to these experiments and how they interact with incentive compatibility. Game-theoretic experiments often involve repetition, viz., repeated play, against the same or different opponents. In fact, Table 18.1 below shows that every experiment in *JEPS* involving strategic interaction included multiple rounds. Lee [2007] conducts a survey of economic experiments involving repetition and highlights three issues that need to be considered: (1) Learning; (2) Boredom; and (3) Payment mechanisms.

Learning is one of the primary reasons to include repetition in an experiment, particularly in complex decision environments involving multiple players. Binmore [2007a, p. 1] states this explicitly when listing three conditions that define a favorable environment in which to conduct game-theoretic experiments, one of which is that, "Sufficient time is available for trial-and-error learning." While there is general acceptance in experimental economics that repetition promotes learning, there is no consensus about what constitutes "sufficient time," whether subjects should be paid monetary incentives during the learning process, and whether subjects should receive feedback between rounds for learning to occur. Clearly feedback supports learning but this does not imply that no learning can take place without feedback. Similarly, while most experimental economists think that monetary incentives tend to increase learning effort and speed, others argue that monetary incentives may encourage subjects to adopt strategies and stick with them, rather than experimenting with new, and sometimes better, strategies (see the discussion in Lee [2007]). In addition, while repetition can promote trial-and-error learning, excessive repetition can lead to boredom and fatigue, which may cause more (subjects experimenting with strategies to relieve boredom) or less (subjects sticking to a particular strategy) variance in subject behavior.

Salient and payoff-dominant monetary incentives are the logical solution to boredom concerns, but the payment mechanisms used to provide these rewards ultimately determine the incentive compatibility of an experiment, as discussed above. CSS and ACH agree that when subjects take part in a repeated game with the same partners and receive feedback, RLIM is inappropriate because it assumes independence between rounds, which cannot be the case by design. Thus, pay-all is the natural payment mechanism for these experiments, as long as researchers are willing to model repeated-game effects, wealth effects, and portfolio effects in statistical analyses.

Another approach suggested by CSS is the use of impure OT, where subjects take part in a number of hypothetical rounds before completing one round for actual payment. This design raises the issue from above though, about whether learning is best supported by providing monetary incentives or not. A related but different approach is adopted by Sherstyuk, Tarui, and Saijo [2013] in the context of an indefinitely repeated game, where a continuation probability determines whether the interaction continues for another round or not. Sherstyuk, Tarui, and Saijo [2013] show theoretically and empirically that RLIM is not incentive compatible in these experiments, whereas pay-all and a last-round payment mechanism[29] are incentive compatible under the assumption of risk neutrality. Furthermore, the last-round payment mechanism is incentive compatible even under risk aversion. Another strength of the last-round payment protocol is that it is immune to endgame effects because in an indefinitely repeated game, subjects do not know when the final round will take place. This incentivizes subjects to treat each choice as though it is for payment, and promotes learning on the basis of feedback received each round. In addition, the last-round mechanism does not produce wealth effects or portfolio effects.

Table 18.1 Review of Lab Experiments in the Economic Tradition in JEPS

Study	Sample (Size)	Within-subject or between-subject	Number of rounds	Matching	Economist?	Payment Mechanism	Salience?	Dominance?	Game Theory Program	Incentive Compatible?	The Trinity?
Al-Ubaydli, McCabe, and Twieg [2014]	Students in Fairfax, VA, USA (144)	Both	3	Random rematching between each round	Yes	Pay-all	Partial, ECUs (7,000 points = $1)	No	Preference refinement	Unlikely	Theory and Design: Yes Econometrics: Partial
Woon [2014]	Students in Pittsburgh, PA, USA (110)	Both	35	Random rematching between each round	Yes	RLIM (6 out of 30 rounds were paid in Part 1, and 1 out of 5 rounds in Part 2)	Partial, ECUs (100 points = $1)	No	Applied	No	Theory and Design: Yes Econometrics: No
Cason and Mui [2015]	Students in West Lafayette, IN, USA and Caulfield East, VIC, Australia (450)	Both	36	Partner matching for 12 rounds at a time but then rematching after each set of 12 rounds	Yes	Pay-all	Partial, ECUs (8 points = $1)	Questionable	Applied	Unlikely	Theory and Design: Yes Econometrics: No
Battaglini and Mechtenberg [2015]	Students in Princeton, NJ, USA and Berlin, Germany (324)	Both	30	Random rematching between each round	Yes	RLIM	Yes (All amounts stated directly in USD)	Questionable	Preference refinement	No	Theory and Design: Yes Econometrics: Partial
St-Vincent, Blais, and Pilet [2016]	Mostly students in Montreal, Canada, and Brussels, Belgium (252)	Both	24	Partners design	No	Pay-all	Partial, ECUs (20 points = 1CAD)	No	Atheoretic	Unlikely	Theory: Tenuous Design and Econometrics: Yes
Sauermann [2016]	Students in Cologne, Germany (120)	Both	20	Partners design	Yes	Pay-all	Partial, ECUs (1000 points = €1)	No	Preference refinement	No	Theory and Design: Yes Econometrics: No

Study	Subjects (n)		Rounds	Matching		Payment mechanism	Stakes				Trinity
Rogers [2017]	Students in Abu Dhabi, United Arab Emirates (109)	Both	Varied on the basis of subject choices	Individual decision making	No	Pay-all and/or RLIM depending on treatment	Yes (All amounts stated directly in AED)	No	N/A	Questionable	Theory and Design: Partial Econometrics: No
Lorenz, Paetzel and Tepe [2017]	Students in Oldenburg, Germany (80)	Both	6	Random rematching between each round	Yes	Average payoff across all rounds	Partial, ECUs (1 point = €0.005)	No	Preference refinement	No	Theory and Design: Partial Econometrics: Yes
Zhang [2018]	Students in Northern and Southern Italy (371)	Both	3	Random rematching between each round	No	Pay-all but with no feedback between rounds (only at the end of the experiment)	Partial, ECUs (20 points = €1)	No	Preference refinement	Unlikely	Theory and Design: Yes Econometrics: Partial
Kingsley and Muise [2018]	Students in Amherst, MA, USA (105)	Both	25 (Broken down into 3 phases)	Partners design	Yes	Pay-all	Partial, ECUs (20 points = $1)	No	Applied and Preference refinement	No	Theory and Design: Yes Econometrics: Partial
Bassi [2019]	Students and staff at the University of North Carolina at Chapel Hill, NC, USA (166)	Both	20 (Broken down into 2 phases)	Individual decision making	Yes	RLIM	Partial, ECUs (1000 points = $0.20)	No	n/a	Questionable	Theory: Tenuous Design: Good Econometrics: No
DeScioli and Kimbrough [2019]	Students in Burnaby, Canada and Cambridge, MA, USA (200)	Both	20 (But with four periods per round)	Partners design	Yes	Pay-all	Yes (All amounts stated directly in USD)	Questionable	Applied	Unlikely	Theory and Design: Yes Econometrics: Partial
Morton and Ou [2019]	Students in New York, NY, USA (200)	Both	24	Partners design	Yes	RLIM	Yes (All amounts stated directly in USD)	Questionable	Applied and Preference refinement	Unlikely	Yes

Source: Authors' construction.

Notes: RLIM = random lottery incentive mechanism; ECUs = experimental currency units; Trinity = the theory-experimental design–econometric trinity.

Consequently, we think this payment mechanism should be used more widely in games where it is applicable.

The preceding discussions show that the debate over the incentive compatibility of different payment mechanisms in experimental economics is not settled. Nevertheless, we will attempt to discern the incentive compatibility of each lab experiment in *JEPS* drawing on the insights from CSS, ACH, Lee [2007], and Sherstyuk, Tarui, and Saijo [2013].

4.   A REVIEW OF LAB EXPERIMENTS IN *JEPS*

Table 18.1 provides a detailed summary of the thirteen articles employing lab experiments in the economic tradition published in *JEPS* since the inaugural issue in 2014. The articles are classified according to a number of criteria, including: sample size and composition; whether a within-subject or between-subject experimental design was adopted; the number of rounds in which subjects took part; the matching protocol that was used in the study; whether the research team included an economist; the payment protocol that was used; whether the experiment satisfied Smith's precept of salience and promoted dominance; the game theory research program to which the study was (most) sympathetic; whether the experiment was incentive compatible; and whether the study embodies the theory-experimental design-econometric trinity. We discuss each of these elements, focusing on specific studies, below.

All of the studies in Table 18.1 were run exclusively with university students, except for St-Vincent, Blais, and Pilet [2016] who recruited from a sample of students and non-students, and Bassi [2019] who conducted her experiments with university students and staff members. The majority of studies (8 out of 13) were conducted, at least in part, in the USA, with the remaining studies either partly or wholly run in Europe (5), Canada (2), Australia (1), and the United Arab Emirates (1). Sample sizes vary from 80 to 450 subjects, with a mean of approximately 200 subjects across all studies.

Experiments can be classified as within-subject studies, between-subject studies, or a mixture of both. A within-subject experimental design is one where each subject is exposed to all experimental manipulations, viz., treatments, whereas a between-subject design is one where treatments are applied between or across subjects, implying that subjects are only exposed to some of the experimental manipulations. A design combining both features means that participants are exposed to within-subject treatment variations, but some treatments vary only on a between-subject basis. For example, in Al-Ubaydli, McCabe, and Twieg [2014] participants were exposed to within-subject variation in natural resource income over the course of the experiment, coupled with between-subject differences in the level of communication and monitoring, and the order in which natural resource income varied. Table 18.1 shows that every study adopted an experimental design combining both within-subject and between-subject elements.

The number of rounds in which subjects took part over the course of the experiment varied markedly across studies from a low of three in Al-Ubaydli, McCabe, and Twieg [2014] and Zhang [2018], to a high of 36 in Cason and Mui [2015]. As 11 of the 13 studies were game-theoretic in nature, the protocol that was used to match subjects in the experiment is relevant. A partners design, as the name suggests, randomly and anonymously groups subjects at the start of the experiment, and subjects remain in their groups throughout the experiment. With a random rematching protocol, also referred to as a strangers design, subjects are randomly and anonymously rematched at the start of each round of the game. The purpose of the random rematching design is to allow subjects to gain experience and learn about the strategic interaction, without the potential confounding effect of playing a repeated game with the same partners.[30] Of the 11 game-theoretic studies in Table 18.1, five adopted the random rematching protocol, five adopted the partners matching protocol, and Cason and Mui [2015] used a hybrid design where subjects played 12 rounds with the same partners, but were then randomly rematched after each set of 12 rounds.

Every paper published in *JEPS*, barring three, has at least one coauthor with a PhD in economics. This datum shows the extent to which lab experiments in political science are joint projects with economists. As discussed earlier, RLIM and pay-all are the most common payment mechanisms in experimental economics, and experimental political science is no different. Specifically, seven studies used the pay-all mechanism, five studies used some variant of RLIM, and one study, Lorenz, Paetzel, and Tepe [2017], paid subjects on the basis of their average earnings across all rounds in the experiment. This latter payment mechanism is rare in experimental economics because it clearly undermines salience (subjects have to understand how their choices map to rewards, which are then used in the calculation of an average) and dominance (the rewards for each choice are diluted by averaging them across all choices).

With regard to salience, there is widespread use of experimental currency units (ECUs), which are converted into monetary rewards at the end of an experiment, in experimental political science. ECUs undermine salience by introducing an additional cognitive burden in decision making because subjects have to understand how the choices they, and other subjects, make are transformed into ECUs, and then how these ECUs are transformed into money. Only four of the studies in Table 18.1 used actual monetary prizes, the remaining nine studies used ECUs that converted at different rates, listed in the table, into monetary rewards. Two of these nine studies, Cason and Mui [2015] and St-Vincent, Blais, and Pilet [2016], were conducted across countries, which has been used as a justification for ECUs (see, for example, Roth et al. [1991]) so as to hold the nominal amounts presented to subjects in the experiment constant, and, through variations in the ECU exchange rate, also hold the real earnings of subjects constant across locations. However, even in these cases, we see no justifiable reason for using ECUs unless researchers believe that experimental subjects are susceptible to money illusion, both in terms of the natural currency and the ECU, where money illusion refers to the (faulty) idea that nominal, as opposed to real, values influence behavior. Furthermore, even if all subjects suffer from money illusion, the extent to which they do would be heterogenous in a sample, thereby introducing an additional confound to the interpretation of results. Thus, researchers in experimental political science should do away with ECUs because they introduce confounds in data interpretation and analysis, and undermine salience by blurring the link between actions and (real) rewards.

While dominance is conceptually distinct from salience, experiments in which the link between actions and rewards is tenuous also tend to score low in terms of dominance. After all, if subjects have to do additional calculations to determine the mapping between choices and rewards, this extra cognitive effort clearly requires larger rewards for dominance to hold. As Harrison [1989, 1992, 1994] points out, this is particularly problematic if the payoff function is relatively flat around the optimal decision. Table 18.1 shows that all of the studies in which salience is only partial are subject to payoff-dominance issues.

Consider, for example, Woon [2014] who conducted a lab experiment based on the theoretical model of Maskin and Tirole [2004] to determine whether their prediction of a "pandering" equilibrium[31] holds. Woon used ECUs with an exchange rate of 100 points = $1, and ran different payoff treatments: a 25/175 treatment, where the politician's electoral payoff (175) was seven times larger than her policy payoff (25); and a 50/150 treatment, where the politician's electoral payoff (150) was only three times larger than her policy payoff (50). On the basis of the subjects' observed behavior in the experiment, Woon [2014, p. 192] calculates that in the 50/150 treatment the expected value of pandering is 129, whereas the expected value of not pandering is 134, and (correctly) concludes that "observed voting behavior does not produce sufficiently strong reputational incentives for politicians to pander."

However, Woon [2014, p. 192] then performs the same calculations for the 25/175 treatment and finds that the expected value of pandering is 150.5, whereas the expected value of not pandering is 123, leading him to conclude that "the incentives are sufficiently strong." While the incentives may be strong in point-space (150.5 − 123 = 27.5), in dollar-space the difference in expected values from pandering and not pandering is only $0.275. In addition, only six of the 30 rounds (1-in-5) in Part 1 of the experiment were randomly selected for payment, and in only 15 of these 30 rounds was the subject the politician, implying that any particular choice by the subject in the role of politician was payoff-relevant with a probability of 0.1. Consequently, the actual expected value difference from pandering in comparison to not pandering on a particular choice is only $0.275 × 0.1 = $0.0275. Finally, the calculations required to determine this expected value difference are complex and require optimal updating of beliefs over the course of the experiment, suggesting that players had very little incentive to perform them given the trivial difference in forgone income from adopting the sub-optimal strategy of not pandering.

As another example, but one which satisfies salience, consider Experiment I of Morton and Ou [2019], who investigated whether public voting, in comparison to secret ballots, increases the likelihood that subjects vote in a prosocial manner. The experiment involved within-subject variation: each type of voter (type A and type B, which was fixed for each subject across all rounds) was exposed to three different types of elections (elections C, E1, and E2) for eight rounds each, where the distribution of payoffs varied depending on whether party A or party B won the election, which itself was determined by a random dictator rule. The experiment also incorporated between-subject variation: subjects either took part in secret ballot elections, secret ballot with information elections, or public voting elections.

In each of the 24 rounds of the experiment, subjects had to choose whether to vote for party A, vote for party B, or abstain. Casting a vote cost $2, while abstaining cost nothing. Focusing on the control election (Election C, Morton and Ou [2019, p. 144]), if party A wins: an A-type subject earns $20, and a B-type subject earns $5. By contrast, if party B wins: a B-type subject earns $20, and an A-type subject earns $5. In each group of 10 voters, which remained constant throughout the experiment (a partners design), there were 6 A-types and 4 B-types. Conditional on choosing to vote, voting for your party clearly dominates voting for the other party. But because voting is costly, subjects must decide whether to vote for their party or abstain.

Morton and Ou [2019, Appendix A] show that the game has a unique, symmetric mixed strategy Nash equilibrium where A-types vote for party A with a probability of 0.345 and, therefore, abstain with a probability of 0.655, and B-types vote for party B with a probability of 0.520. Clearly, devising these optimal strategies requires subjects to expend serious

cognitive effort, or learn-by-doing over the course of the experiment. In relation to dominance, the question is whether subjects were adequately incentivized to adopt these optimal
strategies. As mentioned above, if party B wins, then an A-type subject forgoes $15 ($20–$5
from not voting, or $18–$3 from voting) in expected income, and the same holds for a B-
type subject if party A wins, which would seem to suggest that subjects did indeed have an
incentive to devise or learn these optimal strategies.

However, in the mixed strategy equilibrium above, the payoff consequences if a subject
deviates from optimality, e.g., an A-type voting for party A with probability 0.4, 0.5, or even
1, are very small given the stochastic nature of the outcome, which is driven by the mixing
behavior of all other subjects, and the random dictator rule that determines the outcome of
the election. In addition, as only one out of 24 rounds was selected for payment, this implies
that the marginal loss associated with a single instance of suboptimal behavior is negligible.
In fact, when one considers the other election types (E1 and E2) in addition to election C,
the payoff consequences of deviating from optimality are even smaller for an A-type, although the same is not true for a B-type, because the A-types only lose $5 if party B wins in
election E1, and only $7 if party B wins in election E2. Thus, even though the experimental
design of Morton and Ou [2019] would superficially appear to satisfy dominance, given the
large difference in earnings depending on whether your party or the other party wins the
election, the complex solution to the problem, the outcome's inherent randomness, and
the fact that any individual round is payoff-relevant with a probability of only 1/24 = 0.042,
implies that the experiment has questionable dominance properties.

The preceding discussion highlights a potential issue with the use of RLIM. Specifically,
unless the forgone income associated with suboptimal behavior is high, or the RLIM selection probability is high, RLIM (arguably) has poor payoff-dominance characteristics. To see
this, suppose that a particular suboptimal choice leads to a loss of $3, which is an amount
that should incentivize most university students to take the choice seriously. However,
suppose this particular choice only has a 1-in-10 chance of being selected for payment. This
implies an expected loss of only $3 × (1/10) = $0.30 from that suboptimal choice, which may
not be enough to incentivize subjects to expend the cognitive effort required to choose optimally. Davis and Holt [1993] emphasize the fact that RLIM dilutes incentives and argue that
it should not be employed to reduce subject payment costs in an experiment. Specifically,
Davis and Holt [1993, p. 452] argue that, "if there are ten decisions, only one of which is to be
selected to determine earnings, then each decision is 1/10 as important as it would be with
straight monetary payments. Therefore the potential payoff for each decision should be ten
times higher than the case where the subject receives payments for all decisions."

While this RLIM "dilution" argument is correct theoretically, the extent to which it binds
empirically depends on whether subjects subscribe to the isolation hypothesis. If subjects
do indeed isolate then they will treat each choice as if it is the only choice that needs to
be made, implying they will not dilute monetary incentives by taking into account the
RLIM selection probability. Thus, the expected loss of $0.30 from suboptimal behavior in
the RLIM example above, may be treated as though it is an actual loss of $3.00, thereby
promoting payoff dominance.

However, a major issue with the isolation hypothesis is the potential for heterogeneity
across subjects: some subjects may isolate completely and ignore the RLIM selection probability altogether, others may isolate partially and only factor in moderate incentive dilution due to RLIM, while others may not isolate at all. At least with pay-all, subjects know

that every decision is payoff-relevant, and isolation heterogeneity should not, therefore, exist. Consequently, we do not think use of RLIM is a panacea for payoff-dominance issues, and that appeals to the isolation hypothesis should be replaced with experimental design choices that are cognizant of flat maxima.

For example, suppose an experimentalist estimates that a payoff-difference of $2 from an optimal as opposed to a suboptimal choice will engage full subject attention and effort. Suppose further that the experimentalist is willing to pay $30 per subject in monetary incentives. The experimentalist can then choose to run a 10-round, pay-all experiment where the expected payoff from choosing optimally in each round is $4, while the expected payoff from choosing suboptimally is $2. Alternatively, the experimentalist can use a 10-round, RLIM experiment where the expected payoff from choosing optimally in a round is $40, while the expected payoff from choosing suboptimally is $20. This RLIM design is robust to isolation heterogeneity, even for subjects who fully dilute incentives by multiplying period payoffs by the RLIM selection probability.[32] Assuming that average payment per round is $3 for pay-all and $30 for the randomly selected choice under RLIM, both designs lead to costs of approximately $30 per subject, and payoff-dominance issues are neutralized. As we have pointed out consistently, the holism of testing does not prevent successful efforts to eliminate confounds.

Unfortunately, none of the studies in Table 18.1 appear to have seriously taken payoff-dominance issues into account in their experimental designs. For example, Cason and Mui [2015] and Battaglini and Mechtenberg [2015], whose experiments are rated "questionable" in Table 18.1 in terms of their payoff-dominance characteristics rather than simply "no," used pay-all and RLIM payment protocols, respectively, but the level of incentives, and, more importantly, the difference in payoffs from optimal as opposed to near-optimal choices, does not promote payoff dominance. In Cason and Mui [2015] the largest payoff difference for players 2 and 3 in a single round is $0.75, which may not prompt serious engagement with the task. By contrast, in Battaglini and Mechtenberg [2015] there is a payoff difference of $5 from a suboptimal choice in a single round, but because there is only a 1-in-30 chance of payment, the actuarial payoff difference from a suboptimal choice is only $0.17. Thus, lab experiments in political science should place greater emphasis on payoff dominance, particularly when testing theory. This is a moral that holds for experimental economics as well on our view.

Of the game-theoretic experiments in Table 18.1, five can be classified as following the preference refinement program, three as forming part of the applied game theory program, and two which are a mixture of the preference refinement and applied programs. For example, Sauermann [2016] conducts an experiment on committee decisions under majority rule and explicitly invokes social preferences as an explanation for the result that in approximately 55% of committee decisions, choices were made that were not (directly and immediately) in a player's self-interest. By contrast, Woon [2014] is a clear example of the applied game theory program because he solves for the perfect Bayesian equilibrium of the strategic interaction, accepts the standard payoff bridging principle, and determines the extent to which subjects reach the equilibrium. Kingsley and Muise [2018] combine elements of both programs because they set up and solve their model assuming the standard payoff bridging principle, but then explore the possibility that prosocial motivations affected behavior in the game by analyzing subject communication during the experiment.

In terms of motivating subjects to reveal their preferences truthfully, Table 18.1 suggests that all of the studies have potential incentive-compatibility issues. Consider, for example, the experimental design of Battaglini and Mechtenberg [2015] which used RLIM, and where subjects received feedback after each round that was contingent on their behavior in the round. As discussed earlier, this experimental design motivates subjects to experiment with strategies earlier in the game to devise optimal strategies for use later in the game. In Battaglini and Mechtenberg's [2015] punishment treatments, subjects have a clear incentive to experiment with punishment earlier in the game to determine the effect that it has, and whether it should be adopted, therefore, in later rounds. This incentive could have been removed by using the strategy method to elicit subjects' full strategies and then feed this information back to the players after each round, as suggested by ACH.

As another example, consider the experimental design of Sauermann [2016], which used partner matching, the pay-all mechanism, provided each subject with information on every other player's cumulative earnings over the course of the experiment, and the full distribution of other players' payoffs from both the status quo and the proposed point in two-dimensional policy space at each stage of the experiment. This design almost certainly features complementarities at the top because even though a subject might prefer point A to point B if that decision was made in isolation, the subject may choose point B over point A under the pay-all mechanism if, say, point B gives the subject with the lowest cumulative payoff a higher payoff in that round. Such a strategy may indeed be optimal if it leads to reciprocation later in the experiment, implying that the experimental design is not eliciting "truthful" per-period behavior. In addition, Sauermann [2016] does not take into account the repeated-game nature of the interaction, and instead uses 20-period or 10-period averages of committee decisions, in statistical analyses. Thus, the design is susceptible to wealth effects, portfolio effects, and repeated game effects, but these are not incorporated or adjusted for in the analyses.

Rogers [2017] and Bassi [2019] also have questionable incentive-compatibility characteristics. In both cases, subjects were required to make choices between lotteries using a multiple price list risk preference design, with RLIM used to select one of the choices for subject payment in Bassi [2019], and used to select one of the choices either for subject payment or payment to a local charity in Rogers [2017].[33] As discussed earlier, RLIM paired with a risk preference task creates a compound lottery for subjects because RLIM randomly selects one of the lottery choices, and then the selected lottery is resolved for subject payment.[34] Thus, RLIM is only theoretically incentive compatible if subjects satisfy ROCL and independence. The experimental designs of Rogers [2017] and Bassi [2019] do not allow us to determine whether these axioms are satisfied, and the results of CSS suggest that subjects do not subscribe to the isolation hypothesis, implying that claims to behavioral incentive compatibility are not warranted. In addition, CSS find that with either variant of RLIM adopted by Rogers [2017] and Bassi [2019] (the prior information and no prior information versions, respectively) elicited preferences are significantly more risk averse relative to the OT mechanism. Brown and Healy [2018], by contrast, contend that presenting all of the risk preference choices in a list (Rogers [2017]), as opposed to presenting them separately as single decisions (Bassi [2019]), is more likely to undermine incentive compatibility. In any event, the incentive compatibility of these experiments is open to question, thereby leading to the "questionable" categorization of these studies' designs.

The final column of Table 18.1 lists the extent to which each study incorporates the theory-experimental design-econometric trinity. Morton and Ou [2019] is the only study that fully promotes the trinity, and it stands out because the experimental design was motivated directly by theory, and the statistical analyses were structured by the theory and informed by the experimental design. Specifically, Morton and Ou [2019] solve for the unique, symmetric mixed strategy equilibrium of their strategic interaction assuming entirely self-interested subjects, and then solve for the mixed strategy equilibrium under the assumption that with probability θ subjects always vote for the prosocial choice, while with probability $1-\theta$ they vote in a self-interested manner. Their econometric approach is linked directly to the theory and experimental design, particularly through their use of a finite mixture model to estimate the proportion of types (prosocial and self-interested) in their sample.

A noteworthy pattern that emerges from Table 18.1 is that eight out of the 13 studies had a very tight link between theory and experimental design. For example, Al-Ubaydli, McCabe and Twieg [2014] ran an experiment, using a virtual world environment that investigated the resource curse under different levels of institutional "quality." Their experimental design was based directly on the theoretical model of Torvik [2002], which Al-Ubaydli, McCabe and Twieg [2014] simplified for use in a lab experiment. Thus, there is an impressive link between theory and design in this experiment.

However, the statistical analyses of Al-Ubaydli, McCabe, and Twieg [2014] are inappropriate because they first averaged the data and then used these point estimates as data in subsequent statistical analyses. As Harrison et al. [2018] make clear, using a point estimate of a statistic as data ignores the sampling variability of the estimate, and does not allow one, therefore, to draw valid statistical inferences. In addition, Al-Ubaydli, McCabe, and Twieg [2014] use ordinary least squares (OLS) to estimate a model of rent-seeking behavior, despite the fact that the dependent variable is discrete and bounded, implying OLS is not appropriate for the data generating process.

Thus, the sad corollary of the pattern identified above is that the majority of studies in *JEPS* do not promote the third component of the trinity: rigorous statistical analyses that are grounded in theory and motivated by the study's experimental design. As highlighted above, an issue that is germane to experimental political science is the use of *estimates*, e.g., averages, *as data* for subsequent statistical analyses, despite the fact that this discards information on the sampling variability of the estimate, and leads to a large loss in statistical power by reducing the number of observations for analysis. For example, Cason and Mui [2015], Sauermann [2016], Kingsley and Muise [2018], and DeScioli and Kimbrough [2019] all adopt this approach. A reason that is often cited for averaging experimental data is to avoid the problem of *session effects*, which refer to correlation in subject responses within an experimental session. However, Fréchette [2012] shows that averaging session data is no panacea for this problem. Thus, while averages can be useful descriptively, we see no justification for using estimates as data in statistical analyses.

Other statistical issues include: estimating a linear probability model (Zhang [2018]), which has poor statistical and inferential properties such as predictions that fall outside the unit interval, as opposed to a logit or probit; analyzing simple counts of data (Rogers [2017] and Bassi [2019]) as opposed to estimating structural econometric models that have been prominent in the literature since Hey and Orme [1994] and Harless and Camerer [1994]; reporting coefficient estimates as opposed to marginal effects, which prevents one from determining whether effect sizes are substantively significant or not (Battaglini and Mechtenberg

[2015]); and using a pooled probit model when a random effects probit model would have been more informative, because it takes into account the panel nature of the data set and correlation in the standard errors over time (Woon [2014]).

To sum up this section, Table 18.1 provides a systematic account of the current state of lab experiments in the economic tradition in political science. Specifically, it shows that: lab experiments tend to be dominated by US researchers, most experiments recruit a relatively large number of subjects, experimental designs tend to incorporate both within-subject and between-subject variation, and matching protocols in game-theoretic studies are roughly evenly split between random rematching and the partners design. In addition, economists feature prominently in the literature, most designs employ either the RLIM or pay-all in-centive mechanisms, and game-theoretic experiments predominantly follow the preference refinement research program, but with a nontrivial number of applied game theory studies.

With regard to the more substantive experimental design features in Table 18.1, lab experiments in political science overuse ECUs and this prevailing practice should be avoided because it undermines salience. Similarly, the vast majority of studies are subject to payoff-dominance issues, particularly if subjects under RLIM calculate expected payoff differences from their choices as opposed to focusing on each choice in isolation. Finally, the experiments are subject to incentive-compatibility issues, and, although there tends to be a tight connection between theory and experimental design, the statistical analyses often do not do justice to the data generating process.

5. CONCLUSION

Lab experiments in the economic tradition have become a common tool in modern empirical political science. They are informed by the methodology of economic experiments originally developed by Smith [1976, 1982] in the context of market experiments, and then broadened to encompass decision-theoretic and game-theoretic studies. It is a worthwhile endeavor, therefore, to assess the current state of lab experiments in political science through the lens of the philosophy and methodology of experimental economics.

The publication of *JEPS* in 2014 provides an ideal vehicle for this appraisal because it is the flagship journal for experimental political science of the American Political Science Association, it published a set of reporting guidelines for experimental research in political science (see Gerber et al. [2014] for the original guidelines, Mutz and Pemantle [2015] for a critique, and Gerber et al. [2015] for the rejoinder), it adopted and promoted a set of guidelines for ethical experimental research (Morton and Tucker [2014]), and its current and former editors are some of the preeminent experimental political scientists.

Our review of the articles in *JEPS* shows that lab experiments in the economic tradition are the third most prevalent form of experiments in political science. Specifically, we identified 13 articles that could be classified as lab experiments in the economic tradition, and our review sought to evaluate them by the standards of experimental economics.

To this end, we introduced and discussed Smith's [1976, 1982] precepts for creating a controlled microeconomic environment in the lab, the theory-experimental design-econometric trinity, issues raised by the holism of testing, experimental tests of game theory, and the two game-theoretic experimental research programs identified by Bardsley et al.

[2009]. We then discussed a number of possible inferential confounds: Harrison's [1989, 1992, 1994] payoff-dominance critique; the use of monetary incentives in experiments; the importance of adopting payment mechanisms that are incentive compatible; and issues specific to strategic interactions.

In Table 18.1 we presented a systematic review of the 13 articles in *JEPS* by providing detailed descriptive information on each study, and evaluating the articles according to the criteria mentioned above. In relation to these criteria, we found that lab experiments in political science overuse ECUs and this undermines salience. In addition, the studies are susceptible to payoff-dominance issues because the forgone income from suboptimal behavior tends to be low, particularly if subjects do not view each choice in isolation. Similarly, the experimental designs do not place enough emphasis on incentive compatibility, so the extent to which subjects' responses should be regarded as reflecting their preferences is questionable. Most of the game-theoretic studies follow the preference refinement research program, but there are also some examples of the applied game theory research program (and hybrids of the two). Finally, whereas most studies closely integrate theory with experimental design, the third component of the trinity, viz., rigorous statistical analysis, tends to receive less emphasis.

Our intention in conducting this review was not to take cheap shots at the methodology of lab experiments in political science from the "commanding heights" of experimental economics, but instead to flag issues that experimental political scientists may want to take on board when designing and analyzing future studies. After all, the extent to which these principles of experimental research are embodied in current experimental economic practice is deeply debatable. As Harrison [2010, p. 52], in a discussion of the "anomalous" finding that the provision of complete information can make outcomes less efficient, puts it, "I do not see this as an odd behavioral result, so much as another reminder of theoretical and behavioral insights that were once well known, but appear now to have been equally well forgotten." Thus, when designing experiments in the future, let us not forget these crucial philosophical and methodological issues.

To close on a positive note, we identified four articles in *JEPS* that ran additional experiments to test the robustness of their main results. For example, Woon [2014] and Bassi [2019] both investigated the effect of contextual framing in supplementary experiments, Morton and Ou [2019] ran additional experiments to check for order effects, learning effects, and experimenter-demand effects, and Zhang [2018] ran experiments in the North and South of Italy to mitigate self-selection effects. The value in running these additional experiments cannot be understated from a philosophy of science perspective, particularly because they are typically relegated to supplementary materials, so the incentives for individual researchers to conduct them are low. While not uncommon in experimental economics, that more than one-quarter of the articles we surveyed included these additional robustness checks is a noteworthy and encouraging feature of current experimental political science practice from which experimental economists can learn.

Notes

1. See Deaton and Cartwright [2018] and Bédécarrats, Guérin and Roubaud [2020] for reviews.
2. Kinder and Palfrey [1993] devote approximately half of their book on the experimental foundations of political science to experiments in the psychology tradition.

3. To avoid having to use the qualifier "in the economic tradition," every subsequent reference to lab experiment refers to lab experiments in the economic tradition.

4. See Plott [1979] and Wilde [1980] for other early contributions to the philosophy and methodology of experimental economics. For more recent contributions, see Friedman and Sunder [1994], Roth [1995], Guala [2005], Holt [2009], and Fréchette and Schotter [2015].

5. In individual decision-making experiments, agents do not interact with each other, but they do "interact" with the institution that determines their final experimental outcome, i.e., the payment mechanism.

6. "Game value" refers to nonmonetary "rewards" that subjects may receive from experimental outcomes. For example, subjects may assign game value to winning an item in an experimental, common-value auction, and may therefore overbid for the item relative to its intrinsic value, leading to the so-called *winner's curse*, instead of trying to maximize the difference between the value of the item and what they end up paying for it, which determines their monetary reward for the task.

7. For example, Bohm [1984, p. 137] asks, "If a given mechanism can be shown to work (which in itself is difficult to establish) in one, two or three laboratory tests, how can we be sure it will work in the fourth instance when we want an important decision to be determined by it?"

8. Econometrics is the statistical analysis of economic data.

9. Davis and Holt [1993, p. 526] make a similar argument: "Since the way an experiment is designed prominently affects the claims that can be made from results, some prior consideration of statistical analysis can dramatically increase what may be learned from an experiment." Moffatt [2016, p. 1] concurs: "Needless to say, the type of econometric approach that is chosen is often, and justifiably, dictated by the type of experiment that has been conducted, and by the types of research questions being addressed."

10. An alternative approach would be to risk-neutralize behavior in these games using the binary lottery procedure proposed by Roth and Malouf [1979].

11. Fiorina and Plott [1978] is a classic example in political science where experimental design was directly informed by theory.

12. McKelvey and Palfrey's [1992, 1995, 1998] development of quantal response equilibrium exemplifies the value of the trinity.

13. Whether this is the exception or the norm in experimental economics is debatable. For example, in the *Handbook of Experimental Economic Methodology*, in which Harrison, Lau and Rutström [2015] appears, Niederle [2015] explicitly argues against the structural econometric approach to analyzing experimental data in favor of clever experimental design to isolate outcomes of interest. As Schotter [2015, p. 68] asks, "Why infer when one can observe?" Harrison, Lau, and Rutström [2015, p. 327] provide a direct response to this question, "If we are to understand why certain comparative static outcomes occur, or do not, we need to know what moving parts of the underlying theory are misspecified, as well as if there need to be more 'moving parts' added to the theory. Quite apart from the value of knowing this from a descriptive point of view, normative inferences demand knowledge of this kind if they are to be more than black box behavioral assertions." Similarly, in *Experimetrics: Econometrics for Experimental Economics*, Moffatt [2016, p. 7] stresses that one of his principle goals is, ". . . to encourage the wider use of fully structural models . . . ." While we are sympathetic to the notion of using clever experimental design to, say, test comparative static predictions of theory, we agree with Harrison, Lau and Rustrŏm [2015] and Moffatt [2016] that structural econometrics is an essential tool for the modern experimental economist.

14. See Cooper and Kagel [2015] for a review.
15. See the *Journal of Economic Behavior & Organization* (2010) special issue on "Issues in the Methodology of Experimental Economics" for a spirited debate about the validity of these two game theory research programs. In particular, see Wilson [2010] and Binmore and Shaked [2010a] for pointed critiques of the preference refinement program, the replies by Fehr and Schmidt [2010] and Eckel and Gintis [2010], and the rejoinder by Binmore and Shaked [2010b].
16. There is an extensive and successful literature in our view that shows the big Lakatosian picture to be a mess. This is no surprise since Lakatos made minimal adjustments to Kuhn, whose enormous import is beyond question, but who was also often enormously vague (Hands [2001]) and, at his worst, also a sophomoric skeptic.
17. We are reminded of the story, perhaps apocryphal, of the philosopher going through airport security in the US immediately after 9-11 who responded to the agent's question of whether he was sure that no one else had had access to his bags before check-in with, "I am not sure I have a foot." He was, perhaps appropriately, taken away for questioning.
18. Bardsley et al. [2009, p. 80–82], drawing on von Winterfeldt and Edwards [1982], refer to this instead as the *flat maximum critique*, because if the payoff function in an experiment is relatively flat around the maximum, as represented by Experiment A in Figure 18.3, then subjects may be unwilling to expend the required cognitive effort to move from a near-optimal decision to an optimal decision. Thus, in these cases, evidence against the null hypothesis m_o in the vicinity of the optimum is weak at best.
19. Fudenberg and Levine [1997] develop a different but complementary framework for calculating subjects' expected losses from suboptimal behavior in game-theoretic experiments. Specifically, they calculate the minimum loss required to rationalize experimental observations given that subjects' beliefs incorporate off-the-equilibrium-path prediction errors. Similar to Harrison [1989, 1992, 1994], they find that average losses are small, ranging from $0.03 to $0.64 per player, across a variety of games with experimental payouts of $2–$30. In addition, Wilcox [1993] develops a simple theory of decision costs to model subject behavior in lab experiments where the level of task complexity and the expected benefits from making particular choices vary. He concludes that "payoff dominance worries are increasingly justifiable as designs become increasingly complex" [Wilcox 1993, p. 1416].
20. This percentage drops to 15% when Hertwig and Ortmann [2001] apply more stringent inclusion criteria.
21. Bardsley et al. [2009] cite Read [2005] for also endorsing this view, but as Harrison [2011, p. 186], in a review of Bardsley et al. [2009], points out, "Read (2005) is a wonderful, blunt satire of the arguments in favor of using hypothetical rewards, although in this chapter he is read as seriously advocating the positions he so brilliantly undermines."
22. As RLIM randomly selects one choice for payment in an experiment, it has the desirable feature of eliminating the potential for *wealth effects*, i.e., changes in behavior during the course of an experiment due to changes in wealth.
23. Kahneman and Tversky [1979] proposed an isolation hypothesis for choice between lotteries, which posits that people disregard common components of two lotteries, and only focus on their distinct elements. Isolation is clearly relevant to the RLIM payment mechanism because all prior choices in a RLIM experiment are common components of the subject's payment lottery, implying they will focus purely on the current choice and ignore all past, and potential future, choices if they subscribe to the isolation hypothesis.

24. CSS actually focus on three different forms of RLIM: (1) RLIM with prior information, where subjects are presented with all decision problems prior to making each choice; (2) RLIM with no prior information, where subjects make each choice without having seen all decision problems; and (3) RLIM where each choice is played out after it is made, but only one of these choices is randomly selected for payment at the end of the experiment. We abstract from these differences when discussing RLIM below, despite the fact that CSS show that the differences are *not* empirically innocuous.

25. CSS, again, focus on different variants of the pay-all mechanism, which they refer to as pay all sequentially (PAS), pay all independently (PAI), pay all correlated (PAC), and PAC/N where the total payoff derived under PAC is divided by the number of choices, N, that were made. CSS [p. 218] acknowledge that PAS is the most commonly used payment mechanism in strategic settings, e.g., games, markets, etc., which is why we focus exclusively on this mechanism in our discussion, and simply refer to it as "pay-all."

26. Wealth effects are not an issue if subjects are risk neutral or if they satisfy constant absolute risk aversion (CARA) because in these cases risk attitudes do not change as a function of wealth. By contrast, wealth effects are an issue theoretically if subjects satisfy decreasing absolute risk aversion (DARA), implying they take on more risk as they get wealthier, or increasing absolute risk aversion (IARA), implying they take on less risk as they get wealthier.

27. CSS analyze choice patterns under different payment mechanisms to determine whether they distort choices relative to OT. Harrison and Swarthout [2014, p. 431–433] critique the almost-exclusive focus on choice patterns in this literature, arguing that there is a limit to what can be inferred from choice patterns alone. Consequently, Harrison and Swarthout [2014] estimate structural models of choice under risk to identify the latent preferences of subjects as revealed by their experimental choices. These structural models provide an ideal econometric basis under which to test whether different payment mechanisms have a significant impact on elicited risk preferences.

28. When adopting this approach, it is clearly crucial to explain to subjects that they will be given all of this information after every decision, so that they understand there can be no benefit from experimenting with strategies earlier in the game. If subjects fail to grasp this then salience and incentive compatibility are undermined.

29. The last-round payment mechanism, as the name suggests, pays out subjects on the basis of their choices in the last round of the game.

30. There is also the perfect/complete strangers design where subjects are never randomly rematched with someone with whom they interacted in the past. Some researchers even push this idea further to ensure that, for example, subject A is only matched with other subjects who have never been matched with prior partners of subject A. In other words, if subject A is matched with subject B in round 1, and subject B is matched with subject C in round 2, subject A will never be matched with subject C (or rematched with subject B). This design is used to ensure that no indirect strategic considerations come into play in the experiment.

31. In a pandering equilibrium, the incumbent politician, despite her knowledge of the actual state of the world, panders to the voter by choosing the policy that the voter, given her limited knowledge of the state of the world, believes is best.

32. For those subjects who isolate completely, this RLIM design is payoff-dominance overkill, but as there will tend to be heterogeneity in the extent to which subjects isolate,

this design mitigates concerns about whether payoffs are sufficiently large for subjects to make optimal, as opposed to near-optimal, choices.

33. The majority of subjects in Rogers [2017] completed the multiple price list risk preference task and the bomb risk elicitation task (BRET). In another treatment, subjects only completed the BRET. Thus, the discussion above is specific to subjects who took part in the multiple price list risk preference task.

34. Rogers [2017] and Bassi [2019] used two different versions of RLIM. In the terminology of CSS, Rogers [2017] used RLIM with prior information, given that subjects were presented with all decision problems prior to making each choice. By contrast, Bassi [2019] used RLIM with no prior information, where subjects made each choice without having seen all decision problems.

REFERENCES

Al-Ubaydli, O., K. McCabe, and P. Twieg (2014): "Can More Be Less? An Experimental Test of the Resource Curse," *Journal of Experimental Political Science*, 1, 39–58.

Azrieli, Y., C. P. Chambers, and P. J. Healy (2018): "Incentives in Experiments: A Theoretical Analysis," *Journal of Political Economy*, 126, 1472–1503.

Azrieli, Y., C. P. Chambers, and P. J. Healy (2020): "Incentives in Experiments with Objective Loteries," *Experimental Economics*, 23, 1–29.

Banerjee, A. V., and E. Duflo (2009): "The Experimental Approach to Development Economics," *Annual Review of Economics*, 1, 151–178.

Bardsley, N., R. Cubitt, G. Loomes, P. G. Moffatt, C. Starmer, and R. Sugden (2009): *Experimental Economics: Rethinking the Rules*. Princeton, NJ: Princeton University Press.

Bassi, A. (2019): "Weather, Risk, and Voting: An Experimental Analysis of the Effect of Weather on Vote Choice," *Journal of Experimental Political Science*, 6, 17–32.

Battaglini, M., and L. Mechtenberg (2015): "When Do Conflicting Parties Share Political Power?," *Journal of Experimental Political Science*, 2, 139–151.

Beattie, J., and G. Loomes (1997): "The Impact of Incentives Upon Risky Choice Experiments," *Journal of Risk and Uncertainty*, 14, 149–162.

Bédécarrats, F., I. Guérin, and F. Roubaud (2020): *Randomized Control Trials in the Field of Development: A Critical Perspective*. Oxford: Oxford University Press.

Binmore, K. (2007a): *Does Game Theory Work? The Bargaining Challenge*. Cambridge, MA: MIT Press.

Binmore, K. (2007b): *Playing for Real: A Text on Game Theory*. New York: Oxford University Press.

Binmore, K., and A. Shaked (2010a): "Experimental Economics: Where Next?" *Journal of Economic Behavior & Organization*, 73, 87–100.

Binmore, K., and A. Shaked (2010b): "Experimental Economics: Where Next? Rejoinder," *Journal of Economic Behavior & Organization*, 73, 120–121.

Bohm, P. (1984): "Revealing Demand for an Actual Public Good," *Journal of Public Economics*, 24, 135–151.

Brown, A. L., and P. J. Healy (2018): "Separated Decisions," *European Economic Review*, 101, 20–34.

Camerer, C. F., and R. M. Hogarth (1999): "The Effects of Financial Incentives in Experiments: A Review and Capital-Labor-Production Framework," *Journal of Risk and Uncertainty*, 19, 7–42.

Cason, T. N., and V.-L. Mui (2015): "Individual Versus Group Play in the Repeated Coordinated Resistance Game," *Journal of Experimental Political Science*, 2, 94–106.

Chen, Y., and J. O. Ledyard (2010): "Mechanism Design Experiments," in *Behavioural and Experimental Economics*, ed. by S. N. Durlauf, and L. E. Blume. London: Palgrave Macmillan, 191–205.

Chetty, R., A. Hofmeyr, H. Kincaid, and B. Monroe (2021): "The Trust Game Does Not (Only) Measure Trust: The Risk-Trust Confound Revisited," *Journal of Behavioral and Experimental Economics*, 90, 1–14.

Cooper, D. J., and J. H. Kagel (2015): "Other-Regarding Preferences: A Selective Survey of Experimental Results," in *The Handbook of Experimental Economics, Volume 2*, ed. by J. H. Kagel, and A. E. Roth. Princeton, NJ: Princeton University Press, 217–289.

Cox, J. C., V. Sadiraj, and U. Schmidt (2014): "Asymmetrically Dominated Choice Problems, the Isolation Hypothesis and Random Incentive Mechanisms," *PLoS ONE*, 9 (e90742), 1–3.

Cox, J. C., V. Sadiraj, and U. Schmidt (2015): "Paradoxes and Mechanisms for Choice under Risk," *Experimental Economics*, 18, 215–250.

Cubitt, R., C. Starmer, and R. Sugden (1998): "On the Validity of the Random Lottery Incentive System," *Experimental Economics*, 1, 115–131.

Davis, D. D., and C. A. Holt (1993): *Experimental Economics*. Princeton, NJ: Princeton University Press.

Deaton, A., and N. Cartwright (2018): "Understanding and Misunderstanding Randomized Controlled Trials," *Social Science & Medicine*, 210, 2–21.

DeScioli, P., and E. O. Kimbrough (2019): "Alliance Formation in a Side-Taking Experiment," *Journal of Experimental Political Science*, 6, 53–70.

Dickson, E. S. (2011): "Economic Versus Psychology Experiments: Stylization, Incentives, and Deception," in *Cambridge Handbook of Experimental Political Science*, ed. by J. Druckman, D. P. Green, J. H. Kuklinski, and A. Lupia. New York: Cambridge University Press, 58–72.

Dorling, J. (1979): "Bayesian Personalism, the Methodology of Scientific Research Programmes, and Duhem's Problem," *Studies in History and Philosophy of Science Part A*, 10, 177–187.

Duflo, E. (2006): "Field Experiments in Development Economics," in *Advances in Economic and Econometrics: Theory and Applications*, ed. by R. Blundell, W. Newey, and T. Persson. New York: Cambridge University Press, 322–348.

Eckel, C., and H. Gintis (2010): "Blaming the Messenger: Notes on the Current State of Experimental Economics," *Journal of Economic Behavior & Organization*, 73, 109–119.

Fehr, E., and K. M. Schmidt (1999): "A Theory of Fairness, Competition, and Cooperation," *Quarterly Journal of Economics*, 114, 817–868.

Fehr, E., and K. M. Schmidt (2010): "On Inequity Aversion: A Reply to Binmore and Shaked," *Journal of Economic Behavior & Organization*, 73, 101–108.

Fiorina, M. P., and C. R. Plott (1978): "Committee Decisions under Majority Rule: An Experimental Study," *The American Political Science Review*, 72, 575–598.

Fréchette, G. R. (2012): "Session-Effects in the Laboratory," *Experimental Economics*, 15, 485–498.

Fréchette, G. R., and A. Schotter (2015): *Handbook of Experimental Economic Methodology*. Oxford: Oxford University Press.

Friedman, D., and S. Sunder (1994): *Experimental Methods: A Primer for Economists*. New York: Cambridge University Press.

Fudenberg, D., and D. K. Levine (1997): "Measuring Players' Losses in Experimental Games," *Quarterly Journal of Economics*, 112, 507–536.

Gerber, A., K. Arceneaux, C. Boudreau, C. Dowling, S. Hillygus, T. Palfrey, D. R. Biggers, and D. J. Hendry (2014): "Reporting Guidelines for Experimental Research: A Report from the Experimental Research Section Standards Committee," *Journal of Experimental Political Science*, 1, 81–98.

Gerber, A. S. (2011): "Field Experiments in Political Science," in *Cambridge Handbook of Experimental Political Science*, ed. by J. N. Druckman, D. P. Green, J. H. Kuklinski, and A. Lupia. Cambridge: Cambridge Universiy Press, 115–138.

Gerber, A. S., K. Arceneaux, C. Boudreau, C. Dowling, and D. S. Hillygus (2015): "Reporting Balance Tables, Response Rates and Manipulation Checks in Experimental Research: A Reply from the Committee That Prepared the Reporting Guidelines," *Journal of Experimental Political Science*, 2, 216–229.

Gerber, A. S., and D. P. Green (2012): *Field Experiments: Design, Analysis, and Interpretation*. New York: Norton.

Guala, F. (2005): *The Methodology of Experimental Economics*. Cambridge: Cambridge University Press.

Hands, D. W. (2001): *Reflection without Rules: Economic Methodology and Contemporary Science Theory*. Cambridge, MA: Cambridge University Press.

Harless, D. W., and C. F. Camerer (1994): "The Predictive Utility of Generalized Expected Utility Theories," *Econometrica*, 62, 1251–1289.

Harrison, G. W. (1989): "Theory and Misbehavior of First-Price Auctions," *American Economic Review*, 79, 749–762.

Harrison, G. W. (1992): "Theory and Misbehavior of First-Price Auctions: Reply," *American Economic Review*, 82, 1426–1443.

Harrison, G. W. (1994): "Expected Utility Theory and the Experimentalists," *Empirical Economics*, 19, 223–253.

Harrison, G. W. (2010): "The Behavioral Counter-Revoluion," *Journal of Economic Behavior & Organization*, 73, 49–57.

Harrison, G. W. (2011): "The Methodological Promise of Experimental Economics," *Journal of Economic Methodology*, 18, 183–187.

Harrison, G. W. (2013): "Field Experiments and Methodological Intolerance," *Journal of Economic Methodology*, 20, 103–117.

Harrison, G. W., A. Hofmeyr, D. Ross, and J. T. Swarthout (2018): "Risk Preferences, Time Preferences, and Smoking Behavior," *Southern Economic Journal*, 85, 313–348.

Harrison, G. W., M. I. Lau, and E. E. Rutström (2015): "Theory, Experimental Design, and Econometrics Are Complementary (and So Are Lab and Field Experiments)," in *Handbook of Experimental Economic Methodology*, ed. by G. R. Fréchette, and A. Schotter. New York: Oxford University Press, 296–338.

Harrison, G. W., and J. A. List (2004): "Field Experiments," *Journal of Economic Literature*, 42, 1009–1055.

Harrison, G. W., and E. E. Rutström (2008): "Risk Aversion in the Laboratory," in *Research in Experimental Economics: Volume 12. Risk Aversion in Experiments*, ed. by J. C. Cox, and G. W. Harrison. Bingley: Emerald, 41–196.

Harrison, G. W., and J. T. Swarthout (2014): "Experimental Payment Protocols and the Bipolar Behaviorist," *Theory and Decision*, 77, 423–438.

Hertwig, R., and A. Ortmann (2001): "Experimental Practices in Economics: A Methodological Challenge for Psychologists?," *Behavioral and Brain Sciences*, 24, 383–451.

Hey, J. D., and C. Orme (1994): "Investigating Generalizations of Expected Utility Theory Using Experimental Data," *Econometrica*, 62, 1291–1326.

Holt, C. A. (1986): "Preference Reversals and the Independence Axiom," *American Economic Review*, 76, 508–515.

Holt, C. A. (2007): *Markets, Games, & Strategic Behavior*. Boston, MA: Pearson.

Howson, C., and P. Urbach (2005): *Scientific Reasoning: The Bayesian Approach*. La Salle, IL: Open Court.

Kagel, J. H., and D. Levin (2010): "Auctions (Experiments)," in *Behavioural and Experimental Economics*, ed. by S. N. Durlauf, and L. E. Blume. London: Palgrave Macmillan, 14–22.

Kahneman, D., and A. Tversky (1979): "Prospect Theory: An Analysis of Decision under Risk," *Econometrica*, 47, 263–291.

Kinder, D., and T. R. Palfrey (1993): *Experimental Foundations of Political Science*. Ann Arbor, MI: University of Michigan Press.

Kingsley, D. C., and D. Muise (2018): "More Talk, Less Need for Monitoring: Communication and Deterrence in a Public Good Game," *Journal of Experimental Political Science*, 5, 88–106.

Kittel, B., and R. B. Morton (2012): "Introduction: Experimental Political Science in Perspective," in *Experimental Political Science: Principles and Practices*, ed. by B. Kittel, W. J. Luhan, and R. B. Morton. UK: Palgrave Macmillan, 1–16.

Kuhn, T. (1962): *The Structure of Scientific Revolutions*. Chicago, IL: University of Chicago Press.

Lakatos, I. (1978): "The Methodology of Scientific Research Programmes," in *Philosophical Papers, Volume 1*, ed. by J. Worrall, and G. Currie. Cambridge: Cambridge University Press, 8–101.

Lee, J. (2007): "Repetition and Financial Incentives in Economics Experiments," *Journal of Economic Surveys*, 21, 628–681.

Lorenz, J., F. Paetzel, and M. Tepe (2017): "Just Don't Call It a Tax! Framing in an Experiment on Voting and Redistribution," *Journal of Experimental Political Science*, 4, 183–194.

Maskin, E., and J. Tirole (2004): "The Politician and the Judge: Accountability in Government," *American Economic Review*, 94, 1034–1054.

McDermott, R. (2011): "Internal and External Validity," in *Cambridge Handbook of Experimental Political Science*, ed. by J. N. Druckman, D. P. Green, J. H. Kuklinski, and A. Lupia. Cambridge: Cambridge Universiy Press, 27–40.

McKelvey, R. D., and T. R. Palfrey (1992): "An Experimental Study of the Centipede Game. (Includes Appendix)," *Econometrica*, 60, 803–836.

McKelvey, R. D., and T. R. Palfrey (1995): "Quantal Response Equilibria for Normal Form Games," *Games and Economic Behavior*, 10, 6–38.

McKelvey, R. D., and T. R. Palfrey (1998): "Quantal Response Equilibria for Extensive Form Games," *Experimental Economics*, 1, 9–41.

Moffatt, P. G. (2016): *Experimetrics: Econometrics for Experimental Economics*. London: Palgrave.

Morton, R. B., and K. Ou (2019): "Public Voting and Prosocial Behavior," *Journal of Experimental Political Science*, 6, 141–158.

Morton, R. B., and J. A. Tucker (2014): "Experiments, Journals, and Ethics," *Journal of Experimental Political Science*, 1, 99–103.

Morton, R. B., and K. Williams (2010): *Experimental Political Science and the Study of Causality. From Nature to the Lab.* Cambridge: Cambridge University Press.

Mutz, D. C., and R. Pemantle (2015): "Standards for Experimental Research: Encouraging a Better Understanding of Experimental Methods," *Journal of Experimental Political Science*, 2, 192–215.

Niederle, M. (2015): "Intelligent Design: The Relationship between Economic Theory and Experiments: Treatment-Driven Experiments," in *Collective Decision Making: Applications from Public Choice Theory*, ed. by G. R. Fréchette, and A. Schotter. New York: Oxford University Press, 104–131.

Plott, C. R. (1979): "The Application of Laboratory Experimental Methods to Public Choice," in *Collective Decision Making*, ed. by C. S. Russell. Washington, DC: Resources for the Future, 137–160.

Read, D. (2005): "Monetary Incentives, What Are They Good For?," *Journal of Economic Methodology*, 12, 265–276.

Rogers, J. (2017): "Nothing to Lose: Charitable Donations as Incentives in Risk Preference Measurement," *Journal of Experimental Political Science*, 4, 34–56.

Roth, A. E. (1995): "Introduction to Experimental Economics," in *The Handbook of Experimental Economics*, ed. by J. H. Kagel, and A. E. Roth. Princeton, NJ: Princeton University Press, 3–110.

Roth, A. E., and M. W. K. Malouf (1979): "Game-Theoretic Models and the Role of Information in Bargaining," *Psychological Review*, 86, 574–594.

Roth, A. E., V. Prasnikar, M. Okuno-Fujiwara, and S. Zamir (1991): "Bargaining and Market Behavior in Jerusalem, Ljublana, Pittsburgh, and Tokyo: An Experimental Study," *American Economic Review*, 81, 1068–1095.

Sauermann, J. (2016): "Committee Decisions under Majority Rule Revisited," *Journal of Experimental Political Science*, 3, 185–196.

Schotter, A. (2015): "On the Relationship between Economic Theory and Experiments," in *Handbook of Expeirmental Economic Methodology*, ed. by G. R. Fréchette, and A. Schotter. New York: Oxford University Press, 58–85.

Sherstyuk, K., N. Tarui, and T. Saijo (2013): "Payment Schemes in Infinite-Horizon Experimental Games," *Experimental Economics*, 16, 125–153.

Smith, V. L. (1976): "Experimental Economics: Induced Value Theory," *American Economic Review*, 66, 274–279.

Smith, V. L. (1982): "Microeconomic Systems as an Experimental Science," *American Economic Review*, 72, 923–955.

St-Vincent, S. L., A. Blais, and J.-B. Pilet (2016): "The Electoral Sweet Spot in the Lab," *Journal of Experimental Political Science*, 3, 75–83.

Stanford, K. (2017): "Underdetermination of Scientific Theory," in *The Stanford Encyclopedia of Philosophy*, ed. by E. N. Zalta. Stanford: Stanford University. https://plato.stanford.edu/archives/win2017/entries/scientific-underdetermination/.

Starmer, C. (2000): "Developments in Non-Expected Utility Theory: The Hunt for a Descriptive Theory of Choice under Risk," *Journal of Economic Literature*, 38, 332–382.

Starmer, C., and R. Sugden (1991): "Does the Random Lottery Incentive System Elicit True Preferences? An Experimental Investigation," *American Economic Review*, 81, 971–978.

Torvik, R. (2002): "Natural Resources, Rent-Seeking and Welfare," *Journal of Development Economics*, 67, 455–470.

von Winterfeldt, D., and W. Edwards (1982): "Costs and Payoffs in Perceptual Research," *Pyschological Bulletin*, 91, 609–622.

Wilcox, N. T. (1993): "Lottery Choice: Incentives, Complexity and Decision Time," *The Economic Journal*, 103, 1397–1417.

Wilde, L. (1980): *On the Use of Laboratory Experiments in Economics*. Dordrecht: Reidel.

Wilson, B. J. (2010): "Social Preferences Aren't Preferences," *Journal of Economic Behavior & Organization*, 73, 77–82.

Wilson, M. (2006): *Wandering Significance: An Essay on Conceptual Behaviour*. Oxford: Oxford University Press.

Woon, J. (2014): "An Experimental Study of Electoral Incentives and Institutional Choice," *Journal of Experimental Political Science*, 1, 181–200.

Zhang, N. (2018): "Institutions, Norms, and Accountability: A Corruption Experiment with Northern and Southern Italians," *Journal of Experimental Political Science*, 5, 11–25.

PART 3

···

PURPOSES AND USES OF POLITICAL SCIENCE

···

PART 3, *Purposes and Uses of Political Science*, explores how specific purposes play a role in identifying, selecting, and deselecting aspects of the political phenomena investigated as well as the opportunities and limitations this implies for using political science knowledge. Differences in perspectives and conceptualization when inquiring into political phenomena might reflect the underlying diversity of phenomena but also may reflect the different purposes researchers have. The plurality and contextuality this implies raise questions about how political science knowledge can be used. One issue concerns extrapolation, the extent to which the results of specific studies can be transferred to other contexts and be used by, for example, policymakers to inform interventions. Political science knowledge is not only used for interventions. Another aim is, for instance, to make reliable predictions. This requires sufficient causal knowledge, which might be a challenge due to, inter alia, the ubiquity of causal fragility, underdetermination, and noise. Aspects of causality, prediction, and extrapolation have received much attention in the philosophy of science, and this part of the Handbook explores how political science research might benefit from this work in reflecting on its purposes and uses.

....

CHAPTER 19

PHILOSOPHY OF SCIENCE ISSUES IN CLIENTELISM RESEARCH

....

HAROLD KINCAID, MIQUEL PELLICER, AND EVA WEGNER

CLIENTELISM—roughly the distribution of resources from politicians to voters in exchange for influence on electoral behavior—remains a widespread phenomenon globally and is not just found in less developed countries. While clientelism has been around as long as there have been electoral processes and longer (it probably emerged from landlord-tenant relations), it has received a renewed burst of interest with a burgeoning empirical and theoretical literature from political scientists in the last two decades. This chapter discusses aspects of this recent literature. The discussion is framed in terms of developments in the philosophy of science and philosophy of social science and current debates over clientelism. The hope is to advance both a bit in the process.

Section 1 describes briefly some basic ideas from contemporary approaches in philosophy of science and philosophy of social science. The rest of the chapter then takes up topics in clientelism research where philosophy of science issues are lurking.

Section 2 concerns definitions of clientelism. We document a large range of accounts in the literature. Those definitions are sometimes unclear in key ways, often do not provide anything like a formal definition in terms of necessary and sufficient conditions, and invoke different parameters across definitions. We argue that a plurality of definitions, definitions which are often informal in nature, is not *necessarily* a problem *if* research is cognizant of how it picks out clientelistic phenomena and does so in empirically fruitful ways. To advance that end we chart a set of different parameters that can be found in various definitions of clientelism. Research would be improved, we argue, if work explicitly identified which of the elements of clientelism we sketch (or others) are being investigated. Clientelism is a complex phenomenon, and communication, debate, evidence, and so on would all be advanced if the particular components of clientelism at issue are made as explicit as possible.

Section 3 discusses explanatory frameworks in clientelism research. We break the topic into different parts: first, the general questions about clientelism that are being asked, second, the broad type and system of causes and the specific proposed causal factors that instantiate them, and third questions about evidence raised by alternative possible explanations. Again, our hope is to clarify debates that are sometimes at cross purposes and unclear on basic presuppositions.

Section 4 concludes and raises questions worth further investigation.

1   A PHILOSOPHY OF SCIENCE APPROACH

This section sketches some general ideas from the philosophy of science and philosophy of social science (more details are developed in Chapter 1). These ideas are then applied and hopefully fleshed out and supported in applying them to political science research on clientelism. Most empirical work in political science works with at least implicit philosophy of science assumptions; the goal here is to be explicit about those assumptions with the hope of clarifying and improving debate within the field. This is an overriding goal of the volume as a whole.

The dominant approach in contemporary philosophy of science and the one adopted here is naturalism. "Naturalism" takes on many different meanings, but here the key idea is that philosophy of science and philosophy of social science are continuous with the sciences themselves. This means that philosophy of science issues are ultimately empirical and tested against scientific practice—we ask whether some abstract philosophy picture of science fits what political scientists do and/or suggests how their work might be clarified. That is not to deny that getting clear on concepts is a good thing, and that the sciences, especially the behavioral and social sciences, raise what might be called philosophical questions. Still, naturalists deny that there is some special independent source of knowledge that comes from philosophy that is not already scientifically embedded.

Naturalism in the sense we use here inspires other ideas. The empirical nature of philosophy of science fits well with what we might call "contextualism" (Williams 1999; Kincaid 2003). Contextualism asserts that we are never really in the situation of evaluating all our knowledge at once—that we are always making claims against a background of knowledge that is taken as given. Thus, judgments about good science are likely to be complex, local judgments. Justification is always relative to a specific context, which is specified by the questions to be answered, the relevant error probabilities to be controlled, the background knowledge that is taken as given, etc. A priori universal rules for good inference, good explanation, and the like are hard to find and unlikely to do much work even if found. "Don't contradict yourself too much" may be universal guidance but it is not very helpful; scientific virtues like "simplicity" often are really empirical, substantive claims rather than formal logical virtues.[1] Instead, arguing for scientific success, progress, and error requires making an empirical case that will generally depend on lots of discipline and context-specific details.

Several other ideas are likely fellow travelers with naturalism and contextualism. Some that will be of use in this chapter are:

> *Antiessentialism about theories*: theories are not unified, monolithic entities and there is much
> more to science than theories. Work in the history and sociology of science (Kuhn 1962;
> Beller 2001), analyzes of the role of models in science (Giere 1988; Cartwright 1999) and other
> work in science studies give us reason to believe that 'theories' have diverse interpretations
> across individuals and applications, are often not a single axiomatizable set of statements,
> and involve differing kinds of extra-theoretical assumptions and devices in the process of

explaining. From much of that same work we also learn that skills, material culture and social organization of expertise are essential to science.

Contextual elements in explanation: work on the logic of questions and answers and associated discussions of the pragmatics of explanation show the important role of context in explanation (Belnap and Steel 1976). It is useful to think of an explanation as an answer to a question. Questions are incomplete until contrasts classes of its terms are filled in (Why did Adam {as opposed to Eve} eat{as opposed to throw} the apple); that is done according to the context dictated by the interests and knowledge of the audience (Garfinkel 1981; van Fraassen 1980). A further contextual element suggests what kind of answer the question requires. Thus, what constitutes an adequate answer is not going to be a purely formal or logical matter determined by conceptual analysis of the 'logic of explanation'. Debates in the social sciences over methodological individualism or other constraints on adequate explanation are accordingly empirical and contextual.[2]

Holism of theories, evidence, and explanation: Critics of positivism argued forcefully that testing is always holistic. Bringing hypotheses to data always requires background theory about experimental set up, the distribution of errors in observations, and more. When hypotheses conflict with data it is thus unclear who is the guilty party: it may be the hypothesis that errs, but blame might also be due to bad company in the form of mistaken background assumptions. Contextualism builds on this fundamental insight. Yet, it is a deep mistake to conclude--as much postmodernist commentary has--that this holism shows that judgments about good science are necessarily indeterminate, purely sociological, and the like. In fact, the holism of testing suggests just the opposite.[3] A web of dependencies provides for a variety of independent tests.

Ruling out alternatives: Testing is not just holistic in that any test involves multiple assumptions, but it is also what you might call "contrastive." A hypothesis might fit the evidence and yet not be believable because other hypotheses might explain the evidence equally well. This is easily seen from Bayes' theorem analyzing the value of evidence in evaluating a hypothesis H:

$$p(H/e) = \frac{p(e/H) \cdot p(H)}{p(e/H) \cdot p(H) + p(e/H) \cdot p(H)}$$

We clearly have to evaluate the plausibility of the alternatives to H to assess how well E supports H. This point does not require any commitment to Bayesianism in general but is simply good scientific common sense: your theory is better supported if you give evidence against competitors.

The contextual value of mechanisms: The idea that social science should provide mechanisms is widespread. However, it seems that what we mean by mechanisms and what their role is depends on a number of contextual or local elements. A mechanism might be an intervening cause or the underlying individual details of some macrolevel social phenomena. Mechanisms might strengthen explanation and evidence, they might be essential, or they might obstruct or be inessential to explanation and evidence (Kincaid 2012).

These general philosophy of science ideas will be part of our analysis of current clientelism research at various places in the following. Hopefully, they will both help clarify the empirical issues and be made more concrete in the process.

2 DEFINING CLIENTELISM

This section concerns definitions of clientelism. Political scientists differ in what they take clientelism to be and in how they think it should be explained. We first survey a variety of definitions given by researchers. They differ and could be more explicit, so we outline a set of parameters about which they directly or indirectly make assumptions. That set of parameters goes some way toward clarifying the different perspectives separating researchers. We then argue, instantiating the philosophy of science framework sketched above, that these differences are not automatically worrisome once made explicit. Differences in definitions can reflect underlying diversity of phenomena or diversity of knowledge interests; they need not reflect deep epistemological differences over how to do clientelism research. We discuss a range of recent typologies proposed by clientelism researchers that seek to capture this diversity. Last, we highlight how typologies that are built inductively from existing research can capture both contextualism and provide structure.

It is worth discussing at some length how researchers define clientelism. That will make clear the diversity involved and also provide a base for us to sort out parameters and ambiguities.[4]

"We define clientelism as the discretionary distribution of public resources by politicians" (Golden, Nazrullaeva, and Wolton 2020, p.1)

Clientelism is "nonprogrammatic distribution combined with conditionality" where "the party offers material benefits on the condition that the recipient returns the favor with a vote or other forms of political support." (Stokes et al. 2013, p. 13)

"Clientelist vote buying" is "the distribution of rewards to individuals or small groups during elections in contingent exchange for vote choices. Rewards are defined as cash, goods (including food and drink), and services." (Nichter 2014, p.316)

Clientelism is "the direct exchange of a citizen's vote in return for direct payments or continuing access to employment, good, and services" but "patrons provide private goods or club goods to their clients" (Kitschelt and Wilkinson 2007, p. 2 and p. 109)

Electoral clientelism is "the allocations of private and material benefits to voters during elections". It is "not a transaction" (Kramon 2018, p. 3) but is "informational." (p. 11)

Clientelism involves "material benefits contingent on citizens political support" and a "citizen promises that he or she will provide (or has provided) political support" (Nichter 2018, p. 9 and p. 70).

The "key elements of clientelistic relationship [are] dyadic relationships, contingency, hierarchy, and iteration" (Hicken 2011, p. 290)

"the core attributes of clientelism [are] . . . an exchange in which individuals maximize their interests...involves longevity, diffuseness, face to face contact and inequality" and are different from "vote buying and corruption" (Hilgers 2012b, p. 162).

Clientelism is an "exchange relationship in which a powerful actor trades resources for political support from less powerful actors" (Shefner 2012, p.44).

General clientelism is "a personalistic relationship of power in which a divisible benefit is exchanged for political support" (Aspinall and Sukmajati 2019, p. 3-4).

"A patron-client relationship is a vertical dyadic relationship that is established between two persons of different power status" (Yaghi 2019, p. 119).

"Clientelistic exchanges are electoral strategies where politicians rely on electoral intermediaries to incentivize voters to support a particular candidate." Incentives can be "positive and negative" (e.g., threats) (Mares and Young 2019 p.33 and p.35.)

"Iteration is the major characteristic of clientelism" (Ruiz de Elvira, Schwarz, Weipert-Fenner 2019, p.9)

Clientelism is "a strategy of political mobilization in which politicians solve or promise to solve voters' problems in exchange for their political support." (Szwarcberg 2015, p.2)

These definitions are sometimes unclear at key points and invoke different properties that are taken to be constitutive of clientelism. Some notion of a conditional exchange features in many definitions but scholars often add on other elements to their definition or conception of clientelism while a number also fully dispense with the notion that clientelism is an exchange.

At least the following different elements and questions seemed involved in the quotations above:

1. Is clientelism a contingent relationship? in both directions? for promised or actual behavior? Is exchange the same as contingency?
2. Who or what stands in a clientelistic relation? individual politicians and individual voters, individual politicians and individual brokers and then the latter with individual voters, parties and individual voters, individual politicians and groups of voters, and the latter two relations mediated by a broker cover most of the possibilities.
3. What behavior on the part of voters do patrons try to influence? individual votes in the immediate future? individual votes over time? individual kinds of other electoral support such as campaigning and making donations? immediate future or over time? For all the above, separate questions result if we substitute the often more realistic "promised" as a qualifier to the behavior in question.
4. As the above two questions imply, is the client-patron relation one shot or repeated?
5. Questions 3 and 4 reframed where "individual voters" is replaced by "brokers," e.g., do politicians have one shot or ongoing relations with brokers?
6. "Politician" can also be replaced by "brokers" in questions 2 and 3, e.g., do brokers have ongoing or one-shot relations with voters?
7. Is the relationship voluntary?
8. Is the relationship mutually beneficial? Are relationships with punishment as outcomes beneficial and/or voluntary?
9. Do the benefits from clientelist relations have to go to identifiable individuals? If not, is pork barrel politics an instance of clientelism?
10. Do patrons have to have greater power than clients? Brokers greater power than clients?

These ten questions have answers that can logically vary independently of each other, and most of the questions themselves have subcomponents. Theoretically, there are an enormous number of possible different definitions based on the elements listed here, and the literature has occupied a fair amount of the resulting hyperspace as the quotes above show. Iteration, power differences, one on one relationships, brokers, promises of electoral support, verified votes, club goods, voluntariness and more are all seen as necessary conditions in all kinds of different combinations and seen by others as not essential to clientelism. Sometimes it is not clear whether these elements are being invoked; sometimes an explicit definition is given only a little later for it apparently to be dropped or changed. Researchers often identify elements they take to be necessary but do not say if those elements are supposed to be sufficient or if they are part of a set of elements that is sufficient.

What are the implications of this plethora of actual and possible definitions for political science work on clientelism? On traditional positivist[5] conceptions of science, this clientelist work may seem a mess. Shouldn't we first clearly define major concepts and then move on to tying them to observable events?

Some political scientists do hold the view that there is a correct definition of clientelism and that there are individually necessary and jointly sufficient conditions for particular behaviors truly being clientelism. This is clearly expressed in worries, typical of political science, about "conceptual stretching" (e.g., Hilgers 2012b or Nichter 2014). Several attempts have been made to narrow down the definition, either by making the contingency of the clientelistic exchange the one necessary condition of clientelism (Stokes et al. 2013, Nichter 2014, 2018), by going back to the roots of clientelism research and defining as clientelism only those relations that display longevity, diffuseness, face to face contact and inequality (e.g., Hilgers 2012b), or by extracting specific traits as the "essential" or "core" (Hicken 2011, p. 4) elements of clientelism from the body of research on the topic.

As noted in Section 1, explicit definitions in the form of necessary and sufficient conditions are certainly to be valued. However, the naturalist approach of Section 1 suggests things are not this simple. Much science proceeds without definitions involving necessary and sufficient conditions. Many scientific concepts are hard to define in that way. The concept of "gene," for example, still defies any definition in terms of jointly sufficient necessary conditions (Moss 2003) that covers all uses in biology. However, in applications biologists have been quite empirically and explanatorily successful. A similar situation holds for more ordinary everyday concepts—necessary and sufficient definitions are often unavailable. Since political science often has to build on ordinary language concepts, it is no surprise it runs into similar problems. However, we get on successfully in ordinary life nonetheless just as much good science does.

So, the question is how we deal successfully with less than perfect, often different, definitions? One approach (coming from psychology and artificial intelligence) suggests we use concepts that rely on family resemblance and protoypes (see Goertz 2006). The family resemblance idea in practice can work in diverse ways. Some elements can be necessary, with any of the others providing sufficiency. No element may be necessary, but the number of elements may be set, e.g., "any three of the following." A looser, more general approach basically identifies a cluster of properties found in typical cases and thus groups phenomena by how similar they are to the prototypical properties. There are ways using fuzzy set theory (Ragin 2000) to formalize such judgments. Political science has generally led the way in investigating such methods, but they are almost nonexistent in the study of clientelism. In the end, such methods do not eliminate the need for qualitative similarity judgments in any case.

The contextualism defended here also suggests an alternative pragmatic approach to the definition of clientelism. The test of a definition is what we can do with it.[6] The short story is that the more extensive, tight and clearly formulated are the ties of a concept to a body of theoretical and empirical work the more successful the concepts are. Those ties can be broken down into horizontal and vertical connections as it were, with horizontal ties being relations to other phenomena and their categorization and explanation, and vertical ties being either connections to "lower" more observable phenomena and higher ones to more general phenomena and categories. Definitions ideally get fleshed out by specification of further elements closer to observable data and indicators, even if we do not claim that they provide "if and only if" translations. In these ways the holism of testing, theory and evidence is a virtue.

In the past ten years, research on clientelism has combined prototype and pragmatic approaches to provide typologies or classifications of clientelism (e.g., Stokes et al. 2013, Nichter 2008, 2014, 2018, Kitschelt and Wilkinson 2007, Hutchcroft 2014, Mares and Young 2019, Berenschot and Aspinall 2020, among others). Moving away from providing a single definition of clientelism, researchers seek to identify characteristics that distinguish clientelism from programmatic politics and different types of clientelism from each other. This has led to distinctions of clientelism that takes place at election time ("electoral clientelism" or "one-shot clientelism") and clientelism that involves repeated interactions outside elections ("relational clientelism") (e.g., Nichter 2018 or Yildirim and Kitschelt 2020); scholars have also proposed to distinguish clientelism at the group level (e.g., "meso-particularistic") from clientelism at the individual level (microparticularistic; Hutchcroft 2014); between different types of electoral clientelism, such as abstention, turnout, and vote-buying (Nichter 2008 as well as Gans-Morse et al. 2014); clientelism that is based on positive inducements (e.g., "policy favors") from clientelism that involves negative inducements (e.g., "policy coercion") (Mares and Young 2019); or more broadly, different forms of patronage systems ("party-centered" vs. "community-centered"; Berenschot and Aspinall 2020).

These typologies, although mostly deductive, are typically closely tied to an author's background knowledge on clientelism and often linked to a specific empirical project. This makes them often context-specific, such as Mares and Young's (2019) typology capturing clientelistic exchanges in Eastern Europe, Nichter's (2008) and Stokes et al.'s (2013) capturing "machine politics" or Hutchcroft's (2014) capturing electoral politics in Southeast Asia. The connectedness to context makes them better-suited to guide and organize empirical work in that context—the price is a proliferation of typologies, types, and discriminating factors, that, akin to the proliferation of definitions and understandings of clientelism, do not speak much to each other or build on each other. Again, the absence of such a shared understanding might not be a problem if researchers do not try to sell their typology as the definitive one.

Ultimately, we want a definition—or a typology—that picks out something of interest in the world. It may pick out properties or more broadly causes, causal processes, etc. (and properties or attributes are probably explicated largely in terms of their causal effects). Those properties and causes need to be stable enough and sufficiently contained that we can use them in building explanations of social phenomena. There does not have to be just one way to pick out such stable causes and properties. Afterall, the natural sciences often get on quite well with fundamental concepts such as "gene" that get can be fruitfully used in different ways to pick out useful patterns in the world. Even temperature and H_2O admit such flexibility (Chang 2008, 2012).

One way to identify stable clientelist phenomena comes from seeing which characteristics consistently group together. Pellicer et al. (2020) have shown one way to make progress on this task by developing a typology that is fully inductive and based on ethnographic research on clientelism from all world regions. Taking as the basis ethnographic accounts of clientelism has the advantage of producing a typology closely linked to real-existing empirical phenomena; using accounts from all world regions allows the typology to be potentially more comprehensive than existing ones that are based on a particular context.

Pellicer et al. (2020) develop a coding scheme for capturing characteristics of the clientelistic exchanges described in this literature. The coding scheme seeks answers to many of the ten questions mentioned above for each exchange (e.g., who stands in the clientelistic relation? what are they exchanging? is there coercion? is there iteration?). They use cluster analysis to uncover types of clientelism; by design, each type uncovered in such a cluster analysis differs from the others as much as possible while all the observations (exchanges) that form part of a cluster (type) are as similar as possible. The result is a typology where each type is defined by a rich set of characteristics in terms of the who, what, and how of the exchange. We can think of this set of characteristics as potentially providing multiple sufficiency combinations (in the logic of "family resemblance concepts") for concept membership in a type of clientelism (Barrenechea and Castillo 2019).

Overall, our view on concept definition allows for a certain defensible pluralism. If we give up the idea of finding the "true" definition of the concept, then we can allow that there may be multiple legitimate and useful ways to define. Plurality might result in several different ways, both objective (in the world) and descriptive (in our ways of describing) as suggested by the work on typologies. Perhaps the simplest cases are when there are multiple different causal processes going on and different definitions pick out different components. In addition, our conceptual tools can also be various. We may have different, noncontradictory ways of describing and grouping phenomena, both of which are useful but useful for different purposes. We may also sometimes apply a *single* description differently depending on contexts, e.g., just as "genes" are different kinds of molecular arrangements in different biological circumstances. Note, however, that the pluralism we defend does not eliminate the need to be as clear and specific about the notion of clientelism at use as possible in any particular study.

Thus, we should not be surprised to see different definitions of clientelism. They may be compatible and unproblematic in the ways just described. Of course, they may also be signs of trouble. Maybe there are different definitions because there are not stable phenomena to investigate or because we have not yet found the conceptual tools to pick them out. We think the work by Pellicer et al. (2020) shows one way this can be approached. Any approach will require being as clear about concepts as is possible and ideally will help provide detailed account of their ties with other concepts and data so that we can argue that plurality is unproblematic.

Even if providing a definition of political clientelism is at the same time difficult and sometimes unnecessary, there are nevertheless instances where it may be useful for researchers. We thus develop a possible definition that speaks to the ambiguities in the ten points above. We do not claim that this definition captures all and only the things that have been clientelism at some time or another. However, we think it does pick out standard phenomena that clientelism researchers are interested in.

We first discuss the main ingredients of our definition and then state below. We believe political clientelism is a linkage between a political actor (the patron) and one or a group of citizens (the clients) that has three essential components. First, the patron provides some type of resource and the client provides political support. Second, there is mutual agreement that the main rationale for the exchange is an expectation of conditionality. Third, the patron is more powerful than the client(s).

The linkage may be direct or mediated by a broker, and may involve a one-off or repeated interactions. We allow for the linkage to involve one citizen or a group of citizens which may or may not be organized formally (for example, as a political party or neighborhood association).

The first condition distinguishes political clientelism from other types of clientelism. Political clientelism requires the client to provide some form of *political* support. The political actor may be an incumbent, a candidate, or an actor that conducts or seeks to conduct politics in the broad sense, such as a feudal lord. The type of political support given by the client(s) may be voting, or campaigning, or rallying around the patron for defense. The type of resources given by the patron are also very broad, from material resources to more immaterial ones such as the promise of insurance or protection. Our definition also allows for coercion from the part of the patron in the sense that the resources the patron gives may be the continuous enjoyment of valued goods that would otherwise be withheld.

The second condition is the heart of the definition of clientelism. It requires a mutual understanding that the main motive for each actor to provide its side of the exchange is the expectation that the other side will also fulfill her part of the exchange. We do not require in our definition that the exchange is immediate, or truly materializes. Any party to the exchange may eventually not fulfill their side of it. What is important is that there is a consensus from the part of the two sides that the motives for each party to give is to receive in exchange. This distinguishes clientelism from other linkages between political actors and citizens. For instance, the distribution of goods at political rallies where politicians might try to buy votes would only be considered clientelism if citizens understand the provision of goods in this way. Pork barrel and special interest politics would not qualify as clientelism if the main rational for the politician to deliver pork was the fact that the beneficiaries live in the area that the politician represents. However, there can be clientelism involving a group of citizens, as long as there is mutual agreement that the group will support that politician mainly because she will provide goods to the community, and the politician will provide goods to the community mainly because the community will support him; whether in the end all members of the community support the politician or not is irrelevant, what matters is that each party understands that they and the others behave mainly to fulfill the exchange.

The third condition, that the patron ought to be more powerful than the clients rules out some cases that appear at odds with the usual understanding of the term. Specifically, it is possible to conceive of conditional exchanges where the political actor receives political support by a citizen who is more powerful than her. For instance, the actor providing political support may be a powerful regional entrepreneur, and the political actor may be a local politician that reciprocates with some political favoritism. However, if it is clear that the businessman is more powerful than the politician, we would typically think of the politician being the client and businessman being the patron. This would then not be a case of political clientelism, as the patron provides political support, not the client.

We consider these three conditions as identifying a distinct phenomenon often labeled as "political clientelism." On the basis of this discussion we think it is useful to study political clientelism defined as:

> Political *clientelism is a type of linkage between a citizen or group of citizens (client(s)) and a more powerful political actor (the patron), in which the patron provides resources and the client provides political support, and where there is a mutual understanding that the main motivation for each party to provide goods is the expectation to receive in exchange.*

3 EXPLANATORY FRAMEWORKS AND EVIDENTIAL CONSTRAINTS

Turning next to issues about the *explanation* and evidence of clientelism, we look at the possible questions we might want explanations to answer and possible methodological or normative constraints we might want on answers to those questions (as discussed in Section 1). We sketch a general framework for thinking about the causes of clientelism. The first topic concerns just what about clientelism we want to explain, the second we discussed in Section 1 when we described relevance relations for answering questions, the third concerns the range of causal factors that might be relevant, and the last problems of evidence in clientelism research.

Explanations we saw can usefully be viewed as answers to questions. Clientelism research aims to answer a variety of different questions. However, those different questions are not always explicitly distinguished by researchers. Yet, doing so is important in assessing the evidence for clientelistic explanations and to avoid debates at cross purposes. So, it is important to distinguish which of the following we want an explanation of clientelism to describe:

- What explains the extent of clientelism?
- What explains the origin of clientelism?
- What explains the persistence of clientelism?
- What explains the forms of clientelism?
- What explains the changes in the extent and forms of clientelism?

These are independent questions in that answers for any one of them may not provide answers to the others. So, for example, we might have good evidence about the specific factors supporting clientelism and at the same time reason to think those factors are historically time bound, etc. Modernization theory makes such claims.

When the definition of clientelism and the question to be asked about it is set, then the next task is to begin to spell out what proposed explanations look like. We assume that the primary sense of explanation is causal explanation. Thus, we are asking what the causal explanations of clientelism look like. We break this question into two parts: what are the general kinds of causal factors and what possible forms might they take in specific cases? We will be discussing all five questions listed above, at least indirectly. Extent, persistence and forms of clientelism are the most direct focus.

The kinds of causal factors are usually organized by supply side and demand side factors. Paradigm demand and supply side factors would be the motivations of individual voters and politicians. Income maximization for voters and maximizing the probability of reelection or election for politicians are natural motives to attribute if we think of economic notions of supply and demand. A broader conception of supply and demand factors also includes other, non-material motives, for example psychological needs for status or social acceptance. Beyond individual motivations, there are distal and background causes that would be relevant to supply and demand explanations.

Figure 19.1 provides a schema for thinking about categorizing explanatory factors in clientelism. The particular definition of clientelism to be used and the specific question(s) about clientelism have to be decided. That sets the kind of elements that go into the client and patron behavior boxes. Those elements are the result of motivational and social and political factors. Clientelism is explained when the existing practices are explained by the combination of social and political causes and the interactions of client and patron behavior. Of course, in practice there can be considerable back and forth in determining elements, definitions, questions, etc., but Figure 19.1 gives a framework for thinking about the complexities.

The schema of Figure 19.1 is a simplification. It is purposely abstract so that multiple definitions and explanations are possible. The elements of this schema can be instantiated in multiple ways. The goal here is to put some order into the web of clientelism literature, a prerequisite for sorting out explanatory claims and assessing evidence.

Obviously, any version will have to decide first on the question to be asked. That means at least one and possibly all from the list above, depending on how wide an account is claimed to be. The important point is that explanations may answer some but not all relevant questions.

The various components of definitions and explanatory factors listed in Figure 19.1 are divided into supply side and demand side elements. This is a common parlance in the literature (e.g., Medina and Stokes 2002, Diaz-Cayeros and Magaloni 2003, Pellicer et al. 2020). It usefully organizes different elements and helps point out ways in which extant accounts of clientelism can be incomplete. For example, until recently, the clientelism literature

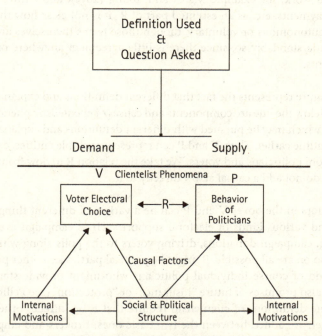

FIGURE 19.1. A framework for thinking about explaining clientelism. Definitions and questions asked pick out what is to be explained. Explanatory factors are organized in terms of the factors influencing the supply and demand for clientelism (signified by the directed arrows) which result from voter and politician behavior that has a range of causes.

has short changed the demand side of the clientelism (see Pellicer et al. 2020; Hicken and Nathan 2020). Researchers that are now taking up the demand side indeed argue that any explanation of the persistence of clientelism will be incomplete if client motives are not well understood, or oversimplified as in standard supply side accounts (e.g., Nichter 2018 or Pellicer et al. 2020).

The definition of clientelism spells out the components of the two boxes and the relation R between them. Probably the most invoked and basic definition takes box V to be a vote for an individual politician who is described in box P who transfers something of value to the voter. R is then described as an "exchange."

However, the phenomena are not all this simple for multiple reasons:

- The basic definition itself hides various decisions that need to be made. A prime question is whether R is an exchange and the transfer is a payment for the vote. We noted above that some researchers do not conceptualize R as an exchange and/ or propose a host of other things that are exchanged instead of payments and votes. Accounts of clientelism that see individual feelings of obligation rather than instrumental self-interest also are not obviously exchanges. This, as in all the complications we mention, is an empirical issue about motives, etc., not a semantic issue about the "right" definition.

- R might be interpreted differently even when it is called an "exchange." "Mutually beneficial" and "voluntary" or "autonomous" are often used adjectives. However, some good work, for example Mares and Young (2019), allow threats to withhold benefits, payments, etc. as an essential part of R. It is not clear how that relationship counts as autonomous or voluntary, though those terms themselves are generally left vague—understandably so, since there is little agreement anywhere on their precise requirements.

The top of the figure represents the fact that different definitions and explanatory questions may be asked. Below the line are components and causes of clientelistic phenomena, various components of which may be pursued with different definitions and explanatory questions such as those outline earlier. Thus, V and P can represent multiple entities, e.g., brokers and parties, aside from politicians and voters. We take the relation R to flow from the traits of V and P and thus do not add a causal arrow directly to it.

- The behaviors in the boxes V and P can be a variety of different things. For V, voter turnout and various kinds of electoral support such as campaign event attendance, canvassing, campaign donations, driving voters to the polls along with a six-pack of beer, and so on are all possible. P might be political parties and other partisan groups, brokers, and of course individual politicians who might provide standard material goods but also promises of future "insurance" or "protection" (see Pellicer et al. 2020).

- While some definitions of clientelism require that R be "direct," other actors could be and often added between the two basic ones. Brokers and employers are obvious candidates. There would presumably be clientelistic relations of some sort between the intermediaries and patrons and the intermediaries and clients. This could again be described with the standard terminology of exchanges, mutually benefits, and so on.

We should note again that multiple definitions are not necessarily a sign of confusion or problematic. They do not need to be eliminated for one "right" definition, especially for one judged by ordinary language. Rather they need to be judged by their empirical success as sketched earlier.

The causal boxes of Figure 19.1 and their causal arrows are, of course, simplified placeholders. Given the complexity and diversity of the phenomena—clientelism—and the diversity of causal factors, many more arrows, elements, and boxes could be added. Even so, the diagram does have some content. It also makes individual motivation an essential part of the story which is not always the case in clientelism research. It makes it possible for there to be social and political causes that are not obviously supply or demand factors. These can influence the behavior of **V** and **P** directly and thus the character of **R**, or indirectly by impacting on the internal motivations of voters and politicians. For example, large-scale structural elements such as the nature of the political system and the distribution of income and wealth can be causes that are in the background.

An illustrative instantiation of the above might be a single district voting system, weak parties, large poverty concentration and little ethnic identification. Those combined with maximizing clients and patrons might result in vote buying among swing voters with relatively high success because programmatic redistribution has little chance of success and the marginal utility of the bribe is high. There is quite some work that focuses on such background causes either that either directly or indirectly affect clientelism (e.g., Pellicer and Wegner 2013 on electoral systems, Stokes et al. 2013 on poverty and modernization, Corstange 2016 on political competition, Shami 2012, Pellicer et al. 2021 on the isolation of a community).

Whether and when any particular model of the above causal factors and others successfully explain is an empirical issue. However, there are some general considerations about what causal explanations should be like that we can raise here. We look at requirements that we must have *theories* that describe clientelism's causes, at specific types of causality that might or might not be adequate for explaining clientelism. And at the types of evidence required to confirm theory and refute others.

4 Theories

A requirement for adequate explanation that is quite common across political science is that there is a theory used to answer the explanation-seeking question regarding the *phenomena* (be it about the extent, the persistence, the origin, the form, etc. of the phenomena). The work cited above explicitly claims to present theories of the clientelist phenomena explained. We think this requirement needs to be qualified.

What do clientelism researchers mean by "theory"? Explicit answers are very rare. Actually, clarifications of what is meant with the word "theory" are very rare across political science.[7] This suggests that we are dealing with assumptions that are taken for granted. Perhaps what lies behind the appeal for theory is a roughly positivist idea of "a set of abstract interconnected statements, consisting of assumptions, definitions and empirically testable hypotheses" (Sanders 2010, p. 25), probably with a friendly amendment that some of the statements are lawlike generalizations and the interconnections are deductive. Perhaps that is an ideal which "theory" expresses.

Clientelist research generally does not provide theory in these senses. Fortunately, it need not do so. Considerable work over considerable time from the history, philosophy and social studies of science has shown that much science works without theory in the sense Sanders describes. Science is rather messier than the theory ideal. We have seen that explicit definitions are sometimes lacking. Not surprisingly, a deductively organized set of generalizations are also not always present in good science. Instead, science is often a much more piecemeal affair. Causal claims are made, but they may have a narrow scope and not fully formalized deductive organization. Models there are, but they are often known to be wrong in fundamental ways and often have an analogical character. Multiple models, sometimes consistent and sometimes not, often are used for the same phenomena. It is not that theories with explicit definitions and deductively organized laws are thought a bad thing, but much science does not work that way.

Political science in general is probably no exception. The work on clientelism certainly is not. Much work on clientelism proposes theories but in most cases the word theory could be substituted with "argument" or "mechanism". Thus, "theory" is typically used to denote some partial causal processes or mechanisms that advocates think explains much of the phenomena. This much more limited sense of "theory" is used across the sciences and thus it is no criticism of clientelism research that it does the same.

However, two caveats are in order. To say that theories in the substantial sense of Sanders are not necessary for good science is not to say anything goes. Providing explicit, clear claims remains essential for science and this standard is certainly not always met in clientelism research. A second, important caveat is that political science and with it work on clientelism often assumes that differing theories have to be incompatible. That does not necessarily hold for theories in the weaker sense of descriptions of causal processes or mechanisms for several reasons. First, as we have seen different but compatible definitions and/or questions may be at issue. Second, causal mechanisms cited by researchers may just be parts of a complex system where other causal paths could be described.

It is not uncommon for clientelism researchers to propose "new," "novel," or "alternative" theories. That juxtaposition is often unnecessary and causes unnecessary confusion. Theories as they show up in clientelism research can sometimes give partial explanations that are extended by other theories which then make the explanation less partial. Complaints that clientelism research ignores the demand side clearly illustrate this point. Accounts that ignore demand are not therefore wrong but rather partial and incomplete. Even if the notion of a "complete" explanation seems suspicious (it smacks of "the one true description of the world"), we can nonetheless practically speak about being able to answer more or fewer questions with a particular account. New or alternative theories *may* answer more questions better, but our point is that sometimes new or alternative theories may just be identifying other aspects and questions about clientelistic phenomena instead of replacing previous work.

5 Causes

If causes are now generally agreed to be the basis of explanation,[8] how causation works remains controversial. Though they are seldom explicitly addressed, two key issues surface in clientelism research: complex causality and functional causes.

"Complex causality" as we use the term here refers to causal relations that are not well captured by a set of individually acting sufficient causes. Independently acting causes are those that have an effect regardless of other causes or, more strongly, that have constant effect *size* regardless of presence, absence or size of other causes. The independent variables in regression equations are generally thought of in this way. Mackie's (1980) INUS account presents a clear case: the cause can be a set of factors, some of which are necessary but not sufficient for the effect and others that are not necessary—the effect can happen without them—but do result in the effect when combined with the necessary connection. There are many related complexities. A factor may be a moderating cause when the effect of another variable depends on the level of the moderating cause. Numerous causal expressions used by social scientists reflect some form of complex causality: "thresholds," "forcing," "shaping," etc., and many appeals to "context" in explanation are also deviating from the idea of independent sufficient causes.

Causation in the case of clientelism may often be complex in these ways. Political science has been a leader in developing methods for thinking about complex causality (Ragin 1987, 2000). These methods, however, have yet to have an influence on clientelism research. Yet, the study of clientelism would be a fertile ground for these methods. Stokes et al. (2013) account of the end of vote-buying in the United Kingdom and the United States can be thought of representing complex causality. Their explanation focuses on the coming together of several conditions (increase in size and wealth of electorate, a less discernible vote, and cheaper mass communication) that made vote-buying unattractive for parties. They emphasize that as one of these conditions took longer to be fulfilled in the United States (votes remained more discernible for a longer time in the United States because of immigration), the decline in vote-buying was delayed. This highlights the idea that complex causality is at play.

Functional explanations are another potentially controversial issue in clientelism research regarding causality. Functional explanations are often indicated linguistically by phrases like "x exists in order to y," "x exists because it does y," and related constructions. They are as widespread as they are controversial across the social sciences (Kincaid 1996, 2006, 2020). Classical examples are Marx's claims that the state functions or exists to protect the interest of the ruling class and Durkheim's assertion that the division of labor functions to promote social solidarity. There are two elements to these explanations: (1) the claim that some social practice has characteristic effects and (2) that it exists because it does. The second kind of claim has seemed mysterious if there is no mechanism based in individual choice, plans, goals and so on—it seems to be free-floating teleology.

These explanations by goals served are quite common in clientelism research, though never recognized as such that we know of. Here are some examples:

- voters "declare support to signal their own credibility" and "request benefits to screen politician credibility" (Nichter 2018);
- "clientelism . . . acts as a pressure relief valve . . . giving formal democratic processes time to develop" (Hilgers 2012a);
- clientelism declines when "its institutional arrangements become fetters stifling the material possibilities of economic performance" (Kitschelt 2007, p. 299);
- clientelism has "filled cultural, institutional, and economics functions across a variety of economic and political systems" (Roniger 2007, p. 26); and

- "electoral clientelism exists in order to signal candidate viability and that they favor redistribution" and to "facilitate elite cooperation" (Kramon 2018, p. 16)

Despite skepticism from philosophers and social scientists alike (Elster 1989), there is nothing inherently wrong with the above qua explanations. The second, controversial element can be fleshed in entirely causal terms. So x exists to y if (a) x causes y and (b) x persists because it does so. At one time t_1 we evidence that x caused y and then that fact causally explains y presence in the next period t_2. Evolutionary selectionist accounts work this way: Some trait contributes to fitness and then that fact causes the trait to exist in future generations. However, selection is just one type of mechanism. There can be other causes of persistence and the social sciences have produced some compelling examples (Kincaid 2006). So, the question is whether clientelism provides reason to believe claims like b.) about clientelist practices. That is a question of evidence and discussed in the next section.

Evidence

We turn finally to look at some philosophy of science issues about evidence as they surface in the clientelism literature. The goal is again to see what philosophy of science perspectives might have to say and how they might be made more nuanced and concrete. First, we discuss the epistemic issues raised by potentially unclear definitions and theories and hypotheses. Then we turn to questions about evidence raised by alternative possible explanations, the need for mechanisms, and causal inference. None of these discussions claims to be decisive but rather to illustrate questions that the clientelism literature has not pursued in detail and suggests routes for clarification.

Here is an evidential maxim, mentioned earlier, that is trivially obvious: unclear definitions, theories and hypotheses make well-confirmed results difficult. Any discussion of evidence in clientelism research must take this platitude seriously. The sheer number of possible definitions and causal factors muted in the literature makes this worry unavoidable.

As discussed, many definitions of clientelism are unclear at key points. Every definition has to—by definition!—have unexplained elements. However, they can be more or less clear about terms with standard meanings within a discipline and about logical relationships between terms. At the very least, the entities in the clientelistic relation are often unclear. Are "voters" individual voters or can they be groups of voters? Are "politicians" individual politicians or can they be parties? or brokers? We have seen that these are core topics in clientelism research but what they mean for a specific author often only becomes obvious when looking at the hypotheses, or even only at the point of the empirical measures.

We saw in section 1 in our common sense Bayesianism that evidence consistent with a hypothesis is inconclusive unless it is inconsistent with reasonable competing explanations. Like much social research, especially observational research, theories of clientelism frequently face problems ruling out reasonable competing explanations. Of course, doing so requires having hypotheses and theories in the first place that are clear enough that we can say what competing explanations might be. Even given that clarity, holism of testing and underdetermination of theory by data can make ruling out alternatives difficult. Further, ruling out alternatives assumes that the theory at issue and its alternatives are sufficiently clear that we judge the latter to be incompatible with the former. Ruling out alternatives is made more difficult by lack of clarity.

A first important question is whether any given theory of clientelism is actually incompatible with some other accounts advocated in the literature. Or, put more accurately, whether all the pieces or elements of a given theory are incompatible with those of other accounts, since theories are not monolithic wholes. As noted above, it is standard in the clientelism literature to assert, at least implicitly, that the research presented represents a competitor to other existing accounts. That is often wrong and unfortunate. Clear debates and empirical and conceptual progress are not promoted when false juxtapositions are made.

One way that claims for exclusivity can fail is because of the plurality of definitions, targets of explanation, and questions asked that we described in the previous section. Theories that try to answer one specific explanatory question need not compete with theories that try to answer others. Theories with different definitions of clientelism may just be picking out different phenomena and thus not be inconsistent. And theories sharing definitions and questions might nonetheless take the entities involved to be different—one theory might be an account of parties and voter organizations and another be about individual politicians and individual votes. How often and where this happens in the clientelism literature is beyond our purview here. Nonetheless, it is an issue worth considering.

Another route to unneeded conflict comes from assuming that my favorite causes in my theory are incompatible with other ones. So, take theories that focus on the informational signals of clientelistic handouts (e.g., Kramon 2018, Muñoz 2014, or Chauchard 2018). These theories have been one of the most relevant contribution to clientelism research in recent years. However, they are probably best seen as a potential addition rather than as a substitute to existing account on the motivations of clients. If a handout from a politician gives me information about electability and thus motivates me to vote for her, that doesn't preclude me from at the same time also being motivated by the direct material payoff or by norms of reciprocity, fairness, etc.. Information about electability, for example, gives me information about the probability of a candidate being able to bring public goods to my community by being elected. I could be a pure maximizer of my material well-being and have both direct payoffs and indirect payoffs (e.g., via public goods) as arguments in my utility function. Information from handouts would affect my subjective probabilities concerning the latter; they do not prevent direct payoffs from being in my utility function. These theories need not be exclusive and many hypotheses, and in fact evidence may be consistent with both signaling causes and causes of other kinds—for example, incumbents may provide lower amounts of handouts vis-a-vis challengers because they have established reciprocal relations, trust, etc. Researchers typically specify observable implications of their theory and argue for it to be confirmed if they find evidence that is consistent with that theory but spend far less effort to discuss other theories with which that same evidence would also be consistent.

These alternatives or complements to different "theories" in clientelism research are really about mechanisms, primarily demand side ones. We saw above in Section 1 there are multiple factors in assessing how important mechanisms are as evidence. Key are how much confidence we have in our mechanisms story and how much our theories, definitions, and hypotheses presuppose or assume about them. There is some benefit for clientelism research to be clear about what mechanisms are or are not supposed to be operative. We sketch some possible areas where this is so.

We have already seen that individual motives of maximizing redistribution via public goods does not rule out other motives. In general, we think that there is much work to be done on specifying and testing motives in clientelism research. The needs here reflect a common situation in the social sciences where multiple individual-level stories are possible and differentiating evidence difficult. But it would be good if these limitations were acknowledged and addressed more explicitly.

To give an important example, consider the widespread claims in the literature about the channels by which poverty leads to demand for clientelism, and thereby to its persistence (Stokes 2009; Stokes et al 2013).[9] At least three types of channels have been proposed and mostly taken for granted. The first channel linking poverty to clientelism concerns the greater marginal utility the poor will find in any additional income and the fact that it will make buying poor votes cheaper than others for politicians (Dixit and Londregan 1996). The second relates to risk aversion—with poor voters said to be more risk averse and thereby more concerned about the uncertainty of redistributive policies promised by programmatic parties (e.g., Desposato 2006). And in the third channel, time attitudes matter. "Poor and uneducated citizens discount the future, rely on short causal chains, and prize instant advantages such that the appeal of direct, clientelist exchanges always trumps that of indirect, programmatic linkages promising uncertain and distant rewards to voters" (Kitschelt 2000, p. 857).

Risk, time and marginal utility attitudes thus are individual-level mechanisms that are thought to explain the role of poverty for clientelist behavior. While all these channels sound plausible, such appeals to risk, time, and marginal utility attitudes are thrown together and mostly not backed up by empirical evidence. We note some examples here. First, the Dixit and Londregan 1996 article on which the marginal utility channel is based is routinely cited in work on clientelism. However, Dixit and Londregan 1996 is a formal model that proposes the theoretical argument but does not show direct evidence in its favor. To the best of our knowledge, the specific role of marginal utility in linking poverty to demand for clientelism has never been empirically tested. Second, risk and time attitudes are usually not distinguished (e.g., in Stokes 2009 or Kitschelt 2000). This makes sense because promises of programmatic redistribution are both risky (the programmatic party might not win, it might renege on the promise, or other actors might veto redistribution) and accrue in the future (after electoral victory and a lengthy legislation process). However, risk aversion and time discounting are different individual preferences and programmatic politics can show independent amounts of delay and uncertainty. Therefore, as a motive for clientelism demand, time discounting is distinctive from risk aversion and thus they correspond to two distinct mechanisms. Third, clientelism research has struggled to operationalize risk or time attitudes empirically so that they are in line with the standard meaning of the concepts. Perceptions of the riskiness of programmatic politics, for example, have been operationalized as trust in politicians or as beliefs about how risky implementing an untested policy is; these are perceptions about the probability of success of programmatic policies which capture first and foremost the expected value of such policies, not their riskiness. Risk attitudes are mostly not explicitly measured, although Nichter (2018) has recently made some advances in distinguishing between risk and time preferences and in measuring them closer to current best practices in clientelism research.[10]

Two other sets of issues about mechanism come from evidence for functional claims and general considerations about causal evidence. Using the account given earlier, functional explanations require showing that x's effect y at one time is a causal factor in x's persistence into the next time period. It is possible to provide evidence for that relation directly using standard statistical correlations between the two events (see Kincaid 1996, 2006. That is seldom done on behalf of functional explanations in the social sciences and clientelism research is no exception. Alternatively, or in addition, evidence tracing a mechanism from the effects of x to its persistence would provide some support.

However, none of the functional ascriptions in the clientelism that we know of do much in this regard—they do not provide causal links between effects and persistence. Kramon's claim that clientelism buys off elites or Kitschelt's assertion that clientelism declines when "its institutional arrangements become fetters stifling the material possibilities of economic performance" (Kitschelt 2017, p. 299) have no elaborated mechanism connecting effects and persistence. Functional explanations may sometimes be less macro and perhaps shorthand for individual motives that could be identified. Nichter's claim that voters "declare support to signal their own credibility" and "request benefits to screen politician credibility" (Nichter 2018) could conceivably be cashed out in terms of individual beliefs and preferences. As usual, these possibilities need to examined case by case in empirical detail.

There are, of course, still other issues about evidence in clientelism research that we have not discussed. However, we hope to have shown that approaching these issues in systematic way from an applied philosophy of science perspective can help pinpoint issues that clientelism researchers should take seriously.

6 CONCLUSION

There has been a renewed interest in clientelism during the last decades. Many monographs and journal articles have been published on different aspects of clientelism, frequently in top outlets. We have learned a lot about many specific aspects of clientelistic relations in different world regions. Moreover, there are probably more researchers and research projects on the topic than ever before, so the field is likely to continue thriving in the foreseeable future. In this context, it is useful to take a step back and consider what insights philosophy of science can provide about the current state of clientelism research (regarding definitions and explanations of clientelism). In this chapter we have sought to contribute to this reflection adopting major perspectives in contemporary philosophy of science: naturalism and contextualism.

As researchers in the clientelism literature have pointed out, there is a multitude of definitions of clientelism. This is often considered a shortcoming of the literature that shows its lack of clarity and requires a solution. We argue that a multitude of definitions is, as such, not a problem, as long as these definitions capture empirically relevant stable phenomena and as long as the parameters in which the definitions differ is made explicit. Different definitions can legitimately reflect different empirical phenomena operating in different contexts. Recent efforts in the clientelism literature to provide typologies that explicitly put structure into the different types of clientelism are helpful in this respect. Among these typologies, inductive ones that are derived from empirical observed clientelistic relations are particularly useful. When delimiting their object of inquiry the field might be better served by researchers being transparent about the specific parameters that delimit the specific phenomenon they are studying (and if possible relating to existing types of clientelism) rather than proposing their own definition of clientelism.

Just as there can be different definitions or types of clientelism, there can also be different causal questions we may ask about clientelism—different aspects of clientelism we seek to explain (its extent, its persistence, etc.). These different types of clientelism and questions asked generally lead to different explanations. We believe this diversity of explanations of clientelism can be accommodated into a useful template. We propose a broad, general, explanatory framework that can be used to organize research on clientelism. This framework requires the researcher to be clear about the definition of clientelism used and the aspect of clientelism to explain. The framework conceptualizes clientelism as a relation between actors whose behavior depends on internal motivations, broad social and political structures, and the interactions between these.

Our framework makes explicit the diversity of definitions and explanatory questions that can be asked about clientelism, but also the diversity of causal paths and interactions that may operate when trying to explain these. We believe it would be useful for researchers to acknowledge this diversity and the implications this diversity has for the status of their argument. It is common in clientelism research to examine one single causal argument, elevate it to the level of a theory, label it as "novel" or "alternative", and test it in isolation. We believe progress in the field could be more solid if this partiality were recognized and more attention were devoted to embedding this part into the whole. Failure to do so may lead to erroneous inferences. Finding support for one's argument does not imply that it is correct and the others are wrong. Different explanations may have overlapping empirical implications. Evidence supporting one partial mechanism may actually be the result of other causes or factors. Or several mechanisms may be at work at the same time.

Moreover, complex causality often implies that the specific mechanism that a researcher considers interacts with other mechanisms. Instead of emphasizing the difference and uniqueness of one's mechanism, researchers may focus more on how their explanations complements and interacts with other explanations.

In sum, the plurality we find in clientelism research is not necessarily a bad thing. It probably reflects a plurality of empirical clientelism phenomena, of questions that can be asked, and of causal explanations. The field could benefit from embracing this plurality, attending to it, and giving it structure. This would be helped by researchers clarifying where their research fits into the whole in terms of definitions and questions and embedding their individual partial mechanisms into larger explanatory frameworks.

ACKNOWLEDGMENTS

Thanks to Jeroen Van Bouwel, Ward Berenschot, and the audience at the Philosophy and Methodology Workshop at Washington State University for helpful comments. Part of the research in this chapter was funded by the German Research Foundation (DFG) as part of the project "The demand side of clientelism" (PE 2423/3-1).

NOTES

1. See Sober (1989) on simplicity in phylogenetic inference for example.
2. On arguments for this view about individualism, see Kincaid (1996, 1997, 2015).
3. For example, if I know there is some casual relation between A, B, and C but only have observations on their correlations, I am in a bind in deciding what causes what. But if it turns out that a fourth cause D is involved, then I can use their partial conditional correlations ("vanishing tetrads") to make causal inferences.
4. We are by far not the only one's pointing out the diversity of definitions and usages of the term "clientelism." See, for example, the recent reviews by Hicken and Nathan (2020), Golden et al. (2020) or Nichter (2014).
5. See Chapter 25 for discussion of positivism. As that chapter shows the term must be used with care because of the diversity of connotations beginning with the original positivists themselves.
6. The test is not whether we can show the definition fits with ordinary usage. As we have seen, those concepts themselves are not neatly definable. Moreover, there is no special status given to the concepts of common sense in any case, for we know that good science often proceeds independently of them and that humans' expressed self-descriptions can be poor guides to their behavior.
7. Representative perhaps is Marsh and Stoker (2010) which has almost no explicit discussion of what theory is, despite the title.
8. "Generally" might seem to suggest that interpetivists are in the minority which is probably in fact true. However, there is no reason that interpretivist points cannot be recognized while finding that meaningful actions have causal explanations. See Chapter 11 and Kincaid (1996).
9. On the role of poverty for clientelism, see Berenschot (2018) for a different perspective. Berenschot finds that in Indonesia, clientelism is more prevalent in relatively richer areas and argues that this results from state-dependent development.
10. Nichter (2018) measures risk aversion with an incentivized game where respondents are asked to select between two bags, one giving a small payout (R$2) with 100% probability and the other a 50:50 change of a very small payout (R$0.20) and a high one (R$5). Time preferences are measured with an unincentivized question about receiving a prize tomorrow or a 10% higher prize in three months.

REFERENCES

Aspinall, E. and Sukmajati, M. (eds.). 2019. *Electoral Dynamics in Indonesia: Money Politics, Patronage, and Clientelism at the Grass Roots.* Singapore: NUS Press.

Barrenechea, Rodrigo, and Isabel Castillo. 2019. "The Many Roads to Rome: Family Resemblance Concepts in the Social Sciences." *Quality & Quantity* 53 (1): 107–130.

Beller, M. 2001. Quantum Dialogue. Chicago: University of Chicago Press.

Belnap, N. and Steel, T. 1976. *The Logic of Questions and Answers.* New Haven: Yale University Press.

Berenschot, W. 2018. "The Political Economy of Clientelism: A Comparative Study of Indonesia's Patronage Democracy." *Comparative Political Studies* 51 (12): 1563–1593.

Berenschot, W., and Aspinall, E. 2020. "How Clientelism Varies: Comparing Patronage Democracies." *Democratization* 27 (1): 1–19.

Cartwright, N. 1999. *The Dappled World*. Cambridge: Cambridge University Press.

Chang, H. 2008. *Inventing Temperature: Measurement and Scientific Progress*. Oxford: Oxford University Press.

Chang, H. 2012. *Is Water H₂O?* Berlin: Springer.

Chauchard, S. 2018. "Electoral handouts in Mumbai elections: The cost of political competition." *Asian Survey*, 58 (2): 341–364.

Corstange, D. 2016. *The Price of a Vote in the Middle East: Clientelism and Communal Politics in Lebanon and Yemen*. New York: Cambridge University Press.

Desposato, S. W. 2006. "How Informal Electoral Institutions Shape the Brazilian Electoral Arena," in Helmke, G. and Levitsky, S. (eds) *Informal Institutions and Democratic Politics*. Baltimore: JHU Press, pp. 56–68.

Diaz-Cayeros, Alberto, and Beatriz Magaloni. 2003. "The Politics of Public Spending. Part I–The Logic of Vote Buying." *Prepared as a Background Paper for the World Bank World Development Report* 1 (26949): 1–44.

Desposato, Scott. W. 2006. "How informal electoral institutions shape the Brazilian legislative arena," in Helmke, G. and Levitsky, S. (eds) *Informal Institutions and Democracy: Lessons from Latin America*. JHU Press, pp. 56–68.

Dixit, A. and Londregan, J. 1996. "The Determinants of Success of Special Interests in Redistributive Politics." The Journal of Politics, 58 (4): 1132–1155.

Gans-Morse, Jordan, Sebastian Mazzuca, and Simeon Nichter. 2014. "Varieties of Clientelism: Machine Politics during Elections." American Journal of Political Science 58 (2): 415–43.

Elster, J. 1989. *Explaining Technical Change*. Cambridge: Cambridge University Press.

Garfinkel, A. 1981. *Forms of Explanation*. New Haven: Yale University Press.

Giere, R. 1988. *Explaining Science*. Chicago: University of Chicago Press.

Goertz, Gary. 2006. *Social Science Concepts: A User's Guide*. Princeton University Press.

Golden, M., Nazrullaeva, E. and Wolton, S. 2020. Politics in Poor Places? Clientelism and Elections in Democracies (May 16, 2020). Available at SSRN: https://ssrn.com/abstract=3602680.

Hicken, A. 2011. "Clientelism." *Annual Review of Political Science* 14: 289–330.

Hicken, A. and Nathan, N. L. 2020. "Clientelism's Red Herrings: Dead Ends and New Directions in the Study of Nonprogrammatic Politics." *Annual Review of Political Science* 23: 277–294.

Hilgers, T. 2012a. "Democractic Processes, Clientelistic Relationships, and the Material Goods Problem," in Hilgers, T. (ed.), *Clientelism in Everyday Latin American Politics*. New York: Palgrave McMillan, pp. 3–22.

Hilgers, T. 2012b. "Clientelistic Democracy," in Hilgers, T. (ed.), *Clientelism in Everyday Latin American Politics*. New York: Palgrave McMillan, pp. 161–187.

Hutchcroft, P. 2014. "Linking Capital and Countryside: Patronage and Clientelism in Japan, Thailand, and the Philippines," in Diego Abente Brun & Larry Diamond (ed.), *Clientelism, Social Policy, and the Quality of Democracy*, Baltimore: Johns Hopkins University Press, pp. 174–203.

Kincaid, H. 1996. *Philosophical Foundations of the Social Sciences*. Cambridge: Cambridge University Press.

Kincaid, H. 2006. "Functional Explanation and Evolutionary Social Science," in Risjord and Turner, *Handbook for the Philosophy of Science: Philosophy of Anthropology and Sociology*. Dordrecht: Elsevier, pp. 213–249.

Kincaid, H. 2012. "Mechanisms, Causal Modeling, and the Limitations of Traditional Multiple Regression," in Kincaid, *Oxford Handbook of the Philosophy of the Social Sciences*. Oxford: Oxford University Press.

Kincaid, H. 2003. "Contextualism, Explanation and the Social Sciences," *Philosophical Explorations* 7 (2005), 201–219.

Kincaid, H. 2020. "The Empirical Issues in Functional Explanation in the Social Sciences," in Hufendiek, R., James, D., and van Riel, R. (eds.) *Social Functions in Philosophy: Metaphysical, Normative, and Methodological Perspectives*. Routledge Studies in Contemporary Philosophy. London: Routledge, pp. 18–28.

Kitschelt, H., 2000. "Linkages between citizens and politicians in democratic polities." *Comparative Political Studies*, 33 (6-7), 845–879.

Kitschelt, H. and Wilkinson, S. 2007. *Patrons, Clients and Policies*. Cambridge: Cambridge University Press.

Kitschelt, Herbert. 2007. "The Demise of Clientelism in Affluent Capitalist Democracies." In *Patrons, Clients, and Policies*, edited by Herbert Kitschelt and Steven Wilkinson. Cambridge: Cambridge University Press, pp. 298–321.

Kramon, E. 2018. *Money for Votes: The Causes and Consequences of Electoral Clientelism in Africa*. Cambridge: Cambridge University Press.

Kuhn, T. 1962. *The Structure of Scientific Revolutions*. Chicago: University of Chicago Press.

Mackie, J. 1980. *Causation: The Cement of the Universe*. Oxford: Oxford University Press.

Mares, I. and Young, L. 2019. *Conditionality and Coercion: Electoral Clientelism in Eastern Europe*. Oxford: Oxford University Press.

Marsh D. and Stoker, G. 2010. *Theory and Method in Political Science*. London: Palgrave MacMillan.

Medina, L. F., and Stokes, S. 2002. "Clientelism as Political Monopoly." Paper prepared for the 2002 Annual Meeting of the American Political Science Association, Boston.

Moss, L. 2003. *What Genes Can't Do*. Cambridge, MA: MIT Press.

Muñoz, P. 2014. "An informational theory of campaign clientelism: The case of Peru." *Comparative Politics*, 47 (1): 79–98.

Nichter, Simeon. 2008. "Vote Buying or Turnout Buying? Machine Politics and the Secret Ballot." *American Political Science Review* 102 (01): 19–31.

Nichter, Simeon. 2014. "Conceptualizing Vote Buying." *Electoral Studies* 35: 315–327.

Nichter, Simeon. 2018. *Votes for Survival: Relational Clientelism in Latin America*. New York, N.Y.: Cambridge University Press.

Pellicer, Miquel, Eva Wegner, Markus Bayer, and Christian Tischmeyer. 2020. "Clientelism from the Client's Perspective: A Meta-Analysis of Ethnographic Literature." *Perspectives on Politics* 1–17. doi:10.1017/S153759272000420X.

Pellicer, Miquel, Eva Wegner, Lindsay J Benstead, and Ellen Lust. 2021. "Poor People's Beliefs and the Dynamics of Clientelism." *Journal of Theoretical Politics* 33 (3): 300–332.

Pellicer, M. and E. Wegner. 2013. "Electoral Rules and Clientelistic Parties: A Regression Discontinuity Approach." *Quarterly Journal of Political Science* 8 (4): 339–371.

Ragin, C. 1987. *The Comparative Method*. Berkeley: University of California Press.

Ragin, C. 2000. *Fuzzy Set Social Science*. Chicago: University of Chicago Press.

Roniger, L. 2007. "Favors, "Merit Ribbons, and Services," in Hilgers (ed.), *Clientelism in Everyday Latin America Politics*. New York: Palgrave Macmillan, pp. 25–41.

Ruiz de Elvira, L. 2019. "Introduction: Networks of dependency, a research perspective," in Ruiz de Elvira, L., Schwarz, C., and Weipert-Fenner, I. (eds.), *Clientelism and Patronage in the Middle East and North Africa*. New York: Routledge, pp. 1–17.

Sanders, D. 2010. "Behavioral Analysis," in Marsh and Stoke (eds.), *Theory and Method in Political Science*. London: Palgrave MacMillan, pp. 23–42.

Shami, M. 2012. "Collective action, clientelism, and connectivity." *American Political Science Review*, 106 (03): 588–606.

Shefner, J. 2012. "What is Politics For? Inequality, Representation, and Needs Satisfaction Under Clientelism and Democracy," in Hilgers, T. (ed) *Clientelism in Everyday Latin American Politics*. New York: Palgrave Macmillan, pp. 32–54.

Sober, E. 1989. *Reconstructing the Past*. Cambridge: MIT Press.

Stokes, S. 2009. Political Clientelism. Boix, C. and Stokes, S. (eds). *The Oxford Handbook of Comparative Politics*. Oxford: Oxford University Press, pp. 604–628.

Stokes, S., Dunning, T., Nazareno, M., and Bursco, V. (2013). Brokers, Voters, and Clientelism. Cambridge: Cambridge University Press.

Szwarcberg, M. 2015. *Mobilizing Poor Voters. Machine Politis, Clientelism, and Social Networks in Argentina*. New York: Cambridge University Press.

Van Fraassen, B. 1980. *The Scientific Image*. Oxford: Clarendon Press.

Williams, M. 1999. *Groundless Belief*. Princeton, NJ: Princeton University Press.

Yaghi, M. 2019. "Neoliberal Reforms, Protests and Enforced Patron-Client Relationships in Tunisia and Egypt," in Ruiz de Elvira, L., Schwarz, C., and Weipert-Fenner, I. (eds.), *Clientelism and Patronage in the Middle East and North Africa*. New York: Routledge, pp. 118–142.

Yıldırım, Kerem, and Herbert Kitschelt. 2020. "Analytical Perspectives on Varieties of Clientelism." *Democratization* 27 (1): 20–43.

CHAPTER 20

EXTERNAL VALIDITY IN PHILOSOPHY AND POLITICAL SCIENCE

Three Paradoxes

MARÍA JIMÉNEZ-BUEDO

1. EXTERNAL VALIDITY: ITS ORIGINS AND DIFFUSION ACROSS DISCIPLINES

THE distinction between internal and external validity was conceived by Donald T. Campbell as part of an admirable and sustained methodological effort directed at understanding the pitfalls of research analysis and causal inference in the social sciences. The project, developed gradually through the second half of the twentieth century, was of both a theoretical nature and an applied one. Theoretically, it consisted of the systematic study of causal inference in relation to different research designs and it included discussions of the limits and advantages of randomized designs versus their alternatives. In its pragmatic dimension, it served to pave the way to what we now know as the Evidence Based Policy movement, as it evaluated, consulted and inspired myriad field try-outs of ameliorative programs (many of which were related to remedial education) and eventually gave rise to the Campbell Collaboration, which was born as a sister organization in the Social Sciences to the Cochrane project in Medicine.

Within the massive methodological legacy left by the Campbellian project, a particularly important bit was the conceptual work on validity, which had its roots in Campbell's previous solo work on psychological test validation (Heukelom 2011). Campbell's first distinction between internal and external validity came in the form of two questions that a researcher ought to ask herself in assessing the success of an experiment: Internal validity would be a response to the question "did in fact the experimental stimulus make some significant difference in this specific instance?" (1957, 297), and external validity was defined as "to what populations, settings, and variables can this effect be generalized?" (p. 297). Later on, Campbell and Stanley (1963) revised these concepts, but it is Cook and Campbell's

(1979) definitions that became the new standard. Cook and Campbell reformulated the original internal/external distinction and embedded it within a four-fold typology that also included statistical conclusion validity and construct validity.

In Cook and Campbell's (1979) (for years the research design manual of reference in many social scientific disciplines), internal validity "refers to the approximate validity with which we infer that a relationship between two variables is causal or that the absence of a relationship implies the absence of cause" whereas external validity "refers to the approximate validity with which we can infer that the presumed causal relationship can be generalized to and across alternate measures of the cause and effect and across different types of persons, settings, and times."

Cook and Campbell's validity typology, and in particular the internal-external types, spurred some controversy among contemporary methodologists, who thought of it as ambiguous (see, for example, (Hammersley 1993)). It also competed against alternative validity typologies, notably by Cronbach's (1982), whose criticisms Cook and Campbell finally integrated in the idea that experimental results needed to be tested systematically for robustness across units, treatments, observations and settings (Cronbach 1982; Shadish, Cook, and Campbell 2002). Despite the controversy, though, the distinction was taken up by the practitioners (especially social scientists) along with Campbell and collaborators' canonical experimental methodological manuals (most notably, Cook and Campbell 1979). Their classification and analysis of common "threats to validity" (or the list of common confounding factors that cannot always be entirely offset by randomization) are still regularly used by social scientific experimentalists.

In 2002, and coinciding in time with a newly found interest in experimentation in other social sciences, notably economics, Campbell's last collaboration comes out (actually, posthumously, since Campbell died in 1996) in the impressive volume by Shadish, Cook, and Campbell (2002). There, internal validity is defined as "refer[ring] to inferences about whether the observed covariation between X (the presumed treatment) and Y (the presumed outcome) reflects a causal relation from X to Y" (p. 38), and external validity is defined as the "degree to which a causal relationship found in a given study generalizes across various persons, settings, treatments, measures, and so forth." The authors continue to emphasize the idea, already present in their 1979 opus, that the internal and external validity are embedded in a four category typology, where statistical conclusion validity is defined as the "validity of inferences about the correlation (covariation) between treatment and outcome," and construct validity is defined by "the validity of inferences about the higher order constructs that represent sampling particulars" (p. 38). They also revisit and update a number of threats to valid inference that were previously not considered in the 1979 volume.

Through the years the Campbellian validity classification became the standard in the specialized literature on research design in social sciences and gradually permeated the language of what was then a still restricted domain of social scientific experimentation, mostly limited to psychology and some areas in educational research. As experimentation became more popular in neighboring fields, the distinction between internal and external validity eventually came to be widely used in other social sciences, in biomedical domains and increasingly in policy making circles, and it has now become part of the standard vocabulary of these disciplines as well as that of the corresponding philosophical debates.

Validity: From Typology to Dyad

The Campbellian validity system became increasingly popular and penetrated the jargon of social scientists, but in this popularization Campbell's validity typology did not always travel intact. As it became increasingly known in broader circles, it often ended up losing some of its components; in this way, internal and external validity are frequently cited as a self-containing dyad, without reference to statistical conclusion validity or construct validity.

Morton and Williams (2008, 2010), a leading tandem of methodologists in experimental political science and authors of one of the more influential manuals in the discipline, have rightly and repeatedly noted one of the dangers of using the distinction between internal and external validity in this way, since they think this usage conflates statistical conclusion validity and construct validity with internal validity. According to these authors, political scientists have adopted a simplistic and outdated view of validity based on the early division of Campbell (1957), in which internal validity refers to the robustness of experimental results *within* the experimental data and external validity refers to how robust experimental results are *outside* the experiment.

For Morton and Williams, this view is reductive, since there are actually many ways to measure the validity of empirical research, both experimental and observational. According to Morton and Williams, when political scientists refer to internal validity they are often referring to three things as a whole: internal validity proper, statistical conclusion validity, and construct validity. In fact, at some point Campbell himself proposed a relabelling (1986) of internal validity as *local molar causal validity*, in order to emphasize that internal validity was meant to refer to causal inferences limited to the context of the particular treatments, outcomes, times, settings, and persons studied in a particular research design. The term *molar* was there to reflect that these tended to be a complex package, tested only *locally* for some brute sense of *causal* efficacy.

Political scientists are not alone in this conceptual sliding, as something rather similar has happened in the field of philosophy of science, even though it is a discipline in which conceptual accuracy is valued over other intellectual goals. In the case of Philosophy of Science, the terms internal and external validity got gradually passed on to the discipline also around the turn of the century. The terms were most notably popularized by Nancy Cartwright (1999, 2007), especially in regard to her ideas on the type of evidence needed to inform policy decisions. Another crucial contribution in this regard was by Francesco Guala (1999, 2003, 2005), who has discussed extensively the concept of external validity in reference to the practices of experimental economists and the problem of "artificiality" in the lab. Perhaps because both sets of problems (evidence for interventions, and artificiality of experimental settings) were connected to the broader issue of extrapolation, it is around this time that the notion of external validity becomes associated with extrapolation and often used interchangeably in some of the philosophical circles interested in social scientific practices. The "problem of external validity" thus became part of the philosophical lingo of those interested in extrapolation and the policy implications of causal evidence (see for instance the debate between Guala and Steel on extrapolation and the role of analogical reasoning; Steel 2008, and its continuation in Steel 2010 and Guala 2010).

At present, and when used in a philosophical context, the terms external and internal validity tend to be used without reference to the broader typology in which Campbell and his collaborators inserted them. Often, the philosophical use is not limited to the original experimental context but generalized to the relation between model and target, case study to universe of interest, or animal models to humans. In the philosophical discussion then, internal and external validity often acquire broader, less specific meanings than those intended by their originator: internal validity is often invoked to convey the idea of reliability of inferences about genuine causal relations within a study, and external validity is associated with the idea of the generalizability of findings, thus outside a study. In other words, internal validity has come to mean a notion that deals with all issues pertaining to causal identification whereas external validity relates to all that has to do with generalization of findings. It is worth reminding ourselves that this is how Campbell's typology itself started, but that he eventually found this to be a conceptual partition that mingled too many different issues together, thus the subsequent four-fold typology he proposed. The fact that philosophers and many social scientists have again reduced the typology to a dyad does suggest that there is a persistent need for a heuristic that allows us to think in terms of the inside versus the outside of an experiment, or that at least, that both philosophers and social scientists seem to find that this inside/outside distinction is a particularly useful way to think about experiments and their inferential power. The distinction between internal and external validity seems to have fulfilled this role, despite the fact that the Campbellian pragmatic project in which they originated and its subsequent conceptualizations were different. As noted, Campbell's project was geared to a rather pragmatic aim: that of systematically reviewing for "common threats" to validity. These systematization of threats were lists of confounders that are often present in the context of social scientific investigations and can bias or impede causal inference. Examples are selection or attrition (for internal validity), low statistical power (for statistical conclusion validity), treatment diffusion or inadequate explication of constructs (for construct validity), or the context-dependent mediation (for external validity).

As a result of this gradual shift in meaning of the terms from the Campbellian pragmatic labels to the more general notions, internal and especially external validity are often used in ambiguous ways, and both of these terms often lack fixed definitions within the relevant literatures or debates. This, in turn, explains a series of confusions or misunderstandings, especially regarding the often polysemic notion of external validity.

In the following pages the problem of external validity is analyzed by dividing it in two separate problems. One is a properly philosophical-scientific problem, and it deals with the difficulties of extrapolation in the social sciences, and in particular, the difficulties of extrapolating the results of experiments in political science. A second dimension is conceptual, and it deals with the ambiguities in the way this term "external validity" is constructed. I argue that these ambiguities have given rise to misunderstanding or contradictory statements in the literature that I refer to as the "three paradoxes of external validity." I argue that in addition to the conceptual ambiguities surrounding the notion of external validity, there is also a problem of conceptual overload and the very many conceptual demands (where external validity is made to mean different things for different people). I conclude this chapter by noting that despite the conceptual problems, the internal/external validity distinction seems to have fulfilled an important heuristic role that helps researchers and philosophers distinguish between the "inside" and the "outside" of an experiment.

2. The Problem of External Validity in Philosophy and in Political Science

In this section I go over how "the problem of external validity" has been conceptualized both in Philosophy and in Political Science, respectively. I then go on to describe the debate over the alleged advantages of field experiments vis a vis the problem of external validity. I end this section by introducing the first two paradoxes of external validity before I go into the last section, dealing with the third paradox.

2.1 The Problem of External Validity in Philosophy

As we saw in the previous section, since the turn of the century, and as experimental methods made their way gradually through social scientific disciplines that had until then described themselves as nonexperimental, the language of internal and external validity became popular both among social scientists and among the philosophers of science interested in them. In the philosophy of science literature this resulted from the coincidence of two separate developments.

The first such development was internal to the discipline: the experimental turn in the philosophy of science that emerged in the 1980s, by putting the emphasis on the practices, rather than the theories, had managed to bring new avenues to an otherwise declining debate between realists and their critics, prominently exemplified in Hacking's work (1983). These philosophers had contributed to the idea, now widespread, that experiments had a privileged status in the scientific pursuit of knowledge, notably, causal knowledge. It had, however, done so at the expense of more applied concerns, such as the problem of extrapolation. In this way, these philosophers still lacked a "general, convincing account of how such knowledge—gained in special, highly controlled circumstances—could be applied in circumstances where the special conditions d[id] not hold" (p.1070; Guala, 2010), to the point that Guala labeled this a "minor scandal" in the philosophy of science. First Guala (1999, 2005), and then Daniel Steel in his (2008) *Across the Boundaries*, brought this issue to the center of the philosophical discussion (Russo 2010). Steel provided a general account of extrapolation that was meant to successfully address what he considered to be the two main challenges that any account of extrapolation faces: the extrapolator's circle and the problem of difference. The extrapolator's circle is the problem faced by the scientist who, in order to successfully apply the knowledge extracted in the analysis of the model, needs knowledge about the target system that she does not yet have: the image of circularity tries to express the bind in which the extrapolator finds herself. She wants to extrapolate to gain knowledge about the target, yet to do so, she needs knowledge about the target. In turn, the problem of difference is the challenge of explaining how extrapolation succeeds despite the causally relevant differences between the model and the target.

Steel's account is aimed to apply across the sciences (both natural and social), and is based on the close observation of existing scientific practices of extrapolation. According to Steel, scientists are able to extrapolate by using the method of comparative process tracing: Steel defends the idea that we may infer that a result obtained in a primary location (e.g., model or laboratory conditions) can be extrapolated to target systems if, by comparing crucial nodes in the causal chain, we are able to examine and compare the similarities and differences in the relevant causal mechanisms and show that based on this comparison, an inference about the causal effect in the model can be expected to hold in the target. According to Steel's account, then, in order to extrapolate from model to target, scientists need to focus on those (crucial) causal nodes in which the mechanisms are most likely to differ in model and target.

A second development explaining the rise of the notion of external validity is, in contrast, external to the discipline, and lies in the Evidence Based Policy movement, a series of institutional initiatives set out to improve the evidential standards of policy makers. In practice this has translated most notably in the promotion of randomized controlled trials (RCTs) as the supposed "gold standard" in the design and evaluation of policy innovation.

As the EBP movement has become mainstream and its associated RCT enthusiasm has progressed, an increasing number of commentators have tried to caution against some of its bolder hopes or ambitions. Deaton and Cartwright (2018), for example, have discussed the many ways in which the value of RCTs' evidence is often overstated. They defend the idea that RCTs are a useful method among many, but that they should not be thought of as the research "gold standard." First, because RCTs are susceptible of bias. For example, in cases of differential experimental attrition among the experimental groups, or, in cases in which treatment blinding fails and impacts results, RCTs will provide biased estimates of the causal impact of treatment on the output variables. Second, Deaton and Cartwright (2018) also call for caution by underlining the fact that RCT results cannot often translate into immediate "applicability" for policy purposes: causal processes often require highly specialized economic, cultural or social structures that enable them to work, and we often lack a theory about which "supporting factors" are important (i.e., additional factors that function along with the treatment to create the observed outcome). RCTs, according to these authors, cannot tell us if what works "there" (in the trial), will also work for us "here" (or in other situations of interest). The second of these criticisms, which has received an enormous degree of attention, has often been framed in terms of "external validity." Thus, in the Cartwrightian picture, RCTs are (albeit with qualms) "good" on internal validity, meaning that they are good tools to identify genuine causal effects, but they are eminently poor on external validity, meaning that they are not good at telling us how to extrapolate their findings to other relevant contexts.

We can thus summarize the developments that brought the notion of external validity to the fore of the philosophical discussion: a general renewed interest in experimentation as a privileged route to causal knowledge, and the commentary on the Evidence Based Policy movement and the associated predominance of RCTs. Though intimately associated, we can say that the two developments are also distinct from each other.

Interestingly, Khosrowi (2019) has knitted these two traditions together, by considering whether some of the recent strategies proposed by econometricians for extrapolating causal effects from experimental to target populations (notably, Hotz et al. 2005; Muller 2014, 2015) suffer from the extrapolator's circle.

Khosrowi distinguishes between two types of extrapolative movements: attributive and predictive. Attributive extrapolations take place when a given researcher attributes (in the target) observed effects to a given cause based on the observation of that same causal relation elsewhere. Both the effects and the cause have been already observed in the target, and by extrapolation, a connection between both effect and cause is *attributed*. Predictive extrapolation, in turn, aims to foresee the effects of future interventions based on previous ones, in cases in which neither the intervention nor its effect have yet been observed. According to Khosrowi, the latter type of extrapolation, i.e., predictive, characterizes the type of setting faced by econometricians involved in the EBP movement. Their strategies to tackle this kind of predictive extrapolation (typically involving the use of supplementary evidence consisting of quantitative observational data), do suffer from the problem of the extrapolator's circle, following Khosrowi's argument: these strategies require so much knowledge about the target population that the causal effects to be extrapolated could be identified from information about the target alone. Khosrowi finally argues that the solution to this problem can be for econometricians and EBP advocates in general to be open to considering integrating different types of evidence (namely, including qualitative evidence). While acknowledging that qualitative evidence suffers from its own limitations, Khosrowi argues that it can nevertheless supplement extrapolative inferences that would otherwise face the choice between the extreme burden of gathering too much evidence on the target or to rely on "hope alone."

2.2 The Problem of External Validity in Political Science

The developments that are behind the spread of thinking of experiments and extrapolation in terms of "external validity" in Political Science mirror those of Philosophy, though they have some particularities explained by the characteristics and recent history of the discipline.[1]

The most direct cause of the introduction of discussion of external validity in Political Science has probably been the (causal) identification revolution in the Social Sciences at the turn of the twenty-first century, a name often preferred within political science to that of the "credibility revolution" in Economics (Angrist and Pischke 2010), even though both developments share a number of characteristics. In political science, the identification revolution was characterized by the rapid adoption of new methods aimed at surmounting the increasingly apparent limitations of regression analyses in asserting causal relations. The limitations of regression analysis came from the "often non-random distribution of observations, problems of endogeneity and omitted variable bias, and the complex causal relationships that abound in the social, political and economic world." (Morgan 2016). These problems became central to empirical political scientists who, in turn, began to explicitly address them with better causal identification procedures, like the renewed emphasis on research design, new statistical methods based on experimental reasoning such as instrumental variables or the potential-outcomes framework (such as Neyman-Rubin's model), and increasingly, with the deployment of experimental designs, thus surmounting a decades-long resistance that tended to resist them as costly or simply unfeasible.

With the identification revolution, political science came to make room for the idea that experiments were not only feasible, but actually superior to other research methods. Again, the same idea that swept many fields, also became prominent in political scientific circles: RCTs as the "gold standard." But with this newly earned status, the same "external validity problem" critique that had been pushed against RCTs in other fields emerged in political science with similar impetus.

Borrowing often from development economics designs, RCTs in political science focus on political independent variables or outcomes (such as turnout or vote choice) and are fielded *within a given community*. While scholars most concerned with correctly identifying genuine causal relations may be satisfied, those concerned with "generalizability" of results are typically not, because a common refrain is that one does not know if such results would be found in larger samples, or simply, in other samples. Some commentators thus frame this in terms of the "problem of external validity" and argue that experimental results may not be externally valid because a different sample in another part of the country would behave differently for a variety of theoretical reasons.

Dani Rodrik, a political economist who is influential amongst political scientists, has formulated these criticisms in ways that resemble Cartwright and Deaton's critique, the bottom line being that randomized field experiments should not be considered superior to other forms of evidence, including qualitative evidence in the form of interviews with informants and observational evidence in general. According to him, "it is actually misleading to think of evidence from randomized evaluations as distinctly "hard" in comparison to other kinds of evidence" (2008, p. 5). The reason is that "the typical evaluation will have been carried out in a specific locale on a specific group and under specific experimental conditions. Its generalizability to other settings is never assured—this is the problem of "external validity"—and it is certainly not established by the evaluation itself." For this reason, evidence from randomized field experiments, "need not be more informative than other types of evidence which may have less airtight causal identification but are stronger on external validity (because of broader geographical or temporal coverage). In practice internal validity—just like external validity—is not an either-or matter; some studies do better than others on this score, . . . and deserve more of our attention on that account. But this preference has to be tempered with a consideration also of external validity" (p. 5).

This critical view of RCTs based on their lack of external validity contrasts with the position, also often found in the literature, that asserts that field experiments have a comparative advantage in terms of their external validity by virtue of taking place in the field, i.e., in a more natural milieu relative to lab experiments. This is basically Donald Green's(a leading contributor and methodologist in experimental political science) line of reasoning. In a 2009 piece (De Rooij et al. 2009, p. 390), Green and his coauthors make this explicit by arguing that: "Field experiments, randomized trials conducted in a naturalistic setting, strive for greater external validity than lab experiments. Field experimentation attempts to approximate as closely as possible the conditions under which a causal process occurs. Ideally, subjects are unaware that they are part of an experiment, the interventions are similar or identical to the interventions they would experience in everyday life, and the outcome measures are the behavioral or institutional consequences of real-world significance."

Just a few years before, and drawing on pioneering work by Gosnell (1927) that had been thought as an early oddity, or more often, ignored, Donald Green, together with Alan Gerber had started an entire research program using field experimentation in political science to understand voting mobilization[2]. The Get Out The Vote (GOTV) experiments turned into a very fruitful intellectual venture by shedding light into the measurement of the impact of campaigning on the vote share of different parties. This was a question that until then had offered particular resistance to be studied with observational data, in part, due to the strategic nature of campaign spending. Gerber and Green (2000b), by tackling the question experimentally, were able to offer empirical estimates of these effects and inaugurated the experimental era in the discipline, also as leading methodologists and promoters of experimental methods and projects (Druckman et al. 2011).

Green et al.'s idea that field experiments have a comparative advantage in terms of external validity relative to lab experiments resonates with the controversy that took place around the 2010s between those who defended the superiority of lab versus field experiments in terms of external validity and those who thought that the idea had no basis. In the camp of the advocates of field experiments, on the one hand, Levitt and List, in a series of influential articles (Levitt and List, 2007a, 2007b, 2008) raised their concerns over the generalizability of most of lab economics experiments. This kind of concern led many to favor field over lab experiments on the basis that the former, by occurring in more realistic settings, are more relevant to policy making, even if they are, perhaps, less tightly controlled. This argument has been countered by Falk and Heckman (2009) and Camerer (2003) on the basis that laboratory experiments produce more controlled manipulations, and that these, ultimately, are a better (even if more distant) basis for extrapolation.

This controversy was important in itself, as it involved leading figures in the related disciplines holding opposing views about seemingly crucial matters regarding the inferential role of experiments, yet, it is also important in that it is intimately connected with two extant contradictions in the literature.

2.3   Two Paradoxes Regarding External Validity

The first such contradiction has been identified by Jiménez-Buedo and Miller (2010) and it regards the way in which the relationship between internal and external validity has been characterized. While the then standard view in the literature claimed that internal and external validity stood in a trade-off relation with each other (the basic intuition being that the more one secures internal validity in an experiment, the more artificial the environment, and the less generalizable the results, see Brehn et al. 1999; Smith and Mackie 1999, Guala 2005), this idea long coexisted with the (prima facie incompatible) view that internal validity was a prerequisite or a necessary condition to external validity (for accounts of this latter contention see Lucas 2003, Hogarth 2005 and Thye 2000). Jiménez-Buedo and Miller (2010) detail the possible interpretations of the mechanisms behind a supposed trade-off between internal and external validity and argue against each of them as responsible for a generalized phenomenon. They consequently advocate for the abandonment or the reformulation of the notion of the trade-off between internal and external validity.

The second contradiction can be formulated as a paradox in regard to the relation between field experiments and external validity: on the one hand, field experiments have been criticized for their lack of external validity (Deaton and Cartwright2018, Rodrik 2008). On the other hand, field experiments have been proposed as a solution to the lack of external validity of lab experiments (De Rooij et al. 2009, Levitt and List 2007ab, 2008).

A possible explanation for this apparent contradiction can be traced by looking into a piece by Nagatsu and Favereau (2020), who have described the recent history of field experiments in economics as coming from two distinct intellectual traditions. The first strand in field experimentation can be seen as an extension of laboratory experiments, whereas the second strand instead is instead heir to a long-standing tradition from social sciences, i.e., the Campbellian tradition of field tryouts of ameliorative programs. According to the authors, these two strands were developed in order to solve different methodological issues, and the two strands face different types of external validity problems. The first strand began as a response to the criticisms of lab experiments as too "artificial," or too different from naturally occurring situations, which led researchers to promote a series of lab-in-the-field experiments aimed at naturalizing the experimental tasks (Harrington and List 2004). The second tradition was however unconcerned with artificiality and instead aimed at correctly identifying causally the effects of different policies on the outcomes of interest. As such, this experimental tradition was concerned with controlling for the biasing effects of unobservable variables through randomization. Rather than artificiality, the issue for this strand is the generalizability of the findings. Thus, in Nagatsu and Favereau's interpretation of these debates, both *artificiality* and *generality* are two types of external validity problems. Building on Sugden's functional analysis of experiments as exhibits for empirical investigations, the authors propose a hybridization of both strands of experiments, in order to strengthen both types of external validity.

Nagatsu and Favereau's historical argument points to the fact that the concept of external validity represents two different sets of problems (artificiality and generality) in two different intellectual strands. Nagatsu and Favereau provide a plausible historical explanation for the variation in the use of "external validity," there are many further conceptual issues and polysemy that they do not address. We turn to these in the next section.

3. The Problems with External Validity

As we have mentioned in the previous section, the term "external validity" was ultimately devised, by its intellectual father, as one term among a typology of validity. This typology itself was part of the bigger Campbellian project, itself a methodological guide for social scientists relating causal identification questions to optimal designs. Within it, the validity typology could, among other things, serve as a heuristic: a checklist aimed at assessing the extent to which a given design is able to identify or filter away all the possible confounders that threaten a researcher's capacity to correctly isolate the effect of interventions on the outcomes of interest. Within it, the terms internal and external validity (and especially the latter) eventually developed lives of their own, and they came to be rather universally adopted as a dyad that users found convenient to express a distinction between the inside and the outside of an experiment or study (a distinction between the genuine causal isolation within an experiment on the one hand, and the applicability of this knowledge outside of the experiment). In the case of internal validity, the notion became synonymous with that of the tightness of the causal conclusions identified by a given design. In the case of external validity, matters were ipso facto more complicated definitionally, because the "outside" of an experiment is, inherently, a very complex, diverse, and layered locus. As a result of this, external validity was bound to mean different things for different people but as we saw, the increase in its use coincided with a growing interest in the problem of extrapolation, and soon enough, a number of issues regarding extrapolation became to be known as "the problem of external validity."

Recently, there seems to be a growing unease with the formulation of extrapolation in terms of the "problem of external validity." Reiss (2019) for example, has claimed that the current reasoning in terms of external validity is based on an undue methodological pre-eminence of experimental methods over alternatives, and that the idea of external validity puts excessive emphasis on knowledge about the inferential source at the expense of the knowledge of the target, thus it encourages poor reasoning about evidence. Also, Deaton and Cartwright (2018) have found problems in some of the current interpretations of external validity in relation to the travelling of evidence from Randomized Controlled Trials and have deemed the term ambiguous.

Within experimental political science, Rebecca Morton and Kenneth Williams (2008), leading methodologists in the subfield, have expressed their malaise regarding current uses of the term, which they think are often based on an outmoded way of understanding external validity (i.e., as disembedded from Campbell's full four-tier typology). According to these authors, incorrect usages of the term are manifested, for example, when experiments are criticized for the lack of external validity relative to other methods. They argue that external validity is a problem for all data generating methods, regardless of whether they are observational or manipulational (as in experimental). Following closely Shadish, Cook, and Campbell's definition, Morton and Williams (2008) argue that external validity (or the question of whether causal inferences established in an empirical analysis hold over variation in persons, settings, treatment variables, and measurement variables) is akin to our capacity to reproduce a result over different datasets, regardless of whether they are observational or experimental:

> Do the results from one dataset generalize to another? This is a question that is of importance for any empirical researcher, regardless of whether the dataset is experimental or observational. If we study, for example, voter turnout in Congressional elections, can we generalize from that study to turnout in mayoral elections or elections in Germany or elections held in a laboratory? Yet, most political scientists rarely worry about the external validity issue with observational data but do worry about it with experimental data. Political scientists typically assume that external validity means that the dataset used for the analysis must resemble some "natural" DGP [data generating process]. (2008, p. 344–345)

We can interpret Morton and Williams' concern with this type of criticism of experiments as being related to what we articulate as a third paradox of external validity.

3.1 A Third Paradox of External Validity

It is generally agreed that experimental methods are superior in their capacity to discern between spurious correlations and genuine causal relations and yet, it is in virtue of this epistemic advantage that we somehow also demand more out of them in terms of a different aspect: we demand that they also help us in the extrapolation process in ways that we do not demand other (observational) methods. In other words, experimental methods, by being particularly good at something, somehow set for themselves a higher bar in everything else, which then ends up being used as an argument about the limitations of experimental methods, and even, sometimes, as an argument against them. This again relates to the ambiguities of the term "external validity" and its intermittent equivalence to the notion of extrapolation: the problem of extrapolation of findings is a challenge for all forms of evidence including even those that have particular advantages with respect to causal identification, such as experimentation. In this sense, it is somehow infelicitous that experiments have come to be often associated (especially, but not only, in the popular accounts and grey literature of reports, white papers, and evaluations) with a problem, that of extrapolative inferences, that is common to all forms of scientific knowledge.

3.2 Doing Away with External Validity?

Morton and Williams have later proposed a "deconstruction" of the term external validity, since they think that a lot of what political scientists call "external validity" is, in fact, something else. According to Morton and Williams, external validity is sometimes confused with construct validity, and sometimes with a quality of experiments that they classify as ecological validity, defined as the *similarity* of the methods, materials and settings of the research to a given target environment. External validity, according to Morton and Williams, also relates to the question of replicability: how often and in what conditions do the results of a given study replicate across different measurements, methods, settings, etc.?

> It is a mistake to equate external validity with whether a given dataset used to establish a particular causal relationship resembles the natural DGP (which can never be accurately measured or observed). Instead, establishing whether a result is externally valid involves replication of the result across a variety of datasets. For example, if a researcher discovered that more informed voters were more likely to turnout in Congressional elections and then found that this is also true in mayoral elections, in elections in Germany, and in an experiment with control and manipulation as well, then we would say the result showed high external validity. The same thing is true about results that originate from experimental analysis. If an experiment demonstrates a particular causal relationship, the establishment of whether that relationship is externally valid is accomplished by examining whether the relationship exists across a range of experimental and observational datasets and not whether the original experimental dataset resembles a hypothesized version of the natural DGP. (2008, p. 345)

In order to avoid some of the ambiguous interpretations of the term, some experimentalists trained in the Morton and Williams tradition do away with the term "external validity" in the discussion section of their papers altogether. Some researchers trained in this tradition have sometimes avoided the term in their articles, and so Michelitch (2015) for example, discusses ecological and construct validity on the one hand, and causal validity on the other, in the discussion section of her well-known field experiment studying whether economic discrimination among different ethnic and political groups changes with the electoral cycle (as exemplified by the differential change in the rates charged by local taxi drivers to different riders in the city of Accra during the 2008 Ghana election).

3.3 Conceptual Overload and Conceptual Ambiguities

In this way, and summing up: on the one hand, the term "external validity" seems to be useful to some researchers to discuss matters of extrapolation (and in particular, it seems to have been useful to many philosophers dealing with this relatively understudied aspect of experimental findings). Yet, on the other hand, the term seems to be subject to too many interpretations (Jiménez-Buedo, 2011), which should be of concern to those preoccupied with conceptual rigor, and creates room for confusion when researchers speak across purposes by referring to different meanings of the term unknowingly. After all, the task that we seem to collectively demand of the term, (i.e., to define, simultaneously, the generalizability of experimental findings; generalizability of causal claims; the phenomenon of extrapolation widely; the policy relevance of experimental results; the scope of average treatment effects; the relative artificiality of experimental settings) seems to be too large a challenge for any one particular concept. This thus seems to be a clear case of conceptual overload; no single concept can serve so many purposes.

But beyond that, there seems to be some conceptual ambiguities embedded in the notion of external validity that do not depend so much on its uses, but were instead there from the beginning, and embedded in the very way in which the concept was constructed. In particular we focus here, drawing on previous work (Jiménez-Buedo, 2011), on the object of which external validity should be predicated.

From the beginning, there has been ambiguity as to what constitutes a proper object of external and or internal validity (whether it is experimental designs, experimental results, or inferences from experiments). Different researchers in the relevant literature use the term differently, and the same author can use it in multiple ways, so we hear references to the external validity of experimental results, the external validity of inferences, or more commonly to references to the external validity of experiments. So, what is it that can be susceptible of being either internally or externally valid? Is it a given experiment (meaning a one-time event in its uniqueness and materiality)? Or, is it instead a type of experiment, i.e., a given experimental design? Is it instead the experimental results, or the data stemming from an experiment? Or rather, should the experimental inferences that we draw from those data be the only viable candidates for validity?

Campbell and his collaborators are not without responsibility for this confusion. Mark (1986) and Hammersley (1993) record that the distinction was initially set out to define experimental designs, but it became increasingly associated with inferences from the experiment. Shadish, Cook, and Campbell (2002) address this ambiguity: "Validity is a property of inferences. It is not a property of designs or methods, for the same design may contribute to more or less valid inferences under different circumstances. For example, using a randomized experiment does not guarantee that one will make a valid inference about the existence of a descriptive causal relationship." However, and though they admit that "it is wrong to say that a randomized experiment is internally valid or has internal validity" they dispense themselves and others the licence to "occasionally speak that way for convenience" (p. 34).

Though defended for its supposed handiness, Shadish, Cook and Campbell's terminological relaxation has other problems, for the economy of language associated with attaching the terms internally/externally valid to an experiment assumes a correspondence between experiments and the inferences we can make from them. This, in turn, represents a simplistic view of experiments, assuming away the fact that for any given experiment (and its associated results), different researchers may draw different conclusions (i.e., they will draw different inferences) depending on their different background knowledge. It instead presents a scenario in which each experimental design comes with a set of attached (valid or invalid) inferences that we may draw from its results. This picture might not be too distorting in some applied settings, in which there often is a straightforward, commonsensical connection between an experimental design and the types of inferences that its results allow. Yet, this view does not represent the relation between inferences and experimental interventions more broadly: in many experimental paradigms, mainly when the construction of theory is at stake (i.e., in theoretically oriented experiments), an experimental design and its associated results can have very divergent interpretations, depending on the different observers' background knowledge and orientation (Jiménez-Buedo, 2011; Jiménez-Buedo and Russo, 2021).

Shadish, Cook and Campbell actually acknowledge that the proper object of the validity typology is inferences from experiments, but this solution has problems of its own, as has been argued in Jiménez-Buedo (2011). If external validity is to be reserved to qualify the inferences from an experiment, rather than the experiment itself, then that means that some inferences from the experiment can only be internally valid, while some can only be externally valid, and so on. But this soon falls into trouble too, as we see exemplified next in Sullivan's account of validity.

Sullivan's position illustrates well the difficulties that come with reserving the use of the internal/external dyad to refer to inferences from an experiment, or as she calls them, interpretive claims (2009, 535, emphasis added): "A claim about an effect produced in a laboratory is internally valid, if and only if that claim is true about the effect produced in the laboratory. A claim about a phenomenon of interest outside the laboratory is externally valid, if and only if that claim is true about that phenomenon." Note that in her account, the type of inferences that can be internally valid are inferences about the experimental results as they apply to the experiment, whereas it is inferences about the phenomenon of interest which can be externally valid. Though consistent, this use of the internal/external validity dyad can render the dichotomy unnecessary, or redundant: in her account inferences are either internal or external depending on what they are predicated upon, but this means that a given inference cannot be *simultaneously* externally and internally valid (or invalid). Think, for example, about the phenomenon of interest: it can only be external, so little is added by asking of them whether they are "externally valid," rather than asking only whether they are, tout court, valid. This means that, for a given inference we can say whether it is valid or invalid and whether it is external or internal, but the distinction "internal/external" does not do any particular job on its own, other than re-stating the inference's domain. To illustrate this, think of a well-known lab experiment trying to detect whether physical similarity between voters and candidates helps the electoral prospects of the latter (Bailenson et al. 2008).

The experiment consists in presenting participants with different pictures of prospective candidates (in the treatment condition, the images digitally blend the candidate's features with those of the experimental subject, whereas the control blends the candidate's features with those of a different person, unknown to the subject). The results of the experiments showed that among weakly partisan or independent participants, there was an effect by which they tended to favor candidates that "resembled" them (through the artificial morphing of their pictures). What is internally or externally valid about this? If we were to use the labels in the way described by Sullivan (and following Campbell's own prescription), we would have the following: An inference about the phenomenon of interest (namely: voters favor candidates that physically resemble them) could be externally valid (or invalid). In turn, an inference about what goes on in the lab (subjects favor the candidates whose pictures are morphed with the subjects' features) could be internally valid (or invalid). Because the inferences cannot be simultaneously external and internal (they are predicated upon different objects), what is really relevant is whether they are valid or invalid, rather than whether they are (trivially) external or internal. This is not to deny that researchers might actually enjoy having a concept that distinguishes between two types of inferences that can be made from an experiment (though Morton and Williams and Campbell himself thought that subsuming all inferences under only two groups was not a good strategy). But if this is the role of the internal/external distinction, it does seem to fall short of the more ambitious epistemic connotations that people seem to attribute to these terms when we speak about the internal and external validity of experiments to refer, more broadly, to the problems of causal identification and extrapolation.

This chapter has tried to show that the conceptual problems of the term "external validity" are not only based on lenient or unclear uses of the terminology, but appear to have roots in the very way the terms were devised or constructed. Philosophers, political scientists (and other social scientists), experimenters in biomedics, and even a few natural scientists have in recent years used the notion of external validity in order to discuss the inferential import of their or others' experimental designs, to talk about the interpretation of their results, to assess the scope of their causal claims that stem from those results or simply to discuss the problems of extrapolation that are inherent to scientific research. Clearly, "external validity" has accommodated some conceptual demand, and even too many demands. It has been, in this sense, a successful term. This chapter however does advise some caution with the use of the notion of external validity, and invites some reflection on whether in this case conceptual success should be measured by metrics other than those of use or "catchiness."

NOTES

1. Here I focus on empirical political science. My particular focus are the subfields of political science where the goal is a broadly empiricist one: comparative politics, international relations, and political economy, which cuts across the other two (there is also the subfield of International Political Economy, that for some purposes has its own, autonomous, standing).

2. Though lab experiments and even quasi-experiments had been implemented before in political science, full randomized field experiments had been a neglected tool in the discipline until the turn of the century (Gerber and Green 2000a; see also Hofmeyr and Kincaid (chapter 18 in this volume) for an analysis of lab experiments in political science).

REFERENCES

Angrist, Joshua D., and Jörn-Steffen Pischke. 2010. "The credibility revolution in empirical economics: How better research design is taking the con out of econometrics." *Journal of economic perspectives* 24.2: 3–30.

Bailenson, Jeremy N., Shanto Iyengar, Nick Yee, and Nathan A. Collins. 2008. "Facial similarity between voters and candidates causes influence." *Public Opinion Quarterly* 72.5: 935–961.

Brehn, S. S., S. M. Kassin, and S. Fein. 1999. *Social Psychology*. Boston: Houghton Mifflin.

Camerer, Colin F. 2003. "Behavioural Studies of Strategic Thinking in Games." Trends in Cognitive Sciences 7.5: 225–31. https://doi.org/10.1016/S1364-6613(03)00094-9.

Campbell, D. T., and J. C. Stanley. 1963. *Experimental and Quasi-Experimental Designs for Research*. Chicago: Rand McNally.

Campbell, Donald T. 1957. "Factors Relevant to the Validity of Experiments in Social Settings." Psychological Bulletin 54.4: 297–312. https://doi.org/10.1037/h0040950.

Cartwright, Nancy. 1999. *The Dappled World: A Study of the Boundaries of Science*. Cambridge: Cambridge University Press.

Cartwright, Nancy. 2007. *Hunting Causes and Using Them: Approaches in Philosophy and Economics*. Cambridge: Cambridge University Press.

Cook, T. D., and D. T. Campbell. 1979. *Quasi-Experimentation: Design and Analysis Issues for Field Settings*. Chicago: Rand MacNally.

Cronbach, L. J. 1982. *Designing Evaluations of Educational and Social Programs*. San Francisco, CA: Jossey-Bass.

Deaton, Angus, and Nancy Cartwright. 2018. "Understanding and Misunderstanding Randomized Controlled Trials." Social Science & Medicine 210 (August): 2–21. https://doi.org/10.1016/j.socscimed.2017.12.005.

Falk, A., and Heckman, J. J. 2009. Lab experiments are a major source of knowledge in the social sciences. *Science* 326(5952), 535–538.

De Rooij, Eline A., Donald P. Green, and Alan S. Gerber. 2009. "Field experiments on political behavior and collective action." *Annual Review of Political Science* 12: 389–395.

Druckman, J. N., Green, D. P., Kuklinski, J. H., and Lupia, A. (Eds.). 2011. *Cambridge Handbook of Experimental Political Science*. Cambridge: Cambridge University Press.

Gerber, A. S., and Green, D. P. 2000a. The effects of canvassing, telephone calls, and direct mail on voter turnout: A field experiment. *American political science review*, 94.3, 653–663.

Gerber, Alan S., and Donald P. Green. 2000b. "The effect of a nonpartisan get-out-the-vote drive: An experimental study of leafletting." *Journal of Politics* 62.3: 846–857.

Gosnell, H. F. 1927. *Getting out the vote*. Chicago: University of Chicago Press.

Guala, Francesco. 1999. "The problem of external validity (or "parallelism") in experimental economics." *Social science information* 38.4: 555–573.

Guala, Francesco. 2003. "Experimental Localism and External Validity." Philosophy of Science 70.5: 1195–1205. https://doi.org/10.1086/377400.

Guala, Francesco. 2005. *The Methodology of Experimental Economics*. Cambridge: Cambridge University Press.

Guala, Francesco. 2010. "Extrapolation, analogy, and comparative process tracing." *Philosophy of Science* 77.5: 1070–1082.

Hammersley, Martyn. 1993. "Abandoning Internal and External Validity: A Response to Swanborn." Quality & Quantity 27.2: 217–18. https://doi.org/10.1007/BF01102735.

Harrison, Glenn W., and John A. List. 2004. "Field experiments." *Journal of Economic literature* 42.4: 1009–1055.

Heukelom, Floris. 2011. "How Validity Travelled to Economic Experimenting." *Journal of Economic Methodology* 18.1: 13–28. https://doi.org/10.1080/1350178X.2011.556435.

Hogarth, R. B. 2005. "The challenge of representativeness design in psychology and economics." *Journal of Economic Methodology* 12: 253–263.

Hotz, V. J., Imbens, G. W., & Mortimer, J. H. 2005. "Predicting the efficacy of future training programs using past experiences at other locations." *Journal of Econometrics* 125: 241–270.

Jiménez-Buedo, M. and L. Miller. 2010. "Why a trade-off? The Relationship between the Internal and External Validity of Experiments." *Theoria*. 25: 301–321.

Jiménez-Buedo, M. 2011. "Conceptual Tools for Assessing Experiments: Some Well-Entrenched Confusions Regarding the Internal/External Validity Distinction." *Journal of Economic Methodology* 18.3: 271–82. https://doi.org/10.1080/1350178X.2011.611027.

Jiménez-Buedo, María, and Federica Russo. 2021. "Experimental practices and objectivity in the social sciences: re-embedding construct validity in the internal–external validity distinction." *Synthese* 199.3: 9549–9579.

Khosrowi, Donal. 2019. "Extrapolation of causal effects–hopes, assumptions, and the extrapolator's circle." *Journal of Economic Methodology* 26.1: 45–58.

Levitt, S. and J. A. List. 2007a. "Viewpoint: On the Generalizability of Lab Behaviour to the Field." *Canadian Journal of Economics* 40.2; 347–370.

Levitt, S. and J. A. List. 2007b. "What do Laboratory Experiments Measuring Social Preferences Reveal about the Real World." *Journal of Economic Perspectives* 21.2: 153–174.

Levitt, S. and J. A. List. 2008. "Homo Economicus Evolves." *Science* 319.5865: 909–910.

Lucas, J. W. 2003. "Theory-Testing, Generalization and the Problem of External Validity." *Sociological Theory* 21: 236–253.

Mark, Melvin M. 1986. "Validity Typologies and the Logic and Practice of Quasi-Experimentation." *New Directions for Program Evaluation* 1986.31: 47–66. https://onlinelibrary.wiley.com/doi/10.1002/ev.1433.

Michelitch, Kristin. 2015. "Does electoral competition exacerbate interethnic or interpartisan economic discrimination? Evidence from a field experiment in market price bargaining." *American Political Science Review* 109.1: 43–61.

Morgan, Kimberly J. 2016. "Process Tracing and the Causal Identification Revolution." New *Political Economy* 21.5: 489–492. https://doi.org/10.1080/13563467.2016.1201804.

Morton, Rebecca B., and Kenneth C. Williams. 2008. "Experimentation in political science." *The Oxford Handbook Of Political Methodology*, pp. 339–356. https://www.oxfordhandbooks.com/view/10.1093/oxfordhb/9780199286546.001.0001/oxfordhb-9780199286546.

Morton, Rebecca B., and Kenneth C. Williams. 2010. *Experimental Political Science and the Study of Causality: From Nature to the Lab*. Cambridge: Cambridge University Press.

Muller, S. M. 2014. *Randomised Trials for Policy: A Review of the External Validity of Treatment Effects* (Southern Africa labour and development research unit working paper 127). University of Cape Town.

Muller, S. M. 2015. Causal interaction and external validity: Obstacles to the policy relevance of randomized evaluations. *The World Bank Economic Review* 29.1: S217–S225.

Nagatsu, Michiru, and Judith Favereau. 2020. "Two strands of field experiments in economics: a historical-methodological analysis." *Philosophy of the Social Sciences* 50.1: 45–77.

Reiss, Julian. 2019. "Against External Validity." *Synthese* 196.8: 3103–3121. https://doi.org/10.1007/s11229-018-1796-6.

Rodrik, Dani. 2008. "The new development economics: we shall experiment, but how shall we learn?" Paper prepared for the Brookings Development Conference, May 29–30, 2008.

Russo, F. 2010. "Comparative process tracing: Yet another virtue of mechanisms?" *Journal of Economic Methodology* 17.1: 81–87.

Shadish, William R., Thomas D. Cook, and Donald T. Campbell. 2002. *Experimental and Quasi-Experimental Designs for Generalized Causal Inference*. Boston, MA: Houghton, Mifflin and Company.

Smith, E. R. and Mackie, D. M. 1999. *Social Psychology*. Philadelphia: Psychology Press.

Steel, Daniel. 2008. *Across the Boundaries. Extrapolation in Biology and Social Science*. Oxford University Press.

Steel, D. 2010. "A New Approach to Argument by Analogy: Extrapolation and Chain Graphs." *Philosophy of Science* 77.5: 1058–1069.

Sullivan, Jacqueline A. 2009. "The Multiplicity of Experimental Protocols: A Challenge to Reductionist and Non-Reductionist Models of the Unity of Neuroscience." *Synthese* 167.3: 511–539. https://doi.org/10.1007/s11229-008-9389-4.

Thye, S. R. 2000. "Reliability in Experimental Sociology." *Social Forces* 78: 1277–1309.

CHAPTER 21

CONTEXT, CONTEXTUALIZATION, AND CASE-STUDY RESEARCH

ATTILIA RUZZENE

1. INTRODUCTION

ACCORDING to some observers of the field, qualitative methods have recently experienced a "renaissance" in several areas of political science (Bennett & Elman 2007a; Gerring 2007; Mahoney 2007). The areas invested by this turn include, but are not limited to, subfields such as comparative politics, international relations, and American politics (Bennet & Elman 2007a). In the early 2000s, a new generation of qualitative studies was born distinguishing itself from previous qualitative works for the broader range of publications, for a higher methodological awareness, and for a closer association with quantitative methods and formal modeling. This remarkable surge of the qualitative is driven by several factors. First is the recognition that political phenomena which are "complex, relatively unstructured and infrequent" lend themselves to be studied less through quantitative than through qualitative approaches (Bennett & Elman 2007b). Second, the professionalization of qualitative scholarship triggered a deeper epistemological reflection on its methods. Finally, there is nowadays a shared awareness that complementarities arise from studying the same phenomenon through a variety of approaches employed either jointly or sequentially (George & Bennett 2005).

Civil war is a case in point. The study of civil war has attracted considerable, and increasing, attention on the part of political scientists. In reviewing four books on civil war, Sidney Tarrow remarks how a first wave of quantitative-oriented studies on civil war, starting approximately in the Sixties, has been followed by a second wave of qualitative-oriented studies in the early 2000s (Tarrow 2007). Essential as it was for providing a first understanding of civil war, this first wave of studies suffered from major lacunae pertaining to issues such as over-aggregation of data, problems of unit heterogeneity, and unaccounted regional-level variability (2007: 589). To Tarrow, these gaps are inherent to large-N studies and, as such, cannot be filled by enlarging the data set or by strengthening the quantitative measures; rather they required to (re)turn to case-study research. Similar observations are offered by Nicholas Sambanis (Sambanis 2004). Sambanis was the primary investigator in the Case Study Project on Civil Wars whereby twenty-one case studies on civil war onset and war avoidance are employed to develop and qualify causal inferences drawn from the Collier-Hoeffler and Fearon-Laitin models of civil war. In his view, case studies complement and benefit the formal-quantitative approach because, by expanding theory and making it more fine-grained, eventually improve its accuracy.

Two points can be elicited from the discussion above. First is the acknowledgment that context matters for political phenomena. Pooling events of civil war in a single model does not lead to sufficiently accurate explanations of the phenomenon since it varies across contexts in relevant respects. Second is the confidence that qualitative methods, specifically case-study research, can enhance our understanding of how context matters and what are the relevant respects in which it does so. These suggestions are *prima facie* hardly disputable. Indeed, case studies are imbued with information that attests to the specificity and variability of social phenomena. However, converting this case-specific information into knowledge of context is not straightforward. In this chapter I refer to this practice as *contextualization*, and offer an account of how it is pursued, and to what extent, in case-study research. I will do so by drawing a distinction between two techniques of data analysis, *process tracing* and *process embedding*, and analyze their interplay in the construction of a case study. Whereas *process tracing* is amply discussed in methodological debates in political science, *process embedding* is so far unacknowledged as a self-standing procedure of data analysis.

The chapter is structured as follows. In Section 2, I examine how the notion of context is understood in political science and the reasons given in support of its relevance for understanding political phenomena. In Section 3, I discuss contextualization in case-study research by drawing a distinction between *process tracing* and *process embedding*. In Section 4, I illustrate the distinctive role of *process embedding* vis-à-vis process tracing and will do so by discussing a few case studies on civil war. In Section 5, I offer some considerations on how far case studies can go in delivering knowledge of context and why, and to what extent, such knowledge should not be forsaken. In section six I conclude.

2. THE RELEVANCE OF CONTEXT IN POLITICAL SCIENCE

In the last decades, several scholars argued that understanding context[1] should be a prominent concern for political scientists. The growing awareness that context influences political phenomena in nontrivial ways prompted the development of measurement procedures, research designs, and theorizations that reflect this influence (Adcock & Collier 2001; Falleti & Lynch 2009; Goertz 1994; Goodin & Tilly 2006; Locke & Thelen 1995). In political science, context is understood almost invariably as a causal construct with two distinguishable meanings. A first meaning traces back to John Mackie's notion of causal field (Falleti & Lynch 2009, Goertz 1994). In this view, context consists of those background conditions that are necessary for the explanatory variable of interest to produce the effect. Hence, both the context and the explanatory variable qualify as INUS conditions,[2] the distinction between them being mostly pragmatic. Alternatively, context is understood as (a set of) factors influencing the relationship between the explanatory variable and the outcome, and thus the way in which the former affects the latter (Goertz 1994).[3] When political scientists claim that outcomes depend on context, they typically conflate these two meanings.

These two meanings of context survived recent trends in the field. It has been voiced from many quarters that political science is undergoing a mechanistic turn. In the new paradigm, the search for causal mechanisms is a prominent, if not defining, feature of political science inquiry. It is now common knowledge that conceptualizations of mechanism proliferate in the social sciences (Mahoney 2001, 2007; Hedstrom and Ylikoski 2010). Mechanisms are sometimes understood in antithesis to universal laws; some other times they are understood as intermediate variables between the cause and the effect; and yet other times they are treated as complex structures responsible for emergent phenomena. Despite the plurality of concepts, the "mechanismic worldview" (Gerring 2008) finds convergence in seeing mechanisms, however understood, as a fundamental part of the causal furniture of the world and of our best scientific explanations. In this view, context is that which enables, impedes, or modifies the mechanism operation, that is, its capacity to bring about the outcome *and* the way it does so.

Once more, context plays a twofold causal role. On the one hand, it enables the operation of the mechanism, meaning that the mechanism only works when contextual conditions are right. I shall refer to this notion of context-as-*interactor*. On the other hand, context affects the ways in which the mechanism operates and impacts on the outcome either quantitatively or qualitatively. I shall refer to this notion of context as *modifier*. In either case, context has deep causal significance and knowledge of it is paramount for fulfilling goals that are valuable for political scientists. In what follows, I briefly present a few scholars who openly argue that contextual knowledge not only improves, but in fact permits, credible explanation of political phenomena, sound policy evaluation, and valid extrapolation. Furthermore, these contributions testify to the three claims made in the previous paragraphs. That is the centrality of mechanisms to political reasoning, the fact that context is mainly understood in causal terms, and the twofold nature it possesses.

Falleti and Lynch (2009) claim that the explanation of political phenomena acquires credibility only if the role of context is accounted for. In their view, explanation in political science consists in the identification of the mechanism responsible for the outcome of interest. However, mechanisms are explanatory only when combined with a characterization of the context in which they operate and an account of the way in which the mechanism and the context interact in bringing the outcome about. The causal effect observed on the outcome of interest depends in fact not only on the mechanism, but on its interaction with the context in which the mechanism is situated. Explanations that disregard the role of context lose credibility not only because they erroneously attribute the outcome uniquely to the mechanism but also because they are liable of faulty generalization. If the outcome depends on the interaction between the mechanism and the context, it follows that when the context changes in relevant respect, the outcome also changes, even if the operating mechanism remains the same. In this view, the mechanism on its own neither fully explains the outcome nor does it enable valid inference about causal impact on the outcome.

Pawson and Tilley defend an approach to policy evaluation grounded on realist principles (Pawson and Tilley 1997, 2004). Realist evaluation is based on program theories, that is theories articulated according to the following conceptual matrix:

(CMO) outcome = mechanism + context

The assumption underlying the matrix is that causal outcomes are engendered by mechanisms acting in context. Policies consist in introducing so-called mechanisms of change into "preexisting social contexts" (1997: 70). The theory on which the program builds formulates hypotheses about how these mechanisms of change overturn, counteract or transform the social processes in place. These social processes result from the interaction between prevailing conditions and currently operating mechanisms which sustained the problem the policy addresses. Mechanisms of change must thus "break into" current social processes and produce the intended change without a major transformation of the prevailing social conditions. It is these conditions that most of the time account for the failure or success of the policy, and their enabling or disabling effect on the mechanism of change must therefore be at the core of evaluation. Accordingly, the task of a realist evaluation is to identify, articulate, test and refine conjectured CMO configurations (1997: 77).

Assessments of external validity are notoriously challenging for the social scientist interested in the extrapolation of scientific findings. This challenge becomes particularly pressing when the scientific finding whose external validity is at stake is a policy claim; that is, a claim about the efficacy of a given intervention. Interventions can be conceived as policy mechanisms, the extrapolation of which raises two main issues concerning matters of context. On the one hand, when the inner working of the policy mechanism is rather well known and possesses some degree of stability, concerns about external validity translate into concerns about their portability (Falleti & Lynch 2009; Woolcock 2013). Context matters here because whether the mechanism is portable, that is generalizable to other settings, depends on whether the original and target contexts are "analytically equivalent" (Falleti & Lynch 2009: 1160). On the other hand, when policy mechanisms are *complex*, the policy mechanism does not possess inner stability and decisions about implementation requires the use of discretion on the part of the implementing agent (Pritchett & Woolcock 2002: 194). In this case, contextual knowledge is also central but for quite different reasons. Whereas in the former case, it serves to assess whether the original and the target context are equivalent, here it serves to find effective ways to modify and adapt the policy mechanism to the characteristics of the target setting.

3. CONTEXTUALIZATION IN CASE-STUDY RESEARCH

The increasing attention paid by political scientists to causal mechanisms and to the role of context in political phenomena goes a long way in explaining the recent calls for a more extensive and conscious use of case-study research. Two features are invariably regarded as characterizing this research approach: the in-depth character of the investigation and its sensitivity to context (Crasnow 2019; Morgan 2012; Yin, 2009, 2015). The former is easily understood within a mechanistic framework. The inquiry into mechanisms requires opening the black box of causation; and case studies offer an avenue for this type of inquiry by digging into the details of a single case while handling a variety of evidential sources (George & Bennett 2005; Gerring 2007). As Gerring points out, even if there is no necessary connection between the study of causal mechanisms and case study investigation, "a strong affinity" exists between the two (Gerring 2008: 173). Whereas the relationship between case studies and mechanisms has been amply investigated and theorized, context sensitivity, despite broadly consensual, has been mainly taken as self-explanatory.

Roughly speaking, context sensitivity is equated to the permeability of case-study research to particulars of the case (Crasnow 2019). This suggestion might be unproblematic when looking at cases as *complex wholes* and to case-studying as tying together different bits and pieces of evidence to make sense of that complexity (Crasnow 2019; Morgan 2012). In this view, drawing a neat distinction between contextual and case-specific knowledge might be even nonsensical. However, insofar as case studies are taken as informative about causal mechanisms and the context in which they are situated, this is a sensible distinction to make. In other terms, if context is the causal construct understood by political scientists, how does one build knowledge of context from a collection of case-specific information? The discussion below aims at providing a tentative answer to this type of questions. In this chapter, I will confine my analysis to single case studies and thereby exclude small-n, comparative, and cross-case research. Furthermore, I will focus on case studies of an analytic kind that are directed to develop causal explanations of outcomes of interest.

In single case studies directed to provide causal explanations of outcomes of interest, contextualization, that is the conversion of case-specific information into knowledge of context, is achieved by employing jointly two strategies of data analysis, namely *process tracing* and *process embedding*. Whereas process tracing is amply discussed in the methodological debate in political science,[4] process embedding is so far unacknowledged as a self-standing procedure of data analysis. Therefore, the characterization below is primarily aimed at defending the relevance of such a distinction. It does so by first disentangling the epistemic goals the two strategies aim to achieve and then highlight three evidentiary principles that govern the application of process embedding.

- Process tracing is a strategy of data analysis that:
  - Addresses *first order* causal questions: How does the outcome come about?
  - Epistemic result: Identification of the causal mechanism (M)[5] leading to the outcome of interest (O)
- Process embedding is a strategy of data analysis that:
  - Addresses *second order* causal questions: Why the mechanism operated *as it did* in the case at hand?
  - Epistemic result: Identification of processes[6] in the neighborhood of M (N_m) that *causally fit* M or its components

Process embedding achieves its epistemic goals with the help of three evidentiary principles. These principles govern contextualization in single case studies and help convert case-specific information into evidence for contextual processes:

1. *Generality and Sequentiality*: Whereas process tracing focuses on the mechanism bringing about the outcome of interest, process embedding targets processes unfolding

in the setting in which the mechanism is situated. The first evidentiary principle governing the relationship between process tracing and process embedding distinguishes particular facts pertaining to the mechanism and general facts pertaining to the surrounding processes. The generality principle thus organizes facts according to what is broader in scope, larger in scale, or unfolding within a longer time span. The principle of *sequientiality* orders pieces of evidence according to what is temporally prior to what. The two principles operate simultaneously, that is pieces of evidence are ordered with respect to each other both according to their temporality *and* their generality.

2. *Coherence*:[7] Process tracing and process embedding jointly aim at relating the mechanism to its context as a part of the whole. Like inserting a piece in a jigsaw puzzle, also in this case one seeks for coherence between the former and the latter. Coherence between particular facts referring to the mechanism and general facts referring to the context can be searched in a variety of directions. Conditions of coherence have a heuristic function and help drawing the boundaries of N_m within which relevant processes can be found. Here are a few such conditions:

- Spatial contiguity
- Temporal continuity
- Systemic relation
- Symbolic connection
- Network relation

3. *Causal fitness:* The principle of causal fitness here defended resonates with similar notions used to describe certain features of causal relations (Woodward 2010). Broadly speaking, it refers to the "explanatorily adequate" amount of details included in the description of a causal relationship. Translated to the case at hand, we can say that process embedding identifies processes in N_m that *causally fit* M or its components by accounting for M, or M components, specifics. Specifics might pertain to the temporality of the mechanism, such as the specific moment in which the mechanism operates; its spatiality, such as its location or distribution; and more in general, the detail of its instantiation and functioning. In particular, contextual processes explain why the mechanism displays these specific features *rather than* others, and thus why it triggered in that specific moment rather than earlier or later than that, or why a specific component of the mechanism had that specific value rather than a different one.

The principles highlighted above guide contextualization; however, they are contingent not only on the identification of the main causal mechanism but also on pragmatic features of the study itself. How to delimit the neighborhood of M, and thereby applying the principles of coherence and causal fitness, depends in the first place on the type of mechanism identified and second on what specific features of the mechanism are in need of contextualization as understood above. Ultimately these are issues that depend on the subject matter of interest, the theoretical inclination of the researcher, and the specific debate one is addressing.

In the next section, I will illustrate what type of findings process embedding delivers. I will do so using as examples a few case studies on civil war and disentangling the mechanism identified by way of process tracing from contextual processes identified by process embedding. The point of the discussion is highlighting the explanatory role that the latter plays with respect to the former.

4. PROCESS EMBEDDING IN CASE STUDIES ON CIVIL WAR

The studies discussed in this section all focus on civil war. As mentioned in the introduction, civil war was chosen as it is an area of research which not only has received increasing attention in the last decades but has also experienced a surge in the use of qualitative methods, and case-study research more specifically. The studies below vary along many dimensions among which the extent to which they are theory driven, the research purpose they have, and also the type of mechanism they suggest, be it a chain of events, a set of variables, or a piece of theory. Nevertheless, they all provide a causal explanation of the outcome of interest which can be understood as mechanistic to some extent. They also engage to some extent in process embedding aimed at situating the mechanism at hand in some context regarded as relevant either for pragmatic or theoretical purposes. I use them for illustrative purposes, namely highlighting the explanatory role process embedding plays vis-à-vis process tracing identification of mechanisms. Meanwhile, I identify the relevant contextual conditions, which will ground the discussion in section five.

4.1. Historically Constructed Political Identity as *Context for* Inter-State Conflicts in Former Yugoslavia

Gagnon (1994) studies the inter-state conflicts sparked in former Yugoslavia in the early Nineties. Against conventional wisdom, Gagnon argues that violent conflicts fought along ethnic lines are caused by within-group, rather than external, dynamics. He claims that "the external conflict, although justified and described in terms of relations with other ethnic groups . . . has its main goal within the state, among members of the same ethnicity" (1994: 131). According to the mechanism described by Gagnon, ruling elites resort to conflictual policies when domestic threats arise; namely, challenger elites seek to mobilize the population majority in a way that threatens the economic or political structure on which the rulers' power is based (1994: 135). When rules of the game forbid the use of force against political opponents, ruling elites whose power basis is at risk typically respond by shifting the focus of the political debate away from issues where they feel most threatened. Specifically, they define collective interest in other terms and create an image of threat to that very interest.

How collective interest is constructed by ruling elites, says Gagnon, depends on the context. In Serbia, collective political interest was defined as the survival of the Serbian people and the image of an external threat as directed to that interest because historical processes made Serbian identity politically salient. Since the struggle against the Ottoman Turks, the Serbian national myth played a central role first in the expansion of the Serbian state in the nineteenth and early twentieth century, then in Yugoslav politics until 1941, and then during the second world war (1994: 141). Furthermore, in the Yugoslav republics ethnic identity used to determine the distribution of certain positions according to the size of each ethnic group. These processes among others constituted what Gagnon defines as the "historical construction of political identity in terms of ethnics identity" (1994: 141).

Processes pertaining to the historical construction of political identity explain why Serbian ruling elites leveraged a specifically ethnic identity when shielding off domestic threats emanating from challengers to the economic and political status quo. The national-ethnic identity was salient, and thus exploitable by ruling elites, because it had acquired political force throughout historical processes that maintained that identity alive and politically significant. Thus, it became *the* identity around which to organize the collective interest and construct the image of an external, rather than domestic, threat. Eventually, it informed the cleavage along which the subsequent war was to be fought.

4.2. Sectarian Political System as *Context for* the Civil War in Lebanon

Makdisi and Sadaka (2005) study the civil war which broke out in Lebanon in 1975 and ended in 1990 shortly after an accord of national reconciliation was signed in Taif, Saudi Arabia. Both internal and external factors are responsible for the chain of events leading to the war outbreak and its duration. Among the former, Makdisi and Sadaka include religious fractionalization in the country (2005: 59). Three main religious communities coexist in the Lebanese society, Christian Maronites, Muslim Sunnis, and the Muslim Shi'a together with a plurality of minor groups. Religious militias coalesced around two main warring camps and were joined by other Lebanese secular groups and foreign parties. Even though very heterogeneous in terms of groups involved, the opposition between the two camps was broadly drawn along confessional lines featuring Christian Maronites on the one side and Muslim (Shi'a and Sunni) on the other.

Makdisi and Sadaka show how the confessional dimension of the war found its roots in the sectarian political system in place in Lebanon since 1943. The constitution contemplated that religious communities had to be equitably represented in public employment and cabinet posts (2005: 61). The system thus organized the distribution of power according to a sophisticated schema of sectarian rules. It assigned the main political positions in the country to the three leading communities namely, a Maronite Christian was given the role of president of the republic, a Shiite Muslim the role of speaker of the house, and a Sunni Muslim the premiership. Cabinet posts were apportioned among the six main religious communities and similar arrangements were adopted for the allocation of parliamentary seats and many positions in the public administration. Even though the Maronite community was overall favored given the strong executive power held by the president, the arrangements were conceived and implemented in a way that preserved the balance among communities and prevented any single political, religious, or politicoreligious groups from raising to hegemony (2005: 62).

The sectarian political system explains why religious fragmentation could play such an important role in the Lebanese civil war. The system regulated the distribution of political power directly, and economic power indirectly through the assignment of positions in the public administration. When tensions and dissatisfaction started mounting among various communities in the years before the war due to the worsening of their relative economic conditions, these were voiced by political leaders as calls for a change in the sectarian system. Muslim and secular parties found common grounds in fighting against the status quo represented by the political system in its current shape on the presumption that changes in the system sectarian formula would have led them to acquire major economic opportunities. For these reasons, Makdisi and Sadaka suggest that the underlying political system enabled religious fragmentation to acquire causal prominence in the events leading to war.

4.3. Power Vacuum in Northern Iraq *as Context* for Escalating Political Violence between PKK and the Turkish State

Sezgin (2013) studies the escalation of ongoing political violence in the conflict between the Kurdistan Workers' Party (PKK) and the Turkish state in the period between 1992 and 1995. The conflict started approximately in 1984 causing significant losses in both human and economic terms; however, the intensity of violence increased radically after 1992. Sezgin traces the mechanism leading to such escalation back to Turkey's foreign policy: by changing the transnational landscape in which PKK operated, this policy brought about the emergence of "opportune moments" for PKK—moments in which the perceived likelihood of success is enhanced (2013: 173)—leading in turn to a radical escalation of violence. Between 1991 and 1992, in fact, Turkey started intense military incursions in northern Iraq to destroy PKK sanctuaries. Turkish massive air attacks, however, caused casualties in Iraqi Kurdish villages alienating the civilian population and fostering the alliance between Iraqi Kurds, their leaders, and PKK. Ultimately, this strengthened PKK resistance which started fighting the Turkish military on the open battlefield (2013: 182).

Sezgin shows how the transnational landscape in which PKK operated was shaped by processes unfolding at that time in neighboring Iraq. Iraq was involved in the Persian Gulf War after the invasion of Kuwait in 1990. Severely defeated in the Gulf War, the Iraqi regime had to deal with the concurrent Kurdish uprising in the north of the country. The repression perpetrated against Kurd insurgents by Iraqi forces and the ensuing massive number of refugees led to the adoption of a United Nations resolution that established a No-Fly Zone and Safe Heaven for Kurds in northern Iraq. By preventing Iraqi forces from entering the area, these processes generated a power vacuum in the Kurdish Inhabited Area (KIA) in Northern Iraq; that is a situation in which no provincial or regional political authority had effective control.

The PKK found a new harbor in this situation from which it could have access not only to humanitarian supply but also to recruitment potential among Iraqi Kurds. The processes leading to the creation of a power vacuum in KIA thus shaped the environment in which PKK was operating. In the absence of political control, PKK was free to enshrine in the area, reap its resources, and move freely across the border. The conditions characterizing such power vacuum explain why the transnational landscape in which PKK was operating at that time changed as it did, namely it featured an emergent collaboration between the PKK and Iraqi Kurds when the Turkish state intensified its attacks against PKK sanctuaries in Northern Iraq. This fostered alliance provided PKK with the opportunity to respond to Turkish attacks with stronger resistance thereby engaging in fighting on the open battlefield.

5. PROCESS EMBEDDING: WHAT IS IT GOOD FOR?

The discussion of the cases above suggests three considerations. The first regards the role that process embedding plays vis-à-vis process tracing in a single case study. The second concerns the role that the contextual knowledge delivered by process embedding plays vis-à-vis the conceptualization of context as discussed in section two. The third regards the relevance of contextualization in case studies for the broader aims of scientific practice, and in particular policy-making. I will address these issues in turn.

In single case studies that identify causal mechanisms for outcomes of interest, process embedding offers explanations of why the mechanism operated *as it did* in the case at hand. These explanations refer to processes unfolding in its neighborhood that account for the way in which the mechanism is concretely instantiated. In other terms, they respond to contrastive questions about the case-specific details of the mechanism. As an example, consider the case of inter-state war in former Yugoslavia discussed above. The mechanism explaining the inter-state ethnic war can be succinctly summarized as follows:

(a) Domestic challengers threaten ruling elites' basis of economic and political power.
(b) Elites shift the focus of debate away by constructing collective interest in other terms.
(c) Elites create an image of threat to collective interest as defined in (b).
(d) Elites resort to conflictual policies to defend collective interest.

In this case, process embedding responds to the question: Why Serbian ruling elites constructed collective interest in ethnic—rather than religious, class, or political—terms? Similarly, in the case of the Lebanese civil war, contextual processes explain why religious, rather than ethnic, fragmentation was causally relevant to the war. In the case of conflict between PKK and the Turkish state instead, the relevant question is why the transnational landscape in which PKK operated featured an alliance with Iraqi Kurds rather than Syrian or Iranian Kurds. The relevant contrast class to which the questions above refer is not necessarily fully spelled out and it either emerges from the case itself or is part of background knowledge.

Incidentally, two things can be noted. Process embedding addresses contrastive questions concerning parts of the mechanism, rather than the whole of it. These could be the components responsible for triggering the causal chain, jointly or alone, or could be some intermediate components. Furthermore, it is now clear how process tracing and process embedding differ. Whereas the former accounts for the causal arrangement of the parts in the mechanisms, explaining how they are causally connected, the latter accounts for their specific instantiation, explaining why a given component instantiated as it did rather than in a different way. These remarks make patent the subordinate position of process embedding in case study research. It not only depends on process tracing identification of the causal mechanism, but is also secondary to it; meaning by this that the causal explanation of the outcome of interest stands or falls independently of the contribution provided by process embedding. This fact can partially explain why the degree of contextualization is so various across case studies and most often incomplete.

The second reflection concerns what it means saying that in case-study research process embedding identifies the *context* for phenomena of interest. In section two, we pointed out an inherent ambiguity in the notion of context as it is used in political science. Context sometimes refers to conditions that enable or prevent the mechanism from functioning; in other terms, these are factors necessary under the circumstances for the mechanism to bring about the outcome of interest. In this case, we defined context-as-*interactor*. Some other times instead, context refers to conditions that modify the mechanism operation. That is, the context affects the mechanism functioning and the ensuing outcome either quantitatively or qualitatively. In this case, context is defined as a *modifier*. The question thus is: what does it mean to say that the historical construction of political identity is *context for* the inter-state war in former Yugoslavia; that the sectarian political system is *context for* the Lebanese civil war; or that the power vacuum in Northern Iraq is *context for* the escalation of violence between PKK and the Turkish state?

Single case studies retain the same ambiguity in the meaning of context highlighted above. Provided that claims of necessity are beyond the reach of a single case study, it is fair to acknowledge that contextual evidence and background knowledge jointly suggest an interpretation in either sense. Sometimes contextual processes seem necessary under the circumstances for the mechanism operation; some other time, they simply seem to act as modifier. In the case discussed by Sezgin, the power vacuum in Northern Iraq *enabled* the escalation of violence following Turkish military incursions against PKK in that area. In the absence of that power vacuum, in fact, PKK could not have rooted so firmly in the region, have access to military and human resources there, and find the support it eventually needed to fight back the Turkish army with increasing violence. In the case discussed by Gagnon, instead, the evidence suggests that the historical construction of political identity in ethnic terms *affected qualitatively* the operation of the mechanism and the ensuing outcome. That is, it affected the way in which the interest of Serbian people was constructed and the ethnic cleavage along which the war was eventually fought. However, nothing suggests that a different way of constructing that interest would not have been found by ruling elites eager to defend the basis of their power from domestic threats.

The preceding discussion suggests that contextual conditions in single case studies explain why the mechanism operated in a specific way in the case at hand and do so either as interactor or as modifier for the mechanism itself. Thus, in both cases they are *second order* causes, meaning that contextual conditions in single case studies do not act upon the outcome directly; their action in this respect is indirect and is filtered by the mechanism. What good does come from such knowledge? Specifically, what good does come from it when the purpose is ultimately practice-oriented and directed to the extrapolation of causal claims, that is the assessment of external validity, or intervention in target settings? The question is neither redundant nor obvious. The reason is that typically first order causes are regarded as prominent for these purposes, that is causes that have a direct effect on the outcome of interest in conjunction with the main explanatory variable. Once their presence is ascertained in the target settings, considerations about second order causes of a processual nature seem to complicate the matter in unnecessary ways.

The distinction between context-as-interactor and context as modifier is relevant here. Let us first consider the case of contextual conditions as interactor for the mechanism. In this case, the evidence suggests that contextual conditions enable or prevent the mechanism from functioning, and their presence or absence in the target setting is therefore decisive for the intended goal. In this respect, they must be regarded on par with first order causes, which are necessary under the circumstances for producing the outcome of interest. Things are different when it comes to the context as modifier. In this scenario, case-specific evidence and background knowledge give us reason to believe that the mechanism would work anyway even though differently than it would in the present conditions. Whether the quantitative or qualitative difference one would eventually observe on the outcome is relevant depends ultimately on the case at hand. In this sense, context as modifier seem not to matter in a fundamental way, even if it can be helpful for instance for predictive purposes. We know for instance that if in a region where conditions for civil wars are present there is a historical insistence on ethnic identity as a politically relevant factor, the civil war could easily take an ethnic bent.

However, things look a bit different when we start thinking of those contextual conditions in terms of sociohistorical processes as those brought to light in the cases discussed in this chapter. Even if we cannot generalize from this point, it is plausible that many mechanisms of interest to political scientists find roots in this type of processes. Thinking of contextual conditions in terms of processes shifts in an important way the perspective on questions of external validity and intervention in target settings. We often think of these tasks as a matter of *setting the conditions right* or *fixing the background conditions* to achieve the intended outcome. However, if contextual conditions are sociohistorical processes, intervention and extrapolation then rather consist in *disembedding* and *reembedding* policy mechanisms. In this view, an intervention modifies or replaces existing mechanisms, and consequently implies the alteration or disruption of the processes related to it; processes which extend in time and space and interact in multiple ways. Disembedding has thus far-reaching consequences beyond the outcome, and the case, of interest. In a similar vein, reembedding implies not only the disruption of existing processes but also the search for causal fit between them and the new mechanism.

6. CONCLUSION

In this chapter, I discuss contextualization in case-study research, and illustrate the output of this process by looking at studies on civil wars. Recently, political science has been invested by a return to the use of qualitative methods and, specifically, case studies. I suggest that the *renaissance* of the qualitative might be due to the increasing attention of political scientists to causal mechanisms and to the context in which they are situated. Well-known features of case-study research such as its in-depth character and context sensitivity might then explain why it is regarded as a fruitful strategy of inquiry into political phenomena. However, whereas there is much debate on how case studies can help identify causal mechanisms, how case-specific information is converted into knowledge of context is an issue so far left unattended.

I argue that contextualization in case-study research, that is the conversion of case-specific information into knowledge of context, is pursued by the joint use of process tracing and process embedding. Process tracing is a well-known strategy of causal inference that is directed to the identification of causal mechanisms. Process embedding is instead directed to identify processes unfolding in the mechanism neighborhood that causally fit the mechanism or its components. Whereas process tracing explains how the outcome of interest is brought about, process embedding is directed to explain why the mechanism operated as it did under the circumstances. It thus addresses contrastive questions regarding the mechanism specifics. To this end, its application is governed by three main evidentiary principles, namely generality, coherence, and fitness.

Even though contextualization is pursued through the joint application of process tracing and process embedding, the latter presupposes the former while the opposite is not the case. Process embedding has thus an ancillary role in the explanation of political phenomena as testified by the intermittent and incomplete degree of contextualization, as understood here, in case-study research. Nevertheless, contextualization is consequential when the inquiry is practice-oriented. Case studies suggest that contextual factors are causes of the second order with respect to the outcome of interest either as interactor or as modifier for the mechanism at hand. In the former case they are on par with first order causes that are jointly necessary for the mechanism to bring the outcome about. In the latter case, their role is less prominent but might be equally important since it points out how a given mechanism might operate in the setting of interest and, in turn, affect the outcome either qualitatively or quantitatively.

Lastly, understanding the context in terms of sociohistorical processes rather than background conditions might shift the way we problematize the practice of extrapolation and intervention in the social sciences. When treating the context as the set of background conditions that must be in place for the mechanism to operate and the intended outcome to obtain, the paramount concern is checking whether conditions are *right* in the target setting. At the level of intervention, this view legitimizes actions directed to *rectify* or *fix* the background conditions in the target setting in such a way as to enable the smooth unimpeded operation of the mechanism there. However, when background conditions are in fact processes of the kind described in this paper, they cannot be easily turned into the target of actions directed to their rectification. Thus, thinking of extrapolation and intervention as directed to disembed and reembed policy mechanism demands a very attentive and careful look at the context and the processes that constitute it. There are empirical, practical, and ethical reasons for recommending this sensitivity to context, which however deserve separate scrutiny and further inquiry.

NOTES

1. The context refers here uniquely to the subject of inquiry. It ignores the context of inquiry which is relevant for the research purpose, the research question, the background beliefs and presuppositions, and so on. For these considerations see Goodin & Tilly (2006).
2. An INUS condition is a nonredundant insufficient component of an unnecessary sufficient set for the outcome (see Mackie 1965, 1974).
3. In quantitative research, these two meanings are distinct by referring to interaction terms in the former case and moderators in the latter.
4. For a discussion of process tracing in political science and social science more in general see Beach & Pedersen 2019; Bennett & George 1997; Collier 2011; Crasnow 2017; George & Bennett 2005; Little 1991, 1998; Mahoney 2015; Steel 2004, 2008; Waldner 2015.

5. In what follows, my understanding of mechanism is very liberal and includes chains of events, complex structures, their abstract description, and so on. Process-embedding is described here in broad strokes and equally applies to any conceptualization of mechanism.

6. As I intend it here, process is a generic for mechanism. This terminological choice is mostly dictated by clarity purposes (distinguishing the main mechanism, which explains the outcome of interest, from those which are somehow ancillary to it).

7. Standards of coherence have been regarded as relevant for case study research by Morgan (2012) and Morck & Yeung (2011).

REFERENCES

Adcock, R. & D. Collier. 2001. Measurement validity: A shared standard for quantitative and qualitative research. *American Political Science Review* 95: 529–546.

Beach, D., & Pedersen, R. B. 2019. *Process-tracing methods: Foundations and guidelines.* University of Michigan Press.

Bennett, A. & C. Elman. 2007a. Qualitative methods: The view from the subfields. *Comparative Political Studies* 40: 111–121.

Bennett, A. & C. Elman. 2007b. Case study methods in the international relations subfield. *Comparative Political Studies* 40: 170–195.

Bennett, A. & A. George. 1997. *Process tracing in case-study research.* Washington, DC: MacArthur Program on Case Studies.

Collier, D. 2011. Understanding process tracing. *PS: Political Science & Politics* 44(4): 823–830.

Crasnow, S. 2017. Process tracing in political science: What's the story? *Studies in History and Philosophy of Science* Part A 62: 6–13.

Crasnow, S. 2019. Political science methodology: A plea for pluralism. *Studies in History and Philosophy of Science Part A* 78: 40–47.

Falleti, T. G., & J.F. Lynch. 2009. Context and causal mechanisms in political analysis. *Comparative Political Studies* 42: 1143–1166.

Gagnon, V. P. 1994. Ethnic nationalism and international conflict: The case of Serbia. *International Security* 19: 130–166.

Goertz, G. 1994. *Contexts in international politics.* Cambridge University Press.

George, A. L. & A. Bennett. 2005. *Case studies and theory development in the social sciences.* MIT Press.

Gerring, J. 2007. *Case study research. Principles and practices.* Cambridge University Press.

Gerring, J. 2008. The mechanismic worldview: Thinking inside the box. *British Journal of Political Science* 38: 161–179.

Goodin, R. E., & C. Tilly (Eds.). 2006. *The oxford handbook of contextual political analysis.* Oxford University Press.

Hedström, P., & Ylikoski, P. (2010). Causal mechanisms in the social sciences. *Annual Review of Sociology* 36: 49–67.

Little, D. 1991. *Varieties of social explanation. An introduction to philosophy of social science.* Westview press.

Little, D. 1998. *Microfoundations, methods and causation. On the philosophy of social sciences.* Transaction Publisher.

Locke, R. M. & K. Thelen. 1995. Apples and oranges revisited: Contextualized comparisons and the study of comparative labor politics. *Politics & Society* 23: 337–367.

Mackie, J. 1965. Causes and conditions. *American Philosophical Quarterly* 2: 245–264.

Mackie, J. L. 1974. *The cement of the universe: A study of causation*. Clarendon Press.

Makdisi, S. & R. Sadaka 2005. The Lebanese civil war, 1975–90. In *Understanding civil war: Evidence and analysis*, Vol. 2. Collier P. & N. Sambanis ed. The World Bank: 59–86.

Mahoney, J. 2001. Beyond correlational analysis: Recent innovations in theory and method. *Sociological Forum* 16(3): 575–593.

Mahoney, J. 2015. Process tracing and historical explanation. *Security Studies* 24(2): 200–218.

Mahoney, J. 2007. Qualitative methodology and comparative politics. *Comparative Political Studies* 40: 122–44.

Morck, R., & Yeung, B. 2011. Economics, history, and causation. *Business History Review* 85: 39–63.

Morgan, M. S. 2012. Case studies: One observation or many? Justification or discovery? *Philosophy of Science* 79: 667–677.

Pawson, R. & N. Tilley. 1997. *Realistic evaluation*. London: Sage.

Pawson, R. & N. Tilley. 2004. Realistic evaluation. Unpublished manuscript.

Pritchett, L. and M. Woolcock. 2002. Solutions when the solution is the problem: arraying the disarray in development. *World Development* 32: 191–212.

Sambanis, N. 2004. Using case studies to expand economic models of civil war. *Perspectives on Politics* 2: 259–279.

Sezgin, I. C. 2013. The link between the foreign policy of states and escalating political violence: Turkey and the PKK. *Critical Studies on Terrorism* 6(1): 167–188.

Steel, D. 2004. Social mechanisms and causal inference. *Philosophy of the Social Sciences* 34: 55–78.

Steel, D. 2007. *Across the boundaries: Extrapolation in biology and social science*. Oxford: Oxford University Press.

Tarrow, S. 2007. Inside insurgencies: Politics and violence in an age of civil war. *Perspectives on Politics* 5: 587–600.

Yin, R. 2009. *Case study research. Design and methods*. Los Angeles: SAGE.

Yin, R. K. 2015. *Qualitative research from start to finish*. Guilford publications.

Waldner, D. 2015. Process tracing and qualitative causal inference. *Security Studies* 24(2): 239–250.

Woodward, J. 2010. Causation in biology: stability, specificity, and the choice of levels of explanation. *Biology & Philosophy* 25(3): 287–318.

Woolcock, M. 2013. Using case studies to explore the external validity of 'complex' development interventions. *Evaluation* 19: 219–248.

CHAPTER 22

······································

PREDICTION, HISTORY, AND POLITICAL SCIENCE

······································

ROBERT NORTHCOTT

1. Introduction and Main Claims

······································

WHAT methods are appropriate for political science?[1] I argue for prediction and contextual historical work, and that these two methods each favor narrow-scope explanations. The arguments apply to field sciences generally, but I concentrate on political science.[2]

The structure of the paper is as follows: in this section, I state some basic distinctions and then my main theses and targets. In Section 2, I make the case for what has been called "scientific prediction". In Sections 3 to 7, I examine the implications for scientific prediction of a series of methodological challenges, namely underdetermination, causal fragility, and noise. In Section 8, I discuss what role is left for theory, and in Section 9, I illustrate this role via an example. Finally, in Section 10, I consider the scope for political science to offer policy advice.

1.1 Different Types of Prediction

The word "prediction" is ambiguous. Two distinctions are important:

(1) *Forward-looking* prediction: predictions about future data; versus *Retrospective* prediction: predictions about past data.

(2) *Simple* prediction: the attempt simply to predict future or past outcomes; versus *Scientific* prediction: the attempt to empirically test particular theories or models.

Often, scientific prediction concerns the impact of varying just one focal variable, holding other variables constant or in some other way controlling for confounders. Scientific prediction may also concern conditional predictions, such as what will happen if a policymaker intervenes in a certain way.

I borrow the term "scientific prediction" from Dowding and Miller (2019).[3] Dowding and Miller discuss only the second of the above distinctions explicitly, although they implicitly nod to the first distinction as well by defining nonscientific prediction to encompass only forward-looking prediction. I keep the two distinctions distinct.

To clarify the relations between the different kinds of prediction: first, scientific prediction is a subset of simple prediction. A simple prediction is in addition scientific only if it concerns data gathered in certain epistemologically propitious conditions, namely those conditions suitable for testing a theory or model. Second, scientific prediction, and simple prediction generally, can be either forward-looking or retrospective. Retrospective simple prediction is just description of the past.

1.2 Different Types of Explanation

There is a difference of degree between:

Wide-scope explanations, which apply to many cases; versus

Narrow-scope explanations, which are very local or contextual and that, in the limit, may apply only to a single case.[4]

An explanation might or might not be derived from a theory or model (Section 8). Theories and models themselves vary in scope, but what matters for our purposes is the scope of explanations (Section 8).

Throughout, I have in mind *causal* explanations. This is not because I rule out other kinds of explanation but rather is because causal explanations are the kind of explanation usually offered in political science.[5] For the most part, the relevant models are causal too.

1.3 Main Theses

I argue that, in political science:

Thesis (1): While any kind of prediction is desirable, scientific prediction is especially so.

Thesis (2): Usually, the purpose of scientific prediction is fulfilled only by forward-looking prediction or by contextual historical work.

Thesis (3): Usually, narrow-scope explanation is favored.

1.4 Targets

Some widespread practices in political science fall foul of the above theses:

(1) A lack of emphasis on forward-looking prediction.
(2) Forward-looking predictions, when they are made, being wide-scope.
(3) Wide-scope retrospective testing, such as much large-N statistical work.
(4) Resources being devoted to "pure theory," in other words devoted to building up a repertoire of wide-scope models divorced from frequent empirical application.

2. Scientific Prediction Is Desirable

Causal knowledge is central to political science, as it is to most sciences, because it is the key to explanation, intervention and extrapolation. The standard template for causal inference is to change one variable while keeping all else equal. Scientific prediction typically concerns the results of just such changes, and therefore delivers causal knowledge.

Simple prediction, by contrast, is concerned purely with actual outcomes, which in field environments are typically the result of many different variables varying all at once. Therefore, simple predictions that are non-scientific do not deliver causal knowledge even when accurate. Thus, Thesis 1: Scientific prediction is especially desirable.

Confirmation of theory is useful for purposes other than causal inference too (Dowding and Miller 2019). Therefore, because it is the means to get confirmation of theory, scientific prediction is useful for these other purposes too.

3. Underdetermination

Suppose that candidate X wins an election. There are likely many plausible explanations of why X won. This creates a problem of underdetermination: the mere occurrence of the same headline fact, namely that X won, cannot by itself discriminate between the many different explanations of that fact. This problem is likely to be especially acute if an explanandum is qualitative, as when we seek to explain merely who won an election rather than by exactly how much. But even in quantitative cases, as when we seek to explain X's margin of victory, the bar is often lowered, because only a partial or approximate fit with the data is demanded: a model may be endorsed even though it "explains" only some but not all of the relevant variation.[6] Such a lowered bar might be cleared by many models, and so the underdetermination problem remains.

One solution to underdetermination is forward-looking prediction. If you have to stick your neck out in advance, that removes the possibility of fudging awkward outcomes after the fact.[7] Many models or pundits might be able to explain the outcome of one election, even of five elections, relatively plausibly. But few are able to predict five correctly in advance. Lucky guesses, although possible of one election, are much less likely of five, especially if the target of prediction is quantitative. Insisting that accurate prediction be forward-looking discriminates between competing models more effectively than does allowing accurate prediction to be retrospective.[8]

Logically speaking, indefinitely many models fit any given body of evidence. But methodologically speaking, the key issue is whether those different models, in addition to being logically possible, are also plausible or to be taken seriously. It is at this methodological level that the confirmational asymmetry between forward-looking and retrospective prediction carries bite.[9]

4. CONTEXTUAL HISTORICAL WORK

Forward-looking prediction is not the only solution to the underdetermination problem. A second solution is if there are *no plausible alternative* explanations, in which case the mere fact of retrospective fit is decisive: if no other plausible theory or model can accommodate the past evidence then the fact that your model can tells strongly in its favor. In political science though, this situation applies only rarely. It is hard to prove this claim in a non-anecdotal way but, as with the election example, in political science there are usually many plausible explanations after the fact (Dowding 2016).

A third solution to the underdetermination problem is more promising: we may gather *additional evidence* that favors one explanation over others (Northcott 2019).[10] If so, there is no need to rely on forward-looking prediction to break an epistemic tie. Additional evidence may favor, say, one explanation of an election result over others. This evidence might take the form of post-election interviews of voters, or of comparisons of vote shares in different districts cross-referenced by potentially explanatory demographic and economic variables.

Happily, gathering such additional evidence is usually possible.[11] It is what historians do all the time. Such additional evidence is often idiographic; that is, it often concerns causal relations that are sui generis and local. The explanations that result thus tend to be specific to the particular case, appealing to local details. So, contextual historical work leads to narrow-scope explanations. Sui generis local details are typically not included in wide-scope models or theories, which seek to capture factors that recur across contexts.

Thus, combining this and the previous section, Thesis 2: Usually, the purpose of scientific prediction is fulfilled only by forward-looking prediction or by contextual historical work. We therefore face a choice: either to make forward-looking predictions, or else to engage in historian-like detailed sifting of the evidence.

Thus, also, one "half" of Thesis 3: Usually, contextual historical work favors narrow-scope explanations. (For why forward-looking prediction does too, see Section 5 below.)

This endorsement of contextual historical work brings with it a challenge: is reliable causal inference possible in singular historical cases? The ubiquity of historical controversies suggests that the problem of underdetermination is still present. Formal techniques of causal inference, such as experiments or statistical analysis, are usually inapplicable. In reply, how skeptical do you want to be? Take Holocaust denial, which implies a denial of many singular causal claims. Setting aside the ugly moral and political dimensions, the skepticism behind Holocaust denial is untenably extreme *epistemologically*, at least with respect to many basic facts of the case. Total skepticism with respect to mundane causal inferences about individual human actions or the social world, is similarly extreme: such inferences are, like observation itself, although fallible, usually reliable. Historians' causal inferences, usually backed up by copious archival and other evidence, and by well-supported background knowledge, are just extensions of these everyday procedures.

Some historical controversies do persist nevertheless. If, after contextual historical work, it remains underdetermined which explanation is correct, then the only epistemic tie-breaker left is forward-looking prediction: which explanation's predictions are borne out?

Often, this tie-breaker is unavailable, perhaps because the relevant events occurred long ago. If so, we are stuck: we must concede that we do not know which explanation is correct.

Total skepticism about narrow-scope historical causal inference would negate this section's argument for narrow-scope explanation. (I present other arguments for narrow-scope explanation shortly.) A more reasonable partial skepticism leaves the endorsement of contextual historical work less widely applicable rather than negated, and therefore this section's argument for narrow-scope explanation also less widely applicable. What is at stake is whether contextual historical work can obviate the need for forward-looking prediction when confirming an explanation. When forward-looking prediction is very difficult, as it often is (Section 6), what is at stake is therefore whether political science can succeed. If we deny the possibility of narrow-scope historical causal inference, we deny most of political science.

5. Causal Fragility

Consider, for a moment, an example from physics. Coulomb's Law describes the electrostatic force between charged particles. Although a particular charged particle's trajectory may not be predicted accurately by Coulomb's Law because of the presence of other forces, Coulomb's Law does identify one of the forces present, and so it does explain the charged particle's motion partially.[12] How is this explanatory claim warranted? By the predictive success of Coulomb's Law in a different context, namely a laboratory experiment, combined with a *stability* assumption that the causal relation demonstrated in the other context is still present in our context (Cartwright 1989).

Label the opposite of such causal stability, *causal fragility*. It tells against wide-scope explanations twice over.

The first reason is metaphysical: causal fragility means that causal relations themselves are not wide-scope. Therefore, explanations based on those causal relations likewise cannot be wide-scope.[13]

The second reason is epistemological: if causal relations are fragile, then even if empirical warrant is achieved in one context, fresh empirical warrant is required again for each new context. Empirical warrant can no longer be deferred; it must be prioritized continuously. A wide-scope explanation cannot automatically be imported, in the manner of Coulomb's Law, on the back of success in other contexts. A model's claim to have identified a causal relation in the field is not established by that model's empirical success in the laboratory.

Thus, if causal fragility is usual in political science, then Thesis 3: Usually, narrow-scope explanation is favored.

Causal relations are often stable in sciences such as laboratory physics, Coulomb's Law being a paradigm example. What about in field sciences such as political science? It seems that in field sciences causal relations are indeed usually fragile: they tend not to generalize easily (Northcott forthcoming).

Consider political elections. The causal relations between demographic variables and voter preference change from election to election, and even during elections and between different regions. The causal relations between demographic variables and voter enthusiasm change frequently too, as do those between economic variables and election outcomes, and between likelihood to vote and answers about that to opinion pollsters (Northcott 2020).

Field scientists' own practice often implicitly assumes that causes are fragile. A famous study showed that, in one circumstance, raising the minimum wage increases employment (Card and Krueger 1994). But in other circumstances, it does not: say, when the minimum wage is already very high, when it is raised by a large amount, or when economic conditions are different. In response, crucially, rather than search for countervailing causes that outweigh the original employment-increasing one, instead researchers just assume that the original employment-increasing cause no longer obtains (Reiss 2008, 173–176). This response is arguably typical in economics, and it implicitly assumes causal fragility.

Causal fragility extends beyond just the social sciences. It is arguably typical of ecology (Elliott-Graves 2018; Sagoff 2016), of field biology more widely (Dupré 2012), and of data science too (Pietsch 2016). In complex systems generally, an explanation that works today often does not work tomorrow. A significant predictor of causal fragility seems to be just that we are in a context of unshielded field phenomena.

Further evidence for the ubiquity of causal fragility is the ubiquity of the problem of external validity. In social science, external validity can rarely if ever be assumed (Levitt and List 2007; Reiss 2008, 92–96): results from laboratory experiments are notoriously unreliable in the field, presumably because of the huge range of new contextual cues and inputs in a field environment. In other words, causal relations discovered in the laboratory are fragile. Again, scientists' own practice often implicitly concedes the point. When field operation of a mechanism really needs to be ensured, extensive contextual testing and simulation is demanded, as in the design of the US government auctions of electromagnetic spectrum in the 1990s (Alexandrova 2008; Alexandrova and Northcott 2009).

Similar remarks apply not just to external validity but also to extrapolation generally. The causal relations underpinning policy interventions or field trials in one context typically cannot just be assumed to carry over to another; they are too fragile for that (Cartwright 2019, Khosrowi 2019, Cartwright and Hardie 2012, Steel 2008).

6. NOISE

A familiar difficulty in field sciences is to distinguish signal from noise. Unshielded environments are typically "noisy" in the sense that it is hard to isolate the impact of one factor alone. A model might posit that X causes Y, so to test the model we must measure the impact of X on Y. But if other factors A, B, and C also impact on Y, then scientific prediction is more challenging than simply predicting Y after a change in X, because we need to shield off or control for the influence of A, B, and C too.[14] In field settings, such shielding off is difficult, and therefore so is scientific prediction.

Political science is not a laboratory science; it is concerned with noisy, unshielded field environments, and so scientific prediction is difficult. There are some well-known workarounds. One is natural experiments, when processes outside the investigator's control happen to divide a sample into treatment and control groups in the same way that an experimenter would have. Others include quasi-experiments, randomized field trials, and laboratory experiments (Northcott 2019). For the many occasions when experiments are not possible, an array of statistical techniques have been developed to try to infer causes from non-experimental data. These various workarounds have different strengths and weaknesses, but they all share two serious difficulties. The first difficulty is scope: practical and ethical limitations mean there is only a limited range of political questions that experiments can usefully elucidate, while statistical methods require large samples and so are difficult to apply to explanatory claims that are narrow-scope. The second difficulty is external validity (Section 5): only rarely do causal inferences from an experimental or other context extrapolate reliably to a new context.

The problem of noise therefore has several consequences. First, scientific prediction can be achieved only by forward-looking rather than retrospective prediction. In a shielded environment, matters can be set up so that only one (salient) model or theory is under test, as in controlled experiments, thereby overcoming the problem of underdetermination, thereby enabling retrospective scientific prediction. But political science rarely concerns shielded environments. Neither can statistical surrogates often fill the gap. Thus, retrospective scientific prediction cannot be achieved, and the first disjunct of Thesis 2 is reaffirmed: forward-looking prediction is favored.

Second, because forward-looking scientific prediction is difficult, usually we must fall back on the second disjunct of Thesis 2, namely contextual historical work, which in turn (Section 4) favors narrow-scope explanations. Thus, Thesis 3: usually, narrow-scope explanation is favored.

Third, narrow-scope explanation is favored via another route too. Wide-scope explanations inevitably miss sui generis local causal relations, and so typically identify only some of the causal relations present in a given field situation. There is no shame in that: in noisy environments, such partial explanations are often the best that can be hoped for. But a partial explanation requires empirical warrant just like any other explanation, and given such explanations' empirical inaccuracy this warrant must be imported from empirical success elsewhere. Applications of Coulomb's Law outside the laboratory, for example, import warrant from the Law's empirical success inside the laboratory. Causal fragility threatens this "imported warrant" strategy because empirical warrant from elsewhere may not travel (Section 5). The ubiquitous difficulty that noise creates for accurate scientific prediction now threatens the "imported warrant" strategy in a new way: it is likely that there is no full empirical success *any*where, and thus no empirical warrant anywhere available to *be* imported. There is no analogue of the successful Coulomb laboratory experiment (Northcott 2017, MS).

To illustrate the difficulty: many competing models seek to explain election results. Suppose that one model says election results are caused by GDP growth in the preceding year. In any actual election, likely many other factors too are causally relevant, so the GDP model will be explanatory at best only partially. If we could somehow tweak a polity so that only GDP was altered and then see how this tweak impacted an election result, then we could test the GDP model and *only* that model. Obviously, such an election experiment is impossible: which is precisely the point. Because of noise, there is no successful scientific prediction anywhere, either in the context at hand or in other contexts. The GDP model's partial explanation is left without warrant (Northcott 2015).[15]

The only solution is empirical accuracy in the case at hand. In a noisy environment with many ever-changing and sui generis causal relations, this implies a causal description—and thus an explanation—that is narrow-scope.[16]

Overall, the problem of noise therefore provides new support for Thesis 2: either forward-looking prediction or contextual historical work is required. It also provides new support, in two ways, for Thesis 3: narrow-scope explanation is favored.

The problem of noise is closely related to the problem of *overfitting*. In fields such as machine learning and statistics, a model normally has a number of free parameters, which leaves considerable flexibility when fitting the model to data. The problem of overfitting is that tweaking parameter values to ensure maximal fit with every idiosyncratic detail of past data often reduces predictive accuracy with respect to future data. How close a fit, then, should we aim for? It is hard to know. At root, overfitting is an underdetermination problem caused by noise: because data are noisy, a precise fit with a model is implausible.

A standard solution to overfitting is to test competing models on data not used in those models' formulation or calibration. If free parameters must be fixed in advance of this testing, then "cheating" is made impossible, i.e., the free parameters cannot be adjusted to fit outcomes after the fact.

This solution is effective. But because the data used to test between competing models need only be independent of model estimation, there is no necessity for the relevant predictions to be forward-looking. Does this solution therefore undercut Thesis 2, which favors forward-looking over retrospective prediction? No. If an explanation is narrow-scope, then usually there is not a large stock of relevant past data available, and so the only predictions available for countering overfitting are forward-looking ones. In political science, successful explanations usually are indeed narrow-scope. Therefore, in political science Thesis 2's favoring of forward-looking over retrospective scientific prediction is (usually) endorsed.

7. Laboratory Versus Field Sciences

Laboratory sciences avoid the problems discussed in this paper. Shielded, controlled experiments avoid the underdetermination and noise problems, and the causal relations that laboratory sciences deal with seem to be less fragile.[17] As a result, wide-scope theories and models succeed empirically, as do wide-scope explanations derived from them. Retrospective prediction is sufficient. Explanations derived from Newtonian force models are a paradigm case: they are wide-scope and they can be satisfactorily tested by retrospective evidence.

Just the opposite is true of field sciences: the problems of underdetermination and noise are not avoided, and causes tend to be fragile. As a result, forward-looking prediction is favored. If forward-looking prediction is too difficult, then only contextual historical work will do. Only narrow-scope explanations succeed. Theses 2 and 3 apply. And they apply to political science because political science is predominantly a field science.

8. THE ROLE OF THEORY

A hallmark of science is that it has ambition beyond singular explanations: it also aims for wide-scope theory. But if forward-looking scientific prediction is usually infeasible because of noise and causal fragility, then usually we must turn to contextual historical work, for which, in unshielded field environments, wide-scope theory is ill-suited. What role, then, can be salvaged for theory?

We should not be blinded by famous physics: not all theories are universal regularities written in mathematical form. Theoretical work in political science is better understood via the *toolbox* view, according to which theories are individual items in an overall repertoire or toolbox. No theory is thought to apply universally or across a whole sample, but any one or more theory might apply in any given case (Cartwright 1999, Northcott forthcoming). In political science, a "theory" in this sense will typically be a causal model or mechanism. In a complementary vein, scientific explanation is not taken to require universal laws; instead, explanation requires only causal relations, whose scope may sometimes be very local (Woodward 2003).

Theory development consists in the expansion and refinement of this toolbox. This expansion and refinement cannot be done in an empirical vacuum: by applying models from the toolbox to real cases, we both sharpen our sense of when a particular model is likely to be applicable, and also sharpen the model itself by learning from experience what aspects of it gain empirical traction (Ylikoski 2019). Such work is essential. Insulation from empirical application is seriously harmful.[18]

Many times, models from the toolbox are putatively wide-scope. Does this vitiate the conclusion that explanations in political science are usually narrow-scope? No, because even if a model is wide-scope, it may still deliver an explanation that is true of only a few cases, i.e., that is narrow-scope. It is true that contextual-historical work inevitably draws on background knowledge, and this background knowledge may in turn draw on wide-scope theory. But any explanation is a particular combination of such knowledge, and may apply only narrowly.

Because a given toolbox model typically applies only to some or a few cases in a sample, the use of large-n statistical methods that assume otherwise is problematized. I cannot do full justice to this issue here. But it is a mistake, for example, to use a statistical regression to test simplistically whether a toolbox model "is confirmed" in a sample as a whole.

Within the toolbox view, there is an important distinction between two ways in which a model leads to an explanation. On the *causalist* view, relations between terms in a model correspond to causal relations in the world, and so causal explanations can be read directly off the model, at least in successful cases. On the rival *heuristicist* view, the role of a model is more indirect. A model or models may helpfully suggest new categories or lines of enquiry to explore, but supplementary empirical work is required to develop an eventual causal hypothesis that is not itself derivable from the model or models. It is this eventual causal hypothesis that furnishes the explanation. The original model or models are not themselves tested; instead, the demand for testing is transferred to the eventual causal hypothesis.[19]

When should we adopt a causalist view and when a heuristicist one? The less idealized and the more contextual a model, the more likely it is we can read off actual causes from it directly, and so the more likely it is that a causalist view is appropriate. And the more contextual a model, the more likely that an explanation derived from it is narrow-scope. Explanations achieved via the heuristicist route, meanwhile, are usually narrow-scope too, because of the reliance on contextual empirical investigation over and above the original (typically wide-scope) model. Either way, usually we end up with explanations that are narrow-scope, in accordance with Thesis 3.

In summary so far: because of underdetermination and causal fragility, and because both experiments and accurate forward-looking prediction are difficult, investigation in field sciences should usually be contextual-historical. Explanations are usually narrow-scope (Sections 2 to 7). This tells against theories understood as applying everywhere. But it does not tell against theories understood as per the toolbox view, which are endorsed so long as they are not developed in isolation from empirical application. In this way, there is still a role for theory, for scientists usefully to develop it, and for cross-contextual scientific achievement.

9. An Exemplar of Theory at Work: Della Porta on Political Violence

Donatella della Porta's *Social Movements, Political Violence, and the State* (1995) is a highly influential study of political violence in 1960s and 1970s Italy and Germany.[20] It is well known for, among other things, emphasizing the nonideological determinants of violent actors' behaviors. Della Porta's primary goal is well-evidenced causal explanations and to this end she adopts, in effect, a contextual-historical approach.

Despite this, her book is famous for being innovative theoretically. How so? Like game-changing work in history and field sciences generally, she provides new categories and outlooks that successors are obliged to consider. A bedrock of her approach is explanatory pluralism, by which she means a willingness to incorporate multiple theoretical approaches, and to add new ones of her own, whenever these pay their way by enabling new causal explanations to be identified.[21] This is the toolbox view in action.

For example, what explains the behavior of violent groups? Some previous work focused on broad sociological determinants, such as the scope within a polity for expression of political frustrations; other previous work focused on rational-choice explanations of what tactics might best achieve a group's ideological goals. Della Porta deviates from both of these. She examines organizational dynamics at the group rather than society level, and even though those dynamics are "irrational" in the sense of not being driven by the groups' ostensible ideological goals (1995, 116–133). Her analysis begins with arrests by police. These arrests disproportionately weaken those groups that are organized loosely, creating a selection effect in favor of groups that are more centralized and compartmentalized. This leads to reduced recruitment, and so to subsequent evolution becoming dominated by internal factors. Targets are chosen to achieve internal goals such as discipline or self-defense (robberies, shoot-outs during arrests, punishment of "traitors") rather than, as earlier, external goals such as propaganda or campaigning (actions against unpopular factories or businesses). The emphasis on self-defense rather than recruitment leads to tactics becoming increasingly lethal and bloody. Ideology evolves accordingly, becoming decreasingly comprehensible to outsiders, with less emphasis on propaganda for external consumption and more emphasis on internal integration. The more underground and sealed off a group becomes, finally, the less effectively it influences wider society, because of its isolation.

The toolbox approach informs all of della Porta's book. Throughout, theory is developed and sharpened via detailed empirical engagement with her Italy and Germany case studies. One fruitful new category of hers is the *policing of protests* (1995, 56). Policing tactics serve as a downstream proxy for deeper state factors and institutional features, such as police organization, the nature of the judiciary, law codes, and constitutional rights. This simplifies the empirical tracking of the state's influence on the (already theorized) "political opportunity structure," because the connection between policing and social movements is conveniently direct. It also enables policing itself to be analyzed in a subtler way than before. Policing tactics became more hardline often not because of internal dynamics within the police but rather because of external political decisions (which the police tried to resist), contrary to much previous theory (1995, 77–78). Other political explanations too are revealed or supported. Examples include (1995, 76–78): how hardline state and police attitudes rose and fell with the attitude and strength of the moderate "old left"; how political polarization strengthened the hand of hardliners on both sides; how, in the long run, hardliners declined in influence; and how the tactics of the protestors influenced the tactics of the police.

This rich explanatory detail is made visible by della Porta's theoretical innovations. Her theories are not formal models; rather, they are qualitative and verbal. Her use of these theories is often heuristicist rather than causalist, bringing into view new categories or ways of seeing things rather than specifying causal hypotheses directly.[22]

Della Porta is explicitly against the possibility of universal theory or wide-scope explanation (1995, 210). "Political violence" and "radicalism" enter into causal relations that are fragile. These causal relations vary with: leftist versus rightist protest movements; democratic versus authoritarian political environments; class versus ethnic bases; and different organizational models, forms of action, and ideologies and goals. Large-n studies would fatally gloss over these heterogeneities, and so would miss many causal explanations. The implicit aim of such large-n studies, namely to confirm or discover a wide-scope causal generalization, is futile in this domain (1995, 14–20). Della Porta takes her own explanations to apply only to leftist, class-based groups in a democratic environment. At the end of her book, she cautiously examines how well these explanations might transfer to the case of the ethnically based civil rights movement in the United States in the 1960s and 1970s. Again, detailed empirical engagement is the only way to tell (1995, 210–215).

10. POLICY ADVICE

Policy advice is inevitably (in part) forward-looking. Therefore, it requires forward-looking prediction, yet in field sciences forward-looking prediction is difficult. Does this imply a counsel of despair? Not always.

To warrant an intervention, we require a confirmed causal model. There are two routes to that. The first route is induction: perhaps the most convincing warrant for forward-looking predictive confidence is past forward-looking predictive success, combined with confidence that the context is sufficiently stable. At the macrolevel, such as predicting civil wars, the predictive record in political science is disappointing (Tetlock 2005; Ward et al. 2010). This mandates caution, except when there is a record of success.

The second route to predictive confidence is local knowledge. Combined with relevant background knowledge, local knowledge can warrant forward-looking predictions when it is detailed enough to establish that there are few significant unmodelled causes, that there is sufficient causal stability, and that outcomes are predictable at all in the sense of not being too sensitive to unknowable details (Sterelny 2016).[23] This route obviously favors local-level predictions. For example, local knowledge may warrant a confident prediction of who will win an election in a particular new district, even if at the national level the election result is in doubt.

Generally, we should expect warranted interventions usually to be narrow-scope. This is because they require confirmed causal knowledge, which we should expect usually to be narrow-scope for the same reasons that causal explanations are.

11. CONCLUSION

There is hope, but only via empirical success. Usually, that means via contextual history or via forward-looking prediction. Usually, it also means narrow-scope explanations, and not seeking to confirm wide-scope explanations via retrospective prediction. Warrant for policy interventions will usually be narrow-scope too.

NOTES

1. My focus in this paper is on epistemological rather than ideological or political considerations.
2. By "field sciences" I mean non-laboratory investigations of systems that are not engineered artefacts.
3. Dowding and Miller's distinction between scientific and non-scientific prediction is fruitful. (They label nonscientific prediction "pragmatic".) As they note, within philosophy of science this distinction was noted by Popper (1989), among others. See also Salmon (1981) and Watkins (1968).
4. Exactly how we should individuate "cases" here is no doubt itself contextual.
5. There is a literature on the relation between causal and *structural* or *functional* explanations. I do not discuss it here.
6. Not all explanations are derived from models (Section 8), but the points in the text carry over *mutatis mutandis*.
7. Howson and Urbach (1993) and Worrall (2014), among others, give formal Bayesian demonstrations of this point. A similar conclusion can be demonstrated in non-Bayesian ways too.
8. At least for the most part. The advantage is epistemic and contingent rather than logically necessary. But, while there are cases in which forward-looking prediction is not favored, in political science it usually is.

9. A recent movement in political science seeks to prioritize forward-looking prediction (see Dowding and Miller 2019 for references). As per Section 2, I agree with Dowding and Miller that forward-looking prediction should in addition be scientific.

10. Formally, this is a version of the no-plausible-alternatives solution, but now with respect to an augmented body of evidence.

11. Formally, such gathering of additional evidence enables retrospective scientific prediction because the additional evidence can be used to test one explanation against another.

12. See (Northcott 2012, 2013) for the relevant sense of partial explanation.

13. This is true even if the causal relations *in a model* are wide-scope. A causal model being wide-scope does not imply that those causal relations are wide-scope in the world, nor that an explanation derived from the model is wide-scope (Section 8).

14. It is because field environments are typically noisy that simple prediction is typically not scientific: simple prediction takes account of the impact on Y not just of X but also of A, B, and C.

15. The GDP model's wide-scope prediction is not empirically confirmed in the particular case. Because of noise and causal fragility, this is the frequent fate of wide-scope predictions. In principle, evidence collected across many elections could favor some wide-scope models over others, thus alleviating underdetermination. But this method would have to assume that the relevant causal structures are stable across many elections, which is dubious.

16. Another way to see the same point: noise means that any empirically accurate explanation is likely multifactor. Any multifactor explanation is more likely than a single-factor explanation to be narrow-scope, because it contains more factors (and interactions between them) that are potentially sensitive to a change in context.

17. This may well not be mere coincidence: sciences whose causal relations are stable have more to gain from investigating via laboratory experiments. But I do not explore that suggestion here.

18. A common criticism of orthodox economic theory is precisely that it has been developed too remotely from empirical application (Northcott 2018; Northcott and Alexandrova 2015; Farmer 2013). Some strands of theory in political science may be vulnerable to the same criticism.

19. The heuristicist view was originally inspired by cases of successful auctions in which the eventual auction mechanism is not derived, or derivable, from auction theory alone, but rather requires extensive supplementary experimental and practical development (Alexandrova 2008; Alexandrova and Northcott 2009).

20. Over 1,500 citations, according to Google Scholar.

21. Della Porta employs *mixed methods* in a similar spirit. Individual actors' life histories, in the form of qualitative analysis of interviews, form part of her evidence base; she uses various quantitative data too, for instance about the number of acts of violence; in addition, she uses archival research, such as consultation of official records. These various forms of evidence each pay their way by supporting particular causal inferences in the service of della Porta's larger explanatory ambitions.

22. "Recent studies on social movements *provide the main categories* for the explanatory model of political violence in Italy and Germany that I am going to develop here." (della Porta 1995, 9, emphasis added)

23. There is principled reason to expect predictability to require local knowledge. The literature on the extrapolation of a model from one context to another, including from the past

to the future, concurs that such extrapolation requires detailed knowledge of the target context (Cartwright 2019; Khosrowi 2019; Cartwright and Hardie 2012).

REFERENCES

Alexandrova, A. (2008). "Making Models Count," *Philosophy of Science* 75, 383–404.

Alexandrova, A., and R. Northcott (2009). "Progress in Economics," in D. Ross and H. Kincaid (eds) *Oxford Handbook of Philosophy of Economics*, 306–337. Oxford.

Card, D., and A. Krueger (1994). "Minimum Wages and Employment: A Case Study of the Fast Food Industry in New Jersey and Pennsylvania," *American Economic Review* 84, 772–793.

Cartwright, N. (1989). *Nature's Capacities and their Measurement*. Oxford: Oxford University Press.

Cartwright, N. (1999). *The Dappled World*. Cambridge: Cambridge University Press.

Cartwright, N., and J. Hardie (2012). *Evidence-Based Policy: A Practical Guide to Doing It Better*. Oxford.

Cartwright, N. (2019). *Nature, the Artful Modeler*. Chicago: Open Court.

della Porta, D. (1995). *Social Movements, Political Violence, and the State*. Cambridge: Cambridge University Press.

Dowding, K. (2016). *The Philosophy and Methods of Political Science*. Basingstoke: Palgrave Macmillan.

Dowding, K., and C. Miller (2019). "On Prediction in Political Science," *European Journal of Political Research* 58.3: 1001–1018.

Dupré, J. (2012). *Processes of Life*. Oxford: Oxford University Press.

Elliott-Graves, A. (2018). "Generality and Causal Interdependence in Ecology," *Philosophy of Science* 85.1: 1102–1114.

Farmer, D. (2013). "Hypotheses Non Fingo: Problems with the Scientific Method in Economics," *Journal of Economic Methodology* 20.4: 377–385.

Howson, C., and P. Urbach (1993). *Scientific Reasoning: The Bayesian Approach* (2nd edn). Chicago: Open Court.

Khosrowi, D. (2019). *Extrapolating Policy Effects*. PhD dissertation, University of Durham.

Levitt, S., and J. List (2007). "What Do Laboratory Experiments Measuring Social Preferences Reveal about the Real World?" *Journal of Economic Perspectives* 21, 153–174.

Northcott, R. (2012). "Partial Explanations in Social Science," in H. Kincaid (ed.) *Oxford Handbook of Philosophy of Social Science*, 130–153. Oxford: Oxford University Press.

Northcott, R. (2013). "Degree of Explanation," *Synthese* 190.15: 3087–3105.

Northcott, R. (2015). "Opinion Polling and Election Predictions," *Philosophy of Science* 82, 1260–1271.

Northcott, R. (2017). "When Are Purely Predictive Models Best?" *Disputatio* 9.47, 631–656.

Northcott, R. (2018). "The Efficiency Question in Economics," *Philosophy of Science* 85.5, 1140–1151.

Northcott, R. (2019). "Prediction Versus Accommodation in Economics," *Journal of Economic Methodology* 26.1, 59–69.

Northcott, R. (2020). "Big Data and Prediction: Four Case Studies," *Studies in History and Philosophy of Science* 86, 96–104.

Northcott, R. (forthcoming). *Science for a Fragile World*. Oxford: Oxford University Press.

Northcott, R., and A. Alexandrova (2015). "Prisoner's Dilemma Doesn't Explain Much," in M. Peterson (ed) *The Prisoner's Dilemma*, 64–84. Cambridge: Cambridge University Press.

Pietsch, W. (2016). "The Causal Nature of Modeling with Big Data," *Philosophy and Technology* 29, 137–171.

Popper, K. (1989). *Conjecture and Refutations*, revised edition. London: Routledge.

Reiss, J. (2008). *Error in Economics: Towards a More Evidence-Based Methodology*. London: Routledge.

Sagoff, M. (2016). "Are There General Causal Forces in Ecology?" *Synthese* 193, 3003–3024.

Salmon, W. (1981). "Rational Prediction," *British Journal for the Philosophy of Science* 32.2, 115–125.

Steel, D. (2008). *Across the Boundaries*. New York: Oxford University Press.

Sterelny, K. (2016). "Contingency and History," *Philosophy of Science* 83.4, 521–539.

Tetlock, P. (2005). *Expert Political Judgment*. Princeton, NJ: Princeton University Press.

Ward, M., Greenhill, B., and K. Bakke (2010). "The Perils of Policy by P-Value: Predicting Civil Conflicts," *Journal of Peace Research* 47.4, 363–375.

Watkins, J. (1968). "Non-Inductive Corroboration," in I. Lakatos (ed) *The Problem of Inductive Logic*, 61–66. Amsterdam: North-Holland Publishing Co.

Woodward, J. (2003). *Making Things Happen: A Theory of Causal Explanation*. Oxford.

Worrall, J. (2014). "Prediction and Accommodation Revisited," *Studies in History and Philosophy of Science* 45, 54–61.

Ylikoski, P. (2019). "Mechanism-Based Theorizing and Generalization from Case Studies," *Studies in History and Philosophy of Science* 78, 14–22.

PART 4

POLITICAL SCIENCE IN SOCIETY
Values, Expertise, and Progress

PART 4, *Political Science in Society: Values, Expertise, and Progress*, focuses on the interactions between political science and society; scrutinizing how the embeddedness of political science in society influences the selection of research problems, for instance, or leads to certain approaches being favored over others, the specific social and institutional dimensions of scientific practice as well as how value judgments present in political science are dealt with. The discussions concerning value freedom, value judgments, and biases in political science are felicitous sites for PoPS, being a meeting ground for philosophical explication and political analysis. Linked to these debates about values are the questions of expertise, and what role someone knowledgeable about scientific findings and evaluations can play in a democratic society. Pertinently, disagreements about values also challenge our ideas about what we should consider progress in political science.

CHAPTER 23

....

TAKING FEMINISM SERIOUSLY IN POLITICAL SCIENCE
A Cross-Disciplinary Dialog

....

SEASON HOARD, LACI HUBBARD-MATTIX,
AMY G. MAZUR, AND SAMANTHA NOLL

1. INTRODUCTION

TAKEN together, feminist approaches in Political Science provide an exemplar of the new research that this volume is charting out. First on the political science radar in the late 1970s through the study of women in politics and today referred to as gender and politics, this area of study has expanded the very definition of the political through a diverse range of epistemologies—e.g., empirical, interpretivist, postmodern, standpoint, deconstruction, postcolonial—not typically associated with political science research.[1] At the heart of this feminist scholarship is a "problem-driven" (e.g., Shapiro 2002) approach where empirical analysis and theory-building are aimed at helping to solve the full range of "wicked" problems that confront contemporary society;[2] a goal that has become increasingly important in political science in recent years. For example, the "Perestroika" movement in American political science in the early 2000s sought to diversify the discipline through a more problem driven approach, which had been dominated by "objective and value-free (sic)" behavioralism (Monroe 2005.

Gender and politics research has been highly successful with several active scholarly associations and numerous international journals. It engages over 1,000 scholars across the globe who publish and work in this area.[3] Thus, as we argue throughout the chapter, gender and politics research that uses feminist approaches has much to offer "nonfeminist" political science to make it a richer, stronger and, arguably, a more scientific field.[4] At the same time, despite over 40 years of feminist efforts to "gender" political studies, nonfeminist political science, the "malestream," remains remarkably unaffected by feminist work, even when feminist scholars directly engage with that work (Mazur 2012; Celis et al. 2013; Aherns et al. 2018).

Feminist political studies are interdisciplinary, often eschewing the typical conventional boundaries in the social sciences (Celis et al. 2013; Siim 2004; Ackelsberg 2014). As such, the epistemological diversity and interdisciplinary overlap, make feminist political studies a rich terrain for feminist philosophy of science. Moreover, while on one hand feminist political scholars think about epistemology in terms of the concrete pursuit of better knowledge production, methodology, theory and results in research; on the other hand, feminist philosophers of science seek to explain the flawed nature of scientific practice and suggest new less biased ways of doing science through feminist epistemology. Simply put, feminist political scientists seek to do better science and feminist philosophers of science seek to reveal better science. In this chapter, we bring together these two different disciplinary lenses in dialog to map out feminist political science and its potential for contributing to nonfeminist political science and, in doing so, to achieve the following goals.[5]

(1) To place gender and politics research on the philosophy of political science agenda as an exemplary area of cutting-edge research that pushes the boundaries of established political science.
(2) To show the full breadth and depth of this new interdisciplinary and international approach to the study of politics from a philosophy of science perspective.
(3) To show how the epistemological richness and core shared principles of the quite ontologically diverse approaches of the field provide an unprecedented opportunity to make both feminist and nonfeminist political science more sound and more successful in solving current 'wicked' problems of injustice and inequality.

Our chapter begins with some basics from a political science perspective; the common principles of feminism used by feminist political analysts, an illustration of the contributions of feminist political science in Feminist Comparative Policy, and a closer look into the persistent resistance of nonfeminist political science to taking feminist work seriously. Next, we cover the basics from the purview of philosophy of science including an introduction to feminist philosophy of science and an overview of the three prominent feminist epistemologies identified by feminist philosophers of social science that are foundational for feminist political science. The following section shows how feminist political science has put into action these epistemological pillars in actual research through an examination of taxonomies of feminist approaches in political science that reflect the increasing epistemological diversity of the field. The final section takes a deeper dive into critical feminist theory by showing how it informs the diversification of the full range of feminist approaches, and most importantly provides the theoretical underpinnings for the necessary critique of the inherent power biases of many feminist approaches. We conclude the chapter with a discussion of the broader lessons learned from applying such a critical and ontologically diverse perspective to feminist approaches for both feminist and nonfeminist political science and suggest future steps for taking more seriously feminist approaches in political science.

2. The Basics through a Political Science Lens

What's Feminist about Feminist Political Analysis

While for many feminist analysts it is not crucial, or even desirable, to present a definition of feminism, for empirically inclined feminist scholars it is of fundamental importance to identify the operational definition of feminism in order to advance research agendas. We can pinpoint some key ideas of feminism while granting that there are different families of feminism that share certain central characteristics, depending on the context in which the concept is used (McBride and Mazur 2008). In this perspective, feminism is a "family resemblance" (Goertz 2019) concept, rather than a classical one based on hierarchically defined categories that reflect the core ideas of western feminism.[6] With these lessons about concept stretching in mind, the operational definition of feminism used here was developed from a review of over 300 published works on feminist policy in post industrial democracies (Mazur 2002). The complex definition includes a certain understanding of women as a group within the context of the social, economic, and cultural diversity of women; the goal of advancing women's rights, status or condition as a self-identified group in both the public and private spheres; and the desire to reduce or eliminate gender-biased hierarchy or patriarchy that underpins basic inequalities between men and women in the public and private spheres.

Any feminist epistemological approach in the social sciences takes into consideration, on some level, this three-fold definition with regards to ontology, methodology and methods, theory-building and the production of knowledge, and its relation to nonfeminist knowledge building. More concretely, there is a common understanding across all feminist approaches that established knowledge creation is biased, because of gender-based hierarchies within the established scientific community that produces male-domination. This bias excludes the serious consideration of issues related to the complex processes of gender as they are intertwined with sex, and in more recent years with race/ethnicity, age, sexuality, disability, etc.—"intersectionality"[7]—in analysis and/or theory. This patriarchal/gender-biased/androcentric nature of social science[8] goes hand in hand with the fact that scholars tend to be predominantly men, while women tend to be excluded from the process of knowing and studying and from actual studies as objects of analysis. To do gender analysis from a feminist perspective, therefore, is to first develop a critique of established epistemological and methodological norms and then bring women, and for some feminists, men with feminist goals, "male allies," into the research process as well as gender as an object of analysis and theorizing. Ultimately, the inclusion of feminist actors and ideas stands to improve established knowledge cumulation and the scientific process.

The Promise of Feminist Political Science: The Example of International Comparative Feminist Policy Research

The standard operating procedure in feminist political science, particularly outside of the United States, has been to develop large-scale international projects including researchers

Table 23.1 International Comparative Feminist Policy Research Projects 1995 to the Present

RNGS (1995–2011). Research Network on Gender Politics and the State http://libarts.wsu.edu/poli sci/rngs (e.g., McBride and Mazur 2010)

EGG (2002–2005). Enlargement, Gender and Governance: The Civic and Political Participation and Representation of Women in Central and Eastern Europe http://www.qub.ac.uk/egg/ (e.g., Galligan et al. 2007)

MAGEEQ (2003–2007). Policy Frames and Implementation Problems: The Case of Gender Mainstreaming http://www.mageeq.net/ (e.g., Verloo 2007)

QUING (2006–2011). Quality in Gender Equality + Policies http://www.quing.eu/ (e.g., Verloo and Walby 2013)

FEMCIT (2006–2010). Gendered Citizenship in Multi-Cultural Europe: The Impact of Contemporary Women's Movements http://www.femcit.org (Halsaa et al. 2012)

VEIL (2006–2009). Values Equality and Differences in Liberal Democracies http://www.univie.ac.at/veil/ (e.g Special Issue in *Social Politics* on Veiling)

GEPP (2013 to the Present). Gender Equality Policy in Practice Network http://www.csbppl.com/gepp/ (Engeli and Mazur 2018 and 2021)

from a multitude of countries; to secure high budget grants from prestigious scientific funders; to publish findings in top ranked journals and books at top shelf presses; and to produce policy reports from that research for government bodies—like the EU, UN, World Bank, and NGOs—the Rand corporation, IDEA, and IPU. Many of these projects, according to Mazur (2012) are situated in the feminist field of study called Feminist Comparative Policy and closely related to the Comparative Politics of Gender.[9]

Table 23.1 presents the more institutionalized international projects that have a formal title and infrastructure; at least a dozen additional studies have received significant funding and have produced collective publications without creating a formal group. All of these studies have the following common features.

- a problem-driven approach where the very design of the project is to develop sound and systematic cross-national studies that focus on understanding how to address persistent gender inequities and through that research to propose potential solution;
- gender is a fundamental "category of analysis" (Scott 1986);
- the centrality of issues of patriarchy, the persistence of gender-biased norms in study designs;
- operationalization of both feminist and nonfeminist theory; and
- comparative theory-building based on either qualitative approaches or, more recently, mixed methods designs that include qualitative and quantitative analysis.

Indeed, many feminist analysts argue that there is a certain methodological pragmatism, driven by the problem-driven approach of these studies, that is shared by researchers who work in this area. This means that staking out methodological and epistemological positions is less important than conducting useful research on the highly complex dynamics and determinants of gender equality policies. McBride and Mazur capture this methodological pluralist approach in their discussion of how the Research Network on Gender Politics and the State approached its comparative study of state feminism,

> [W]e were willing to consider whatever methods would help answer the core question of the study: if, how, and to what degree do women's policy agencies achieve *state feminism* through bringing women's movement interest into government affairs. Part and parcel of this open-mindedness toward methodology was an understanding that qualitative and quantitative approaches could be useful in developing a systematic cross-national and longitudinal study of the dynamics and drivers of state feminism. (2010: 35–36)

While earlier feminist policy studies focused on Western European and North America, more recent projects have included Central Eastern Europe and other regions of the world, moving the field from midrange to more macro theory-building endeavors to answer the "big questions" of democracy, gender equality, and representation.[10] These big questions involve how bringing-in women's movements actors and interests into the democratic process can actually make stable democracies more democratic and to help emerging democracies achieve stability. Including countries from across the globe provides the unprecedented opportunity to see how different cultural, political contexts produce different outcomes in achieving maximum democratic performance and for promoting successful and meaningful gender equality policies. Moreover, developing culturally sensitive analytical concepts that "travel" across time and space as well as increasing the number of observations promotes more macro theory that can apply to a larger number of cases. These studies, thus, can provide more informed and more scientific answers to the perennial big questions being asked by political science as a whole.[11]

Midrange feminist comparative policy studies therefore suggest some key factors that must be taken into consideration as hypotheses/potential drivers in producing authoritative policy responses in any macro theory of gender, policy, and the state, such as discourse/ideas, institutions, women's movements, or partisan politics. Increasingly, studies find sectoral differences are more important in explaining policy outcomes than national or regional policy styles (e.g., Htun and Weldon 2018; McBride and Mazur 2010). While individual studies claim the explanatory power for specific factors and often make them drivers and objects of analysis, many other studies show that pathways to feminist success in policy are actually quite complex, often being comprised of different "configurations" of factors, and in some cases with different pathways leading to the same outcome; thus the logic and methods of Qualitative Comparative Analysis (Rihoux and Ragin 2008) has been increasingly employed by these feminist projects (e.g., McBride and Mazur 2010; Muriaas et al. 2020).

Resistance: Up Against the "Glass Wall"

While feminist analysts have made strong and clear efforts to dialog and build on established political science concepts and research in order to address the inherent biases and silences of existing research, little "malestream" work in political science considers the plethora and wealth of feminist scholarship on similar or adjacent topics. As Mazur (2012) asserts in the area of comparative public policy, there is a "glass wall" between feminist and nonfeminist political science in this area of study.

> [T]he potential of newer feminist scholarship to improve knowledge and theory building in the "mainstream" is at best mitigated, if not all together thwarted by an opaque glass wall. The wall blurs the true nature of feminist approaches and prevents constructive cross-fertilization between feminist and nonfeminist scholars, even when feminist scholars seek to directly contribute to research and theory-building that is not explicitly feminist (533).

Feminist studies in political science more generally observed early on that there is a "profound gender blindness"; also echoed in more recent reviews of feminist work (e.g., Aherns et al. 2018, Celis et al. 2013, Ackerly and True 2018). The bottom line is that while feminist approaches to concepts may have "much to offer" and many feminist analyses have contributed "to building bridges between different approaches in political science" (Kantola and Lombardo 2017: 2), the uptake of gender and politics scholarship in the nonfeminist world of political science has been incremental and piecemeal at best and more often than not, ignored. For example, an important textbook on political science methodology makes no reference to the methodologically rich gender and politics scholarship (Gerring 2012). This echoes Ackerly and True's (2018: 266) findings of gender silences and blindness across their review of methodology textbooks in the social sciences as well.

The glass wall can be observed at work in many other subfields of political science. For example, in critical theory as well as in international relations. Here, feminist analysts are still in the stage of challenging "seemingly unproblematic concepts and framings" in nonfeminist work in this area, as Prügl and Tickner (2018) assert. To be sure there are instances where male political scientists have held up feminist work as an example and have integrated it into nonfeminist scholarship,[12] these are exceptions to the rule, however, and the glass wall has persistently remained intact.

3. The Basics through a Philosophy of Science Lens: The Three Feminist Epistemologies

We now turn to mapping out feminist philosophy of science and the three epistemological traditions in feminist research that were identified in the 1980s by Sandra Harding in her classic book *The Science Question in Feminism* as well as other feminist scholars— standpoint, empirical, and postmodern. This classic taxonomy has been a major touchstone for understanding feminist approaches to knowledge and research across many different disciplines in the physical, biological and social sciences and the humanities. The categorization is essential to understanding the potential contributions that feminist political science can make to political science as a whole (Mazur 2012). Before launching into a discussion of each feminist epistemology, it is important to understand the critical disciplinary context from which they were elaborated.

Feminist Philosophy of *Science (FPS): A Brief Introduction*

FPS is a multidisciplinary branch of feminist scholarship that began in the 1960s with the goals of critiquing sexist science, advancing women in the sciences, and critically evaluating methods of scientific inquiry (Richardson 2010: 337).[13] It is highly interdisciplinary, with roots firmly in philosophy, feminist science studies, and the social sciences. In particular, the field actively creates new epistemologies and reforms aspects of dominant modes of inquiry so that they serve the interests of underrepresented groups (Anderson 2019; Harding 1987). As Richardson (2010) so aptly notes,

> feminists have forged scholarship that explicitly reflects upon the ethics and conditions of academic knowledge production, is grounded in the experiences and knowledge of subordinated peoples, and advances research and values associated with emancipatory politics. (346)

In particular, FPS extensively explores how gender does and should influence our conceptions of knowledge, the situated subject, and practices of inquiry (Anderson 2019).

In this vein, FPS has produced a robust literature discussing the ways that dominant practices of knowledge production, justification, and creation have systematically disadvantaged women and members of other historically marginalized groups and FPS scholars have worked tirelessly to reform these modes of knowing so that they support the interests and goals of women and other historically disadvantaged social groups. Thus, feminist philosophy of science contributes to both critiquing the natural and social sciences and the creative project of building new epistemologies to form the foundation of feminist scholarship (Richardson 2010).

Since this work is largely done from a position of the historically marginalized, the theoretical tools developed in this field are diverse and highly sensitive to values and basic commitments that guide research in the sciences. In fact, FPS (as well as feminist science studies and feminist metaphysics) has a long history of identifying and challenging potentially problematic assumptions used in the social sciences in order to improve the quality of research being done. Even basic concepts used in scientific practice did not escape critique, as theorists, such as Keller (1985), Bleier (1984), and Rosser (1987), challenged the traditionally held scientific values of simplicity, explanatory unification, and consistency. They argued that these values should be replaced or modified (depending on the value and theorist) to better help scientific fields recognize bias and move beyond their problematic past (Kourany 2010; Longino 1994).

The central epistemological concept that informs all subfields of FPS is the situated knower. Thus, the insight is that knowledge is situated or reflects the particular social positionality of the subject (Anderson 2019; Hundleby 2012; Richardson 2010). A person's social location largely consists of social identities (race, gender, ethnicity, sexual orientation etc.) and the social roles and relationships necessitated by these roles (political party, occupation, religious affiliation etc.). These different aspects of identity place the knower in different social roles that include distinct powers, duties, goals, and interests and thus provide unique knowledge about the world. In this context, gender (as distinct from biological sex) is a way that we are socially situated, often from a very young age (Haslanger 2000).[14] FPS scholars are highly interested in how gender situates subjects. There are three main approaches in FPS that have been utilized to answer this question: feminist standpoint theory, feminist empiricism, and feminist post-modernism (Anderson 2019). Basic commitments concerning how gender situates knowers also uniquely informs how each approach addresses central issues in FPS. These approaches, as well as their commitments, will be briefly described below. Though it should be noted that the first two epistemologies will be given more space, as post-modernism will be explored in more detail in the last section of the chapter.

What Is Standpoint Theory?

As Harding (2004) details, standpoint theory developed during the 1970s and 1980s as a feminist critical theory concerned with knowledge production and practices of power. Its intent is to explain

> the surprising successes of emergent feminist research in a wide range of projects—"surprising" because feminism is a political movement and according to the conventional view . . . politics can only obstruct and damage the production of scientific knowledge (1).

While work in this subfield can vary, scholars using standpoint methodologies generally begin from the position that knowledge is socially situated. Additionally, some standpoints, especially those occupied by marginalized groups, can provide an epistemic advantage, in that they provide access to previously suppressed truths. To put it simply, being socially situated often provides people with epistemic authority. Harding (2004) states this last point succinctly when she writes that "social and political disadvantage can be turned into an epistemic, scientific and political advantage" (7–8). The field illuminates the connections between social power, the political, and the production of knowledge. It is located between the twin pulls of the traditional epistemological commitment that abstract and universal knowledge is possible and the commitment that knowledge claims are only fully understood in the social contexts that give rise to them, as those contexts are permeated with assumptions and metaphysical commitments. Here the accepted thesis is that the ways that power relations impact knowledge do not need to be understood as always problematic. Objectivity is not always threatened by subjectivity; in contrast, socially situated knowledge can be objective. Starting research from the lives of women (and/or increasing the numbers of diverse voices involved in scientific inquiry) actually strengthens the standards of objectivity (Harding 2004). As Harding (1993) argues, it can be marshaled to address "the causes of the immense proliferation of theoretically and empirically sound results of research in biology and the social sciences that have discovered what is not supposed to exist: rampant sexist and androcentric bias (49). Today, standpoint theory continues to inform and contribute to the further development of methodological and theoretical thought (2). Indeed, it challenges the assumption that scientific inquiry represents universal human interests, by illustrating how inquiry not sensitive to social situatedness represents the standpoint of the privileged.

What Is Feminist Empiricism?

Feminist empiricism also begins from the position that knowledge is socially situated; however, as its name intimates, it is deeply connected to the philosophical tradition of empiricism. While empiricism has a robust history, it can be generally understood as an epistemic approach in scientific inquiry built on the claim that experience should be the primary justification for knowledge (Creath 2017; Richardson 2010). Classical empiricists, such as John Locke and David Hume, largely held the view that experience should be described in fixed terms (Anderson 2019). Quine pushed back against this assumption, revolutionizing empiricism with his idea that observations are not theory-neutral but theory-laden. Feminist empiricists built on this turn, but they largely reject Quine's "sharp division between facts and values," as this cannot be sustained when epistemology is truly naturalized. According to Hundleby (2011),

> feminist demands for attention to women's experiences suggest that empiricism can be a prom-
> ising resource . . . Yet feminists also value empiricism's purchase on science and the empiricist
> view that knowers' abilities depend on their experiences and their experiential histories. (28)

Feminist empirical scholars take on the large task of determining how feminist commitments can and should inform empirical inquiry and how traditional methods and scientific values could be improved. To put it succinctly, these scholars see social situatedness as a resource that can be harnessed to advance knowledge production.

Although, the feminist empirical project calls for substantial revisions to empiricism, this approach is attractive to feminist scholars, largely due to the prominence of these methodologies in contemporary scientific disciplines (Hundleby 2011). In short, empiricism provides feminists with a robust point of departure (as well as justification for their projects) from which to do their work, as emancipatory science is an important component of the history of empiricism (Okruhlik 2017; Anderson 2019). Indeed, building on the strengths of scientific inquiry is imperative for the development of what Harding (1986) calls feminist "successor science projects" (10). As feminist empirical scholars embrace the social situatedness of knowledge production, they take history, sociological components, and feminist science seriously. In this vein, many feminist empirical scholars conceptualize science as a socially embedded activity (Harding 2004).

Anderson (2019) labels one of the most common critiques of feminist empiricism the "paradox of bias." This critique focuses on how feminist philosophy of science is committed to addressing sexist and androcentric biases in the sciences. However, if we accept this justification, then the subsequent argument that scientific inquiry should be informed by situated knowers is problematic. Is bias problematic or can scientific inquiry be improved if we incorporate insights gleaned from certain biased positions? Feminist empirical scholarship includes strategies to address this critique. This work explores how biases are not always in conflict with scientific best practices, and, indeed, are not necessarily epistemically bad (Anderson 2019; Antony 1993). For example, Longino (2001) argues that single theories are problematic because they can never capture all of reality, as different scientific approaches capture different patterns that are useful for different purposes.

What Is Feminist Postmodernism?

In general, feminism postmodernism is an intellectual tradition that is rooted in French and German poststructuralist and postmodernist theories, such as Heidegger, Foucault, Lacan, Irigaray, etc. While feminist empiricism largely accepts the basic apparatus of scientific inquiry, feminist post modernism embraces the skeptical project, or the desire to critique the Enlightenment project of producing universal, objective, or ultimate "Truth" writ large (Anderson 2019; Flax 1987; Hutcheon 1989). As Flax 1987) argues,

> the criticisms towards the "grand theories" associated with modernity, from Marxism and feminism to the questioning of the modernization and dependency theories . . . lead to a growth of the post-modern consciousness. (8)

This consciousness stresses the idea that concepts are not fixed; they are partial, local, contingent, and historically influenced (Anderson 2019). In short, they are not universal—they shift and are embedded in larger social systems. We communicate our ideas through language and, for this reason, we grasp concepts not as Platonic "forms," but as socially constructed concepts that get their meaning from all other signs in the system of discourse. Additionally, the choice of what scientific work to pursue is an exercise of power; thus, scientific research cannot be separated from systems of power. Two lessons gleaned from this literature that is of particular importance for feminist scholars include the following: (1) That universal claims concerning women and gendered categories are problematic, and (2) that a single epistemically privileged position does not exist (Anderson 2019). These skeptical projects are supposed to serve critical functions in the political context. It also performs the creative project of prompting alternative possibilities that may not be visible in the scientific landscape that historically embraced certainty.

4. Putting Feminist Philosophy of Science in Action in Political Science: Towards More Epistemological Diversity

In large part inspired and echoing the developments of feminist epistemologies traced in the previous section, feminist approaches to study political phenomena have diversified considerably over the past thirty years, especially considering gender and politics as an organized sub-field of political science did not begin until the 1970s. Today, gender and politics is an interdisciplinary and methodologically pluralist subfield within political science that engages with both feminist and nonfeminist literatures, although intersections between nonfeminist and feminist research have been largely one way. While feminist research remains marginalized within the discipline, feminist political science also has some important silences and gaps that have been pointed out by "critical" and postmodern feminist theorists. This section presents how feminist political analysts have understood the epistemological developments in the discipline over the years and have traced the increasing diversification of approaches that have been used by self-identified political scientists and scholars of politics.

Mapping Feminist Approaches in Political Science, 1980s–2010s

The early classifications focused on the growth of the study of gender and politics within the discipline, adopting the three phases of research identified in women's studies (e.g. Carrol

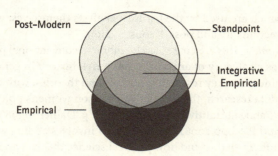

FIGURE 23.1. Mapping the Integrative Feminism Approach

and Zerilli 1993; Black 1989; Sapiro 1981). The first phase began with adding an ignored subject to old research and inquiries, "add women and stir"; the second transitioned to looking at women alone in both public and private spheres, and the third moved away from only looking at women to using the complex concept of gender as the central "category of analysis" (Scott 1986). Harding and others also suggested the application of the three epistemological strands of feminism occurred in stages, which started with empirical feminism before employing other epistemologies to put into action the more transformative standpoint and postmodern approaches (Harding 2004; Hawkesworth 2006).

More recent analyses of the field have shown that these phases of research often co-exist and that political science as a whole is still heavily dominated by what may be interpreted as the first phase, adding the study of women to existing theories or studies without changing the operating premises, particularly in research focused on the United States. Mazur (2012) builds on Harding's foundational work by mapping the overlap of the three strands to identify an "integrative empirical" approach that combines constructive/critical approaches with empiricism as shown in Figure 23.1. The taxonomy highlights both the distinctiveness of each strand as well as a shared common ground. Mazur (2012) argues that this common ground is where work in Feminist Comparative Policy is found. Intemann (2010) also identifies a "convergence" between empirical and standpoint approaches in philosophy of science more generally speaking.

Highlighting the Diversity of Feminist Approaches in Current Political Science

A more recent classification developed by Kantola and Lombardo (2017) is especially useful for understanding feminist political science because it highlights the epistemological diversity of gender and politics, the common ground across the different theoretical and research orientations in the field as well as how the different approaches provide unique perspectives that can improve political analysis. The goal of Kantola and Lombardo's (2017) taxonomy is not only to highlight these diverse and oft overlapping approaches, but to also show how they are actually used by feminist political analysts in actual studies and in doing so to present the larger implications and contributions of future political analysis. Shifting from Harding's three pillared taxonomy, the authors identify five different approaches based on the core concepts which are used by the feminist analysts themselves: women, gender, deconstruction, intersectionality and post deconstruction.

Approach One: Women. This area of research embraces conventional political science and focuses on women as a category of analysis. It has a rich history in gender and politics research, bringing women into key research questions and theories, with examples including candidate gender quota research, the broader research on women's political representation including descriptive and substantive representation (e.g. Dahlerup 1988; Childs and Krook 2009; Franceschet and Piscopo 2008). This approach involves adding women as a variable in research to determine whether and how political science theories and propositions must be adapted to accommodate women as a group. For example, examining the behavior of women representatives in the legislature to determine if women are more likely to substantively represent women.

Approach Two: Gender. Kantola and Lombardo (2017) argue that this second approach captures the essence of gender; defined in its complex form of the social construction of men/ male and women/female as self-identified individuals and where these identities are in asymmetric power relations with each other. They identify three features of this approach.

> (i) [the]need to understand gender always in relation to wider societal structures in order to understand domination and inequalities that are by definition structural; (ii) analytically, the need to study gender as a complex socially constructed relation between masculinities and femininities, . . . and (iii) epistemologically, approaching gender from a "critically realist" perspective, which means that deep gender structures are socially constructed but at the same time are considered real. (27)

Thus, a gender approach utilizes "gender as the category of analysis" (Scott 1986) that examines social relationships and the social construction of gender in various areas.

Many of the large-scale international feminist research projects mentioned above take a gender approach. For example, RNGS examines the impact of women's policy agencies in postindustrial democracies in terms of their ability to get mainstream policy actors to talk about gender roles and norms or "gender" policy debates and help feminist policy actors who speak for women into the policy debate (e.g. McBride and Mazur 2010). The assumption here is that without these base considerations of the social construction of gender included in policy discussions that policies could not effectively tackle the complex causes of gender inequities often which came from gender biases that excluded women and favored men. Again, illustrating the overlap between these categories that often occurs, many scholars, especially comparative politics of gender scholars, embrace more established political science approaches. In fact, comparative scholars often devote considerable attention to conceptualization and operationalization of key feminist concepts for hypothesis testing and theory building (see Goertz and Mazur 2008). Additionally, scholars utilizing a gender approach also often specifically examine the behavior of women, such as RNGS scholars analyzing the policy frames presented by women's movement actors. However, an important distinction between the women approach and the gender approach is that the gender approach moves beyond adding women as a variable to political science research questions through using gender as a category of analysis to understand how it structures and impacts political phenomena.

Another example of this approach is a recent effort made by Benstead to introduce a new multidimensional measurement of patriarchy.

> "Patriarchy" is increasingly part of the political science lexicon, especially in relation to the Middle East and North Africa. Yet political scientists often under-conceptualize patriarchy and fail to draw on existing feminist theory, hindering explanation of the mechanisms sustaining gender inequality. By engaging with Kandiyoti's "patriarchal bargain," which sees gender relations as the outcome of negotiation, and Sadiqi's "private" and "public" patriarchy, political scientists can capture the multidimensional and intersectional nature of patriarchy and better integrate their work within institutional approaches to political science. (2020: x)

Approach Three: Deconstruction. This research area also focuses on gender, but in more complex and critical ways. As Lombardo and Kantola (2017) explain,

> gender is constructed in discourses and practices that privilege some representations of the problem/solution of gender inequality over others and constructs subjects in specific gendered ways (33).

This approach involves recognizing that gender has no distinct and universally agreed upon definition. Instead, gender has multiple constructed meanings that are debated and contested in public discourse. These approaches often center on the discourse used by political actors, examining how some interpretations of gender and solutions to gender equality are favored while others are ignored (Lombardo and Kantola 2017). The large international research project, MAGEEQ exemplifies the deconstruction approach. The group developed a specific technique to assess the gendered content or "discourse" of government documents in European Union countries that formally implemented gender equality policies in order to trace empirically the extent to which policy administration and implementation are gender biased (Verloo 2007). Researchers have used the Critical Frames Analysis to examine multiple meanings of gender and interpretations of gendered relationships that are present in policy discourse with a particular focus on interpretations of gender that are "privileged" over others that reproduce specific gender inequalities and gender biases.[15]

Approach Four: Intersectionality. This approach has its origins in Black, lesbian, and post-colonial feminist critique. It examines the overlap and interrelationships between multiple inequalities, such as race, gender, and class, and the resulting marginalization and domination that occurs from this intersection (e.g. Crenshaw 1991; Hill Collins 2019). It is important to note that intersectional approaches arose to critique the tendency in feminist research and women's movements to treat women as a homogenous group with identical concerns and issues, which in actuality emphasized the experiences of a limited group of women, upper class white women, over all of the other diverse groups of women from different backgrounds. Thus, intersectional approaches may include gender as a category of analysis, but further seek to understand and dismantle power dynamics within gender. As race, class, and other identities intersect to create further inequalities between women, gender equality requires examining how these overlapping identities create further inequalities both between men and women, but also between women as a group. As noted by Lombardo and Kantola (2017), when examining research on institutions, a gender approach may analyze how institutions are gendered and recreate gender through division of labor, interactions and activities (e.g., Acker 1992), while an intersectional approach may examine how race and gender intersect within institutions to create different expectations, activities, and interpretations of activities for black women (e.g., Hawkesworth 2006).

Examples of intersectionality approaches in feminist political science research include the QUING project which examines European Union gender equality policy using an intersectional approach, of which one focus was on how intersectionality might improve gender-based violence policy in the EU (Lombardo and Agustin, 2016) and the political representation of women of color (e.g., Mügge and Erzeel 2016). The Gender Equality Policy in Practice Network (GEPP) asks its researchers to identify the different groups that come forward in the implementation of gender equality policies and for which intersectional interests they are speaking to assess overall representation in the post adoption processes (Engeli and Mazur 2018), In other words, understanding how all of these vectors of inequality intersect, and different interpretations of these inequalities, can produce a deeper understanding of the critical process of public policy and better policy outcomes as well as improve equality for minority women; a major tenet of problem driven research.

Approach Five: Postdeconstruction. More than an approach to research, it is a debate centered on feminist new materialism that focuses on how affect, emotions, and bodily material impact gender and politics. Kantola and Lombardo (2017) contend that while these debates are substantial in larger feminist theory and discourse, they are not often utilized in feminist political science but could provide unique perspectives and research questions in political analysis.

Contributions and Critiques. Kantola and Lombardo's classification is helpful for highlighting the common ground across feminist political analysis. Although the approaches have different analytical foci and methodological tools, they share a critical perspective that interrogates current research, theory and practice within the discipline. The five approaches are not exhaustive, as mapping all the feminist approaches in political science would be a herculean task, but they provide a useful framework for examining not only debates within each approach but also the overlap between different perspectives as scholars across these approaches adopt the tools, research questions, and theories of other approaches to examine political phenomena. Additionally, as noted by the authors, androcentrism still dominates political science despite the contributions of feminist scholars, which leads to some of these approaches being privileged while others are marginalized (Kantola and Lombardo 2017). This five-fold classification not only helps with understanding the diversity of feminist political analysis and its potential contributions to the field, but aids in identifying those approaches that are marginalized within both the gender and politics subfield and the broader field of political science. At this time, the authors contend that the women and gender approaches dominate, and due to this empiricism also dominates political analysis.

A limitation of this taxonomy, which is acknowledged by the authors, is that some epistemologies, such as postcolonial feminist work, do not have their own classification but are included (or can be included) in multiple approaches. For instance, postcolonial feminism is included in both the intersectionality and deconstruction approaches. While potentially highlighting the overlap between important research and theorists working in the broader gender and politics field, this may also serve to further marginalize these approaches. By not including postcolonial feminism as a separate approach, scholars adopting this framework may inadvertently ignore these important critiques in their own analyses which is a problem already experienced by scholars who are from and work on the Global South. While focus on women and gender has grown considerably over the past

50 years, Global South scholars are severely underrepresented in leading gender and politics journals (Medie and Kang 2018). Medie and Kang (2018) not only argue that the marginalization of the Global South needs to be addressed by examining the global order more in gender and politics research, but by building a more inclusive community of scholars.

The classification adopted by Kantola and Lombardo (2017) does not easily address these concerns despite its many strengths. Creating an additional approach for postcolonial feminism and approaches used by these scholars, may help ensure that this important work does not get lost among the cacophony of research in a single approach that often privileges scholars focused on other regions. The various feminist approaches, while quite diverse, can improve science within the discipline through their shared critical focus. Likewise, feminist researchers should consider marginalization of certain feminist approaches, scholars, and foci within feminist political analysis itself to also improve research within this area. We now turn to a more systematic critique of feminist political analysis from within the purview of critical feminist theory.

5. Getting Critical About Feminist Approaches to Research: The Critical Feminist Project

The case made by this chapter that feminist political science is necessarily a critical project is not universally accepted within critical theory. For instance, Michael Thompson (2017) argues that feminist theory[16] is incorrectly considered a critical theory as theorists have conflated the technical term critique with the word critical. Others (Agger 2013; Hill Collins 2019) argue that feminist theory is one of the core aspects of contemporary critical theory. This chapter highlights the ways in which feminist political science specifically and political science broadly is at its best when it is a critical self-reflective project. A discussion of the origins of critical theory as well as an analysis of the shared aspects of critical projects demonstrates that it is appropriate to consider feminist academic work as a part of the critical theory project. And in doing so, makes the overall contributions of feminist work to political science sounder and more scientific.

Critical theory finds its origins with the Early Frankfurt School especially in the work of Max Horkheimer and Theodor Adorno. As a discipline, critical theory focuses on the connection between knowledge production and the creation of power-relations and hierarchies. For instance, Horkheimer et al. (2002) interrogate several aspects of modernity including the connection between the culture industry and the individual. Using a critical lens they demonstrate how people are formed by the culture industry. They turn the assumption that popular culture rather than being an expression of identity and freedom forces its spectators into sameness.[17] They take their critical project one step further and connect the culture industry to economic impotence and inadequacy.

Their focus on the production of knowledge and the creation of hierarchies is a foundational aspect of critical theory. Specifically, what holds critical theory together is the agreement that meaning rather than being natural and immediate is instead necessarily contextual, embedded in power relations, and contingent on knowledge production. (Tyson 1999). More specifically critical theory argues,

> that there is always a theory underlying cultural expression and interpretation, even if, and perhaps especially when, such expression and interpretation deny adamantly or ignore wholly its theoretical positioning. (Hall 2013: 107)

In other words,

> [W]hen science or traditional social theories uncritically produce knowledge that naturalizes and normalizes the social order, they disempower people. Thinking critically about such rules enables people to both unmask societal rules that foster passivity and to refuse to accept them. (Hill Collins 2019: 61)

Thus, critical theory is a necessary project in order to avoid passivity and to engage in praxis that combines theory with practice in a way that empowers vulnerable and marginalize groups. This focus exemplifies another key element of critical theory as a self-reflective or inward-looking discipline. To avoid dissonance, work done through the critical theory lens must acknowledge that it also occurs within power relations and thereby creates hierarchies that must also be viewed and analyzed from the critical perspective. Thus, critical theory is an ongoing project as each new theory, methodology, and approach can prevent new concepts and power relationships from being acknowledged, unpacked, and combatted. A final concern of critical theory is that of reification. Knowledge production as done by researchers reifies concepts creating them as material and fixed when in fact they are flexible and immaterial.

By focusing on the standpoint of marginalized people feminist political science is, as established by this chapter, a critical project. This project also includes an investigation of the power structures of Capitalism/Marxism (Hartmann 1979; Leeb 2007) the categories of the political (Okin 2008), the state/nation (Sihna 2017), and terrorism (Caverero 2009), as well as the way in which knowledge is produced in these areas (Bartky 1992; Butler 1990). Indeed, the presentation of this list provides an opportunity to demonstrate a major aspect of critical theory. By creating a list and deciding which elements to include the authors have privileged some feminist projects over others. There are thousands of works that could have been chosen and several different approaches that could have been appropriately listed. The list chosen produces an authoritative list of feminist critical projects and privileges those while entirely ignoring others. For instance, the list as it was written ignores work done by post-colonial and queer theorists who have made substantial contributions to both feminist theory and political science in order to demonstrate this point. However, including these topics does not negate the point that now other important aspects have been ignored.[18] The very presentation of taxonomies of feminist approaches in the previous section can be critiqued from this perspective as privileging one conceptualization over another; meaning that other feminist approaches are silenced and marginalized.

Feminism historically as a discipline demonstrates the importance of critical approaches as feminist critical theorists and feminist scholars have pushed the discipline to consider the ways in which not only the work done by nonfeminist scholars, but their own work as well reifies and recreates problematic hierarchies and dualism. Feminism at its beginning was a critical project. By demonstrating how the patriarchy had worked to reify gender and to create power relations and hierarchies where one sex was created as a second and inferior one (Beauvoir 1953) feminists demonstrated how current treatment of sex/gender in academic work and beyond (public policy, popular culture, religious institutions, etc.) made women a priori the second and inferior body. However, as was quickly illustrated by Black Feminist theorists (Lorde 1984; Collins 2019; Roberts 1997) the original work done by white feminists propped-up racial hierarchies by privileging white feminist projects over that of others.

These observations led to the term intersectionality which is integral to feminist and critical projects. In fact, they took this argument one step further by demonstrating that not only did liberal feminism ignore many of the people who were marginalized they created further hierarchies by exacerbating established racial hierarchies where privileged (white) women were able to fulfill their goals as feminists (obtaining employment and economic independence) through a reliance on the intimate work done in the home by women of color reifying their bodies in the caring relation. (Threadcraft 2016). Similarly, Marxist feminists (Hartmann 1979; Leeb 2007) demonstrate the way in which traditional Marxism reifies the inferiority of working-class women and devalues domestic labor because it has largely been seen as part of the feminine sphere.

Another direction taken by critical post-colonial theorists demonstrates this same trend in feminist work that *lumped* together all "women of the third world" thus creating a "homogenous sociological grouping characterized by common dependencies or powerlessness (or even strengths) that problems arise—we say too little and too much at the same time" (Mohanty 2003: 25). By saying too much and too little in the same moment the agency of those involved is lost. What connects these various feminist projects is their critical self-reflective nature.

Not all feminist approaches should be considered equally critical. As has been demonstrated by the continuing self-reflective dialogue. What this chapter demonstrates is that feminist approaches when they are at their best incorporate aspects of critical theory including an emphasis on avoiding the glorification of concepts that justify dominant power relations. For instance, the categorizations created by those that study gender and politics exist within power relations that result in creating new or exacerbating old power distributions. What is distinct about critical approaches is that they equally apply to themselves. Being overly critical or reifying abstractions creates new hierarchies. For example, as Hill Collins asserts, without serious self-reflection, "intersectionality could easily become just another social theory that implicitly upholds the status-quo" (2019: 2). Furthermore, as she highlights the project of critical (social) theory reifies certain power relations in that it is academics or the educated elite that are most likely to claim the mantel of critical social theorists "as well as being the most likely to receive the benefits of the practice" (Hill Collins 2019: 4).

6. CONCLUSIONS: LESSONS LEARNED AND NEXT STEPS

In mapping out the diverse approaches of feminist political studies through a dialog between philosophy of science, political science and critical theory, this chapter has been able to hone in on the great potential of feminist political analysis to strengthen political science research: to help identify insights about power structures and exclusion in the larger community that can be harnessed to advance knowledge; to enhance the tools used to identify bias in order to strengthen the objectivity of scientific inquiry (and thus guard against "bad" science); and to increase the awareness of the power implications of concepts, measurement indicators.

From the example of feminist comparative policy, with the infrastructure and funding of large-scale comparative and international projects and its problem-driven and methodologically pluralist approach, we have seen important theoretical and methodological contributions to nonfeminist and feminist work alike. These feminist policy studies have shown how gender considerations of state structures and public policy can enhance understanding of democratic performance and, hence, theories of democracy, more generally speaking, have suggested that sectoral differences may be more important in understanding policy outcomes than national patterns and have shown the importance of developing concepts that travel across cultural boundaries. However, the persistent glass wall continues to block these feminist contributions for making their mark on nonfeminist policy studies.

Moreover, power imbalances within feminist research circles weaken those contributions, particularly for scholars and research from the global south on the international scene. Indeed, applying a critical theory approach allows us to be more watchful of the underlying power structures and intersectional biases reified in feminist as well as nonfeminist research. Hence, there is much room for improvement in order for feminist political science to be taken more seriously. Some future steps to consider include, publish feminist work in nonfeminist political science outlets; include feminist scholars in the design of new studies and projects outside of a gendered purview; include feminist theorists in empirical feminist projects; and include scholars from the global south into international projects. As long as feminist researchers keep positionality, considerations of power and exclusions on their radar, the field will be able to overcome many of the internal weaknesses we have identified. Similarly, the growth, success and diversity of feminist scholarship make the field stronger and more able to overcome barriers between feminist and nonfeminist work on politics. We have seen that certain parts of malestream political science have proven to be more open to dialog with feminist work, including the editors of this volume. Thus, the critical collective feminist project in political science stands to build from these developments to continue its progress towards being taken more seriously by nonfeminist political science and in doing so to become a more meaningful, scientific and influential area of study. In the final analysis, our cross disciplinary dialog between feminist political scientists and feminist philosophers has provided the much-needed platform from which to reveal the promises and pitfalls of taking feminism more seriously in political science.

ACKNOWLEDGMENTS

Many thanks to the Handbook editors for their constructive feedback and support. We also greatly appreciate Sharon Crasnow for pushing us to better showcase how the differences between political science and philosophy of science perspectives can provide a better understanding of feminist political science and its contributions.

NOTES

1. For excellent assessments of the field of gender and politics, see Carroll and Zerilli (1993); the *OUP Handbook on Gender and Politic*s (2013) and the inaugural issue of the *European Journal of Politics and Gender* (2018). Here we use interchangeably the terms feminist political science, feminist political studies and feminist approaches to political science, all part and parcel of gender and politics as a field of study.

2. As Head (2008) argues, "Some of the most difficult policy problems of the modern era have been described as complex, intractable, open-ended and 'wicked.'"

3. The European Conference on Gender and Politics affiliated with the Standing Group on Gender and Politics of the European Consortium of Political Research (https://ecpr.eu/Events/157) has been held on a biannual basis since 2009 and now hosts over 700 feminist researchers. The standing group is one of the most active subgroups of the ECPR and launched a new journal in 2018, the *European Journal of Political and Gender*. Similarly, the Women and Politics section of APSA maintains a large membership—800 plus—and has since 2005, published its own journal as well *Politics and Gender*. Other feminist journals that dialog with gender and politics research include *Journal of Women, Politics and Policy*, *International Journal of Feminist Politics* and *Social Politics*.

4. Increasingly, many feminist scholars who are "normatively interested in gender struggles and [attentive] to social epistemologies" (Ackerly and True 2018: 263) differentiate between feminist and nonfeminist analysis. On one hand, feminist scholars seek to bring gender meaningfully into scientific endeavors to promote more gender just societies. On the other, nonfeminist analysts tend to ignore gender, in its full complexity, as a significant analytical object and the issue of gender justice in politics or the discipline itself. There is a sexual division of labor between these two approaches: feminist scholars are for the most part women, with an increasing number being self-identified as transgender, and nonfeminist scholars are predominantly men.

5. Samantha Noll and Laci Hubbard-Mattix are philosophers who work in feminist philosophy of science and bioethics (Noll and Hubbard-Mattix 2019; Noll 2018 and 2017). Season Hoard and Amy Mazur are political scientists who work in Comparative Feminist Policy (Hoard 2015) and have written on epistemological issues in feminist political science (Mazur and Hoard 2014). All four work together in the School of Politics, Philosophy and Public Affairs at Washington State University, which has provided an intellectual home to nurture and pursue this cross disciplinary dialog.

6. Whether the tenets of western based feminism can "travel" (Sartori 1970) outside of countries associated with western culture, e.g., Western Europe and North America, is a question for research. Some argue that feminist ideas can be found outside of the western context with modifications that take into consideration the particular context, i.e. Islamic feminism, developmental feminism. Others argue that it is not a useful concept in settings outside of the western post-industrial world.

7. For more on intersectionality as an empirical concept and research agenda in political science see, for example, Weldon (2008) and Mügge and Montoya (2018). For epistemological origins and applications of intersectionality see below.

8. These three concepts represent variations on the same theme of male-domination with patriarchy being used to address the underlying gendered power relations and institutional outcomes within cultural, social and political systems. The terms androcentric and gender-biased indicate that a given system is male dominated and based on notions

of masculinity. For some, using the term gender-biased or gender hierarchy is a softer concept than patriarchy; a strategic choice made even to avoid alienating nonfeminist audiences. The concept androcentrism, rather than patriarchy, is used in feminist epistemological discussions of how established scientific communities have been male-dominated and defined in terms of masculine/sexist notions of research questions, knowledge cumulation, methodologies (e.g., Harding 1986).

9. For more on the Comparative Politics of Gender, see the special issue of *Perspectives on Politics* (March, 2010).

10. Following from R. K. Merton's (1949) notion of mid-range or meso theory, this approach to theory-building can take place across categories of countries or sectors of policy, for example. Hypotheses from these studies can then be assessed in larger more macro level studies across different groups of countries or different sectors of policy.

11. Current examples of these global feminist studies include Htun and Weldon's (2018) well-funded study of women's rights across the globe and the work of the new group under Laurel Weldon's leadership at Simon Fraser University working on the impact of women's movements worldwide, with funding from the Gates Foundation. Muriaas et al. (2020) conducted a global study, based at the University of Bergen and financed by the Norwegian Science Foundation, on the impact of gendered electoral financing on women's representation.

12. In conceptualization and mixed methods see Lieberman (2009) and Goertz (2019); in work on welfare states see Pierson (2000).

13. For the most recent survey of feminist philosophy of science see Crasnow and Intemann (2020).

14. Though it should be noted here that feminist critiques include questioning the distinction between gender and biological sex and the position that biological sex is somehow distinct from socially constructed concepts. Please see Richardson's *Sex Itself* (2013) as an example of the many treatments in the literature.

15. See for example the forthcoming special issue in *European Journal of Gender and Politics*, "Do Frames and Ideas Matter in Gender Equality? A Comparative Analysis".

16. Interestingly, Thompson also includes deconstructionism as well as postcolonial theories as those that have been incorrectly placed under the umbrella of critical theory.

17. For an excellent history of critical theory broadly see chapter 2 of Patricia Hill Collins (2019) *Intersectionality as Critical Social Theory*.

18. See Mohanty (2003) for an excellent demonstration of feminist decolonizing critical theory and Josephson and Marques (2017) for an analysis of queer theory in political science.

References

Ackelsberg, Martha. 2014. "Political Science as an Interdisciplinary Exploration." *Polity.* 46(1):115–121.

Acker, Joan. 1992. "Gendered Institutions: From sex roles to gendered institutions." *Contemporary Society.* 21:565–569.

Ackerly, Brooke and Jacqui True. 2018. "With or without Feminism? Research gender and politics in the 21st Century." *European Journal of Politics and Gender.* 1(1) 259–279.

Agger, Ben. 2013. *Critical Social Theories.* Oxford: Oxford University Press.

Aherns, Petra, Karen Celis, Sarah Childs, Isabelle Engeli, Elizabeth Evans and Liza Mügge. 2018. "Politics and Gender: Rocking Political Science and Creating New Horizons. *European Journal of Politics and Gender*. 1(1) 3–16.

Anderson, Elizabeth. 2019. "Feminist Epistemology and Philosophy of Science,'" In *The Stanford Encyclopedia of Philosophy*, edited by N Zalta. https://plato.stanford.edu/entries/feminism-epistemology/.

Antony, Louise. 1993. "Quine as Feminist: The Radical Import of Naturalized Epistemology." In *A Mind of One's Own: Feminist Essays on Reason and Objectivity*, edited by Louise Antony and Charlotte Witt. Boulder, CO: Westview Press.

Benstead, Linsday J. 2021. "Conceptualizing and measuring patriarchy: The importance of feminist theory" *Mediterranean Politics*. 26 (2) 234–246.

Bleier, Ruth. 1984. *Science and Gender: A Critique of Biology and Its Theories on Women*. New York: Pergamon.

Bartky S. 1992. Foucault, Femininity and the Modernization of Patriarchal Power. *Magyar Filozofiai Szemle*. (3–4):434–445.

Beauvoir S de. 1953. *The Second Sex*. [1st American ed.]. New York: Knopf.

Black, N. 1989. *Social Feminism*. Ithaca, NY: Cornell University Press.

Butler J. 1990. *Gender Trouble: Feminism and the Subversion of Identity*. New York, NY: Routledge.

Carroll, S.J., and Zerilli, L.M.G. 1993. "Feminist Challenges to Political Science." In A.W. Finifter (Ed.), *Political Science: The State of the Discipline II*. Washington DC: American Political Science Association. 55–79.

https://plato.stanford.edu/entries/logical-empiricism/ Cavarero A. 2009. *Horrorism: Naming Contemporary Violence*. New York: Columbia University Press.

Celis, Karen, Johanna Kantola, Georgina Waylen and S. Laurel Weldon. 2013."Introduction. Gender and Politics: A Gendered Discipline." In *The OUP Handbook of Gender and Politics*. Edited by Waylen, Georgina, Karen Celis, Johanna Kantola and S. Laurel Weldon. New York, New York: Oxford University Press. 1–25.

Childs, S., and Krook, M. 2009. Analyzing Women's Substantive Representation: From Critical Mass to Critical Actors. *Government and Opposition*, 44(2), 125–145.

Crasnow, Sharon and Kristen Intemann. eds. 2020. *Handbook of Feminist Philosophy of Science*. Routledge.

Creath, Richard. 2017. "Logical Empiricism." Edited by N Zalta. *The Stanford Encyclopedia of Philosophy*. https://plato.stanford.edu/entries/logical-empiricism/.

Crenshaw, Kimberle. 1991. "Decriminalizing the Intersection of Race and Sex: A Black Feminist Critique of Antidiscrmination Doctrine, Feminist Theory, and Antiracist Politics." *University of Chicago Legal Forum*, 1989:1 (139–167).

Dahlerup, D. 1988. From a Small to a Large Minority: Women in Scandinavian Politics. *Scandinavian Political Studies*, 11(4), 275–298.

Engeli, Isabelle and Amy G. Mazur eds. 2021. *Gender Equality and Policy Implementation in the Corporate World: Making Democracy Work in Business*. Oxford: Oxford University Press.

Engeli, Isabelle and Amy G. Mazur. 2018. "Taking Implementation Seriously in Assessing Success: The Politics of Gender Policy in Practice" with Isabelle Engeli. *European Journal of Gender and Politics*. 1(1), 11–29.

Flax, Jane. 1987. "Postmodernism and Gender Relations in Feminist Theory." *Signs: Journal of Women in Culture and Society* 12 (4): 621–43. https://doi.org/10.1086/494359.

Galligan, Y., Clavero, S. and Calloni, M. 2007. *Gender, Politics and Democracy*, Opladen and Farmington Hills: Barbara Budrich Publishers.

Gerring, John. 2012. *Social Science Methodology: A Unified Framework*. Cambridge: Cambridge University Press.

Goertz, Gary. 2019. *Social Science Concepts: A User's Guide*. Princeton: Princeton University Press.

Goertz, Gary and Amy G. Mazur, eds. 2008. *Politics, Gender, and Concepts: Theory and Methodology*. Edited with G/ary Goertz. Cambridge: Cambridge University Press.

Franceschet, S., and Piscopo, J. M. 2008. Gender Quotas and Women's Substantive Representation: Lessons from Argentina. *Politics and Gender*, 4(3), 393–425.

Hall, Donald. 2013. "Gender and Queer Theory" In *The Routledge Companion to Critical and Cultural Theory*. Routledge. 107–119.

Halsaa, Beatrice, Sasha Roseneil and Sevil Sumer, eds. 2012. *Remaking Citizenship in Multicultural Europe*. Houndsmill, Basingstoke, Hampshire: Palgrave MacMillan.

Harding, S. 1986. *The Science Question in Feminism*. Cornell University Press.

Harding, Sandra. 1987. "Introduction: Is There a Feminist Method." In *Feminism and Methodology*. In S. Harding, ed. Bloomington: Indiana University Press. 1–15.

Harding, S. 1993. "Rethinking Standpoint Epistemology: What Is Strong Objectivity? In Feminist Epistemologies. Alcoff, Linda and Elizabeth Potter, eds. New York and London: Routledge. 49–82.

Harding Sandra, ed. 2004. *The Feminist Standpoint Theory Reader: Intellectual and Political Controversies*. New York: Routledge.

Hartmann, H. I. 1979. The Unhappy Marriage of Marxism and Feminism: Towards a more Progressive Union. *Capital & Class*, 3(2), 1–33.

Haslanger, Sally. 2000. "Gender and Race: (What) Are They? (What) Do We Want Them to Be?" *Noûs* 34 (1): 31–55.

Hawkesworth, M. 2006. *Feminist Inquiry: From Political Conviction to Methodological Innovation*. New Brunswick, NJ: Rutgers University Press.

Head, Brian W. 2008. "Wicked Problems in Public Policy". *Public Policy*. 3(2) 101–118.

Hill Collins, Patricia. 2019. *Intersectionality as Critical Social Theory*. Raleigh-Durham, NC: Duke University Press.

Hoard, Season. 2015. *Gender Expertise in Public Policy: Toward A Theory of Policy Success*. Palgrave/Macmillan.

Horkheimer M, Adorno, Theodor W., Schmid Noerr, Gunzelin, Jephcott, E. F. N. 2002. *Dialectic of Enlightenment: Philosophical Fragments*. Stanford, California: Stanford University Press.

Hundleby, Catherine E. 2012. "Feminist Empiricism." In *Handbook of Feminist Research: Theory and Praxis*, Sharlene Hesse-Biber, ed. Thousand Oaks, CA: SAGE Publications. 28–45. https://doi.org/10.4135/9781483384740.n2.

Hutcheon, Linda. 1989. "Feminism and Postmodernism." In *Donna: Women in Italian Culture*. Ada Testaferri, ed. Toronto: Dovehouse Press. 25–37.

Htun, Mala and Laurel Weldon S. 2018. *The Logic of Gender Justice: State Action and Women's Rights Around the World*. Cambridge: Cambridge University Press.

Intemann, Kristen. 2010. "Twenty-five years of Feminist Empiricism and Standpoint Theory: Where are we now?" *Hypatia: A Journal of Feminist Philosophy*. 25 (4): 778–96.

Kantola, J and Lombardo, E. 2017. *Gender and Political Analysis*. London: Palgrave.

Keller, Evelyn Fox. 1985. *Reflections on Gender and Science*. New Haven: Yale University Press.

Kourany, Janet. 2010. *Philosophy of Science after Feminism*. New York: Oxford University Press.

Leeb, Claudia. 2007. "Marx and the Gendered Structure of Capitalism," *Philosophy & Social Criticism* 33(7): 833–859.

Lieberman, Evan. 2009. "Bridging the Qualitative-Quantitative Divide: Best Practice in the Development of Historically Oriented Replication Databases." *Annual Review of Political Science* 7: 57, 37–59.

Lombardo, E. and Kantola, J. 2017. *Feminism and Political Analysis*. Palgrave/Macmillan.

Lombardo, E. and Agustin, L.R. 2016. "Intersectionality in European Union Policymaking: the Case of Gender-Based Violence." *Politics*, 36:4. 364–373.

Longino, Helen. 1994.."In Search of Feminist Epistemology." *The Monist* 77: 472–85.

Longino, Helen 2001. *The Fate of Knowledge*. Princeton: Princeton University Press.

Lorde, Audrey. 1984. Sister Outsider: Essays and Speeches by Audrey Lorde. Crossing Press Malpas, Simon and Wake, Paul.

Mazur, Amy G. 2012. "A Feminist Integrative and Empirical Approach in Political Science: Breaking Down the Glass Wall." In The *Oxford University Press Handbook on Philosophy of Social Sciences*. Edited by Harold Kincaid. Oxford: Oxford University Press. 533–558.

Mazur, Amy G. and Season Hoard. 2014. "Gendering Comparative Policy Studies: Towards Better Science." In *Comparative Policy Studies: Conceptual and Methodological Challenges*. Edited by Isabelle Engeli and Christine Rothmayr. London: Palgrave. 2014. 205–236.

McBride, D. E., and Mazur, A. G. 2010. *The Politics of State Feminism: Innovation in Comparative Research*. Philadelphia: Temple University Press.

McBride, Dorothy and Amy Mazur. 2008. "Women's Movements, Feminism and Feminist Movements." In Goertz and Mazur, eds. *Politics, Gender and Concepts*. Cambridge: Cambridge University Press. 219–243,

Medie, Peace A. and Alice J. Kang. 2018. "Power, Knowledge and the Politics of Gender in the Global South. *European Journal of Politics and Gender*. 1(1) 37–54.

Merton, R.K. [1949] (1968), *Social Theory and Social Structure*. Reprint. New York: Free Press.

Mohanty CT. 2003. *Feminism Without Borders: Decolonizing Theory, Practicing Solidarity*. Raleigh-Durham, NC: Duke University Press.

Monroe, Kristen Renwick (ed). 2005. *Perestroika: The Raucous Rebellion in Political Science* Yale, CT: Yale University Press.

Mügge. Liza and Celeste Montoya. 2018." Intersectionality and the Politics of Knowledge Production." *European Journal of Politics and Gender*. 1(1) 17–36.

Mügge, L.M. and Erzeel, S. 2016. "Double Jeopardy or Multiple Advantage? Intersectionality and Political Representation." *Parliamentary Affairs*, 69:3 (499–511).

Muriaas, Ragnhild, Vibeke Wang and Rainbow Murray, eds. 2020. *Gendered Electoral Financing: Money, Power and Representation in Comparative Perspective*. Routledge.

Noll, Samantha. 2018. "Nonhuman Climate Refugees: The Role That Urban Communities Should Play in Ensuring Ecological Resilience." *Environmental Ethics* 40 (2): 119–34.

Noll, Samantha. 2017. "Food Sovereignty in the City: Challenging Historical Barriers to Food Justice." In *Food Justice in US and Global Contexts: Bringing Theory and Practice Together*, Ian Werkheiser and Zachary Piso, New York: Springer. 95–111.

Noll, S. and L. Hubbard-Mattix. 2019 "Health Justice in the City: Why an Intersectional Analysis of Transportation Matters for Bioethics, *Essays in Philosophy*, 20 (2), 1–16.

Okin, Susan M. 2008. "Gender, the public and the private." *Revista Estudos Feministas*, 16 (2), 305–332.

Okruhlik, Kathleen. 2017. "Feminist Accounts of Science." In *A Companion to Philosophy of Science*, Newton-Smith W H (ed) 134–42. New York: Blackwell.

Prügl, Elizabeth and Ann Tickner. 2018. "Feminist International Relations: Some Research Agendas for a World in Transition." *European Journal of Politics and Gender.* 1(2): 75–92.

Pierson, Paul. 2000. "The Three Worlds of Welfare State Research." *Comparative Political Studies.* 33(67) 791–821.

Richardson, Sarah S. 2010. "Feminist Philosophy of Science: History, Contributions, and Challenges." *Synthese* 177 (3): 337–62. https://doi.org/10.1007/s11229-010-9791-6

Rihoux, B. and Ragin, C. C. (eds) (2008). *Configurational Comparative Methods. Qualitative Comparative Analysis (QCA) and Related Techniques*, Applied Social Research Methods series, Thousand Oaks and London: Sage.

Roberts, Dorothy. 1997. Killing the Black Body. Vintage Book.

Rosser, S. 1987. "Feminist Scholarship in the Sciences: Where Are We Now and When Can We Expect a Theoretical Breakthrough?" *Hypatia* 2 (3): 5–17.

Sapiro, Virginia. 1981. "Research Frontier Essay: When are Interests Interesting? The Problem of Political Representation of Women." *The American Political Science Review*, 75:3 (701–716).

Sartori, Giovanni. 1970. 'Concept Misformation in Comparative Politics'. *American Political Science Review*, 64: 1033–1053.

Scott, Joan. 1986. "Gender a Useful Category of Historical Analysis." *American Historical Review.* 91: 1053–1075.

Shapiro, I. 2002. "Problems, Methods, and Theories in the Study of Politics, of What's Wrong with Political Science and What to Do About It?" *Political Theory* 30 (4): 596–619.

Sinha, Mrilanini. 2017. *Colonial Masculinity: The 'Manly Englishman' and the 'Effeminate Begali' in the Late Nineteenth Century.* Manchester, UK: Manchester University Press.

Siim, Birte. 2004. "Towards a Contextual and Gender Sensitive European Political Science?"

Thompson, M.J. 2017 "Introduction: What is Critical Theory" In *The Palgrave Handbook of Critical Theory.* Edited by Michael J. Thompson. Palgrave McMillian. 1–14.

Threadcraft, Shatema. 2016. *Intimate Justice: The Black Female Body and the Body Politic.* Oxford: Oxford University Press.

Tyson, Lois. 1999. *Critical Theory Today: A User-Friendly Guide.* Garland

Weldon, Laurel. 2008. "Intersectionality." In *Politics, Gender and Concepts: Theory and Methodology*, eds. Goertz and Mazur, 193–218. Cambridge: Cambridge University Press.

Verloo, M. 2007. *Multiple Meanings of Gender Equality: A Critical Frame Analysis of Gender Policies in Europe.* Central European University Press.

Verloo, Mieke and Sylvia Walby. eds. 2013. "Intersectionality in the Equality Architecture." Special Issue *Social Politics. 19(4).*

CHAPTER 24

HOW TO DEAL WITH VALUES IN POLITICAL SCIENCE?

JEROEN VAN BOUWEL

1. INTRODUCTION

PHILOSOPHY of science has a long tradition of debating the relation(s) between science and values. The general trend among recent contributions to this debate is to acknowledge that values, including social, political, economic, ethical values, do influence the scientific process, unavoidably, and that this should not necessarily be considered epistemically problematic. The question rather becomes: under what conditions is the influence of these values justifiable?

Kevin Elliott (2017) offers us a good overview of the current state of the science and values debate. He demonstrates convincingly, using a lot of lively examples, how science is permeated with value judgments and distinguishes five avenues for value influences, connected to five questions that regularly show up and whose answers shape scientific research:

(a) What research topics to prioritize?
(b) What specific questions to raise, methods to use, assumptions to make?
(c) What are the aims of inquiry in this particular context (weighing a variety of theoretical and practical goals, e.g., a quick or inexpensive fix rather than a slower, more detailed result)?
(d) How to deal with questions of uncertainty (e.g., when is the available evidence sufficient for particular sorts of conclusions)?
(e) How to report and frame the conclusions of scientific research (e.g., what terminology, categories, or metaphors to employ in providing scientific information, what not to report)?

Doing science implies answering these questions and thus making value judgments, be it implicitly or explicitly. In this chapter, I consider the presence of these value judgments in science as a given, as the starting point.[1] The next question is: Under what conditions is the influence of values in science justifiable? Elliott (2017: 10) stipulates three conditions that "appear to be particularly important for bringing values into science in an appropriate fashion" and "why some influences appear to be more justifiable than others": value influences should be (1) made as *transparent* as possible, (2) *representative* of our major social and ethical priorities, and (3) scrutinized through *engagement* between different stakeholders, *inter alia*, citizens, policymakers, communities, or other scientists.

Elliott's three conditions can be considered as three different strategies of dealing with values in science; some philosophers have defended one of those strategies as sufficient to deal with values in science, and others, combinations of them. In this chapter, I evaluate those three conditions with respect to discussions in political science. My objective is threefold: (1) to introduce and evaluate Elliott's proposals about how to deal with values in science, (2) to discuss examples taken from contemporary political science debates in order to examine how dealing with values plays out in practice, and (3) by doing so, engaging political scientists to question how best to deal with value influences as well as to contribute to further developing Elliott's proposals and the science and values debate which could benefit from more political and social analysis.

2. THE TRANSPARENCY CONDITION

2.1 General Questions about the Transparency Condition

Elliott's first condition, *transparency*, is a frequently mentioned condition or requirement when discussing how to deal with values in science. The general idea is for scientists to be as clear as possible about their "data, methods, models, and assumptions so that others can identify the ways in which their work supports or is influenced by particular values" (Elliott 2017: 14).

Transparency obviously has benefits, contributing to the credibility and legitimacy of knowledge claims (cf. Lupia and Elman 2014: 20). However, the transparency requirement also raises some general questions, e.g., *(a) How much information do we have to share about our choices and judgments?* There might be cases in which the transparency requirement can be fulfilled smoothly with concise info. However, when we think, for instance, of political scientists measuring democracy or economists calculating GDP, these calculations imply many choices and judgments. Explaining one particular value choice might already be hard, not to speak of enumerating the alternative choices one might have opted for. What if we combine all of these choices and possible interactions between them? Would it not become too cumbersome? *(b) To what extent can you make value judgments transparent?* Are value choices not engrained in our scientific tools, in the history and path dependency of disciplines (choices made a long time ago pushed the discipline in a certain direction and closed off possible alternative tracks)? How deep and how far back can we go? This leads us to the following question: *(c) To what extent are scientists aware of their own values, value judgments, background assumptions?* Many history of science studies show how scientists projected values typical of their historical context into science, most likely being unaware of it.

(d) Does more transparency lead to more or less trust in science? Besides raising questions about the extent to which scientists can and should make value judgments transparent, one can also wonder how more transparency about values would affect the standing of science with the public. Some empirical studies actually seem to show that transparency about values reduces the perceived credibility of scientists. One study by Kevin Elliott himself with coauthors examined how citizens look at scientists who publicly acknowledge value influences. The authors conclude that their "results provide at least preliminary evidence that acknowledging values may reduce the perceived credibility of scientists within the general public, but this effect differs depending on whether scientists and citizens share values, whether scientists draw conclusions that run contrary to their values, and whether scientists make policy recommendations" (Elliott et al. 2017: 1).

However, it seems to me that this should not immediately be reason for despair among defenders of transparency requirements. The reduction in perceived credibility might be a consequence of a public being brought up with an ideal of value-free science. This public perception could be shifted by a learning process, for instance, adjusting the image of science as value-free by acknowledging the unavoidable influence of values in science (as we are doing in this chapter). Trust and credibility might also be increased by engaging citizens in science (as I discuss in Section 6 below).

(e) Might a transparency requirement needlessly restrict scientists' methodological options or skew the scientific community? Besides looking at the possibilities of being transparent and what the consequences on the public's trust in science are, one can also ask what the impact of a transparency requirement on the scientific community as a whole might be and on the distribution of options and opportunities among the members of that community. Let me address question *(e)* by examining a recent debate in political science.

2.2 The Transparency Condition in Political Science

The Introduction of the Transparency Condition in Political Science

In October 2012 the American Political Science Association (APSA) amended its *Guide to Professional Ethics in Political Science* following the suggestions of the *Data Access—Research Transparency* (DA-RT) initiative. Section 6 of the Ethics Guide of APSA became: "Researchers have an ethical obligation to facilitate the evaluation of their evidence-based knowledge claims through data access, production transparency, and analytic transparency so that their work can be tested or replicated" (2012: 9). In the subsections 6.1 to 6.3 of the Guide one finds some further specifications about what *data access, production transparency*, and *analytic transparency* exactly mean and the formalities it implies.

In 2014, the DA-RT initiative led to the *Journal Editors' Transparency Statement* (JETS). This statement was signed by more than twenty editors of political science journals who pledged to commit their journals to the principles of data access and transparency. In some quarters, JETS was received with a lot of skepticism and worries, given the central role journal publications (and bibliometrics) play in the discipline—be it in allocating research funding, appointing faculty, ranking departments, and so on.

In reaction, the *Qualitative and Multi-Method Research* (QMMR) section of the APSA started up a participatory *Qualitative Transparency Deliberations* (QTD) process in 2015.

The QTD process is driven by the concern that journals implementing the new data access and research transparency (DA-RT) requirements risks being incompatible with the plurality of logics of inquiry in the field of political science.[2] Therefore, the benefits and costs of the DA-RT transparency requirements, especially for the qualitative empirical approaches in political science, have to be scrutinized according to the QTD initiators.

The Reception of the Transparency Condition in Political Science

Unsurprisingly, the idea of transparency requirements has been received differently depending on the research approach one is working in. This is illustrated in the report written by political scientists Marcus Kreuzer and Craig Parsons (2018) as part of the QTD. They distinguish five research approaches (or traditions, as they call them), namely, the (1) frequentist/experimentalist tradition, (2) Bayesian/process-tracing tradition, (3) comparative historical tradition, (4) modern constructivist tradition, and (5) interpretivist tradition. For each approach, *transparency* can be more or less problematic and/or filled in differently. The further you go down the list of traditions, from (1) to (5), the more skeptical researchers become about the transparency requirements as proposed by the DA-RT initiative.

Let me here just mention some characteristics and worries of these different research traditions with respect to the transparency requirements in order to make my social-epistemological points. For a more comprehensive characterization of the traditions and their reception of the DA-RT requirements, I refer the reader to the full Kreuzer and Parsons (2018) report.

(1) *The frequentist/experimentalist tradition* consists of experimentalists and proponents of statistical analysis who conceptualize the social world as analogous to the physical world and within which evidence is contextless and lacks any specific historical coordinates. This tradition gets along fine with the DA-RT requirements—these requirements closely reflect the methodology of this tradition.

(2) *The Bayesian/process-tracing tradition* has a more conditional and contextual view on knowledge production than (1). The interpretation of evidence depends on an analysis of preceding knowledge claims, the consideration of alternative explanations as well as the concrete context of evidence. Therefore it has a more encompassing understanding of transparency than (1), having to be transparent about the additional conditional and contextual dimensions. Nonetheless, all of this is still well in line with the DA-RT requirements.

(3) *The comparative historical tradition* has a bit more complex temporal sequencing compared to the former two traditions and also pays more attention to context. Researchers in this tradition are often seeking a whole chain of evidence that must support a hypothesis, with transparency practices involving a series of informal judgments elaborated in detailed historiographies, extended footnotes, or lengthy book reviews. Scholars in this tradition tend to endorse DA-RT requirements—the chain of evidence must be observable—but they worry about its practical limits; making all steps taken transparent (starting from far back into the research design) may be cumbersome in practice and contribute little to compelling results.

(4) *The modern constructivist tradition*, just like tradition (5) below, considers human action to be operating through interpretive social constructs, be it ideas, norms, identities, cultures, etc. These constructs are then considered as interpretive, human-made ideational filters through which people perceive themselves, their surroundings, and shape their actions. Accordingly, scholars in the modern constructivist tradition focus on thick evidence of discourse and action and pay detailed attention to the meaning of this evidence in its precise social context. For scholars studying politics in these socially constructed contexts "the connotation of transparency—seeing through obstructions to reveal reality—suggests a misleading confidence in objective process and results" (Kreuzer and Parsons 2018: 10).

(5) *The interpretivist tradition* (with methods like ethnography, participant observation, and genealogy) shares the emphasis on social construction and, moreover, acknowledges that scholars too only access the world through social constructs, rejecting correspondence theories of truth, instead constructing coherent narratives. Here as well evidence is characterized as thick, detailed, taking into account socially constructed contexts. The notion of making available "raw data," as present in DA-RT, strikes interpretivists as odd: in their view, data never have the autonomous status implied by "rawness," and should be read in holistic, relational, and intersubjective contexts as much as possible. In general, Kreuzer and Parsons conclude that: "It surely makes sense for interpretivists to reject the DA-RT vision of transparency, because a core point of the interpretive tradition is that we cannot ever "see" through our socially-constructed filters. When scholars rooted in the frequentist/experimental tradition exhort interpretivists to articulate "transparency standards," interpretivists perceive a "tyranny of light" that is at best naïve, and more likely to be a move to delegitimize their work" (2018: 11).

Thus, having briefly reviewed the reception of DA-RT among different research traditions, one has to acknowledge that there is considerable discontent with and opposition to DA-RT principles, in particular with respect to their inappropriateness for some qualitative research methods. Let us use this DA-RT case in political science to formulate some concerns about the transparency condition.

2.3 Concerns about the Transparency Condition

First, although proponents of DA-RT label the initiative as "epistemologically neutral" (cf. Lupia and Elman 2014: 20), it seems hard to defend, given the differences among research traditions discussed above. As the discussion of the reception among research traditions also illustrates, the transparency requirements rather risk intentionally or unintentionally discounting certain established approaches as being science or good scholarship. Rather than neutral, it might be skewing the scientific community as well as *hamper scientific pluralism* (cf. Section 3.3 below).[3]

Second, in combination with JETS, the DA-RT initiative might have serious consequences. Once journals subscribe to the transparency requirements as formulated in the APSA Ethics Guide, some methods might lose their status, because important journals stop publishing studies that use those methods.[4] Methods might become underdeveloped, lower in the hierarchy, neglected. (This might affect both research and teaching, as social scientists teach some but not all methods to their students.) Thus, methodological options might become more restricted, which also influences the choice of research question, or even what can be questioned—epistemologically constraining what questions can be raised, and what values might prevail with respect to Elliott's (b)-question above. Reducing methodological choices might then "hinder political science's ability to address important political questions" (Monroe 2018: 142) as well as make "an implicit value judgement about which questions are important to be addressed." (Reiss 2017: 145) This scenario with transparency requirements advocated by JETS—*implemented into journals -> restricting methods -> not able to address certain important questions*—is an example of what I call *hampering scientific pluralism*.

Third, these questions and concerns about transparency have led to pleas for replacing research transparency with less demanding conditions. Some suggest *openness* or *explicitness*. Kreuzer and Parsons write in their report: "It therefore makes sense to substitute research transparency with a more expansive, less formalized term like research explicitness. Especially prominent in posts on our group's forum . . . is the interpretive tradition. It rejects the notion of research transparency, but may be open to explicating their research methods to be consistent with other ways of critically evaluating scholarly interpretations and explanations" (2018: 1). The general idea seems to be that it is important to have scientists clarify and discuss the important choices they make and the value influences that are part of their practice (going beyond the value-free ideal), but that transparency is *too demanding*, *unnecessary* or *utopian* an aim. (And on the basis of our discussion here, we can add that DA-RT transparency might also be *counterproductive*.)

Within the QTD process, there is also a group that proposes to develop "Community Transparency Statements" (CTSs) as an alternative to the current general DA-RT guidelines. CTSs would articulate guidelines for both authors and reviewers appropriate to diverse forms of (quantitative and qualitative) inquiry, guidelines that would be considered reasonable by the respective research communities (as well as promoting transparency consistent with the discipline's pluralism, according to the CTSs advocates). CTSs are at least laudable in that they would result from an active reflection on institutional implications of transparency. However, it seems to me that even if CTSs are apt for smaller communities, the general questions about transparency requirements (cf. Section 2.1) still apply. Next, are we not going to see discussions along the lines of Section 2.2—about how the transparency requirement affects specific research methods differently—within the smaller communities too? Furthermore, I wonder how generalist journals would deal with a variety of transparency conditions in CTSs: How to decide which CTS is applicable? How to trade-off quality between them? Will there be any implicit ranking or hierarchy between the CTSs?

Fourth, besides these suggestions about qualifying the transparency idea in DA-RT, there are also critics of DA-RT who wonder why the focus should be so exclusively on *transparency and data access,* or even whether we should have a transparency condition altogether. Why not highlight other standards like *intellectual engagement*, which might also be a route to more transparency, or *public relevance*, what are the important and interesting questions the public wants to see addressed? (*Intellectual engagement* and *public relevance* are a lot more social, social-epistemic, than DA-RT, the latter being more about rigorous reporting, see Section 3.2.) What is it in contemporary political science that selects *research transparency and data access* as the main focus? Even if it is a good thing to have transparency, the question according to those critics is whether it really is the most important problem, deserves the highest priority at the moment, and whether increased research transparency should be obtained via DA-RT. And, why measure the quality of research with one decisive epistemic criterion like transparency?

Fifth, the emphasis on transparency and replicability as present in the DA-RT initiative is linked to a bigger story in the sciences in which replication is an overarching epistemic criterion to measure the quality of research results. This focus on replication as the criterion and the best strategy to achieve reliable outcomes has been criticized, e.g., by Leonelli (2018: 131) who argues that (1) the "convergence of results can be obtained in the absence of reproduction, and (2) a different, yet crucial function of reproducibility consists in helping researchers to identify relevant variants in the first place." Penders et al. are also critical of replication as the decisive epistemic criterion arguing that replication is a criterion that "cannot be extended everywhere, since the epistemic content of fields, as well as their accountability infrastructures, differ." Moreover, there are limits to replicability in all fields, but in some, and that would include large parts of political science, "these limits severely undermine the value of replication to account for the value of research." (2019: 1) They use Fricker's (2007) idea of *epistemic injustice*—pointing at problems that resonate with the Kreuzer and Parsons report: "If fields of research exist for which replication is an unreasonable epistemic expectation, then policies for research that universalize the replication drive will perpetrate (some might say perpetuate) an epistemic injustice, ghettoizing the non-empirical humanities and hermeneutic social sciences as either inferior research or not really research at all" (Penders et al. 2019: 2).

The demand for more transparency as advocated by the DA-RT initiative is one possible strategy of dealing with value influences in political science, causing concerns and downsides which I have tried to illustrate here. Elliott combines the demand for transparency with conditions of representativeness and engagement which we discuss in sections 4 and 6. Let us first discuss some philosophical ideas that will help us in evaluating ways of dealing with value influences in political science.

3. VALUE INFLUENCES AND SOCIAL-EPISTEMIC PRACTICES

3.1 Philosophers Dealing with Value Influences in Science: Kinds, Roles, Norms

Within philosophy of science, at least three different ways of dealing with values in science have been developed (I am not discussing possible combinations of those three ways here).

(1) The first focuses on different *kinds* of values, allowing some of these kinds to be present in science and others not. Take, for instance, the distinction between "acceptable" *epistemic values* (like *predictive accuracy, internal coherence, external*

consistency, unifying power, fertility, and *simplicity*) and "unacceptable" *nonepistemic values* (see McMullin 1983). It turns out to be very hard to identify the exact list of epistemic values (and their relative weight) as well as to clearly distinguish them from nonepistemic values (see, e.g., Rooney 1992). Moreover, it is doubtful whether nonepistemic values could at all be eliminated from science and questionable whether nonepistemic values are necessarily detrimental to science. Therefore, philosophers developed alternative ways to deal with values.

(2) One alternative is to focus on the *roles* values are allowed to play in science (often distinguishing different stages in science, some in which values do play an acceptable role while in other they should not be allowed). Douglas (2009), for instance, distinguishes an *indirect role* from a *direct role* of values. In the stage of evaluation of evidence, an indirect role of values is acceptable in evaluating whether available evidence is sufficient to support a hypothesis, while a direct role of values, where values are considered as a form of evidence or as reasons in themselves to accept a hypothesis, is unacceptable. In the stage of choosing research topics, on the other hand, a direct role of values is acceptable. Whether a distinction qua *roles* succeeds in erecting a barrier between acceptable (integer) and unacceptable (politicized) science has been questioned too (e.g. Brigandt 2015).

(3) A third way explored by philosophers is to stipulate the *norms* that individual scientists and/or the scientific community (incl. its relations with other stakeholders) have to live up to in dealing with values in science. Longino's (2002) demand for critical interaction between approaches respecting four norms would be an example of such an approach, with the norms being: (1) recognized avenues for criticism; (2) uptake of criticism, community response; (3) shared standards; and, (4) tempered equality of intellectual authority. Let us look further into this third way by considering transparency.

3.2 Transparency via DA-RT or via Social-Epistemic Norms?

One of the three strategies Elliott suggested to deal with values in science is transparency. How that would work exactly—how a transparency requirement is being implemented—can be subject of discussion. You could either consider the individual scientists themselves as responsible for being transparent or you could situate the responsibility on the social level stipulating the norms that a scientific community should live up to.

Skepticism about transparency understood as individual scientists themselves being open about their value influences is not new. Ernst Nagel wrote in 1961:

> Although the recommendation that social scientists make fully explicit their value commitments is undoubtedly salutary, and can produce excellent fruit, it verges on being a counsel of perfection. For the most part we are unaware of many assumptions that enter into our analyses and actions, so that despite resolute efforts to make our preconceptions explicit some decisive ones may not even occur to us. But in any event, the difficulties generated for scientific inquiry by unconscious bias and tacit value orientations are rarely overcome by devout resolutions to eliminate bias. They are overcome, often only gradually, through the self-corrective mechanisms of science as social enterprise. (Nagel 1961: 489)

In the last sentence, Nagel suggests a more social take on dealing with value influences, a track that has been developed over the years in social epistemology and that I will follow here.

Nagel's critique seems still very relevant to DA-RT which focuses on individual researchers having an ethical obligation to be transparent. We have already considered the problematic impact of DA-RT on the distribution of opportunities among the members of the scientific community as well as on the community as a whole (also see Section 3.3 below). Now we might also consider the importance of discussion, social interaction and correction to "realize" transparency, i.e., a solution focusing on the social level of a scientific community considering, among others, social characteristics like hierarchy, representativeness, and diversity (something I do in Section 4).

3.3 Scientific Pluralism and the Focus on Social-Epistemic Constellations

In Section 2.3, I mentioned the risk of *hampering scientific pluralism*. Let me explain what it means and why it would be bad for science. *Scientific pluralism* is a normative endorsement of there being *plurality* in science—this could be a plurality of forms of explanation, methods, kinds, styles of reasoning, systems of knowledge, and so on. Following scientific pluralism, it is important to make scientific practice, and the conditions it is supposed to live up to (e.g., Elliott's three conditions), congruent with the multiple goals science has, the different interests and range(s) of questions it might have to address as well as to avoid hampering or counteracting plurality in science.

In this chapter, I am not zeroing in on the plurality of forms of explanation or kinds or styles of reasoning, rather I want to focus on social-epistemic constellations; analyze social-epistemic norms and practices that characterize the scientific community, and evaluate to what extent certain social-epistemic practices hamper the consideration of certain questions, interests, goals, and methodological options. These social-epistemic practices could concern scientific journals or publishing in general, hierarchies in scientific disciplines, the establishment of disciplinary quality criteria,[5] interactions between scientific communities and citizens, and so on. The hampering could consist in directly blocking the entry for others that want to join, but also in sustaining a disciplinary structure that discourages interaction or promotes self-imposed isolation (cf. Van Bouwel 2009). The hampering is closely related to how we deal with value influences, as I try to illustrate in this chapter; it is linked to questions (a)–(e) in Section 1, i.e., determining research topics and resource allocation, how projects are to be pursued, the particular aims, the weight of different pieces of evidence, and how research results should be used.

Why should we avoid *hampering* scientific pluralism? I argued in earlier work that we need a plurality of well-developed approaches in a discipline to answer the different (kinds of) questions –and underlying interests/goals– scientists and other citizens (will) have in the best way possible—both accurately and adequately (cf. Van Bouwel 2003, 2014). Moreover, in searching for the best possible questions and answers in science, having a plurality of approaches or perspectives is also needed to ensure the desired mutual, transformative criticism among approaches (cf. Longino 2002). To summarize, we should avoid hampering scientific pluralism in order to (a) maximize the number of *questions* (effectively) answerable as well as (b) foster a multiplicity of *perspectives* to ensure mutual criticism. Both seem imperative to get the best out of science.

4. THE REPRESENTATIVENESS CONDITION.

4.1 General questions about the representativeness condition

Having sketched the general social-epistemic framework within which we discuss Elliott's conditions for dealing with values in science, let us now consider the second condition, representativeness. The general idea is that values brought into science "should be *representative* of our major social and ethical priorities" (Elliott 2017: 10). In his book, Elliott is sometimes referring to "our major social and ethical priorities" and sometimes to "fundamental ethical principles" (2017: 106) when stipulating what values brought into science should be representative of. There seems to be some tension between *priorities* and *principles* that might lead to conflicting guidance (cf. Van Bouwel 2021), but I will not discuss that here. Let us follow Elliott: "When clear, widely recognized ethical principles are available, they should be used to guide the values that influence science. When ethical principles are less settled, science should be influenced as much as possible by values that represent broad societal priorities." (2017: 14-15)

Elliott (2017) offers us some examples of how to understand (the lack of) representativeness, for instance: (a) the pharmaceutical industry's research priorities do not represent the needs of the world's citizens (p. 171); (b) manufactured doubts about tobacco use, industrial chemicals, and climate change represent concerns of a few wealthy corporations, not of the broader public (p. 106); and, (c) in more general terms: "Industry values are likely to be less representative of the general public's interests . . . when companies are testing the public-health or environmental impacts of products that generate a great deal of money for them" (Elliott 2017: 106). In these cases concerning public health and the environment, deciding what values should be considered (not) "representative" might be relatively easy; distinguishing a general interest in line with our major social and ethical priorities from special interests, not being representative, is not too hard here.

However, there are more difficult cases. It seems that we do not always agree on what our major social and ethical priorities are or our ethical principles (which is not a problem per se, of course, we can be value pluralists).[6] Elliott does not suggest any (democratic) procedure to decide on priorities and principles and thus on what values are representative. Neither do we learn about how opposing viewpoints about value judgments are to be accommodated or how scientists would be accountable. Let us address these issues with representativeness by looking at scientific practice.

4.2 The Representativeness Condition in Political Science

As mentioned above, in his book Elliott discusses more straightforward examples concerning public health and the environment. However, sometimes scientific practice might be more complicated; there are many instances where the picture is more complex than having general *versus* special corporate interests. There might be disagreement about "our major social and ethical priorities" or different interpretations about what our major priorities should be.

When looking at the social sciences, for instance, these different ideas about priorities, different values, interests, goals, are reflected in there being different research approaches or "schools". When you address a certain topic, you might get many angles, different questions, and different answers. Think, for instance, of experts addressing questions about the desirability of "free trade" (nicely tackled by Reiss 2019; in arguing against Jason Brennan's epistocracy, Reiss shows how social scientists can have different priorities and values incarnated in different schools, and rationally disagree) or experts in international relations theory debating "why states cooperate" (realist, liberal, Marxist, constructivist answers will vary). In cases where you do not get different answers, where there seems to be a lot of agreement, homogeneity, or talk about consensus, at least be wary of social processes within scientific disciplines (as I will clarify below).

Representativeness, Consensus, and Hierarchy in the Social Sciences

What would representativeness mean in the social sciences? Making choices on the basis of our "major social and ethical priorities"? There are lots of choices to make and questions to be answered in shaping scientific research, as the five questions mentioned in Section 1 illustrate. However, there is quite a surprising degree of consensus or homogeneity in some of the social sciences. Does this mean "our major social and ethical priorities" are represented?

Economics, for instance, shows a remarkable amount of consensus (cf. Rodrik 2015). It is important to take sociological characteristics of the discipline into account when evaluating this consensus. Fourcade et al. (2015) document how economics is characterized by a steep internal hierarchy (referring to the significance of top five journals for rankings, hiring; networks dominated by "stars" and top departments; the governance of the discipline being highly concentrated; etc.). This creates a reinforcing loop as power concentration hampers the development of critical resources, mutual criticism, and new perspectives. The dominance of a small group of economists trained at a small selection of top departments does raise the question of whether the consensus in economics is rather the reflection of the sociological make-up of the field than evidence for high-quality knowledge or representativeness (cf. Van Bouwel 2021).

Political science is less hierarchical and less consensual than economics, according to Fourcade et al. (2015). However, just like in economics, we find critiques (often highlighting sociological characteristics) about *monocultures* arisen in top-ranked schools and journals (McNamara 2009), the *slow death of pluralism* (Phillips and Weaver 2011), the *homogenizing* effects of graduate schools (Cox 2009), and so on.[7] What would such conformity, homogeneity, and premature consensus imply for "representativeness" in political science?

Does the consensus then signal that we have "our major priorities" represented? Or, vice versa, would a lack of consensus mean that the condition of representativeness is not fulfilled? Taking the social-epistemic characteristics in economics highlighted above into account, it might be doubted that consensus signals in this case that we have "our major priorities" represented. (While having a consensus among scientists might be a marker for the reliability of certain findings if reached independently, when consensus stems from a very dominant small group of closely intertwined scientists trained at a very limited number of universities, one can question the value of that consensus.) Moreover, might this social-epistemic constellation not be constraining certain kinds of questions to be raised and interests to be addressed?

Consider, for instance, particular social groups having questions and interests that are not well represented in the majority of the population or at universities. Their questions and interests may be excluded, marginalized, or otherwise not heard in some way—in such a way that they do not exist (becoming a case of *hermeneutical injustice* in Fricker's (2007) terminology). To steer clear of that scenario, we can evaluate social-epistemic practices (in line with Section 3.3 above) by looking at (a) whether they make it difficult for certain kinds of questions and interests to be considered—the questions and interests important to particular social groups being underrepresented—as well as (b) whether they hamper (mutual) criticism of decisions about what questions and interests to consider—due to the lack of particular kinds of perspectives in conversations. (Notice that the emphasis is on lifting the social-epistemic hampering, making the invisible visible, rather than advocating that all questions and all interests should be served.)

Underrepresentation in Political Science

Let me illustrate these general epistemological points with three short examples: the first about questions in international political economy, the second about perspectives on central banking, and the third about women in political science.

Questions in international political economy (IPE). While increasing representativeness might imply more plurality, more plurality does not necessarily entail that the representativeness condition is satisfied. Let us look at an example in International Relations (IR). The *Teaching, Research, and International Policy (TRIP)* project is a rich source to study plurality and the relative weight of different approaches in IR. Collaborators of the TRIP project wrote a summary article in 2018 (cf. Maliniak et al. 2018). One of their conclusions was that TRIP "reflects a diverse discipline in which a variety of theoretical paradigms are taken seriously" (p. 475). As concerns diversity, "we outlined two specific indicators of diversity in the discipline: a broad range of topics and regions studied, and variation in theoretical, epistemological, and methodological approaches across and within countries. The TRIP data describe a discipline that is diverse in some ways—breadth of topics and regions studied and theoretical approaches to scholarly research—but less diverse in others—including epistemological and methodological approaches" (p. 471).

When looking more closely at the *variation in approaches* and *the broad range of topics and regions,* however, one has to beware of "nominal pluralization" (comparable to "nominal democratization"). While Maliniak et al. (2018) is very informative and relatively positive with respect to how diverse the field of International Relations is, I think we have to add an important aspect when analyzing the representativeness of values in IR, namely: What are the exact questions raised about those *topics and regions*? As discussed in Section 1, values influence the questions that get asked in scientific research, even if in many cases researchers might not be aware of the way values influence their decisions to specify questions in one way rather than another (and, consequently, serve the interests of some individuals, groups, or institutions rather than others). Specifying questions involves decisions on the choice of contrast,[8] the time frame, the place of relevance/application, and so on (cf. Van Bouwel 2003). Different values, interests, and aims could lead to very different questions about the same topic.

Let us, for instance, have a look at the *Global/International Political Economy* topics (representing 9.7% of all IR research) mentioned among the topics in TRIP and more specifically the analysis of globalization (understood as a phase of expansion of market capitalism resulting in an intensification of international exchanges, whether trade in goods, services, capital or people). Analyzing the way in which questions concerning globalization have been specified, there seems to be an unspoken agreement that IR works mainly for elite policymakers. Henry Farrell and Jack Knight (MS) write: "Scholars disagree over how international relations ought be useful, but largely agree about whom it ought be useful to—policy elites. This obviously makes it hard for scholars to detach themselves from elite perspectives."

Robert Keohane, one of the prominent researchers in IPE, states himself:

> Those of us who have celebrated as well as analyzed globalization share some responsibility for the rise of populism. We demonstrated that an institutional infrastructure was needed to facilitate globalization, but this infrastructure was constructed by and for economic elites. They pursued a path of action favored by academics such as [Keohane himself and Joseph Nye], building multilateral institutions to promote cooperation, but they built these institutions in a biased way. Global finance and global business had a privileged status, and there was little regard for the interests of ordinary workers. (2016)

Keohane acknowledges that IR scholars might have contributed directly to the plight of the liberal order.

Thus, in formulating and specifying their research questions about globalization, the unspoken consensus within IR scholarship (in particular IPE) seems to have been to align questions with the interests and aims of elite policymakers. This raises questions of representativeness because interests and concerns of important constituencies, of "ordinary people" or actors other than elites, are not represented. I return to this IPE example in Section 6.

The social-epistemic constellation of the study of central banks. Let us look at a second example taken from political economy. While the former example focused on neglected questions and interests, this one zooms in on a lack of plurality of well-developed perspectives. Dietsch, Claveau, and Fontan (2018) document how major central banks became dominant in the world-wide central bank-related research community, and this centrality of central banks is worrisome: "Since they control much of the material resources and symbolic capital, we have reason to suspect that research is skewed and that some types of criticism are muted in comparison to an alternative social context where testimonial expertise on central banking would be more broadly shared." (p. 87) On the one hand, it is positive that central banks participate in the research community, because one wants (a) the topics that are actively researched to be aligned with the interests of practitioners; (b) open channels of communication for research critical of consensual beliefs of bankers to reach their ears; and (c) the data and practical knowledge of the regulatory experts that can inform research (cf. Dietsch et al. 2018: 90).

506 JEROEN VAN BOUWEL

On the other hand, the (steadily growing) dominance of central banks inside the research community hampers mutual criticism (to challenge and modify any beliefs and values they may hold), both the amount of criticism as well as its variety. For researchers working at the central bank, there is the risk of direct censure and career considerations that might inhibit criticism or make radical criticism less likely. For researchers working at other institutions, there are different incentives: having your work recognized by central banks has become a marker of expertise; there is evidence that expressing strong criticism can end up with being side-lined by central banks; and, collaborators of central banks are also often gatekeepers in academia, *inter alia*, of journals. That concerns the amount of criticism. Next, looking at the variety of criticism, we notice low diversity within the community, not only along the gender dimension and qua ethnicity, but also qua professional (often having worked for major financial firms) and theoretical backgrounds (overwhelmingly trained in mainstream economics). Dietsch et al. write: "This uniformity of perspective is a significant reason for the myopia of the central banking community in the years leading to the great financial crisis" (2018: 95, also see Fligstein et al. 2017; Riles 2018 for similar findings on the uniformity of perspective). They conclude that a community lacking well-developed alternative perspectives, hampering mutual criticism in this way "does not optimally serve the people" (p. 99). We could also add that it raises serious questions about representativeness.

Women in political science. For a third short example of how certain kinds of questions and interests are being constrained due to social-epistemic practices, one can look at the underrepresentation of women in political science. Examining the social-epistemic constellation of the field, one observes a high ratio of men to women in important positions in political science and most subfields being clearly male-dominated (see, e.g., Shames and Wise 2017; Engeli and Mügge 2020). This gender imbalance, as well as women facing an unwelcoming environment (cf. Mazur 2012; Chapter 23 in this volume), *(a)* make it less likely that the concerns and questions of women are heard in political science research meaning that the interests of half of society often fail to be considered in determining in what direction political science research has to be developed; and, *(b)* limit the quality and scope of mutual criticism in the discipline as a unique and valuable perspective remains underrepresented.

Reconsidering Representativeness

A significant representation of dissenting perspectives is important for mutual criticism as Longino notes: "A diversity of perspectives is necessary for vigorous and epistemically effective critical discourse. The social position or economic power of an individual or group in a community ought not determine who or what perspectives are taken seriously in that community. . . . The point of the requirement is to ensure the exposure of hypotheses to the broadest range of criticism. . . . Not only must potentially dissenting voices not be discounted; they must be cultivated" (2002: 131–132). Increasing the number of perspectives that interact critically—exercise mutual criticism—raises the number of ways that knowledge can be challenged and tested. Considering the importance of critical interaction between well-developed alternative perspectives, as articulated by Longino, we must conclude that political science foregoes important opportunities of mutual criticism by leaving important questions and challenging perspectives underdeveloped and underutilized. Incorporating more different, diverse perspectives increases the range and effectiveness of critical interaction in the discipline, positively affecting group decisions and deliberations, as empirical research has been backing up (see, e.g., Page 2007; Intemann 2009; Phillips 2017).

Thus, changing the distribution of perspectives (including values and power) within the discipline seems to be key to improve the collective epistemic outcome. Ensuring social-epistemic practices that are open to a variety of different interests, questions, and goals is important for both the one being represented as well as for the one not being represented (with respect to a particular value)—there is a common interest to optimize mutual criticism (in the sense that it benefits both overrepresented and underrepresented perspectives).

4.3 Concerns about the Representativeness Condition

Elliott's idea that the values brought into science "should be representative of our major social and ethical priorities" is ambiguous. Following the reasoning I developed in section 4.2, I suggest modifying Elliott's stipulation of representativeness. In discussing representativeness in social science, we notice quite some variation in what "our major priorities" are, more so than Elliott acknowledges. Thus, rather than "our major priorities," it seems important that the questions, values, and interests of diverse sets of the population are represented—some of which are clearly underrepresented and hampered in political science nowadays. Second, to assure optimal mutual criticism—also of the value influences present in the respective perspectives—we should take into account the makeup of the discipline as a whole and ensure that a range of diverse approaches or perspectives is being sufficiently developed, not being hampered. So, a focus on the distribution of perspectives is imperative.[9] Not ensuring substantial mutual criticism (or transformative criticism as Longino calls it) or not representing a range of important questions implies an epistemic loss, a suboptimal collective epistemic outcome. Moreover, this mutual criticism could also affect what we understand as "our priorities," and it could modify what we consider as most valuable, what turns out to be "false needs" or what values do not stand the test of being held accountable to available evidence.

5. Social-Epistemic Practices and Pluralism in Political Science

Modifying the condition of *representativeness* in the way I have suggested in Section 4, might raise worries. Would it not lead to some form of extreme relativism? Would an alignment of values between certain scientific approaches or perspectives and certain groups of citizens not eventually result in a number of isolated research approaches—each consisting of a particular scientific community teamed up with likeminded stakeholders—that are not engaging any longer with each other because any scientific disagreement might be explained away as a difference in value judgment or in epistemic interest? Here as well we should focus on social-epistemic practices to consider how plurality goes hand in hand with some form of productive interaction among different approaches or perspectives.[10]

In earlier work, I developed the idea that the interaction between different approaches can be made explicit in terms of models of democracy, focusing on three models in particular: *consensual deliberative democracy*, *agonistic pluralism*, and *antagonism*. Using these models of democracy helps us to clarify different ideals about the interaction—the social-epistemic practices—among the plurality of research approaches (considering the plurality of values and representativeness). I argued that it is the *agonistic confrontation* that brings about the desired (epistemically) productive interaction between a plurality of approaches, rather than *consensual deliberation* or *unproductive antagonism* (cf. Van Bouwel 2015). In order to avoid antagonism, there is a need for a *common symbolic space* and for *agonistic channels* to express grievances and dissent, to deal with conflicts through agonistic confrontation (cf. Mouffe 2005). Lack of those tends to create the conditions for the emergence of antagonism.

Now, how could we understand the idea of *agonistic channels* in science? Let me suggests at least four arenas: (a) making explanation-seeking questions explicit, i.e., specifying research questions within a common symbolic space when debating what is the better explanation; you learn about the respective epistemic interests, the underlying values and you make disagreement explicit as well as debate which values are legitimate (cf. Van Bouwel 2014); (b) citizen engagement with science (cf. Van Bouwel and Van Oudheusden 2017); (c) joint symposia; (d) scientific journals.

Let us consider here how scientific journals could work as agonistic channels and return to the DA-RT discussion in political science. There exists an APSA-journal called *Perspectives on Politics* that was started up in 2003 in response to Mr. Perestroika (a movement of researchers calling for more pluralism in political science). In Section 2.1, I mentioned the 2014 *Journal Editors' Transparency Statement* (JETS). The (then) editor of the journal *Perspectives on Politics*, Jeffrey Isaac, did not sign JETS, considering it a threat to pluralism and writing that the journal "was the hard-won achievement of a coalition of academic political scientists seeking greater openness and pluralism within the discipline," an example of keeping the agonistic channels open.

Isaac is not arguing against transparency, but rather questioning whether a lack of transparency is really the main problem contemporary political science faces and whether imposing the new norms of transparency may come at a cost to taking intellectual risks in tackling interesting and important questions. Isaac writes:

> The one-size-fits-all expectations articulated in the DA–RT statement do not fit much of what *Perspectives on Politics* publishes. The strong prescriptivism of the statement is too heavy-handed to suit our journal's eclecticism. Perhaps most importantly, our journal operates on a distinctive epistemic premise: that the primary "problem" with political science research today is not that there needs to be more replicable research, "replication studies," and specialized inquiries, but that there needs to be broader discussions, and research projects, that center on ideas that are interesting and important. (2015: 276)

Isaac advocates for a political science that is driven by what is interesting, what are the important questions, rather than by applying a preferred method or strictly abiding by DA-RT prescriptions. Isaac's plea resonates with my understanding of the representativeness condition as he emphasizes the importance of political science addressing "public concerns, public interests, and public groups to which political science speaks and ought to speak" (2015: 277). He writes that what political science most needs now is "new and interesting work that speaks to the real political concerns facing the students we teach—and most of us spend most of our professional time teaching students—and the world in which we live" (2015: 277). The emphasis on real political concerns and currently neglected research questions rather than on DA-RT does not imply that it necessarily comes at the cost of transparency. Transparency might be brought about through mutual criticism in a social-epistemic constellation like the one sketched above following Longino's work, rather than through a list of DA-RT rules that according to Isaac produces professional narrowness and intellectual exclusion. The picture that arises is one of a question-driven scientific pluralism that is keeping the agonistic channels open to avoid ending up with a number of isolated, noninteracting research approaches as well as enabling interaction between approaches to illuminate value-laden aspects of scientific practice and to consider how best to deal with them.

A last issue that remains for Isaac is: How will we decide what the public concerns and the important research questions are? Isaac invokes the work of John Dewey to tackle this issue: "how should political scientists, and political science as an organized discipline, relate to—speak to, but also listen to—the complex and power-infused world that it both inhabits and take as its object of study?" (2015: 277). Dewey himself called for a lively and continuing dialogue between social scientists and the general public, writing that the shoemaker knows how to make a shoe, but it is the public who knows where the shoe pinches. Such a continuing dialogue between social scientists and the public about what the questions should be, what convincing evidence is available to answer them as well as why some values would be more important than others would require a political science discipline that is not standing apart from society. This brings us to Kevin Elliott's third condition, scrutinizing value influences through *engagement* between different stakeholders.

6. THE ENGAGEMENT CONDITION

6.1 General Questions about the Engagement Condition

The general idea of Elliott's engagement condition is that value influences in science be scrutinized by engaging with a wide variety of stakeholders; other scientists, but also citizens, communities, policymakers, and so on, to identify value-laden aspects of science and consider how to deal with them. Elliott writes:

> By "engagement," I mean efforts to interact with other people or institutions in order to exchange views, highlight problems, deliberate, and foster positive change. Four forms of engagement appear to be particularly promising . . . each . . . can help to highlight the ways that values are explicitly or implicitly influencing science. They also provide opportunities to challenge or critique value influences that run counter to people's needs and priorities. Finally, they provide opportunities to reflect on the values that would better serve social needs and to incorporate those values in scientific practice. (2017: 138)

The four forms of engagement Elliott distinguishes are: (1) Bottom-up initiatives, where citizens or community groups take the initiative to engage with scientists; (2) top-down initiatives, where there is a formal exercise engaging the public to give input (about important value judgments in science); (3) interdisciplinary engagement between scientists with diverse backgrounds; and, (4) engagement with institutions, laws, policies that structure the practice of scientific research. General questions we should raise here are: How are these forms actually realized in practice and when can they be considered successful? Due to space constraints, I address these questions only with respect to forms (1) and (2) in political science.

6.2 The Engagement Condition in Political Science

Bottom-Up Initiatives

When Elliott (2017) discusses the benefits of bottom-up engagement, he refers to the many interesting initiatives that are part of so-called *citizen science*—a thriving area. It is important to emphasize that *citizen science* is more than citizens (merely) contributing by, e.g., counting birds, with agendas mainly set by scientists and citizens just helping out. It can also be conceived as a (sometimes collaborative, sometimes oppositional) dialogue between scientists and citizens in which scientists are expected to be responsive to citizens' questions and critiques.

Citizen science in this latter understanding could involve: (a) original research questions grown directly out of the questions and concerns of citizens; (b) identifying relevant variables and sources of data, informed by local knowledge, that professional scientists would miss; (c) using innovative methods, including DIY instruments; and, (d) citizens' questions and methods that often, implicitly or explicitly, challenge the adequacy of standard scientific approaches or point at important research left undone (cf. Cavalier and Kennedy 2016). Hence, this citizen engagement explicates and questions (often implicit) value influences in current scientific research as well as diversifies the values that inform scientific inquiry. It makes science more open and deliberate about its own values.

There are many good examples to be found of bottom-up citizen science initiatives, e.g., in the environmental sciences—think of local communities aiming to address public health concerns related to environmental pollution. In political science, however, citizen-led bottom-up initiatives by which citizens bring up new research questions for political scientists to answer or question certain value influences dominant in current research—similar to what we see in environmental science—are hard to find. One would think discrepancies between the lived experience and the official narratives—backed up by political scientists—could be used to question research and/or make dominant values explicit. It happens somewhat in economics, e.g., the student organization *Rethinking Economics* or *The Economy* (ecnmy.org, a British charity) highlighting the shortcomings of current economics and the disconnect between economics and the public (and its problems). We might see more of it in political science in the future.

Top-Down Initiatives

A second form of citizen engagement highlighted by Elliott (2017) are so-called top-down initiatives. Typical examples are citizen summits, consensus conferences, future panels, and scenario workshops. These are exercises or formats set up by scientists, governmental organizations, and others that aim to foster a dialogue between the citizens and scientists to elicit public input on scientific issues and to scrutinize value influences in current science. As we have mentioned above, there have recently been calls for more engagement and dialogue between political scientists and the public. Isaac (2015), for instance, wrote about the importance of addressing the real political concerns we are facing in today's world. Citizen engagement seems to be one option to find out about what important questions the public wants to see addressed (and what questions have been neglected by political science), but how to establish this engagement?

In order to address this question in political science, let us consider the proposals of Farrell and Knight (2019, MS). They refer to the comments of Keohane (quoted above in Section 4) about the little regard for the interests of ordinary workers in International Political Economy (IPE) and they search for better ways to engage the public. Inspired by Dewey, they are calling for *a continuing dialogue* between social scientists and the public (cf. Isaac above). This call for more dialogue is part of a larger change of direction suggested by Farrell and Knight as an answer to IPE having "missed" the upsurge of political populism. According to them, a better IPE would require a reorientation in which IR scholars: **(a)** no longer solely identify with elite perspectives; **(b)** widen their perspectives, investigating the hidden interdependencies that shape social and political life; **(c)** engage in a dialogue with broader –existing and nascent– publics serving a variety of interests and values.

(a) The first suggestion is to dissociate from the elite perspective on the world economy— an exclusive perspective that is no longer tenable. It boils down to questioning the value influences in the existing approaches in IR. These approaches typically analyze international institutions and policies of global openness mostly in terms of efficiency and overall wellbeing, while ignoring distributional issues, the public's perceptions of fairness, the citizens' sense of financial vulnerability, and so on. Questioning these particular value influences, scholars could go beyond identifying solely with elites, also identifying with and listening to publics that are cut out of decision-making. According to Farrell and Knight, this would entail, e.g., doing more research on the consequences of globalization for the fabric of domestic communities, or on the consequences of free movement of global capital for taxation and domestic corruption. In short, to interrogate what has been mostly occluded both by existing approaches and the elite consensus they inform.

(b) A second suggestion stipulates what kind of knowledge political scientists should be looking for. According to Farrell and Knight (MS), mainstream IPE has given rise to "a body of theory that starts from abstract claims rather than the material circumstances of interdependence; a set of claims that justify rather than interrogate existing arrangements, truncate democracy where it conflicts with the presumed benefits of international institutions and trade liberalization, and are badly suited to grappling with the power relations and inequality that globalization have given rise to; all these help explain why international political economy has lost touch with the problems of ordinary people." Following Dewey, they suggest a different account of the role and responsibilities of political scientists. Instead of starting from posited abstract rules and general laws, political scientists should elucidate the complex causal relationships of interdependence, making

visible otherwise obscured interdependencies that shape our lives. As such, political science makes itself "useful by providing an understanding of the complex webs of interdependence, their implications, and (once needs have been initially identified), the best ways to solve them. This will be useful to publics—both nascent publics that might not identify their common interests at all, were it not for the initial impetus of grounded and accessible social science research, and existing publics, whom social scientists ought engage in a continuing dialogue where goals and the best means to achieve those goals are defined and redefined in response to experience." (Farrell and Knight, MS)

(c) This brings us to a third aspect of Farrell and Knight's reorientation, namely the need for direct engagement with broader publics, serving a variety of interests and values. The role of IR scholars is not only to inform the public on the basis of their expertise, to provide precise knowledge about interdependencies through which new publics may come into being,[11] but also to engage in a dialogue with the publics to become informed about the practical problems they experience. Learning about the problems different publics face through dialogue, scholars can fold these back into their research and think through institutional changes that could address these problems linked to the interdependencies of action. Following Dewey, scholars should see themselves as engaged in a continuing dialogue, a fundamentally democratic project in which all participate to the full extent of their abilities in identifying and effectively solving problems: "The commitment to problem-solving and experimentation entails a deep commitment to power equality and to *democratic* forms of problem-solving that map directly onto the problems of interdependence and the publics they give rise to. In this way, Dewey's normative conclusions follow directly from the logic of his explanatory goals." (Farrell and Knight, MS) It requires attention to the asymmetries of power that might hinder participation and thus distort experimentation as well as dissociation from exclusive elitist interests and values. Thus, through the dialogue with broader publics, a pragmatist IPE is capable of serving a variety of interests and values.

This ambitious agenda definitely deserves our attention (not in the least because it pays explicit attention to dealing with values). The question that remains somewhat underdeveloped at the moment (in comparison with formats we see in other scientific disciplines), however, is how exactly Farrell and Knight envision implementing the idea of a continuing dialogue in political science. They give us some hints, recognizing that there are few existing institutions that support that kind of dialogue at the moment, but there are historical precedents:

> An earlier model of expertise sought to 'educate citizens no less than to advise policymakers' through institutions such as *the Foreign Policy Association*, the *Institute of Pacific Relations*, and even (in its earlier incarnation) the *Council on Foreign Relations*, engaging with a variety of communities across the United States. However, it has fallen nearly completely moribund among international relations scholars. Were this model to be revived in the modern era, it could build on newer communicative opportunities, such as the *Monkey Cage* blog at the *Washington Post*, to reach broad audiences and to supplement more direct forms of public conversation. It could also engage with other nascent publics, such as the *Black Lives Matter*

movement, which has started to craft its own understanding of the global economy and how it affects the lives of African-Americans. (Farrell and Knight, MS)

Such a dialogue does not need to be restricted to groups on the left, of course, the pragmatist commitment is to democracy and equality of voice, rather than to particular voices within democracy. Nor does it mean that scholars should become activists. Rather it means "that they need to engage directly in public debate so as to elucidate and *publicly* explain the 'intricate network of interactions' through which human actions have complex consequences, as well as learning what people actually believe and are concerned with." (Farrell and Knight, MS)

Considering the Benefits

Let me articulate three takeaways from the citizen science literature which could advance a dialogue and are worth taking into account when evaluating citizen engagement in political science (especially in relation to dealing with value influences). They concern (a) scientific literacy and the deficit model, (b) the epistemic productivity of the dialogue model, and, (c) legitimacy.

(a) Scientific literacy and the deficit model. Farrell and Knight (2019) mention Jessica Green's (2018) call for a problem-and-public focused approach to international relations as a parallel argument to their own. Green argues that

> public engagement should be recognized as part of our roles as teachers and scholars. Making complex ideas readily digestible for a lay audience is perhaps the most difficult kind of teaching, one that should be acknowledged not only as a public service, but also as evidence of excellence in teaching. Being an advocate and an expert should not be mutually exclusive. (Green 2018)

While it is undoubtedly beneficial to increase the scientific literacy of the public and decrease the gap between experts and citizens, it is important to highlight that the literature on citizen engagement has moved beyond the so-called deficit model. Engagement should not just be about figuring out ways to get the public to listen better to experts and coming to agree with scientists. Moreover, increased literacy does not necessarily imply increased agreement with dominant views of scientists, see e.g. Yale's cultural cognition project.

In Lupia and Aldrich (2015), a report of the APSA task force to improve communication with the public, the emphasis is very much on amplifying the voice of political scientists, not on interaction or dialogue with the public. Their view rings through in how they understand political science: "Political science as a corporate entity engages in two principal tasks: the creation of knowledge and the dissemination of knowledge." (2015: 1) A view in which the discipline is standing apart from society with the public consuming the knowledge political science disseminates, rather than being engaged or co-creating. The citizen science literature criticizes this too unidirectional model and suggests more productive models.

(b) Epistemic productivity of the dialogue model. Rather than a deficit model, Farrell and Knight aim for a dialogue model, in which scientists engage more directly with the public to find out what the important questions are as well as to develop perspectives different from

the elitist one. First, the dialogue engenders new questions; the engagement of citizens can help to specify a particular question or problem in more accurate ways than scientists alone; citizens—and their lived experience—most affected by certain political problems are well-placed to provide relevant information and explicate important questions. Second, the dialogue also decreases the risks of conformism and premature consensus, actively cultivates alternative perspectives, and changes the distribution of perspectives which makes the social-epistemic constellation more conducive for critical interaction (improving the collective epistemic outcome).

(c) Legitimacy. Besides increased epistemic productivity, a positive impact on the legitimacy of the discipline (lowering skepticism and mistrust) is often being invoked. This is also part of the project of Farrell and Knight who refer to a legitimacy crisis: "International relations—and in particular international political economy (IPE)—is undergoing a legitimacy crisis. This crisis has been precipitated by surging economic populism and the associated threat to the approach's core understanding of global politics." Problems of legitimacy can, for instance, appear when there is a too large discrepancy between the political science dominant narrative on globalization and the lived experience of citizens. Heather Douglas (2017: 91-92) writes: "social and ethical values legitimately shape the attention of scientists to certain topics or questions. But if what scientists care about asking does not align with what members of the public care about knowing, statements based on the findings can be greeted with skepticism, because the public thinks the scientists are not answering the crucial questions." . . . "The values of those citizens and the values of the scientists are not aligning, producing skepticism about what scientists are reporting." Sorting out these value conflicts is one of the promises of citizen engagement in science. Citizens might point at "conflicts of interest", e.g. scientists mainly being theory- or method-driven in their research, tackling questions that fit into their favorite theory or method.[12] Citizens might advance questions that are more broadly shared by other citizens; they might open up to new angles, possessing some advantages over professional scientists as they might be more aware of existing realities in specific social communities, and so on.

The advocates of DA-RT claim that following the DA-RT guidelines will also help political science to achieve legitimacy (cf. Lupia and Elman 2014). In that case, legitimacy is linked to following the prescribed rules for research transparency. However, there is no consideration whether the political scientists actually address questions citizens want to see addressed (the research agenda is decided by experts, the value influences as highlighted by Elliott are not acknowledged), so it is questionable whether DA-RT provides us with a satisfactory answer to the problem Douglas pointed at in the previous paragraph.

6.3 Concerns about the Engagement Condition

Although there are some initiatives and promises as discussed above, citizen engagement is clearly less developed in political science in comparison to other disciplines. Examples in other sciences show how citizen engagement helps identify neglected questions, reveal implicit values, question established assumptions, suggest alternatives, reduce the gap between scientists and citizens, and so on. However, a lot of open questions remain concerning engagement as a strategy of dealing with values in science. For instance: When is the engagement condition satisfied? When have we sufficiently engaged stakeholders in scrutinizing value influences? Who has (not) to be engaged? Who interprets the views of the citizens, of the ones being engaged with? Would all views count just as heavily? When can we say the engagement exercise is completed? These are big questions and a generalizable model for engagement does not seem in sight. One way forward, it seems to me—and well in line with Dewey's penchant for experimentation—is to scrutinize concrete formats of engagement and see how they tackle these questions, e.g., NIH consensus conferences, participatory technology assessments (NanoSoc) or the deliberative workshops of the Citizens' Economic Council, investigating the social-epistemic dynamics, how they decide on group composition, what are the strengths and weaknesses of the respective formats with respect to different purposes, and so on (see, e.g., Van Bouwel and Van Oudheusden 2017).

7. CONCLUSION

We have discussed three different ways of dealing with values in science. A first one emphasizes that scientists need to acknowledge and be transparent about value influences, a second one that value judgments should be made in a responsible manner representative of society's values, and, a third one that citizens should be engaged to critically reflect on the values being used. For each of these three—Elliott's conditions—we have seen different ways of understanding and implementing them, general questions that should be raised and concerns to be dealt with.

Value influences are unavoidably present, even if often very subtly, in the questions scientists ask, assumptions underlying their analyses, choices of methods, standards of evidence for drawing conclusions, or the communication of their results. Rather than denying these value influences, we'd better try to make them explicit, so we can acknowledge, criticize, and develop ways to deal with them. This will also help identifying value influences that are illegitimate or insupportable.

In developing ways to deal with value influences, I emphasized the importance of taking the social-epistemic constellation of scientific communities into account. To critically evaluate value influences, I argued for focusing on social-epistemic practices and norms to be applied in scientific communities, rather than on (the virtues of) individual scientists—the individual scientist that acknowledges value influences risks losing credibility, while a community with the right social-epistemic constellation might both assure scientific pluralism and maintain scientific objectivity.

Specifically for political science, in discussing contemporary debates like DA-RT, I illustrated how a strategy of dealing with values, the *transparency* requirement, might play out in scientific practice and have an impact on the diversity of questions and perspectives as well as the power distribution within a discipline. It is interesting to see how political scientists –scholars of power negotiations and democracy– organize their debates about these impacts. As philosophers of science are paying attention to the social and political as well as to (dispersing) power in analyzing ways of dealing with values, political scientists might weigh in. Philosophers can learn a lot from them.

The discussion of *citizen engagement* and *representativeness* also taught us that including diverse perspectives might not be merely *politically* motivated, i.e., the inclusion resulting in a greater understanding of the broad spectrum of human needs, desires, and important questions, but it can also be motivated *epistemically* because it improves the collective epistemic outcome. Failing to include is then not only a political injustice, but also an epistemic failure. However, some understandings of *representativeness* and *transparency* do not cultivate diverse perspectives, hamper scientific pluralism and prevent us from getting the best—epistemically most productive—out of political science as shown by the examples in this chapter.

Lastly, in the study of politics, science's role might be considered, e.g., in discussing the merits of technocratic government. When bringing in science in the political discourse, understanding different ways of dealing with value influences often becomes central, just as is the role of the scientist/expert in dialogue (or not) with the public. Hopefully, the discussion of Elliott's strategies of dealing with values is helpful for political scientists in this respect too, and, more generally, advances the debates about the social-epistemic set-up of science and society.

ACKNOWLEDGMENTS

I would like to thank Mark Brown, Harold Kincaid, Amy Mazur and the participants in the *PoPS Handbook* workshop at Washington State University (September 2019) for their comments and valuable feedback on an earlier version of this chapter.

NOTES

1. Value influences are also being discussed with respect to, inter alia, *data collection* (Zahle 2018) and *measurement* (Kincaid 2007; Reiss 2017). Let me furthermore add the definitions of *value* and *value judgement* Elliott (2017) works with: "Broadly speaking, a value is something that is desirable or worthy of pursuit." (p. 11); "Value judgements are scientific choices that cannot be decided solely by appealing to evidence and logic." (p. 12).
2. Besides the questions about incompatibility with epistemological diversity, DA-RT also raised questions about ethical, legal, financial and practical aspects or constraints under which many researchers have to work. One can wonder about how to achieve transparency while meeting ethical and legal obligations to protect human subjects, for instance, in cases where clandestine political opponents in an authoritarian regime inform one's research. Financially, questions arise about how the costs associated with archiving some forms of evidence would affect research(ers). Here, I focus on the epistemological aspects of DA-RT drawing on Van Bouwel (2021).
3. I question in the first place the transparency condition as understood by the DA-RT initiative here, a condition that is stipulated in an Ethics Guide. However, one could value transparency without seeing a need for DA-RT; transparency might perhaps be brought about by social interaction or mutual criticism (cf. below). The latter might then be more epistemologically neutral, or, at least, less hampering.

4. I write *important* journals as there is a social-epistemic constellation to be taken into account in which there is a hierarchy between journals. I return to the impact of hierarchy when discussing representativeness in Section 4.

5. See, for instance, the striking epistemic impact of the introduction of standardized quality evaluation exercises (e.g. Pardo-Guerra 2020 showing how these exercises made the British social sciences more homogeneous and epistemically less diverse).

6. I am supposing here that Elliott discusses his representativeness idea in the context of a democratic society.

7. These examples are taken from a lively debate about the future of International Political Economy (cf. Phillips and Weaver 2011). It is interesting to see how many contributors to this debate focus on the interplay between the sociological and the epistemic, i.e., the hierarchy among scholarly journals, graduate schools, disciplinary associations and their epistemic impact on the choice of methods, research questions, the openness to input from outside, etc.

8. When specifying explanation-seeking questions, we do not simply ask "Why f?" but rather "Why f rather than c?" We choose a contrast class. This insight is often illustrated by an anecdote regarding the bank robber Willie Sutton. When asked why he robbed banks, Sutton replied: "Because that's where the money is." While the questioner might have had the following question in mind: "Why do you rob banks, rather than leading an honest life?" Sutton answered a question with a different contrast class: "Why do you rob banks, rather than ice cream parlors or grocery stores?"

9. It does not mean that the distribution of perspectives within the scientific community is the only issue to pay attention to; reliable methods for evidence gathering and analysis are obviously important too. The point is rather that the value of contributions of individual scientists applying reliable methods also depends on the make-up of the community, therefore it is imperative to analyze how certain social-epistemic constellations hamper scientific pluralism.

10. *Epistemically productive* is being understood here in terms of our capacity to answer our questions effectively, i.e. answering important questions in the best way possible as well as minimizing epistemic loss.

11. "to become a true public, those actors who are indirectly affected by a given set of consequences need to be informed about it. A lively intelligence about their situation and shared interests translates an inchoate grouping of people into a public—an organized entity that can reason collectively about its shared interests and how to promote them" (Farrell and Knight, MS).

12. The conflicts of interests and value conflicts between scientists and citizens raise a series of interesting questions, e.g., to what extent scientists in a more democratically organised science might be asked to support values or political causes they may personally oppose, see Schroeder (2017).

References

APSA Committee on Professional Ethics, Rights and Freedoms (2012). *A Guide to Professional Ethics in Political Science*. The American Political Science Association.

Brigandt, I. 2015. "Social values influence the adequacy conditions of scientific theories: Beyond inductive risk." *Canadian Journal of Philosophy* 45(3): 326–356.

Cavalier, D. and E. Kennedy (eds.) 2016. *The Rightful Place of Science: Citizen Science.* CSPO.

Cox, R. 2009. "The 'British School' in the global context." *New Political Economy* 14(3): 315–328.

Dietsch, P., Claveau, F. and C. Fontan. 2018. *Do central banks serve the people?* Polity.

Douglas, H. 2009. *Science, Policy, and the Value-Free Ideal.* University of Pittsburgh Press.

Douglas, H. 2017. "Science, Values, and Citizens." In: M. Adams, Z. Biener, U. Feest and J. Sullivan (eds.) *Oppur Si Muove: Doing History and Philosophy of Science with Peter Machamer.* Springer, pp. 83–96.

Elliott, K. 2017. *A Tapestry of Values: An Introduction to Values in Science.* Oxford University Press.

Elliott, K., A. McCright, S. Allen, T. Dietz. 2017. "Values in environmental research: Citizens' views of scientists who acknowledge values" *PLOS ONE* 12(10): e0186049.

Engeli, I. and L. Mügge.2020. "Patterns of Gender Inequality in European Political Science." In: T. Boncourt, I. Engeli, and D. Garzia (eds.) *Political Science in Europe: Achievements, Challenges, Prospects.* Rowman & Littlefield, pp. 179–198.

Farrell, H. and J. Knight. 2019. "How Political Science Can Be Most Useful." *The Chronicle of Higher Education*(March 10). Washington DC: The Chronicle of Higher Education Inc. https://www.chronicle.com/article/How-Political-Science-Can-Be/245852.

Farrell, H. and J. Knight. MS. "Reconstructing International Political Economy: A Deweyan Approach." Unpublished Paper.

Fligstein, N., J. Stuart Brundage and M. Schultz. 2017. "Seeing Like the Fed: Culture, Cognition, and Framing in the Failure to Anticipate the Financial Crisis of 2008." *American Sociological Review* 82(5): 879–909.

Fourcade, M., E. Ollion, and Y. Algan. 2015. "The Superiority of Economists." *Journal of Economic Perspectives* 29(1): 89–114.

Fricker, M. 2007. *Epistemic Injustice: Power and the Ethics of Knowing.* Oxford University Press.

Green, J. 2018. "Why We Need a More Activist Academy." In: *The Chronicle of Higher Education.* Washington DC: The Chronicle of Higher Education Inc. https://www.chronicle.com/article/why-we-need-a-more-activist-academy/.

Intemann, K. 2009. "Why diversity matters: Understanding and applying the diversity component of the NSF's broader impacts criterion." *Social Epistemology* 23(3-4): 249–266.

Isaac, J. 2015. "For a More *Public* Political Science." *Perspectives on Politics* 13(2): 269–283.

Keohane, R. O. 2016. *International Institutions in an Era of Populism, Nationalism, and Diffusion of Power.* The Warren and Anita Manshel Lecture in American Foreign Policy, Harvard University. Available at: https://wcfia.harvard.edu/lectureships/manshel/2016/transcript (2016).

Kincaid, H. 2007. "Contextualist Morals and Science." In: Kincaid, H., J. Dupré, and A. Wylie (eds) *Value-Free Science? Ideals and Illusions.* Oxford University Press, pp. 218–238.

Kreuzer, M. and C. Parsons. 2018. *Epistemological and Ontological Priors: Varieties of Explicitness and Research Integrity. Final Report of QTD Working Group I.1, Subgroup 1.* APSA Section for Qualitative and Multi-Method Research. (on www.qualtd.net).

Leonelli, S. 2018. "Re-Thinking Reproducibility as a Criterion for Research Quality." *Research in the History of Economic Thought and Methodology* 36: 129–146.

Longino, H. 2002. *The Fate of Knowledge.* Princeton University Press.

Lupia, A. and C. Elman. 2014. "Openness in Political Science: Data Access and Research Transparency: Introduction" *PS: Political Science and Politics* 47(1): 19–42.

Lupia, A. and J. Aldrich. 2015. "How Political Science Can Better Communicate Its Value: 12 Recommendations from the APSA Task Force." *PS: Political Science and Politics* 48(S1): 1–19.

Maliniak, D., S. Peterson, R. Powers and M. Tierney. 2018. "Is International Relations a Global Discipline? Hegemony, Insularity, and Diversity in the Field." *Security Studies* 27(3): 448–484.

Mazur, A. 2012. "A Feminist Empirical and Integrative Approach in Political Science: Breaking Down the Glass Wall?" In: H. Kincaid (ed.) *The Oxford Handbook of Philosophy of Social Science*. Oxford University Press, pp. 533–558.

McMullin, E. 1983. "Values in science." In: P. Asquith and T. Nickles (eds.) *Proceedings of the 1982 Biennial Meeting of the Philosophy of Science Association*. Philosophy of Science Association, pp. 3–28.

McNamara, K. 2009. "Of intellectual monocultures and the study of IPE." *Review of International Political Economy* 16(1): 72–84.

Monroe, K. R. 2018. "The Rush to Transparency: DA-RT and the Potential Dangers for Qualitative Research." *Perspectives on Politics* 16(1): 141–148.

Mouffe, C. 2005. *On the Political*. Routledge.

Nagel, E. 1961. *The Structure of Science: Problems in the Logic of Scientific Explanation*. Harcourt.

Page, S. 2007. *The Difference: How the Power of Diversity Creates Better Groups, Firms, Schools, and Societies*. Princeton University Press.

Pardo-Guerra, J. P. 2020. "Research Metrics, Labor Markets, and Epistemic Change: Evidence from Britain, 1970–2018." *SocArxiv*. doi: 10.31235/osf.io/yzkfu.

Penders, B., J. Holbrook and S. De Rijcke 2019. "Rinse and repeat: understanding the value of replication across different ways of knowing." *Publications* 7(52): 1–15.

Phillips, N. and C. Weaver (eds.) 2011. *International Political Economy. Debating the Past, Present and Future*. Routledge.

Phillips, K. 2017. "What Is the Real Value of Diversity in Organizations? Questioning Our Assumptions." In: S. Page (ed.) *The Diversity Bonus: How Great Teams Pay Off in the Knowledge Economy*. Princeton University Press, pp. 223–245.

Reiss, J. 2017. "Fact-Value Entanglement in Positive Economics." *Journal of Economic Methodology* 24(2): 134–149.

Reiss, J. 2019. "Expertise, Agreement, and the Nature of Social Scientific Facts or: Against Epistocracy." *Social Epistemology* 33(2): 183–192.

Riles, A. 2018. *Financial Citizenship. Experts, Publics, and the Politics of Central Banking*. Cornell University Press.

Rodrik, D. 2015. *Economics Rules: The Rights and Wrongs of the Dismal Science*. W.W. Norton.

Rooney, Ph. 1992. "On values in science: Is the epistemic/non-epistemic distinction useful?" In: D. Hull, M. Forbes, and K. Okruhlik (eds.) *Proceedings of the 1992 biennial meeting of the Philosophy of Science Association*. Philosophy of Science Association, vol. 2, pp. 13–22.

Schroeder, A. 2017. "Using Democratic Values in Science: An Objection and (Partial) Response." *Philosophy of Science* 84(5): 1044–1054.

Shames, S. and T. Wise. 2017. "Gender, Diversity, and Methods in Political Science: A Theory of Selection and Survival Biases." *PS: Political Science & Politics* 50(3): 811–823.

Van Bouwel, J. 2003 *Verklaringspluralisme in de sociale wetenschappen*. (Ph.D. thesis, Ghent University.)

Van Bouwel, J. 2009. "The Problem with(out) Consensus. The Scientific Consensus, Deliberative Democracy and Agonistic Pluralism." In: J. Van Bouwel (ed.) *The Social Sciences and Democracy*. Palgrave Macmillan, pp. 121–142.

Van Bouwel, J. 2014. "Explanatory Strategies beyond the Individualism/ Holism Debate." In: J. Zahle and F. Collin (eds.) *Rethinking the Individualism/Holism Debate*. Springer, pp. 153–175.

Van Bouwel, J. 2015. "Towards Democratic Models of Science. The Case of Scientific Pluralism." *Perspectives on Science* 23: 149–172.

Van Bouwel, J. 2021. "Are transparency and representativeness of values hampering scientific pluralism?" In: P. Hartl and A. Tuboly (eds.) *Science, Freedom, Democracy*. Routledge, pp. 181–205.

Van Bouwel, J. and M. Van Oudheusden. 2017. "Participation Beyond Consensus? Technology Assessments, Consensus Conferences and Democratic Modulation." *Social Epistemology* 31(6): 497–513.

Zahle, J. 2018. "Values and Data Collection in Social Research." *Philosophy of Science* 85: 144–163.

CHAPTER 25

POSITIVISM AND VALUE FREE IDEALS IN POLITICAL SCIENCE

....

HAROLD KINCAID

DEBATES about positivism and value free inquiry have animated methodological debates in political science for more than a half century. Unfortunately, the debates have often been muddled and rhetorical. Conducted at high levels of abstraction, many critiques of positivism and value neutrality have aimed at positions not clearly held by anyone. However, there is a quite defensible moderate position between the extremes of operationalism and mechanical objectivity, on the one hand, and postmodernist social constructivism, on the other. Important open issues remain about methods and values in political science, but they are more local, empirical ones, not giant issues in "epistemology."

This chapter argues for these diagnoses in three steps. I first sort out in Section 1 claims about positivism in philosophy and positivism in the social sciences—what was the original positivism and what is positivism taken to be by political scientists, past and present. Section 2 evaluates various positivist approaches in political science from the perspective of contemporary philosophy of science, in particular claims about value freedom. Section 3 applies the morals of the first two sections to the expanding current research in political science on clientelism. Clientelism nicely poses the main questions about positivism and values. I argue it supports my claims that it is not grand philosophical questions about epistemology that should concern us. Instead, more mundane but still important local, contingent, and empirical questions need to be answered.

1. POSITIVISM AND ITS DISCONTENTS

....

"Positivism" is one of those terms that is often used but not defined. Doctrines are associated with the term differently according to time, place, discipline, and the context of debate. The doctrine often means one thing to its critics and another to its sympathizers. This is true in political science, but it is true across the social sciences and in philosophy, where logical positivism has its origins.[1] Actually systematically sorting out what has been meant by the term would require a nuanced and long study in intellectual and, no doubt, social history. Something much shorter will have to do here.

Some of basic ideas associated with logical positivism and logical empiricism as it originated in philosophy are the following:

- All claims are either empirical or analytic
- Empirical claims are those expressible in terms of sensory experience
- Analytic claims are logical and a priori
- Claims of metaphysics, ethics, and other areas, which are neither empirical nor analytical, are meaningless and cannot provide objective knowledge of the world
- There is a clear and sharp distinction between claims about facts and claims about values
- Theoretical claims in science are either expressible in terms observation or are simply claims about logical entailment between concepts
- Scientific theories can and should be made into formal systems with axioms, definition, theorems and the like
- If it is to contribute to knowledge, philosophy will consist of clarifying the logic of the sciences
- There is one scientific method across the sciences, including the social sciences
- The sciences can and should be unified both by their common method and by their reduction to physics
- The main goal of science is the production of laws relating observables
- Explanation is the subsumption of events under covering laws

Other associated doctrines that might be added to the list are operationalism—the claim that the only defensible theoretical claims are those that can be defined in terms of the procedures to measure them—and behavioralism, which makes observable behavior paramount in some sense in the social and behavioral sciences.

There is no doubt that some subset of these ideas, in some interpretation, is associated with the original logical positivists. However, careful scholarship over the last 20 years has demonstrated that the actual views of those associated with 20th century positivism generally held views more complex and more sophisticated than those on the above list—so much so, in fact, that they sometimes held views nearly exactly opposite of the standard list (Cartwright et. al 1996).

I will not try to go over the full details and the supporting historiography.[2] However, here are some highlights that illustrate how "so not positivist" the positivist could be:

- Carnap's views show strong parallels to those of Thomas Kuhn, whose *Structure of Scientific Revolutions* (1962) was published in the Encyclopedia of Unified Science edited by Carnap, Neurath, and Morris. For later Carnap, everything about science and knowledge revolves around a choice of language, and those choices cannot be determined from outside. There is no uniquely correct logic and no universal principle of verification. Subjecting results to the court of public experience is a pragmatic matter, justified by the fact that other ways of deciding things produce endless controversies. Metaphysical notions can well be part of a language of science, though those are not languages Carnap prefers for various, largely pragmatic, reasons.

- Neurath 1.) rejected reduction to physics and methodological individualism (Neurath 1973, p. 333), 2.) had a picture of scientific unity that saw various quasi-autonomous scientific inquiries to be related in different piecemeal ways (Cartwright et. al 1996), with it being important to interconnect history, sociology and economics (Neurath, 1973, p. 345), 3.) rejected operationalism and verificationism, saying only that claims in the social sciences had to be related to observation "in one way or the other" (Neurath,1973, p. 347), 4.) thought that the social sciences were like geology or meteorology with few general laws (Neurath 1973, pp. 363, 371), 5.) argued that data essentially involved theory (Neurath 1973, p. 391), 6.) claimed that social science had to take into account the subjective meaning of actors (Neurath 1973, p. 393), and 7.) held that the social processes in science and social science in particular needed to be studied social-scientifically (Neurath 1973, p. 402).

Further differences from the perceived standard positivist positions can and have been documented at length (Creath 2020; Richardson and Uebel 2007; Richardson 1998). Doing so is not necessary for my purposes. The moral is clear that from its start, positivism was a diffuse doctrine having different meanings and purposes according to social context, in particular the interwar social upheavals of early 20th century Europe. Thus, when we come to look at positivism in past and current political science, we should expect that a similar contextualizing is essential. However, I cannot pretend to do a decent history here. My goal has to be limited to an accurate description of some of the main theses associated with positivism in political science.

To get to the current meanings of positivism in political science, a two-pronged approach is helpful: I look at what so called positivists actually say and see what ideas are attacked by those criticizing what they call positivism. Identifying positivist ideas in political science is confounded by the overlap with "behavioralism." Behavioralism, which must be kept separate from psychological behaviorism, is closely associated with positivism as instantiated in political science. I will thus discuss them together.

Behavioralism and positivism more generally is described by its advocates as advocating some version of the following:

- uniformities in observable political behavior can be discovered and expressed as lawful generalizations
- those uniformities and generalizations must be tested by empirical observations of behavior
- political science cannot be successful without general theory (Easton 1993)
- political science policy recommendations should follow from political science theory
- political science qua science should be value free or value neutral
- political science should be integrated with other social sciences
- political science should study individual behavior, but not exclusively, and should do so in the context of political institutions
- quantitative methods are central to political science but do not supplant other methods

These ideas were interpreted differently by different individuals and did not constitute an all-or-nothing unit. As Seidelman and Harpham (1985, p. 8) note, "attempts at coming to any complete definition of behavioralism are probably futile given the diversity of those who followed its banner." As I will detail below, these are not quite the radical claims that are often attacked as "positivist." Just to be clear I will refer to "behavioral positivism" to refer to this group of ideas in political science.

The second way to delineate positivism and behavioralism in political science is through its critics. There were two organized movements that I will call "antipositivist." The New Political Science movement of the 1960s is one. It sought above all to develop a political science that was politically committed. That meant it was opposed to value free science. It may have had some other antipositivist strands but they were not consistently formulated. The Perestroika movement of the 2000s focused on changing the organizational structure of political science, especially in the United States, to allow for greater publication of qualitative political science as well more training venues for qualitative work. It was also against an overemphasis on rational choice models (and to that extent antitheoretical) and for greater methodological pluralism. So, these two movements rejected value free science (in some sense) and an overemphasis on quantitative research.

Aside from these well-known quasi-organized movements within political science, antipositivism critiques have been consistent for at least the last three decades. I will use two more or less representative examples: Smith et. al.'s *International Theory: Positivism and Beyond* (1996) and Bevir and Blakely's *Interpretive Social Science: An Anti-Naturalist Approach* (2018).

Among the claims in Smith et. al (1996) are:

- a rejection of the positivist claim "that there can be such a thing as a political neutral analysis of external reality" (p. 6)
- "theories . . . define our ethical and practical horizons." (p. 13)
- positivism is the view that "methodology and ontology are licensed in so far as they are empirically warranted" (p. 17) and "observation and experience are the central criteria by which one judged scientific theories" (p. 13)
- positivism in social sciences embodies the standard views of the logical positivists that statements are meaningful only if they are empirically verifiable or true by definition, there is a strict separation between observations and theory, that there is a foundationalist, i.e. certain and infallible basis to knowledge in direct observation, that science is about producing regularities, and naturalism (the same methods apply to the natural sciences and the social sciences) (p. 15–17)

These are echoed 30 years later by Bevir and Blakely (2018) who say that:

- "naturalism's most serious limitations results from its disavowal of ethical engagement" (p. 12)
- antinaturalist and antipositivists in the social sciences in general believe that human belief and actions are holistic in nature, human beliefs continually change and modify, individuals are embedded in a social background, that social science should not seek general causal laws, and predictive power should not be the goal of social scientific research (Chpt. 2)
- positivist social science is "premised on theories purporting foundationalist truth" (p. 61)

- positivist social science does not realize that "social science concepts must refer to objects constituted in part by meanings or beliefs." (p. 68).
- "the construction of an ideal scientific language outside all of history is simply not possible" (p. 79)
- "naturalism . . . is the search for the one absolute level of analysis" (p. 82).

The description of "positivism" by political scientists is pretty consistent over the three decades involved. In sum, positivist political science according to its critics asserts that good social science is value free, is based on direct observation that is theory free and certain, is about producing laws and prediction, gives explanations that are ahistorical and asociological, is reductionist and individualist, and takes its own results to be independent of social factors.

I have quoted extensively from the original logical positivists, the advocates of behavioralism in political science, and their antipositivist critics to show the diverse set of views that are often at cross purpose or criticize a position nobody holds. I note first that the positivist doctrines attacked by antipositivists in political science have little connection to what the real positivists claimed. Most of what Bevir and Blakely reject was likewise rejected by Carnap and especially Neurath. That error, of course, does not count directly against their claims that positivism as they understand it has an important and misguided role in political science. However, the view held by the behavioralist positivists as I called them are quite different than the positivist views attacked from the interpretivist approach in current political science.

2. Evaluating Positivist Debates

Which kind of positivism if any is actually at work in political science? Which ones are plausible and helpful and which not? The section provides answers to these questions, building on prior work (Kincaid 1996, 1998, 2006). Of course, these debates are large. But I can sketch a position which I think is widely shared in philosophy of science. I break the topics down into naturalism, the role of observation and quantification, interpretivism, the place of theories and regularities, and value freedom.

Naturalism

Clearly, defenders of behavioralist positivism advocated some form of naturalism and currently it is probably a widely held view in political science. As in all these debates, the first issue is exactly which theses are being asserted and denied. Naturalism in one form says that the social sciences can use the methods of the natural sciences. A stronger version says they *must*. However, "the methods of the natural sciences" can be multiple things. For example, some natural science has a large role for experiments (molecular biology, particle physics) and others do not (geology, cosmology); where there are experiments, some achieve control by randomization (clinical research) and some generally do not (molecular biology). At a fine-grained level, the natural sciences do not themselves all have the same method.

It is useful I think to distinguish abstract and concrete scientific virtues (Kincaid 1996). "Tested against experience" is an abstract virtue; "tested by a double blind randomized clinical trial" is a concrete realization of that abstract virtue. So naturalism about the social sciences I would argue is best thought of as asserting that broad scientific virtues are relevant—or, more strongly, essential—for the social sciences. That view does not require physics worship or ignoring the complexity of human affairs. It is quite plausible, even if it is a more minimal claim.

Observation

The claim that observation is essential is ambiguous. The view commonly attributed to positivism makes observation the source of infallible knowledge, entirely theory independent, and the source of all meaning for theoretical terms which must be defined in terms of observational descriptions. Neither the original logical positivists nor the behavioralist positivists in political science generally hold such things.

Again, these claims can admit more concrete or abstract renderings, ensuring more or less substantive content. A minimalist thesis that only skeptics may reject—and the antinaturalists such as Bevir at time seem to be radical skeptics—asserts that claims in political science about political reality should be evaluated in part against observation or experience. That does not require operationalism, infallibility about observational knowledge, the definability of all meaningful terms in observational language, and so on. One can strengthen the claim about observation somewhat by requiring that there be some specified connection to observation when theories are evaluated. We know now that many concepts—across the sciences—describe family resemblances and that they are not definable in necessary and sufficient conditions. Nonetheless, there is reason to worry about concepts and claims that have no clear relation to observational experience. Put alternatively, it is not a bad thing epistemically to have concepts and claims that have precise entailments about what we should observe. Relatedly, contra antipositivists quoted above, positivists old and new do not generally claim there is an ideal language for science or for political science. Nonetheless, it is hard to argue that rational debate and belief is not furthered by clearly describing what claims are, and are not, being asserted.

All this said, there are certainly tendencies in political science that have probably erred in the direction of overly positivist demands about observation and its role. Probably both the original positivists and the behavioralists sometimes pushed views implausibly close to the simplistic positivist pole. Or, perhaps more accurately, they adopted one realization of the abstract virtues of observability and testability to the exclusion of other, plausible instantiations. The focus on statistical testing of quantitative data to the exclusion of any other evidence illustrates this tendency. Statistical inference is often treated as if it were an a priori logic of science that told us what to believe given the data (Kincaid 1998; 2000). Only evidence that can be expressed numerically is taken to be real evidence.

While these tendencies may still exist, political science has moved far beyond these tenets as has the philosophy of science. Mixed methods (Goertz 2017), qualitative comparative analysis (Ragin 1987), process tracing and case studies, and ethnographic data are often used. These are realizations of the abstract idea that hypotheses are "tied" to data. The general attitude among those doing such work is not that their results are entirely beyond the pale of scientific standards, broadly construed. We still want to ask of such studies how hypotheses are linked to data, how competing explanations of the data are ruled out, and other such general questions of reliable investigative method.

Interpretivism

We can ask the above questions about nonquantitative data. That is why the antinaturalist arguments like those espoused by Bevir and Blakely are mistaken. They stem in large part from Taylor's (Taylor 1971) old argument that explanation is about subjective meaning and subjective meaning cannot be investigated because meanings are holistic and require interpretation. Decisive objections to these arguments have been given long ago (Henderson 1991; Kincaid 1996), but they still have some purchase in political science it seems.

The response to interpretivist arguments as blanket criticisms of quantitative political science are multiple. First, it is not clear that all of political science is about or must make use of subjective meanings. Are voting results and factors influencing it like income matters of subjective meaning? A reasonable answer is that they are not or not to such an extent that they rule out standard scientific practices such as asserting clear hypotheses, gathering relevant data, ruling out competing explanations, and the like. Macropolitical studies of parties and states can be at the level of the whole; individual behavior and thus subjective meanings may add to evidence and explanation, but barring a strong methodological individualism, are not essential (Kincaid 1996, 1997). The concepts we use in describing political behavior, institutions, practices and so on may have ties to subjective meanings and we might like to include subjective meanings as evidence and as part of explanations, but this does not mean that we always have to appeal to them.

Second, holism of meaning and interpretation do not exclude standard scientific virtues. After all, all data in the sciences require interpretation and are described in ways that have ties to broader conceptual nets. Actually, the holism of hypothesis, evidence and measurement provide the key to testing interpretations. If there are complex interrelations between claims and independent evidence about those claims and their interconnections, then we can leverage those connections to provide independent evidence that bears differentially on different parts of the net. If, for example, I have multiple measures making different assumptions that agree on the value of another variable, then I have evidence for it. If I have competing causal models consistent with the data, but they share some common causal relations, then I have evidence for those.

Research in political science that tackles meanings, attitudes, etc. still must and can meet standards of evidence. Political scientists work hard to do so. There are many such efforts across political science. Thus, consider survey research first followed by ethnographical field work. Survey research as used in political science almost always involves eliciting answers from participants. In that sense, it is always about meanings. However, the area of survey research has long been aware of possible confounding and misinterpretation.

A part of the problem in interpreting survey response is not directly about meanings but about accuracy of self-reports. Income is a prime example. Obviously, researchers have to spell out what they mean by income. But even then there is an entire little industry improving measures of income. Multiple measures are used; the effect of different measures on predictions are investigated.

These same kind of methods are used in the more interpretative aspect of survey practice (Schwarz et. al 2008). Question order is varied to see if it makes a difference. Social desirability bias is investigated by using list experiments, for example. Various kinds of question framing issues have been raised, and again, their influence on answers investigated, perhaps most rigorously in recent survey experiments (Brady 2000). The effect of different framings on the predictive connection with other variables can also be investigated.

Political ethnography likewise is generally quite aware of ways that investigation can go wrong and practitioners follow general standards of evidence. In political science, ethnography invokes mixed methods as does much of political science research (Baiocchi and Connor 2008). Interviews are combined with surveys, case studies, and even experiments to draw conclusions. The ethnographic work can provide lower-level detail, subjective experience, and other such "value added" pieces to a project as well as suggesting and/or questioning the meaning of central theoretical concepts in a study (Rhodes 2016). Anybody who has done focus groups knows that they can provide ways of conceptualizing phenomena that had not previously occurred to investigators.

These interpretative methods are subject to broad, abstract standards that hold of all empirical inquiry. As a major advocate of the interpretive approach puts it:

> All debates are subject to the provisional rules of intellectual honesty, such as established standards of evidence and reason; we prefer webs of interpretation that are accurate, comprehensive and consistent. Reconfirmation is also integral. (Rhodes 2016, p. 176)

These are the requirements of any science.

This conclusion that interpretive work should and can meet ordinary scientific standards gets lost sometimes in the rhetoric used by practitioners of ethnography and other interpretivist inspired work. This rhetoric divides the possible approaches into two entirely dichotomous possibilities: 1.) positivism in an extreme form that believes in indubitable observational facts into which theories can be translated and inferences produced by an a priori universal logic of science or 2.) entirely idiographic narratives of meaning with no need to worry about falsifiability and other such evidential issues. For example, the introduction to the Bevir and Rhodes (2016) volume on interpretive social science consistently sets out the alternatives in this way. Buts these are not the only two alternatives. We know now that good natural science is not a matter of brute data and universal a priori methods. However, we can still have disciplined inquiry and distinguish good and bad work. Interpretivist practices look entirely different from other sciences only when the latter are given a positivist caricature.

Thus, interpretivist arguments seem best taken as useful warnings. Ignoring subjective understandings may lead to misleading or incomplete explanations. Ignoring the interpretive assumptions needed to understand beliefs, attitudes, and so on may lead to bad inferences. Interpretivism raises concern about badly executed naturalist social science, not the enterprise itself.

Laws and Theories

Positivists such as Hempel certainly emphasized laws. Formalizable theories were important for Carnap. Current philosophy of science has found that things are more complicated and variegated in real scientific practice.

Finding a conceptual account of laws—necessary and sufficient conditions—turned out to have apparently insuperable problems.[3] Describing laws as "universal" in various forms allowed trivializing counterexamples. Also, accounts of laws used other terms such as "natural kinds" that are as much in need of explication as the concept of scientific law. Numerous counterexamples to Hempel's notion of explanation as deduction from laws arose (Salmon 2006).

Recent work shifts away from the notion of laws as universal necessities and instead focuses on causes and models. Cartwright's (1983) *How the Laws of Physics Lie* was seminal in this regard. It is quite clear that much science is about a patchwork of different causes and that if we want to think of laws, it probably should be as those parts of science picking out causal factors (Kincaid 2004). Models are used to get at those factors, but it seems that much natural science works pragmatically with different models for different explanatory purposes (Morgan and Morrison 1999), an idea foreshadowed in part by the ur-positivist Carnap in his notions of multiple frameworks.

Once we move from a focus on laws to a more piecemeal accounts of causal processes and multiple models, the ideal of sciences as primarily expressed as a formalizable theory has less purchase. This was a central conclusion of Kuhn with his notions of a paradigm, something that is both more and less than an axiomatizable theory. Talk in political science of "theories," not surprisingly, is often just a mention of some specific casual mechanisms or, as in game theory, models of certain kinds.

None of this entails that the positivist ideal of clearly formulated theoretical claims with specifications of their ties to evidence is wrong. Like lots of ideals, it is great when you can get it but it should not let the best be the enemy of the better. Science across the spectrum—physics included (Cartwright 1983; Williams 2008)—does not produce the highly formalized theories some positivists thought essential to science, but science nonetheless provide well-confirmed explanations of complex phenomena.

To finish this discussion, I want to emphasize that positivism in some sense has and continues to have some influence in political science (and across the social sciences), and that influence is often detrimental. A prime example is over emphasis on and misinterpretation of the quantitative multiple regression framework (Kincaid 2000; 2012) which occurs across the social sciences. Multiple regression methods are often taken as (1) providing scientific-style generalizations and (2) applying an a priori logic of science via statistical inference. The kind of generalizations produced are taken to be regularities and thus instantiations of Humean type laws.[4] An ambiguous attitude is taken toward causality: sometimes it is eschewed in roughly the positivist sense as unscientific and metaphysical and at other times regression coefficients are thought to represent causal effects and causal effect sizes. The inferences from regression are often treated as mechanical—a p-value or R-squared value is thought to tell us if the results are believable and to embody logical rules of scientific inference.

All this is wrong, of course. Something can be statistically significant and both causally trivial and not believable and causally significant, statistically insignificant (think $p < .051$), and believable. Multiple regressions maybe sometimes give us limited generalizations, but getting causes out of them is not possible simply by looking at p values and regression coefficients (Kincaid 2012, 2021).

Values and Objectivity

Debates about value neutrality are central to debates over positivism and they are also crucial in their own right. As in the above discussion, the main conclusions I will draw are that there are multiple issues at stake with different implications.

The key questions we have to ask about value ladenness include the following parameters (Kincaid, Dupre and Wylie 2007):

- Are values necessary or contingent?
- What kind of values are involved—epistemic or nonepistemic?
- Are values used in the science or are they implied from scientific results given other value assumptions?
- What part of science are values involved in: determining what problems and questions to pursue, in determining the evidence, in explanation, in fundamental categories, and so on?
- And, for each of the above, if true, what are the implications for objectivity, etc.

These elements are fairly obvious but also easily ignored. So, to explain, we may see political science that we think involves values, but those values may not be essential to the research. The theoretical hypotheses, the auxiliary assumptions about data generating process, and so on can be formulated without reference to or presumptions about value issues. If I my world view leads me to see conservatism as deviant and thus to devote greater research effort to it, I exhibit a certain kind of bias. But that bias is not inevitably or essentially part of the evidence gathered—the evidence may be objective even if only a specific set of questions are asked, ones that reflect the investigator's political attitudes. Clark and Winegard (2020) make a case for this kind of bias in political science.

There are also various *kinds* of values that can be involved in political science—political, moral, pragmatic, and epistemic (values such as reliability, simplicity, etc.). Which kind of value is involved makes a difference for the implications we might draw, for example, about objectivity. Also, value implications are often follow from scientific results only by adding other, normative assumptions. Evidence, for example, that elected representatives secure material goods for their constituencies may or may not be ruled as undemocratic and corrupt depending on other value assumptions about democracy.

A further consideration concerns *where* values are involved in science. It is one thing for questions of social welfare to determine which political science questions are pursued and a rather different matter when values are involved in deciding what the evidence is, for example. Finally, for all the factors listed above, we have to ask what implications they have for the objectivity, evidential grounds, etc. for results in political science.

It should be obvious that the question whether political science is value laden is potentially many different questions with possible different answers. Values influencing the research topics pursued do not directly speak to the objectivity of results; value implications following from those results when external value judgments ground those implications do not challenge the objectivity of the results themselves.

I would argue that even when value judgments are at the heart of evidence and explanation, the implications are not obvious. Suppose I use a specific, value-laden conception of democracy in empirical work. If I am explicit about those values and how they are involved in indicator choice, etc., does that mean my results are just asserting a political position? It seems not. Being explicit about essential values thus can still produce a relativized objectivity. Of course, there is no guarantee that we are explicit about values; for this, reason social studies of social science, exemplified by feminist research (see Mazur et. al, Chapter 23, this volume), are especially valuable.

Finally, moral and political values may be essentially involved at the heart of science—in evidence and explanation—but nonetheless produce good epistemic results. Longino (1990) makes a case for the positive role of nonepistemic values in promoting epistemic objectivity. Again, the moral is that identifying the role and implications of values in science requires a careful and nuanced look at specific scientific practices and that there different degrees of value involvement with differing effects that need to be specified. Chernoff (2005) is a useful presentation of aspects of this overall view about political science.

3. Debates in the Concrete: Illustrations from Clientelism Research

I finish my discussion of positivism and value freedom with a more detailed analysis of some political science research illustrating many of my points above. I focus on clientelism research. Clientelism has been a major concern to political scientists for obvious reasons: it is a widespread phenomenon both temporally and globally and it raises important normative concerns. Thus, it makes a good case study for the topics of this chapter. (In addition, Chapter 19 of this volume discusses philosophy of science issues in clientelism research in detail, so these two chapters are complimentary).

The relevant morals from the above discussion of positivism, values and political science I want to illustrate here are:

- theories in any formal sense are often not involved in good research
- important concepts may succeed without strict definitions in terms of necessary and sufficient conditions
- clarity on concepts used and claims made is an essential component of successful investigation
- generalizations are possible but often limited in scope to specific contexts, instead evidence is given for specific causal mechanisms
- a variety of evidence from quantitative to qualitative is possible and needed, but it all has to meet basic evidential standards
- values can be involved in multiple ways in political science research, but their role must be examined case by case and their implications can differ

Clientelism research is diverse in what it studies and how it does. The diversity fits well with the picture of scientific practice pictured above where investigation may be less about generalizations and more about contextual causal processes, and where a web of different kinds of evidence is advanced. As is shown in detail in Kincaid et. al (Chapter 19, this volume), researchers work with a diversity of definitions of clientelism and focus on different aspects of complex causal processes. Clientelism is given different definitions along at least these parameters:

- to what extent is a clientelistic relation contingent or voluntary?
- who stands in clientelistic relations? individuals only? elected officials and voters? parties and voters? elected officials, brokers and voters?
- what behaviors are influenced? voting? campaigning? donations? promised voting?
- are clientelistic relations one shot or repeated?
- are clientelistic inducement to identifiable individuals, collections of voters, or social organizations?

The causal factors used to explain are likewise diverse. They can be divided into supply side and demand side factors, between the reasons that politicians, parties, etc. offer benefits and between the reasons that individuals accept benefits. They may involve internal motivations, social structural causes, or both.

So, we see in the clientelism research the "dappled" picture (Cartwright 1999) invoked above. Subjective experience is included in work on the "demand side" as an important corrective to more institutional, macro accounts. Generalizations are possible, but they are piecemeal. While researchers talk in terms of "theory," what they in fact produce is much more like causal mechanisms whose operation depends on context. There is certainly no essentialism about definitions, with people providing loose characterizations of the phenomena to be investigated. Indeed, a dose of positivism might be good for the field in order to keep clear more precisely its explanatory targets and factors.

The kinds of evidence invoked in clientelism research is also varied. So, consider two recent examples of good work in the area, Nichter's (2018) *Votes for Survival* and Kramon's (2018) *Money for Votes*. Both use large surveys, structured interviews, and experiments. The surveys cover both attitudes and reports of relevant events. One of the surveys, the AfroBarometer, is a long-standing enterprise with a history of careful checking for biases in results. Some of the experiments are incentivized in the economist's sense: individuals receive material benefit designed to elicit honest answers (see Hofmeyr and Kincaid, Chapter 18 in this volume, on the rationale for these). These are mixed methods approaches that gather evidence running from the very qualitative and micro to the quantitative and macro. They illustrate the sort of reasonable middle way between positivism on the one hand and extreme interpretivism on the other.[5]

Is clientelism research value free or value neutral? That question, I would argue, is misguided. Instead, clientelism research illustrates the framework for thinking about facts and values described above where value-leadenness raises multiple, independent issues. Values are involved, but in different ways and with different implications.

There are numerous assertions in the literature that clientelism is a bad thing, generally on the grounds that it undermines democracy in some way. But that assertion raises complex issues which fall roughly into two, partly interrelated categories: in what ways is democracy undermined and what are the implications for such values claims for actual research? One way that democracy might be undermined is by threatening public, and thus democratic, control of expenditure, hiring, etc. Another way democracy might be undermined is by taking away the voice or input of individual voters.

Both these possible routes to the normative evaluation of clientelism depend on nonobvious empirical assumptions or presuppositions. Consider pork-barrel projects—funding sent to the home districts of powerful legislators as is common in the United States. Such funding violates ideals of rule-based public administration that can be part of notions of democracy. However, those grounds for condemning pork projects assume that the alternative will be rule-based collective decision-making. Yet that may well not be the case. It is not even clear that there is a sharp distinction between rule-based public administration and pork. Large parts of government funding decisions are the result of collective bargaining between legislators seeking to promote their own interests. Pork-barrel projects in the United States are voted on, albeit often at late stages in the legislative process when voting against specific items may be difficult or impossible. Specific funding decisions turned over to bureaucracies—such as scientific agencies—do not guarantee rule-based neutrality either.

Moreover, worries that clientelism violates voter expression are seemingly at odds with most definitions of clientism by researchers. Clientelism is generally taken to involve "contingent" exchange where autonomous, noncoercive choice is meant. That kind of choice does not involve violations of free expression in some sense. Perhaps it may do so compared to the situation where voters have sufficient income such that what a politician offers is not worth the cost of being bought. Yet that hypothetical situation does not describe most cases of clientelism. Ethnographic work on clientelism like that of Auyero (2007), for example, emphasize the extent to which individual autonomy is realized in clientelistic relations.

However, these empirical issues are judged, it seems clear that empirical clientelism research does not *always* depend on value judgments that threaten to make the results of research political or moral statements rather than empirical ones. Survey results of self-reports on gifts from politicians, ethnographic studies of the relation between politicians, brokers, and voters, and many other kinds of evidence in clientelism research do not in any obvious way depend taking a stance on whether such practices are "undemocratic," etc. In fact, researchers using these types of evidence can and do take different normative stances on whether the practices they study are political desirable or undesirable.

No doubt there is much more to say about how values surface in clientelism research—about which kind of values show up and where. Differing ideas about autonomous choice described above are one example where more careful analysis is needed. My discussion here is just a sketch and a beginning for doing more decisive and subtle investigation.

4. CONCLUSION

Discussions of positivism in political science have been constant but also at cross purposes. I have distinguished three variants of positivism: 1.) the views mostly held by the original positivists such as Neurath and Carnap, 2.) positivism in its most extreme and commonly used sense that makes very strong claims about meaning, operationalism, etc., and 3.)

the views advocated by behavioralists in political science and affirmed today in different variants by many political scientists. Interpretivist critics, I argued, generally target 2.), a view almost nobody holds. Those critics are right that some political science empirical practice does act as if there was a logic of science and that science is all about laws. However, there is a nonpositivist position that is not committed to 2.), has similarities to what the behavioralists actually wanted, and is defensible as a postpositivist, post-Kuhnian philosophy of science. Some political science follows this defensible post-Kuhnian approach, but where, how, and how successfully must be decided case by case.

ACKNOWLEDGMENTS

Jeroen van Bouwel and Fred Chernoff made very helpful comments on an earlier draft.

NOTES

1. Comte of course is part of the larger story of positivism in general, but that aspect is beyond my purview here.
2. For a manageable and sensitive survey, see Creath (2020).
3. See Lange (2000) for one of the best attempts to provide a noncircular account.
4. There is a large debate about the nature of laws (Lang 2000). Hume's real view would certainly not count the very restricted regularities produced by social science statistical methods as laws, but finding a clear dividing line between "accidental" regularities and those that make real laws has not been easy.
5. This does not mean this work could not also use what I called a "dose of positivism." These can be clarified, especially the extent to which they conflict with the accounts of others, and the bearing of the evidence more precisely specified; this is argued for clientelism in Chapter 19.

REFERENCES

Auyero, J. 2007. Routine Politics and Violence in Argentina. Cambridge: Cambridge University Press.

Baiocchi, G. and Connor, B. 2008. The Ethos in the Polis: Political Ethnography as a Mode of Inquiry. Sociology Compass 2/1: 139–155.

Bevir, M. and Blakely, J. 2018. Interpretive Social Science: An Anti-Naturalist Approach. Oxford: Oxford University Press.

Bevir, M. and Rhodes, R. (eds.). 2016. Routledge Handbook of Interpretive Political Science. London: Routledge.

Brady, H. 2000. Contributions of Survey Research to Political Science. PS: Political Science and Politics. 33 (1): 47–55.

Cartwright, N. 1983. How the Laws of Physics Lie. Oxford: Oxford University Press.

Cartwright, N. 1999. The Dappled World. Cambridge: Cambridge University Press.

Cartwright, N., Cat, J., Fleck, L., Uebel, T. 1996. Otto Neurath: Philosophy between Science and Politics. Cambridge: Cambridge University Press.

Chernoff, F. 2005. The Power of International Relations Theory. London: Routledge.

Clark, C. and Winegard, B. 2020. Tribalism in War and Peace: the Nature and Evolution of Ideological Epistemology and Its Significance for Modern Social Science. Psychological Inquiry 31 (1): 1–22.

Creath, Richard. 2020. "Logical Empiricism." In The Stanford Encyclopedia of Philosophy (Summer 2020 Edition), Edward N. Zalta (ed.). Stanford: Stanford University Press. https://plato.stanford.edu/archives/sum2020/entries/logical-empiricism/.

Easton, David. 1993. "Political Science in the United States: Past and Present." In Discipline and History: Political Science in the United States, James Farr and Raymond Seidelman (ed.). Ann Arbor: University of Michigan Press, pp. 291–310.

Goertz, G. 2017. Multimethod Research, Causal Mechanisms, and Case Studies. Cambridge: Cambridge University Press.

Henderson, D. 1991. "On the Testability of Psychological Generalizations." Philosophy of Science 58: 586–607.

Kincaid, H. 1996. Philosophical Foundations of the Social Sciences: Analyzing Controversies in Social Research (Cambridge: Cambridge University Press, 1996).

Kincaid, H. 1997. Individualism and the Unity of Science: Essays on Reduction, Explanation, and the Special Sciences (Lanham, MD: Rowman and Littlefield, 1997).

Kincaid, H. 2000. "Formal Rationality and Its Pernicious Effects on the Social Sciences," Philosophy of Social Science 30: 67–88.

Kincaid, H. 2006. Excorsizing Hidden Positivist Demons, Methodological Innovations Online (2006) 1(1) 14–18 DOI: 10.4256/mio.2006.0003

Kincaid, H. 1998. "Positivism in the Social Sciences," Routledge Encyclopedia of Philosophy (London: Routledge University Press, 1998), Vol.7, pp. 558–561.

Kincaid, H. 2004. "Are There Laws in the Social Sciences: Yes." In Contemporary Debates in the Philosophy of Science, ed. Christopher Hitchcock (Blackwell, 2004), pp. 168–187.

Kincaid, H. 2012. "Mechanisms, Causal Modeling, and the Limitations of Traditional Multiple Regression." In H. Kincaid (ed.), Oxford Handbook of the Philosophy of the Social Sciences (Oxford University Press 2012), pp. 46–64.

Kincaid, H. 2021. "Making Progress in Causal Inference in Economics." In H. Kincaid and D. Ross, Modern Guide to the Philosophy of Economics. Elgar, pp. 28–65.

Kincaid, H., Dupre, J., Wylie, A. 2007. Value-Free Science: Ideal or Illusion? Oxford: Oxford University Press.

Kramon, E. 2018. Money for Votes. Cambridge: Cambridge University Press.

Kuhn, Thomas S. 1962. The Structure of Scientific Revolutions (1st ed.). University of Chicago Press.

Lange, M. 2000. Natural Laws in Scientific Practice. Oxford: Oxford University Press.

Longino, H. 1990. Science as Social Knowledge. Princeton: Princeton University Press.

Morgan, M. and Morrison, M. 1999. Models as Mediators. Cambridge: Cambridge University Press.

Neurath, O. 1973. Empiricism and Sociology. D. Reidel: Boston.

Nichter, S. 2018. Votes for Survival. Cambridge: Cambridge University Press.

Ragin, C. 1987. The Comparative Method: Moving Beyond Qualitative and Quantitative Strategies. Berkeley: University of California Press.

Rhodes, R. 2016. "Ethnography." In Bevir, M. and Rhodes, R. (eds). Routledge Handbook of Interpretive Political Science. New York: Routledge, pp. 171–185.

Richardson, A. 1998. Carnap's Construction of the World. Cambridge: Cambridge University Press.

Richardson, A. and Uebel, T. 2007. The Cambridge Companion to Logical Empiricism. Cambridge: Cambridge University Press

Salmon, W. 2006. Four Decades of Scientific Explanation. Pittsburg: University of Pittsburgh Press.

Schwarz, N., Knauper, B., Oyserman, D., and Stich, C. 2008. The Psychology of Asking Questions. Leeuw, E., Hox, J, and Dillman, D. (eds). International Handbook of Survey Methodology. New York: Psychology Press. pp: 18–34.

Seidelman, R., Harpham, E. 1985. The Disenchanted Realist. Binghamton: SUNY Press.

Smith, S., Booth, K., and Zalewski, M. 1996. (eds.) International Theory: positivism and beyond. Cambridge: Cambridge University Press.

Taylor, C. 1971. "Interpretation and the Sciences of Man." The Review of Metaphysics 25: 3–51.

Wilson, M. 2008. Wandering Significance. Oxford: Oxford University Press.

CHAPTER 26

POLITICAL EXPERTS, EXPERTISE, AND EXPERT JUDGMENT

JULIAN REISS

1. INTRODUCTION

SCIENCE affects politics, and through politics, our lives, at unprecedented levels. Scientists produce predictions about what the climate will look like in 2050, and they make recommendations which policies will help to ascertain that the climate in 2050 will not be too different from the climate today. Scientists develop new medical treatments and influence, through expert panels, the government in its decisions which of these new treatments will be allowed to be marketed and, in some countries, which will be paid for by the health services. Scientists tell us not only how many and which people have to be affected for an infectious disease to count as a "pandemic," they also deliver tools to make the disease visible in asymptomatic individuals, develop medicines meant to curb its spread, and make recommendations about which policy responses to adopt. Scientists create and examine theories about the origins of the universe and of species that enter textbooks and through these affect the minds of nearly all school children. Scientists test hypotheses about virtually every aspect of social life, and the results of many these are used to justify this or that policy as "evidence-based."

It is not implausible to assume that the scientists who are engaged in these activities "know what they are talking about." They have been trained in applying the scientific method or methods most appropriate to their domain, and the institutional structures within which they operate make sure that their results are, at least on average, not fabricated or accidental. The idea that scientific knowledge is genuine knowledge has much prima facie plausibility. The question is whether it translates into legitimizing the elevated role experts play in contemporary democracy.

The nature of expert judgment and the role of experts in society are thus core issues in political science. If policy makers want to make rational decisions about which of a range of policy options to implement, they will want to know which option is most likely to succeed in advancing the policy goal. But the answer is rarely plain. If it was, all policy debate would concern goals: Is freedom more important than equality? How much growth shall we sacrifice now in order to lower the chances of catastrophic climate change in the future? Is the preservation of national identity a worthwhile aspiration? It is obvious neither to voters nor to policy makers whether introducing or raising minimum wages is or isn't an adequate means to achieve a living wage for all, or whether mRNA vaccines do or do not constitute threats to health and safety.

Scientific experts may help to produce and disseminate knowledge requisite to addressing issues such as these. At least in principle, there should be a fact of the matter whether (say) the provision of transfers or securing strong property rights is a better means to alleviate poverty, which should be open to empirical investigation. If so, scientific experts should be able to determine what this fact is and thus be able to advise governments about the most effective means to reach the desired ends.

There are, however, a number of obstacles to assigning the role of policy adviser to experts. Experts, like everybody else, have private interests. An expert claiming that a vaccine is safe might have received payments from the company that produces the vaccine; one who is claiming that minimum wages do not lower employment might think (or say) so for political reasons; one who advises against transfers might be wedded to an economic theory, an implication of which is that "transfers don't work." Interests affect advice in many different ways, and outright lying is only the most egregious form of acting on private interests. Experts might also fail in an epistemic sense. Perhaps experts are no better than average citizens to predict the effects of policy interventions. Perhaps the effects of policy interventions are inherently unknowable. Perhaps some experts are more reliable than others, but it is impossible for policy makers and the general public to tell which ones are which. If any of these reasons applies, it would be hard to justify using expert policy advice. Moreover, in a liberal democracy, all citizens should participate equally in political matters. But experts, it seems, contribute twice to political outcomes: first, as voters, and second, as advisors. Some commentators thus reject certain roles for experts in democracies on egalitarian grounds even if, counterfactually, the experts were motivated exclusively by public interests and had genuine knowledge of policy effectiveness.

The bulk of this chapter will address normative considerations about the role of experts in democracies. Specifically, I will focus on expert advice concerning questions such as:

- Is nuclear power an adequate means to battle climate change?
- Do mRNA vaccines possess an acceptable risk/benefit profile?
- Is it a good idea to introduced or raise minimum wages?
- Which immigration policy is best for our country?
- Can a trade war be beneficial?
- Should schools be closed to help "flatten the curve"?

The answers to such questions require not only technical considerations concerning causality and efficacy but also evaluative considerations concerning efficiency, the weighting of costs and benefits, the handling of risk and uncertainty, and the desirability of policy ends. I will therefore refer to them as "technical-evaluative" issues.

Sheila Jasanoff says about technical-evaluative issues (Jasanoff 2006):

> In offering opinions on such contested and indeterminate issues, scientists can no longer stand
> on firmly secured platforms of knowledge. The questions contemporary policymakers ask of
> science are rarely of a kind that can be answered by scientists from within the parameters
> of their home disciplines. Scientists instead are expected to function as experts, that is, as
> persons possessing analytic skills grounded in practice and experience, rather than as truth-
> tellers with unmediated access to ascertainable facts. Accordingly, the technical expert's
> attributes often include, but are rarely limited to, mastery of a particular area of knowledge.
> What politicians and society increasingly expect from experts in decision-making processes
> is the ability to size up heterogeneous bodies of knowledge and to offer balanced opinions,
> based on less than perfect understanding, on issues that lie within nobody's precise disci-
> plinary competence. Judgment in the face of uncertainty, and the capacity to exercise that
> judgment in the public interest, are the chief qualifications sought today from experts asked to
> inform policymaking. In these circumstances, the central question is no longer which scien-
> tific assessments are right, or even more technically defensible, but whose recommendations
> the public should accept as credible and authoritative.

The main topic of this chapter is the role of expert judgments concerning technical-
evaluative decision-making in democracies. Before delving into the normative discussion,
let me discuss the very notion of "expertise."

2. DEFINING EXPERTISE

Defining expertise is extraordinarily difficult. There are no (relatively widely) accepted
definitions, nor is there agreement on the phenomenon that is to be characterized. Alvin
Goldman, one of the most widely read contributor to the literature on expertise from within
analytical philosophy, for example, defines an expert as "someone who possesses an extensive fund of knowledge (true belief) and a set of skills or methods for apt and successful deployment of this knowledge to new questions in the domain" (Goldman 2001: 92). Whereas
Goldman insists that at least that kind of expertise that is relevant to epistemology is partly
propositional in nature, Hubert and Stuart Dreyfus reject the idea that experts are sources
of information and build a model of expertise that focuses on expert skills, on "knowing
how" rather than "knowing that" (Dreyfus and Dreyfus 1986).

For our problem neither characterization will do. "True belief" is a non-starter as an
element in a definition of *scientific* expertise. No matter what one's stance in the realism/
anti-realism debate is, it should be uncontroversial to say that *past* scientists got most
things wrong. However, the idea that scientists such as Tycho Brahe, Isaac Newton, Joseph
Priestley and Charles Lyell weren't genuine scientific experts, even though their belief
systems contained a large number of beliefs now considered to be false, is preposterous.
Moreover, whether or not a scientist is on the right side of some scientific controversy (even
of most or all of them) seems immaterial to his status as an expert. Controversies are fought
and debates held *among* scientific experts, not *between* scientific experts and non-experts.
(Cf. Collins and Evans' discussion of Joseph Weber's role in the early gravitational waves
dispute in Collins and Evans 2007: 131).

And while I agree that a variety of skills are involved in expert practice (such as skill in solving mathematical equations, running regressions, or persuading audiences), experts in the sense relevant here are rarely consulted because they have these kinds of skills. Policy makers want *judgments* from experts, judgments they believe improve their own ability to form good judgments. The possession of the right kind of skill set is therefore at best an indicator of the thing we want, but not the thing itself. The argument that a certain skill set is a reliable indicator of good judgment has not been made by the Dreyfuses.

Considering the examples the Dreyfuses take as paradigmatic—airplane pilots, chess players, automobile drivers, adult learners of a second language (Dreyfus and Dreyfus 1986: 20)—does not make it very plausible that there should be a link between a skill set and the relevant good judgment. Why should, for instance, an above-average ability to recognize patterns—a skill shared by expert chess players and medical doctors among others—enable the skill-possessing individual to predict whether British beef was safe for consumption during the BSE crisis or what measures government should take to fight the COVID-19 epidemic? I will come back to this issue below.

A definition similar to that of the Dreyfuses is given by Peter Dear (Dear 2004: 206–207; emphasis in original):

> One who is experienced is an expert, and an expert knows things by virtue of being experienced in the relevant ways of the world. A farmer is experienced in the ways of crop growing or cattle; a banker in the ways of finance; or an auto mechanic in the ways of car engines, all by virtue of having experienced such things often and routinely . . . An expert, in other words, is someone who is reckoned to be *likely* to be experienced in the relevant matters . . . In effect, shared experience relies on the ability to recognize a kind of attribute or property that people ("experts") can be said to possess. Expertise thus resembles "tacit knowledge," as understood by scholars in science studies.

The problem with any experience-based definition of expertise is that the truth-makers of statements such as "British beef is safe for consumption," "Nuclear power should be the preferred means to battle climate change" and "Free trade is good for a nation" are not observable. There is no way to experience them directly. Even if one believes that all knowledge is inferential, as I do (Reiss 2015), judgments about technical-evaluative matters is far more indirect than knowledge about crop growing and car engines. Technical-evaluative judgment is not experience-based.

More promising is Reiner Grundmann and Nico Stehr's relational conception of expertise, which they summarize as follows (Grundmann 2017: 27):

> [E]xperts mediate between the production of knowledge and its application; they define and interpret situations; and they set priorities for action. Experts are primarily judged by clients, not necessarily by peers (professional or scientific); and they rely on trust by their clients.

Despite its promise, Grundmann and Stehr's characterization has shortcomings. A first problem is that it is vastly under-specified: the authors don't tell us, for example, *how* experts mediate between knowledge production and application (or what makes them different from models, which are also said to "mediate" between knowledge production and application, see Morgan and Morrison 1999), for which qualities they are judged by their clients or under what conditions clients trust them (though see Stehr and Grundmann 2011).

Collins and Evans reject the relational conception of expertise, pointing to a second problem from which it suffers (Collins and Evans 2007: 2–3 and 54):

> Relational approaches take expertise to be a matter of experts' relations with others. The notion that expertise is only an "attribution"—the, often retrospective, assignment of a label—is an example of a relational theory. The realist approach adopted here is different. It starts from the view that expertise is the real and substantive possession of groups of experts and that individuals acquire real and substantive expertise through their membership of those groups.
>
> Relational theories of expertise face a problem of dealing with frauds and hoaxes. If expertise is attributed to a hoaxer, there is little more to say about it—the relevant topological location in the network has been achieved. The problem for a relational or attributional theory is to distinguish hoaxes and frauds (before they are exposed) and genuine exercises of expertise. A pure relational conception then might be descriptively successful in that it picks out those individuals as experts who society identifies as such, but it has no normative bite. If society errs by regarding a hoaxer as expert, the theory errs with it.

Collins and Evans' "realist approach" takes socialization into the right group as essential to the formation of expertise (Collins and Evans 2007: 3):

> Acquiring expertise is, therefore, a social process—a matter of socialization into the practices of an expert group—and expertise can be lost if time is spent away from the group. Acquiring expertise is, however, more than attribution by a social group even though acquiring it is a social process; socialization takes time and effort on the part of the putative expert.

Unfortunately, the hoaxer problem reappears in slightly altered form here. What if the whole field is a hoax so that socialization into the group makes an individual a hoaxer rather than an expert whose advice we have good reason to influence our judgments? Collins and Evans recognize the problem. While their earlier work acknowledged, but did not try to solve the problem (e.g., Collins and Evans 2002: 252), a recent book tackles it head-on by characterizing Western science as a "form of life" the participants in which share certain "formative aspirations." The formative aspirations are essentially values to which scientists tend to subscribe or aspire, but not strict criteria according to which an analyst can neatly parse activities into "scientific" and "non-scientific." Among the values Collins and Evans discuss are observation, corroboration/falsification, the Mertonian values (communism, universalism, disinterestedness, organized skepticism), honesty, integrity, and clarity (Collins and Evans 2017: Ch. 2).

I doubt that this characterization of a "form of life" is sharp enough to distinguish genuine science from hoaxes—it seems to me, for instance, that many astrologists believe that they endorse these values and probably so did the alchemists at the time of the scientific revolution. But more importantly, Collins and Evans want to sever the link between the values they ascribe to the scientific form of life and truth—this is their takeaway from what they call the "Second Wave of Science Studies," social constructivism (Collins and Evans 2002: 239). Thus, they write (Collins and Evans 2017: 49):

> There is one fundamental value to science that is so central and obvious that it is easy to miss. This is that the form of life of science is driven by the desire to find the truth of the matter, along with the belief that the truth of the matter can be found. The view associated with Wave Two is that the truth of the matter cannot be found, that there are only interpretations and

perspectives and that it is naïve to steer one's desire and actions by the attempt to find the truth of the matter.

But why would we take someone's advice seriously if the advice is not reliable? Collins and Evans answer (Collins and Evans 2017: 65):

> Because they know what they are talking about. . . . A person who knows what they are talking about has studied, or spent much time getting to know, the thing in question. Such a person "knows" in the sense of having a long and intimate acquaintance with the thing—they are familiar with the thing in the way that they are familiar with people that they know. They are the people who have made the observations in matters where the observable is at stake.

However, as argued above, the truth-makers for the claims at stake here are not observable and inferred very indirectly. Ultimately, Collins and Evans defend an experience-based conception of expertise which suffers from the same defects as Peter Dear's.

The last conception I want to review here before making my own attempt is Roger Koppl's. In his economic model of expertise an expert is simply someone who gets paid for their opinion (Koppl 2018: 8). As a descriptive account this is surely plausible. Unless the clients are crazy or for some other reason not under full control of their wallet, to pay someone for their opinion means to value the opinion, and as liberals we might want to leave it to the client to decide what the reasons are for valuing someone's opinion. The putative expert "gets it right most of the time," "has the right kind of socialization," "has the right kind of experience/knows what s/he is talking about" and "I trust him/her" are all equally good reasons for valuing the opinion.

The problem is of course that quacks and hoaxers get paid for their opinions, and while (in a liberal society) this is fine at the individual level, it is less plausible when it comes to expert advice for policy. It does not seem right to use taxpayer money to consult astrologers for predicting whether the outbreak of a new virus will lead to an epidemic or whether the use of some substance will turn out to be safe for long-term consumption. For these purposes we want to use a different method than to "follow the money."

The most defensible account of expertise that is in my view most defensible in the context of technical-evaluative decision-making comes from an account of *moral expertise*. This is no accident: as we will see below, judgment in technical-evaluative matters requires, in part, the same capacities as moral judgment. And: technical-evaluative and moral judgments share the feature that their subject matters are not observable, and that inferences about them are fairly indirect.

According to Brad Hooker, a moral expert is someone who "might be expected to provide arguments which, if examined carefully, would persuade reasonable people and produce convergence in their moral views" (Hooker 1998). However, he cautions (1998: 509; emphasis in original):

> The criterion of success in moral arguments cannot be mere success in convincing people (after all, sophistry can be good at convincing people). Rather, the arguments must be ones *whose careful examination* would resolve moral disagreements.

This is the right approach, except that many moral disagreements will not be resolved by arguments. There are many routes to persistent moral disagreement. Mine is through value pluralism (Reiss 2020). Individually and collectively, humans value more than one thing: health and material well-being, spirituality and sanctity, friendship and loyalty, freedom and autonomy, tradition and hierarchy, justice and equality, to name but a few things. While most (albeit by no means all) of us will recognize each item on the list as a valuable thing, we disagree on their relative importance, on what to give priority when different goals clash. Famously, some of us will prioritize freedom over equality, others equality over freedom. Moreover, each item on the list is subject to multiple interpretations. Negative or positive freedom? Equality of what? Which account of well-being is correct? Which account of justice? And so on. Moral disagreement is persistent because there are persistent differences of opinion on how to interpret and prioritize different values.

Since technical-evaluative decision making requires value judgments, the resolution of disagreements cannot be the success criterion. I will offer a slightly modified definition. The modification concerns two aspects of Hooker's definition. I agree with relational theories in so far as expertise requires social recognition to count as such. This is only a necessary, not a sufficient condition, because of the problem of hoaxters. But an opinion is not an expert opinion merely because it would withstand scrutiny if examined. The expert must have actually proven the possession of expertise to the community in order to be recognized as an expert by the community.

The second aspect that requires modification is also motivated by the problem of hoaxters. As Hooker explains, it is not enough merely to persuade others. After all, this is exactly the thing at which hoaxters are good. Being able to withstand *critical* examination is therefore key. "Critical" in the sense used here carries with it a whiff of objectivity. Critically to examine an expert opinion would mean, for instance, to examine whether it follows deductively from accepted premises, or whether it is sufficiently supported by evidence, whether the all known alternative explanations have been ruled out and so on. While surely there is no cast-iron fact of the matter whether a given piece of evidence is relevant to the matter at hand, how much evidence is needed or even whether a given argument is deductively valid, there are clear cases of bad arguments, and that is all that is needed here. An expert does not give, time and again, bad arguments.

These two modifications yield the following definition:

> *Definition Expert.* An expert (in the sense relevant to technical-evaluative decision-making) in a subject S is an individual whose arguments about S have, on balance, withstood critical scrutiny by the public.

An individual is thus an expert on S if he or she has offered judgments on S and defended these judgments using arguments that members of the public—which can include peers, journalists, policy makers, citizens—have criticized, but these criticisms have, on balance, not been successful. I qualify with "on balance" because experts can of course make mistakes. They just shouldn't make mistakes all the time.

My definition is subject to a number of fairly obvious shortcomings. Let me briefly discuss two of them. One is its vagueness. How many times does a person's opinion have to withstand criticism in order for the person to be an expert? I have no answer to that question. This is after all a matter of inductive learning—we want past success to be indicative of future success. There are no straightforward rules for how this works. Various philosophers of science have pointed to one-shot experiments or observations sufficient to confirm a general principle (e.g., Cartwright 1989, Norton 2021). An analogous situation concerning expertise might be one where someone, hitherto a novice in some field, makes a strong case for a prediction that is extremely unlikely but comes out true anyway. (The "making a strong case" for the prediction is essential as we don't want the prediction to be accidentally correct.) But in most cases, we will want a longer and more varied track record. I therefore take the vagueness of the definition to be an asset rather than a drawback. It allows for the notion of an expert to change with the details of a situation.

The other shortcoming is that I have said nothing about the institutional setting within which the critical examination to take place. That the institutional setting matters for effective criticism has been a longstanding theme in the philosophy of science from Karl Popper to Helen Longino and beyond. I will add nothing to that debate here except to note that I envisage an institutional setting that does enable and encourage effective criticism so that the public can use that information for expert identification.

3. THE ROLE OF EXPERTS IN A DEMOCRACY

In his essay "The Scientization of Politics and Public Opinion," Jürgen Habermas develops three ideal-typical models for the role of scientific experts in a democratic society (Habermas 1987). Both the decisionistic model and the technocratic model build on a clear functional separation of expert and policy maker. The decisionistic model derives its name from the fact that "political action cannot rationally justify its own premises. Instead a decision is made between competing value orders and convictions, which escape compelling arguments and remain inaccessible to cogent discussion" (Habermas 1987: 63). Moving beyond Habermas, I would maintain that the decisionistic model is defined by a constellation in which the political decision maker (whether the voter or the democratically elected representative) decides (1) whether to follow scientific experts to begin with; (2) which expert or experts to follow; and (3) how and to what extent the scientific expertise makes a difference to the political decision.

> In the technocratic model the constellation is reversed in that the politician becomes the mere agent of a scientific intelligentsia, which, in concrete circumstances, elaborates the objective implications and requirements of available techniques and resources as well as of optimal strategies and rules of control. If it is possible to rationalize decisions about practical questions . . . and thus the problems of decision in general are reduced step by step, then the politician in the technical state is left with nothing but a fictitious decision-making power. (Habermas 1987: 63–64)

Again moving beyond Habermas, the technocratic model is defined by a constellation in which (1) there is a predetermined process of expert appointment; (2) there is a predetermined process of expert opinion formation; and (3) the policy maker is bound by the expert opinion that results from this process.

The functional separation of experts and policy makers is given up in the *pragmatistic model*. About it, Habermas says (Habermas 1987: 66–67; emphasis in original):

> [The] interaction [between policy makers and experts] not only strips the ideologically supported exercise of power of an unreliable basis of legitimation but makes it accessible *as a whole* to scientifically informed discussion, thereby substantially changing it.

[. . . In this model] reciprocal communication seems possible and necessary, through which scientific experts advise the decision-makers and politicians consult scientists in accordance with practical needs. Thus, on the one hand the development of new techniques is governed by a horizon of needs and historically determined interpretations of these needs, in other words, of value systems. [. . .] On the other hand, these social interests, as reflected in the value systems, are regulated by being tested with regard to the technical possibilities and strategic means for their gratification.

As we will see, there are a number of subtypes of the pragmatistic model, so I will leave a more precise characterization until later.

In a widely cited article, Stephen Turner drew attention to what he calls "the problem with experts" (Turner 2001). There are two aspects to the problem. The first arises from concerns with democracy and equality. The recognition of experts in a democracy violates norms of democratic equality because experts, if their opinions are given any weight in technical-evaluative decision-making, wield illegitimate power. (When I speak of "democracy" here I mean no more than the general idea that group decision making is characterized by a kind of equality among the participants as in "One person—one vote"; cf. Christiano 2018.)

The other aspect of the problem arises from the idea of state (or government) neutrality: "if the liberal state is supposed to be neutral with respect to opinions—that is to say that it neither promotes nor gives special regard to any particular beliefs, world views, sectarian positions, and so on—what about expert opinions?" (Turner 2001: 124). Either way, giving experts a special role in democratic society appears to violate democratic norms and therefore both the technocratic and the pragmatistic model stand in need of justification.

Though most contributions to the contemporary literature on experts elaborates and defends one version or another of the pragmatistic model, one can find support for decisionism and technocracy. It is easy to see why. Experts are humans and as such prone to error, subject to private interests, overconfidence and many other biases. Marshal Ferdinand Foch predicted, in 1918, that "Airplanes are interesting toys, but of no military value" (Pickover 1998: 249). Famously, Irving Fisher, according to Joseph Schumpeter, the United States' "greatest scientific economist" (Schumpeter 1951: 223), stated a few days before the 1929 stock market crash that "Stock prices have reached what looks like a permanently high plateau." The failed predictions of Nobel prize winning economists Paul Krugman and Joseph Stiglitz alone could turn one into an avid skeptic of expertise (on Krugman, see Smith 2018; on Stiglitz, Epstein 2018). Cases of expert failure such as these certainly support the decisionist's case in favor of keeping experts at bay.

On the other hand, the technological, scientific, social, environmental, and public health challenges society faces appear to be too complex for the average citizen to grasp well enough to form a rational opinion about technical-evaluative issues. Arguably, nuclear energy, artificial intelligence, climate change, quantitative easing and vaccination, to mention but a few examples, are all issues the subtleties of which are well understood, if at all, only by relatively small groups of experts. When polities make decisions about the future energy mix, the regulation of autonomous cars, how to respond to financial and environmental crises and whether to mandate vaccination or not, there is a pressure on decision makers at least to consider carefully what experts say. As David Estlund puts it, "The idea of democracy is not naturally plausible. The stakes of political decisions are high, and the ancient analogy is apt: in life-and-death medical decisions, what could be stupider than holding a vote?" (Estlund 2008: 3).

In his book *Expert Failure*, Roger Koppl has developed an economic model of expertise that fits into the decisionistic category (Koppl 2018). His model provides a two-by-two typology of relations between experts and decision-makers or nonexperts the dimensions of which are (X) the degree of competition among experts; and (Y) the degree of autonomy of the nonexpert (Koppl 2018: 190). Social structures in which the expert decides for the nonexpert are called "Rule of experts" when the expert has monopoly power and "Quasi-rule of experts" when there is competition among experts. Examples of the former include central planning of economic activity and central bank monetary policy, examples of the latter, school vouchers and representative democracy. Social structures in which the non-expert decides autonomously are called "Expert-dependent choice" when there is just one expert and "Self-rule or autonomy" when there are many. Examples of the former include religion in a theocratic state, of the latter, periodicals such as *Consumer Reports* and the market for venture capital. Koppl's main contributions are economic arguments to the effect that expert failure is less likely, *ceteris paribus*, when more experts compete for the attention (or money) of the non-experts (a view defended also by Gebhard Kirchgässner, see Kirchgässner 1999, 2003) and the more autonomous non-experts are in their decision-making. Applied to polities, competition among experts and autonomous democratic decision-making leads us, of course, to the decisionistic model.

Technocratic ideas go back to Francis Bacon (Farrington 1949), Henri de Saint-Simon (Bell 1999: 76), and, in a sense to be explained in a moment, John Stuart Mill (Estlund 2003), and have recently been revived in the guise of arguments in favor of epistocracy. The term "epistocracy" refers to the "rule of the knowers." Suffrage is thus not universal but instead restricted to individuals with college degrees or who have passed a competence test. A technocracy is a kind of epistocracy, one which restricts suffrage to those knowers who have the requisite technical or technical-evaluative expertise. Mill was an early epistocrat who argued that more votes should be given to better educated citizens (Mill 1861/1991).

Jason Brennan is the most vocal recent defender of epistocracy (Brennan 2011, 2013, 2016). According to Brennan, citizens have the right to be governed competently, but democratic voters tend to be incompetent (the latter claim is based on empirical evidence from sources such as Somin 2013). If voters are, by and large, "ignorant, irrational, misinformed nationalists" (this is the title of Chapter 2 of Brennan 2016), then they are likely to make bad political decisions from which citizens must be protected. It is a short step from here to a full-fledged technocracy. All that is needed is a claim to the effect that only technical-evaluative experts are competent voters.

It is not obvious, however, that the latter claim is true. Brennan rests his case on social science/policy examples such as "free trade/open borders/no price controls. . . are good for a nation." To him, the idea that someone with an economics or political science degree should have better judgment on questions such as these seems incontrovertible. In a recent paper I have argued that the claim that there is a link between social science knowledge and good judgment in political-evaluative matters is not only not obviously true, it is most likely false (Reiss 2019). Among the reasons are fact/value entanglement (of which I will say a little more below), persistent disagreement about values, which feeds through to factual opinions due to fact/value entanglement, and the absence of widely shared methodological standards in the social sciences. There is also at least some evidence that experts don't outperform laypeople in tasks that appear relevant to good political judgment such as the forecasting of political outcomes (e.g., Tetlock 2006).

Brennan derives his epistocratic conclusions from what he calls the "competence principle." It reads (Brennan 2011: 704):

> It is unjust to deprive citizens of life, liberty or property, or to alter their life prospects significantly, by force and threats of force as a result of decisions made by an incompetent or morally unreasonable deliberative body, or as a result of decisions made in an incompetent and morally unreasonable way.

Even if we accept this principle (though it might seem awfully *ad hoc* to some readers), it won't yield the desired result when there are few reasons to think that experts are competent. Moreover, there are reasons to believe that experts are actually *less* competent than ordinary citizens because research shows that individuals' opinions tend to rigidify as they become more knowledgeable. Jeffrey Friedman refers to this phenomenon as "the spiral of conviction" (Friedman 2020: Ch. 5). Epistocracy (with or without a technocratic element) cannot be justified by the competence principle.

As mentioned above, most recent contributions to the debate about the role of experts defend one version or another of "pragmatistic model" in that they advocate interaction between experts and policy makers within a deliberative outlook (e.g., 2003b, Jasanoff 2003a, Wynne 2007, Brown 2009, Fischer 2009, Collins and Evans 2017, Levy and Peart 2017). It is therefore fruitful to distinguish among different, essentially pragmatistic, models. Darrin Durant has provided such a typology that distinguishes Collins and Evans' 'Rawlsian" from Sheila Jasanoff's and Brian Wynne's "Habermasian" approach (in a narrower sense) (Durant 2011).

Collins and Evans argue that one major contribution of "Wave Two" of science studies was the idea that policy making involving technical(-evaluative) matters can and should include a broader range of actors than certified specialists. But "Wave Two" provided no resources to address the question where inclusion should stop (Collins and Evans 2002). "Wave Three" is to make up for that lacuna. One of the results of "Wave Three" is a "periodic table of expertises" that distinguishes different kinds of expertise such as contributory, interactional, and referred expertise (Collins and Evans 2007). The main intellectual problem of "Wave Three," according to Collins and Evans, is to defend the view that "it is better to give more weight to the opinions of those who, literally, *know* what they are talking about [i.e., scientific experts]" (Collins and Evans 2017: 11) in the light of the main result of "Wave Two," viz., social constructivism and its rejection of truth as a viable aim for science. I have described their vision of "elective modernism," their attempt to manage the dilemma, in Section 2 above. Here let me focus on the institutional aspect of their proposal.

Collins and Evans advance a model for the role of scientific experts in society in which a novel institution—called "The Owls"—reviews the scientific state-of-the-art on a topic of interest and certifies the quality and strength of the consensus on that topic. What is important is that the polity is autonomous in deciding whether to follow or implement the scientific consensus on a topic (Collins and Evans 2017: 159; emphasis in original):

> What distinguishes elective modernism from technocracy is that recognizing expert advice is not the same as endorsing or accepting it. Under elective modernism, policy-makers are under no obligation to adopt any of the policies put forward by experts, and may reject all of them if they so choose.

There is, however, an important rule of conduct that applies to situations in which political institutions over-rule the expert verdict. The rule is that it must be done openly and it must be clearly stated that it is happening. The technical consensus must never be disguised or distorted so as to make the political decision easier. This does not reduce the range of policy options being considered, but it does restrict the kinds of *justifications* policy-makers can offer. If, say, experts have reached the verdict that a certain compound is safe to use for consumption or as a pesticide, policy-makers may ban it anyway but, according to the proposal, they could not ban it because experts are uncertain or have found it to be unsafe (see also Weinel 2010: 68–85).

Arguably, then, Collins and Evans' model is an instance of Koppl's "expert-dependent choice" where the nonexpert does not have to follow the expert advice and the expert committee has a monopoly. However, the nonexpert's autonomy is restricted by restricting the kinds of justifications for their decisions policy-makers can give.

Durant points out that both Rawls and Habermas "presuppose that there must be restrictions on political discourse within a liberal democracy and on the kinds of issues appropriate for different decision-making arenas" (Durant 2011: 695) such as those given by Rawls' "veil of ignorance" and Habermas' "ideal speech situation." Rawls uses his construct to bracket evaluative questions concerning the good life, about which citizens are unlikely to agree, so that an "overlapping consensus" about the fundamental institutional arrangement can be reached. In a similar vein, Collins and Evans aim to keep science as free from societal values as possible, not the least because they want to protect science from "the wrong kinds of social values" and hope that the scientific values of elective modernism can help to protect democracy (Collins and Evans 2017: Ch. 1). Another Rawlsian aspect of their model is the justification of (evaluative-)technical decisions based in public reason.

Jasanoff and Wynne advance two different criticisms of Collins and Evans' project: a contextual and a normative one (Durant 2011: 694). The contextual criticism challenges the view that politics can be as neatly separated from science as Collins and Evans suggest. One reason is fact/value entanglement. All of Collins and Evans' supposedly "technical" questions in fact have mixed factual and evaluative components. This is why I prefer to refer to the relevant decision-making as "technical-evaluative." There is no fact of the matter whether British beef is safe to eat, much less whether you should eat it (as they put it). Facts play into that judgment but so do evaluations of how much risk "you" as an individual or "society" is willing to take, if it is "society," who to include and how to aggregate individual risk profiles, how to balance the increasing cost of continuing an investigation and reducing uncertainty optimally, which methods to use to produce the relevant evidence and calculations, what it means to take a decision rationally, and, perhaps most fundamentally, what the right framing of the issue is. It is certainly not obvious that scientists are always the best people to answer these questions.

This takes us directly to the normative criticism, which holds that Collins and Evans' project is anti-democratic in that it prevents citizen participation which can serve to establish limits of expert power (e.g., Jasanoff 2003a: 394, 397). Jasanoff and Wynne offer a participatory model, in which diverse publics are represented in a deliberative process of scientific belief formation. Their model is therefore closer to Habermas' discursive democracy that accepts, among other things, that value judgments can be a legitimate subject of the deliberation.

Both versions of the pragmatistic model have to answer Turner's challenge that giving experts a special role in society violates democratic norms. Collins and Evans's defense of their "Rawlsian" version of the model derives mainly from the idea that it is part and parcel of "elective modernism" to try to keep science and politics as separate as possible, to bracket off political considerations from the process of scientific belief formation. In their proposal scientific experts enjoy a certain authority because they "know what they are talking about." I have argued above that the desire to keep science as free from politics as possible is optimistic at best, and more likely harmful because value judgments are so deeply entangled with more purely scientific questions in the technical-evaluative realm. The intuitive idea that "it is better to give more weight to the opinions of those who, literally, know what they are talking about" (Collins and Evans 2017: 13) does not have any pull when it comes to technical-evaluative matters.

Perhaps more contentiously, even if scientific experts "knew what they are talking about," their opinions should not weigh more than those of other citizens in a liberal democracy. Take the individual citizen as an analogy. Arguably, it would be irrational for her to ignore the technical-scientific consensus on matters of personal relevance to her (presuming, as we have, that there are cases of relevant technical-scientific consensus). But would it be justified to force her to believe the technical-scientific consensus or to give it more weight than other opinions? Certainly not, for all the well-known reasons: for all we know, the scientific experts may be wrong and the citizen right; there may be legitimate difference in opinion about relevance; forcing her to believe an opinion, whatever that may be, infringes on her autonomy—which may be justified in some cases (say, when the citizen is drunk or enraged) but not a matter of principle. Likewise, polities shouldn't be required, against people's will, to take any opinions into account even if there are reasons to believe that these opinions are in fact superior.

In Jasanoff's Habermasian model expertise is regarded as an instance of "delegated authority," analogous to other forms of delegated authority such as that given to administrative agencies (e.g., Jasanoff 2003b: 158). To her, this means that expert committees should be "representative" in two distinct senses (Jasanoff 2003b: 161):

> Perhaps the best way to conceive of expert bodies, then, is as a mini-republic of ideas, in which trustworthy governance requires a multiplicity of views to be represented, or at least given some chance to express themselves. Non-representative expert groups, no less than non-representative governments, can scarcely claim to speak with authority for the complex territories they seek to manage. It is important, then, for expert deliberations to include not only the full range of views that bear on the technical issues at hand, but also voices that can question the disciplinary assumptions and prior issue-framings of the experts being consulted.

There are two types of problem with this proposal, practical and principle. The practical problems relate to the notion of "representation": whose views are included (a) in the "full range of views that bear on the technical issues at hand" and (b) among the "voices that can question the disciplinary assumptions and prior issue-framings"? There are no obviously correct answers to either of these questions, and all answers that would suggest themselves appear problematic in one way or another. Durant, for example, points out that Jasanoff's (and Wynne's) proposals are subject to well-known criticisms of identity politics (Durant 2011: 706).

This is not a problem for either the decisionistic or the technocratic model. On the decisionistic model, technical-evaluative decisions are a matter of democratic decision making. Every voter chooses (a) whether to listen to experts; (b) which expert or experts to listen to; and (c) the extent to which to follow the expert or experts. In a sense the problem reappears at the individual level, but that problem is not a problem for policy. The technocratic model presupposes that there is a scientific consensus on technical-evaluative matters. That consensus is unlikely when it comes to technical-evaluative decisions is a major reason for rejecting the technocratic model. However, if there is a consensus, the practical problem does not arise because representation is not an issue.

The problem of principle is that expertise legitimization and delegated authority are disanalogous in one important respect. A delegated authority might have considerable discretion with respect to the concrete means to implement in the pursuit of process goals. By contrast, it should not have discretion with respect to the underlying goals themselves. This is why we speak of a principal-agent *problem* when the agent (delegate) substitutes his own goals for those of the principal. This is also at the core of Milton Friedman's critique of corporate social responsibility. (Even if we do not want to follow Friedman in his conclusions, this premise in his argument seems correct.) It is one thing to delegate authority to a management or an administration that, because of its knowledge, skill, or place in the network of social relations, is likely to achieve a superior result. It is quite another to ask a third party what goals one should pursue in the first place. However, deliberation about goals is an important ingredient in the process of expert knowledge creation.

4. CONCLUSIONS

The most defensible model of the role of experts in society is the decisionistic one. It is more consistent with the democratic norms of equality and state neutrality, it fares better at preserving the autonomy of citizens, and it is less likely to generate expert failure. Many readers will baulk at the suggestion. Decisions about whether to eat British beef, regard anti-misting kerosene as safe, and what to do about climate change are important indeed. There is something counterintuitive in leaving them to the mob. But many decisions democratically organized polities make are important, and we have become used to thinking that democracy is a superior form of government all things considered.

Plato, famously, uses the image of the ship of state and compares government to navigation by the sea captain. Similarly, Brennan compares political judgment to the judgments plumbers make about plumbing, pilots about piloting, and surgeons about surgery. Plato argues that good government is rule by political expertise, democracy is rule by the many, most of whom do not have political expertise, and so democracy cannot be good government (Sørensen 2016). Similarly, Brennan argues that most voters are incompetent, citizens have the right to be ruled competently, and so the vote should be restricted to competent individuals such as him.

Today most people would bemoan Plato's and Brennan's anti-democratic conclusions. And yet, they would place higher weight to expert opinions when it comes to decisions that have a technical aspect. I hope to have shown here that this is inconsistent. For a democrat, only the decisionistic model of expertise is defensible.

References

Bell, Daniel 1999. *The Coming of Post-Industrial Society: A Venture in Social Forecasting.* New York: Basic Books.

Brennan, Jason 2011. "The Right to a Competent Electorate." *Philosophical Quarterly* **61**: 700–724.

Brennan, Jason 2013. *Epistocracy within Public Reason. Philosophical Perspectives on Democracy in the 21st Century.* Ann Cudd and Sally Scholz, Eds. New York: Springer, 191–204.

Brennan, Jason 2016. *Against Democracy.* Princeton, NJ: Princeton University Press.

Brown, Mark 2009. *Science in Democracy: Expertise, Institutions, and Representation.* Cambridge, MA: MIT Press.

Cartwright, Nancy 1989. *Nature's Capacities and Their Measurement.* Oxford: Clarendon.

Christiano, Tom 2018. *Stanford Encyclopedia of Philosophy.* Edward Zalta, Ed., Stanford, CA: Metaphysics Research Lab, Stanford University.

Collins, Harry and Robert Evans 2002. "The Third Wave of Science Studies: Studies of Expertise and Experience." *Social Studies of Science* **32**(2): 235–296.

Collins, Harry and Robert Evans 2007. *Rethinking Expertise.* Chicago: Chicago University Press.

Collins, Harry and Robert Evans 2017. *Why Democracies Need Science.* Cambridge: Polity Press.

Dear, Peter 2004. Mysteries of State, Mysteries of Nature. Authority, Knowledge and Expertise in the Seventeenth Century. *States of Knowledge: The Co-production of Science and the Social Order.* Sheila Jasanoff, Ed. London, Routledge: 206–224.

Dreyfus, Hubert and Stuart Dreyfus 1986. *Mind Over Machine: The Power of Human Intuition and Expertise in the Era of the Computer.* New York (NY), Free Press.

Durant, Darrin 2011. "Models of Democracy in Social Studies of Science." *Social Studies of Science* **41**(5): 691–714.

Epstein, Gene 2018. "Continually Mistaken, Chronically Admired." *City Journal*, September 20, 2018. https://www.city-journal.org/joseph-stiglitz-venezuela-16181.html.

Estlund, David 2003. Why Not Epistocracy? *Desire, Identity and Existence. Essays in Honor of T.M. Penner.* Naomi Reshotko, Ed. New York: Academic Printing & Publishing.

Estlund, David 2008. *Democratic Authority.* Princeton: Princeton University Press.

Farrington, Benjamin 1949. *Francis Bacon: The Philosopher of Industrial Science.* New York: Henry Schuman.

Fischer, Frank 2009. *Democracy and Expertise: Reorienting Policy Inquiry.* Oxford, Oxford University Press.

Friedman, Jeffrey 2020. *Power without Knowledge: A Critique of Technocracy.* Oxford: Oxford University Press.

Goldman, Alvin 2001. "Experts: Which Ones Should You Trust?" *Philosophy and Phenomenological Research* **63**(1): 85–110.

Grundmann, Reiner 2017. "The Problem of Expertise in Knowledge Societies." *Minerva* **55**: 25–48.

Habermas, Jürgen 1987. The Scientization of Politics and Public Opinion. *Toward a Rational Society: Student Protest, Science, and Politics*. Cambridge, Polity Press.

Hooker, Brad 1998. Moral Expertise. *Routledge Encyclopedia of Philosophy*. Tim Crane, Ed. Taylor and Francis. https://www.rep.routledge.com/articles/thematic/moral-expertise/v-1.

Jasanoff, Sheila 2003a. "Breaking the Waves in Science Studies." *Social Studies of Science* **33**(3): 389–400.

Jasanoff, Sheila 2003b. "(No?) accounting for expertise?" *Science and Public Policy* **30**(3): 157–162.

Jasanoff, Sheila 2006. Judgment under Siege: The Three-Body Problem of Expert Legitimacy. Democratization of Expertise? *Exploring Novel Forms of Scientific Advice in Political Decision-Making*. Sabine Maasen and Peter Weingart, Eds. Berlin, Springer: 209–224.

Kirchgässner, Gebhard 1999. On the Political Economy of Economic Policy Advice. *The Transfer of Economic Knowledge*. Ernst Mohr, Ed. Cheltenham, Edward Elgar: 13–31.

Kirchgässner, Gebhard 2003. Empirical Economic Research and Economic Policy Advice: Some Remarks. *Economic Policy Issues for the Next Decade*. Karl Aiginger and Gernot Hutschenreiter, Eds. New York (NY), Springer: 265–288.

Koppl, Roger 2018. *Expert Failure*. Cembridge, Cambridge University Press.

Levy, David and Sandra Peart 2017. *Escape from Democracy: The Role of Experts and the Public in Economic Policy*. Cambridge, University of Cambridge Press.

Mill, John Stuart 1861/1991. *Considerations on Representative Government*. Buffalo (NY), Prometheus Books.

Morgan, Mary S. and Margaret Morrison, Eds. 1999. *Models as Mediators. Perspectives on Natural and Social Science*. Cambridge, Cambridge University Press.

Norton, John 2021. *The Material Theory of Induction*. Calgary, University of Calgary Press.

Pickover, Clifford 1998. *Time: A Traveler's Guide*. Oxford, Oxford University Press.

Reiss, Julian 2015. "A Pragmatist Theory of Evidence." *Philosophy of Science* **82**(3): 341–362.

Reiss, Julian 2019. "Expertise, Agreement, and the Nature of Social Scientific Facts or: Against Epistocracy." *Social Epistemology* **33**(2): 183–192.

Reiss, Julian 2020. "Why Do Experts Disagree?" *Critical Review* **32**(1–3): 218–241. Doi:10.1080/08913811.2020.1872948.

Schumpeter, Joseph 1951. *Ten Great Economists from Marx to Keynes*. Oxford, Oxford University Press.

Smith, John 2018. "Paul Krugman the lord of wrong predictions." *BPR Business & Politics* Retrieved 6. March, 2020. https://www.bizpacreview.com/2018/01/22/paul-krugman-lord-wrong-predictions-592049/.

Somin, Ilya 2013. *Democracy and Political Ignorance: Why Smaller Government Is Smarter*. Palo Alto (CA), Stanford University Press.

Sørensen, Anders Dahl 2016. *Plato on Democracy and Political technē*. Leiden, Brill.

Stehr, Nico and Reiner Grundmann 2011. *Experts: The Knowledge and Power of Expertise*. New York (NY), Routledge.

Tetlock, Philip 2006. *Expert Political Judgment: How Good Is It? How Can We Know?* Princeton, Princeton University Press.

Turner, Stephen 2001. "What is the Problem with Experts?" *Social Studies of Science* **31**(1): 123–149.

Weinel, Martin 2010. Technological Decision-making under Scientific Uncertainty: Preventing Mother-to-child Transmission of HIV in South Africa. PhD Thesis, Cardiff School of Social Sciences, Cardiff University.

Wynne, Brian 2007. "Public participation in science and technology: Performing and obscuring a political-conceptual category mistake." *East Asian Science, Technology and Society* **1**(1): 99–110.

CHAPTER 27

....

PROGRESS IN INTERNATIONAL POLITICS
The Democratic Peace Debate

....

FRED CHERNOFF

1. INTRODUCTION

....

THIS chapter focuses on one subfield of political science, international relations (IR), and asks if there has been, or can be, progress in the pursuit of knowledge. Because of the substantive and methodological diversity of the subfields in political science, the chapter's focus is on IR rather than on political theory, political institutions, or comparative politics. The chapter considers the question of progress by examining the democratic peace debate, one of the most important topics of recent decades. It describes liberalism and realism, their debate over the connection between democracy and peace and progress therein. It then raises constructivist worries that cast doubt on whether there is legitimate progress akin to that in the natural sciences. The chapter seeks to show how some of the constructivist criticisms, especially ~~about~~ concerning the meanings of key terms, capture something of real importance, but that a proper perspective on their claims does not necessarily show divergence from the natural sciences.

The meaning of the term "democracy"

The term democratic peace (DP) will be used throughout the chapter to include scholarly works that use the terms "democracy," "liberal democracy," "republican government," and even "libertarianism." There are various aspects of democracies that authors have focused on when discussing these related terms, such as fair elections, separation of powers, free press, etc. The core debate over the past fifty years has increasingly come to focus on "mature liberal democracies" and their differences from other types of state. The contemporary debate has separated the connection between democracy and peace into two distinct claims. The monadic hypothesis states that democracies are inherently more peaceful than nondemocracies. And the dyadic hypothesis states that pairs—or dyads—of democracies

Table 27.1 Central hypotheses in the Democratic Peace Debate	
DP Hypotheses	
Monadic Hypothesis	Democratic states go to war less often than other types of state
Dyadic Hypothesis	Pairs of democracies go to war with one another less often than other pairs of states

are more peaceful towards one another than other sorts of dyads—i.e., two nondemocracies or one democracy and one nondemocracy (see Table 27.1).

The Imperative of Progress

The importance of thinking about progress in the academic study of international relations (IR) can be seen clearly by considering the negation, that progress is not an important matter to political scientists and IR scholars. Were this established, academic researchers would go forward in their careers aware that their empirical findings are no better those they are arguing against. They would be compelled to accept that their efforts are not in any sense *better* than what has come before. If what others have previously found is all there is to know in a given area, then it would make little sense to engage in new research. Authors who most vigorously embrace the possibility of progress are usually those who believe that there is a strong parallel between the natural sciences' methods of study the social sciences' methods, a position known as *naturalism* in the philosophy of social science.

After outlining the development of major theoretical debates in IR (Section 1) and the democratic peace debate conducted by mainstream naturalists in IR (Section 2), the chapter will consider criticisms of that debate by constructivists and poststructural theorists outside of the naturalist or positivist framework (Section 3). Two hallmarks of progress in science are *cumulation of knowledge* and, when disputes arise, the scholarly community *approaching consensus*. The chapter discusses further how the two long-standing opposing camps in IR, liberals and political realists rarely agree on substantive principles of IR; but the two sides managed to display both of the natural science hallmarks just noted, *cumulation* as they built on one another's research, which paved the way for an approach to *consensus* (Section 4). The chapter connects constructivist concerns as well as natural science-like achievements to the pragmatic aspect of explanation, which involves careful attention to the context in which theories and explanations are presented and the questions they are intended to answer (Section 5). Section 6 offers some conclusions, as well as some caveats to the argument of this chapter.

2. Great Debates in International Relations

For over two thousand years, military commanders, political leaders, jurists, philosophers, theologians, and historians have pondered and written about international politics. They composed the writings that have come to the twenty-first century as classics. World War I exceeded virtually all others in size, and introduced terrifying new dimensions of combat, especially aerial attack and indiscriminate weapons of mass destruction. Many thought that civilization itself could not survive another such war. It has only been since the end of World War I that the academic study of IR has been recognized as a distinct field in its own right. The first university chair of international relations was established in 1919 at the University of Wales at Aberystwyth.

The history of the study of IR since the 1930s is often described as dominated by three so-called great debates. The case study of this chapter, the democratic peace, is impacted by the central issues of all three debates. The first debate was between supporters of political realism and idealism or liberalism (both characterized more fully in the next section). Political realism has historically been the dominant position among political leaders and scholars, and directs those who subscribe to it to expect conflict between states. Realists claim Sun Tzu, Thucydides, and other major figures from antiquity as forebearers. Realists have regularly faced challenges on empirical grounds, that they are factually wrong about the cycles of violence, and on moral grounds, that their theory lends justification to immoral violence. In the aftermath of World War I, and again after World War II, there were important policy decisions to be made, and the way those decisions would go would depend upon which theory policy-makers adopt. If policy-makers accept realism, they would be likely to rely on greater armaments and military alliances. In contrast, if they should accept idealism-liberalism, according to which solutions for large-scale war are conceivable, they would likely try to strengthen the League of Nations and the UN, as well as to place greater reliance on international treaties and to work toward the strengthening of international law. We might add that it is sometimes erroneously believed that realists recommend the use of force freely to solve problems of foreign policy. Realist theory sees the use of force as legitimate, but only appropriate when it enhances national interest more than undercuts it. The three most important realists since World War II are Hans Morgenthau, Kenneth Waltz, and John Mearsheimer. The former opposed the Vietnam War and the latter two opposed the US invasion of Iraq.

The second debate began in the 1960s as behavioral social science made its way into IR. Proponents of quantitative methods argued that, by relying on traditional modes of argument, IR found itself debating the same questions for centuries without natural-science-like resolution or progress. Any future progress would require researchers to learn to focus on objectively observable behavior and reproduceable tests. Defenders of the traditional approach argued that much of what is important in the study of world politics cannot be captured simply by counting certain observable actions, and that essential factors like military morale, leadership and much else could never be quantified.

The third debate arose in the late 1980s and has continued since. The rise of interpretivist and constructivist social scientists have challenged the mainstream of realists and liberals and their notion of what the state is, especially that the state is something that can be spoken of and studied in an objective way. These scholars argue that states are a human construct and have no fixed identity over time. Norms shape the goals that states seek, and norms change significantly over time. The agents in the international system are not metaphysically distinct from the international system itself; both affect the character of the other, and every action has the potential to change the state and the system.

As the sections below show, the first debate impacts DP studies because the DP hypotheses contradict a core realist principle; that all states seek the same ends and behave in the same ways. The second debate impacts DP studies because DP proponents can point to what appears to be natural-science-like *progress* in part as a result of quantitative methods. And some of the most recent criticisms of DP hypotheses derive directly from the constructivist-interpretivist camp that emerged in the third debate.

The Enduring Theoretical Rivals

The dominant approach to the study of international conflict over the centuries has been some form or other of political realism. But that line of theory has consistently been challenged, especially by various versions of idealism and liberalism. Textbooks over the past three-quarters of a century have tended to cast the field of IR as divided into three traditions: realism, idealism-liberalism, and a third theory—initially Marxism, and after the Cold War, constructivism. It is useful to have contrast between realism and liberalism clearly in mind before examining the impact of the DP debate.

Political realism. Those who support political realism claim to be following the intellectual path of Thucydides, the contemporary historian of the Peloponnesian War, as well as Niccolò Machiavelli, Thomas Hobbes, and others. Three of the core principles of political realism are the following. First, that states are the most important actors, and analytical focus should be fixed on them; second, states seek their own self-interest and understand their interests in terms of power. There is no way to create more overall "power" in any system. The result, on the realist view, is that states evaluate their options within a relative-gain and zero-sum framework. Consequently, for one state to acquire more power, others must be equivalently reduced. This principle also entails that all states are motivated similarly—whether the state is communist, capitalist, socialist, democratic, or monarchical. Third, the environment in which states operate lacks any legitimate government or hierarchical authority, and a lack of hierarchy is termed *anarchy*. Because power is never equal among all states, there are greater and lesser powers in any system. Because the system is zero-sum, and states seek power, there will be conflicts. And because there can be no authoritative among states, there is no mechanism to prevent continued escalation. The result is that *realists expect recurrent war.*

Idealism-Liberalism. Through most of the modern world, political realism has been opposed by idealists and liberals. There is no widely accepted definition of these two terms, and thus no widely accepted distinction between them. Indeed, the same individual is cited as the principle intellectual figure in both idealism and liberalism, Immanuel Kant.1 While the term "idealism" was much more common through most of the twentieth century, from about the 1970s onward, liberalism is the term primarily employed to denote the contrasting theoretical position.

There is a difference at least in connotation, which is that *idealism* is more often used to convey a theory that is morally superior to realism, producing greater justice and liberty; this can take the form in which idealism is sometimes seen as a theory of the way the world should be. Liberal theories are often used to claim that the proper policies can lead states to achieve a (morally or just materially) better world, where people may live longer and happier lives, in part owing to the reduction or absence of war. One can also conceivably advance the liberal democratic peace claim on self-interest grounds without resorting to any claim of moral superiority, e.g., by arguing that when citizens are ultimately responsible for decisions of war and peace, as in a democracy, they will choose peace much more often than monarchs and autocrats do, because the citizens pay the financial and personal costs of war. The many liberal theories over the centuries have denied one or more of the three core realist principles described above. Some liberals argue that actors other than states are important; because individuals all have inherent moral obligations, they can consider moral goodness in their decisions; or international institutions like the League of Nations and UN make a difference in world politics. They can reduce the likelihood of war in a variety of ways that will lead states that maximize self-interest to choose paths that avoid war. In this way they can fundamentally alter, if not erase, the effects of the absence of a world government. Some liberals even argue that world government is possible.

Marxism. For much of the post–World War II period, the third theory was Marxism. Many states in the international system formally adopted some form of Marxist-Leninist socialist form of government. Marx and Lenin based their theories on notions of inevitable class conflict. Marx saw class conflict within each capitalist society; the wealthy capitalist class would exploit the workers in increasing degrees until the latter would rise up in internal revolution in which workers' parties would come to rule the society. Eventually each great power society would be ruled by workers parties and would see that the interests of workers in one society were in harmony with those of others. After finishing socialist states' wars against capitalist states, as the latter have tried, and will try, to prevent socialism from prevailing, socialist societies would live together in peace. Lenin drew from the same set of class conflict concepts as Marx, but argued that in the new environment of imperialism, the wealthy industrialized capitalist states now must be seen as a "class" of rich states exploiting the "class" of poor less industrialized societies. The latter should coalesce like workers must in industrial, capitalist states.

Constructivism. As the Cold War was coming to an end, and more clearly after it ended, Marxism was no longer widely accepted nor viewed as a comparable third theory of IR. In part, many people believed that Marxist principles had been empirically shown to be flawed by virtue of the fact that nearly all of the states that were forced into socialism under Soviet control rejected socialism as soon as they had the chance, Russia included. At this time a new alternative theoretical approach gained more attention in major IR journals and textbooks. It came to be termed "constructivism." The term, like political realism and liberalism, covers a wide range of different specific theories. As we will see in more detail in Section 3, constructivists question the nature of the social world that liberals, political realists, methodological traditionalists and behavioralists claim to study. Constructivist theorists hold that states and the system of states are socially constructed and that their basic identities and core interests change over time. The states and the system interact, and over time the interactions can shape both the states and the structure of the system. As a result there is no clear ontic separation between "agents and structures." Moreover, states do not have a fixed nature that permits researchers to be able to study them objectively. Most constructivists argue that there are no cause-and-effect relationships in IR of the sort that natural scientists identify. In their view researchers in the social sciences are confronted with subject matter that is more like a text or a work of art that has to be interpreted than inanimate objects following timeless laws.

3. THE DEMOCRATIC PEACE DEBATE

The democratic peace (DP) debate has been the subject of exceptionally intense focus in IR. A principle aim of this section is to illustrate the ways in which liberals and political realists interacted in academic journals and books, particularly the way in which they carefully addressed one another's arguments rather than simply "talked past" one another. The section will attempt to lay out the main points of the arguments for the DP position; the ways in which political realists developed arguments seeking to show that factors other than "democracy" can explain the patterns of war and peace; and the ways in which liberal theorists responded in point-by-point critiques of the realists' counter-arguments.

All of the top-ranked journals published papers supporting or opposing the DP hypotheses. Over a hundred authors, including nearly all of the most influential figures,[2] have contributed to the debate in a relatively brief time span. The intensity was a result of the magnitude of the stakes—both theoretical and practical. On the theoretical side, given that a core realist principle is that all states are driven by the same power-seeking motivations, the liberal claim that one set of states behaves in a different way on fundamental issues of war and peace flatly contradicts realism. Realists assure us that any systematic differences in behavior are due to factors like power resources, geography, or alliances. Sustaining any of the DP claims would deal a severe and high-profile blow to the core of realism.

The policy stakes were similarly momentous. The end of the Cold War and the collapse of the USSR, the dissolution of the Warsaw Pact, and the breakup of Yugoslavia, brought nearly 30 new regimes into Europe and Central Asia. These states were now able to choose their own destiny. Of course, the US and NATO members hoped to nudge them into friendly orientations. But if helping former Soviet states democratize would also significantly decrease the chances of war over the long haul, then NATO members would be willing to devote much more energy and greater resources to democratize them.

Origins of DP hypotheses. Scholars typically trace the origins of the DP claims to Thomas Paine's *Common Sense* in 1776, and especially to Kant's 1795 *Essay on Perpetual Peace* (Kant 1939). Kant argued that if states with republican constitutions and attendant separation of powers came to dominate the system, wars would cease to be fought—provided that certain other conditions were met, including the development of genuine free trade and the creation of a dispute-resolving federation of republican states. Among the "articles" for perpetual peace contemporary liberals have stressed the three just noted as key, which they refer to as the Kantian tripod or triangle (see Kant; Bohman and -Bachman 1997). While Kant believed a system of such states would behave peacefully toward one another, he had to rely entirely on a theoretical argument because there were so few republican states that fit his requirements.

Throughout the twentieth century, more democracies appeared. The first important quantitative studies of IR were written by Quincy Wright in 1942 and Lewis F. Richardson in 1960. They dealt with many factors potentially connected to war, including "democracy." The first quantitative study specifically of DP hypotheses were written by Dean Babst. He published two very short papers (ten pages combined) in 1964 and 1972, asking "whether there are certain types of governments which do not make war against each other" (Babst 1964: 9). It seemed reasonable to him, "purely impressionistically," that these could be the governments that were elected by voters. So, he tested whether states that have elective governments, as well as stable borders, were statistically unlikely to go to war with similar states; he found that they were. Babst was thus testing the dyadic hypothesis.

Intensifying debate: 1975–2000. It is impossible to survey the hundreds of DP publications in a few pages (see Haas 2014 bibliography). One way to get a sense of the contours of the debate is to examine a dozen of the most influential publications in the prime years of the debate.3 We begin by noting that in the 1960s J. David Singer at the University of Michigan initiated a project, the Correlates of War (COW), to compile and code factors thought to be associated with the onset of war. The COW database, still growing, is widely used in the study of IR. Singer was soon joined by Melvin Small in the project. In 1972, Singer and Small published *The Wages of War: 1816-1965, A statistical handbook.* They dealt with the DP question in their 1976 paper in the *Jerusalem Journal of International Relations*, which drew on the COW database, that tested the statistical associations of a range of variables with the onset of war. Democracy was one of the variables they included. They found a positive association with peace, but, as the study was preliminary, they speculated that when further tests were conducted it would be likely to prove spurious.

R. J. Rummel was also engaged in DP studies at the same time. In his five-volume study of war, Rummel defended both the monadic and dyadic hypotheses (1975–1981). In 1983 Rummel published a paper in the highly ranked *Journal of Conflict Resolution* in which he tested three DP hypotheses, and found them all to be statistically significant. Rather than "democracy," Rummel used the term "libertarianism," which he defined in terms of degrees of civil liberties. One of the tests included both civil liberties and economic freedom. Also in 1983, Michael Doyle published papers that seemed to bring the debate to center stage in the field of IR theory (Doyle 1983a, 1983b). His two-part article "Kant, Liberal Legacies, and Foreign Affairs" in *Philosophy and Public Affairs* was followed in 1986 by "Liberalism and World Politics," in the *American Political Science Review*, the flagship journal of the American Political Science Association. At this point the DP claims had received enough high-profile attention that it seemed to force political realists to come to the defense of their theory.

Two important tests of the dyadic hypothesis were published in 1992, one by Stuart Bremer in *JCR* (1992) and the other by David Lake in *APSR* (1992) . Bremer considered the factors that are most often statistically associated with the onset of war by research studies and used a series of multivariate tests, from which he was able to see the degree to which various factors increased or decreased the probability of war. As many studies have found, the most statistically important factor is sharing a border (or being separated by less than 150 miles of water). But democracy was also statistically very important; democratic dyads are only one-third as likely to go to war as any other type of dyad. Lake argued not only that the dyadic hypothesis is right, but also began to extend the research tradition by testing the claim that democracies are more successful than autocracies when the two states engage in war with one another.

The most recognized and prolific defender of DP claims, along with Doyle, is Bruce Russett. Often with various co-authors, Russett published extensive tests of, and explanations for, the dyadic DP hypothesis. In his 1993 book *Grasping the Democratic Peace*, Russett aimed to show, among other things, that "there are no clearcut cases of sovereign, stable democracies waging war with each other in the modern international system" (1993: 11). Russett's definition of "democracy" was utilized by subsequent authors. He used a dichotomous variable, based on the Polity II dataset (Gurr 1989). The Polity coding uses a zero-to-ten scale measuring autocracy, and another measuring democracy. Russett's dichotomous variable combined the two scales to define a threshold level to qualify as a "liberal democracy" (1993: 76–79).

In 1993 Russett, with Zeev Maoz, published an extremely influential article in the *APSR*—at one point the most downloaded article in that journal's history. By 1993, scholars had strong doubts about the monadic hypothesis, but there was considerable empirical support for the dyadic hypothesis. The *APSR* paper tested models that could explain both why the dyadic hypothesis is true and the monadic hypothesis false. Maoz and Russett considered two mechanisms that could account both for democracies' reluctance to fight one another and for their tendency to go to war, overall, as often as other states do. The "norms" explanation holds that democratic regimes are based on norms of compromise and peaceful resolution of internal disputes. These norms guide democracies when they interact with other regimes with similar norms. But when nondemocratic regimes approach conflict with democracies, and when the use of force is a live option, the democracies have no choice but to respond with force. The "structural" explanation is based on the fact that leaders of democracies must gain public support for war in order to use force. When two democracies are engaged in a dispute, the leaders on both sides must build internal support for any violent policy choice, but since the building of such support is a slow process, it provides time for tensions to dissipate and for leaders to resolve conflicts peacefully.4

Replies after Maoz and Russett. One of the distinctive aspects of the DP debate is that the replies and rebuttals after 1993 were so precisely targeted on elements of the works they were criticizing. Realists responded with both process-tracing historical narratives and a barrage of statistical arguments and critiques. Christopher Layne's 1994 process-tracing paper looking at four historical cases. Layne argued that the peaceful resolutions in all four cases resulted because at least one side was inhibited by national interest and maintaining power, not joint democracy. That is, democracy cannot be shown to be a cause in any of the four cases. Layne maintained that even if a statistical association can be shown by looking at historical cases, correlation does not prove causation. Layne charges that the literature supporting DP hypotheses "fails to establish a causal link" (Layne 1995: 38; Risse-Kappen 1995: 491).

Realists' statistical replies argued that DP studies left out other, more important variables; and if they had been included, they would provide better explanations for war and peace. The COW database used by these authors had been expanded to cover states from 1500 onwards. Realists point out that in almost that entire half-millennium span, up through 1945, democracies were rare. Between 1500 and 1945 there were so few democracies that it would be statistically unlikely for any two of them to go to war against one another, no matter what inclinations they had. In his 1994 paper in *International Security*, David Spiro points out that through the first thirteen years covered by the original COW dataset, 1816–1829, there were only two liberal democracies, the United States and the Swiss Confederation (1994, 66); war between them was materially impossible regardless of any other factors. Spiro makes the case, soon supported by Farber and Gowa in 1995 in *International Security*—and in 1997 by their paper in the *Journal of Politics*—that after World War II, the new democracies were concentrated in European and Asian states under threat from the Soviet Union (Farber and Gowa). They were peaceful towards one another, as realists would expect, because they had a common enemy. States like Belgium and the Netherlands were at peace in 1970, 1971, 1972, etc., primarily because both feared attack by the Soviet Red Army, not because both were democracies. Spiro, like Farber and Gowa, thus argues that the Cold War alliance system was more causally responsible for peace among the many democracies after 1945. Realist theory is quite able to explain peace and cooperation between states that fear a common great power enemy.

Another criticism we see among realists, including (Layne 1994: 38), is that there is no such thing as "democratic peace theory"; that is, there is no legitimate theory, only an empirical regularity (Layne 1994: 38). And some authors argue that if there is no sustainable theoretical-causal mechanism that can be established, then the regularity is likely spurious. The final example of a very influential paper in this period is that of Mansfield and Snyder, also in *International Security* in 1995, who distinguish recently formed democracies from mature democracies, and argue that the former are especially war-prone; even more war-prone than states overall.

Rebuttals to the Realist Criticisms

DP supporters addressed the wave of realist criticisms in the mid-1990s with carefully focused, often point-by-point, responses. Owen presented powerful criticisms of Layne's interpretation of the cases in a reply in the same number of *International Security* as Layne's paper. In his 1995 correspondence, "And Yet it Moves" in *International Security*, Russett (1995: 164–175) deals directly with Layne's historical interpretation of the causal forces restraining the US and Britain from war. In that correspondence, and again in his 2001 book with John R. Oneal, *Triangulating Peace*, Russett replies to the critique that the democratic peace was merely an "artifact of the Cold War" (caused by widespread fear of the USSR) by adding tests of democratic dyads peaceful relations both prior to World War I and in the interwar period (Russett and Oneal 2001). Thompson and Tucker (1997) and Maoz (1998) also address the "artifact" critique.

Some of the DP supporters responded to Mansfield and Snyder's argument that democratizing countries are especially war-prone by acknowledging that the argument is well-founded, but that it does not violate the democracy explanation. They agreed that the causal forces that prevent democracies from fighting one another—namely, entrenched institutions of compromise and negotiation—are in fact absent in newly democratized countries. Thus, the formulation of the dyadic hypothesis was generally circumscribed to refer to "mature liberal democracies." Gibler (2012) later made the case that border stability brings about peace far more effectively than does democracy and that stable borders even bring about democracy. Back in 1964, in his first, brief paper, Babst specified that the causal process to which he referred required that the states have stable borders. So, he seemed aware of the separate cause-and-effect processes involved in border instability.5

Some critics argue that other factors decrease the probability of war more than joint democracy. But DP defenders do not have to show that joint liberal democracy is the only factor that decreases the probability of war. It is widely accepted that the factor most statistically associated with pairs of states going to war is proximity—sharing a land border or being separated by no more than 150 miles of water. Indeed, Kant, Russett, Doyle and others argue on behalf of the Kantian tripod—democracy, international institutions, and economic interdependence—as efficacious in promoting peace. The question for DP

Table 27.2 Realist and liberal theories' factors affecting war and peace	
Factors affecting war and peace behavior	Realist or liberal*
Proximity-common land or sea border	Realist
Democracy	Liberal institutionalist
Economic interdependence and trade	Liberal institutionalist
Presence of International Institutions	Liberal institutionalist
Great power status	Realist
Power differentials	Realist
Alliance ties	Realist
Industrialization	Realist and liberal
Pre- versus post-cold war epoch	Realist

*Liberal institutionalists do not deny that some realist factors can promote war, but they hold that the Kantian tripod (the presence of democracy, trade, certain sorts of institutions) can ameliorate the impulse to solve conflict through violence.

defenders is whether joint democracy reduces the chance of two states going to war regardless of whether they are near to or far from one another. Consequently, DP supporters controlled for other variables like great power status, power differentials, geographic distance/proximity, alliance ties, pre-versus post–Cold War era, regime stability, industrialization/nonindustrialization, military spending, and economic growth. These studies have often found very different results depending on methodology and included variables, which has caused criticism.

Progress in Science

Some have claimed that the democratic peace debate has focused on empirical evidence and both sides built on the other's critiques by improving evidence collection and methods of analysis. In these respects it has progressed in ways akin to what we see in the natural sciences Jack Levy's widely quoted assessment is that the "absence of war between democracies comes as close as anything we have to an empirical law in international relations" (Levy 1988: 662). Has IR indeed progressed to the point of having established a scientific-style empirical law? The concept of "scientific progress" has, of course, been widely debated, though the different schools of thought generally agree on what innovations in science constitute progress. (Examples would include Galileo over Ptolemy, Harvey over Galen, Einstein over Newton.) Although there is debate over just what progress means, there are several points that are generally accepted. One is that science must be cumulative (at least within the practice of Kuhnian "normal science"). And the other is that there must be some way—that is, some set of criteria—that will allow scientists to determine which hypothesis or theory to be more acceptable than rivals. It is easy to see why so many philosophers of science that accept these if we imagine someone presenting a paper at a scientific conference or at the Philosophy of Science Association meeting who claims to define a new area of study that is a legitimate science, but that is not cumulative—every contribution stands on its own and there is no way to extend, expand, or find new sources of evidence for any existing claim in that "science." And the same holds if the paper presenter acknowledges that when competition arises between mutually exclusive claims, either empirical or theoretical, there is simply no way to discern which should be accepted.

Beyond these widely held conditions, there is debate over which precise theory of good scientific practice has the most validity, either in terms of what ideally is good science or what best reflects existing good science. Among IR theorists who contest these issues, the account of scientific progress most cited in IR debates is that of Imre Lakatos. Put briefly, Lakatos accepted the basic idea of Karl Popper (a mentor of his at LSE) that truly scientific statements or theories must be "falsifiable"—which means that one must be able to imagine an observation that would force a theory's supporters to acknowledge that it is false. If the theory allows its supporters to reinterpret or modify it so that apparently falsifying instances can be made consistent with the theory, then the theory is not falsifiable, and therefore not scientific. Lakatos took this idea and developed what he called the "methodology of scientific research programs" (Lakatos 1970). According to Lakatos, scientific research consists of falsifiable theories that may be modified as scientists gain new, and sometimes problematic, observations, or new analytical methods. The series of theories and their modifications is called a "scientific research program." Some principles in the theory are essential to the identity of the research program and some are not. That is, if any of the former were changed, the research program would no longer be *that* research program. Those principles make up the theory's "hard core." The other "auxiliary hypotheses" make up the theory's "protective belt." These latter can be modified to keep the new, revised theory both within the research program and consistent with evidence.

Some ways of modifying the theory constitute good science (progressive research programs) and some do not constitute good science (degenerating research programs). The difference between them, which Lakatos bases on his investigation of the history of science, includes the idea that theory modifications ("theory shifts") that alter the hard core represent a diminution of explanatory power, as they do not legitimately "explain" the anomalous observation. Rather, they show that the theory had no significant scientific substance. Those modifications are indicative of a "degenerating" research program. Moreover, modifications that are "progressive" add explanatory power. One requirement is that the theory and its modifications will lead researchers to consider new hypotheses. These new hypotheses, when established, constitute what Lakatos calls "novel facts." The observed facts are novel in that researchers would not have considered undertaking the necessary steps, or focused their attention in ways to make it possible, to observe them before the modification was made within the research program.

As noted, falsifying evidence led liberals to cease to support the monadic hypothesis. Is this change degenerating or progressive? That is, does abandoning the monadic hypothesis reveal degeneration in IR liberalism? It seems not, since the research program sprang from hard core of the "Kantian triangle" and that position depends only on democracies not going to war against one another, that is, on the dyadic hypothesis, rather than on the claim that democracies fight fewer wars generally than nondemocracies. What about the question of whether it is progressiveness? We might ask if the liberal DP research program satisfies Lakatos's key requirement of identifying "new facts"? After corroboration of the dyadic hypothesis, a large literature developed posing new questions about possible differences that liberal democracy makes with respect to war and peace. New questions were posed: Is the frequency with which democracies win wars different from that of nondemocracies? (Yes, more often, Ray 1998.) Are democracies less likely to engage in conflicts short of

COW-defined war? (Yes, Ray 1993.) Does military superiority play out differently in democratic dyads than other sort of dyads? (Yes, Gelpi and Griesdorf 2001.) Does a higher level of democratization lead to a higher level of success in wars? (Yes.) Does the initiator affect democracies' success? (Yes, Reiter and Stam 1998.)

4. CONSTRUCTIVIST AND POSTSTRUCTURALIST CRITIQUES OF DEMOCRATIC PEACE STUDIES

The third group of contemporary theorists, broadly defined as constructivists, reject nearly the entire approach of IR naturalists. This section will look at the criticisms raised by the various groups within the constructivist school. It begins with "conventional" or "interpretive" constructivists, the position held by most US authors in the constructivist camp. It then discusses the constructivist debt to Critical Theory, and finally describes the view known as poststructuralism in IR, whose adherents argue that the appropriate methods for theorizing about world politics are even farther from naturalism than other constructivists.

All constructivists deny the naturalists' claims that:

   (i)   there is a genuine separation of observer and social subject matter;
   (ii) agents in IR and social structures are distinct;
   (iii) there is objective truth in social theorizing, and facts and values are distinct;
   (iv) there are natural science-like causal relationships;
   (v)   the subjects of study in IR are materially constructed (rather, constructivists say that they are socially constructed);
   (vi) observers in the social sciences can formulate value-free hypotheses and theories.

Constructivists argue that social scientists are not capable of making natural science-like observations that are objective and untainted by their own values. What we can study in the social world is what people and groups *mean* by what they say and what they do. In IR, this becomes the search for the meaning of leaders' statements; the real meaning is often quite different from what a simple surface or literal interpretation would suggest. Consequently, many constructivists see the model for our study of the social world not in the natural sciences, but in the humanities, especially the search for meaning in works of art and literature. Constructivists place little or no emphasis on material factors. This contrasts sharply with political realists and liberals, as the former see material factors as driving states' actions, and the latter regard material factors as important, along with other factors like international institutions, domestic factors like democracy, and social norms. Constructivists regard the realm of world politics as "socially constructed."

Conventional and Interpretive Constructivists

The constructivist scholars closest to naturalists are, as Alex Wendt terms them, "conventional constructivists." This group is associated with Wendt's journal articles and especially his book in 1999, *Social Theory of International Politics*.6 Ted Hopf (1998) and Emmanuel Adler (1997) are among the other constructivists in this school of thought. They hold that material forces have a place in the study of IR, and that some causal claims are justifiable in at least some instances. In contrast, European constructivism denies the legitimacy of causal claims and material forces (e.g., Kratochwil 1989; Pouliot 2008). The strongest opposition to naturalist approaches to social science come from poststructuralists; they thoroughly reject naturalism and positivism. They take a critical view of all academic attempts to encapsulate human action, requiring instead that research retain a steady focus on the researcher's own potential biases, and an emphasis on the researcher's moral obligation to create a better world with any published findings. Scholars on all points of the constructivist spectrum share deep skepticism of both liberals' and realists' DP arguments, as this section discusses.

Constructivism in IR draws on various sources, including what is known as "the English School" of Herbert Butterfield, Charles Manning, Hedley Bull, and Martin Wight (Dunne 2008). The English School authors acknowledge that international anarchy is real, but the anarchy today is not a necessary feature of the international system; anarchy is socially constructed and could have evolved very differently. Rather than the largely zero-sum world we have, the system might have evolved in a way where states look out for one another's interest, or at least work cooperatively to seek the greater good of the entire system. They hold that there is nothing in the concept of "anarchy" that entails the dog-eat-dog struggle for supremacy. Wendt sums up this outlook in the title of one of his papers, "Anarchy Is What States Make of It" (1992).

Constructivist Norms and Democratic Peace

With the above outline of the constructivist approach to IR now in place, the remainder of this section will describe how different strands of constructivism relate to one another and how they provide a set of counter-arguments to the self-described "scientific progress" that naturalist authors claim can be found in the DP debate between liberals and realists. First, we note that at the height of the DP debate, Thomas Risse-Kappen conceded that the empirical evidence for the dyadic hypothesis is persuasive, but said the hypothesis is "undertheorized," as the explanations were inadequate (Risse-Kappen 1995: 492). He argued that social constructivism offers a better explanation for the empirical fact that democratic states rarely go to war with one another, that disputes between democracies rarely escalate, and that democracies overall fight wars as often as do nondemocracies. The question, he says, boils down to, "why does the security dilemma not arise among democracies?" Risse-Kappen says that constructivism is a theory about how IR "forms part of the social construction of reality" rather than a "a substantive theory of international relations" (502). He explicitly mentions four of the above principles (i, ii, v, and vi). Researchers and subject matter are not completely distinct, actors' interests are socially constructed, could have be, en constructed differently, and can change in the future.

In responding to Maoz and Russett's tests of structural and normative "models" for the monadic and dyadic hypotheses, Risse-Kappen says that constructivism builds on, and completes, the norms model. There is no mechanical process guiding liberal democracies with shared norms to avoid war. States socially construct their relationships with others.

They self-identify as "liberal democracies" and come to view others as fitting into their own group. States' internal governance structures are part of the web of communication that takes place between states. Demonstrating that one has democratic structures automatically sends a particular set of signals to other states, which democracies interpret as signals that the sender is part of their group.7 These governance structures gradually create a collective identity among liberal democracies; they become part of the "us" which is against "them." Risse-Kappen says that only when scholars include this aspect of the norms model is it possible to explain why liberal democracies are so aggressive in general, but are not when interacting with states identified as part of their kind.

Wesley Widmaier (2005) follows Risse-Kappen's pattern of using constructivists' principles about the social construction of relationships that make up world politics in order to supplement the liberal account of peace between liberal democracies. He agrees that *perceptions* of other states are combined to constitute an image of world politics, and that that image is what drives decisions to restrain oneself or attack in times of crisis. But Widmaier differs from Risse-Kappen and other constructivists by holding that the perceptions are not uniform throughout a state or society. He argues that the perceptions are processed by sub-societal groups or by individuals. These smaller groups' perceptions are what guide political actors to categorize another state as inside or outside their group. Thus, for Widmaier the constructor of the image is not the society as a whole, but is a subset of a part of the society.

Widmaier gives as an example the US, where different political parties perceive other states in different ways. The differences shape leaders' thinking about whether another state is or is not "like" the US. Democratic leaders tend to see the US as a *social* democracy, and thus see other social democracies around the world as part of the group the US is in. Republican leaders view the US as a *liberal* democracy and thus see a greater connection between the US and liberal democracies. Consequently, they are more prone to place liberal democracies in the "us group" with the US. This is squarely a constructivist analysis because neither material considerations nor unambiguously objective nonmaterial factors drive the perception. Rather, how people see the world and how they "construct" their own society and other states is what influences behavior.

For empirical support, Widmaier analyzes the 1971 Indo-Pakistan war, in which democratic India intervened in the effort of Pakistan, under military rule, to prevent East Pakistan from becoming independent Bangladesh. The constructivist explanation of which states fit into the "us group" was open to social construction. And the Republican Nixon Administration's "tilt" toward Pakistan, and against social-democratic India, could have brought the US to war, Widmaier argues, against democratic India.8 He concludes that it is neither the norms of the *society or state,* nor the structure of democracies' decision-making process that keep democracies from fighting one another, but rather the socially constructed image in the minds of groups smaller than the state, e.g., political parties, that creates the perception of "us" or "them."

Critical Theory and Constructivism

Critical Theory employs a genealogical or historical analysis of ideas and the social forces producing them. The historical-sociological approach to knowledge that Critical Theory requires is "much richer and more nuanced than quantitative analyses" that naturalists have used (Hobson 2011: 1914). Christopher Hobson, a Critical Theory-inspired constructivist, contends that the historical approach reveals that the meanings of "democracy," "war," and "peace" are "heavily contested" and are "diachronically and synchronically variable" (Hobson 2011:1908). This follows also the approach taken by Barkawi and Laffey who "contextualize . . . conceptual histories within processes of global change" (Hobson 1999: 405). The genealogy also exposes an important motivation of DP supporters, given that the exchanges reached their high-point "during the so-called 'the third debate' between positivist and post-positivist perspectives" (Hobson 2011: 1905). Positivists had a strong incentive to show the advantages of their "scientific" approach to producing knowledge.

Hobson sees democracies' extensive use of violence as casting doubt on the reality of the image of democracies as naturally inclined toward peaceful behavior. He says that DP studies manifest positivism's inability to deal with the moral problems that are raised by their policy implications, such as the justification for the invasion of Iraq, and the morality of authorizing killing in order to advance democratic ideals. While someone might argue that DP studies, and the solidity of the findings therein, show IR's scientific character, Hobson argues that the any justification for killing people by reference to some benefit for democracy is a distortion. He argues that the damage it does to the standing or legitimacy of positivist-naturalist IR is far greater than any increase in legitimacy it could gain by its ability to produce "scientific findings." Like most constructivists, Hobson accepts much of the social analysis of Frankfurt School Critical Theory, which applies to all studies of the social world. The Frankfurt School founders saw the Nazi regime present pseudo-scholarship as though it were "science" in a way that was carefully devised to aid Germany's brutal repression in Europe. Hobson maintains that Frankfurt School Critical Theory can address various "ontological, epistemological, and methodological problems that restrict existing work" in DP studies (2011: 1904).

A crucial point to note is that Critical Theorists regard all scholarship as intimately involving a critique of the status quo and of the dominant power structure. The Critical Theory approach involves "immanent critique" of the current socio-political state of affairs. This, they say, is a moral obligation of scholars. Finally, Hobson acknowledges that Critical Theory "lacks the parsimony and elegance of positivist scholarship," and clear policy implications, but overall its application "will far outweigh any potential side effects, especially as it is meant to complement, not replace, current scholarship" (2011: 1922).

Foucault and the Poststructural Critique

Poststructuralist theorists in the tradition of Michel Foucault are those in IR who most vigorously reject naturalism and value-free positivism in the study of IR (Foucault 1984, 2000). Accordingly, they reject both realist and liberal arguments about democratic peace. Foucault's theorizing, drawn from philosophy, history, and social analysis, has had an enormous impact on a diverse set of scholarly enterprises. Foucault developed a range of new concepts, emphasizing the role of language in humans' understanding of the world and of one another. "Structuralist linguistics" posits language as a mediating factor, connecting abstract ideas and reality. In contrast to both traditional Western thinking and structuralism, poststructuralist thinkers like Foucault, Jacques Derrida (1976), Gilles Deleuze (1990), and others, see history and culture as having such a deep and intimate effect on any scholars' understanding that objective truth, as ordinarily understood, is simply not possible.

In IR, poststructuralists are further opposed to realists and liberals because the latter group treat the state with more moral legitimacy than it deserves, particularly in light of the forces of repression that states employ. Indeed, a core interest of Foucault was the effort to identify the sources of control and oppression in society. In modern society the intellectual class works, perhaps unwittingly, to support the forces of repression that every state uses to maintain control. Some poststructuralists even charge that, in order to reinforce the dominant socio-politico-economic interests in society, positivist social science is designed to mislead the public into accepting academia's findings as objective fact.

Scholars such as Richard Ashley (1986), James Der Derian (1987), and RBJ Walker (1993) represent poststructuralism in IR in their rejection of the entire framework of the DP debate. An application of this approach is offered in a recent paper by Rose Shimko, who argues that the study of peace understood in the context of an international system of sovereign states marginalizes the more important question of the use of violence that is required to create and maintain sovereign, territorially defined states. Critical Theorists, along with various other groups, emphasize that it is essential for scholars to reassess their own moral frameworks of analysis. Shimko critically examines "discourses of peace" and argues that IR discussions are shaped by the hegemonic powers in the international system. What peace is, or what it should be conceived to be, needs a fundamental reappraisal with attention to the moral commitments or biases of the researchers who publish their scholarship. The entire framework of the DP debate, what gets written and what gets published, especially in the most prestigious journals and presses, is influenced by the forces that control the most powerful states and seek to maintain the existing order in the international system. One way to view this aspect of poststructuralism is as a moral stance that rejects the illegitimate tools of repression of the state. Claims of legitimacy grounded in the peace-producing effects of one regime-type, liberal democracy, are another way to disguise the moral defects of the global system of nation-states. Poststructuralists regard the moral component as one that cannot be evaded; thus, positivist or naturalist IR theories are taking a moral position, specifically one that gives a free pass to the existing sociopolitical superstructure of repression.

For poststructuralists, the manner in which scholars conceptualize peace is itself a political decision or commitment. Foucault treated the notion of war in a way that allowed him to emphasize the technology of control that was " 'intended to blur the distinction between war and peace, the battlefield and the social sphere' " (Shimko, p. 487, citing Foucault *Discipline and Punish*, p.168). Violence is used for control. And if the violence can be disguised, it is all the more effective. Shimko describes Foucault's view that, in any society, the most important political task is the "unmasking of political violence" (Shimko 2008: 485). The DP debate does not represent intellectual or scientific progress because, as Shimko says, the study of sovereignty and the state are "conceptual dead-ends" (474; see Table 27.3).

Table 27.3 Points of contention between Naturalism and Anti-Naturalist Constructivisms

Naturalism	Objective facts help support cause-and-effect conclusions
Conventional constructivism	Some causal claims
Critical theory	All social analysis must carry immanent critique of the hegemonic powers
Post-structuralism	The state is inherently a repressive construct

5. Background Information, Context, and Explanation

Section 3 brought us to the central topic of this volume, the philosophy of political science, as we just saw that constructivists' criticisms of the DP debate focus on questions regarding the nature of the actors, objective truth, causality, and the possibility of knowledge parallel to that in the natural sciences. These are issues in the philosophy of science that are fundamentally different from realists' and liberals' scholarly works that focus on empirical observations and substantive theory. Constructivists offer a critique of the philosophical framework within which liberals and realists present their arguments for their position and against the other side's.

The liberal-versus-realist DP debate achieved a rare degree of cumulation of knowledge, as each side's arguments and criticisms directly addressed the other's and built upon critiques by responding with precisely targeted and improved arguments. Constructivists offer a range of criticisms of naturalist social science and in particular the claim of scientific progress in the DP debate. This section and the next will attempt to show that constructivists' arguments about the changing nature of key terms in the social sciences have force. But the discussion will also seek to show constructivists are not entirely justified in their conclusion that this negates the naturalists' claim of scientific knowledge in IR based on the progress of the DP debate. That is, natural scientists also have shifting interests, which, over time, can sometimes move their focus to different aspects of the phenomena.

Whether the dyadic hypothesis answers an important question about war and peace depends upon what social scientists regard as qualifying, in general, as an acceptable hypothesis or explanatory answer. The first part of this section makes the case that the social and intellectual context of a debate over a question influences what can be regarded as a good answer. The second part of this section examines the context of the 1960s as it affected how Babst's publication was evaluated in terms of explanatory success, and how the sociopolitical context changed in the aftermath of the Cold War—as the most intense period of the DP debate unfolded. The goal here is to set the stage for a discussion in Section 5 of philosophers of science who endorse the pragmatic/contextualist theory of hypothesis or theory choice. The pragmatic approach to science enables political scientists to evaluate the constructivist critique of naturalists' claims of "progress" regarding the DP debate. It attempts to show that the constructivists' are in accord with pragmatist philosophers of science on the question of context-dependent meanings of terms, but that fact does not demonstrate a divergence from what philosophers of natural science see as progress.

The Context and Background Beliefs Shape What Will Count as a Good Answer to a Research Question

While DP arguments go back to Kant in the eighteenth century, the modern debate has been brief by historical standards. Even in that short span, the context of world politics changed from the Cuban Missile Crisis, which was just months before Babst's paper appeared, to the dissolution of the USSR just prior to Russett's 1993 book and *APSR* paper with Maoz. The pragmatic account of knowledge and theory choice give a prominent role to the context in which a knowledge claim is made. Bas Van Fraassen is the most influential proponent of this account of science (1980, 1989, 2002). He argues that every explanatory theory is devised as an answer to a question, and is offered in the context of a particular historical moment when the relevant research community, as audience, holds (a) specific background beliefs and (b) priorities as to the most important questions to investigate—both of which vary over time. In order for an explanatory answer to be accepted by the audience, it typically will have to answer a question about why a particular event or process took place, *rather than some alternative* event.

Another pragmatist philosopher of science, Peter Achinstein, emphasizes that an utterance is an explanatory answer only if the explainer has the intention of making something understandable to the audience (Achinstein 1971, 1984). The process of explaining is thus a speech act, in Austin's sense (Austin 1962). For Achinstein, as for Van Fraassen, an explanation must answer a question, and the full understanding of the question includes (perhaps implicitly) a contrast class of answers. To use Achinstein's example (1984)—coincidentally about a dyadic war—we can imagine someone observing the American flag flying over Fort McHenry after the British assault and asking, "Why is our flag still there?" But the question without any context can be interpreted in multiple ways.

The simple formulation of this question does not, by itself, tell us all we need to know about what is being asked, and thus what the audience would regard as a legitimate answer. Knowledge of the context, specifically of the questioner's intention and the audience's beliefs and interests are all essential. The questioner might be asking why our flag is still there (1) in contrast *to some other flag* being there, (2) in contrast to why is our flag there *instead of some other sort of object* being there, or (3) in contrast to our flag being *somewhere else (or nowhere)*. Once we establish proper contrast to "Why is our flag still there?" we will be able to clarify just what the question is asking. This in turn enables us to determine what would count as an appropriate answer to the question. If the contrast is (1), then legitimate answers (though not necessarily perhaps correct) might be "Seaman Smyth was about to replace it with the Union Jack but his ship sank just as it entered the port ," or "Captain Morgan intended to hoist the Jolly Roger but fell overboard." A proposed explanatory answer is appropriate only when we know enough about the context to understand what the *contrast class* is (see also Garfinkle 1981; Woodward 2003; Kincaid 1996, ch. 2).

With regard to the contextual research priorities of the audience, Achinstein offers as an example the question about atomic theory that led to Rutherford's 1911 experiment (1984,

286). He argues that, "Rutherford's explanation is good . . . because it answers a causal question about the scattering [of alpha particles] . . . in a way that physicists at the time were interested in understanding the scattering." The subset of physicists working on atomic nuclei, and specifically alpha-scatter, had interests in *specific aspects of* alpha scatter. Those interests constituted a part of the context of Rutherford's choice of an explanatory answer, and constituted a part of the framework for what would count as a superior answer. What the community of researchers is most interested in, and is considering as a plausible answer, will form part of their set of ideas about what will constitute a good explanatory answer, given the empirical results (see Kincaid 2004).

The DP Debate through the Last Third of the Twentieth Century and the Context of Changing Assumptions about Liberal Democracy

How does this help us understand the meaning of the question that the dyadic hypothesis is intended as an answer? Before we turn to the contextual aspect of choosing an explanatory answer, it is useful to consider further the changes in the context of debates about democratic states between 1964, when Babst published his first paper, and perceptions of democracies in the late 1980s, when the DP debate began to gather steam.

Let us for a moment suppose that a scholar offers an empirical demonstration that mature liberal democracies very rarely fight one another. We then ask: have we achieved progress, and have we come to know something that can help policy-makers guide decisions about democracy-promotion? In the 1960s, when Babst published his first paper that began the modern DP debate, many people personally remembered Kaiser Wilhelm's aggression that they regarded as causing World War I, which took 20 million lives. In 1964, anyone over the age of 25 could remember fascist Germany's aggression that cost 50 million lives. And nearly everyone could remember that, within the last two years, the antidemocratic Soviet Union was discovered to be secretly emplacing "offensive missiles" in Cuba, just 90 miles from American soil. In the two world wars Western democracies sought to avoid war, but nondemocratic leaders could not be stopped. And after World War II, the Soviet Union seized control of eastern Europe, worked to aid Mao in turning China communist, and then cooperated with Mao to support Kim Il-Sung's aggression against South Korea.

As surveys of the period show,9 Americans accepted that the Communist Bloc was overtly threatening the free world, and possibly the survival of humanity. An empirical demonstration in 1964, like Babst's, that democracies behave peacefully toward one another was, like all propositions, rooted in a specific context. In American politics in 1964, the principal context was the contrast between democracy and fascism and communism. With that context, if democracies are shown historically to be unusually peaceful in their dealings with one another, Americans and Westerners ask why that is the case. The personal experience that people in the West have of democracy, as background for their understanding of democracies, would leave little mystery about the link between peaceful behavior and democratic regime-type.

Before turning to the role of context in choosing a best answer, we should compare the context of the start of the modern DP debate, with Babst's 1964 paper, to that of the point when the debate intensifies, in the late 1980s. Ronald Reagan became US president in 1981. He promised, and delivered, what he described as the greatest military buildup in American peacetime history. He added harsh anti-communist rhetoric, which was seen by many as provoking the Soviets. His famous August 1984 sound-check incident, "My fellow Americans, I'm pleased to tell you I just signed legislation which outlaws Russia forever. The bombing begins in five minutes" (UPI, August 11, 2014). This struck many people in the US and around the world as showing a very cavalier attitude toward war, even nuclear war. This of course included Western academics who are likely to contribute to DP studies; they were not at all sure of the good-versus-evil contrast of democracy and socialism. Doubts about the peacefulness of democracies and aggression by the USSR were compounded the next year with the rise of Mikhail Gorbachev in the USSR, who soon initiated genuine and far-reaching reforms. The public in Europe even more than in the US saw Reagan as a greater threat to peace than Gorbachev. The perception from the 1950s and 1960s was that the Western democracies were self-evidently more careful in their willingness to initiate major war. The difference in attitudes can be seen by means of various public opinion polls (such as the Roper polls; see Richman, 1991: 136-37).

An important driver of the changed context in the three decades following 1964 is the effect of the Vietnam War. The US had 23,000 troops in Vietnam in 1964. This rose to nearly half a million five years later. And the world was not particularly focused on the US role in Vietnam in 1963–1964.10 A strong majority of Americans did not object to the US involvement in that conflict. In November 1964, only 13 percent or respondents thought the US should withdraw. By April of 1972 a Gallup poll showed that over 70 percent of respondents supported the Senate proposal to withdraw US forces from Vietnam if prisoners are returned. This turn-around in public opinion led many, who may not have thought so after World War II, to realize that democracies can make bad choices in the use of force. The image in the US and around the world of democracies was clearly different from what surveys showed in 1964.

The change in context from 1964 to the 1990s makes clear that any implicit belief in democracy as self-evidently more peaceful than nondemocracies had faded. In 1964, "fear of the threat of communism was 86 percent" (Smith 1983). Democracy was clearly seen as a more just and more peace-loving form of government compared to the alternative forms of government. After a decade of détente, the sense of "enemy" declined, only 40 percent or Americans saw the USSR in that way (Richman 1991: 143). By July 1989, still before the fall of the Berlin Wall, with the many reforms in the Soviet Union instituted by Gorbachev, the percent of Americans who saw the USSR as threatening was a mere 14 percent (Richman 1991: 143). After the fall of the USSR and dissolution of the Warsaw Pact, the danger of alternatives to democracy fell even further and the view of democracy as the peaceful regime-type had become more of an open question. By 1993, opponents could view the dyadic hypothesis as a much more contestable proposition, and one in need of a causal explanation, even though many of them acknowledged the strong statistical regularity. The background beliefs of Babst's audience in 1964 were substantially different from those of the dyadic hypothesis debate audience three decades later. It should not come as a surprise that debates about a causal mechanism arose concurrently with the fall of the Soviet Union, rather than in the 1960s or 70s, when communism was perceived as an existential threat to the survival of democracy.11

5. Constructivist Critique, Pragmatics of Explanation and Naturalist Cumulation, and Approach-to-Consensus

Liberal and realist empirical scholars have, as noted, approached a level of consensus on the monadic and dyadic hypotheses—the former false and the latter true—that is rare in contentious IR debates in which the theoretical and policy states are so high. In the last fifteen-plus years, major IR journals have seldom published papers challenging the dyadic hypothesis or supporting the monadic hypothesis. In this stretch of time publications on the dyadic hypothesis have demonstrated cumulation in view of the fact that they more often build upon the dyadic hypothesis than contest it. New questions about democracies and war are posed, stemming from the well-supported dyadic hypothesis. Given standards of "progress" in at least some major lines of thinking in the philosophy of science, at this point there appears to have been genuine progress that parallels natural science progress.12

Constructivist Critics and the Pragmatist Account of Scientific Enquiry

Critiques of the dyadic hypothesis since the late 1990s are rarely empirical in the mold of the liberal-realist debate. These critiques, for the most part, come from outside of the mainstream naturalist framework. Three related points are in order with regard to those critiques. First, constructivists are usually asking different questions than those that liberals and realists have asked; second, the questions are not just superficially different but are of a fundamentally different sort; and third, outside of the US, especially in Europe, different aspects of war-peace behavior are at the forefront of debate.

To begin with the first: the questions that are of most interest to constructivists are quite different from those asked by mainstream empirical IR researchers. A great deal of scholarly disagreement in all fields arises from opposing factions failing to notice that they are after answers to somewhat different questions. Our understanding of intellectual progress benefits from the work of Van Fraassen and like-minded philosophers, who emphasize the vital need to clarify exactly what question is at stake. As we saw with the question about the presence of "our flag," what *looks like* the same very question in a given language can be intended by the questioners to investigate different aspects of the world. This appears to be the case with conventional constructivists and poststructuralists like Risse-Kappen, Hobson, and Shimko, who are interested in how different societies viewed certain concepts in different times and places. The realist-liberal DP debate, e.g., with the COW database, identified a specific set of traits that were either present or absent in various historical cases. They were typically not focusing on how people "inside" those historical periods conceptualized the terms.

The second point is that constructivists are asking *fundamentally different kinds* of questions. Their questions are generally not substantive empirical questions. The self-description by Alex Wendt, the most influential constructivist (Maliniak, Susan, and

Michael 2012: 42–44), of the nature of his two books is instructive. He describes the first as half philosophy and half IR, and the second as all philosophy. Hobson, discussed above, says, "At the heart of Critical Theory lies the method of immanent critique, a form of analysis that derives 'from a nonpositivist epistemology.' " This clearly involves questions realists and liberals are not asking (2011: 1913, quoting Antonio 1981: 332). Constructivists pose questions, for example, about whether there is an ontic separation between the nation-state and the system of states, about how embedded the meanings of terms are from the genealogy of those terms, about the ability of scholars to evade moral commitments and think in value-neutral terms, and about the possibility of conveying ideas that are disentangled from their own individual human perspective. Sammy Barkin argues that constructivism is a philosophical-methodological stance. Thus, it is not an alternative to, or competitor with, realism and liberalism. In his view, the subject matter of realism and liberalism is so divorced from constructivism that one can be a constructivist and, at the same time, hold either liberal or realist substantive principles. Barkin's core point here is evident in the title of his book on the subject, *Realist Constructivism* (Barkin 2010).

A third point is that IR audiences in geographically different areas prioritize different aspects of questions about democracies' war and peace behavior. Constructivist hold that the meanings of terms vary from one place to another, and from one time period to another. The major journals that have published the most widely read constructivist DP critiques are European. The divide between European and North American political scientists somewhat parallels the divide between the different approaches of Anglo-American philosophers and continental philosophers.

Support for the geographical-divide claim can be seen in the TRIP survey, as it asks scholars in various countries to list journals' importance to their work. The survey reports the percentage of respondents who identify the four top journals in that regard. For the journal *International Security*, the fraction was fairly similar on either side of the Atlantic: for the US 45 percent, for the UK 37 percent, for France 39 percent, and for Denmark 25 percent. But in the case of the journals that published most of the constructivist articles discussed above, the variation was huge. For *The European Journal of International Relations*, only 12 percent of US respondents listed it as one of the top four. But in the UK, the total was 52 percent; Denmark 39 percent; and France 17 percent. For the *Review of International Studies*, in the US it is a mere four percent; while in the UK it is a whopping 37 percent, and France and Denmark were both more than triple the US level, at 14 percent and 15 percent, respectively (Maliniak et al. 2012: 53–54). Again, the pragmatist and contextualist approaches to the ways in which scientists choose the best among several explanatory answers to a question call our attention to how scholarly audiences in different times and/or places can have different priorities about what aspect of a subject is most important to investigate, as the rest of this section shows.

Question Clarity, Consensus, and the Democratic Peace Debate

Another reason for the exceptional approach-to-consensus success in the DP debate was that there was greater agreement about the meaning of the question during the most intense phase of the debate. If two groups of theorists interpret a question differently, they are unlikely to agree on an answer. As was discussed in Section 4, the political context of the DP debate changed significantly between Babst in 1964 and the post–Cold War period of intense debate. Even within the decade of the 1990s there was an explosion of publications. The short time-span increases the chance that divergent scholars would interpret the question similarly, and that their interest in specific aspects would be less variable. We noted in Section 3 Widmaier's remark that notions of "democracy," etc. are contested over time, but in a time span of just ten years the meanings are not likely to shift far. As Achinstein argues, at the time of the Rutherford experiment, the scientific community of particle physicists had a particular interest, which helped the research community agree on the superiority of one explanatory answer. So the closer temporal sequence of works in the DP debate may have enhanced a similarity of focus and framework, which may in turn have helped greater consensus develop as compared to other IR and social science debates.

Databases. One major obstacle to consensus in political science debates is disagreement about what actually happened, i.e., whether a certain outcome does or does not fit an analytical category. Was the Indo-Pakistani Kargil conflict in 1999 a *war*? In 1914 was Germany a *democracy*? Tetlock (2005) offers an extensive discussion of the ways in which theoretically or ideologically opposed groups manage to interpret specific events as confirming their own divergent theories' expectations. When scholars code their own cases, opponents can always challenge the other side's codings as (unintentionally) biased to support the authors' conclusions. The two sides might disagree on whether the Kargil conflict counts as a war or Wilhelmine Germany as a democracy. But by the time Doyle's papers were published in 1983, the COW project was already two decades old and widely used in IR. The COW database was a logical choice for researchers who needed codings for states' participation in wars. As a result, both sides generally used the same databases. The COW database provided a specific definition of "war," namely 1,000 battle deaths within a year of the onset of war. The COW dataset uses a binary variable: states are either at war or not at war. The COW also defines "militarized interstate disputes," for lower level conflict in which states threaten the use of force.

Liberals and realists also had a common database for the variable "democracy." Two widely used databases pre-date the rise of the DP debate, those of Freedom House and the Polity project. There are some differences between them but they were largely in agreement. The Polity project codings became more widely used than those of Freedom House. They are subtler and thus more able to capture the fact that regimes sometimes combine some aspects of democracy and some of autocracy. Polity codes states on both of the scales. Because of the availability and quality of these databases, reviewers for any major journal would expect authors to use one of them and if they did not, the author would bear a clear burden of proof to justify deviations. The fact that there were common databases in use for both the independent variable, *democracy*, and the dependent variable, *peace*, reduced each side's ability to tailor codings to advance its own conclusion; both sides had to use those databases or explain deviations, thus eliminating one of the common reasons for continual disagreement on major empirical questions.

Criteria of evaluation. In the philosophy of science, two broad schools of thought are empiricism and scientific realism, and they are roughly evenly split between the two major philosophy of science approaches to theory choice (listed in note 3). The two philosophical schools emphasize different criteria of theory choice as being paramount. For empiricists, predictive accuracy and empirical adequacy are key criteria, though there are many others. And for scientific realists, the identification of mechanisms and "deep causes" are key. We can imagine a dispute in IR proceeding without resolution over a central principle of IR, like "all states, whether democratic or not, seek power," because the two groups of theorists endorse different criteria of theory choice as the ones that are of greatest weight. But this is not the case, and thus it was not an obstacle. There is no difference between liberals and realists with regard to which philosophy of science tradition to which they subscribe.

One might guess that liberalism and political realism are aligned with opposing philosophical/methodological principles in the philosophy of science; e.g., perhaps all liberals are empiricists and all realists are not. But there is no connection between the substantive IR theories and the schools of thought in the philosophy of social science: some IR political realists are empiricists, and some are scientific realists, and some IR liberals are empiricists and some scientific realists. Major figures in political realism and those in liberalism seem to be more or less evenly distributed between these two broad approaches to the philosophy of science (see Chernoff 2014). For example, Doyle uses scientific realist criteria like "uncovering true causes" and "identification of causal mechanisms," both of which are prominently used by IR's most influential political realist, John Mearsheimer. Maoz and Russett sought causal mechanisms in their 1993 *APSR* paper; indeed, it was essentially a test of two micro-mechanisms, which are the structural and normative explanations. The important empiricist criterion, "empirical adequacy," was employed by nearly all twelve of the authors, both liberal and realist. Six of the twelve employed the next most important empiricist criterion, "predictive accuracy," but the six are divided evenly between realists and liberals. The most influential realist and most influential liberal not included in the above group, Robert Keohane and the late Kenneth Waltz, were both very clearly empiricists. King, Keohane, and Verba's /.*Designing Social Inquiry* (1994) is the most widely used empiricist methodology textbook (see Table 27.4).13

Of the dozen most cited DP authors, five are realist opponents of the DP claims and seven are liberal supporters. Of the seven most oft-invoked criteria by these twelve authors, all were very nearly used equally by the five realists and seven liberal authors. With regard to empirical adequacy, 11 authors make clear use of empirical adequacy, nearly evenly with five liberals and six realists; three criteria were used by six authors total, evenly split between liberals and realists. "Robustness," "falsifiability," and "predictive accuracy" were each used by six authors, evenly split between liberals and realists, specifically, the two criteria of "uncovers true causes" and "identifies mechanisms" were used by five authors, two liberals and three realists. Thus, with regard to the six most frequently used criteria of theory-acceptance, there was nearly and even split between the two liberals and realist.

Table 27.4 Disagreement on meta-theory among most influential figures in realism and liberalism

	Scientific realist	Empiricist
Political realist	Mearsheimer	Waltz
Liberal	Doyle	Keohane

Table 27.5 Key scientific realist and empiricist criteria used
           by top dozen political realist and liberal authors

	Political realist	Liberal
Empiricist criteria		
Empirical adequacy	6	5
Predictive accuracy	3	3
Scientific realist criteria		
Uncovers true causes	3	2
Identifies mechanisms	3	2
Other		
Falsifiability	3	3
Robustness	3	3

A related observation on the tight overlap of the criteria used by the two schools of IR is that the DP debate played out in the most highly ranked IR journals (Maliniak et al. 2012: 52), and it quickly turned quantitative. Both sides in the DP debate relied more and more on statistical analysis of large numbers of datapoints. The fact that the two groups of scholars primarily used statistical analysis to study the empirical claim meant that they shared criteria of adequacy. For the most part, scholars have come to agree that the statistical argument for the association between joint democracy and peace is very firm. There has been cumulation and approach-to-consensus on points that were hotly disputed in the 1980s and 1990s. We ask in the next section whether there are flaws in the liberal position, given that the dyadic hypothesis is now widely accepted (Table 27.5).

7. Caveats and Conclusions

The DP debate is intimately connected to all three Great Debates in IR. Realists and liberals were the clear opponents in the core DP debate (which was the subject of the first debate), that over the dyadic hypothesis. DP studies highlighted the value of quantitative, behavioral methods to solve a problem by approaching consensus (which was the focus of the second debate). And by the latter 1990s, and into the new century, constructivists used the DP debate as a venue to emphasize the value that "critical studies," the socially constructed nature and interconnections between agent and structure, and "immanent critique" add to social enquiry (which is the subject of the third debate).

The central conclusion here is that DP debate shows that the field of political science is capable of what can legitimately be regarded as scientific progress. This can be seen at least with respect to two major hallmarks of progress, *approach-to-consensus* among disputing groups of researchers, and the *cumulation of knowledge*. We see the former by remembering that both realists and liberals largely came to agree over time and multiple interactions that the monadic hypothesis does not stand up to empirical scrutiny, but that the dyadic hypothesis does. And we see cumulation by noting how realists' and liberals' movement toward consensus came about—specifically that some scholars on either side incorporated the critiques of the other side into the next round of research designs, and by noting the development of new hypothesis, and tests of those hypotheses, as scholars came to see the empirical support for the dyadic hypothesis. While this conclusion is significant, there is a danger of loosely extrapolating more progress than is strictly shown by the preceding argument. Section 3 outlined several key constructivist critiques of the naturalists' DP debate, including the persuasive criticism that meanings of key terms can change, even in the course of a fairly brief intellectual discourse like that of the DP debate. But this shift of emphasis does not, as constructivists claim, undermine the conclusion that the DP debate exhibited scientific progress, given the pragmatist philosophy of science analysis of background knowledge and the importance of clarifying the precise question at issue. Nevertheless, several warnings and caveats are in order.

DP progress may not be easily generalizable to other political science or IR issue-areas. Social science disciplines like political science and IR are diverse and varied. Unlike formal sciences like set theory and algebra, or natural sciences like chemistry and astronomy, IR researchers pose a wide variety of types of questions, regarding historical facts, empirical and causal generalizations, interpretive disputes, and moral-normative issues. From the conclusion that the DP debate exemplifies natural-science-like progress along the two dimensions noted, cumulation and approach-to-consensus, it does not follow that progress is equally achievable on all of the other kinds of question just noted.

Policy implications are rarely straightforward. Researchers today know that there are various factors that can be shown empirically to coincide with peace. The most strongly associated factor with peace is geographical distance. But policy decisions cannot do much about geographical location. In contrast, policymakers can indeed attempt to promote democracy, especially in regimes developing new constitutions. The combined efforts of the Western democracies might well be effective on this score; and they appear to have had some successes in the 1990s. If the dyadic hypothesis is true, for policy purposes it would be important to know that it is, in order to make decisions about resource investment in states from Kazakhstan to Ukraine and from Montenegro to Mongolia. American policymakers have drawn inferences using, and misusing, DP results, and there may be more of the latter in the future. One of the lessons from the DP debate is that policy implications can be misdrawn from academic debates. US leaders from Woodrow Wilson to George W. Bush have cited democracies' peaceful interactions.

It might be added that the empirical IR has included extensive work showing the failures of attempts by major powers to impose democracy on societies that have not primarily worked internally for democratic governance structures.14 Anyone truly familiar with empirical IR is not likely to jump from the dyadic hypothesis to the policy conclusion that Western states should use force to bring about democracies in nondemocratic states. It is true, as some poststructuralists charge, that DP results have been developed through empirical research and that research has been misused to justify major mistakes like the Iraq war. But those policy decisions are the responsibility of the policymakers and their skewed knowledge, or ignorance, of empirical IR debates. Russett (2005), a key defender of the dyadic hypothesis, published a harsh critique of US appeal to DP scholarship in his 2005 paper, "Bushwacking the Democratic Peace."

The Timing of the DP Debate. There are several reasons why the DP debate gained prominence when it did. One reason that has not been previously discussed is the pragmatic aspect of scholars' efforts to answer questions that become worthy of study; the pragmatic account emphasizes the importance of context in understanding just precisely what a re-search question is asking. And any implicit assumption of democracies as more peaceful, especially toward one another, that was common during the Cold War seemed to fade after the election of the more bellicose-sounding Ronald Reagan in the US and the ascendency of "glasnost"-supporting Mikhail Gorbachev in the USSR and subsequent end of the Cold War. Democracy as a form of government had been seen in the West as inherently superior to other forms when there was a communist threat, but was open to much more scrutiny when that threat essentially dissolved.

Democracies are often violent. Liberals have largely surrendered the monadic hypotheses; few if any claim that democracies avoid war in general. Some of the important qualifications about democracies and peaceful behavior include the observation that newly democratized states are not peaceful toward other democracies, and evidence shows that they are more war-prone than states generally. Democracies are not peaceful toward nondemocracies, and the violence between them does not arise simply because nondemocracies attack democracies. Furthermore, democracies have fought brutal colonial wars. But the key claim about democracies in the Kantian triangle, given all evidence to date, seems to hold.

All scientific results are subject to revision. Most people see inter-state war as all too fre-quent and the death and destruction abhorrent. But as Spiro pointed out, among the many interactions that states have had over millennia, war is fairly rare. Thus, a small number of wars among democratic dyads would have a significant effect on the statistical argument supporting the DP. This is not an argument against the conclusion that the debate exhibits genuine progress, since new evidence in the most scientific of disciplines can overthrow previous findings. Empirical sciences are fallible. This is a feature of them that cannot be escaped.

Pragmatist contextualism deepens researchers' understanding of questions at issue and holds potential for cumulation and approach-to-consensus. The pragmatist understanding of scientific enquiry, one aspect of which has been summarized here, provides social scientists with a set of methods to enhance the possibility of progress, by focusing attention on the precise question under consideration to help circumvent controversies which all-too-often endure because researchers are arguing past one another, misunderstanding one another's arguments and replies to their own side's scholarship. It also points our attention to the description of the audience's focus and set of scientific or intellectual priorities in an issue-area.

Cumulation and approach-to-consensus in the study of Democratic Peace. Twenty years after Babst's first paper, the DP debate started to get a great deal of attention in IR. Especially with the end of the Cold War, it became a primary focus of the discipline of IR. Soon liberals ceased to defend the monadic hypothesis, accepting historical disconfirmation. Then, after several rounds of point-by-point criticism and responses, most realists ceased denying that democracies have been unusually peaceful toward one another. Such near-consensus outcomes are rare in IR debates. Moreover, most DP-related articles for the past 20 years build upon the accepted fact of the dyadic hypothesis. The discussion above focused on the time-frame of the DP debate, the criteria of theory choice used by the most influen-tial realists and liberals, and pragmatist-contextualist ideas in the philosophy of science. Together these illuminate the *cumulation* we noted, as each side developed more compre-hensive evidence bases and tests, based on the other side's critiques. And those interactions allowed the opposing schools' *approach-to-consensus.* The process looks very similar to the way natural science debates reach resolution over time, which is referred to as scientific progress.

ACKNOWLEDGMENTS

I would like to thank Genevieve McCarthy for expert proofreading and help in the production of the manuscript.

1. Hobson (2011: 1913) identifies Kant also as the primary source of inspiration for the Frankfurt School, discussed in Sec III, which has in turn inspired many constructivists, who are deeply critical of both realists and liberals.
2. The most influential scholars in IR are ranked in Maliniak (2012).
3. The dozen most cited works during the height of the DP debate are by the following authors (and coauthors): Stuart Bremer, Michael Doyle, Henry Farber and Joanne Gowa, Erik Gartzke, David Lake, Christopher Layne, John Mearsheimer, John M. Owen, R.J. Rummel, Bruce Russett with a variety of co-authors especially Zeev Maoz and John R Oneal, Melvin Small and J. David Singer, and David Spiro. See Chernoff (2014, ch. 5).
4. The datapoints studied in the dyadic hypothesis, as in many other areas of IR scholarship are cases consisting of "dyad-years." "Belgium-Netherlands 1950" is an example of one dyad-year; others are "Belgium-Netherlands 1951,"and "Honduras-North Korea 1966."
5. Babst added other qualifications, e.g., that they must be internationally recognized (which eliminates the Confederates States of America from the category, and thus discounts the American Civil War as a counterexample).
6. Along with a number of other influential papers by Wendt. This does not, however, include Wendt's most recent work published in 2015, *Quantum Mind and Social Science.*
7. See also Risse 2000 on "theory of communicative action".
8. Widmaier (2005) overlooks the fact that the US and Pakistan were both members of CENTO, the Central Treaty Organization.
9. Key relationships were in flux. US-Soviet détente began in 1968. And a decade later, in 1978, a Roper Poll showed that 57 percent of Americans believed that the USSR sought world domination. (Smith Summer 1983: 281).
10. See Lunch and Sperlich, 1979, p. 25, citing Hazel Erskine, "The Polls: Is War A Mistake?" *Public Opinion Quarterly* 34 (Spring 1970): 141–142, and Gallup Opinion Index, numbers 56, 59, 61, 69, and 73.
11. This is an interesting contrast to the changing context of threats to democracy two decades later when today there is a substantial literature on threats to democracy coming from domestic forces and political leaders working to strip various democratic institutions (see Mead 2018; Wallender 2018; Levitsky and Ziblat 2018; and Mounk and Foa 2018).
12. Of course, as in the natural sciences, progress at one point does not guarantee that future developments might not undercut the developments that were regarded as progressive.
13. For a comparison of the specific criteria that both sides relied on in this debate, and evidence that other major debates in security studies tend to have less uniformity of both sides of those debates, see Chernoff (2014).
14. Surveyed by Hermann and Kegley (1998) and Pickering and Peceny (2006).

REFERENCES

Achinstein, Peter. 1971. *Law and Explanation: An Essay in the Philosophy of Science.* London: Oxford University Press.

Achinstein, Peter. 1984. "The Pragmatic Character of Explanation." *PSA: Proceedings of the Biennial Meeting of the Philosophy of Science Association* 2: 275–292.

Adler, Emmauel. 1997. Seizing the Middle Ground." *European Journal of International Relations.* 3 (3): 319–363.

Ashley, Richard C. 1986. The Poverty of Neorealism. In *Neorealism and Its Critics*, edited by Robert O. Keohane. New York: Columbia University Press: 255–300.

Austin, J. L. 1962. *How to Do Things with Words.* Cambridge, MA: Harvard University Press.

Babst, Dean. 1964. "Elective Governments: A Force for Peace." *Wisconsin Sociologist* 3 (1): 9–14.

Babst, Dean. 1972. "A Force for Peace." *Industrial Research* 14: 55–58.

Barkawi, Tarak and Mark Laffey. 1999. "The Imperial Peace: Democracy, Force and Globalization." *European Journal of International Relations.* 5 (4): 403–434.

Barkin, J. Samuel. 2010. *Realist Constructivism: Rethinking International Relations Theory.* New York: Cambridge University Press.

Bohman, James and Matthias Lutz-Bachmann. 1997. *Perpetual Peace: Essays on Kant's Cosmopolitan Ideal.* Cambridge, Mass: MIT Press.

Bremer, Stuart A. 1992. "Dangerous Dyads: Conditions Affecting the Likelihood of Interstate War, 1816–1965." *Journal of Conflict Resolution* 36: 309–341.

Chernoff, Fred. 2014. *Explanation and Progress in Security Studies: Bridging Theoretical Divides in International Relations.* Palo Alto: Stanford University Press.

Deleuze, Gilles. 1990. *The Logic of Sense.* Edited by Constantin V. Boundas. Translated by Mark Lester and Charles Stivale. New York: Columbia University Press.

Der Derian, James. 1987. *On Diplomacy: A Genealogy of Western Estrangement.* Oxford, OX, UK; New York, NY, USA: B. Blackwell.

Derrida, Jacques. 1976. *Of Grammatology.* Translated by Gayatri Chakravorty Spivak. Baltimore: Johns Hopkins University Press.

Doyle, Michael W. 1983a. "Kant, Liberal Legacies, and Foreign Affairs, Part 1." *Philosophy and Public Affairs* 12 (Summer): 205–235.

Doyle, Michael W. 1983b. "Kant, Liberal Legacies, and Foreign Affairs, Part 2." *Philosophy and Public Affairs* 12 (Autumn): 323–353.

Doyle, Michael W. 1986. "Liberalism and World Politics." *American Political Science Review* 80 (December): 1151–1169.

Dunne, Tim. 2008. *Oxford Handbook of International Relations.* Edited by Christopher Reus-Smith and Duncan Snidal. Oxford: Oxford University Press: 107–114.

Erskine, Hazel. 1970. "The Polls: Is War a Mistake?" *Public Opinion Quarterly* 34 (1): 134–150.

Farber, Henry S., and Joanne Gowa. 1995. "Polities and Peace." *International Security* 20: 123–146.

Farber, Henry S., and Joanne Gowa. 1997. "Common Interests or Common Polities? Reinterpreting the Democratic Peace." *Journal of Politics* 59: 393–417.

Foucault, Michael. 1984. "Polemics, Politics, and Problemizations.'" In *Foucault Reader*, edited by Paul Rabinow, 381. New York: Pantheon Books.

Foucault, M. 2000. The Subject and Power. In J. Faubion (Ed.), *Michel Foucault: Power.* New York: The New Press.

Garfinkel, Alan. 1981. *Forms of Explanation: Rethinking the Questions in Social Theory.* New Haven, CT: Yale University Press.

Gelpi, Christopher F. and Michael Griesdorf. 2001. "Winners or Losers: Democracies in international crises, 1918–1994." *American Political Science Review.* 95 (3) 633–647.

Gibler, Douglas. 2012. *The Territorial Peace: Borders, State Development, and International Conflict.* Cambridge: Cambridge University Press.

Gurr, Robert Ted. 1990. *Polity II: Political Structures and Regime Change, 1800-1986.* ICPSR: 9236.

Haas, Michael. 2014. *Deconstructing the "Democratic Peace": How a Research Agenda Boomeranged.* West Palm Beach, FL: Publishinghouse for Scholars.

Hermann, Margaret G. and Chales W. Kegley, Jr. 1998. "The U.S. Use of Military Interventions to Promote Democracy: Evaluating the Record." *International Interactions.* 24 (2): 91–114.

Hobson, Christopher. 2011. "Towards a Critical Theory of Democratic Peace." *Review of International Studies.* 37 (4): 1903–1922.

Hopf, Ted. 1998. The Promise of Constructivism in International Relations Theory." *International Security.* 23 (1) (Summer): 171–200.

Kant, Immanuel. 1939. *Perpetual Peace.* New York: Columbia University Press. Originally published, Konigsberg: Friedrich Nicolovius, 1795.

Kincaid, Harold. 1996. *Philosophical Foundations of the Social Sciences: Analyzing Controversies in Social Research.* Cambridge: Cambridge University Press.

Kincaid, Harold. 2004, "Are There Laws in the Social Sciences?: Yes", in *Contemporary Debates in the Philosophy of Science,* C. Hitchcock (ed.), Oxford: Blackwell, pp. 168–187.

King, Gary, Robert O. Keohane, and Sidney Verba. (1994) *Designing Social Inquiry: Scientific Inference in Qualitative Research.* Princeton: Princeton University Press.

Kratochwil, Friedrich. 1989. *Rules, Norms and Decisions, On the Conditions of Practical and Legal Reasoning in International Relations and Domestic Society.* Cambridge: Cambridge University Press.

Lakatos, Imre. 1970. "History of Science and its Rational Reconstructions." *PSA* (East Lansing, Michigan): 91–136.

Lake, David A. 1992. "Powerful Pacifists: Democratic States and War." *The American Political Science Review* 86 (1): 24–37.

Layne, Christopher. 1994. "Kant or Cant? The Myth of Democratic Peace." *International Security* 18 (1): 5–49.

Levitsky, Stephen and Daniel Ziblatt. 2018. *How Democracies Die.* New York: Crown Publishing.

Levy, Jack. 1988. "Domestic Politics and War." *Journal of Interdisciplinary History* 18 (4): 653–673.

Lunch, William L. and Peter W. Sperlich. 1979. "American Public Opinion and the War in Vietnam." *The Western Political Quarterly* 32 (1): 21–44.

Maliniak, Daniel, Susan Peterson, and Michael J. Tierney. 2012. *Teaching, Research, and Policy Views of International Relations Faculty in 20 Countries.* Williamsburg, VA: College of William and Mary.

Mansfield, Edward D., and Jack Snyder. 1995. "Democratization and the Danger of War." *International Security* 20 (1): 5–38.

Maoz, Zeev. 1998. "Realist and Cultural Critiques of Democratic Peace: A Theoretical and Empirical Re-assessment." *International Interaction* 24 (1): 3–89.

Maoz, Zeev, and Bruce M. Russet. 1993. "Normative and Structural Causes of Democratic Peace 1946–1986." *American Political Science Review* 87(September): 624–638.

Mead, Walter Russell. 2018. "The Big Shift: How American democracy fails its way to success." *Foreign Affairs* 97 (3) (May/June): 10–19.

Mounk, Yascha and Roberto Stefan Foa. 2018. "The End of the Democratic Century Autocracy's Global Ascendance." *Foreign Affairs*. 97 (2) (March/April): 29–36.

Paine, Thomas. 1776. *Common sense: addressed to the inhabitants of America, on the following interesting subjects: I. Of the origin and design of government in general, with concise remarks on the English Constitution. II. Of monarchy and hereditary succession. III. Thoughts on the present state of American affairs. IV. Of the present ability of America, with some miscellaneous reflections.: [Two lines from Thomson].* [Providence]: Philadelphia, printed.

Pickering, Jeffrey and Mark Peceny. 2006. "Forging Democracy at Gunpoint." *International Studies Quarterly.* 50: 539–559.

Pouliot, V. 2008. "The Logic of Practicality: A Theory of Practice of Security Communities." *International Organization.* 62 (2): 257–288.

Ray, James Lee. 1993. "Wars between Democracies: Rare, Or Nonexistent?" *International Interactions: Democracy and War: Research and Reflections.* 18 (3): 251–276.

Ray, James Lee. 1998. "Does Democracy Cause Peace?" *Annual Review of Political Science.* 1: 27–46.

Reiter, Dan, and Allan C. Stam III. 1998. "Democracy, War Initiation, and Victory." *American Political Science Review.* 92 (2): 377–389.

Richardson, Lewis F. 1960. *The Statistics of Deadly Quarrels.* Pittsburgh: Boxwood.

Richman, Alvin. 1991. "Poll Trends: Changing American Attitudes Toward the Soviet Union." *Public Opinion Quarterly* 55 (1): 135–148.

Risse, Thomas. 2000. "Let's Argue: Communicative Action in World Politics." *International Organization* 54 (1): 1–39.

Risse-Kappen, Thomas. 1995. "Democratic Peace — Warlike Democracies?: A Social Constructivist Interpretation of the Liberal Argument." *European Journal of International Relations.* 1 (4): 491–517.

Russett, Bruce. 1993. *Grasping the Democratic Peace: Principles for a Post-Cold War World.* Princeton, NJ: Princeton University Press.

Russett, Bruce. 1995. "The Democratic Peace: And Yet It Moves." *International Security* 19: 164–175.

Russett, Bruce. 2005. "Bushwhacking the Democratic Peace." *International Studies Perspectives.* 6 (4): 395–408.

Russett, Bruce, and John R. Oneal. 2001. *Triangulating Peace: Democracy, Trade, and International Organizations.* New York: Norton.

Rummel, Rudolf J. 1975–81. *Understanding Conflict and War.* Beverly Hills, CA: Sage Publications.

Rummel, Rudolf J. 1983. "Libertarianism and International Violence." *Journal of Conflict Resolution* 27: 27–71.

Shinko, Rosemary E. 2008. "Agonistic Peace: A Postmodern Reading." *Millennium: Journal of International Studies.* 36 (3): 473–491.

Singer, J. David, and Melvin Small. 1972. *The wages of war, 1816-1965: a statistical handbook.* New York: Wiley.

Small, Melvin, and J. David Singer. 1976. "The War-Proneness of Democratic Regimes." *Jerusalem Journal of International Relations* 1 (1): 50–69.

Smith, Tom W. 1983. "The Polls: American Attitudes Toward the Soviet Union and Communism." *Public Opinion Quarterly* 47 (2): 277–292.

Spiro, David E. 1994. "The Insignificance of the Liberal Peace." *International Security* 19 (Autumn): 50–86.

Tetlock, Philip. 2005. *Expert Political Judgment*. Princeton, NJ: Princeton University Press.

Thompson, William R., and Richard Tucker. 1997. "A Tale of Two Democratic Peace Critiques." *Journal of Conflict Resolution* 41: 428–454.

UPI. 2014. "Flashback: Reagan jokes about bombing Soviet Union, 30 years ago 'The bombing begins in five minutes,' Reagan joked, unleashing an international outcry." United Press International (August 11).

Van Fraassen, Bas C. 1980. *The Scientific Image*. New York: Oxford University Press.

Van Fraassen, Bas C. 1989. *Laws and symmetry*. Oxford: Clarendon.

Van Fraassen, Bas C. 2002. *The Empirical Stance*. New Haven, CT: Yale University Press.

Wallender, Celeste. 2018. "NATO's Enemies Within: How democratic decline could destroy the alliance." *Foreign Affairs* V. 97, issue 4, (July/Aug) pp. 70–81.

Walker, R. B. J. 1993. *Inside/outside: International Relations as Political Theory*. Vol. 24. New York;Cambridge [England]: Cambridge University Press.

Wendt, Alexander. 1999. *Social Theory of International Politics*. New York: Cambridge University Press.

Wendt, Alexander. 1992. "Anarchy is What States Make of it: The Social Construction of Power Politics." *International Organization*. 46 (2): 129–177.

Wendt, Alexander. 2015. *Quantum Mind and Social Science: Unifying Physical and Social Ontology*. Cambridge, U.K.: Cambridge University Press.

Widmaier, Wesley. 2005. "The Democratic Peace is What States Make of It: A Constructivist Analysis of the US-Indian 'Near-Miss' in the 1971 South Asian Crisis." *European Journal of International Relations*. 11 (3): 431–455.

Woodward, James. 2003. *Making Things Happen: A Causal Theory of Explanation*. Oxford: Oxford University Press.

Wright, Quincy. 1942. *A Study of War*. Chicago: University of Chicago Press.

INDEX

For the benefit of digital users, indexed terms that span two pages (e.g., 52–53) may, on occasion, appear on only one of those pages.

Tables, figures, and boxes are indicated by *t*, *f*, and *b* following the page number